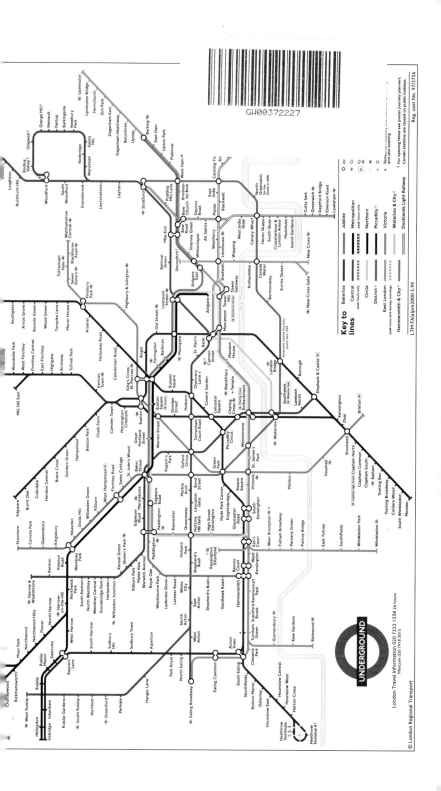

GW00372227

Reg. user No 9/72726

Key to lines

Bakerloo	
Central	
Circle	
District †	
East London	
peak hours and Sunday mornings	
Hammersmith & City †	
Jubilee	
Metropolitan	
peak hours only	
Northern	
Piccadilly †	
Victoria	
Waterloo & City †	
Docklands Light Railway	

† For opening times see poster journey planners.
Certain stations are closed on public holidays.

Service by London Underground Limited early morning and late evening

London Travel Information 020 7222 1234 24 hours
Minicom 020 7918 3015

UNDERGROUND

© London Regional Transport

LTM FAJ a Jpre2000 5.99

London: Westminster and Whitehall

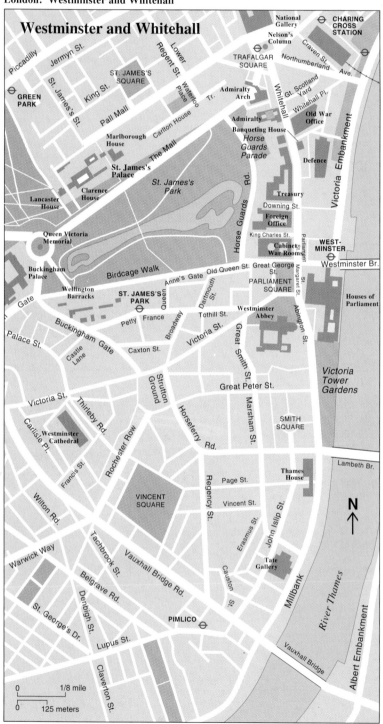

Westminster and Whitehall

Piccadilly
Jermyn St.
St. James's St.
ST. JAMES'S SQUARE
King St.
Regent St.
Lower Regent St.
Waterloo Pl.
Carlton House Tr.
GREEN PARK
Pall Mall
Marlborough House
Carlton House Rd.
The Mall
St. James's Palace
Clarence House
Lancaster House
St. James's Park
Queen Victoria Memorial
Buckingham Palace
Birdcage Walk
Wellington Barracks
ST. JAMES'S PARK
Anne's Gate
Old Queen St.
Queen Anne's Gate
Petty France
Broadway
Dartmouth St.
Tothill St.
Gate
Buckingham Gate
Caxton St.
Palace St.
Castle Lane
Victoria St.
Carlisle Pl.
Thirleby Rd.
Westminster Cathedral
Francis St.
Strutton Ground
Rochester Row
Horseferry Rd.
Victoria St.
Great Smith St.
Great Peter St.
Marsham St.
SMITH SQUARE
VINCENT SQUARE
Wilton Rd.
Tachbrook St.
Vauxhall Bridge Rd.
Regency St.
Page St.
Vincent St.
Erasmus St.
Thames House
Warwick Way
Belgrave Rd.
Denbigh St.
St. George's Dr.
Lupus St.
Claverton St.
Caustin St.
John Islip St.
Tate Gallery
PIMLICO
Vauxhall Bridge
Millbank
Albert Embankment
River Thames
Lambeth Br.
Vauxhall Bridge

National Gallery
Nelson's Column
TRAFALGAR SQUARE
Admiralty Arch
Admiralty
Banqueting House
Horse Guards Parade
Treasury
Downing St.
Foreign Office
King Charles St.
Cabinet War Rooms
Great George St.
PARLIAMENT SQUARE
Westminster Abbey
Victoria Tower Gardens
Houses of Parliament
WEST-MINSTER
Westminster Br.
Whitehall
Gt. Scotland Yard
Whitehall Pl.
Old War Office
Defence
Northumberland Ave.
Craven St.
CHARING CROSS STATION
Victoria Embankment
Horse Guards Rd.
Parliament St.
Margaret St.
Abingdon St.

N

0   1/8 mile
0   125 meters

Soho and Covent Garden

N

1/8 mile

125 meters

Lincoln's Inn Fields

HOLBORN

Southampton Row

Kingsway

Newton St.

Parker St.

Great Queen St.

Drury Lane

Bow St.

Shorts Gardens

Endell St.

Neal St.

Shelton St.

Langley St.

Earlham St.

Long Acre

Floral Pl.

Russell St.

Catherine St.

Theatre Museum

Floral Hall

COVENT GARDEN

Royal Opera

COVENT GARDEN

St. Paul's Covent Garden

King St.

Wellington St.

London Transport Museum

Southampton St.

Maiden La.

Henrietta St.

Lancaster Pl.

ALDWYCH

Aldwych

Waterloo Br.

The Strand

Savoy St.

Savoy Hotel

Victoria Embankment

Cleopatra's Needle

Charing Cross Station

Chandos Pl.

William IV St.

St. Martin-in-the-Fields

Bedfordbury

St.Martins La.

New Row

Garrick St.

National Jazz Center

Monmouth St.

LEICESTER SQUARE

CAMBRIDGE CIRCUS

Charing Cross Rd.

Mercer St.

BLOOMSBURY SQUARE

High Holborn

Bloomsbury Way

Bloomsbury St.

Great Russell St.

New Oxford St.

St. Giles St.

High St.

Shaftesbury Ave.

St. Barnabas in Soho

Sutton Row

Greek St.

Frith St.

Dean St.

Manette St.

Bateman St.

Charles II Statue

SOHO SQUARE

Carlisle St.

St. Anne's

St. Anne's Ct.

Old Compton St.

CHINATOWN

Gerrard St.

Lisle St.

Cranbourne St.

LEICESTER SQUARE

Coventry St.

Irving St.

Orange St.

St. Martin's St.

National Gallery

Whitcomb St.

Haymarket

Regent St.

PICCADILLY CIRCUS

Jermyn St.

Piccadilly

Tottenham Court Rd.

TOTTENHAM COURT RD.

Rathbone Pl.

Newman St.

Great Chapel St.

Wardour St.

Berwick St.

Noel St.

Berners St.

Eastcastle St.

Oxford St.

Poland St.

Lexington St.

Brewer St.

Glasshouse St.

SOHO

Great Marlborough St.

Marshall St.

Carnaby St.

Beak St.

Broadwick St.

GOLDEN SQUARE

Windmill St.

Margaret St.

CAVENDISH SQUARE

HANOVER SQUARE

OXFORD CIRCUS

Argyll St.

St. George St.

Regent St.

New Bond St.

Savile Row

Albemarle St.

Dover St.

Clifford St.

Old Bond St.

Burlington Gardens

Royal Academy

BERKELEY SQUARE

Berkeley St.

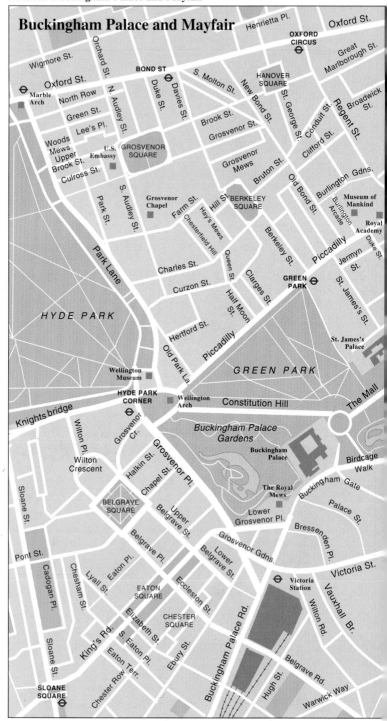

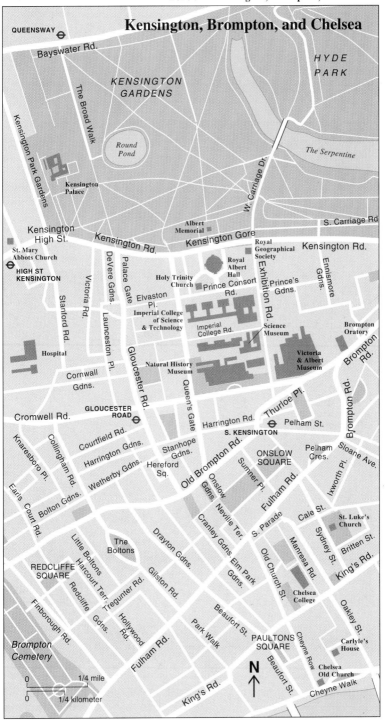

Kensington, Brompton, and Chelsea

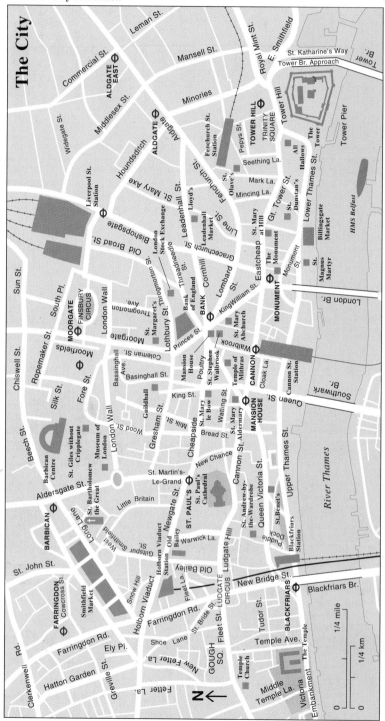

◪ Let's Go writers travel on your budget.

"Guides that penetrate the veneer of the holiday brochures and mine the grit of real life."

—*The Economist*

"The writers seem to have experienced every rooster-packed bus and lunar-surfaced mattress about which they write."

—*The New York Times*

"All the dirt, dirt cheap."

—*People*

◪ Great for independent travelers.

"The guides are aimed not only at young budget travelers but at the independent traveler; a sort of streetwise cookbook for traveling alone."

—*The New York Times*

"A guide should tell you what to expect from a destination. Here *Let's Go* shines."

—*The Chicago Tribune*

"An indispensible resource, *Let's Go*'s practical information can be used by every traveler."

—*The Chattanooga Free Press*

◪ Let's Go is completely revised each year.

"A publishing phenomenon...the only major guidebook series updated annually. *Let's Go* is the big kahuna."

—*The Boston Globe*

"Unbeatable: good sight-seeing advice; up-to-date info on restaurants, hotels, and inns; a commitment to money-saving travel; and a wry style that brightens nearly every page."

—*The Washington Post*

◪ All the important information you need.

"*Let's Go* authors provide a comedic element while still providing concise information and thorough coverage of the country. Anything you need to know about budget traveling is detailed in this book."

—*The Chicago Sun-Times*

"*Let's Go* guidebooks take night life seriously."

—*The Chicago Tribune*

Let's Go Publications

Let's Go: Alaska & the Pacific Northwest 2002
Let's Go: Amsterdam 2002 **New Title!**
Let's Go: Australia 2002
Let's Go: Austria & Switzerland 2002
Let's Go: Barcelona 2002 **New Title!**
Let's Go: Boston 2002
Let's Go: Britain & Ireland 2002
Let's Go: California 2002
Let's Go: Central America 2002
Let's Go: China 2002
Let's Go: Eastern Europe 2002
Let's Go: Egypt 2002 **New Title!**
Let's Go: Europe 2002
Let's Go: France 2002
Let's Go: Germany 2002
Let's Go: Greece 2002
Let's Go: India & Nepal 2002
Let's Go: Ireland 2002
Let's Go: Israel 2002
Let's Go: Italy 2002
Let's Go: London 2002
Let's Go: Mexico 2002
Let's Go: Middle East 2002
Let's Go: New York City 2002
Let's Go: New Zealand 2002
Let's Go: Paris 2002
Let's Go: Peru, Ecuador & Bolivia 2002
Let's Go: Rome 2002
Let's Go: San Francisco 2002
Let's Go: South Africa with Southern Africa 2002
Let's Go: Southeast Asia 2002
Let's Go: Southwest USA 2002 **New Title!**
Let's Go: Spain & Portugal 2002
Let's Go: Turkey 2002
Let's Go: USA 2002
Let's Go: Washington, D.C. 2002
Let's Go: Western Europe 2002

Let's Go *Map Guides*

Amsterdam	New Orleans
Berlin	New York City
Boston	Paris
Chicago	Prague
Dublin	Rome
Florence	San Francisco
Hong Kong	Seattle
London	Sydney
Los Angeles	Venice
Madrid	Washington, D.C.

Let's Go

London

2002

editor and researcher-writer

D. Jonathan Dawid

Julia Stephens map editor
Sarah P. Rotman managing editor
D. Jonathan Dawid, Luke Marion photographers

Macmillan

HELPING LET'S GO

If you want to share your discoveries, suggestions, or corrections, please drop us a line. We read every piece of correspondence, whether a postcard, a 10-page email, or a coconut. Please note that mail received after May 2002 may be too late for the 2003 book, but will be kept for future editions. **Address mail to:**

> Let's Go: London
> 67 Mount Auburn Street
> Cambridge, MA 02138
> USA

Visit Let's Go at **http://www.letsgo.com,** or send email to:

> **feedback@letsgo.com**
> **Subject: "Let's Go: London"**

In addition to the invaluable travel advice our readers share with us, many are kind enough to offer their services as researchers or editors. Unfortunately, our charter enables us to employ only currently enrolled Harvard students.

Published in Great Britain 2002 by Macmillan, an imprint of Pan Macmillan Ltd.
20 New Wharf Road, London N1 9RR
Basingstoke and Oxford
Associated companies throughout the world
www.panmacmillan.com

Maps by David Lindroth copyright © 2002, 2001, 2000, 1999, 1998, 1997, 1996, 1995, 1994, 1993, 1992, 1991, 1990, 1989, 1988 by St. Martin's Press.

Published in the United States of America by St. Martin's Press.

ISBN: 0-333-90607-1
First edition
10 9 8 7 6 5 4 3 2 1

Let's Go: London is written by Let's Go Publications, 67 Mount Auburn Street, Cambridge, MA 02138, USA.

Let's Go® and the thumb logo are trademarks of Let's Go, Inc.
Printed in the USA on recycled paper with biodegradable soy ink.

HOW TO USE THIS BOOK

ORGANIZATION OF THIS BOOK

INTRODUCTORY MATERIAL. The first chapter, **Discover London,** provides a fore-taste of what awaits the intrepid traveler, complete with an overview of the city's various neighborhoods and our top recommendations of those sights, museums, restaurants, and nightspots no visitor should miss. **Life & Times** completes your introduction to London with a roller-coaster ride through its history and culture. Once your appetite is whetted, **Planning Your Trip** gives you all the logistic informa-tion you need to arrive at these shores with tickets, currency, insurance, and steely confidence. **Once in London** picks up at the airport, guiding you into town and explaining how to navigate London's transport, communications, financial, and medical services. If you like it so much you decide to stay, **Living in London** supplies tips on locating long-term accommodations, sorting out visas, and finding work or a program of study. If there's anything else you need, chances are you'll find it listed in our comprehensive **Service Directory.**

COVERAGE. Fairly self-explanatory, the **Sights, Museums, Food & Drink, Nightlife, Entertainment, Shopping,** and **Accommodations** chapters give you everything you need for a successful stay—even Londoners will find something new in our bang-up-to-date listings. Each chapter is organized in the same way, with all the listings arranged according to **neighborhood,** moving in a clockwise circle out from Oxford Circus; this way, you'll soon get a feel for what makes each part of London special and different from its neighbors. **Quicklinks** between each chapter make it simple to instantly locate other types of listings nearby, so if you're looking for a restau-rant close to the British Museum, you'll find it in seconds. Of course, if you know you want sushi, then tables arranging all listings **by type** at the start of each chapter will soon have you on your way. For times when the city gets too much, the **Daytrip-ping** chapter provides a selection of one-day and weekend breaks away from Lon-don into the historic heart of England.

A FEW NOTES ABOUT LET'S GO FORMAT

RANKING ESTABLISHMENTS. In each section (accommodations, food, etc.), establishments are listed in alphabetical order; however, those marked with a Let's Go thumb (🔏) are extra-specially super-duper good, so we put them first.

PHONE CODES AND TELEPHONE NUMBERS. Any number listed without a phone code is a local London number—if you're calling from outside London, that makes it in the (020) code. British phone codes are listed in parentheses when they refer to local codes (e.g. (01223) for Cambridge), but not when the code is an integral part of the number (e.g. 0800 for toll-free calls).

BLACK BARS AND FEATURE BARS. Black bars at times provide wonderful cul-tural insight, at times simply crude humor. In any case, they're usually amusing, so enjoy. **Feature boxes** are more practical, full of tips on how to enjoy London **On the Cheap,** or live it up with **the Big Splurge.**

A NOTE TO OUR READERS The information for this book was gathered by *Let's Go* researchers from May through August of 2001. Each listing is based on one researcher's opinion, formed during his or her visit at a particular time. Those traveling at other times may have different experiences since prices, dates, hours, and conditions are always subject to change. You are urged to check the facts presented in this book beforehand to avoid inconvenience and surprises.

......in Central London

WESTPOINT HOTEL
170-172 Sussex Gardens
Hyde Park London W2 1TP
Tel: (020) 7402 0281
Fax: (020) 7224 9114
www.westpointhotel.com
e-mail info@westpointhotel.com

- ☑ Pleasant central location
- ☑ Convenient for all major sights, museums & theatres
- ☑ Close to all shopping districts, Oxford Street & Piccadilly Circus
- ☑ Clean, comfortable, well-decorated rooms
- ☑ All rooms with ensuite shower, toilet, colour TV & radio
- ☑ Lift to all floors, free daytime luggage room facility
- ☑ 2 minutes from Paddington station & Heathrow Express
- ☑ 4 minutes from Lancaster Court tube station & Airbus

ABBEY COURT HOTEL
174 Sussex Gardens
Hyde Park London W2 1TP
Tel: (020) 7402 0704
Fax: (020) 7262 2055
www.abbeycourt.com
e-mail info@abbeycourt.com

- ☑ Convenient location 2 minutes from Paddington station & Heathrow Express, & 4 minutes from Airbus
- ☑ Easy access to all London's important tourist sights, shopping districts and theatres
- ☑ Ensuite shower and w.c. in all rooms
- ☑ Lift to all floors
- ☑ Each room with colour TV, radio & intercom
- ☑ Car parking by arrangement

SASS HOTEL
11 Craven Terrace
Hyde Park London W2 3QD
Tel: (020) 7262 2325
Fax: (020) 7262 0889
www.sasshotel.com
e-mail info@sasshotel.com

Sass Hotel offers superb value for money accommodations in a convenient, quiet location, just 3 minutes walk from Hyde Park, Lancaster Gate tube station with Heathrow Express is just 5 minutes away. Easy access to all London's famous sights and entertainment.

- ☑ All rooms with ensuite shower, toilet & colour TV
- ☑ Friendly personal service
- ☑ Car parking by arrangement

RATES Per Person per night — FROM £22

	Low Season	High season
Singles	from £48	from £56
Doubles	from £32	from £37
Triples	from £26	from £28
Family Room	from £22	from £24

RATES Per Person per night — FROM £22

	Low Season	High season
Singles	from £48	from £56
Doubles	from £32	from £37
Triples	from £26	from £28
Family Room	from £22	from £24

RATES Per Person per night — FROM £21

	Low Season	High season
Singles	from £35	from £48
Doubles	from £24	from £28
Triples	from £23	from £26
Family Room	from £21	from £24

ALL PRICES INCLUDE COMPLIMENTARY CONTINENTAL BREAKFAST, SERVICE CHARGE & ALL TAXES

Contents

ACKNOWLEDGMENTS

The Let's Go 2002 series is dedicated to the memory of Haley Surti

Let us give thanks. To my beloved wife, Dolly, for taking on the burden of my long absences and increased paunch; to my mother and father, for boundless generosity and unflinching support; to my crazy sister Jools, for stomping and storming the places men dare not tread; to Tim and Preti, for relieving the tedium of lonesome research; to Rita, Dinah, Sheri, Mitra, Karim, Ali, Ebbe, for their assistance, time, and thoughts in London; to Ben, for letting me crash; to Julia, for her tireless map questing; to Sarah, a friend, not a boss; to Melissa and Jen, avatars of the Frame goddess; to Vanessa, for transforming my sugar snaps into photographic magic; to Rebecca, for my twelve pieces of silver; to Anne, for invaluable advice, support, and steel; to David North, Morven Knowles, and the many others at Macmillan UK for invaluable logistical support; and in this, my Let's Go swansong, to all the hundreds of people, friends and comrades, partners in a common cause, who have made my years here a time I will always cherish.

Editor
D. Jonathan Dawid
Research
D. Jonathan Dawid
Photographs
D. Jonathan Dawid, Luke Marion
Managing Editor
Sarah P. Rotman
Map Editor
Julia Stephens

Matthew B. Sussman *Editor, Britain & Ireland*
Kate D. Nesin *Associate Editor, Britain & Ireland*
A. Morgan Rotman *Bath, Oxford, Stratford*
Jennifer A. O'Brien *Canterbury, Salisbury, Cambridge*
Julie M. Dawid *London nightlife*

Publishing Director
Sarah P. Rotman
Editor-in-Chief
Ankur N. Ghosh
Production Manager
Jen Taylor
Cartography Manager
Dan Barnes
Design & Photo Manager
Vanessa Bertozzi
Editorial Managers
Amélie Cherlin, Naz F. Firoz,
Matthew Gibson, Sharmi
Surianarain, Brian R. Walsh
Financial Manager
Rebecca L. Schoff
Marketing & Publicity Managers
Brady R. Dewar, Katharine
Douglas, Marly Ohlsson
New Media Manager
Kevin H. Yip
Online Manager
Alex Lloyd
Personnel Manager
Nathaniel Popper
Production Associates
Steven Aponte, Chris Clayton,
Caleb S. Epps, Eduardo Montoya,
Melissa Rudolph
Some Design
Melissa Rudolph
Office Coordinators
Efrat Kussell, Peter Richards

Director of Advertising Sales
Adam M. Grant
Senior Advertising Associates
Ariel Shwayder, Kennedy Thorwarth
Advertising Associate
Jennie Timoney
Advertising Artwork Editor
Peter Henderson

President
Cindy L. Rodriguez
General Manager
Robert B. Rombauer
Assistant General Manager
Anne E. Chisholm

Discover London

London! It has the sound of distant thunder.
James Bone, 1925

Six letters for seven million citizens; two syllables encapsulating two thousand years. One word, evoking as many different cities as the people you speak it to: the London of kings and the London of drag-queens, of cockney cabbies and bowler-hatted bankers, neighborhood pubs and underground clubs, fish and chips and filled *chaphati*, the capital of Britain and a city of the world. The crown jewel of Britain's sceptred isle lives to a beat all its own, where all partake of the hybrid fruits of a thousand cultural cross-fertilizations. Here is where Jinnah and Gandhi studied; where the Mayflower set sail and Thomas Paine wrote *The Rights of Man;* where Voltaire, Marx, and Freud sought refuge from persecution; where thousands arrive each day to seek a better future. The world's first industrial city, London turned postmodern when her rivals were still modernizing: distinctions between past and future, east and west are meaningless in a place where tradition fuses with innovation and a citizen is as likely to hail from Asia as Essex.

To the visitor, London offers a bewildering array of choices: tea at the Ritz or chilling in the Fridge; Leonardo at the National or Damian at Tate Modern; Rossini at the Royal Opera or Les Mis at the Palace; Bond street couture or Covent Garden cutting-edge—you could spend your entire stay just deciding what to do and what to leave out. This chapter is designed to help put some method into the madness of visiting London. If you know exactly what you want from your trip, skip ahead—otherwise, this introduction should give you some idea of what to expect. Go ahead, turn the page, and discover London.

1

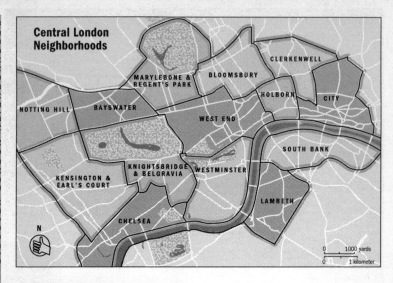

Central London
Neighborhoods

CLERKENWELL

MARYLEBONE &
REGENT'S PARK

BLOOMSBURY

HOLBORN

CITY

NOTTING HILL   BAYSWATER

WEST END

SOUTH BANK

KNIGHTSBRIDGE
& BELGRAVIA   WESTMINSTER

KENSINGTON &
EARL'S COURT

LAMBETH

CHELSEA

N

0   1000 yards
0   1 kilometer

NEIGHBORHOODS

London is often described as being more a conglomeration of villages than a unified city. While this understates the civic pride Londoners take in their city as a whole, it is true that locals are strongly attached to their neighborhoods—in part because each area's heritage and traditions are still alive and evolving, from the City's 2000-year-old association with trade and Westminster's millennial position as the seat of government to Notting Hill's more recent West Indian-inspired Carnival. It's thanks to the feisty independence and diversity of each area that the London "buzz" is continually on the move—every few years a previously disregarded neighborhood explodes into cultural prominence. In the 60s Soho and Chelsea swung the world; the late 80s saw grunge rule the roost from Camden; and in the 90s the East End sprung Damien Hirst and the Britpack artists on the world. More recently South London has come to prominence with the cultural advantages of the South Bank and the thumping nightlife of a recharged Brixton.

THE WEST END

SEE MAP, p. 330-331

NEIGHBORHOOD QUICKFIND: Sights, p. 79; **Museums&Galleries,** p. 139; **Food&Drink,** p. 159; **Nightlife,** p. 190; **Entertainment,** p. 209; **Shopping,** p. 226; **Accommodations,** p. 284, **TRANSPORTATION:** At the hub of London's transportation network, the West End is also surprisingly easy to walk. **Tube:** With numerous stations, the Tube is best for getting in and out of the West End; it's not worth it for one or two stops within the area. **Buses:** The best way to get around. Many routes head from Trafalgar Square to the Strand, Piccadilly, and Charing Cross Rd.; more bus lines converge at Oxford Circus, from where they run south down Regent St. to Piccadilly Circus, west up Oxford St. to Marble Arch, and east to Tottenham Court Rd. Trafalgar Square is also the departure point for most of the **Night Bus** network.

Whether it's shopping, eating, theatergoing, or clubbing, the West End is London's popular (and populist) heartland, with a wider variety of activities than anywhere else in the city. This ill-defined district between royal Westminster and the financial powerhouse of the City was first settled by nobles wanting to be close to both; over time, the neighborhood developed into a patchwork of distinct communities. The well-heeled still live in mansions in prestigious **Mayfair** and socialise in neighboring **St. James's** gentlemen's clubs; on the other side of Piccadilly Circus, a very different type of Londoner frequents a very different type of club in **Soho,** London's nightlife nexus—and, around Old Compton St., its gay ground-zero. **Oxford Street,** which forms Mayfair's northern boundary, has been London's premier shopping street for

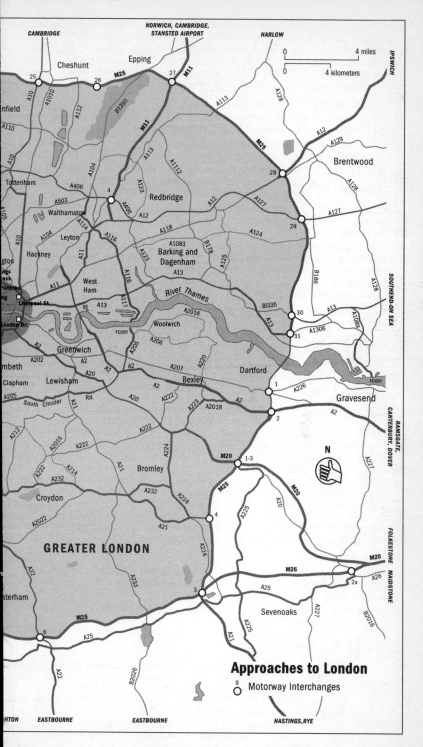

Approaches to London

○ Motorway Interchanges

over 150 years—on the weekend before Christmas, there's barely room to stand. The more fashion conscious head to the boutiques of **Covent Garden,** southwest of Soho, along with crowds of tourists who just hang out in Inigo Jones's piazza. South of Covent Garden, the **Strand** offers glimpses of London's past along with a smattering of theaters and touristy restaurants on its way to to majestic, pigeon-infested **Trafalgar Square,** a reminder of Britain's greater days.

DON'T MISS...

Sights: Soak in the atmosphere—smug St. James's; Oxford St. overload on Saturday; chilled-out Covent Garden in the afternoon; slinky Soho by night; titanic Trafalgar Sq.

Museums & Galleries: Leonardo, Michelangelo et al. at the National Gallery; Monet and Manet at the Courtauld; Tubes and trams at London's Transport Museum.

Food&Drink: Monorail-delivered fusion sushi at Itsu; high tea with a postmodern twist at Ian Schrager's St. Martin's Lane hotel; a truly bazaar experience at Mô's Moroccan tea-room; the piazza cafes of St. Christopher's Place, just yards from Oxford St.

Shopping: the hottest fashions on Floral St., Covent Garden; top DJs' favorite record stores in Soho; window-shopping at the *couture* boutiques on Bond St.; Selfridges, London's favorite department store.

Entertainment: Blockbusters, classic films, and *Sing-a-long-a-Sound-of-Music* in and around Leicester Sq.; jazz legends at Ronnie Scott's; big people, big voices at the Royal Opera and the Coliseum; the funniest funny-men around at the Comedy Store.

Nightlife: The spirit of disco at Sound's *Carwash;* Brazilian dance at the Velvet Room's *Swerve;* chilling on the couches at Freud.

Gay&Lesbian: Old Compton St., the heart of gay London; the labrynthine Heaven, Britain's most famous gay nightclub.

HOLBORN

⚑ NEIGHBORHOOD QUICKFIND: Sights, *p. 88;* **Museums&Galleries,** *p. 142;* **Food&Drink,** *p. 164;* **Nightlife,** *p. 194;* **Entertainment,** *p. 212;* **Shopping,** *p. 232.* **TRANSPORTATION:** *Fairly compact, walking is the easiest way to get around Holborn.* **Tube:** *Holborn and Chancery Lane (closed Su) in the north, Temple (closed Su).* **Buses:** *Dozens run up and down Fleet St., linking Holborn to the City and the West End.*

SEE MAP, pp. 334-335

London's second-oldest area, Holborn was the first part of the city settled by Saxons—"Aldwych," on the western boundary of Holborn, is Anglo-Saxon for "old port." A center of medieval monasticism, today Holborn is associated with two unholy professions: lawyers and journalists. If you thought lawyers had it good at home, wait until you see the **Inns of Court,** colleges-cum-clubs for barristers that have been growing in wealth and power for centuries. Though **Fleet Street** remains synonymous with the British press, the newspapers have since moved on, sapping Holborn of much of its vitality. Home to some sterling sights, after hours there's little to do but sit in one of the many historic pubs once frequented by local lads Samuel Johnson and Samuel Pepys.

DON'T MISS...

Sights: Lawyers in wigs at the Royal Courts of Justice; lawyers in digs in the Temple; the spiritual home of the wedding cake, St. Bride's. **Museums&Galleries:** The incredible maze-museum of architectural innovator Sir John Soane.

Food & Drink: Brilliant British food at the Bleeding Heart Tavern; three hundred years of drinking at Ye Olde Cheshire Cheese.

CLERKENWELL

⚑ NEIGHBORHOOD QUICKFIND: Sights, *p. 92;* **Museums&Galleries,** *p. 143;* **Food&Drink,** *p. 166;* **Nightlife,** *p. 194;* **Entertainment,** *p. 213;* **Accommodations,** *p. 285.* **TRANSPORTATION:** *Walking is the best to get around Clerkenwell.* **Tube:** *Eveything's in walking distance of Farringdon, while southern and eastern parts can also be reached from Barbican.*

Is Clerkenwell the new Soho? With a heady combination of
 SEE MAP, pp. 334-335 nightlife and restaurants fuelled by a growing media presence,

comparisons are hard to avoid. Under the vamped-up guise of "Cityside"—a reference to its position on the boundaries of the City of London—Clerkenwell was the success story of the late 1990s, and if it's no longer cutting-edge cool, that's a bonus: less attitude, more fun. Yet don't go away thinking this is solely a party neighborhood: behind the often grim industrial facade, Clerkenwell is one of London's most fascinating and historic districts. Good food, great bars, *and* historic sights? This tiny neighborhood truly has it all.

DON'T MISS...

Sights: The ancient church of St. Bartholomew the Great; Smithfield, London's largest meat market; a tour of the Charterhouse (W 2pm), a fascinating, living Elizabethan institution.

Food&Drink: Affordable bar food at St. John, British restaurant of the year; artery-hardening breakfasts with beer at the Fox & Anchor, one of London's earliest-opening pubs.

Nightlife: Louder than you thought possible, top dance nights at megaclub Fabric; go football crazy at Cafe Kick's multiple foosball tables.

THE CITY OF LONDON

◪ NEIGHBORHOOD QUICKFIND: Sights, p. 93; **Museums&Galleries,** p. 143; **Food&Drink,** p. 167; **Entertainment,** p. 213; **Accommodations,** p. 285. **TRANSPORTATION:** Public transportation in the City is geared toward getting office workers in and out; within the compact City, walking is easiest. **Rail:** Cannon Street, Liverpool Street, and Blackfriar's, along with London Bridge across the river, provide regular service to commuters. **Tube:** Of the numerous Tube stations, Bank and St. Paul's are within easy reach of most sights. **Buses:** Dozens of routes pass

SEE MAP, p. 334-335

through the City: those from the West End and Holborn arrive along Ludgate Hill and Holborn Viaduct, while Liverpool Street station serves as a terminus for buses arriving from north London.

The City is where London began—indeed, for most of its history, the City was London. Proud of its history and jealous of its traditions, the City's past sits uneasily with its present: once by far the largest urban center in the country, to most Londoners the most important financial center in Europe is an outlying irrelevence. A quarter of a million people may work here during the day, but by night the City's population shrinks to a measly 8000, most of whom live in the 1970s towers of the luxury **Barbican Centre.** Unsurprisingly, not much happens here outside office hours: the only restaurants and pubs that don't close entirely are those aimed squarely at the millions of tourists who outnumber the pigeons at **St. Paul's Cathedral** and daily storm the **Tower of London**—London's two most famous sights. The City's gems are the 24 surviving churches built following the Great Fire of 1666 by Christopher Wren; once a defining aspect of the London skyline, today their spires are largely overshadowed by temples of commerce.

DON'T MISS...

Sights: London at your feet from the top of St. Paul's Cathedral; Elizabeth II's baubles at the Tower of London (though judging from Henry VIII's codpiece, his Crown Jewels must have been even more impressive); the Guildhall, seat of the Lord Mayor's Great Council.

Museums & Galleries: 1969 years of history at the fabulous Museum of London.

Food & Drink: The best of a new breed of Indian restaurants, Cafe Spice Namaste.

Entertainment: Top plays and musical acts in the hard-to-navigate Barbican Centre.

THE SOUTH BANK

◪ NEIGHBORHOOD QUICKFIND: Sights, p. 100; **Museums&Galleries,** p. 144; **Food&Drink,** p. 168; **Entertainment,** p. 214; **Accommodations,** p. 285. **TRANSPORTATION:** Poorly served by public transportation, most South Bank attractions are best reached by walking along the river. **Tube:** The closest station to the South Bank Centre is across the river at Embankment; take the Hungerford foot bridge. Waterloo is convenient for inland attractions, Southwark is closest for Bankside, while London Bridge station provides service for those headed to Borough and Butler's Wharf.

SEE MAP, p. 336-337

Close to the City, but long exempt from its party-pooping laws, this part of London was for centuries London's entertainment center, renowned for its theaters, cock-fighting, bull-baiting, and gentlemanly diversions of a less reputable form. Dominated by wharves and warehouses in the 19th century, devastation wrought by WWII gave the South Bank a chance to reassert its fun-loving heritage. Now, the **"Millennium Mile"** stretches from the twirling London Eye in the west to the swank restaurants of Butler's Wharf in the east, passing by the cultural powerhouses of the Festival Hall, Hayward Gallery, National Theatre, National Film Theatre, Tate Modern, and Shakespeare's Globe Theatre, as well as the quirky riverside shops and eateries of Gabriel's Wharf and the Oxo Tower.

DON'T MISS...

Sights: London—all of it, as seen from the top of the London Eye; HMS Belfast, one mother of a WWII warship; the graceful (and for now purely decorative) span of the Millennium Bridge.

Museums&Galleries: Tate Modern, the world's largest, most unusual modern art museum; the meaning of modernity at the Design Museum; horrors of the past at the Old Operating Theatre and Herb Garret.

Food&Drink: A trio of affordable lunches with brilliant food and great riverside views at the People's Palace, Tate Modern, and Cantina del Ponte; top Turkish treats at Tas.

Entertainment: World-beating drama at the National Theatre, the Old Vic, and the Globe; classics, world music, and jazz at the South Bank Centre; celluloid variety at the National Film Theater and mind-boggling cinematic experiences at the BFI IMAX.

WESTMINSTER

SEE MAP, p. 338-339

⚐ NEIGHBORHOOD QUICKFIND: Sights, p. 106; **Museums&Galleries,** p. 145; **Food&Drink,** p. 169; **Entertainment,** p. 215; **Shopping,** p. 232; **Accommodations,** p. 286. **TRANSPORTATION:** Getting here is not a problem. Victoria, to the west, doubles as a mainline **train** station and (a few minutes' walk away) the London terminus for most long-distance **coach** services. **Tube:** Westminster deposits you near most sights; use St. James's Park for Buckingham Palace. **Buses:** Numerous buses swirl around Parliament Sq. before being catapulted up Whitehall to Trafalgar Sq., down Victoria St. to Victoria, along the Embankment to Pimlico, and across the river into Lambeth.

Home to Parliament, the Prime Minister, and the Queen herself, Westminster exudes power and privilege. But away from the bureaucracy of Whitehall and the Gothic grandeur of the Abbey, Westminster is a surprisingly down-to-earth district, helped by the hundreds of thousands of office workers who make Victoria London's busiest Tube station. **Pimlico,** south of Victoria, is a quiet residential district with some of London's best B&Bs. Don't come here for food, shopping, or—unless you count late-running debates—nightlife; but with some of London's top sights, and with the West End, Knightsbridge, and Chelsea within easy reach, whatever you don't find in Westminster can't be far away.

DON'T MISS...

Sights: The Houses of Parliament seen from Westminster Bridge at dusk; the resting places of England's great and good in Westminster Abbey; the neo-Byzantine splendor of Westminster Cathedral; Inigo Jones's masterpiece, Whitehall's Banqueting House.

Museums & Galleries: The heart of a nation at war in the Cabinet War Rooms; the art of a nation through the ages in Tate Britain.

Accommodations: Stay in the same neighborhood as the Queen: Pimlico's best B&Bs provide red-carpet treatment at down-to-earth prices.

CHELSEA

SEE MAP, p. 346

⚐ NEIGHBORHOOD QUICKFIND: Sights, p. 108; **Museums&Galleries,** p. 146; **Food&Drink,** p. 170; **Entertainment,** p. 215; **Shopping,** p. 232. **TRANSPORTATION:** Are you joking? In a borough where even the poorest resident drives a BMW, public transportation is a low priority—be prepared to walk. **Tube:** Sloane Square, on Chelsea's eastern boundary is the lone stop. **Buses:** Most run from Sloane Sq. down the King's Rd. on their way from Knightsbridge or Victoria.

Chelsea has the cachet of Knightsbridge and Kensington without their stuffiness—the legacy of both the 19th century, when **Cheyne Walk** and surrounding streets hummed to the discussions of Edgar Allen Poe, George Eliot, Dante Gabriel Rossetti, Oscar Wilde, J.M.W. Turner, John Singer Sargent, and James MacNeill Whistler; and the 1960s and 1970s, when the **King's Road** gave the world miniskirts and punk rock. Stifled by a surfeit of wealth, today's Chelsea has little stomach for radicalism—you'll find nothing more shocking than electric-blue frocks on the King's Rd. these days, while local luminaries now include Hugh Grant, Liz Hurley, Britt Ekland, and a string of B-list celebrities and trust-fund kids known collectively as "Sloane Rangers." Nonetheless, somehow Chelsea still manages to retain a little of that old-time glamor, helped along by the presence of numerous modelling agencies around **Sloane Square.**

DON'T MISS...

Sights: The envy of all retirement homes, Christopher Wren's Royal Hospital; the healing plants of Chelsea Physic Garden.

Shopping: A last stand against global brands, the many unique boutiques of the King's Rd.

Entertainment: New plays and iconoclastic classics at the Royal Court; underground jazz in the hard-to-find 606 club.

KNIGHTSBRIDGE & BELGRAVIA

⑦ NEIGHBORHOOD QUICKFIND: Sights, p. 109; **Food&Drink,** p. 171; **Shopping,** p. 233; **Accommodations,** p. 287. **TRANSPORTATION:** Knightsbridge is compact and easy to walk. **Tube:** Knightsbridge station is near all the shops; for Belgravia, you'll need to leg it south from Hyde Park Corner or north from Victoria. **Buses:** Numerous routes converge on Knightsbridge from Piccadilly, Oxford Street, Kensington, and Chelsea, but they all manage to bypass Belgravia.

SEE MAP, p. 338-339

Knightsbridge has been one of London's most desired addresses for centuries—Apsley House, the Duke of Wellington's former abode, revels in the address "No. 1, London." Today, **Knightsbridge** provides the foil to the West End's shopping stranglehold: like the locals, famed department stores Harrods and Harvey Nichols are secure in their sense of superiority. Sloane Street's boutiques, meanwhile, have nothing to envy their Bond Street cousins—if anything, they're even glitzier and more exclusive. **Belgravia,** which occupies the expanse east of Sloane St., is a cultural desert of grand 19th-century mansions occupied by inumerable embassies and consulates, billionaire's penthouses and millionaire's studio apartments.

DON'T MISS...

Sights: Apsley House, proving that real men can have interests beyond football; just opposite, the Wellington Arch, providing a rare glimpse into Buckingham Palace gardens.

Shopping: Harrods—to be seen to be believed, especially the prices; Harvey Nichols, Diana's favorite department store and still the most fashionable; designer collections on Sloane St.

KENSINGTON & EARL'S COURT

⑦ NEIGHBORHOOD QUICKFIND: Sights, p. 112; **Museums&Galleries,** p. 146; **Food&Drink,** p. 172; **Entertainment,** p. 216; **Shopping,** p. 233; **Accommodations,** p. 287. **TRANSPORTATION:** One of central London's larger neighborhoods, you'll need public transport to get around here. **Tube:** Stations are helpfully named: High St. Kensington for the High St.., South Kensington for the South Ken museums, and Earl's Court for Earl's Court. **Buses:** Numerous buses ply the High St. before disappearing up Kensington Church St. to Notting Hill; to get to South Kensington, hop on a #49 or #70.

SEE MAP, p. 340-341

Until recently the stomping ground of Princess Diana, Kensington divides more or less equally between the label-obsessed consumer mecca of **Kensington High St.** in the west and the incredible array of museums and colleges of **South Kensington's** "Albertopolis" in the east—no prizes for guessing which was Di's favorite. The presence of 2000 French schoolkids at the local *lycée* lends a continental feel to parts of South Kensington, with a corresponding number of good, cheap restaurants. Both

High St. and South Ken have a smattering of budget accommodations, but neither can compare with **Earl Court's** "Kangaroo Valley" to the southwest. In the 1960s and 70s the sole preserve of Aussie backpackers and a large gay community, today others have cottoned on to its combination of cheap accommodations and food with good transport links to central London.

DON'T MISS...

Sights: The Royal Dress Collection in Kensington Palace, Diana's former home.

Museums: South Kensington's imperial triumvirate: The Victoria & Albert tops most people's lists, but those with kids shouldn't ignore the Natural History and Science Museums nearby.

Food&Drink: Brilliant *nouvelle* Polish cuisine at Wòdka; tea at the Palace in the Orangery; a taste of France at Raison d'Être in South Kensington's Little Paris.

Shopping: Oxford St. variety without Oxford St. crowds on Kensington High St.

NOTTING HILL

SEE MAP, p. 342

⊠ *NEIGHBORHOOD QUICKFIND: Sights,* p. 113; *Food&Drink,* p. 173; *Nightlife,* p. 195; *Entertainment,* p. 216; *Shopping,* p. 234. TRANSPORTATION: *Getting to Notting Hill is easy; getting around is another matter. **Tube:** Notting Hill Gate serves the south, while Ladbroke Grove deposits you close by Portobello Rd. **Buses:** #52 runs from Ladbroke Grove down to the Gate and Kensington Park Rd. From the West End, #12 and 94 will get you to Notting Hill Gate, while a plethora of buses make the trip up from High St. Kensington.*

For decades one of London's most vibrant, ethnically mixed neighborhoods, in the past few years (helped on by a certain movie) Notting Hill has become a victim of its own trendiness. The rich mix of bohemians, immigrants, and blue-collar workers that sustained its vitality is rapidly being diplaced by a braying crowd of brash yuppies, resulting in rising prices and a diminished community. Only at the edges can you catch glimpses of the old Notting Hill: toward the south, where the ugly 1950s facades of **Notting Hill Gate** do their best to keep yuppieville at bay, and in the north around **Portobello Road** and the Westway, where the vibrant market and numerous low-income housing blocks come together to recreate some of the old Notting Hill magic. Once a year, the whole neighborhood explodes with Caribbean color and sound during the **Notting Hill Carnival,** attended by over 2 million people—following outbreaks of violence in recent years, however, it has been proposed to reroute the carnival through Hyde Park.

DON'T MISS

Shopping: Portobello Market on a Saturday; vintage Westwood, Gaultier, and other outrageous couture at One of a Kind; second-hand everything at the Music&Video Exchange.

Food: Top fish'n'chips at George's; fresh Portuguese pastries at Oporto and Lisboa; taste the latest recipes at Books for Cooks' in-store demo kitchen.

BAYSWATER

SEE MAP, p. 342

⊠ *NEIGHBORHOOD QUICKFIND: Food&Drink,* p. 174; *Entertainment,* p. 217; *Shopping,* p. 236; *Accommodations,* p. 289. TRANSPORTATION: *Bayswater falls into two halves, with most shops and restaurants in the west and accommodations in the east. **Tube:** Bayswater and Queensway for the west; Paddington and Lancaster Gate for the east. Note that there are 2 separate Paddington tube stations: the Hammersmith&City line one is a hike from the mainline station concourse. **Buses:** Plenty of routes converge at Paddington from the West End and Knightsbridge, while the #12 and #94 run along Hyde Park from Marble Arch.*

A dense conglomeration of tall Victorian terraces, Bayswater has neither the fashionable status of Notting Hill to the west, nor the respectability of Marylebone to the east, despite a sterling central position neighboring Hyde Park. Yet as the handsome early 19th-century stuccoed buildings will attest, this was once London's most stylish neighborhood. Its downfall arrived with the Paddington canal and then the railway, and the slums that naturally grew up around them. Today, while the area could hardly be considered seedy, a question mark still hangs over it in the eyes of many Londoners—though not in those of the thousands of travelers who gratefully bed down in the hundreds of B&Bs lining the streets around Queensway and Paddington. Another relic of Bayswater's historically low-cost of living is that it has always been one of the most ethnically diverse London neighborhoods; indeed, it can rightly claim to be the original London home of those two English staples, curries and kebabs. Today, you'll find Arab shops, Thai supermarkets, and Chinese restaurants one next door to the other.

DON'T MISS...

Food&Drink: The original branch of Royal China, still serving up the capitals best *dim sum;* la Bottega del Gelato's fantastic fresh ice-cream.

Accommodations: Some of London's best B&Bs around the transport hub of Paddington Station.

MARYLEBONE & REGENT'S PARK

⚑ NEIGHBORHOOD QUICKFIND: Sights, p. 114; **Museums&Galleries,** p. 147; **Entertainment,** p. 217; **Food&Drink,** p. 174; **Accommodations,** p. 292. **TRANSPORTATION:** The main problem getting around Marylebone is crossing the vast and boring expanse in the middle. **Tube:** Baker St. deposits you conveniently for Marylebone's northern sights, while Bond St. anchors the south. Confusingly, there are two entirely separate Edgware Rd. stations; fortunately, they're not far apart. **Buses:** The best way of getting across Marylebone. 10 routes link north and south via **SEE MAP, p. 344-345** Baker St. (going south) and Gloucester Pl. (heading north), while 7 more ply the Edgware Rd.

Marylebone is an elusive district; easy to find on a map, it lacks cohesion and a sense of identity. Largely residential and respectable, like a pretzel its best parts are the edges—though some have already been chewed off. Oxford St. to the south and beautiful Portland Place to the east have long been co-opted by the West End (see p. 2), but the **Edgware Rd.** to the west still clings tenuously to Marylebone: on this long road, its straightness a clue of its Roman origins, Arabic is spoken more often than English, and kebabs are the default cuisine. Forming the nothern border of Marylebone, **Regent's Park** is a giant and popular expanse of greenery surrounded by elegant Regency terraces. More than London's biggest football practice-ground, the park is home to a panoply of sights from the golden dome of the London Central Mosque to the massive elephant house of London Zoo; nearby, Marylebone Rd. and Baker St. provide tourist thrills, in the shape of the ever-popular Madame Tussauds and the Sherlock Holmes Museum. Yet Marylebone's center is not entirely hollow: Marylebone High St. drives a wedge of trendy shops, cafes, and restaurants on its way from Marylebone Rd. to Oxford St.

DON'T MISS...

Museums: The Wallace Collection, combining one of the world's finest private art collections with Britain's biggest array of medieval armor.

Food&Drink: Some of London's best kebabs at Patogh, an authentic taste of Persia.

Entertainment: The beautiful Wigmore Hall, London's top chamber music venue; if the weather's good, the Regent's Park Open-Air Theatre, with pre-performance barbeque.

BLOOMSBURY

⚑ NEIGHBORHOOD QUICKFIND: Sights, p. 116; **Museums&Galleries,** p. 148; **Food&Drink,** p. 175; **Entertainment,** p. 217; **Shopping,** p. 236; **Accommodations,** p. 293. **TRANSPORTATION:** Though fairly large, Bloomsbury is a pleasant district to walk around. **Tube:** A plethora of stations make Bloomsbury easy to get to from all over London: King's Cross is the system's biggest interchange, while Goodge St. and Russell Sq. are most central for the sights. A word of warning: choose your tube interchanges carefully here. Avoid connections at Warren St., and use Euston **SEE MAP, pp. 344-345** rather than King's Cross to get between the Northern and Victoria lines. Another King's Cross no-no is changing between Circle/Metropolitan/Hammersmith&City lines and Northern/Victoria/Piccadilly, though going from Northern to Piccadilly here is simple. **Buses:** Run mostly north-south, either *between Warren St. and Tottenham Court Rd. stations (along Gower St. heading south, along Tottenham Court Rd. heading north), or between Euston and Holborn along Southampton Pl.*

Home to dozens of universities, colleges, and specialist hospitals, not to mention both the British Museum and the British Library, Bloomsbury is London's undisputed intellectual powerhouse. In the early 20th century, the quiet squares and Georgian terraces resounded to the intellectual musings of the famous Bloomsbury Group, including T.S. Eliot, E.M. Forster, Virginia Woolf, Bertrand Russell, Vanessa Bell, and John Maynard Keynes; today, they house student halls and dozens of affordable accommodations. But don't come here expecting a campus atmosphere: instead Bloomsbury offers a sedate appeal, with fine architecture and some great restaurants.

DON'T MISS...

Sights: The British Library and St. Pancras Station, forming an odd but intriguing architectural contrast; both reward a visit inside.

Museums: The British Museum, in which whole vacations can be swallowed; a past world of playthings in Pollock's Toy Museum, with not a Playstation in sight; great exhibitions of African and Asian art at the Brunei Gallery.

Food&Drink: Da Beppe, serving huge portions of London's best Italian food; Diwana Bhel Poori House, a paradise for vegetarians with great South Indian food at unbeatable prices.

Accommodations: The Generator, taking hosteling into a whole new universe; the Indian YMCA, the best-value half-board deal in town; any of the Georgian B&Bs on Cartwright Gardens.

NORTH LONDON

⊡ NEIGHBORHOOD QUICKFIND: Sights, *p. 118;* **Museums&Galleries,** *p. 150;* **Food&Drink,** *p. 176;* **Nightlife,** *p. 196;* **Entertainment,** *p. 218;* **Shopping,** *p. 237;* **Accommodations,** *p. 298.*
TRANSPORTATION: *Most individual neighborhoods are walkable, once you're there.* **Tube:** *Long distances make this the way to get around. Note that north of Euston you're in Zone 2, while Highgate and Golder's Green are in Zone 3.* **Buses:** *Essential for getting to some out-of-the-way locations. Take advantage of the bus and local-area maps in tube stations and at bus stops to help you find your way.*

Green and prosperous, North London's inner suburbs are some of London's older outlying communities: **Hampstead** and **Highgate** were pleasant country retreats for centuries before urban sprawl engulfed them and still retain their distinct village atmospheres. Of the two, Hampstead is the busier and more urbane, with a long line of intellectual associations from William Hogarth and John Keats to Sigmund Freud and Aldous Huxley. Closer to the center, **Camden Town** and **Islington** were for most of the 19th and 20th centuries grimy, predominantly working-class areas, but in the 1980s their stock shot up and both are now solidly populated with wealthy liberals: Camden Town is home to playwright Alan Bennet, while Tony Blair lived in Islington before making the move to Downing St. Arrive during the weekend in Camden Town and you'd be hard-pressed to notice, though: the gigantic street market is more popular than ever, attracting what looks like half the under-25 population of Europe every Sunday. In Islington the prosperity is more apparent: in recent years Upper St. has become one of London's top eating destinations, with over 100 restaurants within walking distance of Angel Tube. **Maida Vale** and **St. John's Wood** are wealthy northern extensions of Marylebone and Bayswater; particularly picturesque is **Little Venice,** at the confluence of three canals, while the most famous sight in these parts is the fairly unremarkable pedestrian crossing at **Abbey Road.**

DON'T MISS...

Sights: Kenwood House, a picture-perfect country mansion with a great art collection; the hidden pastures of the Hill Garden; a stroll along the Regent's Canal; Looking like it had just flown in on a magic carpet, the ornate Shri Swaminaryan Hindu Mandeer.

Museums: Hundreds of planes at the Royal Airforce Museum; the story of Israel in England at the Jewish Museum; the latest Brit Art at the Saatchi Gallery.

Food&Drink: Funky world-food fun at Giraffe; brilliant bagels at Carmelli's; top Turkish treats at Gallipoli; pancakes at La Crêperie de Hampstead and Tartuf; London's best sushi at Noto.

Shopping: Total weekend madness at Camden market; the zaniest clubwear at Cybercity.

Entertainment: The Next Big Thing at the Dublin Castle; top theatrical action at the Almeida; rock and poetry slams at Shane MacGowan's favorite, Filthy McNasty's Whisky Cafe.

Nightlife: Vox'n'Roll at Filthy MacNasty's; funky dance madness at WKD.

Gay&Lesbian: The King William IV, north London's most popular gay pub; the Black Cap, with a live cabaret six nights a week.

WEST LONDON

*▶ **NEIGHBORHOOD QUICKFIND: Sights,** p. 123; **Food&Drink,** p. 179; **Entertainment,** p. 220; **Accommodations,** p. 299. **TRANSPORTATION:** Though its size is potentially a problem, most sights are easy to get to. You're eating up the Zones here, with Richmond edging into Zone 4. If you've got the time, a **river boat** is the most relaxing way of getting to Richmond and Kew. **Tube:** The District Line does an admirable job of getting tourists to most sights. **Buses:** Invaluable for getting to some of the more obscure sights and also an efficient way of getting between West London neighborhoods.*

Laid out along the river, West London stretches for miles before petering out in the hills and vales of the Thames valley. Here, the river changes tack so often and so sharply that it makes no sense to talk about the north or south bank, and communities have developed almost in isolation from their neighbors. Further from the river, such as at **Shepherd's Bush,** the city reasserts itself: currently the capital of London's antipodean population, were it not for its entertainment this neighborhood would have little to distinguish it from dozens of other drab suburbs. The change comes around **Hammersmith,** with a sharp transition from the urbanity around the Tube station to the pleasant parks and pubs along the Thames. Historically, the western reaches of the Thames were fashionable spots for country retreats, and by the time you reach affluent **Richmond,** the river winds carelessly through the grounds of stately homes and former royal palaces on its way to Hampton Court: this truly is the garden of London.

DON'T MISS...

Sights: Paradise under glass at the conservatories of Kew Gardens; Chiswick House, an Italian villa in the heart of England; the great expanse of Richmond Park.

Food&Drink: Vegetarian delights at the Gate; riverside drinks in the 17th-century Dove.

Entertainment: Being part of a live studio audience at BBC Television Centre; top rock and variety acts at the Shepherd's Bush Empire and London Apollo.

SOUTH LONDON

*▶ **NEIGHBORHOOD QUICKFIND: Sights,** p. 125; **Museums&Galleries,** p. 151; **Food&Drink,** p. 180; **Nightlife,** p. 198; **Entertainment,** p. 220; **Shopping,** p. 238; **Accommodations,** p. 299. **TRANSPORTATION:** Largely bypassed by the **Tube,** overland **rail** makes up the shortfall, with services from Victoria, Waterloo, and London Bridge. **Buses:** From Brixton, the P4 will take you to all the Dulwich sights.*

Few divides are harder to breach than that which separates South from North London: with a few exceptions (notably the South Bank), North Londoners regard everything south of the Thames as inherently disreputable, whilst for their part South Londoners think of their northern neighbors as insufferably arrogant. The truth is that, only really developing in the 19th century, South London lacks a historical center to counterbalance the north, and so can easily appear as an undifferentiated mass of Victorian railway suburbs. Yet this anonymity hides some of London's most dynamic neighborhoods. From a tourist perspective, two South London areas stand out: **Brixton,** which north Londoners invariably associate with the race riots of the early 1980s, is a vibrant melting pot where African, Caribbean, and English traditions collide and fuse—with London's highest concentration of under-40s, it's unsurprisingly home to some thumping nightlife. Neighboring **Dulwich** couldn't be more different: the south's answer to Hampstead, this prosperous hilly village is where Margaret Thatcher has chosen to live out her days.

DON'T MISS...

Museums: The Imperial War Museum, offering a surprisingly balanced view of conflicts since 1914 and a truly impressive array of weapons; Dulwich Picture Gallery, a fantastic collection of Old Masters in one of the first purpose-designed galleries in the world.

Food&Drink: Top vegetarian food and fish in an atmospheric church crypt at Bah Humbug; massive portions of comforting Caribbean food in a used bookstore at Souls of Black Folk.

Entertainment: Headline rock, pop, and world acts at the famous Brixton Academy.

Nightlife: Chilling at Dogstar and the Living Room; serious trance action at the Fridge.

EAST LONDON

 NEIGHBORHOOD QUICKFIND: Sights, p. 126; **Museums&Galleries,** p. 152; **Food&Drink,** p. 180; **Nightlife,** p. 199; **Entertainment,** p. 221; **Shopping,** p. 239. **TRANSPORTATION:** Much of East London is surprisingly central; you're unlikely to get beyond Zone 2. **Tube:** The East End is well served by the Underground. Old St. is best for Hoxton/Shoreditch while Aldgate East and Liverpool St. are nearest Whitechapel sights. Further east, the Tube swings away and the **DLR** takes over: these dinky driverless trains will whisk you all the way down to Greenwich. **Buses:** Useful for getting from the City to the East End, but distances further east work in favor of the Tube and DLR.

At Aldgate, the fabulous wealth of the city abruptly gives way to the historically impoverished **East End.** The divide is centuries old: since both prevailing winds and the river current conspired to waft the pollution of the crowded City eastward, the rich fled to West London just as surely as the poor were obliged to stay in the east. Cheap land together with a proximity to the docks where they arrived made the East End a focal point for immigration: older residents still remember when this was a predominantly Jewish neighborhood, but today it's solidly Bangladeshi. Brick Lane, famed for its market and its restaurants, is now at the center of a new influx: artists and designers busy colonising one of the last affordable outposts of more-or-less central London. East of Whitechapel, the East End remains poor and working-class until you hit **Docklands.** Since the late 1980s, this vast man-made archipelago has been busy building itself up from the abandoned ruins of what was once the world's busiest port into a sort of city-within-a-city: the skyscrapers of Canary Wharf are establishing it as London's second financial center, while people are finally starting to move into the thousands of waterside housing complexes that surround it. Unfortunately, the rebuilding has decimated the area's traditional communities and bulldozed much of its history—there's not much reason to get off the elevated DLR trains as they shuffle you south toward **Greenwich.** Once the favorite residence of Elizabeth I, Greenwich bucks the trend in East London: steeped in history, it's a beautiful district with a wealth of sights. From nowhere in Greenwich or Docklands can you ignore the sight of the massive Millennium Dome, but don't set your heart on visiting it—as planned, this much-maligned attraction closed a year after it opened, in December 2001.

DON'T MISS...

Sights: The painted hall of the Royal Naval College, Greenwich; the sights, sounds, and smells of Brick Lane market in the East End; the soaring skyscrapers of Canary Wharf.

Museums&Galleries: Whitechapel Art Gallery, home to some of London's most avant-garde contemporary art shows; the engrossing National Maritime Museum.

Food&Drink: The US ambassador's personal choice for BBQ, Spitalfields' Arkansas Cafe; unbelievably cheap balti and bagels along Brick Lane.

Nightlife: The hipper-than-thou hangouts of the old Truman Brewery: loosen up with a drink at the Vibe bar, then dance the night away at 93 Feet East.

ASPECTS OF LONDON

> It is difficult to speak adequately of London. It is not a pleasant place...it is only magnificent...It is the biggest aggregation of human life—the most complete compendium of the world.
>   Henry James, 1881

LIVING TRADITIONS

Sometimes, it seems as though nothing changes in London—even the cholesterol-laden English breakfast hasn't killed off London's love of pomp and pageantry. From the **Changing of the Guard** at Buckingham Palace (see p. 68) to the 700-year-old **Ceremony of the Keys** at the Tower of London (p. 73), British soldiers are kept well drilled at marching in step and burnishing their breastplates. Governments come and go, but **Parliament** (p. 70) stays constant: MPs still stay behind red lines meant to prevent sword-fights with their opponents. Less well known, the **Inns of Court** have acted as guardians of England's legal heritage for centuries (p. 88), while the **Royal Hospital, Chelsea** (p. 108), and the **Charterhouse** in Clerkenwell (p. 93) are examples of charitable institutions that have stood the test of time with their honor and heritage intact. No less constant are more recent traditions, from **afternoon tea** at Browns (a mere 160 years old; p. 160) to the scrums that form outside the annual **Harrods** sale (p. 233). Oldest and most enduring of all London customs, though, is the hand-pulled pint of beer served in a cosy **pub** as ancient and historic as any monument.

GREEN LONDON

Big Ben

London is blessed with an incredible variety of parks and open spaces—with all that rain, it's not surprising plants love it! Most famous of London parks are the siamese twins of **Hyde Park** and **Kensington Gardens** (p. 111), the model for city parks around the world. With its own palace, gallery, historic sights, and restaurants, you could spend a whole day here—add horse riding, swimming, boating, and rollerblading, and you might never want to leave. Nearby, **St. James's Park** and **Green Park** (p. 107) were both formerly private palace gardens: genteel and well-kept, they're now a prime spot for picnicking and sunbathing (but beware the pricey lawnchairs). Few parks anywhere can compete with the diversity of **Regent's Park,** with an open-air theater, two boating lakes, a mosque, and even London Zoo.

Bobbies

For all their leafy glory, central London's parks pale beside the bounty on offer in the suburbs. The most impressive formal gardens are those attached to palaces and stately homes, such as **Hampton Court** (p. 244) and **Ham House** (p. 243). Those who prefer their nature more natural will revel in the vast expanse of **Richmond Park** (p. 243), whose thousands of acres offer spectacular views as well as sheltering several hundred deer. Also in Richmond, **Kew Gardens** (p. 124) are a unique botanical resource, preserving thousands of delicate species in vast climate-controlled greenhouses set among perfectly maintained landscaped gardens. For many Londoners, though, there's nothing to beat **Hampstead Heath** (p. 121)—the vast, centuries-old common offers thick woodlands and meadows of waist-deep grass to help you forget about the metropolis around. It also shelters Robert Adam's picture-perfect **Kenwood House,** with a fine collection of Old Master paintings, and the romantic hidden oasis of the **Hill Garden.**

Buckingham

OLD MAN RIVER

London owes its very existence to the Thames, which for almost two thousand years linked this trading city to the rest of the world; in its time it has served as London's main thoroughfare, primary water source, and only sewer—often all at the same time. Today, the mighty river lies dormant, plied only by pleasure craft and tamed by the **Thames Barrier** (p. 131), an astounding feat of engineering that protects London from the devastating tidal surges that have swept through the city in the past. The city's maritime heritage is most evident in the Thames' eastern reaches: **Greenwich** (p. 128) was until recently the headquarters of the Royal Navy, while across the river the ongoing development of **Docklands** (p. 128) is bringing new life to what was once the busiest port in the world. The unique shape of **Tower Bridge** (p. 99) is a legacy of the days when traffic up and down the river was as important as that across it; with around 600 bridge-lifts a year, you still have a good chance of seeing it in action. Reminders of the Thames' past as London's main highway are found in **Traitor's Gate** at the Tower of London (p. 74) and **York Watergate** (p. 88) in Victoria Embankment Gardens. Yet the Thames serves to divide London as much as to unite it: northerners and southerners rarely change places, and the rivalry between the two halves is as deep-seated and bitter as any ancient conflict. Even so, ever since puritanical City authorities forced Shakespeare south of the river to the **Globe Theatre** (p. 102), north Londoners have flocked to the entertainments of the **South Bank** (p. 100). In west London, the Thames takes on another character: peaceful, narrower, and rural, its sweeping curves and loops separate the outer suburbs into a patchwork of towns and villages that once served as country retreats for London-based aristocrats. From the extravagance of **Chiswick House** (p. 124) to more homely **Marble Hill** (p. 243), these western oases are the perfect place to spend hot summer afternoons.

FLAVORS OF EMPIRE

One of the few truly multicultural cities in the world, London has benefited from the end of the Empire as the oppressed peoples of Britain's far-flung domains have come "home" with a vengeance, creating new traditions and rejuvenating large tracts of the capital. For most Londoners, the biggest influence has been on the taste buds: it's often said that London's **Indian** food is better than Delhi's. While most "curry houses" continue to serve a limited range of tried-and-trusted dishes as much influenced by British tastes as Indian, groundbreaking restaurants such as **Cafe Spice Namaste** (p. 167) and **Masala Zone** (p. 159) are bringing the delights of regional Indian cusine to the London palate. South Indian vegetarian restaurants are also a hit with herbivores and meat-eaters alike—try **Diwana Bhel Poori** (p. 175) house for one of the best and cheapest lunches in London. For "balti" cuisine—allegedly invented in Manchester, but none the less tasty for that—you should head to the Bangladeshi community of **Brick Lane** (p. 127).

Thanks to Britain's imperial legacy in Hong Kong, **Cantonese** restaurants in the capital are both plentiful and excellent. **Royal China** (p. 174) is widely considered to have the best *dim sum* in London, though Chinatown's **Harbour City** (p. 161) is close behind. If you judge the authenticity of a restaurant by the outlandishness of its ingredients, you won't be disappointed in **Mr. Kong** (p. 161)—fish lips with sea cucumber, anyone? Softened up by the Chinese, Londoners have proved themselves susceptible to all manner of other Asian delights. **Japanese** food is the success story of the past decade, with noodle bars and conveyor-belt sushi joints on every street corner. Try **Itsu** (p. 161) for the best, most innovative fusion sushi around, though purists should trek out to north London's **Noto Sushi** (p. 179) for the freshest cuts.

Another victim of past British meddling, the **Middle East** has given London some of its best and best-value restaurants. For simple kebabs, it's hard to beat the slow-grilled wonders Iranian **Patogh** (p. 174), with its mouthwatering flatbread, while for a quick meal the glitz of Lebanese takeaway **Ranoush Juice** (p. 174) impresses. The widest variety, though, is on offer at the many Turkish restaurants, such as **Gallipoli** (p. 177) and **Tas** (p. 169)—here, in addition to kebabs, an astounding array of dips, savoury pastries, stews, and bakes will provide even the strictest vegetarian with a Sultan's banquet.

SUGGESTIONS

LET'S GO PICKS: THE LONDON FIFTEEN

London's big tourist draws—the British Museum, the Tower of London, the Changing of the Guard—need no recommendation; they fully deserve their fame. Instead, below we've recommended some of the lesser-known attractions and establishments that we believe best encapsulate the spirit of London.

The London Eye (p. 101). OK, so it's hardly obscure—but the view from the top of this giant observation wheel make it an absolute must-see. Make sure to book tickets in advance!

The Temple (p. 88). Formerly the seat of the Knights Templars, this legal enclave is an oasis of peace and quiet seconds from London's busiest streets.

Sir John Soanes' Museum (p. 142). Designed by the eponymous architect for his own collection, this eccentric museum is as fascinating for its building as its contents.

The Hill Garden (p. 121). Of all London's parks, this hidden garden-within-a-garden is perhaps the most unexpected and most enchanting.

Afternoon Tea (p. 160). Arguably England's greatest contribution to civilisation, this combination of sandwiches, cakes, and delicate teas is best experienced in 5-star surroundings.

Itsu (p. 161). London is sushi crazy, and the craziest sushi are found here, from salmon tartar to green bean and pesto (plus all the usual favorites), delivered on a steel monorail.

St. Christopher's Place (p. 159). Seconds from Oxford St., this pedestrian piazza lined with outdoor cafes is the perfect place for refreshment before hitting the shops.

Ye Olde Cheshire Cheese (p. 165). No mere "heritage inn," this is the real thing: opened in 1667 and barely changed since the days Samuel Johnson held court here.

Portobello Market (p. 234). The rest of Notting Hill may be descending into yuppie hell, but Portobello's market and myriad stores make it the perfect place to pick up a souvenir.

Cyberdog (p. 238). Clubbers need look no further for their clobber: Cyberdog's array of outlandish glo-wear will guarantee you attention on the dancefloor.

The Proms (p. 216). A 2-month classical music festival with a concert every night, it's the atmosphere of thousands standing in the Royal Albert Hall that makes the Proms so special.

The South Bank Centre (p. 214). These acres of gray concrete hide London's top cultural complex, from film and theater to classical, world, and jazz music.

Old Compton St. (p. 83). The heart of gay London, Old Compton St. is animated 24/7, with cafes and bars consistently full to bursting with gay and straight alike.

Fabric (p. 195). The ultimate London superclub. With the best dance DJs around and a soundsystem that could trigger a small earthquake, you'll dance till your ears fall off.

Notting Hill Arts Club (p. 196). At the other end of the scale, the NHAC puts on some of London's most laid-back club nights in an intimate underground space.

KIDS IN THE CITY

There's plenty in the capital to keep the littl'uns occupied. Of the major **sights,** a beefeater tour of the **Tower of London** (p. 73) is a must, as is posing with the Household Cavalry on **Horseguards Parade** (p. 106) and the bearskin-hatted Foot Guards outside **Buckingham Palace** (p. 68). Live animals are always a draw: **London Zoo** (p. 119) is a must, and don't neglect the Queen's horses in the **Royal Mews** (p. 107). While most major **museums** offer themed activity sheets to keep hands and eyes busy, some are naturally bigger hits than others. Robotic dinosaurs and an interactive human biology display make the **Natural History Museum** (p. 146) a firm favorite with children, while the hands-on galleries at the **Science Museum** (p. 147) are specifically tailored to different age groups. Budding engineers are sure to love the planes, tanks, and guns at the **Imperial War Museum** (p. 151) and the **Royal Airforce Museum** (p. 150), not to mention clambering all over the battleship HMS Belfast. Quiet kids might prefer the array of dolls and more sedate playthings at **Pollock's Toy Museum** (p. 149) and the **Museum of Childhood** (p. 153). If the weather's too nice to stay indoors, **Coram's Fields** is a park reserved solely for kids.

When it comes to **food,** don't despair—there is life beyond McDonalds. **Giraffe** (p. 177) is bright, fun, and has a kid-friendly menu, while **Tartuf's** pancake-like concotions are cutlery-free (p. 176). In Lincoln's Inn Fields the **Cafe in the Park** (p. 165) cooks up barbecues all summer long—in inclement weather, head instead to the **Arkansas Cafe** (p. 181). Of the major chains, **Pizza Express** (p. 158) is used to families, and chances are adults will like it too. Good little girls and boys deserve an ice cream from **Marine Ices** (p. 177) or a thick candy shake from **Tinseltown Diner** (p. 167). Note that pubs don't admit kids under 14 inside though they're normally allowed in outside beer gardens. For **entertainment,** try the street performers of **Covent Garden** (p. 84) or, around Christmas time, a traditional **pantomime.** Older kids will love the spectacle at **Shakespeare's Globe Theatre** (p. 215), even if they don't catch every word, while musicals such as the **Lion King** (p. 206) were made with kids in mind.

WALKING TOURS

Each of the following walking tours is designed to last a full day, with about 3-4 hours of sightseeing before lunch and 5-6 hours afterwards; of course, you can always just walk a portion of the tour if you're tired or pressed for time.

CITYSIDE CIRCULAR

Together, the historic districts of Clerkenwell, the City of London, and Holborn offer a fascinating insight into London past, with numerous institutions barely changed since the Middle Ages—along with some of London's trendiest bars and clubs. If it's a weekday, kick off with a hearty breakfast at the **Fox & Anchor** (p. 166), a unique pub whose early opening and meaty menu are both designed to satify the workers from nearby **Smithfield Market** (p. 93), London's main meat market. Take a quick peek at the **Charterhouse** (p. 93), just past the pub, before passing through the center of the market to reach **St. Bartholomew-the-Great** (p. 93), a 12th-century church where Benjamin Franklin once worked as a printer. Continue down Little Britain and turn left to come out into St. Martin's-le-Grand, where you'll find the excellent **Museum of London** (p. 143). Return south down St. Martin's and then turn left into Gresham St., which runs past the vast gothic **Guildhall** (p. 96), from where the Lord Mayor rules the city with a fur-trimmed fist. From here, it's a short jaunt past two of Christopher Wren's most distinctive churches: **St. Mary-le-Bow** (p. 95) and **St. Mary Aldermary** (p. 96), whose completely different styles are a testament to Wren's versatility. If you're feeling peckish by now, St. Mary-le-Bow's Norman crypt holds a good vegetarian cafe, **The Place Below** (p. 168)—it's also where the archbishop of Canterbury holds court. An even more ancient monument awaits just up Queen Victoria St., where the remains of the Roman **Temple of Mithras** (p. 96) have stood for almost 2000 years. Returning down Queen Vic St. and bearing right into Cannon St. will bring you to the City of London's most famous landmark: **St. Paul's Cathedral** (p. 71). If you've got the strength, be sure to climb the 530 steps up to the Golden Gallery for a fantastic view of London. From St. Paul's, walk down Ludgate Hill, which becomes **Fleet St.** (p. 90) after Ludgate Circus. Though the newspapers which made it famous have long since moved out, **St. Bride's Church** (p. 90) is a reminder of when this area was Britain's printing press. The church's unusual steeple may look familiar—it was the original model for the tiered wedding cake. Fleet Street's other association is with the law: nip through the gateway into Middle Temple Ln. to reach the heart of **The Temple** (p. 88), one of Holborn's Inns of Court. Shakespeare once performed in Middle Temple Hall, while Temple Church is the finest surviving medieval round church in Britain. Returning to Fleet St., why not take refreshment at **Ye Olde Cheshire Cheese** (p. 165), a 17th-century pub that was Samuel Johnson's local. Pay a visit to the good doctor's **House** (p. 90) on nearby Gough Sq. before heading north up New Fetter Ln. to reach **Ely Place** (p. 91), a short private road that by a constitutional quirk isn't in London at all, despite geography. Duck through the narrow passage of Ely Ct. (past Ye Olde Mitre pub, another of Holborn's historic drinking haunts) to reach **Hatton Garden,** the center of London's jewelry trade. From here, Greville St. leads back down toward Farringdon Tube station, at the heart of hip'n'trendy Clerkenwell. At the end of your day, consider taking dinner at the **Bleeding Heart Tavern** (p. 165) followed by some chilled-out cocktails at **Match** (p. 194).

THE MILLENNIUM MILE (AND THEN SOME)

One of the lasting successes of the recent millennial hoo-ha has been the re-invention of the South Bank into one of Europe's leading cultural quarters, linked by a riverside walk offering some of the best views in London. But historically Southwark is one of the oldest districts in London, and there's plenty of action away from the river too. Get into the mood by kicking off right in the middle of the river at **Tower Bridge** (p. 99). The views from the top aren't as good as you'd expect, but a tour of the engine rooms is fascinating. From here, take a gander along **Butler's Wharf,** whose bridge-linked warehouses (now bankers' luxury pads) are a reminder of when this was at the heart of the busiest stretch of river in the world. Another echo of the past is found upriver at **HMS Belfast** (p. 104), a WWII-era battleship that saw action on D-Day and in Korea. Kids will jump at the chance to aim the anti-aircraft guns on unperturbed seagulls. Moving inland, skip the terrifying queues at the unfathomably popular London Dungeon and duck though London Bridge station to the truer horrors on display at the **Old Operating Theatre** (p. 104). Next stop is **Southwark Cathedral** (p. 103), whose spanking new visitors center includes a tip-top exhibition on local history; the cathedral itself holds the mortal coil of Ed Shakespeare, Will's brother. Appropriately enough, a further five minutes' walk up the Thames will bring you to **Shakespeare's Globe Theatre** (p. 102), a faithful reproduction of the playhouse where the Bard premiered and performed in many of his plays. By now you must be starving; fortunately, **Tate Modern** (p. 137) has a great cafe with fantastic views of London. Oh, and there's the world's largest modern art museum downstairs, too. Or skip the Tate for now (but don't forget to go back later!) and drive on to **Gabriel's Wharf** (p. 102), a community development of stores, cafes, and restaurants that's bound to tickle the tastebuds of diners and shoppers alike. You're now at the **South Bank Centre** proper (p. 101): the **National Theatre, National Film Theatre, Festival Hall,** and **Hayward Gallery** lie just around the next bend in the river. Why not book tickets for an evening show, then take a lazy turn on the **London Eye** (p. 101), whose 135m wheel offer undisputably the best panoramas in London. When you're back on the ground, wander along **Westminster Bridge** for an equally impressive view of the Houses of Parliament: this is the sight that inspired Wordsworth and Monet.

WALKING WITH ROYALTY

London is littered with the vestiges of royal vanity—this tour alone will take you past four palaces (and London's got four more). There aren't many restaurants on the way, so bring a packed lunch. Start off under Nelson's watchful gaze in **Trafalgar Sq.** (p. 85) before marching down **Whitehall** (p. 106). Now home to various ministries, Whitehall's royal past is evident both in the flashing breastplates of the Queen's Household Cavalry at **Horseguard's,** and Inigo Jones' grand **Banqueting House,** now all that remains of Whitehall Palace, which burned down in 1698. Continuing down Whitehall, say hi to Tony as you pass **Downing Street** before you emerge into Parliament Sq. Here, the **Palace of Westminster**—also known as the Houses of Parliament (p. 70)—was begun by Edward the Confessor back in the 11th century. Edward is buried across the street (along with most of his successors) in **Westminster Abbey** (p. 77)—though MPs, wary of royalty, prefer to worship in **St. Margaret's** (p. 106) next-door. From Parliament Sq., Great George St. leads to **St. James's Park,** originally Henry VIII's private hunting ground; at the far end rises **Buckingham Palace** (p. 68), where the Royal Family has been content to reside since Victoria moved in in 1837. Even so, since 1531 the official seat of royal power has been **St. James's Palace** (now Charles's home; p. 82), just up the Mall from Buckingham. A hike past the palace up Marlborough Rd. will deposit you in **St. James's** (p. 82), London's poshest neighborhood. Pall Mall, home to exclusive gentlemen's clubs, leads from here to **Waterloo Place** (p. 82), where Wellington's statue is overshadowed by his royal boss Frederick, the "Grand Old" Duke of York. March your 10,000 men down the steps back to the Mall to appreciate **Carlton House Terrace.** Another monument to royal vanity, it's built on the site of George IV's Carlton House. Although Nash had just finished building Regent St. as Carlton House's main driveway, George decided that anywhere not called "palace" just wasn't good enough for a king, and moved out; Nash was called in again to redevelop the site as aristocratic townhouses. From here, it's a short trip up the Mall back to Trafalgar Square.

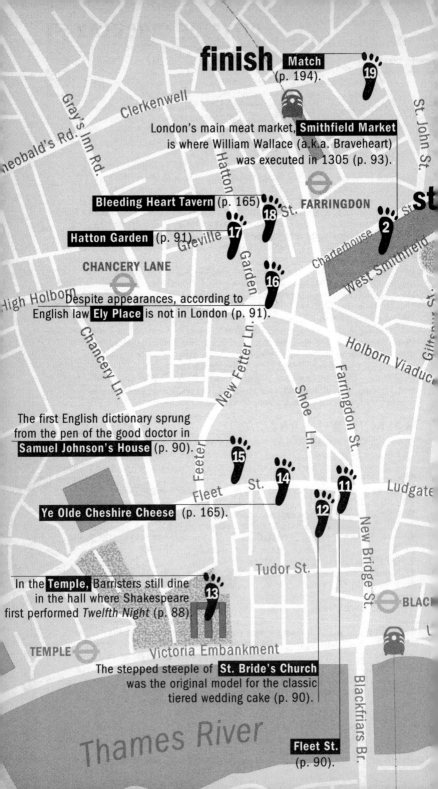

finish Match (p. 194).

19

London's main meat market, **Smithfield Market** is where William Wallace (a.k.a. Braveheart) was executed in 1305 (p. 93).

st

FARRINGDON

2

Bleeding Heart Tavern (p. 165)

18

17

Hatton Garden (p. 91)

CHANCERY LANE

16

Despite appearances, according to English law **Ely Place** is not in London (p. 91).

The first English dictionary sprung from the pen of the good doctor in **Samuel Johnson's House** (p. 90).

15

14

11

12

Ye Olde Cheshire Cheese (p. 165).

In the **Temple,** Barristers still dine in the hall where Shakespeare first performed *Twelfth Night* (p. 88).

13

TEMPLE

BLAC

The stepped steeple of **St. Bride's Church** was the original model for the classic tiered wedding cake (p. 90).

Fleet St. (p. 90).

Thames River

x & Anchor (p. 166).

3

Henry VIII nailed the hands of the **Charterhouse's** monks to the main gate when they resisted his attempt to dissolve the monastery (p. 93).

Chiswell St.

BARBICAN

Beech St.

Long Ln.

Aldergate St.

a Britain

4

Benjamin Franklin worked as a printer in the 12th-century church of **St. Bartholomew-the-Great** (p. 93).

Moorgate

MOORGATE

Moorgate

5

The fabulous **Museum of London** gives the lowdown on 200 years of the city's history (p. 143).

6

Ever since the 12th century, the City of London has been governed from the **Guildhall** (p. 96).

Gresham St.

King St.

ST. PAULS

10

Traditionally, cockneys must be born with the range of the bells of **St. Mary-le-Bow** (p. 168).

BANK

7

The Place Below

9

St.

The **Temple of Mithras** is dedicated to a Persian god popular among the Romans (p. 96).

8

Queen Victoria

MANSION HOUSE

Following the Great Fire of 1666, **St. Mary Aldermary's** parishioners persuaded Christopher Wren to rebuild their church in its old style (p. 96).

CANON ST.

Cannon St.

MONUMENT

ames St.

Wrens masterpiece, **St. Paul's Cathedral** narrowly escaped German bombs in World War WWII (p. 71).

Southwark Br.

London Br.

National Film Theatre

National Theatre

7

SOUTH BANK

Festival Hall

Hayward Gallery

8

Upper Ground

Stamford St.

Hatfields

Blackfriars Rd.

Southwark

In the shell of a former power station, **Tate Modern** is the world's largest modern art museum (p. 137).

SOUTHWARK

Mapham St.

WATERLOO

Cornwall Rd.

Created by a non-profit community developer, **Gabriel's Wharf** is a flower-strewn haven of crafts, boutiques, and pavement cafes (p. 102).

9

Jubilee Gardens

Belvedere Rd.

York Rd.

Waterloo Rd.

Lancaster St. Rd.

10

finish
LAMBETH

LAMBETH NORTH

Westminster

Borough Rd.

London Rd.

The concrete megalith of the **South Bank Centre** harbors one of Europe's premier cultural centres (p. 101).

Lambeth Palace Rd.

Lambeth Palace Gardens

Lambeth Rd.

Bridge Rd.

Geraldine Mary Hemsworth Park

St. George's Rd.

When it comes to views, nothing compares with a spin on the **London Eye** (p. 101).

Kennington Rd.

Brook Drive

Newington Butts

Finish off your day in a state of composure upon **Westminster Bridge** (p.101).

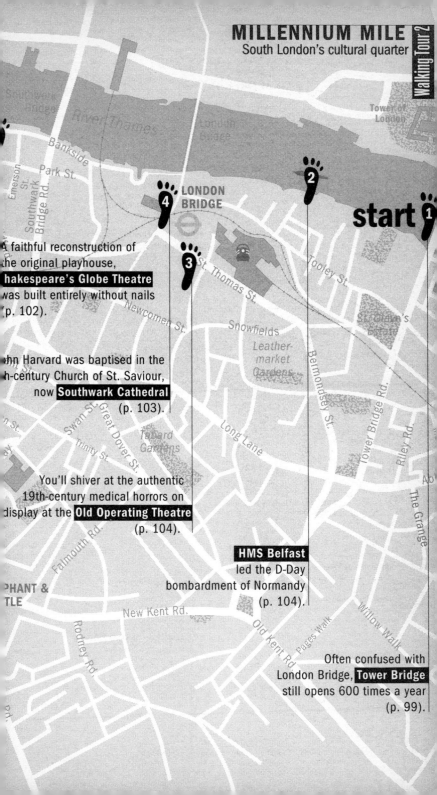

Tower of London

River Thames

Bankside

Park St.

Emerson

Southwark Bridge Rd.

LONDON BRIDGE

start 1

2

4

3

St. Thomas St.

Tooley St.

St. Olave's Estate

Newcomen St.

A faithful reconstruction of the original playhouse, **Shakespeare's Globe Theatre** was built entirely without nails (p. 102).

Snowfields

Leather-market Gardens

Bermondsey St.

John Harvard was baptised in the 13th-century Church of St. Saviour, now **Southwark Cathedral** (p. 103).

Swan St.

Great Dover St.

Trinity St.

Tabard Gardens

Long Lane

Tower Bridge Rd.

Riley Rd.

The Grange

You'll shiver at the authentic 19th-century medical horrors on display at the **Old Operating Theatre** (p. 104).

Falmouth Rd.

HMS Belfast led the D-Day bombardment of Normandy (p. 104).

PHANT & TLE

New Kent Rd.

Rodney Rd.

Old Kent Rd.

Pages Walk

Willow Walk

Often confused with London Bridge, **Tower Bridge** still opens 600 times a year (p. 99).

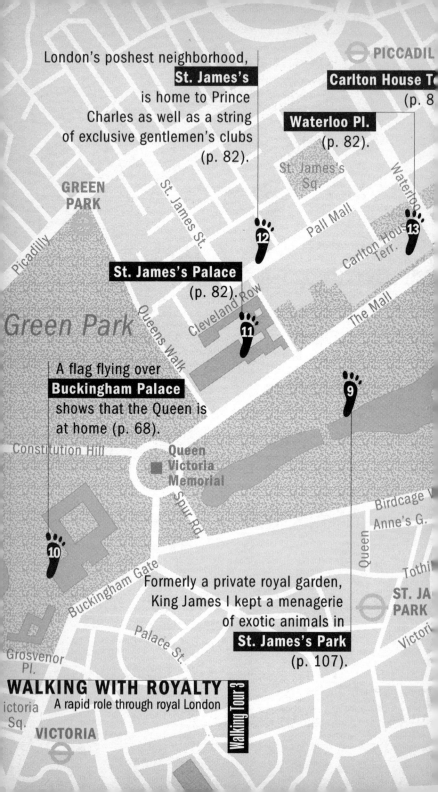

London's poshest neighborhood, **St. James's** is home to Prince Charles as well as a string of exclusive gentlemen's clubs (p. 82).

PICCADIL

Carlton House T (p. 8

Waterloo Pl. (p. 82).

GREEN PARK

St. James's Sq.

St. James St.

Pall Mall

Waterlo

St. James's Palace (p. 82).

Carlton House Terr.

The Mall

Green Park

Queens Walk

Cleveland Row

A flag flying over **Buckingham Palace** shows that the Queen is at home (p. 68).

Constitution Hill

Queen Victoria Memorial

Spur Rd.

Birdcage V

Anne's G.

Queen

ST. JA PARK

Tothi

Buckingham Gate

Formerly a private royal garden, King James I kept a menagerie of exotic animals in **St. James's Park** (p. 107).

Victori

Palace St.

Grosvenor Pl.

WALKING WITH ROYALTY

A rapid role through royal London

Walking Tour 3

ictoria Sq.

VICTORIA

start

London's largest square, pigeons outnumber tourists at **Trafalgar Square** (p. 85).

1

CHARING CROSS   **EMBANKMENT**

2

finish

Whitehall   *Whitehall Pl.*

Whitehall (p. 106).

3   Horse Guards' Ave.

Horseguard's (p. 106).

4

Charles I lost his head outside **Banqueting House** in 1649--literally (p. 106).

5 Downing St.   Richmond Terr.

Wave to Tony as you pass the Prime Minister's house at **10 Downing St.** (p. 106).

Horse Guard's Rd.

WESTMINSTER

St. George St.   Bridge St.   Westminster Br.

Storey's Gate

Big Ben

8

7

6

St. Margaret St.

The Palace of Westminster has been the seat of English government for almost 1,000 years (p. 70).

Great Smith St.

From poets to princes, you'll find them all at **Westminster Abbey** (p. 77).

Margaret's 106)

Great Peter St.

Marsham St.

Abingdon St.

Lambeth Palace Rd.

Once in London

Big and bewildering, London can be confusing to outsiders, not least because the reality is so different from what many expect. Even well-known quirks—driving on the left, ridiculously early pub-closing hours—can come as surprises to those not schooled by years of experience. But once you've mastered London's secrets, you'll find it a remarkably friendly and even—in its own crazy way—logical city.

ARRIVING AND DEPARTING

AIRPORTS

HEATHROW

⌖ Location: *Near Hounslow, west London.* **Contact:** ☎ *0870 000 0123; www.baa.co.uk/main/airports/heathrow/.*

Ugly, sprawling, crowded, and chaotic, Heathrow often feels more like a shopping mall with a runway than the world's busiest international airport. Airlines and destinations are divvied up among its four terminals as follows, although there are a few exceptions—if in doubt, check with the airline.

Terminal 1: domestic flights and British Airways' European destinations, except for flights to Amsterdam, Athens, Moscow, and Paris.
Terminal 2: all non-British Airways flights to Europe with the exception of KLM and Air Malta.
Terminal 3: intercontinental flights, except British Airways, Sri Lankan Airlines, and Qantas.

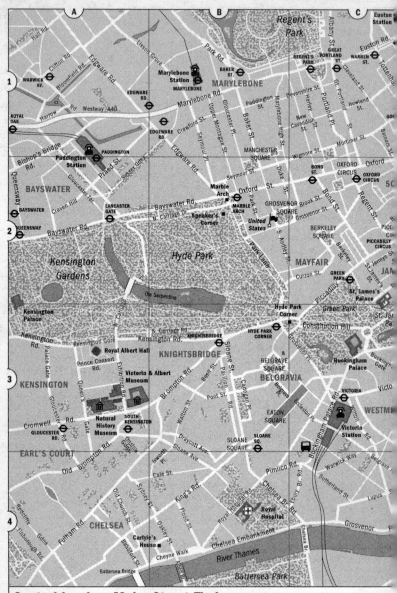

Central London: Major Street Finder

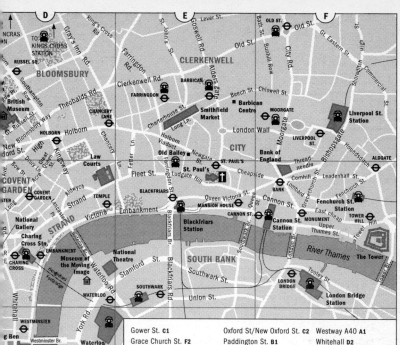

Terminal 4: British Airway's intercontinental flights and services to Amsterdam, Athens, Moscow, and Paris; Air Malta; KLM; Sri Lankan Airlines; Qantas; and any other flights that won't squeeze into terminals 1, 2, or 3.

GROUND TRANSPORTATION

UNDERGROUND. Heathrow's two Tube stations form a loop on the end of the Piccadilly Line: trains stop first at **Heathrow Terminal 4** and then at **Heathrow Terminals 1,2,3** before swinging back towards central London. Note that stairs are an integral part of most Tube stations. (*☎ 7222 1234; www.thetube.com. Zone 6. 40-60min. from central London, every 4-5 minutes. £3.50, under 16 £1.50.*)

TRAIN. The **Heathrow Express** provides a speedy and exhorbitant connection from Heathrow to Paddington Station. An added bonus is check-in facilities at Paddington. Ticket counters at Heathrow even accept foreign currency. (*☎ 0845 600 1515; www.heathrowexpress.co.uk. Wheelchair accessible. 15min., every 15min. daily 5:10am-11:40pm. Railpasses and Travelcards not valid. £12, return £22; £2 extra if bought on the train. Ask about day returns and group specials. Up to 4 kids under 15 free with adult.*)

BUS. The **Airbus A2** crawls from Heathrow to King's Cross, stopping off at various points on the way. (*☎ 0870 575 7777; www.gobycoach.com. 75-90min., every 30min. 4am-8pm. £7, return £10; ages 5-15 half price.*) **National Express** (which operates Airbus) also sends coaches to Victoria Coach Station. (*Contact and prices as above. 40-60min., approx. every 30min. 5:40am-9:30pm Heathrow-Victoria, 7:45am-11:30pm Victoria-Heathrow.*)

SHUTTLE. Hotelink runs shared shuttles from Heathrow to hotels in London. Book at least 48hr. ahead. (*☎ (01293) 552 251; fax 531 131; reservations@hotelink.co.uk; www.hotelink.co.uk. Operates 4am-6pm. £14, return £25.*)

TAXI. With metered fares to central London unlikely to be below $40, and journey times from 50min. to over 90min., you'd have to be rich *and* crazy to take a **licensed taxicab** from Heathrow to London by yourself. If possible, have a a contact in London (hotel and hostel owners will often oblige) book a **minicab** to meet you: expect to pay $25-30 including waiting, parking, and tip.

GATWICK

⚑ Location: *Sussex, 30mi. south of London.* **Contact:** *☎ 0870 000 2468; www.baa.co.uk/main/airports/gatwick.*

Though Gatwick is much further from London, numerous swift and affordable train services often make it quicker and easier to get to. Transport facilities are concentrated in the **South Terminal,** which is linked by a futuristic free monorail shuttle to the newer **North Terminal** (which has better shops and restaurants).

TRAIN. The wonder of rail privatization means that while three train companies run between Gatwick and London, they all charge different prices and tickets are non-transferable between services. The **Gatwick Express** non-stop service to Victoria station would like you to think it's the only train to London—in fact the cheaper **Connex** commuter trains run the same route just as frequently and take only 7min. longer. The main advantage of the Express is that BA and AA passengers can check-in at Victoria. (*Gatwick Express: ☎ 0870 0002 468; www.gatwickexpress.co.uk. 30-35min., every 15min. 5am-midnight and hourly through the night. £10.50, return £20; ages 5-16 half price. Connex: ☎ 0870 603 0405, www.connex.co.uk. 37-42min., every 15-20min. 5am-midnight and hourly through the night. £8.20, return £16.40; ages 5-16 half price.*) Additionally, **Thameslink** commuter trains head regularly to King's Cross, stopping in London Bridge and Blackfriars. Beware that Thameslink stations typically have lots of stairs. (*☎ 0845 7300 400; www.thameslink.co.uk. 50min., every 15-30min. 4am-midnight. £9.80; return £19.60.*)

BUSES, SHUTTLES, AND TAXIS. Gatwick's distance from London means that road services are both slow and unpredictable. The **Airbus A5** takes 90min. to travel to Victoria bus station. (*Contact details and prices as for Heathrow. Hourly 4:15am-9:15pm from Gatwick, 6am-11pm from Victoria.*) The **Hotelink** shuttle offers a pick-up service from Gatwick to London hotels. (*See Heathrow for details.Operates 5am-4pm daily. £20 per person, return £35.*) Taking a **licensed taxi** from Gatwick to London should only be considered if there is no alternative available: the trip will take over an hour, and cost at least £90. **Minicabs** are cheaper ($30-$40) but still leave you at the mercy of traffic. If you've got heavy bags, take the train to Victoria and catch a taxi from there.

STANSTED

⚐ *Location:* Essex, 30mi. north of London. *Contact:* ☎ 0870 000 0303; www.baa.co.uk/main/airports/stansted/.

Half-way between London and Cambridge, Stansted is one of those rare beasts—an airport of architectural merit. However, that doesn't stop it from getting hellishly crowded in high season.

TRAINS. The train station is below the terminal building. The **Stansted Express** offers frequent service to Liverpool St. (☎ 08457 44 44 22; *www.stanstedexpress.co.uk. 42min., every 15-30min. 6am-midnight from Stansted and 5am-11pm from Liverpool St. £13, return £20; ages 5-15 half price.*) **WAGN** runs a slower train along the same route for the same price. (*08457 48 49 50; www.wagn.co.uk. 60-70min., approx. every hour 7am-10:30pm.*)

BUS. The **Airbus A6/A7** runs every 30min. to Victoria station, 24/7. The A6 travels via the West End, the A7 via the City. (*Contact and prices as for Heathrow. 75-100min.*)

LUTON

⚐ *Location:* Bedfordshire, 32mi. north of London. *Contact:* (01582) 405 100; www.london-luton.com.)

The London airport that never quite made it big, Luton serves mostly charter flights and no-frills budget airlines. The **Thameslink** line that links Gatwick to King's Cross also continues north to Luton. (*Contact as for Gatwick. 30-50min.; every 15-30min. 3:21am-12:55am M-Sa, less frequently 6:12am-11:12pm Su. Single £9.50; return £18.*) **Green Line 757** buses link Luton to the West End and Victoria. (*☎ 0870 608 7261. www.greenline.co.uk. 60-105min., every 30min. 8am-8pm, hourly 8pm-midnight and 3am-8am. £8, return £13; ages 5-15 half price.*)

LONDON CITY AIRPORT

⚐ *Location:* Docklands, East London. *Contact:* ☎ (020) 7646 0088 for transport and other info.

London City Airport is built over the former Royal Docks, once the heart of London's trading empire. Today, the main export is pin-striped business men. Every 10min., a **shuttle** makes the 25min. run to Liverpool St. via Canary Wharf, while another route takes 5min. to get to Canning Town. (*Liverpool St./Canary Wharf: 6:50am-9:20pm M-F, 6:50am-1:10pm Sa, 11am-9:20pm Su; £3 to Canary Wharf, to Liverpool St. £6. Canning Town: 6am-10:30pm M-F, 6am-1pm Sa, 10am-10:20pm Su; £2.*) The **#69** bus also runs to Canning Town, while the **#474** stops at Silvertown rail station. (*Both approx. every 10min., 6am-midnight. 70p.*)

Double Decker

Black Cab

Frog Tour

31

TRAIN STATIONS

London's array of mainline stations (9 in all) dates from the Victorian era, when each railway company had its own London terminus. After being unified for most of the 20th century, the 1990s saw the railways broken up and privatized again. Corporate loyalty means that some station staff are unwilling to tell you about rival services. For impartial advice, call **National Rail Enquiries** (☎08457 48 49 50, 24hr.). All London termini are well-served by bus and tube services. If you'll be travelling by public transport when you get to London, you'll almost certainly save with a combined **rail and One Day Travelcard** combination.

BUS STATIONS

Victoria Coach Station (Tube: Victoria), Buckingham Palace Rd., is the hub of Britain's long-distance bus network. **National Express** is the largest operator of intercity services. (☎0990 808 080; www.gobycoach.com.) International services are dominated by **Eurolines,** which offers regular links to all major European cities. (☎0990 143 219; www.eurolines.com.) Much of the area around London is served by **Green Line** coaches, which leave from the Eccleston Bridge mall behind Victoria station. Purchase tickets from the driver. (☎0870 608 7261; www.greenline.co.uk.)

GETTING AROUND

Londoners love to complain, and they love nothing better than complaining about transportation—even the weather gets a better rap. Whether it's overcrowding on the Tube, congested streets, or pollution, nothing is more deeply ingrained in the London psyche than the idea that its transport infrastructure is falling to pieces. For all this, London's transport system remains one of the world's best: there's nary a spot in the city not served by frequent Tubes, buses, or trains. If occasionally you have to wait 20min. for a bus, or squeeze into an overcrowded Tube, that's just part of the fun—and an opportunity to appreciate the fact that, when it comes to politeness under pressure, Londoners are still world-beaters. Oddly enough, what shocks visitors to London the most about transportation seems least important to locals: the expense—count on spending at least £3 per day on travel.

WALKING

Too few visitors to London see any more of the city than the brief sprint from Tube station to sight and back—a pity, because London is a great walking city. One of the city's greatest charms—the fact that every neighborhood has its own distinctive look and feel—can only be appreciated by spending some time just walking around. Just steps from some of London's main thoroughfares there awaits another universe of Georgian terraces laid out around leafy squares, 17th-century churches, and quiet pubs. Elsewhere, the back streets are a hive of cutting-edge boutiques and late-night hangouts. Wherever you go, keep a lookout for the **blue plaques** that adorn the former residences of the great, the good, and the honorably obscure. Since London has shied away from every attempt to impose order on its street plan, a good map is essential to successful walking. Should you wish to venture into parts of the capital not covered by the maps in this book, your best friend will be the pocket-sized **London A-Z.** (Geographer's A-Z Map Company, £5.95.)

As in any big city, it's best to use caution when on foot. While London enjoys a remarkably low level of violent crime, theft is an increasing problem: be on the alert for pickpockets by day, and move in groups at night. Stick to busy, well-lit thoroughfares, especially in unfamiliar areas, and stay away from open spaces after dark. A far bigger menace to most foreigners than crime, though, is the fact that Britons drive on the left—remember to **look right when crossing the road** (except on certain one-way streets, of course). Also be warned that London drivers rarely stop for pedestrian except at marked crossings: jaywalking is an art best left to natives.

PUBLIC TRANSPORT

7 *Operated by Transport for London (www.transportfor-london.gov.uk). 24hr. info, including route advice,* ☎ *7222 1234. Current delays and route changes,* ☎ *7222 1200.*

Local gripes aside, London's public transport is remarkably efficient—and it's getting better. London's new Mayor, Ken Livingstone, is the man who first introduced Travelcards in the 1980s, and scarcely a week goes by without a new initiative to make travel in London easier and cheaper. New fares are generally introduced in January.

ZONES

The public-transport network is divided into a series of concentric zones; ticket prices depend on the zones passed through during your journey. To confuse matters, there's a different zoning system depending on the type of transport. The **Tube, rail,** and **DLR** network operates on a system of six zones, with Zone 1 being the most central. **Buses** reduce this to 4 zones, though Zones 1, 2, and 3 are the same as for the Tube. (Tube zones 4, 5, and 6 are rolled together into bus Zone 4.) Almost everything of interest to visitors is found in Zones 1 and 2.

TRAVEL PASSES

Unless you plan on walking or taking taxis around London, you're almost bound to save money by investing in one of London's range of travel passes. Passes work on the zone system (see above): note that any pass including Zone 4 will be valid throughout the entire bus Zone 4, but will only cover other journeys up to the validity of the last zone covered. (So a Zone 1-4 pass will cover all bus routes in London, but Tube services only up to the Tube zone 4 boundary.) Passes can be purchased at Tube, DLR, commuter rail stations, and newsagents. Beware **ticket touts** hawking second-hand One-Day Trav-

TRAVEL INFO

Transport for London operates a number of **Travel Information Centres** offering information, route maps for all Tube, bus, DLR, suburban railway, and riverboat service. Major TICs can be found at:

Euston Station (open M-Sa 7:15am-6pm, Su 8:30am-5pm.); **Greenwich,** Cutty Sark Gdns. (open daily 10am-5pm); **Heathrow: Terminal 1 arrivals** (open M-Sa 7:15am-10pm, 8:15am-10pm Su); **Terminal 2 arrivals** (open M-Sa 7:15am-5pm, Su 8:15am-5pm); **Terminals 1,2,3 Tube** (open M-Sa 6:30am-7pm, Su 7:15am-7pm), and **Terminal 4 arrivals** (open M-Sa 6am-3pm, Su 7:15am-3pm); **King's Cross Tube** (open M-Sa 8am-6pm, Su 8:30am-5pm); **Liverpool St. Tube** (open M-F 8a-6pm, Sa-Su 8:45am-5:30pm); **Oxford Circus Tube** (open M-Sa 8:45am-6pm, Su 10am-3pm); **Paddington Station** (open M-Sa 7:15am-8:30pm, Su 8:15am-8:30pm); **Piccadilly Circus Tube** (open daily 8:45am-6pm); **St. James's Park Tube** (open M-F 8:15am-5:15pm); **Victoria Station** (open M-Sa 7:45am-7pm, Su 8:45am-7pm); **Waterloo International** (open daily 8am-11pm).

elcards, LT Cards, and Bus Passes: you might save a few pounds, but there's no guarantee the ticket will work, and more importantly it's illegal—penalties are stiff.

Note that all **passes expire** at 4:30am the morning after the printed expiry date.

One Day Travelcards & LT Cards: Valid for bus, tube, DLR, and commuter rail services from 9:30am M-F, all day Sa-Su. Zones 1-2 £4, 1-4 £4.30, 1-6 £4.90; ages 5-15 Zones 1-6 £2. **LT Cards** differ only in being valid before 9:30am; only available M-F. Zones 1-2 £5.10, 1-4 £6.20, 1-6 £7.70; ages 5-15 £2.50/£3/£3.30.

Family Travelcards: For 1-2 adults and 1-4 children traveling together. Validity as for One Day Travelcards. Per person: Zones 1-2 £2.60, 1-4 £2.80, 1-6 £3.20, 2-6 £2.30; ages 5-15 80p.

Weekend Travelcards: Valid 2 consecutive days Sa, Su and public holidays. Zones 1-2 £6, 1-4 £6.40, 1-4 £6.40, 1-6 £7.30 2-6 £5.20; ages 5-15 Zones 1-6 £3.

Season Tickets: Weekly, monthly, and annual Travelcards can be bought at any time and are valid for 7 days, one month, or one year from the date of purchase. Matching **Photocard** required, free from Tube stations with an ID photo. Rates for Zone 1 only are £15.90 weekly, £61.10 monthly, and £636 annually; ages 5-15 £6.60 weekly, £25.40 monthly.

Bus Passes: Only if you won't be using the Tube. **One Day Bus Pass** £2 all Zones, ages 5-15 £1; **Weekly Bus Passes** £9.50 all Zones, ages 5-15 £4. Longer periods available.

Youth and Student passes: those aged 16-17 and full-time students at a London university can buy weekly, monthly, and annual passes at 30% off the adult rate. You must have a "16-17" or "Student" photocard (see below).

Ticket Extensions: If you travel beyond the validity of your pass, you must purchase an **excess fare** at the start of your journey—this will be just the fare from the last point included in your pass to your destination. Failure to do so counts as fare evasion.

TEENAGERS AND STUDENTS

To qualify for child fares, teenagers **aged 14-15** must display a **child-rate Photocard** when purchasing tickets and traveling on public transportation. These can be obtained free of charge from any Tube station on presentation of proof of age and a passport-sized photo. Teenagers **aged 16-17** and full-time **students** at London colleges are eligible for 30% discounts on period Travelcard and Bus passes: you'll need either a "16-17" Photocard (available at Tube stations) or a student Photocard, which must be obtained through the qualifying educational establishment.

SENIORS AND DISABLED TRAVELERS

FREEDOM PASS. London residents aged over 60 (for women) or 65 (for men), or who are registered as disabled, qualify for the free Freedom Pass, which offers unlimited travel on most services after 9am M-F and all day Sa-Su and holidays. A utility bill in your name or driver's licence made out to a London address usually suffices as evidence of residency. To obtain the pass, contact your local council.

DISABLED ACCESS. Traveling by public transport in London with a disability is no joke. The only fully wheelchair-accessible transportation system is the **Docklands Light Railway**. Only 40 of 275 Tube stations are step-free; accessible stations are marked on Tube maps with a wheelchair icon. The situation on **buses** is marginally better: wheelchair-friendly "kneeling buses" are being introduced on many routes, while most newer buses incorporate features to make them easier to use for the elderly and infirm. Those qualifying as London residents can take advantage of **Dial-a-Ride** and **Taxicard** schemes giving free or reduced-rate accessible shuttle-bus and taxi rides all over London: contact your local council for details. For **information** on accessibility on London transport, call ☎7941 4600.

THE UNDERGROUND

🚩 www.thetube.com. For 24hr. travel info, use the TfL information line (see p. 33). **Maps** of the Underground network are available at Tube stations and Transport for London info centers.

Universally known as "the Tube," the Underground provides a fast and convenient way of getting around the capital. Within Zone 1, the Tube is best suited to longer journeys: adjacent stations are so close together that you might as well walk, and buses are cheaper and often get you closer to your destination. If you'll be using the Tube a lot, you'll save money with a **Travelcard** (see p. 33).

NAVIGATING THE SYSTEM. Color coding makes navigating the 12 lines a breeze. **Platforms** are labeled by line name and general direction (north-, south-, east-, or westbound); if travelling on one of the any lines that splits into two or more branches, check platform indicators or the front of the train. Unless you want to be run down by a commuter in full stride, **stand on the right** on escalators.

HOURS OF OPERATION. The Tube runs approximately 6am-midnight daily, giving clubbers that extra incentive to party till dawn. The exact time of the first and last train from each station should be posted in the ticket hall: check if you think you'll be taking the Tube any time after 11:30pm. Trains run less frequently early mornings, late nights, and Sunday.

TICKETS. You can buy tickets from ticket counters or ticket machines in all stations. Each station displays a chart showing how much a ticket costs to any other station in the network. Tickets must be bought at the start of your journey and are valid only for the day of purchase (including return tickets, but excluding carnets).

Keep your ticket for the entire journey; it will be checked on the way out and may be controlled at any time. There's a £10 **on-the-spot fine** for traveling without a valid ticket.

BUSES

⏹ *www.transportforlondon.gov.uk/buses/. For 24hr. travel info, use the TfL information line (see p. 33). Ticket prices are given in the sidebar "Fares Please." Bus maps are available at most Tube stations and at TfL information centers.*

Only tourists use the Tube for short trips in central London—chances are you'll spend half as long walking underground as it would take to get to your destination. If it's only a couple of Tube stops, or if it involves more than one change, chances are a bus that will get you there faster. Excellent signage makes the bus system easy to use even for those with no local knowledge; most stops display a map of local routes and nearby stops, together with a key to help you find the bus and stop you need faster than you can say "mind the gap." Most stops also have their name posted; if you're not sure where to get off, ask the driver or conductor to tell you.

Buses run approx. 5:30am-midnight; a reduced network of **Night Buses** (see below) fills in the gap. Double-deckers generally run every 10-15min., while single-decker hoppers should come every 5-8min. These are very much averages, though—it's not uncommon to wait 30min. only for three buses to show up in a row.

BUS STOPS. Officially bus stops come in two varieties, regular and request: supposedly buses must stop at regular stops (red logo on white background), but only pull up at request stops (white on red) if someone rings the bell, or someone at the bus stop indicates to the driver with an outstretched arm. In reality, it's safest to ring/indicate at all stops. On the older open-platform "Routemaster" buses, you're free to hop on and off whenever you like, but the risk is yours. **Never try to board or alight from a moving bus.**

BUS TICKETS. On newer buses, show your pass or buy a ticket from the driver as you board: state your destination or just say the price. Older buses still use conductors, who make the rounds between stops to collect fares—they have android-like memories for remembering who's already paid. Despite the "Exact change" warnings posted on buses, drivers and conductors give change, though a £5 note will elicit grumbles and anything larger risks refusal. Keep your ticket until you get off the bus, or you face a £5 **on-the-spot fine.** For **Prices,** see the *Fares Please!* sidebar.

NIGHT BUSES. When honest folk are in bed, London's army of Night Buses comes out to ferry party-goers home. Night Bus route numbers are prefixed with an "N";

FARES PLEASE!

TUBE AND DLR FARES

Ticket prices on the London Underground depend on two factors: how many zones traveled (p. 33), and whether you traveled through Zone 1 or not.

For journeys **including Zone 1,** prices are as follows (ages 5-15 given in parentheses):

Zone 1 only: £1.50 (60p)
1-2: £1.90 (80p)
1-3: £2.20 (£1)
1-4: £2.70 (£1.20)
1-5: £3.30 (£1.40)
1-6: £3.60 (£1.50)

The **Carnet** offers 10 tickets for travel in Zone 1 for £11.50. Unlike other Tube tickets, Carnet tickets are valid for a year, not just on the day of purchase.

Outside Zone 1, prices are:

any 1 zone: 90p (40p)
2 zones: £1.20 (60p)
3 zones: £1.70 (80p)
4 zones: £2.10 (£1)
5 zones: £2.30 (£1.10)

BUS FARES

Trips **including zone 1** costs £1; journeys wholly **outside zone 1** cost 70p. Before 10pm, ages 5-15 pay 40p regardless of zones traveled; after 10pm they pay the adult fare.

NIGHT-BUS FARES

Night buses cost £1.50 for journeys **including Zone 1,** and £1 **outside Zone 1.** Note that One Day and Family Travelcards, LT cards, and Bus Passes are valid only for journeys starting before 4:30am of the following day.

All the above ticket prices are valid until at least January 2002.

they typically operate the same route as their daytime equivalents, but occasionally start and finish at different points. Many routes start from Trafalgar Sq. (except on New Year's Eve, since that's where all the celebration happens.) Most Night Buses operate every 30min. or every hour midnight-5:30am, when they miraculously revert to pumpkins.

DOCKLANDS LIGHT RAILWAY

🛈 *Customer service* ☎ *7363 9700 (open 9am-5pm M-F). Docklands travel hotline* ☎ *7918 4000 (24hr.). WAP phone users can find out next train times from all stations at http://dlr.kizoom.co.uk.*

The toylike driverless cabs of this elevated railway have provide a vital link in the transport network of East London. Obvious physical differences aside, the network is basically an extension of the Tube, with the same tickets and pricing structure: within the validity of a given ticket, you can transfer from Tube to DLR at no charge. Those combining Greenwich and Docklands in one day should enquire about **Rail and Sail** tickets (see p. 128). The DLR operates M-F 5:30am-12:30am, Sa and holidays 6am-12:30am, and Su 7:30am-11:30pm.

SUBURBAN RAILWAYS

🛈 *Schedule and fare information* ☎ *08457 48 49 50 (24hr.) and at www.railtrack.co.uk.*

Almost non-existent in the city center, in the suburbs London's commuter rail network is almost as extensive as the Tube—and in much of South and East London is the only option. Services are run by a range of companies: **Thameslink** heads north-south from the Clerkenwell and the City; **Silverlink** runs east-west from Docklands to Richmond via Islington and Hampstead; and **WAGN** trains run from Liverpool St. to Hackney to name but a few. Trains can dramatically cut journey times thanks to direct cross-town links—Silverlink takes 25min. from Hampstead to Kew, a journey that would take an hour by Tube. Trains run less frequently than the Tube—generally every 20-30min.—but service often continues later into the night.

For journeys combining rail travel with Tube and DLR, you can buy a single ticket valid for the entire trip. Travelcards are also valid on most suburban rail services, though not on intercity lines that happen to make a few local stops.

COMMUTER BOATS

🛈 *www.transportforlondon.gov.uk/river/. For 24hr. travel info, use the TfL information line (see p. 33). **Maps** available at piers and TfL Travel Information Centres.*

London's most important transport artery for most of its history, for the last century the Thames has been little used except for pleasure cruises. Nevertheless, a small and growing number of regularly scheduled commuter boats are once more plying the river. Currently three routes are in operation, though only during rush hour: Chelsea Harbour to Embankment via Cadogan (near Tate Britain), operated by **Riverside Launches** *(☎ 7352 5888; 4 boats every morning and 3 every afternoon M-F; £4, return £8; reservations required)*; Cadogan to Blackfriars via Westminster, operated by **Thames Speed Ferry** *(☎ 7731 7671; temporarily suspended at time of press)*; and Savoy Pier (near Waterloo Bridge) to Greenlands (near Greenwich) via Blackfriars, London Bridge, St. Katharine's Docks, and Canary Wharf, by **Collins River Services** *(☎ 7237 9538; 6 boats each morning and afternoon M-F; £1.50-£2.70, ages 5-15 half price; reservations required).*

OTHER FORMS OF TRANSPORT

LICENSED TAXICABS

🛈 **Charges:** *First 405m/87s £1.40, then 20p per 202.5m/43.5s until fare reaches £10.60, then 20p per 135m/29s; 40p per additional passenger, 10p per item of luggage; M-F 8pm-midnight and Sa 6am-8pm 60p surcharge, 8pm Sa to 6am M and holidays 90p.* **Pick-up:** *£1.20 extra. See p. 317 for numbers.* **Lost Property:** *15 Penton St., N1. (☎ 7833 0996). Tube: Angel. Open M-F 9am-4pm.*

As symbolic of London as gondolas are of Venice, "black cabs" are almost as expensive. That's because driving a London taxi is skilled work: your driver has studied for years to pass a rigorous exam called "The Knowledge" to prove he knows the name of every street in central London and how to get there by the shortest possible route. And when considering the expense, remember that all is relative—four people in a cab can save money on the Tube fare over shorter distances.

All three varieties of official black cabs are specially designed for London's narrow streets and can turn on a sixpence—don't be afraid to hail one on the other side of the road. Available cabs are indicated by the blue "for hire" light by the driver and the orange "taxi" sign on the roof; frantic waving and a loud cry of "TAXI!" should do the trick. Taxis are obliged to take passengers anywhere in central London, even just one block, but longer journeys (excluding Heathrow airport) are at their discretion—it's best to negotiate a fare in advance if you're going outside the city. In any case, a **10% tip** is expected. It's possible to order a licensed cab by phone (see Service Directory, p. 317, for numbers), but most people book cheaper minicabs (see below).

North Greenwich Station

MINICABS

▼ For listings of minicab services, see p. 315.

Anyone with a car and a driving license can set themselves up as a "minicab" company: while only licensed cabs can ply the streets for hire, there are no regulations concerning pre-arranged pickups. As a result, competition is fierce and prices are lower than licensed cabs— but unless you know a reliable company, ordering a minicab is something of a crapshoot, though there's rarely any danger involved (not counting the often hair-raising driving skills of many drivers). However, be especially careful with the dodgy drivers that turn up outside **nightclubs** at closing time— note down a number before you go out and call from the club, or arrange to be picked-up in advance. Always agree on a price with the driver in advance; some firms now have a standardized price lists.

Charing Cross

BIKES AND SCOOTERS

▼ For a listing of bicycle and scooter rental shops in London, see the **Service Directory**, p. 311.

Biking in London is not for the faint of heart. A strong motorists' lobby fights against any proposal to give an inch of the crowded streets over to dedicated cycle lanes, while bus drivers take special glee in scaring the living daylights out of bikers who seek refuge in bus lanes. The cyclist cause isn't helped by the fact that the majority of central-London riders are professional couriers bent hell-for-leather on getting to their next pick-up as soon as possible without regard for pedestrians or traffic regulations. When riding, always wear a helmet; you'll probably want a face mask, too.

St. Pancras Station

37

inside
SECRETS TO...

The Royal Mail

1. The Royal Mail was founded in 1516 as **Henry VIII's** private courier service. No doubt he negotiated special bulk rates for wedding invitations.

2. Instead of the country name, British stamps show a profile of the current monarch. This practice dates from the world's first stamp, the **Penny Black** (1840), which bore a silhouette of Queen Victoria.

3. The world's first scheduled **airmail** service was inaugurated in 1911, dramatically speeding the delivery of mail between Hendon and Windsor—a grand distance of 30mi.

4. The Post Office has its own 6mi. underground railway, the **Mail Rail,** which delivers mail from Paddington and Liverpool St. train stations to numerous sorting offices.

5. The initials in the name of the world's most famous ship, the **RMS Titanic,** stand for "Royal Mail Ship." Nine million letters went down with the ship, as did five clerks employed to guard mail at all costs. They were last sighted working in the flooded mail room, desperately trying to save 200 sacks of registered letters.

6. Today, the Royal Mail handles over **77 million** letters and parcels a day, including 3 million international items.

Aside from a brief period in the 1960s, **motor scooters** have never been as fashionable in London as they are in Europe—maybe it's the weather. Undeniably fun and fast, they're also dangerous and unstable, especially in the wet. Expect no mercy from London drivers, either. A driving license is sufficient to drive a 50cc moped; for 100cc you need to have taken Compulsory Basic Training (a government-approved course in handling 2-wheelers); over 500cc you need a special motorcycle licence.

London Cycling Campaign, 30 Great Guildford St. #228 (☎7928 7220, fax 7928 2318; www.lcc.org.uk) ceaselessly works to improve the cyclists' lot in London. They also sell a series of maps detailing cycle routes in London and organize group rides. Open M-F 2-5pm.

London Bicycle Tour Company, Gabriel's Wharf (☎7928 6838; www.londonbicycle.com). Tube: Blackfriars or Waterloo. Organizes regular bike tours of the city. Also rents bikes and roller skates (see p. 68). Open daily 10am-6pm Apr.-Oct.; call ahead Nov.-Mar.

DRIVING

🖅 *For listings of car-rental firms in London, see* **Service Directory,** *p. 312.*

You'd be crazy to drive in central London—unless you have a secret parking spot, leave it to professionals. Various thoroughfares are off-limits to private vehicles during the week, on-street parking is almost non-existent, and off-street parking hideously expensive. Not to mention labyrinthine one-way streets and psychotic van drivers. On the other hand, cars can be invaluable in the outer suburbs and for daytrips—you can be in rolling fields in an hour or less.

The driving age in the UK is 17, though almost no one will rent out cars to those under 23. It may well work out cheapest to organize car rental before you leave from one of the major international companies, most of which offer online booking.

PARKING. Street parking in London is allowed wherever it's not explicitly forbidden or controlled via a set of simple visual cues. If the kerb is free of any written exhortation or colored demarcation, parking is permitted providing that it does not cause an obstruction; stay away from **street corners, bus stops,** and **pedestrian crossings.** It's also illegal to park with any wheels on the pavement (sidewalk). Elsewhere, look out for lines painted on the road parallel to the kerb. A **zig-zag white line** indicates the approach to a pedestrian crossing where parking is forbidden. A **single yellow line** indicates that parking is forbidden during certain hours, usually M-F 8am to 6 or 7pm. **Double yellow lines** indicate that parking is always forbidden. **Red lines** function in the same way, except that penalties are stiffer. **Yellow stripes** painted on the kerb itself control **loading** and **unloading;** single and double stripes control permissible loading hours, while triple stripes forbid loading completely. Simpler to understand are areas marked **resident parking** and **disabled parking;** if you're not in possession of the relevant permit, steer clear. **Parking meters** are a common site in central London, with prices and maximum stays depending on the area; in general, meters are in operation M-Sa 8am-6pm. If the meter is broken, don't park there.

If you fall foul of parking restrictions, a number of things can happen. If you're lucky, all you'll get is a **parking ticket** and a hefty fine. Less fortunately, you could be **clamped;** don't try and tamper with the large metal clamp on your wheel—even if you break free, the authorities will track you down. Worst of all, your car may have disappeared completely—it's probably been **towed,** typically to a distant lot from where it will take you hours and copious amounts of money to release it. Since the only sign that a car's been towed is its conspicuous absence, you'll need to call the local council yourself to check they have it and where it's being held.

KEEPING IN TOUCH

POSTAL SERVICES

⚐ Royal Mail ☎ 08457 740 740; www.royalmail.co.uk. See the leaflet **All you need to know,** available at Post Offices, for details of all domestic and international rates.

The Royal Mail's official monopoly on stamped mail ran out in April 2001, but no-one's expecting it to be knocked off its perch soon—indeed, would-be competitors are nowhere to be found. That's unsurprising when you consider that Britain's post is perhaps the best in the world: you can mail a letter at 5pm secure in the knowledge that it will arrive by 10am the next day almost anywhere in the UK.

RECEIVING MAIL IN LONDON

London enjoys two morning deliveries per day M-F, and one Sa. To ensure speedy delivery, make sure mail bears the full **post code,** consisting of the 2-5 initial characters of the postal district (e.g. W1 in the West End, and WC2 for Holborn), followed by a space and then a number and two more letters that define the street.

POSTE RESTANTE. If you don't have a mailing address in London, you can still receive mail via Poste Restante (the international term for General Delivery). Up to 5 items will be held free of charge at most larger London post offices. To find the address of a participating post office, call the Post Office counter service at ☎ 08457 22 33 44. Mail to Poste Restante should be addressed as follows:

POSTE RESTANTE,
[Post office name],
[Post office street address],
LONDON [Post office postcode],
UNITED KINGDOM
Hold for: [Your name].

FORWARDING MAIL. Call the Royal Mail helpline (see above) for them to send you a redirection form to have mail automatically forwarded, or ask at a post office. The Royal Mail will not forward mail from hotels, hostels, or colleges. (Domestic redirection £6.30 for 1 month, £31.50 per yr.; international £10.60, £60.) A riskier but free method for forwarding mail within the UK is to ask someone at your old address to scribble your new address over the old one on any letters that arrive, and pop them back in the post; if the letter is unopened, no extra postage is required. However this is not guaranteed to work, as the letter may be returned to sender.

SENDING MAIL WITHIN THE UK

Collection times are posted on each postbox; the last weekday collection from most boxes is at around 3-4pm, with late collections in some post offices at 7-8pm. **First Class** mail is delivered the next day (except Su), while **Second Class** takes up to three days. For letters under 60g (2oz), you can insure yourself against rises in postage rates by buying "non-value indicator" stamps, which display only "1st" or "2nd" (class) rather than the purchase price. Current postage rates are valid to April 2002. *(1st class 27p up to 60g, 2nd class 19p. 750g weight limit on all 2nd class mail.)*

SENDING MAIL ABROAD

The Royal Mail divides the outside world into three price bands: Europe, World Zone 1, and World Zone 2. World Zone 2 basically covers the Pacific Rim, including Australia and New Zealand, while World Zone 1 is everything else beyond Europe. **Customs labels** are required for packets and parcels being sent outside the EU.

Airmail letters should get to their destination country within 2 days for Western Europe, 3 for Eastern Europe, and 4 for everywhere else; obviously, the ultimate delivery time is dependent on the receiving mail system. All airmail should bear an "airmail" sticker (available at post offices) or have "PAR AVION—AIR MAIL" clearly marked in the upper-left-hand corner. **Rates:** to Europe up to 20g 36p, 20-40g 50p; to World Zones 1/2 40p for postcards, up to 10g 45p, 10g-20g 65p.

Prepaid airmail packs: The Post Office sells numerous ready-to-post aerogrammes, envelopes, and parcels valid for delivery anywhere in the world. **Aircards** (£1.30) are basically just postcards-with-postage; **Airletters** (40p) are fold-up aerogrammes, suitable for short letters; **Airpacks** (from £5.99 for 500g) are small packets for sending gifts; and **Swiftpacks** (£5.99 for up to 300g) offer an expedited service. All are available at larger post offices.

Surface mail is best for parcels: it's not available for letters within Europe, nor is it much cheaper than airmail for letters to the rest of the world. Delivery times are 2 weeks to Western Europe, 4 to Eastern Europe, and 8 elsewhere. **Letters** to World Zone 1/2: up to 20g 36p, 20-60g 58p. **Small Packet** and **Printed Matter** to anywhere in the world: up to 100g 57p, rising in stages to £1.90 for 450g (about 1lb.)

TELEPHONES

Over 50% of Britons own a mobile phone (cellphone)—and in London the proportion is higher. One result of this, aside from a cacophony of rings, is that public payphones are becoming increasingly scarce—luckily, at the same time an explosion of low-cost calling cards is making calling abroad ever cheaper.

LONDON PHONE NUMBERS

London's phone code is 020; within this area all numbers are 8 digits long. Note that all telephone numbers given in this book are in area code 020 unless otherwise specified. For other common codes and useful numbers, see the "Phone facts" sidebar.

Since London's phone codes have changed four times in the last 15 years, you'll probably encounter some out-of-date numbers while in London. Here's the lowdown on how to convert from the old numbers to the new ones: Starting in the late 1980s, London had two phone codes, **071** and **081**; in the 90s this was changed (oh! progress!) to **0181** and **0171**. To convert these old 7-digit numbers to the new 8-digit number, just prefix 7 (if it was an 0171 number) or 8 (for 0181) to the start of the old number. Prior to 071/081, London's phone code was simply **01**. The rule-of-thumb for converting these is that if the number was in Travelcard Zone 1, use a "7;" if its in zone 3 or higher, use an "8;" and if it's in zone 2, try both. Still confused? Try the online number converter at **www.numberchange.org.**

CALLING WITHIN THE UK

To make a local call, simply dial the number without the area code. For a long-distance call, you must first dial the 3- to 5-digit area code, including the initial zero. (In foreign publications and some websites, the zero is sometimes omitted when the number is quoted with the UK country code: e.g. a London number may be given as starting +44 20 rather than 020.)

Call rates vary depending on the distance called, the time of day, and the telephone company used. Typically rates are highest M-F from 8 or 9am until 6 or 7pm, somewhat lower on weekday evenings, and lowest on weekends.

BT PAYPHONES. The majority of payphones are operated by BT (formerly British Telecom), recognizable by the red-and-blue piper logo. While newer phones typically accept phonecards, coins, and credit cards, many older payphones only accept **BT phonecards** and their bastard offspring, the **Phonecard Plus**. This is essentially a combination BT phonecard and calling card—you can either stick it in a payphone, or call the access number from any land phone. They're tricky, though—payphone calls cost more than calling-card ones. *(Phonecards and Phonecard Plus available from most newsagents and kiosks. Cards available in £3-£20 denominations.)*

If you're paying by **cash,** the minimum deposit is 20p. The **dial tone** is a continuous purring sound; a repeated double-purr means the line is **ringing.** For the rest of the call, the display ticks off in 1p increments; a series of harsh beeps will warn you to insert more money when your time is up. Once you hang up, your remaining phonecard credit is rounded down to the nearest 10p, or unused coins are returned. Payphones do *not* give change—if you use 22p from a 50p coin, the remaining 28p is gone once you put the receiver down. If you want to make another call, transfer remaining credit by pushing the "follow-on call" button—hang up and you'll lose the money. Note that **freephone** (0800 and 0808) and **emergency** calls (999) can be made free from any phone without needing to insert a card or coins.

OTHER PAYPHONES. In addition to BT, a range of other companies operate payphones in central London. To use these, you'll either need the company's special phonecard, or you can often use cash or a credit card. More common are private payphones, often installed in hostels and pubs. Since the owner can set his own rates on these money-gobbling devices, you'll probably save money by heading outside.

CALLING ABROAD

To call abroad from a UK phone, dial the **international access code** (00), the **country code,** the **area code** less any leading zero, and finally the **local number.** Thus to call the Dublin number (01) 234 5678, dial 00-353-1-2345678, where 353 is the Ireland country code. A number of country codes are given in the Essentials bar, *"Phone Facts."*

When calling abroad, remember that most international calls are cheaper M-F 6pm-8am and Sa-Su; calls to Australia and New Zealand are cheaper 2:30-7:30pm and midnight-7am.

i **ESSENTIAL** INFORMATION

PHONE FACTS

USEFUL NUMBERS
All 24hr.

Directory Enquiries: 152 (UK), 192 (international). Both free from payphones, 50p from a land line.

Operator: ☎100. Free.

Reverse-charge (collect) call: 155. Expensive (but not for you).

Talking Pages: 0800 600 900. Say what you need and where, and they'll find it. Free.

COUNTRY CODES
For an international line, dial 00 plus:

Australia 61;
Canada 1;
France 33;
Ireland 353;
Italy 39;
New Zealand 64;
South Africa 27;
USA 1.

Drop the leading zero from the local area code, if applicable.

OTHER UK CODES
Aside from 020, there are a few other UK phone codes you should watch out for:

0800 and 0808 numbers are free.

0845 numbers are charged at the local rate.

0870 numbers are charged at the national (long-distance) rate.

Numbers starting with **09** are premium rate, charging £1-£1.50 per min. or more.

Numbers starting with **07** are mobile phones, costing around 30p per minute to call from a land line (more from a payphone).

PAYPHONES AND REVERSE-CHARGE (COLLECT) CALLS. Payphones are an expensive way to phone abroad—the only thing ticking faster than the money indicator will be your heart as you realize how much it costs. Still, that's nothing compared to the coronary implications of a **reverse-charge** international call—save them for people you really don't like. *(Reverse-charge operator ☎ 155.)*

THE SUNNY SIDE

The Sun is the undisputed master of the visual sound-bite, with a single headline frequently occupying almost the entire page. After the Conservative's shock election victory in 1992, the tabloid declared *"It's the Sun wot won it"* (sic); following Tony Blair's 1997 triumph for Labour, the tagline became *"It's the Sun wot swung it."* Other unforgettable *Sun* headlines include *"Up Yours Delors,"* a xenophobic outburst directed at the then-President of the European Commission, Jacques Delors; and the jingoistic *"Gotcha!,"* following the sinking of the Argentinian troop carrier *General Belgrano* during the 1981 Falklands War.

Scarcely less infamous, or important to *The Sun's* runaway success with the English working man, is its daily *page 3* "feature" of a scantily clad and unnaturally well-endowed woman, normally to a groan-inducing headline of the "fertile Fay tells us about her meaty melons" variety. And this in a newspaper that fumes with indignation at the first hint of impropriety in the government.

PREPAID CALLING CARDS. Probably the cheapest way to call long-distance, an endless variety of oddly named prepaid calling cards are sold in most newsagents and post offices. Whether you go for the Banana card, the Giraffe, or the Girl From Ipanema (just kidding), be sure to check **rates** and **connection charges** before you buy. If you're planning to make one long call, it's best to go for the card with the cheapest rate; for lots of short calls, look for a low connection charge. The 🛢**Hippo card** offers low rates and has no connection charge. *(Available in £5 and £10 denominations.)*

BILLED CALLING CARDS. Convenient, especially if someone else is paying the bill, these calling cards must be set up in your home country before you leave: contact your telephone provider. In the USA, AT&T, Sprint, and MCI all offer their own versions. When in the UK, simply dial the free access number and your account code: you'll then either be able to make a direct-dial call home, or reach an operator who'll make the connection for you. Once a month, the calls will be totted up and a bill sent home—make sure someone's around to pay it! The disadvantage of these cards is that rates are not always low, and they're only good for calling their home country—you can make calls to other countries, but you'll be charged the rate for calling home *plus* the rate from home to other country.

EMAIL AND THE INTERNET

Even though more people are getting connected at home and on the move, the number of cyber-cafes is burgeoning—scarcely a major street in London is without a dedicated internet shop, or at least a regular cafe with a couple of terminals. *Let's Go* lists when internet facilities are available in accommodations, while cybercafes are listed in the Service Directory (see p. 315). One innovation is the BT **Multi.phone**, a souped-up payphone that also offers internet and email access via a touch screen. Multi.phones are being installed in Tube stations and other indoor locations across London, including a number of hotels, hostels, and museums.

PRINT MEDIA

NEWSPAPERS

Although circulation has been dropping in the UK for the last 40 years, newspapers still wield enough power to make and break governments. Best-selling *The Sun* (see *the sunny side* sidebar) claims that its surprise switch from Conservative to Labour handed Tony Blair the 1997 election, there's an element of truth to its claim:

Labour had seemed set for victory in 1992 until the right-wing press turned the tide. But *The Sun* is merely the most popular—and most sensational—of the mass-market **tabloids** that dominate the British newspaper market. The left-leaning *Daily Mirror* tries to even the political stakes, while the *Daily Express*, and the unbelievably unbelievable *News of the World* merely follow in *The Sun's* footsteps. The *Daily Mail* tries and fails to bridge the intellectual gap between the tabloids and the serious, unmanageably large pages of the **broadsheets.** *The Times*, has gone downmarket under the ownership of Rupert Murdoch (who also owns *The Sun*); arch-rival *The Daily Telegraph* retains a more aloof tone. Both are unmistakably right-wing, as is the *Financial Times*, despite being printed on pink paper. Leaning to the left are the *Independent* and the *Guardian*, which includes a daily magazine-style pullout. Most daily papers share their name with an overgrown **Sunday** double; *The Guardian* is the exception: its Sunday equivalent is *The Observer*. These Sunday papers are editorially independent from their sister dailies but share a similar outlook.

Long London's only **local daily,** the tabloid-format but marginally more intelligent *Evening Standard* is published in several editions throughout the day—despite its name, it's available in the morning. The *Standard* was joined in 1999 by its offspring *Metro*, available free in Tube stations M-F (though they're usually all gone by 9am).

MAGAZINES

As you'd expect from a nation of hobbyists, the British are magazine crazy—there's scarcely a subject under the sun (or *The Sun*) that doesn't have its own weekly or monthly publication. **News** magazines are generally published weekly and provide a more in-depth examination of issues than the papers—with a strong political slant. *The Economist* is the most respected and apolitical of the bunch; political hacks get their kicks from the New Labour *New Statesman* and the Tory *Spectator*. For a less reverential approach, *Private Eye* walks a fine line between hilarity and libel.

Lifestyle magazines are the biggest sellers—their advice on living life to the full generally focuses on sex and alcohol. The UK editions of women's mags such as *Cosmopolitan* and *Hello* tend to be more gung-ho than their US counterparts, while men's equivalents *FHM* and *Loaded* leave little to the imagination. Pure **style** magazines range from the ad-laden pages of British *Vogue* to the object-oriented Starck recommendations of *i-D* and *Wallpaper*.

For information on events in London, **music** mags such as *Melody Maker* and that arbiter of cool, *New Musical Express* (or NME) carry details of gigs, and **clubbing** reviews *Mixmag* and *Jockey Slut* give the biz on hot nightspots. Still, the Londoner's bible must be *Time Out* (W), worth every penny of its £2.20 cover price.

BROADCAST MEDIA

Whether on radio or TV, British broadcasting has a strong national identity. While there's no denying the influence from across the Atlantic, it's largely limited to pop music and the occasional show—national resilience is illustrated by the fact that the America's top-rated sitcom, *Seinfeld*, bombed in Britain. In fact, the most popular British programmes (with two "m"s!) are about as far removed from showbiz glamor as possible: the no. 1 soap, *Eastenders*, follows the working-class lives of people in East London; ridiculously long-running radio rival *The Archers* does the same for struggling farmers. As for comedy, the renowned British sense of humor has resulted in some of the world's funniest and least-exportable (see the *funny stuff* sidebar). Lately, British television has had an even wider worldwide impact than normal—*Survivor* and *Who Wants to be a Millionaire* were both British concepts.

RADIO

Two fundamental divisions cut across British radio: public and commercial, and national and local. The national market is dominated by the **BBC's** public offerings, though "the Beeb" or "Auntie" as it's affectionately (or sarcastically) known also has at least one local station available everywhere in the country. Equally, while commercial radio is strongest in local markets, there are a number of national stations. It's largely thanks to the BBC that commercial pop and phone-in shows have not yet achieved total domination of the airwaves: **BBC Radio 4** offers insightful news, com-

FUNNY STUFF

Comedy is central to the British concept of themselves—the number one quality desired in personal ads is "GSOH" (good sense of humour). It's only natural that comedy should rule the British airwaves to an extent unheard of abroad.

Sitcoms are merely the most traditional of a wide range of genres. No subject is deemed unsuitable for parody: *Father Ted* and *The Vicar of Dibbly* send up Catholicism and Anglicanism respectively, classics *Steptoe and Son* and *Rising Damp* got their laughs from lives on the edge of poverty, *Absolutely Fabulous* relentlessly parodied fashion victims, and *Drop the Dead Donkey* turned its sights on the media itself. Most popular shows are regularly re-broadcast. There's even a satellite channel devoted to them.

Celebrity Quiz Shows play on the uniquely British talent for self-mockery—no foreign politician, sportsman, or film star would willingly subject themselves to ritual humiliation on shows like *Have I Got News For You* and *Never Mind the Buzzcocks*. It's crueller than fox hunting.

Absurdity, though, is Britain's biggest contribution to the world of laughs. Even today, no-one knows quite what made Monty Python so funny, while only in the UK they even consider making a show in which a hologram, a cat, a computer, and a lifelong loser get lost in space—the result was that worldwide sci-fi cult classic, *Red Dwarf*.

ment, and analysis all day long, while **Radio 3** is Britain's cultural herald, with often-challenging classical music, literary readings, and radio plays. For a complete listing of radio stations available in London, see the *On the air* Essentials sidebar.

TELEVISION

British television's self-image as "the best in the world" is buckling under the same commercial pressures found in the rest of the Western world, but there's still an astounding variety of shows to be found on the telly's five broadcast channels. This is largely because every television-set owner in Britain is required to purchase an annual "TV licence," the proceeds of which go directly to the BBC—in return, the BBC is not allowed to run advertisements. (Although it's publicly funded, the BBC is independent of the Government.) This guarantees a source of money for serious programming, while also bringing an obligation to satisfy the mass-market tastes of the people who foot the bill—which includes the lower-income groups that advertisers normally scorn. As a result, the publicly-funded **BBC 1** remains more popular than its commercial rivals, and its presence results in an unavoidable upwards pressure on its main commercial rival **ITV**. The BBC's "cultural" channel, **BBC 2**, has a commercial counterpart in **Channel 4**; both mix in-depth news, documentaries, and groundbreaking dramas with test-runs of comedies which, if successful, often transfer to their more populist siblings. Finally, **Channel 5,** which launched in the late 1990s, has yet to carve itself a following—though that can't be said of perky newscaster Kirsty Young.

Satellite TV is also popular. The only major operator is Rupert Murdoch's *BSkyB*, and its endless diet of sports, American dramas, and movies confirms the intelligentsia's worst fears about commercial TV. The popularity of satellite TV has resulted in Britain's bypassing the **cable TV** revolution—large swathes of London aren't even wired up—but things are changing as cable operators start to offer internet services.

MONEY

For pre-departure info, including exchange rates, see **Planning Your Trip,** *p. 265.*

A trip to London can easily break the bank—but it doesn't have to. Always be on the lookout for discounts, especially if you're a student, under 26, or an "OAP" (Old Age Pensioner; women over 60 and men over 65)—you'll never find out if you don't ask. Discount rates for students and seniors are often posted as **concessions** or "concs" on price lists. **Families** should note that children under 5 travel for free on public transportation, while those aged 5-15 get reduced rates (but also see **Family Travelcards,** p. 33). Child rates at sights and museums normally apply to those under 16.

EXCHANGING MONEY

BANKS AND BUREAUX DE CHANGE

Contrary to what you might expect, the best exchange rates are normally found at **banks,** not specialist **bureaux de change** (though on weekends and after 4:30pm M-F, you won't have any choice); look for a spread of no more than 10% between the "buy" and "sell" rates. It's almost always cheaper to exchange large amounts at the same time rather than a succession of small quantities. Beware **"commission-free"** deals—if you have to change a small amount, they're the best option, but for larger sums what you gain in commission you give away in poor rates.

TRAVELER'S CHECKS

🔁 *For information on buying traveler's checks, see **Planning Your Trip,** p. 267.*

Banks often give better rates than the issuing institutions for foreign-denominated **Traveler's Checks,** but you may have to pay a service fee or commission; *bureaux de change* will often give you worse rates and charge commission. Sterling-denominated checks can be exchanged commission-free at issuing institutions and affiliated banks—ask your issuer for a list of affiliates. In department stores and some hotels, you may be able to pay directly in traveler's checks—however, if your checks are foreign-denominated, bear in mind that exchange rates are almost guaranteed to be worse than you'll find on the high street.

CASH (ATM) CARDS AND CREDIT CARDS

🔁 *Cards accepted by establishments are detailed in listings as follows: V for Visa, MC for Mastercard, AmEx for American Express. Discover and Diners Club are rarely accepted, and are not listed.*

Most shops, restaurants, and sights accept payment by credit card, though there's often a £10 minimum purchase; small establishments, market stalls, and takeaways are normally cash only.

CASH MACHINES. If you have a **cash (ATM) card,** chances are it will work in the UK—however, note that British machines only accept **4-digit PINs,** so if yours is longer, check with your bank to see if the first four digits will work in the UK or if you need a new code. Also, UK cash machines do not have letters on the keypad, so be sure to memorize your PIN in numerical form. You'll get the same wholesale exchange rates as credit cards, but beware that many banks levy hefty fees for withdrawing money abroad—up to US$5 a pop. For details of a **common scam** to steal cash cards and PINs, see p. 47.

PAYING WITH PLASTIC. If possible, pay with a credit card—you'll get a much better exchange rate than for cash or travelers checks. On the other hand, it can be harder to keep track of your spending, and **interest charges** can offset any gains if you

---

ⓘ ESSENTIAL INFORMATION

ON THE AIR

POP/INDIE
BBC Radio 1 (98.8FM)
Capital Radio (95.8)
XFM (104.9FM)
Kiss (100FM)

ADULT ROCK
Virgin (105.8FM/1215AM)
Heart (106.2FM)

EASY LISTENING
BBC Radio 2 (89.2FM)
Magic (105.4FM)
Capital Gold (1548AM)

CLASSICAL
BBC Radio 3 (91.3FM)
Classic FM (100.9FM)

OTHER MUSIC
Jazz FM (102.2FM)
Ritz (country; 1035AM)
Choice (soul; 96.9FM)

NEWS
BBC Radio 4 (93.5FM/720AM/198LW)
News Direct (97.3FM)

SPORT
BBC Radio 5 Live! (909AM/693AM)

TALK/LOCAL
BBC London Live (94.9FM)
Thames (107.8FM)
LBC (1152AM)

ENGLISH	AMERICAN
aubergine	eggplant
bangers and mash	pork sausage and mashed potato
bank holiday	public holiday
bap	soft bun
barmy	insane, erratic; hot weather
bathroom	room containing a bathtub
bird (slang)	girl
biro	ballpoint pen
bit of alright (slang)	attractive (of girls)
biscuit	cookie or cracker
bloke	guy
bobby (slang)	police officer
bonnet	car hood
brilliant (exclamation)	awesome
bonkers	crazy
(car) boot	car trunk
braces	suspenders
bum bag	fanny pack
busker	street musician
caravan	trailer, mobile home
car park	parking lot
cheeky	mischievous
cheerio	goodbye
cheers	thanks
chemist	pharmacy
chips	french fries
chuffed	happy
coach	inter-city bus
courgette	zucchini
crisps	potato chips
dicey, dodgy	sketchy
the dog's bollocks (slang)	the best
dosh, dough (slang)	money
drop someone a line	write a letter
durex	(common brand of) condom
ensuite	with bathroom
fag (slang)	cigarette
fanny (obsolete)	vagina

don't pay off the full balance at the end of the month. (Make sure there's someone at home to pay it if you'll be away, or arrange for it to be debited automatically from your bank account.) Depending on your card, you'll also receive some level of **purchase protection**—invaluable if that new gadget stops working when you get home.

CASH ADVANCES. You can also withdraw money from most cash machines and bank tellers with a **credit card,** up to your **cash advance** limit. (To use a machine, you'll need to set up a 4-digit PIN with your card issuer before you leave.) There are often high transaction fees associated with foreign cash advances (up to US$10 plus 2-3%), plus cash advances are normally charged at higher interest rates than purchases, with no grace period for payment until interest kicks in, either.

SALES TAX

The prices of all items sold in Britain include a 17.5% **Value-Added Tax** (VAT), with the exception of books, medicine, food (in stores), and children's clothes, which are VAT-free, and tobacco, alcohol, and certain luxury items, which are taxed at a higher rate. If you lived outside the EU, you may be able to claim some VAT back through the **Retail Export Scheme.** This only applies to articles that are being exported out of the EU; meals and lodging do not qualify. Only larger stores in heavily-touristed areas normally participate in the scheme, and there is often a £50-100 minimum purchase. If the store participates, you will need to request a VAT refund form from the shopkeeper. On leaving the country, take this form and the goods to the Tax-Free Refund desk at the airport, where officers will ensure the items are being exported and stamp your forms; this process can take up to an hour. After going through passport control, mail the form back to the shop, which will then eventually send you a refund (less an administrative fee) by check or credit it to your credit card. This scheme only applies to purchases made three months or less before departure.

HEALTH AND SAFETY

MEDICAL CARE

▼ In an **emergency,** dial 999 free from any phone. For a list of Accident & Emergency rooms in London, see the **Service Directory,** p. 314. For details of how to obtain long-term medical care, see **Living in London,** p. 309.

Medical care in the UK is either part of the government-run National Health Service or is privately administered: often the same doctors and hospitals do both NHS and private work. **EU** citizens, citizens of many **Commonwealth** countries and full-time **students** at British universities are eligible for free treatment on the NHS. Many **US health insurance** plans (but not Medicare) will cover emergency treatment abroad in private clinics, but you may be asked to pay up-front and then apply for a reimbursement to your insurer. If you're unsure whether you have medical cover in the UK, it's best to play safe and buy **travel insurance** (see p. 269) before you leave.

CHEMISTS (PHARMACIES). For minor ailments, such as light burns, blisters, coughs, and sneezes, you can save time by going to a chemist: **Boots** is the biggest chain. If you can't find what you need on the shelves, or are unsure of your symptoms, you'll find a trained pharmacist behind the prescription drugs counter. They'll either recommend medication, or advise you to see a doctor if they think it's serious. Note that chemists are rarely open late or on Sundays: most hospitals have 24hr. pharmacies, but may only serve patients with prescriptions.

MEDICAL EMERGENCIES. In a life-threatening situation, call **999** from any phone to request an ambulance. For less acute situations, most London hospitals run 24hr. **Accident & Emergency** (A&E) or **Casualty** wards. A list of A&E departments in London can be found on p. 314. If your condition isn't judged serious, be prepared to wait for hours, especially on F-Sa nights.

CRIME

🔢 *In case of **emergency**, dial 999 free from any phone.*

If you're a victim of crime, **report it to the police**—not only will it help future travelers, it's normally required if you intend to make an insurance claim afterwards.

VIOLENT CRIME. London is as safe a big city as you're likely to find—by US and even most European standards, violent crime is rare, and police rarely carry anything more dangerous than a truncheon. Nevertheless, while crime levels are low, they're not zero, and those unfamiliar with London will inevitably be at higher risk than locals. While most of London's dodgier neighborhoods—Hackney, Tottenham, and parts of South and East London—are far off the tourist trail, you should take extra care after dark around **King's Cross**, the **East End**, and **Brixton**. Finally, never venture alone into **parks** after dark, and **never admit you're traveling alone**.

THEFT. Violence is just part of the story—when it comes to theft, especially opportunistic crimes such as **pickpocketing** or **bagsnatching**, London's track record is worse than New York's. Here's a 5-point plan to minimize your risk:

ENGLISH	AMERICAN
first floor	second floor
fortnight	two weeks
full stop	period (punctuation)
geezer (slang)	guy
gob (vulgar)	mouth
grotty	grungy
high street	main street
to hire	to rent
holiday	vacation
hoover	vacuum cleaner,
ice lolly	popsicle
interval	intermission
jumper	sweater
knackered (slang)	tired, worn out
knob (vulg.)	penis, awkward person
to knock up	to knock on someone's door
lavatory, loo	restroom
lay-by	roadside turnout
leader (press)	editorial
legless (slang)	drunk
to let	to rent (property)
liberal (politics)	centre-right
lift	elevator
lorry	truck
mad	crazy
mate	pal
motorway	highway
mobile phone	cellphone
naff (slang)	shabby, in poor taste
pants	underpants; bad (slang)
petrol	gasoline
phone box, call box	telephone booth
take the piss, take the mickey (slang)	make fun
pissed	drunk
Paki (derog.)	racial slur for Pakistani or any South Asian.
plaster	generic Band-Aid
poof (vulgar)	gay person
prat (vulgar)	unpleasant person

47

ENGLISH	AMERICAN
prawn	shrimp
pudding	dessert
to pull (slang)	to "score"
public school	prestigious private school
punter	average person, customer
quid (slang)	pound (money)
to queue (up), queue	to stand in line, a line
quay (pron. "key")	river bank
return ticket	round-trip ticket
to ring (up)	to telephone
roundabout	rotary intersection
rubber	eraser
to sack, give the sack	to fire someone
self-catering	with kitchen
serviette	napkin
shag (slang)	sex, to have sex
single ticket	one-way ticket
snog (slang)	kiss
slag (vulgar)	bitch
sod it (vulgar)	forget it
sultanas	a type of raisin
suspenders	garters
subway	underpass
sweets	candy
swish	swanky
ta (slang)	thanks
ta-ta (slang)	goodbye
thick (slang)	stupid
tights	pantyhose
toilet	restroom
torch	flashlight
Tory	supporter of Conservative Party
tosser (vulgar)	see wanker
trousers	pants
vest	undershirt
waistcoat	men's vest
wanker (vulgar)	see tosser
wasted	very drunk
way out	exit
WC	restroom

1. Don't put a wallet in your back pocket, and don't keep all your valuables (money, important documents) in one place.

2. Carry as little as possible and avoid counting money in public. If you carry a handbag, buy a sturdy one with a secure clasp and carry it crosswise on the side away from the street with the clasp against you.

3. Use a money belt and keep a small cash reserve (say £40) somewhere safe.

4. Never leave belongings visibly unattended, especially in a locked car.

5. Don't trust strangers to watch your things (especially if they make the offer).

One common ruse at **cash machines** is for someone to claim you've dropped something. You look down, and sure enough there's a £10 note on the floor—by the time you've picked it up, an accomplice standing behind you—who's already memorized your PIN—has made off with the card and has probably withdrawn your daily limit from a nearby cash machine before you've even realized what's happened.

TERRORISM. With IRA splinter groups ignoring the official cease-fire, terrorism is an ever-present threat in London; however, the risk of injury is minute—you're far more likely to be run over. With a few murderous exceptions, bombers leave warnings and time for evacuation. Some of the bloodiest recent attacks have had nothing to do with Ireland: in 1999 nail-bomb attacks on the largely black Brixton Market and the Admiral Duncan gay pub in Soho killed dozens and maimed many more. While the perpetrator of those atrocities has been brought to book, vigilance is still called for: if you see an abandoned bag or package in a public space, Tube, or bus, *always* alert the nearest police officer or member of staff.

RACISM. London has traditionally prided itself on being an exceptionally tolerant city, but the enormous increase in immigration since the 1950s has taken its toll. While overall London is relatively color-blind, recent years have seen a few horrific attacks take place in some poorer neighborhoods. In **South London,** tensions are worst between black immigrants and poor whites, though there's also friction within the black community between those of West Indian and African origin. In **East London,** South Asians are on the receiving end. These troublespots aside, races mix in London to a far greater extent than in most countries: among second-generation immigrants, there's little cultural distinction between different groups and native Anglos.

DRUGS AND ALCOHOL

The legal **drinking age** in the UK is a complicated beast: technically, it's legal for anyone to drink alcohol in private, but there are numerous regulations regarding who can buy or sell it. To buy alcohol in a **shop**, you have to be at least 18; however it's illegal to buy alcohol on behalf on an underage person. 18 is also the normal drinking age in **bars** and **pubs**, but you can drink in a pub at 16 with food, or even at 14 in a **restaurant.** (Not many restaurateurs know this so don't count on them complying.) Enforcement is lax—you need to look *really* young before anyone will demand I.D.—but punishments are severe. **Smoking** is simpler: you have to be 16 or older.

Drugs are dealt with harshly. Current police policy is to only issue warnings, not arrests, for first-time cannabis offenders, but if prosecuted you could go to jail (or be deported); possession of larger amounts risks you being treated as a dealer, for which penalties are far stiffer. **Ecstasy, cocaine, heroine, amphetamines,** and practically every other mind-altering drug are illegal and possession is subject to strict penalties; you may also be subjected to a blood test. You shouldn't buy drugs anyway, but be especially wary in nightclubs—there have been several cases of poisoning after taking impure ecstasy tablets, and who knows how many people have been duped into buying something no more mind-enhancing than aspirin. If you need to take a drug for **medical reasons,** check that it is legal in the UK, and always carry a prescription or note from you doctor.

ENGLISH	AMERICAN
wellies, Wellington boots	waterproof boots
wicked (slang)	cool
yob (slang)	uncultured person
Yorkshire pudding	eggy pastry served with roast beef
zed	the letter Z

WRITTEN	PRONOUNCED
Berkeley	BAHK-lee
Berkshire	BAHK-sher
Birmingham	BERM-ing-um
Cholmondely	CHUM-lee
Derby	DAR-bee
Dulwich	DULL-ich
Edinburgh	ED-in-bur-ra
Featherstonehaw	FAN-shaw
Gloucester	GLOS-ter
Greenwich	GREN-ich
Grosvenor	GRO-vna
gaol	JAIL
Islington	IHZ-ling-tun
Leicester	LES-ter
Marylebone	MAR-lee-bun
Magdalen	MAUD-lin
quay	KEY
Norwich	NOR-ich
Salisbury	SAULS-bree
Southwark	SUTH-uk
Thames	TEMS
Worcester	WOO-ster

Life & Times

LONDON THROUGH THE AGES

ROMANS TO NORMANS (A.D. 43-1066)

A LEGENDARY START. According to legend, London owes its existence to **Brutus,** a descendant of the Trojan hero Aeneas, who after being banished from Italy arrived in Britain in 1074 B.C. Here he founded a city on the banks of the Thames at a spot he called "New Troy," or Trinovantum, a name it held until a certain King Lud renamed it for himself. While the name of the city was later corrupted to London, Lud himself supposedly still lies in his tomb on the site of present-day Ludgate, near St. Paul's Cathedral.

LONDON BRIDGE, TAKE I. The truth, inevitably, is more prosaic, but on one point myth and fact stand in agreement: London owes its existence to a band of hardy Italian adventurers. In A.D. 43, **Aulus Plautius** landed in Kent with 40,000 battle-hardened Romans and marched north until he found his way barred by the Thames. Pausing here to await the Emperor Claudius, Aulus busied his troops with the building of a bridge. Situated at the lowest navigable point on the river, and soon the center of an excellent network of Roman roads, the crossing naturally became a focal point for trade. Merchants set up on the north bank of the river: London—or rather, Londinium—was born.

GROWING PAINS. London was only 17 years old when it faced the first of the many calamities that would befall it over the next two millennia. After the Romans murdered her husband and raped her daughters, **Boudicca,** Celtic Queen of the Iceni, swore vengeance—and London, a city born of Rome—was a prime target. Unlike the garrison towns established at Colchester, Lincoln, York, and Gloucester, London was an undefended

WILL THE REAL DICK WHITTINGTON PLEASE STAND UP

For centuries, London children have been thrilled by the story of Dick Whittington. Dazzled by tales of London's wealth, young Dick comes to the city to make his fortune, accompanied by his trusty black cat. Life turns out to be tougher than he'd expected, though, and Dick is on the point of leaving London when church bells call him back with the famous cry: "Turn again Dick Whittington, Lord Mayor of London." Back in the city, Dick finds his cat in demand as a champion rat-catcher. Rich at last, Dick marries his former boss's daughter, and is duly elected Mayor an unprecedented three times.

Despite the obvious appeal of this rats-to-riches tale, only the last part of the legend has any truth to it. Richard Whittington came from a wealthy provincial family, while his "cat" was a type of trading ship. Nonetheless, as Mayor (in 1397, 1406, and 1419), Whittington was famed for his generosity, paying for the reconstruction of numerous public buildings and founding a number of charities.

Many of the legend's embellishments can be traced to a 1605 play. For all its lack of truth, the formula was a hit: Dick Whittington is still a staple of the British pantomime scene.

trading outpost; the city was burned to the ground, and its inhabitants massacred. London soon got over this early disaster: with Roman control reestablished, London's commercial preeminence soon led it to become the capital of Britain. In addition to the governor's palace, by the end of the second century London could boast a forum four times the size of Trafalgar Square and a population of 45,000 drawn from all over the Empire.

THE END OF EMPIRE. As Rome's long decline turned into a headlong tumble in the fourth century, British-based potentates launched ill-fated bids for imperial power, sapping Britain of the manpower needed to defend against ever-more-frequent raiding parties of **Picts, Angles** and **Saxons.** With Rome itself in the hands of barbarians, an appeal to the Emperor for assistance in A.D. 410 brought the reply that from now on, Britain would have to fend for itself.

A NEW BEGINNING. In the mid-fifth century, as Angles and Saxons overran southern Britain and began ethnically cleansing their new home of its Celtic inhabitants, refugees flocked to safety behind London's 20ft. thick Roman walls. What happened to them is unknown—history falls silent for 150 years, and when it reopens London is part of the East Saxon kingdom. In 604, on a mission from Rome, **St. Augustine** converted the local king and consecrated the first Bishop of London, **Mellitus.** In the same year, work started on the first **St. Paul's Cathedral.** The City of London's higgledy-piggledy street plan can also be traced to this era: turning the orderly Roman city inside-out, the new inhabitants built their houses on the solid surface of the old Roman roads.

LONDON BRIDGE, TAKE II. London's prosperity brought unwelcome attention: following the example of the Saxons, 9th-century **Vikings** made the transition from raiders to would-be conquerors. In 871, the Danes occupied London; it took **Alfred the Great** 15 years to retake it. Even so, Danes still controlled half of England (the "Danelaw"), and intermittent war continued for over a century. Once more, in 1013, London came under Danish rule when King **Ethelred the Unready** (Old English for "ill-advised") fled to Normandy. This time it was reconquered with the help of a 19-year-old Norwegian, Olaf, who hitched ropes between his fleet and the bridge supports and rowed away hard. The supports gave way, the Danes fell into the Thames, and the song "London Bridge is Falling Down" was born. Even so, when Ethelred died in 1016 the kingdom passed (peacefully) to a Dane, **Canute,** who made London the capital of an empire encompassing England, Denmark, and Norway.

THE MIDDLE AGES (1042-1485)

CONQUEST. Canute's successors held on to England until 1042, when Ethelred's son **Edward the Confessor** became king. London owes its status as a capital to Edward, who wanted to live near his favorite new church, the West Minster; **Westminster** has been home to the English government ever since. Edward's death in 1066 set the scene for the most famous battle in English history. **William of Normandy** claimed that Edward (who grew up in Normandy and was half-Norman) had promised him the throne; **Harold,** Earl of Wessex, disagreed. The difference was resolved on October 14th, at Hastings. By sunset Harold was dead, and William had a new soubriquet. One of William's first actions following the battle of Hastings was to send word to London that he would respect the city's laws and privileges: while Normans soon replaced English nobles at the heads of castles and churches, business went on as normal. Even as the Norman monarchs tried to awe their new capital into submission with the construction of the **Tower of London** and the now-vanished Baynard's and Montfichet castles, London businessmen increased their stranglehold on the economy.

King George II

LONDON BRIDGE, TAKE III. As the monarchy built castles, London was bridgeless for most of the 12th century: one wooden bridge was destroyed by a gale in 1109, and its replacement burned down in 1136. Finally, in 1176 work started on a new bridge—this time in stone. Construction lasted until 1209: problems included diverting the Thames while 20 massive stone piers were sunk into the riverbed. The roadway along the top was lined with shops and houses, and market stalls filled the remaining space: nevertheless, **Old London Bridge** lasted until 1832.

God Save the Queen

INCORPORATION. Desperate for money to finance their wars, Norman kings made numerous concessions to London merchants. London was incorporated in 1191, granting the city a measure of self-governance and independence from the crown: the first Mayor, **Henry FitzAilwyn,** was elected in 1193. His present-day successor, the Lord Mayor, still presides over the 680 acres of the City of London; as a reminder of the power once wielded by the Mayor of London, even today the Queen may not enter the city without his permission.

A CENTURY OF HORRORS. The 14th century was a time of calamity. In 1348, plague arrived, born by rats carried on ships from Europe. The resulting **Black Death** claimed the lives of 30,000 people—perhaps half the city's total population; thousands more died in further outbreaks in

Hyde Park-Queen Elizabeth Gate

53

A NIGHT TO REMEMBER

Americans do it on July 4th, Canadians on July 1st, and the French on July 14th. The British, however, wait until cold, damp November 5th to let off their fireworks. That's the date of **Guy Fawkes Night,** which commemorates the failure of a dastardly plot to blow up the opening of Parliament (and with it King James I) in 1605.

Determined to rid England of its increasingly repressive Protestant government, the Catholic Guy Fawkes and his co-conspirators came within hours of success. The plot was averted only after one of their number wrote an anonymous letter to his brother-in-law, Lord Monteagle, warning him to stay away. Suspicions aroused, a search of the premises led to the discovery of Fawkes setting the fuses on 36 barrels of gunpowder packed into a cellar beneath Parliament.

The anniversary of the plot soon became an annual event marked by the lighting of bonfires and the burning of an effigy of Guy Fawkes. If political correctness has largely put a stop to that last custom, the night is still one of celebration with bonfires, fireworks, mulled wine, and the traditional verse:

"Remember, remember the fifth of November, gunpowder, treason, and plot."

1361, 1369, and 1375. Then, in 1381, came the **Peasant's Revolt.** Incensed by a new poll tax, 60,000 men marched on London. On June 14th the Tower was occupied, and the Archbishop of Canterbury and the Treasurer captured and beheaded. The 14-year-old **Richard II** had no choice but to accept the rebels' demands; the following day he rode out to meet their leader **Wat Tyler** at Smithfield. During a heated discussion, **William Walworth,** the Mayor of London, killed Tyler with a dagger. As the angry mob surged at the royal party, the child-king spurred his horse forward and proclaimed that he would be their leader; incredibly, the crowd believed him. As soon as he was safe, Richard reneged on his promises: the ringleaders were executed, and promises of better conditions withdrawn.

A THORNY PROBLEM. The year 1387 was a double boon for the English language: it saw the publication of **Geoffrey Chaucer's** masterpiece, the *Canterbury Tales*, and the birth of the future **Henry V,** England's first ruler since the Conquest to speak English as his first language. While Henry V proved to be one of England's most capable kings, his son **Henry VI** led England into the quagmire known as the **Wars of the Roses.** As told by Shakespeare, it was in **Middle Temple Garden** (see p. 88) that the protagonists plucked the red and white roses that would serve as their emblems. Tired of Henry's dithering, London's merchants gave full backing to the financially astute future **Edward IV,** whose shared interest in business led them to overlook his equally shared interest in their wives. It was under Edward's patronage that in 1476 **William Caxton** set up a printing press in Westminster; after his death, his aptly named assistant Wyknyn de Worde moved the presses to **Fleet Street** (see p. 90), which remained at the heart of the British printing industry until the 1980s.

It was rumored that Edward's premature death, at 40, was due to an excess of debauchery; in any case, it left the country in the hands of his brother, **Richard III.** Originally installed only as Protector until Edward's own children were old enough to reign, Richard earned universal opprobrium following the mysterious death of the "little princes," whom he had imprisoned in the Tower—for their own safety, of course. Taking advantage of Richard's unpopularity, **Henry Tudor** was able to unseat him in 1485.

THE FLOWER OF CITIES (1485-1685)

THE TUDOR AGE. While the new Henry VII's claim to the throne was tenuous to say the least (his grandmother was Henry V's widow), his dynasty ushered in a golden age of prosperity. Scots poet **William Dunbar,** in London for the marriage of Henry's daughter to James IV of Scotland, wrote "London, thou art the flower of cities all"; yet at the time of his writing, in 1501, the transformation had scarcely begun. In the next century, London's population would quadruple to 200,000, mostly through immigration from rural areas hit hard by agricultural changes and **Henry VIII's** dissolution of the monasteries in 1536. Many of the new arrivals would have found employment on Henry's numerous building projects, including palaces at **Hampton Court** (see p. 244), **Whitehall** (p. 106), and **St. James's** (p. 82); others on the equally luxurious houses that soon lined the Strand between the City and Westminster. The sumptuousness of the court can be seen through the portraits of Henry's court artist, the German **Hans Holbein**.

Despite the desperate marital measures taken by Henry to secure the succession, his only son, **Edward VI,** reigned only six years before dying in 1553 at the age of 15. He was succeeded by his Catholic sister **Mary I,** who earned her nickname "Bloody" through a relentless campaign against the Anglican church established by her father. During her short reign, over 300 Protestants were burned at **Smithfield** (see p. 93).

ELIZABETH'S LONDON. Elizabeth I, daughter of Henry VIII and Anne Boleyn, inherited all the virtues of her father and few of his faults—indeed, her refusal to marry earned her the title "The Virgin Queen." During her 45-year reign, England flourished as never before: it was the age of discovery and adventure, when Francis Drake and Walter Ralegh displayed England's mastery of the seas and thousands set sail to seek their fortunes abroad—backed, naturally, by London capital. Joint-stock companies, such as the **East India Company** spread the risk and rewards of these ventures as shares busily changed hands on the floor of the new **Royal Exchange**, built by Thomas Gresham in 1570 to spare businessmen the indignity of having to make transactions in the streets.

As Drake and Raleigh expanded the horizons of England's world, so dramatists such as **William Shakespeare, Christopher Marlowe,** and **Ben Jonson** expanded her literary horizons. At first plays were performed in the courtyards of London inns, with audiences packed into the galleries. The City authorities, wary of this new form of entertainment, soon sent the actors packing over the river to Southwark, where **James Burbage** had constructed London's first custom-built playhouse, The Theatre, later renamed **The Globe** (see p. 102).

A SCOTTISH KING. Elizabeth's refusal to take a husband led to her cousin James VI of Scotland inheriting the throne as **James I.** If London had loved Elizabeth, it only tolerated James. Closing himself up in Whitehall, James replied to the people's desire to see his face with the riposte "then I will pull down my breeches and they shall also see my arse." Nevertheless, James was not wholly uncaring of the fate of Londoners: he gave his backing to an ambitious project to supply London with fresh drinking water via hollowed-out wooden pipes from a new reservoir in Clerkenwell. Such improvements were all the more necessary as London continued its unchecked expansion: the city was increasingly spilling beyond the city walls and into the future **West End**—

KEY DATES

A.D. 43 Romans bridge the Thames at Londinium

60 Boudicca's rebellion

604 St. Augustine in London

871 Vikings occupy London

1066 Norman Conquest

1176-1209 Construction of Old London Bridge

1189 Incorporation of the city

1269 Westminster Abbey rebuilt and reconsecrated

1348 Black Death kills 30,000—half the city

1381 Peasant's Revolt

1455-1485 Wars of the Roses

1485-1603 Tudor dynasty

1599 Globe Theatre opens

1603-1649 and **1660-1688** House of Stuart

1605 Gunpowder Plot against James I and Parliament fails

1649 Charles I beheaded and Commonwealth declared

1666 Great Fire destroys city

1675-1710 Rebuilding of St. Paul's Cathedral under Wren

1688-9 Glorious Revolution

1714 House of Hanover takes power with George I

1759 British Museum opens

1837-1901 Queen Victoria

1858 The Great Stink

1863 Metropolitan line opens, the first underground railway

1888 Jack the Ripper

1915 German bombs bring WWI to London

1940 The Blitz devastates the City and the East End

1953 Elizabeth II crowned

1960-1968 London swings

2000 Ken Livingstone first democratic Mayor of London

which was preferred since prevailing winds carried the stench and pollution of the growing metropolis eastwards. That the expansion was carried off with such grace is due largely to the architectural genius of **Inigo Jones,** who gave London such Renaissance gems as **Banqueting House** (see p. 106) in Whitehall, the **Queen's House** (see p. 129) in Greenwich, and **Covent Garden Piazza** (p. 84) in the West End.

WAR AND REGICIDE. James's autocratic, high-handed approach in dealing with Parliament, the aristocracy, and not least the Lord Mayor meant that his passing, in 1625, was little mourned; and it soon became obvious that affairs would not get any better under his son, **Charles I.** Beset by military defeat abroad and religious dissent at home, Charles's skirmishes with Parliament over constitutional reform degenerated into the **Civil War** in 1642. London's support for Parliament sealed the king's fate: without the city's money and manpower, his chance of victory was slim. After an abortive stand-off between the king's army and the London militia at Turnham Green at the outset of the war, Charles never threatened London again; when next he returned to his former capital it would be as a captive of **Oliver Cromwell.** The king was tried for treason in Westminster Hall, spent his last night in St. James's Palace, and was executed on the lawn of Banqueting House on January 25th, 1649.

Though Cromwell's firm hand restored the health of the new Puritan-dominated **Commonwealth,** Parliament proved to be as repressive, and unpopular as the King it replaced. Not content with outlawing theater and most other forms of entertainment, it went as far as to ban music in churches and even, in 1652, to abolish Christmas, accused of being a Catholic superstition. More positively, Cromwell permitted the return of Jews to England, who had been expelled under Edward I in 1290.

A TUMULTUOUS DECADE. In 1660, **Charles II** returned from exile in Holland to a rapturous welcome. Among those accompanying him on his return was **Samuel Pepys,** whose diary of 1660s London provides an invaluable eyewitness account of this tumultuous time. The happy-go-lucky atmosphere of the Restoration's early years died in the **Great Plague** of 1665, in which 100,000 Londoners perished. An even worse disaster was to follow: early in the morning of September 2nd, 1666, fire broke out in a bakery on Pudding Lane. By Thursday, when the **Great Fire** was finally extinguished, 80% of London lay in ruins, including 80 churches, 13,000 homes, St. Paul's, the Guildhall, and virtually every other building of note save the Tower.

In the face of this devastating double blow, Londoners proved their resilience. **Christopher Wren** submitted a daring plan to rebuild London on a rational basis, with wide boulevards and sweeping vistas. His grand scheme foundered in the face of opposition from existing landowners, and in the end Wren had to settle for the commission to rebuild **St. Paul's Cathedral** (see p. 71) and 51 lesser churches. The fire itself was commemorated by Wren's simple **Monument** (see p. 99), a 202ft. high column situated 202ft from the spot where the fire broke out.

As London rebuilt, some former refugees discovered that they preferred life beyond the city limits. In the latter part of the century speculators threw up numerous handsome squares and terraces in the West End; **Downing Street** (see p. 106) was the brainchild of George Downing, Massachusetts native, early Harvard graduate, and—appropriately enough—a consummate political fixer.

THE ENLIGHTENED CITY (1685-1783)

A GLORIOUS REVOLUTION. When Charles died in 1685, England was thrown into political crisis by the accession of his Catholic brother **James II.** While James's rule started with a promise of religious tolerance, many believed that he was preparing the way for a return to Catholicism. The alternative seemed clear: the crown should instead pass to Charles II's daughter, Mary, and her husband William of Orange, ruler of the Netherlands. When William landed in 1688, James's support melted away and the last Stuart was compelled to flee. The **Glorious Revolution** ended with the crowning of **William and Mary** as co-equal rulers, and the passing on the **Bill of Rights,** which enshrined Parliament's sovereignty and independence from the Crown.

Under the leadership of the Dutch William, London gradually supplanted Amsterdam as the lynchpin of international trade, an achievement greatly aided by the founding of the **Bank of England** (see p. 98) on the model of the Bank of Amsterdam in 1694. Other future financial behemoths had less obvious beginnings: **Lloyd's of London** (see p. 100) the world's oldest insurance market, started out as Edward Lloyd's coffee shop, where captains congregated to exchange shipping gossip.

PARLIAMENT SUPREME. On the accession of William, Parliament fixed the line of succession to ensure that no Catholic would ever sit on the throne again. The upshot of their tortured reasoning was that in 1714, the dying Queen Anne (Mary's sister) was succeeded by a German prince who spoke no English: **George I,** formerly the Elector of Hanover. By this time, however, most of the business of government was handled by Parliament and in particular the man who invented for himself the role of Prime Minister, **Robert Walpole.** During Walpole's 20 years at the top, many people believed that he had become too powerful: writers such as **Jonathan Swift, Alexander Pope,** and **Henry Fielding** wrote articles criticizing Walpole, while **John Gay's** wildly popular *Beggar's Opera* (1728) simultaneously satirized government corruption and the current fad for Italian operas. Walpole and the King were far more comfortable with the music of **George Frederick Handel,** who had followed his master from Hanover. Handel is best remembered for his English-language oratorios such as the *Messiah* (1741), and his later music is recognized as quintessentially English—something his royal master never achieved.

JOHNSON'S LONDON. When **George III** came to the throne in 1760, Britain had its first English-speaking king in 70 years. Although George is best remembered for losing America and going mad, between the extremes of these two calamities the capable hands of **Pitt the Younger** (only 24 when he became Prime Minister in 1783) restored Britain to robust financial health. Meanwhile, London added an intellectual sheen to its mercantile character. The **British Museum** opened its doors in 1759, and the city eagerly followed the well-publicized doings of **Samuel Johnson,** wit and author of the charmingly idiosyncratic *Dictionary* (1755). Together with his good friend, the painter **Sir Joshua Reynolds,** Johnson founded **The Club** in 1764, an exclusive institution whose members included the actor and theatrical innovator **David Garrick,** historian **Edward Gibbon,** philosopher and free-trade advocate **Adam Smith,** and of course Johnson's famed biographer, **James Boswell,** whose *Life of Johnson* provides an unforgettable portrait of the great man and his age. Reynolds was also the prime mover behind the 1768 foundation of the **Royal Academy of Arts** (see p. 141), whose early members included **Thomas Gainsborough.**

A MODERN CITY. In the latter part of the 18th century, London began to take on many of the characteristics of the present-day city. As the focus of life shifted westwards, **Oxford Street** became the capital's main shopping artery, tempting customers with new-fangled ideas such as window displays and fixed prices. Meanwhile, Scottish architect **Robert Adam,** best known for mansions such as **Kenwood House** (see p. 121), revolutionized city living for the wealthy with **The Adelphi,** the first luxury apartment block. Fellow Scot **William Chambers** did the same for London's workers with the first purpose-built office complex, **Somerset House** (see p. 87). And in 1750, London Bridge—until then the sole crossing over the Thames—acquired a neighbor, **Westminster Bridge,** which in 1802 inspired poet **William Wordsworth's** paen to the beauty of the sleeping city, *Composed upon Westminster Bridge.*

With the trappings of a modern city, London also acquired modern problems, not least among them a massive increase in crime. Much of this could be attributed to the widening gulf between rich and poor, but there was another cause: cheap liquor. **Gin,** invented in Holland in the 17th century, was so cheap and plentiful that by the 1730s consumption had risen to an average of two pints per week for every man, woman, and child in the city. London was becoming a city of alcoholics, and the social evils caused were memorably illustrated in **William Hogarth's** allegorical prints, which oppose *Gin Lane* with the cheerful *Beer Street.* In 1751 Parliament passed the Gin Act, imposing government regulation of the sale of alcohol; as a result, mortality rates dropped dramatically. In the same year magistrate and novelist **Henry Fielding,** together with his brother John, established the **Bow Street Runners,** a band of volunteer "thieftakers" which evolved into the Metropolitan Police. Even so, crime was still prevalent enough that in the 1770s the Prime Minister, the Lord Mayor, and even the Prince of Wales were all robbed in broad daylight.

FROM REGENCY TO EMPIRE (1783-1901)

THE HAPPY PRINCE. There could be no mistaking the Prince of Wales for his staid father. From the moment he turned 21 in 1783, the Prince announced himself through flamboyant opposition to his father's ministers and an utter disregard for convention. When, after overcoming an earlier bout in 1788 (subject of the play and film, *The Madness of King George III*), the King descended into permanent insanity in 1811, the heir to the throne assumed power as the **Prince Regent.**

Unpopular as a wastrel ruler concerned more with his appearance than the state of the country, the Regent's obsession with self-aggrandizement nevertheless brought important benefits to London. Inspired by the changes wrought by Napoleon in Paris, he dreamt of creating a grand processional way leading from Marylebone Park to his residence at Carlton House. **John Nash** was the architect chosen to transform this vision into reality: the result was some of London's best-loved architecture, from the grand **Nash Terraces** surrounding the renamed and remodelled **Regent's Park** (see p. 115), to the great sweep of **Regent's Street** leading up to **Piccadilly Circus** (see p. 83), from where the Haymarket would complete the journey to Carlton House. Alas, all this work was in vain: when the Prince Regent finally became **George IV** in 1820 (five years before the completion of Piccadilly Circus), he abruptly ordered Carlton House demolished, and commissioned Nash to remodel **Buckingham Palace** (see p. 68) for his future residence.

It was the age of the dandy and the aesthete. Fashion was changed for ever when **Beau Brummel,** the king's confidant and self-appointed arbiter of taste, did away with gold braid and lace, and made black the new pink. **Romanticism** announced itself in the works of **Lord Byron** and **John Keats,** while the London they occupied can still be seen in the masterful landscapes of **John Constable** and **J.M.W. Turner.**

UNDERGROUND, OVERGROUND. If the Regency had given London a new face, it was the Victorian age that would supply the infrastructure. By the time the 18-year-old **Queen Victoria** ascended to the throne in 1837, London was already at the heart of the largest Empire the world had ever seen, and its 2-million strong population would add almost another million for every decade of her 64-year reign. Just as the expansion was driven by the new factories of steam-powered manufacturing, so it was made possible by steam-powered transportation. London's first **railway** opened in 1836, connecting London Bridge to the then-distant suburb of Greenwich; by 1876 there were 10 railway companies connecting London to the rest of Britain, each with its own terminal and tracks. Pressure on the capital's roads was relieved with the inauguration of the **Metropolitan Line,** the world's first underground railway, in 1863. Together with the spread of horse-drawn trams, the railways made commuting possible for the first time: once-rural villages such as Islington and Hampstead were rapidly engulfed by the voracious city.

Britain's technological and mercantile might was displayed to the world during the **Great Exhibition** of 1851, the first of the world fairs that plague us to this day. Its six million visitors were dazzled by the vast iron and glass expanse of the **Crystal Palace,** with 14,000 exhibits spread over 23 acres. This showcase of modern engineering aside, though, Victorian architects reacted to the rush of modernization with a return to the distant past. **Gothic** architecture was all the rage, as can be seen in **Charles Barry's** enormous, ornate **Houses of Parliament** (see p. 70), but Victorian eclecticism ran the historical gamut, from the neo-classical friezes of the **Albert Hall** to the Romanesque solidity of the **Natural History Museum** (see p. 146). A similar sensibility motivated painter-poet **Dante Gabriel Rossetti,** who founded the influential **Pre-Raphaelite Brotherhood** and unleashed on the unsuspecting public a wave of highly stylized medieval pastiche and open-mouthed maidens. The general anti-modern feeling of the age was best captured by designer and poet **William Morris,** who founded the **Arts and Crafts** movement in the belief that the Industrial Revolution had destroyed notions of taste and craftsmanship.

THE SATANIC CITY. Many Victorian artistic movements were deeply influenced by the work of visionary poet and artist **William Blake,** who as early as 1804 had written of the "dark satanic mills" spawned by the Industrial Revolution. Working and living conditions for the majority of the capital's inhabitants were appalling, health-care and sanitation almost non-existent. **Child labor** was unregulated until 1886; **cholera**

raged unchecked until the **Great Stink** of 1858 forced Parliament to reform the city's sewers; and air pollution was such that 1879 the capital was shrouded in smog for the entire winter. A more human tragedy struck in 1888, when police searched in vain for serial killer **Jack the Ripper.**

This was the London that inspired **Charles Dickens** to write such urban masterpieces as *Oliver Twist* (1837-1839), and saw **Karl Marx** lead the proto-communist First International, founded in London in 1864. Even so, it was not until the last third of the century that significant progress was made: in 1867, the **Reform Bill** extended the franchise to most of London's working men and 1870 saw the **Education Act** provide schooling for all. Organized labor was also beginning to make headway: in 1889, Marx's daughter Eleanor led gasworkers in a strike which won recognition for the 8-hour day, while in 1893 the working classes found a political voice with the establishment of the **Independent Labour Party.** 1889 also saw the establishment of the **London County Council,** unifying the disparate voices of London's many boroughs and finally providing a cohesive force for change.

Kensington Gardens

THE 20TH CENTURY

THE APEX OF POWER. Although **Edward VII** did not succeed his mother until 1901, Victorian morality had already begun to crumble during the "naughty nineties," when two Irish-born adopted Londoners, taboo-breaking **George Bernard Shaw** and flamboyant **Oscar Wilde,** thrilled theatergoers and shocked the authorities. **Emmeline Pankhurst** struck another blow for progress when she started the Woman's Social and Political Union to win the vote for women, a struggle that lasted until 1928. The stunts pulled off by her and her **suffragettes** were meat and drink to the new **tabloid press,** which had been born with the launching of the *Daily Mail* in 1903 and rapidly became London's main source of news.

Spitalfields Market

The changes wrought on London by steam in the previous century were completed by the advance of **electricity** and **petroleum** power in the new; already by the outbreak of the First World War in 1914, London was recognizably the same city it is today. Red double-decker buses and clean, electrically powered Underground trains delivered Londoners to new department stores such as **Selfridges** (opened 1909) and **Harrods,** which moved to its present site in 1905. Londoners could entertain themselves at one of 30 West End theaters or any of 250 **cinemas,** and from 1905 they could call their friends from the brand new **telephone boxes** mushrooming all over town.

THE LOSS OF INNOCENCE. Londoners greeted the outset of **World War I** in 1914 with jubilant confidence, and recruiting stations

Queen Victoria Memorial, Buckingham Palace

THE MOTHER OF PARLIA-MENTS

Britons regard the reverence Americans accord their constitution with bemusement—after all, they've managed quite nicely without one for centuries. Instead, British democracy rests on a foundation of tradition, legislation, and common sense that has evolved since the barons forced King John to sign the Magna Carta in 1215.

Britons take immense pride in this **"unwritten constitution,"** whose flexibility allowed for a virtually bloodless transition from agrarian monarchy to industrial democracy over the last 350 years. In a dramatic example of its ongoing evolution, 1999 saw over 700 hereditary peers barred from voting in the House of Lords—instead, only government-appointed **life peers**, whose titles are not inherited, will be allowed to sit in the Lords.

Although the once-equitable division of power between the **Crown**, the **Lords**, and the **Commons** formed the model for the US system of president, senate, and house, since the 17th century the Commons has been in the ascendancy.

[continued opposite]

were besieged by eager young men. Yet the horror of modern warfare was soon brought home even to those without relatives in the trenches, when in 1915 the first German **air raid** on London killed 39. From now on, it was clear that London would be in the front line of any European action. If the war forever shattered the moral certitudes of the Victorian era, victory masked the fact that economic power had shifted across the Atlantic. Yet as the boom brought on by the wartime economy came to an end, London began to feel the pain: unemployment rose and in 1926 the 10-day **General Strike** brought the nation to a standstill amid fears of revolution. In the end, though, the main beneficiary of the strike was **radio**; the paralyzing of Fleet Street during the strike made the nation dependent on the new **BBC** for news.

ACTION AND REACTION. While **George Orwell** took the conscious decision to share in the people's plight—his experiences living with the East End poor are chronicled in *Down and Out in Paris and London*—others chose to argue from positions of comfort. Such were the members of the intellectual circle known as the **Bloomsbury Group.** So-called because they met at the house of critic-artist couple **Clive** and **Vanessa Bell** in Bloomsbury, the group was less a school of thought than a group of extremely talented friends. Famous names associated with the group included Vanessa's sister, **Virginia Woolf**, novelist **E.M. Forster**, and revolutionary economist **John Maynard Keynes**; the fringes of the group were populated with no-less extraordinary intellects, including philosopher **Bertrand Russell**, writer **Aldous Huxley**, and poet **T.S. Eliot**. If Bloomsbury represented the intellectual establishment, the same cannot be said of **Unit One**, an association of artists dedicated to dragging a reticent public into the brave new world of modern art: sculptors **Henry Moore** and **Barbara Hepworth** and painter **Ben Nicholson** bewildered Londoners with a universe of semi-abstract forms.

LONDON DEFIANT. London's first showdown with Fascism took place in 1936 at the **Battle of Cable Street,** when a furious local crowd attacked a deliberately provocative march through the Jewish East End by **Oswald Mosley's** Blackshirts. Even so, when **World War II** broke out in 1939, London was ill-prepared: the thousands of gas-masks issued in expectation of German chemical attacks were useless against the incendiary devices of **The Blitz**. Starting on September 7th, 1940, London suffered 57 days of consecutive bombing; regular raids continued until 1941. In 1944, a new rain of death started with the advent of V-1 and V-2 missiles.

By the end of the war, London had suffered destruction on a scale unseen since the Great

Fire. If the all-night vigils of volunteer firefighters had saved St. Paul's, the same could not be said for the House of Commons, Buckingham Palace, or most of the East End. 130,000 houses had been damaged beyond repair, and a third of the City of London flattened.

YEAH BABY, YEAH. The end of the war left Britain economically shattered; with industry in ruins and the country billions of pounds in debt, the government was obliged to continue rationing at home while beating an orderly retreat from the fast-disappearing Empire. Even so, London showed an upbeat face to the world during both the **Festival of Britain,** which transformed a bombed-out wasteland by the river into the **South Bank** arts complex (see p. 101), and the 1953 Coronation of **Elizabeth II.** Slowly, London rose from the ashes of war. In the harsh light of the nuclear age, city planners were eager to sweep away the past and replace it with a rational city of concrete towers that proved as unpopular as they were ugly. But if the architectural opportunities created left by the war were squandered, the cultural ones were not.

Home to thousands of European exiles and American troops during the war, London transformed itself from hidebound Capital of Empire to cosmopolitan city of the world. **Carnaby Street** and the **King's Road** became the twin foci of a London peopled by hipsters and bohemians. Local boys the **Rolling Stones** battled for supremacy with the **Beatles,** who set up in **Abbey Road** in 1964, and **The Who** chronicled the fights between scooter-riding "mods" and quiff-toting "rockers." Somewhat belatedly, in 1966 *Time* magazine announced that London "swings, it is the scene."

REDIRECTION AND REDEVELOPMENT. Swinging London died with the oil shocks of the 1970s. Unemployment rose as conflict between unions and the government resulted in the three-day week in 1974 and the **winter of discontent** five years later. A nation in crisis sought refuge in the strong leadership promised by the "Iron Lady" **Margaret Thatcher,** who was elected Prime Minister in 1979. A polarizing figure in British politics even today, Thatcher's program of economic liberalization combined with a return to "Victorian values" in everyday life brought her into direct conflict with the overwhelmingly Labour-dominated **Greater London Council** and its charismatic leader "Red" **Ken Livingstone.** Thatcher's solution was to simply abolish the GLC, depriving London of its sole unified administrative structure and devolving power to the 33 boroughs.

No less controversial was her other major contribution to London, the redevelopment of **Docklands.** London's docks, ever since Roman times the source of the city's prosperity, had been declining since its dockers had success-

Tradition now demands that the **Prime Minister** and the **cabinet** be Members of Parliament (MPs), while the power of the Lords to initiate and modify legislation has been steadily diminished and the monarchy reduced to a rubber stamp.

Although **general elections** to the Commons must be held at least every 5 years, between elections the government has almost unlimited power. Britain's electoral system means the Prime Minister almost always commands an absolute majority of votes in the Commons, while judges have no power to strike down new laws. As a result, despite the weekly theatrics of **Question Time,** when opposition MPs grill the Prime Minister on his performance, the only real check on government power is the court of public opinion.

Today, though, Britain's traditional constitution is under threat: already legislation passed by the European Union supersedes British law, while since 2000 British judges have been able to strike down legislation deemed incompatible with the European Convention on Human Rights. While some see this as a long-needed change to prevent abuses of power, others regard the transfer of power to an unelected international body with trepidation.

ETHNIC LONDON

While ethnic "ghettos" are rare in London, most communities have a neighborhood focus, where members can find the sights, smells, and sounds (if not the sunshine) of their former homeland.

(South) **Asians**, London's largest ethnic group, are also the most fragmented. Sikhs from the **Punjab** congregate in Ealing; the **East End** is the center of the **Bengali** community; and **Pakistanis** prefer **Walthamstow.**

London's **Black** population is divided into two main groups: those of **Caribbean** origin, whose cultural focus is in **Brixton,** and 160,000 **Africans**, mostly West African in origin, who tend to settle in **West London.**

If few of London's ethnic **Chinese** still live there, they still pack **Soho's** Chinatown on weekends to shop and eat—though these days they're often outnumbered by tourists. From oil-rich Saudis to Lebanese refugees, **Arabs** come together over kebabs and strong black coffee on the **Edgware Road.**

Many ethnic groups in London are harder to spot. The majority of the strong **Jewish** community lead secular lives, though you'll still see plenty of black hats in **Golders Green.** A large number of **Cypriot Greeks** can be found in numerous *tavernas* around **Camden Town.** London's largest foreign-born community is also its least visible—you won't find any **Irish** neighborhoods, but there's good *craic* in any number of Irish pubs around the city (not to be confused with the recent abhorrent torrent of Irish-themed chain pubs).

fully fought off containerization in the 1960s. While they may have saved a few jobs in the long term, the death-knell was sounded: shipping moved to the containerized port downriver at Tilbury, and by 1981, for the first time in almost 2000 years, not a single dock was in operation. Thatcher's response was to make the enormous area—as large as Manhattan—into an "enterprise zone," a study in market forces free from normal planning restrictions. Despite being home to London's first new transport system in a century, the futuristic, driverless **Docklands Light Railway,** a new airport, and Britain's tallest building, the 800ft **Canary Wharf,** Docklands was initially condemned for providing unneeded yuppie housing and ignoring the needs of local communities. Today, however, Docklands is seen as a qualified success, with a near-doubling in population since the scheme's inception in 1981.

INTO THE FUTURE. On March 31st, 1990, an initially peaceful protest by 100,000 against a highly unpopular new tax degenerated into an orgy of destruction. The **Poll Tax Riots** sealed the fate of an increasingly out-of-touch Mrs. Thatcher and led to her replacement, in November, with the lacklustre **John Major.** Real change, though, would have to wait for 1997 and the election of another charismatic reformer, **Tony Blair.** Having rid the "New" Labour Party of most of its socialist baggage, Blair's overriding obsession, it would seem, is with modernity. Eagerly embracing the cultural mini-Renaissance so painfully known as **Cool Britannia,** the new government poured millions into a misconceived plan to make London the "Capital of the Millennium." In the event, the much-vaunted "river of fire" merely fizzled, and thousands of VIP guests had to wait for hours outside the **Millennium Dome.**

Other projects have had more success. Gilbert Scott's 1930s Bankside power station reopened in 2000 as the world's largest modern art museum, **Tate Modern** (see p. 136); if **Norman Foster's** reputation suffered when his **Millennium Bridge,** linking the new Tate to the City, was closed for safety reasons three days after being unveiled, it recovered with the opening of the **Great Court** (see p. 134), an ambitious reworking of the British Museum's central courtyard.

On the political front, London regained a unified voice with the election of maverick Ken Livingstone (see above) as its first-ever directly **elected mayor** in 2000. Relationships with Westminster were soured even before Ken took office, during a bitter primary campaign in which Tony Blair did everything he could to prevent the highly popular Livingstone from winning the official Labour Part nomination. Undaunted, Ken stood as an independent and won by a landslide.

THE LIVING CITY

THE CITY TODAY

SIZE

London today is a city of 7 million people—way down from its pre-war peak of almost 9 million, but still comfortably the largest city in Europe, especially if you include the further 3 million living just outside the boundaries of **Greater London** (so called to distinguish it from the historic square mile of the City of London). Even so, London's enormous size—over 30 miles wide east-west, covering some 650 square miles—has less to do with its population that with the English aversion to apartments: the majority of homes are single-family houses, inevitably with their own patch of garden. Add to this a distrust of city-wide planning and a strong sense of community, and you're left with a sprawling, messy metropolis of proudly distinct neighborhoods—which all adds up to the most vibrant, exciting city in the world.

ETHNIC COMPOSITION

Today, one in three Londoners belong to an ethnic minority, a figure that will rise to 40% in five years' time. Although London's origins as a trading center and port mean that it has always been home to a number of small foreign communities, the first large-scale immigration occurred in the 17th century, as religious persecution sent Protestants from all over Europe seeking refuge in England: 1685 saw the arrival of 30,000 French **Huguenots.** A new wave of persecutions in the 19th century brought 20,000 Russian and Polish **Jews,** many of whom were cheated into believing they had arrived in America, while the rise of fascism in the 1930s saw their numbers swelled by Germans and Austrians. After WWII, Communism sent hundreds of thousands of Central and Eastern Europeans of all creeds spilling into England, including 250,000 Polish refugees. The post-war collapse of the British Empire brought a new type of immigrant: rather than fleeing persecution, these were people who had been brought up in the British system and had been taught to think of Britain as their "mother country"—or at least a source of economic opportunity unheard of at home. If the 250,000 **Irish** and 60,000 **Chinese** in London tended towards the latter, the former was true for many of London's 300,000 **West Indians** and 500,000**Asians** (in Britain, "Asian" always refers to someone of Indian, Pakistani, or Bangladeshi origin). More recently, political upheaval in Britain's former colonies has sent a new wave of refugees to London, including some 160,000 **West Africans.**

Each group of new arrivals followed the same pattern of consolidation and dispersal: first staying in cheap housing near the East End docks where they had landed, then moving on to more affluent neighborhoods—while another boatload of refugees soon erased all evidence of their original community. As the heart of Jewish London shifted from Whitechapel to Golders Green, in North London, in the 1950s, the East End became the focus of the then-new Bangladeshi community. Since then, the docks have since ceased to be the main arrival point for newcomers to London; more recent refugees, such as those from West Africa, tend instead to settle in west London—near Heathrow airport.

CONTEMPORARY CULTURE

MUSIC

The central role London has played on the world music scene since the 1960s needs no introduction. The **Beatles** may have started in Liverpool, but they hotfooted it down to London as soon as possible, where the **Rolling Stones** soon joined battle over the hearts and minds of teenagers everywhere. The scooter-riding **Mod** movement abhorred American-influenced rock'n'roll, preferring introspective ballads by **The Kinks** and **The Who,** who soon expanded into "Rock Operas" such as *Quadrophenia* (1973). This new genre of musical theater had been pioneered five years earlier, when composer **Andrew Lloyd 'Webber** and lyricist **Tim Rice** wrote *Joseph and the Amazing Technicolor Dreamcoat* for a high-school production. Despite such revolutionary beginnings, the duo soon descended into polished populism: Lloyd Webber went on to write such crowd-pleasers as *Starlight Express* and *Phantom of the Opera*, and Rice's collaboration with Disney on films such as *Aladdin* and *The Lion King* has won him three Oscars. Just when it seemed that London music had reached an artistic dead end, it roared back to life in the hands of the **Sex Pistols,** created by Malcolm McLaren to drum up publicity for his King's Road boutique, "Sex."

In the late 1980s the focus of British music swung north to Manchester, before landing back down with a bump in the mid-1990s as groups like **Blur** and **Pulp** fought it out with Manchester-boys-come-south **Oasis.** Meanwhile, musical standards reached a new low with the carefully crafted appeal of the **Spice Girls**—not to be confused with arch-rivals **All Saints,** who take their name from the Notting Hill road where they first recorded. Another nineties phenomenon was the explosive growth of electronic music, born of the rave craze that started in Britain in the late 1980s: bands like **Prodigy, Portishead, Massive Attack,** and the **Chemical Brothers** provide the high-octane power for serious dancing in the capital's mega-clubs.

LITERATURE

Londoners love to read: in the bus, on the tube, or in private, the capital has a love affair with books. A nomination for the annual **Booker Prize** brings instant best-seller status, even though recent winners such as Margaret Atwood's *The Blind Assassin* (2000) or Arundhati Roy's *The God of Small Things* (1997) are anything but easy novels. London's home-grown literature tends to continue the tradition of satire and dry humor started by Jonathan Swift and Samuel Johnson in the 18th century. **Julian Barnes's** *Letters from London* (1995)—a collection of *New Yorker* pieces about life in the capital—provide outsiders with an insider perspective, **Dorris Lessing's** *London Observed* (1993) chronicles London through the eyes of an outsider-turned-insider, and **Martin Amis's** murder mystery *London Fields* (1991) turns the city inside-out. More recently, fictional diaries have been all the rage: **Helen Fielding** charts the trials and tribulations of being young, single, and insecure in the wildly popular *Bridget Jones's Diary* (1999) and its sequel, *The Edge of Reason* (2001), while **Sue Townsend,** whose *Secret Diary of Adrian Mole, aged 13 3/4* was a hit with teenagers in 1989, has followed her hapless protagonist into premature middle age with *Adrian Mole: the Cappuccino Years* (2000).

ART

If there's one thing the varied strands of contemporary London art have in common, it's an uncanny ability to unnerve. Since English art until the 20th century was largely the story of portraiture, it's only fitting that the earliest proponents of the stomach-churning school were figurative: the late **Francis Bacon** (1909-1992), who ghoulishly reworked Velazquez's portrait of Innocent X in his *Screaming Popes* series; and **Lucien Freud** (b. 1922), Sigmund's grandson, whose oddly unrealistic "realist" nudes had more than one stuffy patron headed for the couch. In the 1960s, the eye-strain inducing abstractions of "Op-Art" created by **Bridget Riley** (b. 1931) sent aspirin sales soaring. After going underground in the 1980s, the London art scene reexploded on the national consciousness in 1995 when **Damien Hirst** won Britain's most prestigious artistic accolade, the **Turner Prize.** The controversy crossed the Atlantic in 1999 when New York City mayor Rudolph Giuliani attempted to ban **Sensation,** a collection of works by Hirst and his fellow "Britpack" artists. Sensation had first made headlines at its London opening in 1997, when an enraged member of the public defaced an iconic portrait of serial murderer Myra Hindley by **Marcus Harvey;** Giuliani was more concerned with **Chris Ofil's** image of the Virgin Mary incorporating elephant dung. Other recent works to have provoked a storm include brothers **Jake** and **Dinos Chapman's** sculptures of toy figures engaged in highly unnatural activites and **Rachel Whiteread's** *House,* a concrete cast of the inside of a London townhouse. However, with the turn of the century it seems that shock art has had its day. A sober piece by video artist **Steve MacQueen** beat **Tracey Emin's** unmade bed (complete with used condoms), to the 1999 Turner, and the 2000 prize went to **Wolfgang Tillman,** a German-born but London-based photographer, over **Glenn Brown's** reproduction of a sci-fi bookjacket.

FILM

What do films such as *Superman, Star Wars, Titanic, Eyes Wide Shut,* and *Alien* have in common? Easy—they were all filmed in London. If Hollywood supplies the money and the stars, it's generally London studios such as **Pinewood** and **Elstree** that give blockbusters their stages and special effects. But Hollywood owes more to London than backstage trickery: from the earliest days of film, London-bred stars have been among the biggest names to grace the silver screen. Many distinguished actors first proved their mettle on the London stage before making the difficult transition to celluloid, whether in serious drama—such as **Laurence Olivier, Alec Guinness, Anthony Hopkins, Kenneth Branagh,** and **Ralph Fiennes**—or in the equally demanding world of musical theater (think **Charlie Chaplin** and **Julie Andrews**). Others went almost straight to film, from *Gone with the Wind* vixen **Vivien Leigh** in the 1930s to more recent sensation **Hugh Grant.** There's no shortage to talent behind the cameras, either. From the "master of suspense" **Alfred Hitchcock** and *Lawrence of Arabia* director **David Lean** to art-house hero **Derek Jarman,** adopted son **Stanley Kubrick,** and "Mr. Madonna," **Guy Ritchie,** Londoners have called the shots on some of the world's best-loved movies.

There's no bigger star than the city herself, though: London has been the backdrop to thousands of films. Compare **Austin Power's** modern take on London in the swinging sixties to the the real thing in the Beatles' **A Hard Day's Night,** dance with Edwardian chimney sweeps in **Mary Poppins,** follow **Dracula** through the Victorian night, or experience the sights and sounds of Elizabethan London in **Shakespeare in Love.** For a taste of the contemporary city, think of James Bond landing on the Millennium Dome in **The World is Not Enough,** John Cleese's high capers in **A Fish Called Wanda,** Hugh Grant bumbling through **Notting Hill,** or Ewan MacGregor outwitting the locals at the end of in **Trainspotting.**

SPORT

Londoners have always been sports mad. Medieval Londoner William FitzStephen described **football** (soccer) games being played in the 12th century, and football is still the capital's prime diversion. From August until May, thousands turn out every weekend to see top London teams **Arsenal** (or "Gunners"), **Chelsea, West Ham,** and **Tottenham Hotspurs** ("Spurs" for short). Football is very much a lads game—beer and rude songs are essential parts of the ritual—but violence is more publicized than prevalent, and you'll often see fathers and their young sons (dressed, naturally, in full team "strip" and matching scarf) cheering on their team from the terraces.

Rugby, similar to American Football but without the body armor, is the other main winter sport. Divided into two slightly-differing species, Rugby Union and Rugby League, Union rules the roost in London: **Wasps, Harlequins,** and **Saracens** are the top London teams. A game whose defining characteristic is the **scrum**—in which players lock their heads between team-mates' buttocks and try to push the opposing team off the ball—it should come as no surprise that London also has an all-gay Rugby Union side, the **King's Cross Steelers.** More than football, though, Rugby is a game of international rivalries: even those with no team affiliation follow the ups and downs of England at **Twickenham.**

In spring, by when the rugby fields are little more than expanses of mud, attention turns to **cricket.** A game, according to one anonymous commenter, "which the English have invented in order to give themselves some conception of eternity," cricket is the ideal way to spend long summer days: play starts at 11am and typically run until dusk, with breaks for lunch and tea; matches last one to five days. **Middlesex** and **Surrey** are the main London sides; their grounds, at **Lords** and the **Oval** respectively, are also used to host international **Test Matches,** in which England traditionally lose abysmally. Anything else would be "just not cricket," as they say.

Ironically, the sport which gives London the most international attention is the one Londoners care the least about. Although it has a long and distinguished history in the city (Henry VIII was a keen player in his youth), **tennis**—seen as a snob's game—is something most Londoner's tune into during **Wimbledon** fortnight, then promptly tune out again. More democratic is the **London Marathon,** held every April, which sees over 30,000 runners complete the gruelling 26-mile course from Greenwich, in south-east London, to the final stretch just outside Buckingham Palace.

Sights

The characteristic of London is that you never go where you wish nor do what you wish,
and that you always wish to be somewhere else than where you are.
—Sydney Smith, 1818

ORGANIZED TOURS

Cheesy though it may seem, a good city tour has its advantages: it offers a quick overview of London's major sights and historic neighborhoods, and while few venture off the beaten path, sightseeing from the top of a bus will give you a better sense of London's geography than point-to-point excursions by Tube. However, don't make the mistake of thinking a city tour will give you time to properly see everything—just because your tour has stops at every important sight, it doesn't follow that you'll be able to see it all in a day. Instead, treat a tour as a helpful starting point in trying to plan the rest of your stay.

BUS TOURS

The classic London tour is on an open-top double-decker bus—and in good weather, it's undoubtedly the best way to get a good overview of the city. However, if you're booking in advance, you might prefer to insure against rain and choose a bus with a roof upstairs, since you'll see little from street level. Most operators run hop-on, hop-off services, but be sure to check schedules and how long tickets are valid before purchasing. Tickets are often sold at hotels and by agencies all over London, but be careful—travelers have reported overpaying for tickets and being misled about concessionary and child fares by untrustworthy middlemen. In any case, you can usually by tickets on the bus.

If you baulk at the cost of an organized tour, take a regular bus; you'll miss the commentary, but save pounds—a ticket costs £1, and you can buy an all-day bus pass for £2. **Route #11,** beginning at Liverpool Street station, rides past St. Paul's, Fleet St., the Strand, Trafalgar Sq., Westminster, Sloane Sq., and all of King's Rd. **Route #14** runs past the South Kensington museums, Knightsbridge, Hyde Park Corner, Piccadilly Circus and Leicester Sq., and terminates on Tottenham Court Rd.

The Big Bus Company, 48 Buckingham Palace Rd. (☎ 7233 9533; www.bigbus.co.uk). Tube: Victoria. Choice of live commentary in English or recorded in 12 languages. 3 routes, with buses every 15min. 1hr. walking tours and mini Thames cruise included. Also books fast-track entry tickets to many attractions. Tickets valid 24hr. from first use. £15, kids £7.

London Frog Tours, County Hall (☎ 7928 3132; www.frogtours.com). Tube: Waterloo or Westminster. Frog Tours operates a fleet of amphibious vehicles that follow an 80min. non-stop road tour with a splash into the Thames for a 30min. cruise. Tours depart County Hall, opposite the London Eye. £15, students and seniors £12, kids £9.

Original London Sightseeing Tour (☎8877 1722; www.theoriginaltour.com). 3 different routes, with buses every 6min. in peak season. Also books fast-track entry tickets to many attractions. Tickets vaild 24hr. £12.50, kids £7.50; £1 for online bookings.

WALKING TOURS

For a more in-depth account, you can't beat a walking tour led by a knowledgeable guide. Tours usually focus on a specific aspect of a neighborhood's past, often taking you into parts of London most visitors never see. Prebooking is rarely required—though an umbrella is a good idea!

Original London Walks (☎7624 9255; www.walks.com). The oldest and biggest walking-tour company. Weekly program of 12-16 walks per day, from "Magical Mystery Tour" to nighttime "Jack the Ripper's Haunts" and guided visits to larger museums. Most walks last 2hr. £5, students and seniors £4, under 16 free.

Stepping Out (☎8881 2933; www.walklon.ndirect.co.uk). Emphasis on going off the beaten tracks. The "Historical Cat Walk", tracking famous moggies through the streets, will get cat-lovers purring. £5, concs. £4; full-day and tours including museum entry more.

Streets of London (☎07812 501 418; www.thestreetsoflondon.com). 2hr. tours concentrating on the City of London and Clerkenwell. Tours run late May to Sept. £5, concs. £4.

ALTERNATIVE TOURS

BY BIKE. Organised bicycle tours let you cover plenty of ground while still taking you to places double-decker buses can't go. The **London Bicycle Tour Company** has been operating bike tours for seven years. The pace is leisurely, and tours are designed to keep contact with road traffic to a minimum; prices include bike hire, helmet, and comprehensive insurance. The *Royal West* (Sa 2pm) tour takes you along the South Bank, Chelsea, Kensington, and the West End, while the *East Tour* (Su 2pm) encompasses the City, Docklands, and the East End. *(Tours start from the LBTC store, Gabriel's Wharf. ☎7928 6838; www.londonbicycle.com. Tube: Waterloo or Southwark. Royal West Sa 2pm; East Tour Su 2pm. Both 9mi., 3.5hr. Book in advance. £12.)*

BY BOAT. A trip on the Thames provides an alternative, and in some ways more authentic, overview of London—for centuries, the river was London's main highway. Pick up the *River Thames Boat Service Guide* at Tube stations for comprehensive details of all London's different river services; for an overview of commuter services, see p. 36, for trips upriver to Hampton Court see p. 244, and for services to Greenwich see p. 128. **Catamaran Cruises** operates a non-stop sightseeing cruise with recorded commentary, leaving year-round from Waterloo Pier and Apr.-May from Embankment Pier. *(☎7987 1185; www.catamarancruises.co.uk. July-Aug. £7, seniors £6.30, kids £5; Sept.-June £6.70, £6, £4.70. 33% discount with Travelcard.)*

MAJOR ATTRACTIONS

BUCKINGHAM PALACE

> I must say, notwithstanding the expense which has been incurred... no sovereign in Europe, I may even add, perhaps no private gentleman, is so ill-lodged as the king of this country.
> —Arthur Wellesly, Duke of Wellington, 1828

LOCATION: *At the end of the Mall, between* **Westminster, Belgravia,** *and* **Mayfair. LOCAL QUICKFIND:** *Sights, p. 106, p. 109, and p. 80; Museums&Galleries, p. 145 and p. 139; Food&Drink, p. 169, p. 171, and p. 159.* **CONTACT:** ☎ *7839 1377. www.royal.gov.uk.* **TUBE:** *St. James's Park, Victoria, Green Park, or Hyde Park Corner.*

Originally built for the Dukes of Buckingham, Buckingham House was acquired by George III in 1762, and converted into full-scale palace by George IV, who commissioned John Nash to expand the existing building. Neither George IV nor his successor William IV ever lived in the Palace—with good reason, for when a freshly crowned Victoria finally moved in in 1837, she had to contend with faulty drains and a host of other difficulties. Nash's structure was soon found to be too small for her rapidly growing brood; a solution was found by closing off the three-sided courtyard, concealing the best architecture with Edward Blore's uninspiring facade.

Buckingham Palace

THE STATE ROOMS. The Palace opens to visitors for a two-month period every summer, while the Royals are off sunning themselves; advance booking is recommended. Don't look for any insights into the Queen's personal life— the State Rooms are used only for formal occasions, such as entertaining visiting heads of state; as such, they are also the most sumptuous in the Palace, if not all of Britain. Look for the secret door concealed in one of the **White Drawing Room's** mirrors, through which the Royals enter the state apartments. In addition to further chromatically labeled drawing rooms, you also get to see the **Throne Room,** whose unusual plaster frieze treats the War of the Roses in classical style—Tudor costumes give the game away. The **Galleries** display many of the finest pieces in the outstanding Royal Collection, including works by Rembrandt, Rubens, Vermeer, Van Dyck, and Canaletto, as well as Gobelins tapestries. New from 2001, Liz has also graciously allowed commoners into the **Gardens**—keep off the grass! *(Enter on Buckingham Palace Rd. Tickets available from ☎ 7321 2233, www.the-royal-collection. org.uk, or (from late July) the Ticket Office, Green Park. Open daily early Aug.-Sept. 9:30am-4:30pm. £11, seniors £9, under 17 £5.50, under 5 free, family £27.50.)*

Houses of Parliament

CHANGING OF THE GUARD. The Palace is protected by a detachment of Foot Guards in full dress uniform, (fake) bearskin hats and all. "Changing of the Guard" refers not to replacing the sentries, but to the exchanging of guard duty between different Guards regiments. Accompanied by a band, the "New Guard" starts marching down Birdcage Walk from Wellington Barracks around 10:30am, while the "Old Guard" leaves St. James's Palace around 11:10am. When they meet at the central gates of the palace, the officers of the regiments then touch hands, symbolically exchanging keys, *et voilà*, the guard is

St. Paul's

officially changed. To witness the spectacle, show up well before 11:30am and stand directly in front of the palace; for a less-crowded close-up of the guards, watch along the routes of the troops prior to their arrival at the palace (10:40-11:25am) between the Victoria Memorial and St. James's Palace or along Birdcage Walk. *(Daily Apr.-Oct., every other day Nov.-Mar., provided the Queen is in residence, it's not raining too hard, and there are no pressing state functions. Free.)*

THE HOUSES OF PARLIAMENT

⁊ LOCATION: *Parliament Sq., in* **Westminster.** *Enter at St. Stephen's Gate, between Old and New Palace Yards.* **LOCAL QUICKFIND:** *Sights, p. 106; museums&galleries, p. 145; food&drink, p. 169.* **CONTACT:** *Commons Info Office ☎ 7219 4272; www.parliament.uk.* **TUBE:** *Westminster.* **DEBATES:** *Open to all while Parliament is in session (Oct.-July.); afternoon waits can be 2hr., M-Th after 6pm and F are least busy. Tickets required for Prime Minister's Question Time (W 3-3:30pm).* **Lords** *usually sits M-W from 2:30pm, Th 3pm, occasionally F 11:30am; closing times vary.* **Commons** *usually M-W 2:30-10:30pm, Th 11:30am-7:30pm, F 9:30am-3pm.* **TOURS: British residents:** *Tours held year-round M-W 9:30am-noon and F 2:30-5:30pm; contact your MP to book.* **Overseas visitors:** *Oct.-July, non-residents must apply in writing at least 4 weeks ahead to: Parliamentary Education Unit, Norman Shaw Building, SW1A 2TT (☎ 7219 4600; edunit @parliament.uk). Tours F 3:30-5:30pm.* **Summer tours:** *Open to all Aug.-Sept. M-Sa 9:15am-4:30pm. Reserve through Ticketmaster (☎ 7344 9966; www. ticket-master.co.uk) or in person from mid-July. £3.50.*

The Palace of Westminster, as the building in which Parliament sits is officially known, has been at the heart of English governance since the 11th century, when Edward the Confessor established his court here. William the Conqueror found the site to his liking, and under the Normans the palace was greatly extended, most notably with the addition of Westminster Hall in 1097. Westminster Hall and Jewel Tower (see below) aside, what little of the Norman palace to remain following was entirely destroyed in the massive conflagration of October 16, 1834. The rebuilding started in 1835 under the joint command of classicist Charles Barry and Gothic champion Augustus Pugin. The resulting clash of temperaments resulted in a a masterful combination of classical symmetry with a fairy-tale abundance of crenellations, tracery, and sculpture. Access to the Palace has been restricted since a bomb killed an MP in 1979. If you're unable to gain a place on one of the rare tours don't despair: all are allowed in to see debates while the Houses are in session.

OUTSIDE THE HOUSES. Standing on the Parliament Sq. side of the Palace, **Old Palace Yard** is the triangular area to the right. Once the site of executions, including those of Walter Ralegh and Guy Fawkes, today a statuesque Richard I lords it over parked cars. On the left, **New Palace Yard** is a good place to spy your favorite MPs as they enter the complex through the Members' entrance. Between the two, Cromwell stares out in the general direction of Buckingham Palace.

WESTMINSTER HALL. Behind Cromwell squats this low, unadorned chamber, the sole survivor of the 1834 fire. Unremarkable from the outside, the Hall stuns from within with a magnificent hammerbeam roof, constructed in 1394 and considered the finest timber roof ever made. Originally the setting for medieval feasts, when Henry VIII decamped to Whitehall it was converted into law courts; famous defendants have included Thomas More, and Charles I. These days, it sees use for public ceremonies, the lying-in-state of monarchs, and occasional exhibitions.

DEBATING CHAMBERS. Visitors to the debating chambers must first pass through **St. Stephen's Hall,** which stands on the site of St. Stephen's Chapel. Formerly the king's private chapel, in 1550 St. Stephen's became the meeting place of the House of Commons. The Commons have since moved on, but four brass markers still mark where the Speaker's Chair used to stand. At the end of the hall, the octagonal **Central Lobby** marks the separation of the two houses, with the Commons to the north and the Lords to the south. Access to the **House of Lords** is via the Peers' Lobby, which smug MPs have bedecked with scenes of Charles I's downfall. The ostentatious chamber itself is dominated by the sovereign's Throne of State under a gilt canopy. The Lord Chancellor presides over the Peers from the **Woolsack,** a red behemoth the size of a VW Beetle. Next to him rests the almost 6 ft. **Mace,** which is brought in to open the House each morning. In contrast with the Lords is the restrained **House of Commons,** with simple green-backed benches under a plain wooden roof. This is not entirely due to the difference in class—the Commons was destroyed by bombs in 1941, and rebuilding took place during a time of post-war austerity. The Speaker sits at the center-rear of the chamber, with the government MPs to his right and the opposition to his left. However, with room for only 437 out of 635 MPs, things can get hectic when all are present. The front benches are reserved for government ministers and their opposition "shadows"; the Prime Minister and the Leader of the Opposition face off across their dispatch boxes.

BIG BEN AND VICTORIA TOWER. The **Clock Tower** is universally misknown as Big Ben, which strictly refers only to the 14-ton bell that tolls the hours. The bell is named after the robustly proportioned Sir Benjamin Hall, who served as Commissioner of Works when the bell was cast and hung in 1858. At 98.5m, the southern **Victoria Tower** pips its northern brother by a shade over 2m. Designed to hold the parliamentary archives, inside are copies of every Act of Parliament passed since 1497. A flag flown from the top indicates that Parliament is in session.

ST. PAUL'S CATHEDRAL

⧉ LOCATION: St. Paul's Churchyard, **City of London. LOCAL QUICKFIND:** sights, p. 93; for museums&galleries, p. 143; food&drink, p. 167. **CONTACT:** ☎ 7246 8348; www.stpauls.co.uk. **TUBE:** St. Paul's, Mansion House, or Blackfriars. **AUDIOGUIDE:** £3.50, concs. £3. **TOURS:** M-F 11, 11:30am, 1:30, 2pm; 90min. £2.50, students & seniors £2, kids £1. **OPEN:** M-Sa 8:30am-4pm; open for worship daily 7:15am-6pm. **EVENSONG:** The cathedral choir sings evensong M-Sa at 5pm. Arrive at 4:50pm to be admitted to seats in the Quire. 45min.; free. **ADMISSION:** £5, students & seniors £4, kids £2.50; worshippers free.

St. Paul's continues to dominate its surroundings even as modern usurpers sneak up around it. Sir Christopher Wren's masterpiece is the fifth cathedral to occupy the site; the original was built in AD 604 shortly after St. Augustine's mission to the Anglo-Saxons. Incredibly, Wren's is not the largest of the five: the fourth, "Old St. Paul's," begun in 1087 had a steeple as third as high again as the current 111m dome. By 1666, when the Great Fire swept away it away, Old St. Paul's was ripe for replacement; already in 1663 a commission had met to consider the situation. Even so, only in 1668 did the authorities abandon hope of restoring the old building and invite Wren to design a new cathedral. Church and architect were at loggerheads from the start: when the bishops rejected his third design,Wren simply ignored them and, with Charles II's approval, started building. Sneakily, Wren had persuaded the king to let him make "necessary alterations" as work progressed, and the building that emerged from the scaffolding in 1708 bore a closer resemblance to Wren's second "Great Model," design. Child of one fire, the cathedral only just survived another: on December 29, 1940 St. Paul's was again in flames. Fifty-one firebombs landed on the cathedral, all put out by the volunteer St. Paul's Fire Watch; a small plaque in the floor at the end of the nave honors them.

INTERIOR. The entrance leads to the north aisle of the **nave,** the largest space in the cathedral with seats for 2500 worshippers; here, the enormous memorial to the **Duke of Wellington** completely fills one of the arches. Note that, unlike medieval churches, no one is actually buried in the cathedral floor—the graves are all downstairs, in the crypt. The second tallest freestanding **dome** in Europe (after St. Peter's in the Vatican) seems even larger from inside, its height exaggerated by the false perspective of the paintings on the inner surface. The north transept functions as the **baptistry,** with William Holman Hunt's third version of *The Light of the World* hanging opposite the font; the south transept holds the **Nelson Memorial.** The stalls in the **Quire** narrowly escaped a bomb, but the old altar did not. It was replaced with the current marble **High Altar,** above which looms the ceiling mosaic of *Christ Seated in Majesty.* The altar itself bears a dedication to the Commonwealth war dead of both World Wars, while immediately behind it is the **American Memorial Chapel,** in honor of the 28,000 US soldiers based in Britain who died during WWII. The north quire aisle holds Henry Moore's *Mother and Child.* One month after the sculpture's arrival, guides insisted a plaque be affixed to the base because no one knew what it was. The south quire aisle contains one of the few monuments to survive from Old St. Paul's: a swaddled statue of **John Donne** (Dean of the Cathedral 1621-31).

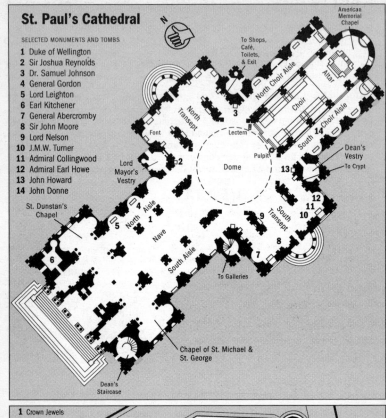

St. Paul's Cathedral

SELECTED MONUMENTS AND TOMBS

1 Duke of Wellington
2 Sir Joshua Reynolds
3 Dr. Samuel Johnson
4 General Gordon
5 Lord Leighton
6 Earl Kitchener
7 General Abercromby
8 Sir John Moore
9 Lord Nelson
10 J.M.W. Turner
11 Admiral Collingwood
12 Admiral Earl Howe
13 John Howard
14 John Donne

N

To Shops,
Café,
Toilets,
& Exit

American
Memorial
Chapel

North Choir Aisle

Choir

Altar

North
Transept

South Choir Aisle

Font

Lectern

Dean's
Vestry

To Crypt

Pulpit

Dome

13

12

11

10

Lord
Mayor's
Vestry

St. Dunstan's
Chapel

North
Aisle

Nave

South Aisle

South
Transept

To Galleries

Chapel of St. Michael &
St. George

Dean's
Staircase

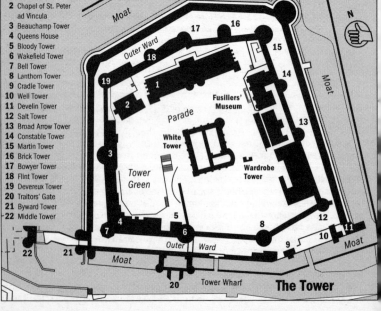

1 Crown Jewels
2 Chapel of St. Peter
   ad Vincula
3 Beauchamp Tower
4 Queens House
5 Bloody Tower
6 Wakefield Tower
7 Bell Tower
8 Lanthorn Tower
9 Cradle Tower
10 Well Tower
11 Develin Tower
12 Salt Tower
13 Broad Arrow Tower
14 Constable Tower
15 Martin Tower
16 Brick Tower
17 Bowyer Tower
18 Flint Tower
19 Devereux Tower
20 Traitors' Gate
21 Byward Tower
22 Middle Tower

Moat

N

Outer Ward

Fusiliers'
Museum

Parade

White
Tower

Wardrobe
Tower

Tower
Green

Traitors' Gate

Byward Tower

Middle Tower

Outer   Ward

Moat

Moat

Moat

Tower Wharf

The Tower

SCALING THE HEIGHTS. St. Paul's dome is built in three parts; an inner brick dome, visible from the inside of the cathedral; an outer timber structure; and between the two a brick cone that carries the weight of the lantern on top. A network of stairs pierce the structure, carrying brave visitors up, up, and away. First stop is the narrow **Whispering Gallery**, reached by 259 shallow steps or (for those in need only) a small elevator—though it's not wheelchair accessible. Encircling the base of the inner dome, the gallery is a perfect resounding chamber: whisper into the wall, and your friend on the other side should be able to hear you. Well, they could if everyone else wasn't trying the same thing. Instead, admire the scenes from the life of St. Paul painted on the canopy. From here, the stout of heart and leg can climb another 119 steps (this time steep and winding) to the **Stone Gallery**, outside the cathedral at the base of the outer dome. The heavy stone balustrade, not to mention taller modern buildings, result in an underwhelming view, so take a deep breath and persevere up the final 152 vertiginous steps to the **Golden Gallery** at the base of the lantern. The view from makes it all worth it, although at busier times it can be hard to see farther than the person in front of you.

PLUMBING THE DEPTHS. In the other vertical direction, the crypt (the largest in Europe) is saturated with tombs of great Britons. **Nelson** commands pride of place, with radiating galleries festooned with monuments to other military heroes, from Epstein's bust of **T.E. Lawrence** (of Arabia) to a plaque commemorating the casualties of the Gulf War; **Florence Nightingale** is also honored here. The neighboring chamber contains **Wellington's** massive tomb, its stark simplicity in contrast to the ornate monument upstairs. The rear of the crypt, now the chapel of the "most excellent Order of the British Empire," bears the graves of artists, including **William Blake, J.M.W. Turner,** and **Henry Moore,** crowded around the black slab concealing the body of **Christopher Wren.** Inscribed on the wall above is his famous epitaph: *Lector, si monumentum requiris circumspice* ("Reader, if you seek his monument, look around"). Also in the crypt are models of St. Paul's various incarnations and the **treasury,** with a glittering collection of plate, cups, and robes, including the Bishop of London's Jubilee cope, a silk robe with 73 churches and St. Paul's Cathedral embroidered upon it with gold silk.

THE TOWER OF LONDON

◢ LOCATION: Tower Hill, next to Tower Bridge, in the **City of London,** within easy reach of the **South Bank** and the **East End. LOCAL QUICKFIND:** sights p. 93, p. 100, and p. 126 respectively; museums&galleries, p. 143, p. 144, and p. 126; food&drink, p. 167, p. 168, and p. 180. **CONTACT:** ☎ 7709 0765; www.hrp.org.uk. **TUBE:** Tower Hill or **DLR:** Tower Gateway. **AUDIOGUIDES:** £3. **TOURS: Yeoman Warder Tours:** Meet near entrance. Every 30min. M-Sa 9:30am-3:30pm, Su 10am-3:30pm; 1hr. **Illustrated Tours:** Meet at Lanthorn Tower. Prisoners & Punishment 9:30, 11:30am, 2:15, 4:30pm; Hidden Life of the Tower 10:15am, 5pm; Attack the Tower 12:15, 3pm. **OPEN:** Mar.-Oct. M-Sa 9am-5:30pm, Su 10am-5:30pm; Nov.-Feb. closes 4:30pm. Last admission 30min. before close. **ADMISSION:** £11.30, students & seniors £8.50, kids £7.50, family (2 adults + 3 kids) £34. Tickets also sold at Tube stations; buy them in advance since queues at the door are horrendous.

The Tower of London, palace and prison of English monarchs for over 900 years, is steeped in blood and history. Conceived by William the Conqueror more to provide protection from than to his new subjects, his wooden palisade of 1067 was replaced in 1078 by a stone structure that over the next 20 years would grow into the White Tower. Richard the Lionheart began the construction of additional defenses in 1189, and further work by Henry III and Edward I brought the Tower close to its present condition. Now 20 towers stand behind its walls, all connected by massive walls and gateways, forming fortifications disheartening to visitors even today. The whole castle used to be surrounded by a broad moat, but cholera epidemics led to its draining in 1843; it's since sprouted a tennis court for the Yeomen Warders. These "Beefeaters"—whose nickname is a reference to their daily allowance of meat in former times—still guard the fortress, dressed in their discinctive blue everyday or red ceremonial uniforms. To be eligible for Beefeaterhood, a candidate must have at least 22 years of service in the forces, as well as a strong appetite for flash photography. All this history and tradition notwithstanding, with 2.5 million visitors a year, the Tower can feel like a medieval theme park at times. To make the most of your visit, buy tickets in advance and arrive as early as possible—before the school buses

RAVENS MISBE- HAVIN'

No one's quite sure how, why, or when ravens took to living in the Tower, but these large black birds have become an integral part of London folklore. According to legend, when the ravens leave, the Tower will crumble and the monarchy will fall. To prevent such calamitous occurrences, Charles II ordered that ravens be kept at the Tower, if not exactly under lock and key, then at least under a very close watch; even today the incumbents have their wings clipped.

There's little reason for the birds to wander far, though—they rival the Beefeaters in popularity and are treated suitably regally, being fed each day on 6oz. of raw meat and blood-soaked biscuits. Even so, some birds seem to prefer life outside; Grog escaped to the Rose and Punchbowl pub in 1981.

Naturally, with all the tourist attention they get, the ravens have to be on best behavior all the time; cantakerous fowl have been given the sack. George was dismissed in 1986 after becoming obsessed with eating TV aerials. The dispatch read "On Saturday 13 Sept 1986, Raven George, enlisted 1975, was posted to the Welsh Mountain Zoo. Conduct unsatisfactory, services therefore no longer required."

unload. To make it easier for visitors to find their way around, the fortress has been divided into seven more-or-less self-contained areas, which can be visited in any order. An enjoyable and popular way to get a feel for the Tower is to join one of the **Yeoman Warders' Tours** (see above), which will fill you in on the history and legends associated with the Tower.

WESTERN ENTRANCE AND WATERLANE. Historically, the main overland entrance to the Tower was over a double system of drawbridges via mini-fortress where the ticket offices now stand; **Lion Tower,** of which only the foundations remain, was the first line of defense, followed by **Middle Tower,** where today tickets are collected and bags searched. After passing over the moat, you enter the **Outer Ward** though **Byward Tower.** The password, required for entry after hours, has been changed every day since 1327. Just beyond Byward Tower, the massive **Bell Tower** dates from 1190; the curfew bell has been rung here nightly for over 500 years. The stretch of the Outer Ward along the Thames is **Water Lane,** which until the 16th century was adjacent to the river. The riverine **Traitor's Gate** was built by Edward I for his personal use, but is now associated with the prisoner who passed through it.

MEDIEVAL PALACE. In this sequence of rooms, archaeologists have attempted to recreate the look and feel of the Tower during the reign of Edward I (1275-1279). The tour starts at **St. Thomas's Tower,** a half-timbered set of rooms above Traitor's Gate named for that early traitor, Thomas Becket. In other rooms, costumed guides regale visitors with stories and demonstrations of medieval palace life. The tour also takes in **Wakefield Tower,** now presented as a putative throne room. Tower lore claims that Henry VI was murdered while imprisoned here in 1471 by Edward IV, though recent evidence suggests he was in fact kept in the adjacent **Lanthorn Tower.**

WALL WALK. The Wall Walk runs along the eastern wall constructed by Henry III in the mid-13th century. The wall is entered via **Salt Tower,** whose long service as a prison is witnessed by the inscriptions scratched out by bored inmates. Presumably some of them came to a sticky end, since the tower is allegedly haunted—apparently dogs refuse to enter it. At the end of the walk is **Martin Tower.** In 1671, the self-styled "Colonel" Thomas Blood nearly pulled off the heist of the millennium. Blood befriended the warden of the tower, where the crown jewels were then kept, and visited him at night with some "friends." They subdued the guard and stuffed their trousers with booty, only to be caught at the nearby docks. Charles II was so taken with Blood's bravado that he awarded the colonel a privileged spot in his court, the moral being, of course, that crime does pay. These days, the Martin Tower is home to a fascinating collection of retired crowns, *sans* gemstones (which have been recycled into the current models) along with paste models of some of the more famous jewels, including the fist-sized Cullinan diamond, the largest ever found at 3106 carats. Scotland Yard mailed the stone third class from the Transvaal in an unmarked parcel, a scheme they believed was the safest way of getting it to London.

CROWN JEWELS. The queue at the Jewel House (formerly Waterloo Barracks) is a miracle of crowd management. Tourists file past room after room of rope barriers while video projections show larger-than-life depictions of the jewels in action. Finally, the crowd is ushered into the vault, past two-foot thick steel doors, and onto moving walkways that whisk them past the crowns and ensure no awestruck gazers hold up the queue. Most of the items on display come from the Coronation regalia; with the exception of the Coronation Spoon, everything dates from after 1660, since Cromwell melted down the original booty. While the eye is naturally drawn to the **Imperial State Crown,** home to the Stuart Sapphire along with 16 others, 2876 diamonds, 273 pearls, 11 emeralds, and a mere five rubies, don't miss the **Sceptre with the Cross,** topped with First Star of Africa, the largest quality cut diamond in the world. Look for the **Queen Mother's Crown,** which contains the Koh-I-Noor diamond. Legend claims the diamond will only bring luck to women.

WHITE TOWER. Originally a royal residence, the Conqueror's original castle has also served as a wardrobe, storehouse, records office, mint, armory, and prison. Visitors are given the option of long or short routes; unless you have trouble with spiral staircases or are particularly pressed for time, take the long version, which starts with the first-floor **Chapel of St. John the Evangelist.** A study in massive simplicity, this 11th-century Norman chapel was probably originally brightly painted. The spacious hall next door was most likely the royal **bedchamber,** with numerous garderobes (medieval toilets) set into the walls. The larger room next door would have been his **Great Hall.** Today it houses a collection of armor and weapons from the Royal collection: one look at Henry VIII's "generous" tournament suit will show why never had any trouble remarrying. The visit then passes through more displays of swords, cannon, and muskets on the second floor, before dropping down two levels to meet up with the start of the short route. This trails through a set of historic misrepresentations, starting with the **Spanish Armory**—torture instruments displayed in the 17th century as being captured from the Spanish Armada (1588), but

Queen Anne

Wall Walk, Tower of London

The Mall

LOCKED UP

Although more famous for the prisoners who died here, the Tower has seen a handful of spectacular escapes. In 1101, the Bishop of Durham, the first prisoner, escaped Henry I by climbing out of a window and sliding down a rope. The Welsh prince Gruffydd ap Llewelyn, was less successful in 1244—his rope of knotted sheets broke and he fell to his death.

Prisoners of special privilege sometimes received the honor of a private execution, particularly when their public execution risked escape or riot. The **Scaffold Site** on Tower Green marks the spot where the axe fell on Catherine Howard, Lady Jane Grey, Anne Boleyn, and the Earl of Essex, Queen Elizabeth's rejected suitor. All these and More (Sir Thomas) were treated to unconsecrated burial in the nearby **Chapel of St. Peter ad Vincula.**

You may be surprised to discover that the Tower's prison role lasted well into the 20th century. During WWI, German spies were exectued in the Outer Ward, while the last prisoner was Rudolph Hess, Hitler's no. 2, who defected by parachuting into Scotland in 1941.

actually from the Tower's own armoury. Finally, you exit via the basement past a display telling how the Victorians "restored" the Tower to their ideal of a medieval fortress, demolishing many of its historic buildings along the way.

TOWER GREEN. The grassy western side of the Inner Ward, site of the Tower's most famous executions (see *Locked Up*, p. 76), is surrounded by a suite of houses that have been home to Tower officials for centuries. The Tudor **Queen's House** (which will become the King's House when Charles ascends the throne) is now occupied by the Governor of the Tower. Nearby, the **Beauchamp Tower** was usually reserved for high-class "guests," many of whom carved intricate inscriptions into the walls during their detention. On the north of Tower Green is the **Chapel Royal of St. Peter ad Vinculum.** Originally just another City church, by the 13th century it found itself well within the Tower walls. Three Queens of England, Anne Boleyn, Catherine Howard, and Lady Jane Grey, are buried here, as well as Catholic martyrs Sir Thomas More and John Fisher. *(Open only by Yeoman tours or after 4:30pm.)* Across the green, **Bloody Tower** is named for the tradition that it was here Richard III imprisoned and then murdered his nephews, the rightful Edward V (aged 12) and his brother, before usurping the throne in 1483. In 1674, the bones of two children were unearthed beneath a nearby staircase and subsequently re-interred in Westminster Abbey. Inside, the tower has been restored to its appearance in the early 17th century, when it housed erstwhile adventurer and treason suspect Sir Walter Ralegh.

FUSILIERS' MUSEUM. Of all the sights in the Tower, this is the least popular—not least because you have to stump up an extra 50p (kids free). Inside, a gung-ho set of rooms extolls the virtues and campaigns of the Royal Fusilier Guards, founded by James II in 1685 to protect the Tower's arsenal.

OUTSIDE THE TOWER. The Tower's jurisdiction extends beyond its walls into the surrounding area, known as the **Liberty of the Tower. Tower Hill** was the traditional site for public beheadings. The last execution was that of 80-year-old Lord Lovat, leader of the Jacobite rebellion, in 1747. *(In Trinity Gardens next to Tower Hill Underground station.)* Between the Tower and the Thames, the **Wharf** offers a view of Tower Bridge and Southwark. Ceremonial salutes are fired from the river bank here on Royal birthdays and during state visits.

CEREMONY OF THE KEYS. As the oldest continuously occupied castle in Europe, the Tower has a wealth of traditions. One of the most popular is the Ceremony of the Keys. This nightly locking-up ritual has been performed every night without fail for over 700 years: At precisely 9:53pm, the Chief Yeoman locks the outer gates of the Tower before presenting the keys to the Governor amid much marching and salutation. *(For tickets, write six weeks in advance with the full name of those attending, a choice of at least three dates, and a stamped addressed envelope or international response coupon to: Ceremony of the Keys, Waterloo Block, HM Tower of London, EC3N 4AB. Free.).*

WESTMINSTER ABBEY

🖪 LOCATION: *Parliament Sq.,* **Westminster;** *access Old Monastery, Cloister, & Garden from Dean's Yard, behind the Abbey.* **LOCAL QUICKFIND:** *Sights, p. 106; museums&galleries, p. 145; food&drink, p. 169.* **CONTACT:** *Abbey ☎ 7222 7110, Old Monastery ☎ 7222 5897; www.westminster-abbey.org.* **TUBE:** *Westminster or St. James's Park.* **AUDIOGUIDES***: available M-F 9:30am-3pm, Sa 9:30am-1pm. £2.* **TOURS:** *90min. guided tours M-F 10, 11am, 2, 3pm; Sa 10, 11am; Apr.-Oct. also M-F 10:30am and 2:30pm. £3, including Old Monastery.* **OPEN: Abbey:** *M-F 9am-4:45pm, Sa 9am-2:45pm; last admission 1hr. before closing; Su open for services only.* **Pyx Chamber and Museum:** *Daily 10:30am-4pm.* **Chapter House:** *Daily Apr.-Oct. 10am-5:30pm, Nov.-Mar. 10am-4pm.* **Cloisters:** *Daily 8am-6pm. Garden Apr.-Sept. Tu-Th 10am-6pm, Oct.-Mar. 10am-4pm.* **ADMISSION: Abbey:** *£6; students, seniors, and ages 11-15 £3; under 11 free; family (2 adults + 2 kids) £12. Entry to services is free.* **Old Monastery:** *£2.50; joint entry with Abbey £1 extra on Abbey prices.* **Cloisters & Garden:** *Free.*

On December 28, 1065, Edward the Confessor, last Saxon King of England, was buried in his still-unfinished Abbey church of the West Monastery; almost exactly a year later, the Abbey saw the coronation of William the Conqueror. Thus even before it was completed, the Abbey's twin traditions as the figurative birthplace and literal resting place of royalty had been established. Almost nothing remains of Edward's Abbey, following a Gothic reworking under Henry III. Later monarchs continued to add to the Abbey, but the biggest change was constitutional rather than physical: in 1540 Henry VIII dissolved the monasteries, expelling the monks and stripping their wealth. Fortunately, Henry's respect for his royal forebears outweighed his vindictiveness against the Pope, and so uniquely among the great monastic centers of England, Westminster escaped destruction and desecration. Instead, the Abbey became a "Royal Peculiar," under the direct control of the crown.

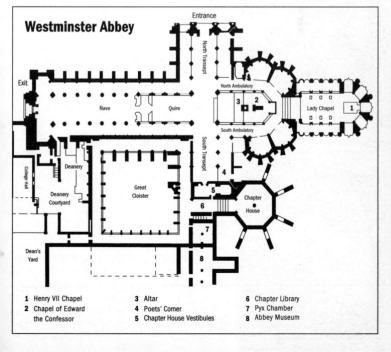

1 Henry VII Chapel	**3** Altar	**6** Chapter Library
2 Chapel of Edward the Confessor	**4** Poets' Corner	**7** Pyx Chamber
	5 Chapter House Vestibules	**8** Abbey Museum

STONED

On Christmas Day, 1950, daring Scottish patriot Ian Hamilton—posing as a visitor—hid himself in Westminster Abbey until it closed. He meant to steal the 200kg Stone of Scone and return it to Scotland. As he approached the door near Poet's Corner to let in his three accomplices, he was detected by a watchman. Hamilton (now a prominent Scottish MP) talked fast enough to convince the watchman that he had been locked in involuntarily.

That same night the foursome forcibly entered the Abbey and pulled the stone out of its wooden container, in the process inadvertently breaking the famed rock into two uneven pieces. Hamilton sent his girlfriend driving off to Scotland with the smaller piece, while he returned to deal with the larger piece. He lugged the piece to his car, and, while driving out of London, happened across his wayward accomplices. The stone was repaired in a Glasgow workyard, but the patriots were frustrated that they could not display it in a public place. On April 11, 1951, Hamilton and Company carried the stone to the altar at Arbroath Abbey where it was discovered and returned to England.

The final chapter of the story is that now-deceased Glasgow councilor Bertie Gray claimed, before he died, that the stone was copied and that the stone that resided in the Abbey was a fake. The British authorities dispute his claim.

INSIDE THE ABBEY

Due to the volume of tourists besieging the Abbey, visitors are obliged to follow a set route. Visitors enter through the **Great North Door** into **Statesman's Aisle,** littered with monuments to 18th- and 19th-century politicians. Prime Ministers Disraeli and Gladstone could not stand each other in life, but in death their figures stand close together. Following the trail around, the **ambulatory** leads past a string of side chapels to the left and the **Shrine of St. Edward** to the right. Around the Confessor's shrine, the **House of Kings** arrays the tombs of monarchs from Henry III (d. 1272) to Henry V (d. 1422). At the far end of the Shrine stands the **Coronation Chair,** built for Edward I; the shelf below the seat was made to house the Scottish Stone of Scone (see *Stoned*, p. 78), which Edward brought south in 1296—the Stone was finally returned to Scotland 700 years later. Stairs lead from the chair to the fan-vaulted **Lady Chapel,** now a Tudor mausoleum. On entering the chapel, a passage to the left leads to a side aisle where **Elizabeth I** lies together with her Catholic half-sister and rival Bloody Mary. Returning to the central part of the Lady Chapel, the nave is dominated by the carved wooden stalls of the **Order of the Bath;** at its end **Henry VII** lies in front of the **Battle of Britain Chapel.** Just before leaving the Lady Chapel, a passageway leads to the south aisle where the tomb of **Mary, Queen of Scots** distracts visitors from the plainer graves of Charles II, William III, Mary II, and Queen Anne.

The south transept holds the Abbey's most famous and popular attraction: **Poet's Corner.** Its founder member was buried here for reasons nothing to do with literary repute—**Chaucer** had a job in the Abbey administration. Plaques at his feet commemorate both poets and prose writers, as does the stained-glass window above. Many of the plaques bear images for puzzle solvers, such as D.H. Lawrence's publishing mark (a phoenix) and T.S. Eliot's symbol of death. You don't need to be buried here to get a fancy monument, as **Shakespeare** (buried in Stratford) attests, nor do you need to be a writer—**Handel** is feted with a freestanding statue, another statue mounted on the wall, and a floor plaque. Outsiders among the *artistes* include Old Parr, who reputedly lived to 152 on a diet of green cheese, bread, and weak ale before expiring shortly after James I honored him with a series of banquets. At the very center of the Abbey, a short flight of steps leads up to the **Sanctuary,** where coronations take place; the stall to the left of the altar is used by the Royal Family. Cordons prevent you from climbing up to admire the 13th-century Cosmati mosaic floor.

After a detour through the Cloisters, including optional visits to the Old Monastery and Gardens (see below), visitors re-enter into the **nave,** the largest uninterrupted space in the Abbey and the part used for daily services. At the western end is the **Tomb of the Unknown Warrior,** surrounded by poppies and bearing the remains of an unidentified WWI soldier from the trenches of Flanders, with an oration poured from molten bullets. Hanging from a column by the tomb is the **US Congressional Medal of Honor,** laid on the grave in 1921 by General Pershing. Just beyond the tomb is the simple grave of a well-known hero, **Winston Churchill.** Stretching eastwards, the North Aisle starts with memorials to 20th-century Prime Ministers before transmuting into **"Scientist's Corner,"** even less of a corner than its poetic equivalent. Isaac Newton's massive monument, set into the left-hand Quire screen, presides over a tide of physicists around his grave in the nave itself, while adjacent in the aisle biologists cluster around would-be pastor Charles Darwin. Just beyond, in the shadow of the Quire, is **Musician's Aisle.** Originally the resting place of the Abbey's organists, including John Blow and William Purcell, its remit has been extended to include the likes of Elgar, Vaughan Williams, and Britten.

OLD MONASTERY, CLOISTERS, AND GARDENS

Formerly a major monastery, the Abbey complex still stretches far beyond the church itself; still on the grounds are the buildings of Westminster School, founded in 1560 by Elizabeth I. Note that all the sights below are accessible through Dean's Yard without going through the Abbey. The **Great Cloisters** hold yet more tombs and commemorative plaques; a passageway running off the southeastern corner leads to the idyllic **Little Cloister,** from where another passage leads to the 900-year-old **College Gardens.** Recent tests have shown that lead contamination makes the herbs grown here unfit for human consumption. A door off the east cloister leads to the octagonal **Chapter House,** the original meeting place of the House of Commons, whose 13th-century tiled floor is the best-preserved in Europe. In 1395, the Abbey succeeded in throwing the MPs out; the faded but still exquisite frescoes of the Book of Revelations around the walls date from this period. Dark and windowless, the **Pyx Chamber** is one of the few surviving parts of the original 11th-century monastic complex. Originally a chapel, it was converted into a treasury in the 13th century. Today the treasure consists of the Abbey's limited silverware collection—the bulk was melted down in the 16th century by Henry VIII. Next door, the **Abbey Museum** is housed in the Norman undercroft. The self-proclaimed highlight of the collection is the array of **funeral effigies,** from the unhealthy-looking wooden models of the 14th century to fully-dressed 17th-century wax versions.

SIGHTS BY NEIGHBORHOOD

WEST END

OXFORD STREET & REGENT STREET

⚑ NEIGHBORHOOD QUICKFIND: *Discover, p. 2; Food&Drink, p. 159; Nightlife, p. 190; Entertainment, p. 209; Shopping, p. 226.*

OXFORD CIRCUS AND AROUND

⚑ Tube: *Oxford Circus.*

SEE MAP, p. 330-331

Oscar Wilde famously quipped that **Oxford Street** is "all street and no Oxford"; there's precious little of beauty or historic interest on London's top commercial thoroughfare. Still, if you're intent on a photo-op with a street lined end-to-end with double-decker buses, it's the place to be. **Regent Street** is at least more imposing, even though none of Nash's original Regency arcades have survived. From November to January of every year, Oxford St. and Regent St. tempt with a festival of **Christmas lights** strung across the street. For some reason, **Oxford Circus** is one of London's most famous landmarks, although it's actually an extremely busy junction where Regent St. and Oxford St. cross. At Christmas, the crowds are so crazy that the police are called in to control the crosswalks.

CARNABY STREET. In the 1960s, Carnaby St. was at the heart of Swinging London, witnessing the rise of youth culture and becoming a hotbed of sex and fashion. After that brief psychadelic high, there followed 30 years as a lurid tourist trap; now it's starting to look as though Carnaby could swing again for the naughty noughties with an influx of trendy boutiques. They may not be heralding a new sexual revolution, but at least they provide an alternative to the mainstream selection of Regent St. Carnaby St. itself is dominated by streetwise, but not exactly exclusive labels such as Diesel, Mambo, and Muji; explore the nearby streets for more cutting-edge items.

ALL SOULS LANGHAM PLACE. John Nash's plan to link Regent St. to Portland Pl. was thrown off by the Langham family, who refused to let him build across their land. Forced to make an ungainly kink in his road at Langham Pl., Nash designed All Souls to soften the bend. Unlike any other church in London, the main building barely brushes against its circular entrance hall, whose central spire pierces a double wedding-cake tier of columns. By combining elements of Classical and Gothic architecture, Nash shocked his contemporaries, but accomplished his aim of creating a church that looked the same from both sides of the bend. A bust of Nash adorns the outside of the entrance hall, to the right of the door.

PORTLAND PLACE

🚇 *Tube: Oxford Circus.*

Perhaps the handsomest street in London, Portland Pl. was first laid out by Robert and James Adam in the 18th century. Of the original buldings, only that at no. 46 survives, and the attraction of today's Portland Pl. lies rather in the great variety of architectural styles to be found, which makes it a natural home for the Royal Institute of British Architects (see below).

ROYAL INSTITUTE OF BRITISH ARCHITECTS (RIBA). RIBA is the most arresting building in Portland Pl., particularly at night when the facade is lit an eerie blue. Completed in 1932—the same year as Broadcasting House (see below)—RIBA was criticized for its continental style. Yet who today would complain at the accusation that it was "gentlemanly...but a gentleman dressed in clothes not bought in England"? Parts of the building open to the public include three exhibition galleries, a bookshop, and a decent cafe/restaurant. *(66 Portland Pl. ☎ 7580 5533. Open M and W-F 10am-6pm, Tu 10am-6:30pm, Sa 10am-5pm. Entrance and exhibitions free.)*

BROADCASTING HOUSE. Guarding the entrance to Portland Pl. from Regent St., the curved facade of this 1931 monument to mass-communications is instantly recognisable to all Britons. Built as the headquarters of the recently formed British Broadcasting Corporation, today Broadcasting House remains the BBC's main centre for radio production. On the facade is Eric Gill's sculpture of Shakespeare's Arial, together with the BBC motto "nation shall speak peace unto nation."

MARBLE ARCH

🚇 *Location: Near the intersection of Park Ln., Oxford St., Edgware Rd., and Bayswater Rd. **Tube:** Marble Arch.*

Looking rather pathetic by itself, Marble Arch was never meant to be a stand-alone monument. Designed by Nash in 1828 as the front entrance to Buckingham Palace, extensions to the Palace soon rendered it useless, so it was moved to the present site as an entrance into Hyde Park. Then new roads cut the arch off, leaving it stranded forlornly on a traffic roundabout. The arch stands close to the site of Tyburn gallows; until 1783 the main execution site in London. Crowds gathered to watch condemned prisoners being hung, drawn, and quartered. The gathered would jeer and throw rotting food at the unfortunate criminals as they rolled in carts to the "Tyburn Tree," which stood at the present corner of Bayswater Rd. and Edgware Rd.

MAYFAIR & ST. JAMES'S

🚇 *NEIGHBORHOOD QUICKFIND: Discover, p. 2; Museums&Galleries, p. 139; Food&Drink, p. 159; Entertainment, p. 209; Shopping, p. 226.*

Mayfair and St. James's are not areas in which *hoi polloi* tourists tend to linger—many would-be sights, such as St. James's Palace and the gentlemen's clubs, are strictly out-of-bounds to all but the most aristocratic; meanwhile, haughty sales assistants and outrageous prices do their best to keep window shoppers on the streets. On the other hand, the combination of wealth and conservatism make the area one of the few in London to retain its historic atmosphere and this, together with its parks its art galleries, makes Mayfair well worth a day's wander.

PICCADILLY

Tube: Piccadilly Circus or Green Park. For details of *Piccadilly Circus,* see Soho, p. 83.

Frilly ruffs were big business in the 16th century. So big, that one tailor made enough money from manufacturing these "piccadills" to build himself a fancy mansion (long since gone) called Pickadill House. The name stuck, though the tailoring industry has sinced move south to Jermyn St. Clogged with traffic, Piccadilly is no longer the preferred address of gentlemen, as it was in the late 18th century, but as home to the Ritz, Fortnum and Mason, and the Royal Academy, it's still posh, with a capital P.

Westminster Abbey

BURLINGTON HOUSE. The only one of Piccadilly's aristocratic mansions to survive, Burlington House was built in 1665, though its current neo-Renaissance appearance dates from a remodeling in the 1870s. Although the Earls of Burlington have long since departed, it still has an aristocratic grandeur about: today, Burlington House is home to numerous regal societies, including the Royal Society of Chemistry, the Royal Astronomical Society, and the **Royal Academy,** heart of the British artistic establishment and home to some excellent exhibitions (see p. 141).

19TH-CENTURY ARCADES. Running off and around Piccadilly on both sides are a number of early covered passageways lined with glass-fronted boutiques. Today, these proto-malls make for a picturesque but anachronistic shopping experience. The oldest is the **Royal Opera Arcade,** between Pall Mall and Charles II St.; the most prestigious the **Royal Arcade,** patronized by Queen Victoria and home of palace *chocolatiers* Charbonnel et Walker; the most famous, and longest, is the **Burlington Arcade,** next to Burlington House (see above) where top-hatted "beadles" enforce the original 1819 laws banning whistling, singing, and hurrying.

Burlington House, Royal Academy

ST. JAMES'S CHURCH PICCADILLY. William Blake was baptised in this building, whose exterior is now darkened by the soot of London's satanic mills. The grime belies the fact that the current structure is largely a post-war reconstruction of what Wren considered his best parish church; the flowers, garlands, and cherubs by master carver Grinling Gibbons fortunately escaped the Blitz. The churchyard is home to a tourist-oriented weekly craft market. *(Enter at 197 Piccadilly or on Jermyn St. ☎7734 4511. Church open daily 8am-7pm. Market Th-Sa 10am-6pm.)*

St. James's Palace

THE ALBANY. Built in 1771 and remodeled in 1812 as a set of gentlemen's chambers, the Albany evolved into an exclusive enclave of literary repute. Lord Byron wrote his epic "Childe Harold" here. Other past residents include Macaulay, Gladstone, and J.B. Priestley. The interior is off-limits to the public, though you might be able to sneak into the entrance hall and read the plaque explaining the Albany's history inside. *(Albany Court Yard, off Piccadilly next to the Alliance & Leicester.)*

ST. JAMES'S

🚇 *Tube: Piccadilly Circus or Green Park.*

Ever since Henry VIII chose St. James's Palace to be the residence of the royal court—foreign ambassadors are still officially received "into the Court of St. James's"—this has been London's most aristocratic address; current occupants include Prince Charles in the Palace itself and the Queen Mum in neighboring Clarence House. Those familiar with the English version of Monopoly will know that **Pall Mall** (rhymes with "Hal shall") is London's most bankable street, lined with exclusive **gentlemen's clubs,** steadfast bastions of wealth, tradition, and male privilege (most do not admit women); more can be found on **St. James's Street.**

ST. JAMES'S PALACE. Built in 1536, St. James's is London's only remaining purpose-built palace (Buckingham Palace was a rough-and-ready conversion job). The massive gateway giving onto St. James's St. is one of the few original parts of the palace to survive; outside, a pair of bearskin-hatted guards stomp and turn in perfect unison. As the statutory home of the Crown, royal proclamations are issued every Friday from the balcony in the interior Friary Court, though since only Prince Charles is around to hear them, you'd think his mum could just phone. Unless your name starts with HRH (or ends with Parker-Bowles), the only part of the Palace you're likely to get into is the **Chapel Royal,** open for Sunday services from October to Easter at 8:30 and 11am. From Easter to September, services are held in the Inigo Jones-designed **Queen's Chapel,** across Marlborough Rd. from the Palace.

ST. JAMES'S SQUARE. One of London's earliest squares, St. James's was laid out in the 1670s; of the original houses, only no. 4 survives. No. 20, designed by Robert Adam, was the home of the Queen Mother from 1906-1920; other famous residents include Prime Ministers Pitt the Elder and Gladstone, both at no. 10, and Dwight D. Eisenhower, who had his HQ at no. 31 from 1943 to '44.

CARLTON HOUSE TERRACE AND WATERLOO PLACE. Sweeping down from Piccadilly Circus, the final stage of Regent St. comes to an abrupt halt at Waterloo Pl., from where steps lead down to the Mall. It wasn't meant to be like this; the whole point of Regent St. was as a triumphal route leading to the Prince Regent's residence at Carlton House, but by the time it was finished the prince (by now George IV) had moved on to Buckingham Palace and had his old house pulled down. The aging royal architect, John Nash, was recommissioned to knock up something quickly on the site; the result was **Carlton House Terrace,** a pair of imposing classical buildings that dominate the northern reach of the Mall. On **Waterloo Place,** between the two terraces, the Duke of Wellington is dwarfed by a vast column topped by his boss (and George IV's brother), the "Grand Old" Duke of York. Presumably his men left him there before marching down again as thanks for docking their wages to pay for the monument.

OTHER MAYFAIR SIGHTS

SHEPHERD MARKET. This pedestrian area just north of Green Park occupies the site of the original **May Fair** that gave the neighborhood its name. A 17th-century version of Camden Market, the infamously raucous fair was closed down in 1706. Later in the century, one Edward Shepherd developed the area as a market (hence the name); today the 18th-century buildings house tiny restaurants, shops, and pubs, giving this corner of Mayfair a village-like charm. Other local charms include those of high-class prostitutes—apparently, this is Mayfair's red light district, though you'd never guess by looking. *(Tube: Hyde Park Corner or Green Park.)*

ROYAL INSTITUTION. Founded in 1799 to promote public understanding of science, the "Ri" counts 14 Nobel laureates among its alumni. Its most famous scientist-in-residence was Michael Faraday, one of the founding fathers of electromagnetism.

Most of the building is out-of-bounds; the exception is the archaic **Faraday museum,** a replica of Faraday's lab along with various bits of equipment that's unlikely to be appreciated except by those with a keen interest in the early history of electromagnetism. *(21 Albemarle St. ☎ 7409 2992. Open M-F 10am-5:30pm. £1, under 13 free.)*

BOND STREET AND SAVILE ROW. The oldest and most prestigious shops, art dealers, and auction houses in the city are found on these streets. **Old Bond Street,** the Piccadilly end of the street, is dominated by art and jewelry dealers, including homegrown luxury megastore Asprey and Gerrard, who stock essentials such as leather Scrabble boards with gold inlay. Versace and Ralph Lauren aside, most of the designer boutiques are found on **New Bond Street,** nearer Oxford St. On the small pedestrian area between the two stands a park bench bearing the bronze weights of best buddies Churchill and Roosevelt. *(Tube: Bond St. or Green Park. Note that Bond St. Tube is not on Bond St.; exit right onto Oxford St., then take the 2nd right onto Bond St.)* **Savile Row,** running parallel to Bond St., is synonymous with elegant and expensive tailoring; less well known is that the **Beatles** performed their last ever live gig on the roof of no. 3, during the filming of *Let It Be. (Tube: Piccadilly Circus.)*

GROSVENOR SQUARE. One of the largest in central London, Grosvenor Sq. has gradually evolved into a North American diplomatic enclave. John Adams lived at no. 9 while serving as the first US ambassador to England in 1785. A century and a half later, Eisenhower established his wartime headquarters at no. 20; memory of his stay persists in the area's nickname, "Eisenhowerplatz." Conforming to stereotype, the attention-seeking, humorless **US Embassy** faces the unassuming **Canadian High Commission** across the square. *(Tube: Bond St. or Marble Arch.)*

NEARBY MUSEUMS & GALLERIES

Exhibition Spaces: ◪ Royal Academy, p. 141; ◪ Institute of Contemporary Art, p. 141.

Commercial Galleries & Auctioneers: Annely Juda Fine Art, Bernard Jacobson, Christie's, Marlborough Fine Arts, Robert Sandelson, Sotherby's, and White Cube: p. 142.

SOHO

◪ *NEIGHBORHOOD QUICKFIND: Discover, p. 2; Food&Drink, p. 160; Nightlife, p. 191; Entertainment, p. 209 ; Shopping, p. 229; Accommodations, p. 284.*

Soho has a history of welcoming all colors and creeds to its streets. Early settlers included French Huguenots fleeing religious persecution in the 17th century, but these days Soho is less gay Paris, more plain gay: a concentration of gay-owned restaurants and bars has turned **Old Compton Street** into the heart of gay London. Soho also has a rich literary past: William Blake and Daniel Defoe lived on **Broadwick Street,** and William Hazlitt spent his last years at **6 Frith Street.** A blue plaque above Quo Vadis restaurant at **28 Dean Street** locates the two-room flat where Karl Marx lived with his wife, maid, and five children while writing *Das Kapital.*

PICCADILLY CIRCUS

◪ *Tube: Piccadilly Circus.*

Five of the West End's major arteries (Piccadilly, Regent St., Shaftesbury Ave., and the Haymarket) merge and swirl around Piccadilly Circus, and at times it seems as though the entire tourist population of London has decided to bask in the lurid neon signs. The central focus of the Circus is the **statue of Eros,** dedicated to the Victorian philanthropist, Lord Shaftesbury: Eros originally pointed his bow and arrow down Shaftesbury Ave., but recent restoration work has put his aim significantly off.

MADAME TUSSAUD'S ROCK CIRCUS. From the Michael Jackson tribute, featuring such authentic memorabilia as "a hat of the type...", to the tasteless mock-cemetery, with plastic headstones inscribed with the names of prematurely-departed rock stars (would Jerry Garcia be grateful to be named on two graves?), this musical waxworks is possibly the most shameless piece of tourist exploitation ever seen. *(London Pavilion. ☎ 0870 400 3030; www.rock-circus.com. Open M-Tu 11am-5:30pm, W-Su 10am-5:30pm. £8.25, students & seniors £7.25, under 16 £6.25.)*

LEICESTER SQUARE

⊠ Tube: *Leicester Sq. or Piccadilly Circus.*

Amusements at this entertainment nexus range from London's largest cinemas to the **Swiss Centre** glockenspiel, whose atonal renditions of anything from folk songs to Beethoven's *Moonlight Sonata* are enough to make even the tone-deaf weep. *(Rings M-F at noon, 6, 7, and 8pm; Sa-Su noon, 2, 4, 5, 6, 7, and 8pm.)* Follow this by having your name engraved on a grain of rice, getting a henna tattoo and sitting for a caricature. In the summer, a small funfair invades the square, adding to the tacky atmosphere.

CHINATOWN. Chinese immigrants first arrived in London in the 19th century, settling in Limehouse, in the East End. It wasn't until the 1950s that immigrants from Hong Kong started moving *en masse* to these few blocks just north of Leicester Sq. Pedestrianised, tourist-ridden **Gerrard Street,** with scroll-worked dragon gates and pagoda-capped phone booths, is the self-proclaimed heart of this tiny slice of Canton, but gritty **Lisle Street,** one block to the south, has a more authentic feel. Chinatown is most vibrant during the year's two major festivals: the Mid-Autumn Festival at the end of September, and the raucous Chinese New Year Festival in February. *(Between Leicester Sq., Shaftesbury Ave., and Charing Cross Rd.)*

OTHER SOHO SIGHTS

SOHO SQUARE. Soho Sq. was first laid out in 1681, bringing urbanity to this former hunting ground. Today it's a rather scruffy patch of green, popular with picnickers and sunbathers. If you're lucky, you might bump into Paul McCartney, whose business HQ is at no. 1 (MPL Communications)—crane your neck for a view of his first-floor office lined with platinum discs. Two monuments to Soho's cosmopolitan past border the square; London's only **French Protestant Church,** was founded in 1550 and **St. Patrick's,** long the focal point of Soho's Irish and Italian communities. *(Tube: Tottenham Court Rd. Park open daily 10am-dusk.)*

ST. ANNE'S. Scholars long argued whether Wren designed St. Anne's (built 1677-85), but WWII bombs put an end to the dispute. For a long time, only the ungainly 1803 bell tower survived among the ruins, but 1991 saw a new church and community center erected on the site. William Hazlitt is buried in the churchyard, while Dorothy L. Sayers lies beneath the tower itself. *(Churchyard accessed from Wardour St.; church via 55 Dean St. ☎ 7437 5006. Churchyard open M-Sa 8am-dusk, Su 9am-dusk.)*

COVENT GARDEN

⊠ TRANSPORTATION: *All listings nearest Tube: Covent Garden.* **NEIGHBORHOOD QUICKFIND:** *Discover, p. 2; Museums&Galleries, p. 139; Food&Drink, p. 162; Nightlife, p. 193; Entertainment, p. 209; Shopping, p. 231; Accommodations, p. 284.*

Covent Garden is one of the few parts of London popular with locals and tourists alike. On the very spot where, 350 years ago, Samuel Pepys saw the first Punch and Judy show in England, street performers still entertain the thousands who flock here summer and winter, rain and shine. It's hard to imagine that for centuries this was London's main vegetable market; only in 1974 did the traders transfer to new, spacious premises south of the river, triggering a fight between locals and commercial developers that ended in a rare defeat for the forces of Mammon.

ST. PAUL'S. Not to be confused with St. Paul's Cathedral, this 1633 Inigo Jones church now stands as the sole remnant of the original square. Its simplicity is attributable to the Earl of Bedford who, running short of funds, instructed the architect to make it "not much better than a barn." Known as "the actor's church" for its long association with nearby theaters, the interior is festooned with plaques commemorating the achievements of Boris Karloff, Vivien Leigh, Charlie Chaplin, and Tony Simpson ("inspired player of small parts") among others. Non-thespians associated with the church include artist J.M.W. Turner, who was baptized here, and master carver Grinling Gibbons, buried in the church. To enter the church, you must first pass through the peaceful **churchyard,** whose leafy gardens belie its status as a plague burial ground—Margaret Ponteous, the first victim of the Great Plague, was buried here on April 12, 1665. *(On Covent Garden Piazza; enter via King St., Henrietta St., or Bedford St. ☎ 7836 5221; www.spcg.org. Open daily 8:30am-4:30pm.)*

THE ROYAL OPERA HOUSE. The Royal Opera House reopened in 2000 after a major expansion—the Piazza's new boutique-lined colonnade is the rear of the ROH's rehearsal studios and workshops. Except in the run-up to performances, the public is free to wander the ornate lobby of the original 1858 theater, as well as the enormous glass-roofed space of **Floral Hall.** From here, take the escalator to reach the **terrace** overlooking the Piazza, with great views of London, plus a chance to peek into the neighboring costume workshop. *(Enter on Bow St., or through "the Link" in the northeast of the Piazza. Open daily 10am-3:30pm. 75min. backstage tours M-Sa 10:30am, 12:30, and 2:30pm; reservations essential. £7, concessions £6. For performances, see p. 245.)*

Picadilly Circus

THEATRE ROYAL, DRURY LANE. Founded in 1663, this is the oldest of London's surviving theaters, though the current building dates from 1812. Charles II met Nell Gwynn here in 1655, while David Garrick ruled the roost in the 18th century. The theater even has a ghost—a corpse and dagger were found bricked up in the wall in the 19th century. This and other pieces of Drury Ln. lore are brought back to life in the actor-led backstage tours. *(Entrance on Catherine St. ☎ 7240 5357. Tours M-Tu, Th-F and Su 12:30, 2:15, and 4:45pm; W and Sa 10:15am and noon. £7.50, children £5.50.)*

SEVEN DIALS. This star-configuration of six streets is a rare surviving example of 17th-century town planning. Thomas Neale commissioned the pillar in the center in 1694, with one sundial facing each street; the seventh dial is the column itself. The original column was pulled down in 1773 to rid the area of "undesirables" who congregated around it; a replica, erected in 1989, has reasserted this role. *(Intersection of Monmouth, Earlham, and Mercer St.)*

Ritziness of St. James's

NEARBY MUSEUMS & GALLERIES
Permanent Collections: 🖾 London's Transport Museum, p. 140; Theatre Museum, p. 141.

Exhibition Spaces: Photographers' Gallery, p. 142.

TRAFALGAR SQUARE & THE STRAND

🚩 *NEIGHBORHOOD QUICKFIND: Discover, p. 2; Museums&Galleries, p. 139; Food&Drink, p. 164; Nightlife, p. 194; Entertainment, p. 209.*

TRAFALGAR SQUARE
🚩 *Tube: Charing Cross or Leicester Sq.*

John Nash first suggested laying out this square in 1820, but it took almost 50 years for London's largest traffic roundabout to take on its current appearance: Nelson only arrived in 1843, and the bronze lions in 1867. If they don't look very

Leicester Square

fierce, it's because sculptor Edmund Landseer's model died during the sittings, forcing him to work from a decomposing animal. Far scarier are the legions of pigeons dive-bombing the square—it's enough to make a Hitchcock fan quake.

Ever since its completion, Trafalgar Sq. has been a focus for public rallies and protest movements, from the Chartist rallies of 1848 to the anti-apartheid vigils held outside South Africa House, on the square's east side, in the early '90s. More joyful congregations gather here on **New Year's Eve** to ring in midnight with the chimes of Big Ben, while April 2001 saw what is hoped will be the first of many open-air **concerts** in the square, featuring REM among others giving tribute to Nelson Mandela. Every December since the end of WWII, the square has hosted a giant **Christmas Tree,** donated by Norway as thanks for British assistance against the Nazis.

NELSON'S COLUMN. It was not until the 1830s that it was proposed to dedicate the square to England's greatest naval victory, and the fluted 51m granite column was only erected in 1839. Before the statue was hoisted into place in 1843, dinner was served to 14 brave (or idiotic) patriots on the column's summit. The reliefs at the column's base were cast from captured French and Spanish cannon, and commemorate Nelson's victories at Cape St. Vincent, Copenhagen, the Nile, and Trafalgar (again).

OTHER STATUES. Nelson is not the only national hero to watch over the square; to prove that the English are not sore losers, **George Washington** keeps a watch from a horse just in front of the National Gallery (see p. 136). The statue of **George IV** in the northeastern corner was originally intended to top Marble Arch (see p. 80). The eastern "Fourth Plinth" was empty until 1999, since when it has hosted changing displays of **modern sculpture:** the first half of 2002 will see Rachel Whiteread's inverted clear resin cast of the plinth itself. To the south of the square, **Charles I** stands on the site of the original Charing Cross (see below). The statue escaped Cromwell's wrath with the aid of one John Rivett, who bought it "for scrap" and did a roaring trade in souvenirs supposedly made from the figure. It was in fact hidden and later sold, at a tidy profit, to Charles II.

ST. MARTIN-IN-THE-FIELDS

🚩 *Location: St. Martin's Lane, in the northeast corner of Trafalgar Sq.; crypt entrance on Duncannon St. Contact: ☎ 7766 1100. Tube: Leicester Sq. or Charing Cross. Open: Market daily 11am-7pm.*

James Gibbs' 1720s creation is instantly recognizable: the then-groundbreaking combination of a Classical portico and a Gothic spire made it the model for countless Georgian churches in Britain and America. George I was the church's first warden, and it's still the Queen's parish church; look for the royal box to the left of the altar. Handel and Mozart both performed here, and the church hosts frequent concerts, often by candlelight (see p. 211). Outside, the churchyard is home to a tourist-oriented **daily market,** while downstairs the **crypt** has a life of its own, home to a popular **cafe** (see p. 164), bookshop, art gallery, and the ever-popular **London Brass Rubbing Centre.** (☎ 7930 9306. Open M-Sa 10am-6pm, Su noon-6pm. Brass rubbing £5-8.)

THE STRAND

🚩 *Tube: Charing Cross.*

Officially known simply as "Strand," this busy road is perhaps the most ancient in London, predating the Romans. Originally a riverside track, shifting watercourses and Victorian engineering have conspired to leave it high and dry; yet as the main thoroughfare between Westminster and the City, it remains as busy as ever. The only reminder of the many episcopal and aristocratic palaces that once made the Strand London's top address are in the street names nearby: Villiers St. recalls George Villiers, Duke of Buckingham, while Essex St. commemorates Elizabeth I's favorite Robert Devereux, Earl of Essex.

CHARING CROSS. This was the last of the 14 crosses erected by Edward I in 1290 to mark the passage of his wife's funeral cortege. Though any Londoner will tell you that "Charing" is a corruption of *chère reine*, French for "dear Queen," it's complete cobblers—the word actually comes from the Old English *ceiring*, meaning a bend in the river. The original cross was destroyed by Cromwell in 1647; the current monument, standing in the middle of the cab rank outside Charing Cross station, is a 19th-century replica. To complete the deception, it's not even in the right place—the original stood at the top of Whitehall on the spot now occupied by Charles I's statue (see Trafalgar Sq., above).

THE SAVOY. Considered the "fairest manor in all England," John of Gaunt's great Palace of Savoy was gleefully destroyed by rampaging peasants in 1381. Five hundred years later, the D'Oyly Carte Opera Company moved into the new **Savoy Theatre,** the first in the world to be entirely lit by electricity, followed soon after by the opening of the **Savoy Hotel.** Managed by César Ritz, it was every bit as decadent as the Palace that once stood on the site. Don't be afraid to wander into the Savoy's grand foyer, second only to the Ritz in popularity for afternoon tea (see p. 164). Be careful as you cross the Savoy **driveway**—this short road running into the Strand is the only street in the UK where people drive on the right. *(On the south side of the Strand.)*

Chinatown Gate

SOMERSET HOUSE. Completed in 1790, Somerset House was London's first purpose-built office block. Originally home to the Royal Academy, the Royal Society, and the Navy Board, the elegant Neoclassical courtyard long induced a shiver of distaste in Londoners as the headquarters of the Inland Revenue. While the taxman still presides over the west wing, most of the building is open to the public. The **Courtauld Institute Galleries** (see p. 139) and the **Gilbert Collection of Decorative Art** (see p. 140) are both compelling, though on sunny days they face strong competition from the spectacular view afforded by the **River Terrace,** also home to an attractive but pricey outdoor cafe. Mid-December to mid-January, the central **Fountain Courtyard** is iced over to make an open-air rink, while Thursday evenings from mid-June to mid-July bring classical music concerts. More activities take place in the **Navy Board Room,** from puppet shows to poetry. *(Strand, just east of Waterloo Bridge. ☎ 7845 4600, events ☎ 7845 4670; www.somerset-house.org.uk. Tube: Charing Cross or Temple. 45min. tours of the building given Tu, Th, and Sa at 11am and 3:15pm. £2.75. Courtyard open daily 7:30am-11pm.)*

Chinatown Streets

ST. MARY-LE-STRAND. The slender steeple and elegant portico of this 1724 Baroque church rise above an island of green in a sea of traffic. Designed by James Gibbs, the church overlooks the site of the original Maypole, claimed by parishioner Isaac Newton for a telescope stand. Inside, the Baroque barrel vault and altar walls reflect not only the glory of God but also Gibbs' Roman architectural training. The anchor-themed prayer cushions are a reminder that the church is dedicated to the Women's Royal Naval Service, or Wrens. *(☎ 7836 3205. Open M-F 11am-4pm. £1 recommended donation.)*

National Gallery

VICTORIA EMBANKMENT

⚑ Location: *North bank of the Thames between Hungerford and Waterloo Bridges.* **Tube:** *Embankment.* **Gardens open:** *Daily 7am-dusk.*

Though few walking or driving here realize it, Victoria Embankment is a remarkable feat of engineering. Using an 8 ft. thick wall, the Thames was pushed back and enough space created to house both the sewers that would put an end to the Big Stinks of the 1850s, and the new-fangled Underground trains that would relieve the congested streets. Both the sewer and the Circle line are still with us, though so too are traffic and pollution. Separated from the river by a busy road and a screen of trees, the thin green line of **Victoria Embankment Gardens** makes a pleasant picnic spot, with frequent live music from the bandstand during summer afternoons. At the rear of the gardens, the **York Watergate** marks the pre-1860 waterline of the Thames. Styled after the Fontaine de Médicis in Paris, it was erected in 1626 as the river entrance to the Duke of Buckingham's mansion. Since the palace's destruction in 1672 and the building of the embankment two centuries late, the watergate has stood as a forlorn reminder of the Strand's glorious past.

CLEOPATRA'S NEEDLE. By far the oldest monument in London, this Egyptian obelisk was first erected at Heliopolis in 1500 BC—making it some 1400 years older than Cleo. How it came to rest by the banks of the Thames is a story in itself: though the Viceroy of Egypt presented it to Britain in 1819 in recognition for their help in booting Napoleon out of Africa, it wasn't until 1877 that it was attempted to ship it to London. The ship sank en route, but a salvage operation recovered the obelisk and it was finally re-erected in 1879. Underneath it is a Victorian time-capsule containing a railway guide, numerous bibles, and pictures of the 20 prettiest British women of the day. The scars at the needle's base and at the (Victorian) sphinx to its right were left by the first-ever bombing raid on London, by German zeppelins in 1917.

NEARBY MUSEUMS & GALLERIES

Major Collections: National Gallery, p. 136.

Other Permanent Collections: ▧ Courtauld Institute, p. 139; National Portrait Gallery, p. 140; Gilbert Collection, p. 140.

HOLBORN

⚑ NEIGHBORHOOD QUICKFIND: Discover, *p. 88;* **Museums&Galleries,** *p. 142;* **Food&Drink,** *p. 164;* **Nightlife,** *p. 194;* **Entertainment,** *p. 212;* **Shopping,** *p. 232.*

SEE MAP, pp. 334-335

Squeezed between the unfettered capitalism of the City and the rampant commercialism of the West End, Holborn at first glance is a crush of streets as busy, dirty, and unattractive as anywhere in the capital—yet it is also home to many of London's most peaceful, attractive, and historic buildings and open spaces. Chief among its hidden marvels are the four **Inns of Court.** These venerable institutions provide apprenticeships for law students and house the chambers of practising barristers in mini-villages of gardens, chapels, and dining halls. Most were founded in the 13th century when a royal decree barred the clergy from the courts, giving rise to a class of professional advocates. Today, students may seek their legal training elsewhere, but to be considered for membership must "keep term" by dining regularly in one of the halls. East of Gray's Inn Rd. a livelier Holborn is apparent, mixing the market cries of **Leather Lane** with the diamond merchants of **Hatton Garden.**

THE TEMPLE

⚑ Location: *Between Strand/Fleet St., Essex St., Victoria Embankment, and Temple Ave./Bouvier St.; numerous (often easily missed) passages lead from these streets into the Temple.* **Tube:** *Temple or Blackfriars.* **Temple Church:** ☎ *7353 3470; open W-Th 11am-4pm, Sa 9:30am-1:30pm, Su 12:45-4pm.* **Middle Temple Garden:** *Open May-Sept. M-F noon-3pm.* **Free.**

South of Fleet St., this labyrinthine compound encompasses the inns of the Middle Temple, to the west, and the Inner Temple neighboring it on the east, separated by Middle Temple Lane—there was once also an Outer Temple, but it has long since gone. All derive their name from the crusading Order of the Knights Templar, who embraced this site as their English seat in 1185. The order was dissolved in 1312, and the property eventually passed to the Knights Hospitallers of St. John, who leased it to a community of common law scholars in 1338. The **Inner Temple** was virtually leveled by bombs in the early 1940s (though you wouldn't think to see it); fortunately the gabled Tudor **Inner Temple Gateway,** between 16 and 17 Fleet St., survived.

TEMPLE CHURCH. Held in common by both Temples, Temple Church is the finest surviving medieval round church, built in the 12th century on the model of the Church of the Holy Sepulchre, Jerusalem. Stained-glass windows, an original Norman doorway, and 10 arresting, armor-clad effigies of sinister knights complete the impressive interior. Adjoining the round church is a rectangular Gothic nave, built in 1240, with an altar screen by Wren (1682).

MIDDLE TEMPLE. The Middle Temple largely escaped the destruction of World War II, and retains some fine examples of 16th- and 17th-century buildings. Just off Middle Temple Ln., **Middle Temple Hall,** closed to the public, still has its 1574 hammerbeam ceiling as well as large wooden dining table made from the hatch of Sir Francis Drake's *Golden Hinde.* Elizabeth I saw Shakespeare act in the premier of *Twelfth Night* here on Groundhog Day, 1601. More Shakespearean legend is attached to **Middle Temple Garden,** south of the hall—according to his *Henry VI,* the red and white flowers that served as emblems throughout the War of the Roses were plucked here.

LINCOLN'S INN

Location: Between Lincoln's Inn Fields and Chancery Lane. **Tube:** Chancery Lane or Holborn. **Gardens:** Open M-F noon-2:30pm. **Free.**

Just to the east of **Lincoln's Inn Fields,** London's largest square and home to Sir John Soane's Museum and the Royal College of Surgeons (see Museums, p. 143), sprawl the grounds of Lincoln's Inn. John Donne, Thomas More, Walpole, Pitt, Gladstone, and Disraeli are but a few of the former Inn-mates. The main gates into the Inn from the Fields deposit you in **New Square,** an open square of houses appearing much as it did when built in the 1690s. Adjacent to the Fields, the neo-Tudor **New Hall** and **Library** (closed to the public) stand among attractive gardens, popular with picnickers. On the other side of the gardens are the **Old Buildings,** including the 15th-century **Old Hall** (closed to the public) where the Lord High Chancellor presided over the Court of Chancery from 1733 to 1873. Dickens drew on his time as a clerk in New Court across the yard when penning the case of

Sir Walter Raleigh

Trafalgar Square

Nelson's Column

Jarndyce and Jarndyce in *Bleak House.* The **Chapel,** whose foundation stone was laid in 1620 by John Donne, sits above a unique open undercroft—once a popular spot for abandoning babies, who would be brought up in the Inn under the surname Lincoln. On the opposite side of the complex from the Fields, a 16th-century **gatehouse** opens onto Chancery Lane.

OTHER INNS

GRAY'S INN. With an appropriately-colored facade on Gray's Inn Rd., Gray's Inn does not inspire joy from the outside—Dickens dubbed it "that stronghold of melancholy." However, if you approach it through the 1688 **gatehouse** on High Holborn, you'll find it's really rather pleasant inside. The **Hall,** to your right as you pass through the archway, retains its original stained glass (1580) and most of its screen, carved from the timbers of a Spanish galleon. Francis Bacon maintained chambers here, and is the purported designer of the **gardens,** the largest of any Inn. Current members include Tony Blair's wife Cherie, a member of the "Matrix" chambers (legal partnership). She knows kung-fu. *(Between Theobald's Rd., Jockey's Fields, High Holborn, and Gray's Inn Rd. Tube: Chancery Lane or Holborn. Gardens open M-F noon-2:30pm.)*

STAPLE INN. Leaning alarmingly over Holborn is the 16th-century half-timbered terrace of Staple Inn. Originally built for wool merchants (hence the name—wool was England's main, or staple, export at the time), the building later became an Inn of Chancery, precursors to the Inns of Court. Today housing offices, stores, and the Institute of Actuaries, passing through the covered passage into the courtyard reveals the wooden facade to be just a front for a brick back. The 1581 hall, with an original hammerbeam roof, is closed to the public, but you can enjoy the sight of the gardens and fountain behind it. *(On Holborn, opposite Tube: Chancery Lane.)*

FLEET STREET

⚑ Location: *Fleet St. is the continuation of the Strand between Temple Bar and Ludgate Circus. Note that Fleet St. is numbered up one side and down the other.* **Tube:** *Temple.*

Named for the one-time river (now underground) that flows from Hampstead to the Thames, Fleet Street's association with the press goes back to the days when Thomas Caxton's successor Wyken de Worde relocated from Westminster to the precincts of St. Bride's church (below). The area long remained a center for publishing, but it was in the 19th century that Fleet St. became synonymous with journalism. Times—or rather *The Times*—have changed, though: following a standoff with printers in 1986, Rupert Murdoch moved all his papers, including *The Times*, to Wapping, Docklands, initiating a mass exodus. Though "Fleet Street" is still used to describe London-based newspapers, the famous facades, such as the *Daily Telegraph's* startling Greek and Egyptian Revival building and the *Daily Express's* Art Deco manse of chrome and black glass, no longer hum to the sound of the presses.

ST. BRIDE'S. The unusual spire of Wren's 1675 church is the most imitated piece of architecture in the world: perhaps taking his cue from the church's name, a local baker tried modelling a wedding cake on the multi-tiered structure. Dubbed "the printers' cathedral" since 1531, when Wyken de Worde set up his press here, it has long been closely associated with nearby newspapermen, bearing numerous plaques commemorating journalists. More literary associations include Pepys, baptized here, and Milton, who lived in the churchyard. The crypt, closed in 1853 following a cholera epidemic, was reopened during the post-Blitz restoration 1952 as a museum; displays include the baker's wife's wedding dress, as well as the remains of a Roman pavement and ditch. *(St. Bride's Ave., just off Fleet St. Open daily 8am-4:45pm. Free.)*

SAMUEL JOHNSON'S HOUSE. Samuel Johnson, a self-described "shrine to the English language," lived in this abode from 1748 to 1759. Here he completed his Dictionary, the first definitive English lexicon, even though rumor falsely insists that he omitted "sausage." He compiled this amazing document by reading all the great books of the age and marking the words he wanted included in the dictionary with black pen. The books he used were unreadable by the project's end. *(17 Gough Sq.; follow the signs down the alley opposite 54 Fleet St. ☎ 7353 3745. The house was closed for restoration at going to press, but should reopen by late 2001; call for hours and prices.)*

PRINCE HENRY'S ROOM. Up an easily missed flight of stairs, this one-room museum offers an insider perspective into the pre-Fire city. Built in 1515, the gabled house was once a Victorian waxworks, mentioned by Dickens in *The Old Curiosity Shop*. In 17th-century the rooms served as offices of the Duchy of Cornwall, then in the hands of James I's son, Prince Henry; it's from this period that the beautiful ceiling originates (1610). Display cases house marginally interesting memorabilia pertaining to local lad Samuel Pepys, but the real treasures are the room itself and the knowledgeable staff, who know everything there is to know about Fleet St. and the surrounding area. *(17 Fleet St. ☎ 7936 2710. Tube: Temple. Open M-Sa 11am-2pm. Free.)*

ST. CLEMENT DANES. Legend places this church over the tomb of Harold Harefoot, a Danish warlord who settled here in the 9th century, though its fame with Londoners derives from its opening role in the famous nursery rhyme *(Oranges and Lemons say the bells of St. Clement's)*. The church has seen many changes since being completed in 1682: in 1720, Gibbs replaced Wren's tower with a slimmer spire, and in 1941 the interior was gutted by firebombs. Restored inside to its ornate white stucco and gilt splendor, it's now the official church of the Royal Air Force. The crypt houses an eerie collection of 17th-century funerary monuments. *(At the eastern junction of Aldwych and Strand. ☎ 7242 8282. Tube: Temple. Open daily 8am-5pm.)*

ST. DUNSTAN-IN-THE-WEST. An early-Victorian neo-Gothic church crammed between Fleet St. facades, St. Dunstan is most notable for its 17th-century clock, whose bells are struck every 15min. by a pair of hammer-wielding musclemen representing mythical Celtic giants Gog and Magog. The statues adorning the porch are saved from the 16th-century Lud Gate that stood nearby. One is recognisably Elizabeth I; the others represent the legendary King Lud, after whom London is supposedly named, and his two equally mythical sons. *(Fleet St., just north of the Temple. Tube: Temple or Chancery Lane.)*

ROYAL COURTS OF JUSTICE

◪ Location: *At the point where the Strand becomes Fleet St.; rear entrance on Carey St.* **Contact:** *☎ 7936 6000.* **Tube:** *Temple or Chancery Lane.* **Open:** *M-F 9am-6pm, last entrance 4:30pm; cases start around 10am, with a break for lunch 1-2pm.* **Free.**

Straddling the official division between the City of Westminster and the City of London is this elaborate neo-Gothic structure, designed in 1874 by G.E. Street. Inside are 77 courtrooms—open to the public during cases—and countless chambers for judges and court staff, not to mention cells for defendants. In the cathedral-like Great Hall, you stand on the largest mosaic floor in Europe; noticeboards here detail the day's business. At the top of the stairs at the rear of the hall is a small exhibition dedicated to the history of legal costume, including the wigs that are a source of endless fascination for tourists.

ELY PLACE

◪ Location: *Off Holborn Circus.* **Tube:** *Chancery Lane.*

Step through the gates separating Ely Place from Holborn Circus, and you're no longer in London. In the 13th century, the Bishop of Ely built a palace here, later appropriated by Henry VIII's. Though the palace is long gone, by a constitutional quirk the street remains outside the jurisdiction of local government (and local police). Shakespeare mentioned Ely Place in *Richard III*, when Gloucester asks the Bishop "My Lord of Ely, when I was last in Holborn, I saw good strawberries in your garden there. I do beseech you, send for some of them." Should you be beseeched, **Strawberry Fayre** is held on the third Sunday in June. Next to Ely Place, **Hatton Garden** (actually a street) is the center of Britain's gem trade, with dozens of diamond merchants proving that all that glitters is not gold.

ST. ETHELDREDA'S. The church of St. Etheldreda is the last remaining vestige of the palace; indeed this mid-13th century building is the sole surviving complete edifice of its age in London. The upper church was badly damaged in WWII and has a fairly plain interior, but the undercroft below is almost entirely original. It was here that Henry VIII held a five-day banquet to celebrate his marriage to Catherine of Aragon in 1531. Today, it's the site for debaucherous cream teas and light lunches. *(☎ 7405 1061. Open M-F 8am-6pm, Sa-Su 9:30am-6pm. Free.)*

NEARBY MUSEUMS & GALLERIES

Permanent Collections: ▥ Sir John Soane's Museum, p. 142; Dickens House Museum, p. 143; Hunterian Museum, p. 143.

CLERKENWELL

SEE MAP, pp. 334-335

▣ TRANSPORTATION: *All sights are nearest Tube: Farringdon.* **NEIGHBORHOOD QUICKFIND: Discover,** *p. 6;* **Museums&Galleries,** *p. 143;* **Food&Drink,** *p. 166;* **Nightlife,** *p. 194;* **Entertainment,** *p. 213;* **Accommodations,** *p. 285.*

Clerkenwell may be the new Soho in terms of louche bars and trendy nightclubs, but in historical terms it's far older. From the 12th century until Henry VIII's break with Rome, Clerkenwell was dominated by the great monastic foundations of which traces can still be found. After a brief period of aristocratic fashionability in the early 17th century, Clerkenwell descended first to the status of an artisan's quarter, and by Victorian times to a notorious slum. The late 20th century saw this progression reversed, with artists taking advantage of cheap rents in the area in the 1980s and propelling it to the height of loft-living trendiness in the 1990s. Not conventionally "beautiful," Clerkenwell remains an intriguing mixture of medieval vestiges and green spaces in a post-industrial district of rather grim converted warehouses.

CLERKENWELL GREEN

Not very green at all—actually just a wider-than-normal street—Clerkenwell Green's interest comes from its strong historical associations. A gathering place for over 900 years, Wat Tyler rallied the Peasant's Revolt here in 1381, and Lenin published the Bolshevik newspaper *Iskra* from no. 37a. The Green's oldest building, dating from 1737, it's now the **Marx Memorial Library.** *(Open M 1-6pm, Tu-Th 1-8pm, Sa 10am-1pm.)* In opposition to these revolutionary tendencies, the 1782 **Sessions House** was formerly the courthouse for the county of Middlesex (which included north London). Reputedly haunted, it's now the enigmatic London Masonic Centre. *(Closed to the public.)*

CLERKENWELL VISITORS CENTRE. The friendly staff of this family-run info center almost seem surprised to see tourists. Nonetheless they offer a wealth of information and leaflets on the area, and hand out the **Clerkenwell Historic Trail,** which leads 2 mi. past sights both fascinating and deservedly obscure. (Tip: leave out everything north of Bowling Green Lane.) The center also doubles as a store selling the wares of local artisans, plus homemade ice cream. *(6 Clerkenwell Close, by St. James's Church. ☎7253 7438. Open M-Sa 11am-6pm.)*

ST. JOHN'S SQUARE

Now bisected by the busy Clerkenwell Rd., St. John's Square occupies the sight of the 12th-century **Priory of St. John.** The Knights Hospitallers (technically the Order of the Hospital of St. John of Jerusalem) were founded in 1113 during the First Crusade, rapidly moving on from tending the sick to fighting the heathens, at first from castles in the Middle East, then gradually pushed back to Rhodes and Malta. Founded in 1140 as the English HQ of the order, 400 years later the priory was the last monastery to be suppressed by Henry VIII. What remains is now in the hands of a distantly related organisation, the British Order of St. John. Unaffiliated to the original order (which still exists, based in the Vatican), this Protestant organization was founded in 1887 to promote first-aid training; its most famous arm is the St. John Ambulance Brigade, which operates in 45 countries worldwide.

ST. JOHN'S GATE. Arching grandly over the entrance to St. John's Sq. is this 16th-century gateway. The small ground-floor museum offers an odd mixture of artefacts relating to the original priory and Knights Hospitallers with hi-tech displays detailing the exploits of the modern-day order in bringing band-aids to the masses. Join a tour to see the upstairs council chamber as well as being taken around the priory church (see below). *(St. John's Lane. ☎7253 6644. www.sja.org.uk/history/visit/default.asp. Tours Tu and F-Sa 11am and 2:30pm; £4., seniors £3. Open M-F 10am-5pm, Sa 10am-4pm. Free.)*

PRIORY CHURCH. On the other side of Clerkenwell Rd. from the gate, cobblestones in St. John's Sq. mark the position of the original Norman church; the current building, 16th century but rebuilt following bomb damage in WWII, lies at the end of a pleasant cloister. Two panels of the 1480 Weston Triptych stand on their original altar, but the real treasure of the church is the crypt, the only surviving part of the original 12th-century priory. *(Open only for tours of St. John's Gate, above.)*

◤ THE CHARTERHOUSE

⚑ Location: *On the north side of Charterhouse Sq.* **Contact:** *☎ 7253 3260.* **Tube:** *Farringdon or Barbican.* **Open:** *Only for 90min. tours Apr.-Sept. W 2:15pm. Free; donation requested.*

An ancient-looking wall and arched gateway separate Charterhouse Sq. from the the Charterhouse itself. Founded in the 14th century as a Carthusian monastery, in 1611 **Thomas Sutton** bought the property and established a foundation for the education of 40 boys and the care of 80 impoverished old men. Charterhouse School rapidly established itself as one of the most prestigious (and expensive) in England, but in 1872 moved to Surrey, leaving the complex to the (still penniless) pensioners. The pensioner-led weekly tour guides you through the grounds and into some of the buildings, including the Duke of Norfolk's Great Hall and the chapel with Thomas Sutton's ornate tomb. If you miss the tour, you can admire the **main gate,** the same wooden door to which Henry VIII nailed the severed hands of the last monks. The small **garden** to the right of the gate, just visible through some thick foliage, occupies the site of the original 14th-century monastic chapel, with the low tomb of monastery founder Sir Walter de Manney.

ST. BARTHOLOMEW THE GREAT

⚑ Location: *Little Britain, off West Smithfield.* **Contact:** *☎ 7606 5171.* **Tube:** *Barbican or Farringdon.* **Open:** *M-F (Aug. Tu-F) 8:30am-5pm, Sa 10:30am-1:30pm, Su 8am-1pm and 2-8pm.*

One must enter through a 13th-century arch, cunningly disguised as a Tudor house, to reach this Norman gem. The current neck-stretching nave was only the chancel of the original 12th-century church, which formerly reached all the way to the street. Hogarth was baptized in the 15th-century font, and at one time Benjamin Franklin worked at a printers' in the Lady's Chapel.. The tomb near the central altar belongs to **Rahere,** who in 1123 founded both the church and the neighboring **St. Bartholomew's Hospital.** The hospital, just across Little Britain, was reconstructed in the 18th century by James Gibbs and is one of London's largest as well as its oldest; within its walls is the 16th-century church of **St. Bartholomew the Less** and a small **museum** on the hospital history (see p. 143).

SMITHFIELD MARKET

⚑ Location: *Between West Smithfield and Charterhouse St.* **Tube:** *Barbican or Farringdon.* **Open:** *M-F 4-10am.*

Smithfield, or "smooth field," first emerged as a market in the 12th century, when cattle were driven here for sale at the annual St. Bartholomew's Fair. Over the centuries the fair became so raucous that 700 years later the Victorians decided to shut it down and turn the market over to dead animals; Smithfield has been London's main source of wholesale meat ever since. Still, the association with butchery predates the Victorians: Wat Tyler, leader of the Peasants' Revolt of 1381, and Scotsman William Wallace (a.k.a. Mel Gibson in *Braveheart*) count among those executed here in the Middle Ages. Today, you're free to wander through the center of the impressive Victorian market hall. The domed corner towers originally held pubs.

NEARBY MUSEUMS & GALLERIES
Permanent Collections: Museum of St.Bartholomew's Hospital, p. 143.

CITY OF LONDON

⚑ *The* **City of London Information Centre,** *St. Paul's Churchyard (☎ 7332 1456; Tube: St. Paul's) offers acres of leaflets and maps, sells tickets to sights and shows, and gives info on a host of traditional municipal events. One of the largest is the* **Lord Mayor's Show,** *held each year on the second Saturday of November. Open Apr.-Sept. daily 9:30am-5pm; Oct.-Mar. M-F 9:30am-5pm, Sa 9:30am-12:30pm.* **NEIGHBORHOOD QUICKFIND: Discover,** *p. 7;* **Museums&Galleries,** *p. 143;* **Food&Drink,** *p. 167;* **Entertainment,** *p. 213;* **Accommodations,** *p. 285.*

SEE MAP, p. 334-335

THE LIVERY MEN

In the Middle Ages, the City was controlled by **guilds** such as the Fishmongers, the Grocers, and the Haberdashers. Also known as **livery companies** after the colorful costumes worn by their members, these associations of craftsmen or merchants regulated business in the capital. No-one could practice a trade unless they were a member of the appropriate guild; yet with skill and hard work, a humble-born freeman might be able to make it to the coveted status of Master Craftsman, and perhaps one day Warden of his guild—or even Lord Mayor.

While their power was broken by the industrial revolution, the guilds survive today—in fact, their number is growing. On January 1st, 2000, the Worshipful Company of Water Conservators became the 101st guild to be recognised.

Originally, each guild had its own **livery hall**, a grand building where new members were invested and feasts celebrated. Fire, war, and changing times have reduced the number of halls to 25. These ancient institutions are usually closed to the public, but occasionally hold open days; some also open during the City of London festival (see p. 213). Contact the **City of London information office** (☎ 7606 3030) for details and tickets.

The City of London (usually shortened to "the City") is the oldest part of London— as its name suggests, for most of its 2000 years this was London, all other districts being merely outlying villages. Yet its appearance is much newer; following the Great Fire of 1666 and the Blitz of 1940-43, very little of that history survives, if not obliterated, then overshadowed by giant temples of commerce. Ancient churches huddle by busy thoroughfares, while others hide in secluded squares; the ruins of a Roman temple lie in the shadow of a modern office block; and above it all ride the dome of **St. Paul's** (p. 71) and the battlements of the **Tower of London,** (p. 73). Yet the 20th century had a more profound effect on the City than the cosmetic rearrangement of the Blitz: as its power in the world of international finance grew, so the City's relevance to ordinary Londoners diminished. The 39 surviving churches and street names recalling the local population or trades once practised there—Lombard St., Jewry, Bread St., Poultry, even Love Lane—are almost the only reminders of the time when this was the beating heart of London. Nowadays, only 8000 people call the City home, and few of the 300,000 who rush in and out every weekday have reason to return on evenings or weekends.

LUDGATE HILL & AROUND

Legend holds that London takes its name from King Lud, a mythical ruler of the city who was buried beneath the Lud Gate, one of the original Roman entryways into the City. As the City's highest spot, Ludgate Hill was the obvious spot to build **St. Paul's Cathedral** (see Major Attractions, p. 71) in the 7th century, whose current incarnation still towers above its surroundings.

OLD BAILEY

🚩 *Location:* Corner of Old Bailey and Newgate St.; public entry via Warwick Passage. *Contact:* ☎ 7248 3277. *Tube:* St. Paul's. *Open:* M-F 10:30am-1pm and 2-4:30pm. *Restrictions:* No cameras, drinks, food, electronics, or large bags; there are no cloakroom facilities.

Technically the Central Criminal Courts, the Old Bailey crouches under a copper dome and a wide-eyed figure of Justice. The current building is the third courthouse on the site; the previous two were incorporated into notorious Newgate Prison, founded in 1180 and only demolished in 1902. Originally, the court only had jurisdiction over the City, and it remains officially in the charge of the Corporation of London—the Lord Mayor is an *ex officio* judge. Some of the most celebrated cases in legal history were heard here: very influential was that of William Penn, accused of unlawfully evangelizing in 1670. After unhelpfully returning a verdict of "not guilty"— allowing Penn to go off and do useful things like founding Pennsylvania—the jury was fined and imprisoned. This led to the establishment of the of the "rights of juries to give their verdict according to their convictions," a principle sorely tested by many of the journalists who camp outside during trials.

ST. SEPULCHRE-WITHOUT-NEWGATE

⚑ Location: *Holborn Viaduct, opposite the Old Bailey.* **Contact:** ☎ *7248 3826; www.stmichaels.org.uk/sepulchre.* **Concerts:** *Occasional M and most Tu-W 1pm; choral evensong Su 3pm. Free.* **Open:** *for concerts and Tu and Th 12am-2pm, W 11am-3pm.* **Free.**

"Without" meaning "outside." Founded in Saxon times but rebuilt in 1450, St. Sepulchre was gutted in the Great Fire; the interior dates from 1670. Captain John Smith, of *Pocahontas* fame, is buried in the aisle. The church has a strong association with music, containing a Musicians' Chapel and a huge pipe organ once played by Handel and Mendelssohn, as well as the 12 "bells of Old Bailey" mentioned in *Oranges and Lemons.* Also in the church is the hand bell of Newgate Prison, rung outside the cells of the condemned on the eve of their execution.

Smithfield Market

ST. MARY-LE-BOW

⚑ Location: *Cheapside, by Bow Ln.* **Contact:** ☎ *7246 5139.* **Tube:** *St. Paul's or Mansion House.* **Concerts:** *Occasional Th 1:05pm. Free.* **Open:** *M-F 6:30am-6pm.* **Free.**

Another Wren creation, St. Mary's is most famous for its Great Bell, which from 1334 to 1874 rang the City curfew at 9pm and the reveille at 5:45am (ouch!). Traditionally, a Cockney is anyone born within their range—Dick Whittington (see p. 52) was meant to have heard them from as far away as Highgate. While he claimed the peal sounded "turn again Dick Whittington, thrice Lord Mayor of London," the nursery rhyme *Oranges and Lemons* settles for the shorter "I do not know." The church had to be almost completely rebuilt after the blitz, but the 11th-century **crypt,** whose "bows" (arches) gave the church its epithet, survived. Since the 12th century, it has hosted the ecclesiastical Court of Arches, where the Archbishop of Canterbury swears in bishops. Today, the court shares space with **The Place Below** restaurant (see p. 168).

Guildhall, City of London

OTHER LUDGATE HILL SIGHTS

ST. MARTIN-WITHIN-LUDGATE. Adjacent to the original Ludgate (demolished 1720), St. Martin claims to have been founded around AD 700 by a shadowy "King Cadwalla." William Penn married here in 1643, but the church was destroyed in the Fire and rebuilt by Wren in 1684. St. Martin's most notable features are the narrow spire, intended as a foil to St. Paul's, and the Grinling Gibbons woodwork inside. *(Ludgate Hill. ☎ 7248 6054. Open M-F 11am-3pm.)*

Barbican Apartments

WRENOVA-TIONS

On the morning of September 2, 1666, fire broke out in a bakery on Pudding Lane. By the time it had burned itself out, three days later, most of the City was a smouldering ruin—including the medieval Old St. Paul's and all but 11 of the City's 87 churches.

Christopher Wren, who had already proposed replacing the dilapidated cathedral, submitted a masterplan for the reconstruction of the entire City on rational lines. Expense and time ruled out this ambition plan (which influenced later proposals for Washington D.C. and Paris), but Wren was commissioned with rebuilding both St. Paul's and 51 new churches to replace those lost.

Of these, 23 survive, along with the towers of six more. Often constrained by tiny or oddly shaped plots of land, no two are alike, ranging in style from perpendicular Gothic to daring domes. Seemingly on every street corner in the City, it's easy to ignore them altogether, and impossible to see them all in a day. If you're pressed for time, don't miss **St. Bride's** (p. 90), **St. Mary-le-Bow** (p. 95), **St. Stephen Walbrook** (p. 98), and of course, **St. Paul's Cathedral** (p. 71).

ST. MARY ALDERMARY. "Aldermary" because it predates nearby St. Mary-le-Bow, this is a rare example of a Gothic Wren church—the conservative parishioners offered £5000 to restore the church to its pre-fire appearance, and Wren obliged. St. Mary's oddest feature is the east wall, built at an angle on account of the path running behind it. *(Corner of Watling St. and Victoria St. Tube: Mansion House. Open Tu-F 11am-3pm. Free.)*

ST. JAMES GARLICKHYTHE. The name refers to the garlic once sold nearby—the 16th-century equivalent of chewing gum. Known as "Wren's lantern" for its high ceiling and many windows, St. James's remains bright even though structural weakness and exterior noise have resulted in the bricking-up of the great east window and those along Upper Thames St. *(Garlick Hill, just north of Upper Thames St. ☎ 7236 1719. Tube: Mansion House or Cannon St. Open M-F 10am-4pm. Free)*

TEMPLE OF MITHRAS. Dwelling incongruously in the shadow of the Temple Court building are the remains of this 3rd-century Roman temple. The foundations, floor, and 2ft. of wall were discovered during construction work in 1954 and shifted up 18ft. to current street level. Artefacts unearthed during the excavation are on display at the Museum of London (see p. 143). *(Queen Victoria St. Tube: Mansion House or Bank.)*

COLLEGE OF ARMS. Like the US Supreme Court, the College upholds the right to bear arms—any male-line descendent of an ancestor with "armorial bearings" registered here is entitled to use them, something George Washington took full advantage of. Intriguingly, his family crest is remarkably similar to the stars and stripes. The Officer in Waiting can assess your claim (for a fee); otherwise, just admire the 17th-century Earl Marshal's Court, lined with paintings of obscure heralds and featuring the Earl Marshal's Throne. *(Queen Victoria St. ☎ 7248 2762; www.college-of-arms.gov.uk. Tube: Blackfriars or Mansion House. Open M-F 10am-4pm. Free.)*

GUILDHALL AND LONDON WALL

GUILDHALL YARD

🖪 Location: *Off Gresham St. Tube: St. Paul's, Moorgate, or Bank.*

Since the founding of the Corporation in 1193, the City has been governed from this site, the centerpiece of which is the Guildhall itself. As the name suggests, this is where the representatives of the City's 102 guilds, from the Fletchers (arrow-makers) to the Information Technologists, meet under the aegis of the Lord Mayor. Excavations in the 1990s revealed the remains of a Roman amphitheater below the Yard; its position is marked by an ellipse on the floor.

GUILDHALL. The vast Gothic hall dates from 1440, though after repeated remodelling in the 17th and 18th centuries—not to mention almost complete reconstruction following the Great Fire and the Blitz—little of the original remains beyond the crypt (closed to visitors) and the walls. The stained-glass windows bear the names of all 673 Mayors and Lord Mayors of the Corporation—the builders foresaw the City's longevity, as there's room for about 700 more. On either side of the wooden Minstrel's Gallery are 9 ft. statues of mythical Celtic giants Gog and Magog. The hall has seen numerous trials, including that of Lady Jane Grey in 1553; these days it hosts banquets and, every third Thursday of the month, public meetings of the **Court of Common Council,** presided over by the Lord Mayor bedecked in traditional robes and followed by a sword-wielding entourage. (☎ 7606 3030. Open May-Sept. M-F 10am-5pm, Sa-Su 10am-4pm; Oct.-Apr. closed Su. Last admission 30min. before closing. Free.)

ST. LAWRENCE JEWRY. The title reflects the fact that this area was known as "Jewry" for its predominantly Jewish population. Built anew by Wren after the Great Fire consumed its 12th-century predecessor, St. Lawrence was again aflame in 1940, after being struck by an incendiary bomb—formally referred to as "action by the King's Enemies." Restored to Wren's original design, St. Lawrence became the church of the Corporation in 1957; look for the Lord Mayor's pew, complete with sword rest. (Gresham St., opposite the Guildhall. ☎ 7600 9478. Open M-F 7:30am-2pm.)

OTHER GUILDHALL YARD SIGHTS. To the right of the Guildhall, is the brand-new **Guidhall Art Gallery** (see p. 144), built with the express purpose of being a permanent companion to the Guildhall—the architects claim it has a "design life of centuries." The **Guildhall Library,** in the 1970s annex and accessed via Aldermanbury, specializes in the history of London, and is open to all. It also houses the **Guildhall Clock Museum** (p. 144). (Entrance on Aldermanbury. ☎ 7332 1839. Library open M-Sa 9:30am-5pm.)

THE BARBICAN

⚑ Location: Between London Wall, Beech St., Aldersgate, and Moorgate. **Tube:** Barbican or Moorgate.

In the aftermath of WWII, the Corporation of London decided to redevelop this bomb-flattened 35-acre plot in the north of the City as a textbook piece of integrated development. Construction took 20 years, starting only in 1962, and the result bears all the hallmarks of its time: 40-storey tower blocks and masses of grey concrete, interlinked by a labyrinthine system of overhead walkways and open spaces. That said, it's not as bad as it sounds: lakes and gardens temper the hardness of the design. The complex's main fault is the difficulty of navigation, still not completely resolved despite the addition of signs and painted lines on the walkways.

BARBICAN CENTRE. Smack in the center of the Barbican is, logically enough, the Barbican Centre, a powerhouse of the arts. Described at its 1982 opening as "the City's gift to the nation," the complex incorporates a concert hall, two theaters, a cinema, three art galleries, and numerous cafeterias, bars, and restaurants—if you can find any of them. The **Lakeside Terrace** is a large piazza with picnic tables, sculpture, and sunken fountains flowing over waterfalls into a giant rectangular lake, opposite the 16th-century church of St. Giles Cripplegate (see below). Most surreal is the level 3 **Conservatory,** a literal concrete jungle—tropical plants burst forth on multiple levels amid ventilation ducts and pipes from the center below, like some post-apocalyptic scenario. (Main entrance on Silk St. From Tube: Moorgate or Barbican, follow the yellow painted lines. ☎ 7638 8891; www.barbican.org.uk. For more information on catching events, see Museums&Galleries, p. 164, and Entertainment, p. 248. Open M-Sa 9am-11pm, Su 10:30am-11pm.)

ST. GILES CRIPPLEGATE. Founded under King Canute in 1030, rebuilt in 1545, St. Giles's survived the Fire unscathed but was gutted in the Blitz. Now restored, it serves as the only link between the Barbican and its past. Milton is buried in the chancel, and Cromwell married here in 1620. (From the Barbican Centre, take the overhead walkway across the lake. Open M-F 10:30am-4pm and Su 7:30am-7pm.)

OTHER BARBICAN SIGHTS. Just behind St. Giles is a well-preserved section of **London Wall,** the city wall built by the Romans and maintained into the Middle Ages. Next to the Barbican Centre, overlooking the lake, is the distinctive and distinguished **Guildhall School of Music**—on hot days you can often hear students practising. At the complex's southwestern corner is the **Museum of London** (see p. 143).

OTHER SIGHTS AROUND GUILDHALL AND LONDON WALL

GOLDSMITH'S HALL. The Goldsmiths are one of the twelve "Great Guilds," originating in the Middle Ages, though the hall dates only to 1835. Today, the Goldsmith's Company remains responsible for assaying (verifying) all gold, silver, and platinum sold in the UK—this is the hall referred to in "hallmarking." The Livery Hall—decorated with oodles of gold leaf, naturaly—is closed except on five days per year: for information and bookings call the City of London Information Centre (☎7606 3030). At other times, you may be able to sneak in for **exhibitions,** held in November and March, and **concerts,** organised by the City Music Society (☎7628 6228). *(Corner of Gresham St. and Foster Ln. ☎7606 7010; www.thegoldsmiths.co.uk. Tube: St. Paul's.)*

NEARBY MUSEUMS & GALLERIES

Permanent Collections: ◼ Museum of London, p. 143; Guildhall Art Gallery, p. 144; Guildhall Clock Museum, p. 144.

Exhibition Spaces: Barbican Art Galleries, p. 144.

BANK TO THE TOWER

"Bank," referring to, of course, *the* Bank—the **Bank of England** (see below). Around this convergence of six streets stand hallowed institutions: the **Stock Exchange,** on Throgmorton St.; the neoclassical **Royal Exchange,** between Cornhill and Threadneedle St., founded in 1566 as Britain's first mercantile exchange; and the 18th-century **Mansion House,** on Walbrook, the official residence of the Lord Mayor.

BANK OF ENGLAND

🔒 *Location: Threadneedle St. Tube: Bank.*

Government financial difficulties led to the founding of the "Old Lady of Threadneedle St." in 1694, as a way of raising money without raising taxes—the bank's creditors supplied £1.2 million, and the national debt was born. The 8ft.-thick, windowless outer wall, enclosing four acres, is the only remnant of Sir John Soane's 1788 building; above it rises the current 1925 edifice. Top-hatted guards in pink tailsuits will direct those who wander into the main entrance to the **Bank of England Museum,** around the corner on St. Bartholomew Lane (see p. 144). The intrepid can try presenting their English banknotes and demanding the "sum of ten pounds" (or five, twenty, or fifty) as promised, but don't hold your breath.

MONUMENT

🔒 *Location: Monument St. Contact: ☎7626 2717. Tube: Monument. Open: Daily 10am-6pm; last admission 5:40pm. Admission: £1.50, child 50p; joint with Tower Bridge Experience (see p. 99) £6.75, child £4.25.*

The only non-ecclesiastical Wren building in the City, this plain Doric pillar topped with gilded flaming urn is a lasting reminder of the Great Fire. Erected in 1677, the 202ft.-tall column stands exactly that distance from the bakery on Pudding Lane where fire first broke out. As the inscription on the outside says, the fire "rushed devastating through every quarter with astonishing swiftness and worse." In 1681, a small addition was made: "but Popish frenzy, which wrought such horrors, is not yet quenched." This anti-Catholic sentiment was removed in 1830. The column offers an expansive view of London, despite the iron bars to prevent suicidal leaps; bring stern resolution to climb its 311 steps.

ST. STEPHEN WALBROOK

🔒 *Location: 39 Walbrook. Contact: ☎7283 4444. Tube: Bank or Cannon St. Open: M-Th 9am-4pm, F 9am-3pm. Free.*

On the site of a 7th-century Saxon church, St. Stephen's (built 1672-9) was Wren's personal favorite and is arguably his finest church. The plain exterior gives no inkling of the breathtakingly wide dome that floats above Henry Moore's mysterious freeform altar (1985). An honorary phone, donated by British Telecom, commemorates current rector Chad Varah, who in 1953 founded the Samaritans here, a hotline that advises the suicidal and severely depressed.

LOWER THAMES STREET

⚑ Location: *Just north of the Thames between London Bridge and the Tower.* **Tube:** *Monument.*

So busy that it must be crossed by overhead walkways, Lower Thames St. passes a number of interesting sights. It starts at **London Bridge,** more interesting for its history than its current bland incarnation. Close to the spot of the original Roman bridge, the first stone bridge across the Thames stood here from 1176 until 1832—and would have survived until today had not 18th-century "improvements" fatally weakened the structure. Its replacement lasted until 1973, when a wealthy American bought it for £1.03 million and shipped it to Arizona. A few steps up Lower Thames from the bridge, **St. Magnus-the-Martyr** proudly displays a chunk of wood from a Roman jetty. According to T.S. Eliot, its walls "hold inexplicable splendor of Ionian white and gold." (☎7626 4481. *Open Tu-F 10am-4pm, Su 10am-1pm.)*

Tower Bridge

ALL HALLOWS BY THE TOWER

⚑ Location: *Byward St.* **Contact:** ☎7481 2928. **Tube:** *Tower Hill.* **Open:** *Church M-F 9am-5:45pm, Sa-Su 10am-5pm; crypt M-Sa 11am-4pm, Su 1-4pm.*

Soon to be dwarfed by a vast new Norman Foster development, All Hallows bears the marks of its longevity with pride. Near the church bookshop stands a Saxon arch from AD 675, and the undercroft "museum" takes you down to stand on a Roman pavement in the crypt, now home to a motley array of local archaeological finds. Samuel Pepys witnessed the spread of the Great Fire from its tower, while American associations include John Quincy Adams, who married here, and William Penn, baptized here in 1644. Numerous model ships and nautical stained-glass motifs recall All Hallow's position as the church of Her Majesty's Customs & Excise force.

Lloyd's

TOWER BRIDGE

⚑ Location: *Entrance to the Tower Bridge Experience is through the west side (upriver) of the North Tower.* **Contact:** ☎7378 1928, lifting schedule ☎7378 7700; www.towerbridge.org.uk. **Tube:** *Tower Hill or London Bridge.* **Open:** *Apr.-Oct. daily 10am-6:30pm; Nov.-Mar. 9:30am-6pm. Last entry 1¼hr. before closing.* **Admission:** *£6.25, concessions £4.25, family £18.25.*

When TV and movie directors want to say "London!," nine times out of ten they settle for a shot of Tower Bridge—which helps explain why tourists often mistaken it for its plainer sibling, London Bridge (see above). Indeed, folklore insists that when London Bridge was sold and moved brick-by-brick to Arizona to make way for a replacement, the Americans thought they were getting Tower Bridge! A marvel of engineering, the steam-powered lifting mechanism remained in use from 1894 until 1973, when electric motors took over. Though clippers no longer sail

Wharf Building

into London very often, there's still enough large river traffic for the bridge to be lifted around 600 times per year—call to find out the schedule. For a deeper understanding of the history and technology behind the bridge, the **Tower Bridge Experience** fills the two towers with video shows, animated puppets, and ghosts, though the most impressive part is the visit to the engine rooms on the south bank. While it's a thrill to be so high over the Thames, don't expect too much of the view from the overhead walkways—iron latticework gets in the way, and the double-walkway design means you can only see the view in one direction at a time.

OTHER BANK TO THE TOWER SIGHTS

ST. OLAVE. This 15th-century church is dedicated to the patron saint of Norway, who as a young man helped King Ethelred defeat the Danes by demolishing London Bridge in 1013, inaugurating a nursery rhyme (see Life&Times, p. 52). An annual service is held in the church for Samuel Pepys, whose office was across the street in Seething Ln. and who is buried here with his wife. According to a 1586 entry in the church's burial register, Mother Goose is also interred here. *(8 Hart St. Tube: Tower Hill or DLR: Tower Gateway. ☎ 7488 4318. Open M-F 9am-5pm.)*

ST. MARY WOOLNOTH. The only City church untouched by the Blitz, St. Mary's confirms the talent of Wren's pupil Nicholas Hawksmoor. The lack of lower windows arises from the lack of open space around the site at the time of its building (1716-1727); even so the domed design results in a light, airy feel. *(Conjunction of King William and Lombard Sts. Open M-F 7:45am-5pm.)*

OTHER LOCAL SIGHTS. The most famous modern structure in the City is **Lloyd's of London,** built by Richard Rogers in 1986 for the organization that grew from a 17th-century coffeehouse to the largest insurance market in the world. With metal ducts, lifts, and chutes on the outside, it wears its heart (or at least its internal organs) on its sleeve. *(Leadenhall. Tube: Bank.)* Less intrusive is the **London Stone,** now indistinguishable (but for a plaque) from other stones nearby. This limestone fragment, possibly a Roman milestone, was once significant enough that a parish (St. Swithun London Stone) was named after it. Life's like that sometimes. *(In the side of 111 Cannon St., opposite the Tube/Rail: Cannon St.)* Only the tower remains of Wren's **St. Dunstan-in-the-East.** The unusual design, with a pointed spire supported on hollow buttresses, is reminiscent of the Warrant Model Wren submitted for St. Paul's Cathedral. The blitzed ruins have been converted into a pretty garden that makes a fine picnic spot. *(St. Dunstans Hill. Tube: Monument or Tower Hill.)* When rebuilding **St. Margaret Lothbury** in 1689, Wren was obliged to follow the lines of the former church, despite its north wall being shorter than the south; the result is a roof that's noticeably off-kilter. Like most of the furnishings, the sumptuous carved-wood screen—one of only two designed by Wren—was saved from other, now-demolished, City churches. *(Lothbury. Tube: Bank. ☎ 7606 8330. Open M-F 8am-4:30pm.)*

THE SOUTH BANK

SEE MAP, p. 336-337

⁊ The **Southwark Information Centre** (☎ 7403 8299; www.sic.southwark.org.uk), at the southern end of London Bridge opposite London Bridge mainline station, sells tickets to a wide variety of sights, shows, and events, books rooms, and gives out a list of local accommodations. Open M-Sa 10am-6pm, Su 10:30am-5:30pm. **NEIGHBORHOOD QUICKFIND: Discover,** p. 7; **Museums&Galleries,** p. 144; **Food&Drink,** p. 168; **Entertainment,** p. 214; **Accommodations,** p. 285.

From the Middle Ages until Cromwell spoilt the party, the South Bank was London's entertainment quarter; banished from the strictly-regulated City, all manner of illicit attractions sprouted in "the Borough," at the southern end of London Bridge. After Civil War, the area's fortunes turned to the sea, as wharves groaned under the weight of cargoes from across the Empire. Yet by the time the docks were succumbing to containerization in the late 1950s, the seeds of regeneration had been sown. From the 1951 Festival of Britain sprang the Royal Festival Hall, the nucleus of the future South Bank Centre and the heart of the new South Bank; the National Theatre followed 20 years later, and recently development has continued at such a pace the South Bank has fully recovered its position at the heart of London entertainment.

THE SOUTH BANK CENTRE

⚑ Location: *On the riverbank between Hungerford and Waterloo Bridges; road access from Belvedere Rd. and Upper Ground.* **Tube:** *Waterloo or Embankment (take the Hungerford foot bridge across the river).* **See also:** *For Festival Hall, Purcell Room, Queen Elizabeth Hall, and National Film Theatre, see Entertainment, p. 214; for Hayward Gallery, see Museums&Galleries, p. 145.*

Sprawling on either side of Waterloo Bridge along the Thames, this symphony of concrete is Britain's premier cultural center. Its nucleus is the **Royal Festival Hall**, a classic piece of white 1950s architecture. The gigantic lobby—whose stepped ceiling is actually the underside of the 2500-seat concert hall—often hosts free events, while the upper-level balconies offer fantastic views up and down the river. Close by the Festival Hall, the **Purcell Room** and **Queen Elizabeth Hall** cater for smaller concerts, while just behind it the spiky ceiling of the **Hayward Gallery** shelters excellent shows of modern art. On the embankment beneath Waterloo Bridge, the **National Film Theatre** offers London's most varied cinematic fare, while past the bridge looms the **National Theatre.** As controversial now as it was when built, whatever you think of the raw concrete exterior, the quality of productions is rarely in doubt. To find out how one of the world's largest, most modern theaters operates, join an hour-long backstage tour. (☎ 7452 3400; www.nationaltheatre.org.uk. Tours M-Sa 10:15am, 12:15 or 12:30 and 5:15 or 5:30pm, depending on performance schedule. £5, students & seniors £4.25.)

LONDON EYE

⚑ Location: *Jubilee Gardens, between County Hall and the Festival Hall.* **Contact:** *☎ 0870 500 0600; www.ba-londoneye.com.* **Open:** *Daily late May to early Sept. 9:30am-10pm, Apr. to late May and rest of Sept. 10:30am-8pm, Jan.-Mar. and Oct.-Dec. 10:30am-7pm; ticket office opens 30min. earlier.* **Tickets:** *Buy tickets from box office in corner of County Hall before joining the queue at the Eye; advance booking recommended. July-Sept. £9.50, seniors & disabled £7.50; Oct.-June £9, £7; under 16 £5 year-round.*

Also known as the Millennium Wheel, at 135m the British Airways London Eye is the biggest observational wheel in the world, taller than St. Paul's and visible from miles around. The Eye has established itself as one of London's top attractions with locals and tourists alike, despite problems during the initial hoist—engineers left the wheel lying at a shallow angle for months, as Virgin Atlantic balloons emblazoned with "BA can't get it up" buzzed overhead. The ellipsoid glass "pods" give uninterrupted views from the top of each 30min. revolution: on clear days you can see to Windsor in the west, though eastward views are blocked by skyscrapers further down the river.

COUNTY HALL

⚑ Location: *Westminster Bridge Rd., by Westminster Bridge.* **Tube:** *Westminster or Waterloo.*

This enormous curved facade facing the Thames was formerly the home of the Greater London Council, the unified city government abolished by Margaret Thatcher for being too socialist. After years as an empty shell, it's been redeveloped for tourism: the upper floors host a Marriott facing the river and a Travel Inn at the rear (see Accommodations, p. 286), while lower levels house the London Aquarium, Dalí Universe (see below), and a McDonald's, which more-or-less sets the tone.

LONDON AQUARIUM. As aquaria go, this is pretty small fry, a maze of windowless, black-painted tunnels neither particularly spectacular nor informative. The main attractions are two 3-story ocean tanks; pollock and bream circle aimlessly in the Atlantic tank, safe from the Pacific's menacing sharks. There is also a beach area where jelly-fleshed rays seem happy enough to be stroked and petted and parents can bully terrified children into picking up crabs and starfish. (☎ 7967 8000; www.londonaquarium.co.uk. Open daily 10am-6pm, last admission 5pm. £8.50, students & seniors £6.50, under 14s £5, family (2 adults + 2 kids) £24.)

DALÍ UNIVERSE. "500 works of art" scream the posters which, accuracy aside, tells you all you need to know about this "gallery": it's quantity that counts, not quality. Almost all the works are multiple-run prints, castings, or reproductions. You'll find a better array of Dalís for free in the Tate Modern (see p. 137), but if melting watches are your thing, spend on. (☎ 7620 2720; www.daliuniverse.com. Open daily 10am-5:30pm. £8.50, students & seniors £6, ages 5-16 £5, family (2 adults + 3 kids) £22.)

THE WAGES OF SIN

While most people are aware of Southwark's illicit past, few know of the essential conniving role played by the Church. Yet from the 13th century to the Civil War in the 17th, much of Southwark was part of the Bishop of Winchester's estate. As church property, this so-called "Liberty of the Clink" was exempt from ordinary English laws—it was pretty much the Bishop's private domain.

Naturally, as God-fearing men, the Bishops cared deeply for the well-being of the local population. Acting, bear-baiting, gambling, and all manner of other activities banned elsewhere were not only permitted, but actively encouraged (and, naturally, taxed).

Most notorious of all were the "Winchester geese"—local prostitutes. Indeed, the Bishop encouraged and profited from prostitution. A strict code of conduct protected both customers and workers: pimping was controlled, with prostitutes free to join and leave "stews" (brothels), while value for money was ensured by the rule that "any whore who takes a man's money must stay with him to the following morning."

To prove that underneath it all he was a God-fearing man, the Bishop went as far as throwing all the prostitutes out on holy days. Presumably, God wasn't looking at other times.

GABRIEL'S WHARF & OXO TOWER WHARF

🔁 **Location:** *Between Upper Ground and the Thames.* **Tube:** *Blackfriars, Southwark, or Waterloo.*

The most colorful new additions to the South Bank result from the unflagging efforts of the Coin Street Community Builders (CSCB), a non-profit development company which has sought to preserve the area as a model of integrated, affordable living. This is perhaps best realized in the many crafts boutiques, bars, and cafes of **Gabriel's Wharf**, a vibrant market-like area with not a multinational in sight—unless you count the **OXO Tower** just a block down the river. Built by a company that once supplied instant beef-stock to the entire British Empire, this Art Deco tower is famous for its clever subversion of rules prohibiting advertising on buildings (the windows spell out "OXO"). The Tower is now enveloped in the brick mass of **OXO Tower Wharf**, another Coin Street development full of tiny boutiques and workshops run by some of London's most innovative young designers, as well as a Harvey Nichols-managed restaurant at the tower's summit whose prices are as stratospheric as the view. Fortunately, a public viewing gallery on the eighth floor allows you to savor the view without paying Harvey Nicks prices.

TATE MODERN AND THE MILLENNIUM BRIDGE

🔁 **Location:** *Queen's Walk, Bankside.* **Tube:** *Southwark, Blackfriars, or (across the bridge) St. Paul's.*

Squarely opposite each other on Bankside are the biggest success and most abject failure of London's millennial celebrations. **Tate Modern** (see Museums&Galleries, p. 137), created from the shell of the former Bankside power station, is the runaway success of recent years, as visually arresting as its contents are thought-provoking. Built to link the Tate to the City—with a grand walkway leading from the northern end right up to St. Paul's—the **Millennium Bridge** outdid even the Dome for underachievement. Like the Dome a Norman Foster project, the bridge was not only completed six months too late for the Y2K festivities, but following a literally shaky debut closed down within days. Engineers promised to fix it in weeks, but a year later no progress had been made; with luck, it will finally reopen sometime in 2002.

SHAKESPEARE'S GLOBE THEATRE

🔁 **Location:** *Bankside, close to Bankside pier.* **Contact:** ☎ *7902 1500; www.shakespeares-globe.org.* **Tube:** *Southwark or London Bridge.* **Open:** *Daily May-Sept. 9am-noon and 1pm-4pm (exhibition only), Oct.-Apr. daily 10am-5pm.* **Admission:** *£7.50, students £6, ages 5-15*

£5, family (2 adults + 3 kids) £23; 50p reduction when no tour operates. **See also:** Entertainment, p. 215.

In the shadow of Tate Modern, the half-timbered Globe rises just 200m from where the original burned down in 1613 after a succesful 14-year run as the Bard's preferred playhouse. Today's reconstruction had its first full season in 1997, and now stands among assorted other buildings of the International Shakespeare Globe Centre. The excellent exhibition inside covers both the story of the rebuilding of the Globe and the life and times of the original version. Other amusements include recordings of famous performances, costumes to try on, and attempts to recreate the English accent of Shakespeare's time. Try to arrive in time for a tour of the theater itself (mornings only during the performance season), where enthusiastic guides will tell you why only cashmere was good for the plaster walls.

OXO Tower

THE ROSE THEATRE

⊞ Location: 56 Park St. **Contact:** ☎ 7593 0026; www.rosetheatre.org.uk. **Open:** Daily 11am-5pm. **Admission:** £4, students & seniors £3, ages 5-15 £2, family (2 adults + 4 kids) £10; £1 off on presentation of a same-day Globe exhibition ticket.

Nearby lie the ruins of the 1587 Rose Theatre, Bankside's first, where both Shakespeare and Christopher Marlowe performed. The site was rediscovered in 1989 during excavations to build a new office block; following a public outcry the block was redesigned so that the remains could be preserved and opened to the public. Not much is left, though the outline is clearly visible; an accompanying 30min. video projection tells the history of Southwark and the site since Roman times.

Tate Modern

SOUTHWARK CATHEDRAL

⊞ Location: Montague Close. **Contact:** ☎ 7367 6700; www.dswark.org. **Tube:** London Bridge. **Open:** Cathedral daily 8am-6pm; exhibition daily 10am-6pm (last admission 5:30pm). **Audioguide:** cathedral tour £5, students & seniors £4, ages 5-15 £2.50. **Photography:** Camera permit £1.50; video permit £5. **Admission:** Cathedral free (£2.50 suggested donation); exhibition £3, seniors & students £2.50, ages 5-15 £1.50, family (2 adults + 3 kids, includes audioguide) £12.

One of London's oldest churches is, paradoxically, its newest (Anglican) cathedral—only in 1905 was the parish church of St. Saviour promoted, even though Christians have worshipped here since AD 606. The cathedral is now the proud home of a spanking new **Visitor Centre**, "The Long View of London" exhibition. Three rooms house hi-tech exhibits, including an "X-Ray wall" where you can search for hidden archeological treasures, as well as locally-found artefacts. Close to the exhibition, the **archeological gallery** is actually a small excavation by the

St. Paul's & Millennium Bridge

103

cathedral wall, revealing a 1st-century Roman road along with Saxon, Norman, and 18th-century remains. The oldest complete part of the **cathedral** itself is the **Retrochoir,** separated from the main choir by a wonderfully carved 16th-century **altar screen** (though the statues are early 20th-century). Adjacent to the 13th-century **north transept,** the **Harvard chapel** commemorates John Harvard, baptized here in 1607. Nearby, the **north aisle** holds the richly painted tomb of John Gower (d. 1408), the "first English poet." Across the 19th-century nave, the **south aisle** bears a window and monument to William Shakespeare; a tablet in the choir commemorates his brother Ed.

HMS BELFAST

🚇 *Location:* At the end of Morgans Ln. off Tooley St. *Contact:* ☎ 7940 6300; www.iwm.org.uk. *Tube:* London Bridge. *Open:* Daily Mar.-Oct. 10am-6pm, Nov.-Feb. 10am-5pm; last admission 45min. before closing. *Admission:* £5.40, students & seniors £4, under 16 free.

This enormous battleship was one of the most powerful in the world when launched in 1938, leading the bombardment of Normandy during D-Day and supporting UN forces in Korea before graciously retiring in 1965. Today the 6 in. guns are trained on a motorway service station 11 mi. away, ready to punish speeding drivers. Kids will love clambering over the decks and aiming the 40mm anti-aircraft guns at dive-bombing seagulls. Inside, almost every room is on show, from the kitchens to the operations room, where waxworks and sound recordings recreate the sinking of the German battleship Scharnhorst in 1943. Dozens of narrow passages, steep staircases, and ladders make exploring the boat a physical challenge in itself.

OTHER SOUTH BANK SIGHTS

VINOPOLIS. This Dionysian Disneyland offers patrons an interactive (yes, that means samples) tour of the world's wine regions. France hogs the limelight, but there are also displays on less well-known viticultural centers—how about Indian champagne? The overall impression is that the curators have sniffed more than they can swallow: the treatment is too shallow to satisfy wine buffs, but too long (at least two hours) for casual visitors. Still, with five generous tastings (from a choice of dozens) included in the price, by the end of the tour you'll be in no state to complain. *(1 Bank End, at the end of Clink St. ☎ 0870 4444 777 (24hr.); www.vinopolis.co.uk. Tube: London Bridge. Open Tu-F and Su 11am-6pm, M 11am-8pm, Sa 11am-9pm. £11.50, seniors £10.50, ages 5-15 (no tastings) £5; book of 5 extra tasting vouchers £2.50.)*

OLD OPERATING THEATRE & HERB GARRET. Bizarrely located in the loft of an 18th-century church is the oldest surviving operating theater in the world. The semicircular design, with tiered observation galleries around the wooden operating table, shows this truly was a theater—and no doubt highly dramatic in those pre-anaesthetics days. A fearsome array of saws and knives accompanies an exhibition on surgical history, highlighting the resistance of Victorian doctors to new-fangled ideas such as "hygiene." In the neighboring **herb garret,** used by the hospital apothecary to prepare medicines (one cure for venereal disease starts "take six gallons of snails"), the calming effect of fragrant herbs is destroyed by a display of old medical instruments, such as a trepanning drill, used to relieve headaches by boring a hole in the skull. *(9a St. Thomas's St. ☎ 7955 4791; www.thegarret.org.uk. Tube: London Bridge. Open daily 10:30am-4:45pm. £3.50, concs. £2.50, kids £1.75, family £8.)*

GOLDEN HINDE. This dinky-looking boat is a full-sized replica of the 16th-century warship in which Sir Francis Drake became the first Englishman to circumnavigate the world. Incredibly, the replica has comprehensively outsailed the original since launching in 1973, clocking up over 100,000 miles, rounding the globe twice, and starring in films from *Swashbuckler* to *Shogun*. Visitors will be able to clamber over the decks until mid-2002, when the ship will once more take to the high seas to ravage treasure galleons, defeat armadas, and generally get in the way of Spanish imperialist designs. *(St. Mary Overie Dock, Cathedral St. ☎ 7403 0123. Tube: London Bridge. Open daily 9am-5:30pm. £2.50, students & seniors £2.10, kids £1.75.)*

HAY'S GALLERIA AND BUTLER'S WHARF. Now paved over, glass-topped, and lined with uninspiring chain stores and restaurants, **Hay's Galleria** was once Hay's Wharf, one of the busiest docks in London. Designed by William Cubitt, the 1857 wharf was frequented by clippers such as the Cutty Sark (see p. 129). Today, a nautical note is struck by *Navigators*, David Kemp's camp kinetic sculpture-fountain. Its water jets pay tribute to Joseph Hay, who founded the first fire brigade here in 1696. *(London Bridge City, off Tooley St. ☎ 7940 7770. Tube: London Bridge.)* Just east of Tower Bridge, **Butler's Wharf** retains some of the look of its heyday along **Shad Thames,** crisscrossed by overhead walkways across which dock porters transferred cargoes between warehouses. Following the demise of the docks, in the 1970s Butler's Wharf became home to London's largest artists' colonies, film-maker Derek Jarman and sculptor André Logan among its residents. The party ended in 1980, when developers moved in: today the wharf is lined with restaurants taking advantage of the fantastic views, including the 🔲Cantina del Ponte (p. 168).

HMS Belfast

LONDON DUNGEON. Most effective of the many instruments of torture on display here is the unbelievably long queue; once in, the dark-ened railway arches tastefully recreate the happy days of Jack the Ripper and the Great Fire of London, with anything else remotely connected to horror and Britain thrown in for effect. In "Judgement Day," visitors are con-victed, sentenced, and hauled off to be exe-cuted for being gullible enough to fall for this gloomy franchise. If you must see it, arrive when it opens or buy tickets in advance. *(28-34 Tooley St. ☎ 0870 846 0666; www.thedungeons.com. Tube: London Bridge. Open daily mid-July to Sept. 10:30am-8pm (last admission), Apr. to mid-July and Sept.-Oct. 10:30am-5:30pm, Nov.-Mar. 10:30am-5pm. £10.95, students £9.50, seniors & children £6.95; advance tickets £1 extra.)*

Hay's Galleria

WINSTON CHURCHILL'S BRITAIN AT WAR EXPERIENCE. A macabre reconstruction of London life during the Blitz. The grand finale, a walk-through recreated bomb site, borders on the tasteless, even if the body parts strewn among the wreckage are meant to be shop dum-mies from a bombed-out clothing store. Skip it and head to the Imperial War Museum (see p. 151) instead. *(64-66 Tooley St. ☎ 7403 3171; www.britainatwar.co.uk. Tube: London Bridge. Open daily Apr.-Sept. 10am-5:30pm (last admission), Oct.-Mar. 10am-4:30pm. £5.95, concessions £3.95, under 16 £2.95, families £14.)*

NEARBY MUSEUMS & GALLERIES
Major Collections: Tate Modern, p. 137.

Other Permanent Collections: Design Museum, p. 144; Clink Prison Museum, p. 145.

Exhibition Spaces: Hayward Gallery, p. 145; Bank-side Gallery, p. 145; Jerwood Gallery, p. 145.

St. Margaret's, Westminster

WESTMINSTER

NEIGHBORHOOD QUICKFIND: Discover, *p. 8;* **Museums&Galleries,** *p. 145;* **Food&Drink,** *p. 169;* **Entertainment,** *p. 215;* **Shopping,** *p. 232;* **Accommodations,** *p. 286.*

WHITEHALL

Location: *Between Trafalgar Sq. and Parliament Sq.* **Tube:** *Westminster, Embankment, or Charing Cross.*

SEE MAP, p. 338-339

A long stretch of imposing facades housing government ministries, "Whitehall" is synonymous with the British civil service. From 1532 until a devastating fire in 1698, however, it was the home of the monarchy and one of the greatest palaces in Europe. Today all that remains are Henry VIII's wine cellars, hidden under the monolithic **Ministry of Defence** and viewable only on written application, and Inigo Jones's **Banqueting House** (see below). Towards the northern end of Whitehall, shortly before Trafalgar Sq., **Great Scotland Yard** marks the address of the former HQ of the Metropolitan Police—although the front entrance (and commemorative plaque) is one block south, at 3-8 Whitehall Pl. Nearer Parliament Sq., where Whitehall changes name to Parliament St., steel gates mark the entrance to **Downing Street.** In 1735, no. 10 was made the official residence of the First Lord of the Treasury, a position that soon became permanently identified with the Prime Minister. The Chancellor of the Exchequer traditionally resides at no. 11, and the Chief Whip at no. 12. However, Tony Blair's family is too big for no. 10, so he's swapped with Gordon Brown next door. Just outside the entrance to Downing St., in the middle of Whitehall, Edward Lutyen's **Cenotaph** (1919) commemorates the dead of WWI.

HORSEGUARDS. Immediately recognizable from the crowds of tourists, this 18th-century building is where the burnished hussars of the Household Cavalry, in shining cuirasses and plumed helmets, guard a shortcut to St. James's Park. While anyone can walk through, only those with a special ivory pass issued by the Queen may drive past the gates. The guard is changed M-F at 11am, Sa 10am, with a dismount for inspection daily at 4pm. Beyond the neoclassical building is the sandy expanse of **Horseguards' Parade,** where the Queen ceremonially reviews her troops during the Trooping of the Colour, which takes place on the second or third Saturday in June.

BANQUETING HOUSE. All that remains of the Palace of Whitehall, Banqueting House was built in 1622 by Inigo Jones for James I. Jones's had hoped to rebuild the entire palace, but the prudent king restricted him to just this one edifice. Essentially a one-up, one-down affair—the vaulted undercroft below and the great hall above—Banqueting House is still used for state dinners. Charles I commissioned Rubens to paint the great ceiling panels with scenes extolling the monarchy; unfortunately for him, Parliament was impressed and on January 27, 1649 Charles stepped out of the window on the first-floor landing onto the scaffold where he was beheaded. The weather vane on the roof tells another tale of Stuart misfortune—James II placed it there to see if the wind was favorable for his rival William of Orange's voyage from the Netherlands in 1688. *(Whitehall, opposite Horseguards. ☎ 7930 4179. Open M-Sa 10am-5pm, last admission 4:30pm. £3.90, students&seniors £3.10, children £2.30.)*

PARLIAMENT SQUARE

Tube: *Westminster.*

Laid out in 1750, Parliament Square rapidly became the focal point for opposition to the government. Today, demonstrators are dissuaded by a continuos stream of heavy traffic, with no pedestrian crossings. Those who make it across will find statues of Parliamentary greats (Lord Palmerstone) and forgotten heros (Ian Smut). Standing opposite the **Houses of Parliament** (see p. 70), Winston Churchill was famously given a turf mohican during the May 2000 anti-capitalist demonstrations. South of the square rises **Westminster Abbey** (see p. 77) while to the west looms the great dome of **Methodist Central Hall,** where the United Nations first met in 1946.

ST. MARGARET'S WESTMINSTER

Location: *Parliament Sq. (☎ 7222 6382).* **Tube:** *Westminster.* **Open:** *M-F 9:30am-3:45pm, Sa 9:30am-1:45pm, Su 2-5pm.* **Free.**

Literally in Westminster Abbey's shadow, St. Margaret's was built for local residents by Abbey monks sick of having to share their own church with laymen; since 1614, it's been the official worshipping place of the House of Commons. The **Milton Window** (1888), to the right of the main entrance above the North Aisle, shows the poet (married here in 1608) dictating *Paradise Lost* to his daughters. Lining the South Aisle, the grey-hued 1966 **Piper Windows** replace those destroyed in WWII; the subdued design is designed not to compete with the **East Window** above the altar. Celebrating the wedding of Henry VIII to Catherine of Aragon, this 1526 Flemish window was originally made for another church, but following the marriage's unhappy ending was dismantled and kept in storage until being bought by St. Margaret's in 1758. Opposite, the **West Window** commemorates Sir Walter Ralegh, executed across the street in 1618 and now lying in the chancel, neighboring the High Altar.

WESTMINSTER CATHEDRAL

⛊ Location: *Cathedral Piazza, off Victoria St. (☎ 7798 9055; www.westminstercathedral.org.uk).* **Tube:** *Victoria.* **Open:** *Daily 7am-7pm.* **Admission:** *Free; suggested donation £2.* **Bell Tower:** *Open 9am-5pm daily Apr.-Nov.; Th-Su Dec.-Mar. £2, concs. £1, family £5.*

Following Henry VIII's break with Rome, London's Catholic community remained without a cathedral for over three centuries until 1887, when the Church purchased a derelict prison as the site from which the new neo-Byzantine church was to rise. Construction began in 1895, but the architect's plan outran available funds; by 1903, when work stopped, the interior remained unfinished. The three blackened brick domes contrast dramatically with the swirling marble of the lower walls and the magnificence of the side chapels. Eric Gill's **stations of the cross** (1918), were criticized for their diagrammatic designs that eschewed tradition; today they are among the Cathedral's most prized possessions. Gill used his own face as the model for Christ's in the 10th station. A lift carries visitors up the striped 273ft. **bell tower** for a view of the Westminster, the river, and Kensington.

OTHER WESTMINSTER SIGHTS

JEWEL TOWER. Cut off from the Houses of Parliament by Millbank, Jewel Tower is a lone survivor of the medieval Palace of Westminster. Built by Edward III in 1365-6, from 1621 to 1869 it was used to store the parliamentary archives (now in Victoria Tower, across the street). These days it houses a small shop and the **Parliament Past and Present** exhibition, which explains the history and workings of Parliament through a series of wall panels. In case you really want to know how many gills there are to a bushel, a room on the top floor displays measures from the Tower's days as home of the Standards Dept. (☎ 7222 2219. *Tube: Westminster. Open daily Apr.-Sept. 10am-6pm, Oct. 10am-5pm, Nov.-Mar 10am-4pm. £1.60, student and seniors £1.20, children 80p, under 5 free.*)

VICTORIA TOWER GARDENS. South of the Palace of Westminster, the magnificent backdrop of makes the gardens a favorite spot for TV crews interviewing politicians. Their task is made slightly more difficult by a cast of Rodin's *Burghers of Calais*, an odd place for such anti-English propaganda. A Neogothic gazebo commemorates the abolition of slavery on British territory in 1834, while a statue of Emmeline Pankhurst recalls the struggle for emancipation. (*On Millbank. Tube: Westminster. Open daily until dusk.*)

THE ROYAL MEWS. Doubling as a museum and a working carriage house, the Mews' main attraction is the Queen's collection of coaches, from the "glass coach" used to carry Diana to her wedding to the four-ton **Gold State Coach.** The attendant guarding the coach is himself a goldmine of royal information, full of tips on when and where to catch glimpses of their Royal Highnesses. Kids will enjoy a chance to get up close to the carriage horses themselves, each named personally by the Queen. Note that, as a working mews, horses and carriages are liable to be absent without notice, and opening hours are subject to change. (*Buckingham Palace Rd. ☎ 7839 1377. Tube: St. James's Park or Victoria. Open M-Th noon-4pm, last admission 3:30pm. £4, seniors £3.60, under 17 £2.60, family £11.80.*)

ST. JAMES'S PARK AND GREEN PARK. The run-up to Buckingham Palace is flanked by two expanses of greenery. **St. James's Park,** acquired along with St.

James's Palace by Henry VIII in 1531, owes its informal appearance to a re-landscaping by Nash in 1827. Across the Mall, **Green Park** is the creation of Charles II; "Constitution Hill" refers not to the king's interest in political theory, but to his daily exercises. Sit on one of the lawn chairs scattered enticingly around both parks and an attendant will magically materialize and demand money. *(The Mall. Open daily 5am-midnight. Lawn chairs available Apr.-Sept. 10am-6pm, June-Aug. to 10pm. £1 for 4hr.)*

ST. JOHN'S SMITH SQUARE. Four assertive corner towers distinguish this unusual example of English Baroque. The church is nicknamed "Queen Anne's Footstool" after the story that when the architect, Thomas Archer, asked the impatient Queen's advice, she upended her footstool and told him "like that." Dickens likened Archer's effort to a "petrified monster." The church stood ruined for years following a bomb hit in 1941, reopening as a concert hall in 1969. While officially the interior is only open for concerts, the staff are usually happy to let people look around if no rehearsals are being held—August is (literally) the quietest time. *(Smith Sq. Tube: Westminster or St. James's Park. ☎ 7222 1061; www.sjss.org.uk. For concert info, see p. 215.)*

NEARBY MUSEUMS & GALLERIES

Permanent Collections: Cabinet War Rooms, p. 145; Queen's Gallery, p. 145; Guard's Museum, p. 146.

CHELSEA

SEE MAP, p. 346

🚇 TRANSPORTATION: *The only **Tube** station in Chelsea is Sloane Sq.; from here **buses** 11, 19, 22, 211, and 319 run down the King's Rd.* **NEIGHBORHOOD QUICKFIND: Discover,** *p. 8;* **Museums&Galleries,** *p. 146;* **Food&Drink,** *p. 170;* **Entertainment,** *p. 215;* **Shopping,** *p. 108.*

The stomping ground of the Sloane Ranger—well-bred, dimwitted aristocratic scions—Chelsea nevertheless retains a unique vibrancy. As wealthy as neighboring Belgravia and Kensington, Chelsea adds a riverside location and a strong artistic heritage. Henry VIII's right-man (and later victim) Sir Thomas More was the first big-name resident in the 16th century, but it was in the 19th century that the neighborhood acquired its reputation as an artistic hothouse: **Cheyne** (CHAIN-ee) **Walk** was home to Turner, George Eliot, Dante Gabriel Rossetti, and more recently Mick Jagger (at no. 48); Oscar Wilde, Sargent, Whistler, and Bertrand Russell lived on **Tite Street;** while Brunel, Mark Twain, Henry James, T.S. Eliot, and William Morris were also Chelsea residents at one time. The latest artist-in-residence is none other than Damien Hirst, who recently purchased a large houseboat moored near Cheyne Walk.

THE ROYAL HOSPITAL

🚇 Location: *Royal Hospital Rd.* **Contact:** *☎ 7881 5204.* **Hospital open:** *M-Sa 10am-noon and 2-4pm, Apr.-Sept. also Su 2-4pm.* **Ranelagh Gardens open:** *May-Aug. M-Sa 10am-12:45pm and 2-8:30pm, Su 2-8:30pm; Nov.-Mar. closes 4:30pm, Apr. 7:30pm, Sept. 7pm, Oct. 5pm.* **Free.**

The Royal Hospital is home to the **Chelsea Pensioners,** who shuffle around the grounds as they have done since 1692, dressed in blue for everyday wear and scarlet for ceremonial occasions. Charles II established the Hospital as a retirement home for army veterans ("hospital" meaning a place of shelter), and the entrance criteria have barely changed since: 20 years' distinguished service or disability. It remains a military institution, with inmates arranged in companies under the command of a retired officer; until 1805 pensioners remained armed and carried out guard duties. Although the gracefulness of the layout is a hallmark of the Hospital's Christopher Wren pedigree, the buildings are severe and restrained as befits a military establishment. The only respite is in the pediment and cupola of the central **Figure Court,** named for Grinling Gibbons's statue of Charles II. French canon from Waterloo guard its open south side, while the north is divided between the **chapel** and the **Great Hall,** where pensioners dine amid royal portraits and captured enemy standards. The outhouses harbor a small **museum,** detailing the history and everyday life of the hospital and pensioners along with a display of medals.

RANELAGH GARDENS. Accessed through the hospital grounds, these gardens were were opened to the public in 1724, and soon became a fashionable spot, with meals served in the enormous Rotunda. When the Hospital repurchased the land in 1805, the Rotunda was demolished and now the gardens are a quiet oasis free of high society—except during the week of the **Chelsea Flower Show,** held May 21-24 in 2002, when the braying masses of the Royal Horticultural Society descend *en masse. (See www.rhs.org.uk for information; tickets to the show must be purchased well in advance.)*

OTHER CHELSEA SIGHTS

SLOANE SQUARE AND THE KING'S ROAD. Mostly just a square, with four sides at 90°, **Sloane Sq.** takes its name from British Museum founder Sir Hans Sloane (1660-1753), who spearheaded the neighborhood's transformation from sleepy backwater to fashionable suburb. Until 1829, the **King's Road,** stretching southwest from Sloane Sq., served as a private royal route from Hampton Court to Whitehall. The 60s were launched here in 1955 when Mary Quant launched the miniskirt on an unsuspecting world; two decades later the Sex Pistols snarled their way out of Malcom McLaren's boutique at the **World's End,** 430 King's Rd. (see p. 233).

CARLYLE'S HOUSE. In his time, the "Sage of Chelsea" Thomas Carlyle was the most famous writer and historian in England—at his death in 1881, admirers purchased the house in which he had lived since 1834 to preserve it as a national monument. The house and garden in which he entertained Dickens, Tennyson, George Eliot, and Ruskin, are more or less as they were during his lifetime. In the attic study, you can see copies of correspondence, including a letter from Disraeli offering Carlyle the Order of the Bath on the grounds that he was the only writer of his time who would without doubt remain a household name. *(24 Cheyne Row. ☎ 7352 7087. Open Apr.-Oct. W-Su 11am-5pm, last admission 4:30pm. £3.50, under 16 £1.75.)*

CHELSEA PHYSIC GARDEN. Founded in 1673 to provide medicinal herbs, the Physic Garden is today a living repository of all manner of useful, rare, or just plain interesting plants, from opium poppies to leeks. It has also played an important historic role, serving as the staging post from which tea was introduced to India and cotton to America. *(66 Royal Hospital Rd.; entrance on Swan Walk. ☎ 7352 5646; www.cpgarden.demon.co.uk. Open early Apr. to late Oct. W noon-5pm, Su 2-6pm; M-F noon-5 during Chelsea Flower Show (late May) and Chelsea Festival (mid-June). £4, students and under 16 £2.)*

CHELSEA OLD CHURCH. Where Cheyne Walk spills onto Chelsea Embankment is this originally Saxon church, restored after WWII to look remarkably new. Fortunately, the bombs spared the southern chapel, designed by Thomas More in the 16th century. Henry VIII is reported to have married Jane Seymour here before the official wedding took place. Just down the street is **Crosby Hall,** a 15th-century hall that was More's residence in Bishopsgate before being moved, stone by stone, to its present position in 1910. *(Old Church St. www.domini.org/chelsea-old-church. Open Tu-F 1:30-5:30pm and for services Su 8, 10, 11am, 12:15, 6pm.)*

NEARBY MUSEUMS & GALLERIES
Permanent Collections: National Army Museum, p. 146.

KNIGHTSBRIDGE & BELGRAVIA

↗ NEIGHBORHOOD QUICKFIND: Discover, *p. 9;* **Food&Drink,** *p. 171;* **Shopping,** *p. 233;* **Accommodations,** *p. 109.*

Now home to London's most expensive stores, it's hard to imagine that in the 18th century **Knightsbridge** was a racy district known for its taverns and its highwaymen, both taking advantage of the area's position just outside the city's jurisdiction. In many people's eyes, gentrification has merely pushed the highway robbery indoors—what else could you call having to pay £1 just to use the loo in Harrods?

SEE MAP, p. 338-339

Squeezed between Knightsbridge, Chelsea, and Westminster, the wedge-shaped district of **Belgravia,** like Mayfair and Kensington before it, was catapulted to respectability by the presence of royalty. When George IV decided to make Buckingham Palace his official residence in the 1820s, developers were quick to throw up suitably grand buildings for aristocratic hangers-on nearby. **Belgrave Square,** the

BEEFCAKE WELLINGTON

Before television, film, and Hugh Grant, the military was a prime source of sex symbols— and few soldiers set pulses racing faster than Arthur Wellesley, Duke of Wellington. Charlotte Brontë fancied the victor at Waterloo so much as a child that she modeled Jane Eyre's Rochester after him. Countess Lavinia Spencer showed her affection in another way, by launching a women-only public subscription to raise funds for a memorial statue. The result was the "Ladies' Trophy," Hyde Park's nude statue of Achilles, cheekily referred to as the ladies' fancy. The statue, London's first public nude, was embroiled in controversy from its creation. Lady Holland wrote saucily: "A difficulty has arisen, and the artist had submitted to the female subscribers whether this colossal figure should preserve its antique nudity or should be garnished with a fig leaf. It was carried for the leaf by a majority...The names of the *minority* have not transpired." Those eager to accuse women of prudery should be advised that it was in fact the gentleman head of the statue committee who insisted on the fig leaf.

setting for *My Fair Lady*, is the most impressive of the set-pieces, now so expensive that the aristocracy has had to sell out to foreign governments—this is embassyland.

APSLEY HOUSE

🖫 **Location:** *Hyde Park Corner.* **Contact:** ☎ *7499 5676; www.apsleyhouse.org.uk.* **Tube:** *Hyde Park Corner.* **Open:** *Tu-Su 11am-5pm.* **Admission:** *£4.50, students&seniors £3, under 18 free.*

Named for Baron Apsley, for whom Robert Adam designed a mansion in 1771, the house later known as "No. 1, London" was bought in 1817 by the Duke of Wellington, whose heirs still occupy a modest suite of rooms on the top floor. On display is Wellington's fine collection of art, much of it given in gratitude by the crowned heads of Europe following the battle of Waterloo. The majority of paintings hang in the **Waterloo Gallery,** where that the Duke would hold his annual Waterloo banquet on the stupendous silver table service donated by the Portuguese government (now displayed in the dining room). X-ray analysis revealed that the famous Goya portrait of Wellington on horseback—the model for a thousand pub signs—was originally of Napoleon's brother Joseph Bonaparte. Wellington's respect for his opponent is evident in the many works of art depicting Napoleon, including Canova's monumental statue of the famously portly Emperor as an improbably muscular nude Greek athlete. In the basement an entire cabinet is filled with Wellington's medals, while another holds the death masks of both Wellington and Napoleon. Also on show here are newspaper caricatures from Wellington's later political career—his nickname "the Iron Duke" comes not from his steadfastness in battle, but from the metal shutters he had put up on the windows to protect himself from egg-throwing political opponents.

THE WELLINGTON ARCH

🖫 **Location:** *Hyde Park Corner.* **Contact:** ☎ *7930 2726; www.english-heritage.org.uk.* **Tube:** *Hyde Park Corner.* **Open:** *Apr.-Sept. W-Su 10am-6pm, Oct. 10am-5pm, Nov.-Mar. 10am-4pm.* **Admission:** *£2.50, students&seniors £1.90, kids £1.30.*

Standing at the center of London's most infamous traffic intersection, the Wellington Arch has long been ignored by tourists and Londoners alike. All changed in April 2001, when the wraps came off a long restoration project and the interior was opened to the public for the first time. When it was built, in 1825, the "Green Park Arch" marked the western boundary to London; in 1838 it was dedicated to the Duke of Wellington, and 8 years later encumbered by a gigantic statue of the Duke, much to the horror of its architect, Decimus Burton. Indeed, the government immediately ordered the statue's removal, but desisted when Wellington threatened to resign from the army. Wellington's statue was finally replaced in 1910 by the even bigger (though not taller) *Quadriga of Peace*, designed by army vet Adrian Joens. Inside the arch, exhibitions on the building's history and the changing nature of war memorials play second fiddle to the two viewing platforms.

BROMPTON ORATORY

⚑ Location: *Thurloe Pl., Brompton Rd.* **Contact:** *☎ 7808 0900.* **Tube:** *South Kensington or Knightbsbridge.* **Open:** *Daily 6:30am-8pm. Solemn Mass Su 11am.* **Free.**

On entering this church, properly called the Oratory of St. Philip Neri, you are transported to a world of ornate Baroque flourishes and lofty domes. London's second-largest Catholic church was built from 1874-1884 under the direction of Herbert Gribble, who deliberately designed a nave wider than St. Paul's. Among the side chapels, two stand out: the Lady Chapel, with a 17th-century Italian altar, and St. Winfred's Chapel, with Whistler's triptych of the English Martyrs. One of the altars was considered by the KGB to be the best dead drop in London—until 1985, agents left microfilm and other documents behind a statue for other agents to retrieve. The church lives up to its reputation for music during its **Solemn Masses,** sung in Latin.

HYDE PARK & KENSINGTON GARDENS

⚑ Location: *Framed by Kensington Rd., Knightsbridge, Park Lane, and Bayswater Rd.; bordered by Knightsbridge, Kensington, Bayswater, Marylebone, and Mayfair.* **Contact:** *☎ 7298 2100.* **Tube:** *Queensway, Lancaster Gate, Marble Arch, Hyde Park Corner, or High St. Kensington.* **Accessibility:** *"Liberty Drive" rides for seniors and the disabled. Call ☎ 07767 498 096; free.* **Activities&Events:** *A full program of music, performance, and kids' activites takes place during the summer; see park noticeboards for details.* **Open:** *Hyde Park daily 5am-midnight, Kensington Gdns. dawn-dusk.* **Free.**

Surrounded by London's wealthiest neighborhoods, giant Hyde Park has served as the model for city parks around the world, including Central Park in New York and Paris's Bois de Boulogne. Henry VIII wrested the land from Westminster Abbey in 1536, and the park remained a royal hunting ground until James I it to the public in 1637. **Kensington Gardens,** contiguous with Hyde Park and originally part of it, was created in the late 17th century when William and Mary set up in Kensington Palace.

THE SERPENTINE. Officially known as the Long Water west of the Serpentine Bridge, the 41-acre Serpentine was created in 1730. From the number of people who pay to row and swim here, you'd think it was the fountain of youth. A

St. James Park

Kensington Gardens

Hyde Park

111

bone-white arch derived from a Henry Moore sculpture stands on the northwest bank, but the best view is from across the water. South of Long Water, some way from the lake itself, the **Serpentine Gallery** displays contemporary art (see p. 147). *(Boating:* ☎ *7262 1440. Open daily, weather permitting, 10am-6pm. £3.50 per person for 30min., £5 per hr.; kids £1, £2. Cash only. Swimming: At the Lido, south shore.* ☎ *7706 3422. Open: Daily late June to early Sept. 10am-5:30pm. £2.70, seniors £1.70, children 60p, family £6.)*

OTHER PARK SIGHTS. Running south of the Serpentine, the dirt track of **Rotten Row** stretches out westwards from Hyde Park Corner. The name is a corruption of *Route du Roi* or "King's Road," as this was the royal route from Kensington Palace to Whitehall; its historical interest derives from being the first English thoroughfare lit at night to deter crime. At the southern end of Hyde Park clusters a group of statues: a **Diana fountain** (the goddess, not the princess); the "family of man"; a likeness of **Lord Byron;** and a fig-leafed **Achilles** dedicated to Wellington (see "Beefcake Wellington," p. 110). At the northeastern corner of the park, near Marble Arch, you can see free speech in action as proselytizers, politicos, and flat-out crazies dispense the fruits of their knowledge to bemused tourists at **Speaker's Corner** on Sundays.

KENSINGTON & EARL'S COURT

SEE MAP, p. 340-341

🖪 NEIGHBORHOOD QUICKFIND: Discover, *p. 9;* **Museums&Galleries,** *p. 146;* **Food&Drink,** *p. 172;* **Entertainment,** *p. 216;* **Shopping,** *p. 233;* **Accommodations,** *p. 287.*

Nobody took much notice of Kensington before 1689, when the newly crowned William III and Mary II decided to move into Kensington Palace and high society tagged along. The next significant date in Kensington's history was 1851, when the Great Exhibition brought in enough money to finance the museums and colleges of South Kensington, converting it from a quiet residential suburb to a powerhouse of the arts and sciences. Blending into Kensington's southwestern corner, **Earl's Court** is a livelier, grimier district that never managed to shake off its reputation as "Kangaroo Valley," earned in the 1960s and 1970s for its popularity with Australian expats.

KENSINGTON PALACE

🖪 Location: *Eastern edge of Kensington Gardens; enter through the park.* **Contact:** ☎ *7937 9561; www.hrp.org.uk.* **Tube:** *High St. Kensington or Queensway.* **Open:** *daily Mar.-Oct. 10am-5pm, Nov.-Feb. 10am-4pm; last admission 1hr. before closing.* **Admission:** *£8.80, students & seniors £6.90, ages 5-15 £6.30, family (2 adults + 3 kids) £26.80.*

In 1689, William and Mary commissioned Christopher Wren to remodel Nottingham House into proper palace. Kensington remained a principal royal residence until George III decamped to Kew in 1760, and is still in use—Princess Diana was the most famous recent inhabitant. Inside the palace is the **Royal Ceremonial Dress Collection,** devoted to the intricate costumes required of courtiers in the 19th and early 20th century. Also on display are a number of the Queen's demur evening gowns and Diana's racier numbers. After the dresses, you enter the **State Apartments,** where monarchs would receive their subjects on official occasions. Hanoverian economy is evident in the *trompe l'oeil* decoration throughout, carried out by William Kent for George I. The palace **grounds,** set apart from the rest of Kensington Gardens, encompass Vanbrugh's grand 1704 **Orangery,** built for Queen Anne's dinner parties and now a popular setting for light lunches and **afternoon teas** (see p. 172).

"ALBERTOPOLIS"

🖪 Location: *Roughly bounded by Hyde Park to the north, Exhibition Rd. to the east, Cromwell Rd. to the south, and Queen's Gate to the west.* **Tube:** *South Kensington or High St. Kensington.*

Spurred on by self-congratulatory exhibitions of French arts and industry in Paris, Prince Albert, Queen Victoria's husband, proposed to hold an "Exhibition of All Nations" in London. On May 1, 1851, the Great Exhibition opened in Hyde Park, housed in the Crystal Palace—a gigantic iron-and-glass structure 1,848ft. long, 408ft. wide, and tall enough to completely enclose mature trees. By the time the exhibition was dismantled a year later, six million people had passed through it—as many as saw the Millennium Dome in 2000—and the organisers were left with a profit of

£200,000. Again at Albert's suggestion, this was used to buy 86 acres of land in South Kensington to be dedicated to institutions promoting British arts and sciences. Even he would be surprised at how his dream has blossomed; today on this land stand not only the quartet of the **Royal Albert Hall,** the **Victoria & Albert Museum** (p. 138), the **Science Museum** (p. 147), and the **Natural History Museum** (p. 146), but also the **Royal College of Music,** the **Royal College of Art,** and the **Imperial College** of Science and Technology, all world-beating institutions in their fields.

ALBERT MEMORIAL. Nightmarish or fairy tale, depending on your opinion of Victorian High Gothic, George Gilbert Scott's canopy recently emerged blinking into the sunlight following 10 years under wraps. At Albert's gilded feet, friezes represent the Four Industries, the Four Sciences, and the Four Continents, themes chosen more for their symmetry than their relation to reality. *(Kensington Gore. Tours Su 2pm and 3pm; 45min. £3.50, concs. £3; reserve on ☎ 7495 0916.)*

ROYAL ALBERT HALL. In contrast to the ornate Albert Memorial across the street, the quietly classical Royal Albert Hall is one of the more restrained pieces of Victorian architecture, though there's nothing restrained about its size. Intended as an all-purpose venue, guests at the 1871 opening immediately noticed one shortcoming of the elliptical design—a booming echo that made it next to useless for musical concerts. This was solved in 1968, when acoustic scientists oversaw the installation of dozens of discs suspended in a haphazard fashion from the dome. In its time, the hall has hosted a full-length marathon, the first public display of electric lighting, and the world premiere of Hiawatha, and it remains a versatile venue holding everything from boxing to rock concerts. It's best known as the seat of the **Proms** classical-music concerts (see p. 216). *(Kensington Gore. Box office ☎ 7589 8212; www.royalalberthall.com. For accessibility info, call 7589 3853.)*

OTHER KENSINGTON SIGHTS

LEIGHTON HOUSE. The home of painter Frederic, Lord Leighton (1830-1896), is a perfect example of all that is endearing and ridiculous in Victorian tastes. Inspired by his trips to the Middle East, Leighton's home is a mix of oriental pastiche, neo-classicicism, and English homeliness. The centerpiece of it all is the Arab Hall, a Moorish extravaganza of tilework and mosaics complete with a fountain. Other rooms, more restrained, contain paintings by Leighton and his contemporaries, including works by Millais and Edward Burne-Jones. *(12 Holland Park Rd. ☎ 7602 3316. Tube: High St. Kensington. 50min. tours W-Th noon; £3. Open W-Su 11am-5:30pm. Free.)*

NEARBY MUSEUMS AND GALLERIES

Major Collections: Victoria & Albert Museum, p. 138.

Other Permanent Collections: Natural History Museum, p. 146; Science Museum, p. 147.

Exhibition Spaces: Serpentine Gallery, p. 147.

NOTTING HILL

🖪 *QUICK REFERENCE: Discover, p. 10; Food&Drink, p. 173; Shopping, p. 234; Entertainment, p. 216; Nightlife, p. 195.*

Notting Hill's best bits are on the outside. At the south, **Notting Hill Gate** is a fairly unattractive road of 1950s facades, it's home to a good range of shops and bars, and retains a definite bohemian feel. To the north, **Portobello Road** around Lancaster Road and the overhead Westway motorway retains a

SEE MAP, p. 342

strong West Indian community, evinced in the many regggae-heavy record stores and market stalls selling Caribbean foods. Intersecting Portobello north of the Westway, **Golborne Road** has its own colorful street scene, with many Moroccan and Portuguese shops and cafes. Fans of modernist architect Erno Goldfinger (see Two Willow Road, p. 120) will be pleased to see another of his uncompromising creations looming at the end of Golborne Rd., the rather forbidding high-rise **Trellick Tower.** If you plan to visit Notting Hill, try to do so on a Saturday, when the world famous **Portobello market** (see p. 234) is held, spreading from Golborne Rd. all the way down Portobello Rd. and the surrounding streets almost to Notting Hill Gate itself. Wear your biggest Bob Marley hat, buy a large plate of international grub from one of the many stalls or takeaways, and eat it sitting on the steps of some media millionaire's villa, being sure to make a copious mess.

MARYLEBONE & REGENT'S PARK

SEE MAP, p. 344-345

⊞ NEIGHBORHOOD QUICKFIND: Discover, p. 11; **Museums&Galleries,** p. 147; **Entertainment,** p. 217; **Food&Drink,** p. 174; **Accommodations,** p. 292.

A tidy district of residential squares, the most popular of Marylebone's tourist attractions cluster along its northern edge. The inexplicably popular Madame Tussaud's, the lawns of Regent's Park, and the tiny Sherlock Holmes Museum can all be found within a few minutes walk of **Baker St.** Tube. A few more attractions cling to the southern boundary near Oxford St.; the uncommonly regular grid between may be void of textbook tourist attractions, but values a wander for its fine 18th-century architecture. Many of the Georgian houses have been home to famous residents; Elizabeth Barrett lived in **Wimpole Street,** while at different times John Milton, John Stuart Mill, and William Hazlitt all called no. 19 **York Street** home. The area's most famous resident (and address), though, never even existed; **221b Baker Street** was of course the fictional lodging house of Sherlock Holmes. 221 Baker St. is actually the headquarters of the Abbey National bank (there was never a 221b). A little further down the street, the **Sherlock Holmes Museum** (see p. 148) gives its address out as 221b, although a little sleuthing will reveal that it in fact stands at no. 239.

MADAME TUSSAUD'S AND THE LONDON PLANETARIUM

⊞ Location: Marylebone Rd. (☎0870 400 3000; www.madame-tussauds.com). **Tube:** Baker St. **Open** M-F 10am-5:30pm, Sa-Su 9:30am-5:30pm. Planetarium shows start every 30min. **Admission:** All tickets sold at both Madame Tussaud's and Planetarium. Madame Tussaud's £11.50, seniors £9, ages 5-16 £8; Planetarium £6.50, £5.10, £4.35; combined ticket £14, £10.80, £9.50. Advance booking (by phone or online) £1 extra; groups (10+) approx. £1 less per person.

Together, Madame Tussaud's and the London Planetarium constitute London's third-largest tourist attraction, a fact which amazes locals even more than the continued survival of Angus Steak Houses. Unless you enjoy spending hours waiting outside, make sure to book ahead, or get together with at least 9 other fellow-sufferers and save time and money by using the group entrance. The Planetarium and Madame T's are internally connected and (on a combo ticket) can be visited in either order—there are ticket offices in both buildings.

MADAME TUSSAUD'S. Back in the 18th century, Mrs. T got her start modelling wax portraits of the stars of pre-revolutionary Paris. It was the storming of the Bastille that led to the creation of today's tourist-eating monster, though: a string of commissions making death masks of guillotined *aristos* (including a freshly beheaded Marie Antoinette, in 1793) laid the foundations for a popular touring exhibition that she brought to England in 1802. Despite its revolutionary beginnings, the display positively fawns over royalty and other more- and less-worthy celebrities. Even after five galleries of steadily lowering expectations, you're guaranteed to be underwhelmed by the would-be grand finale, the rather fleeting **Spirit of London.** Taxicab-style cars whisk you through 400 years of history so quickly that Hamlet's words still echo in your ears as you enter the Victorian age.

THE PLANETARIUM. Like a giant green silicone-filled breast, the Planetarium rises alluringly next to Madame Tussaud's masculine bulk. Those who remember 40min. informative displays with a live narrator will be shocked to find that today's show is a 20min. simulated rocket-ride through the universe. There's no denying that, as cinematic spectacle, the Planetarium is tough to beat, but entertainment values have completely swamped any educational ideals the Planetarium formerly aspired to. Facts (sunspots) are uncritically mixed with fiction (inter-dimensional hyperdrive), and anyone without a physics degree will have a hard time separating the two. It's no better in the "departure lounge;" the display on gravity claims that "while the Earth may eventually fall into the sun, it won't happen for hundreds of thousands of years."

REGENT'S PARK

Location: 500 acres of gardens stretching north from Marylebone Rd. to Camden Town. **Contact:** ☎ 7486 7905; police 7935 1259. **Tube:** Baker St., Regent's Park, Gt. Portland St., or Camden Town. **Open:** daily 6am-5pm Jan., 6pm Feb., 7pm Mar. (8pm after clocks change), 9pm Apr. and Aug., 9:30pm May-July, 8pm Sept., 7pm Oct. (5:30pm after clocks change), 4:30pm Nov.-Dec. **Free.**

Perhaps London's most attractive and most popular park, with a wide range of landscapes from soccer-scarred fields to Italian-style formal gardens. It's all very different from the plans John Nash had in mind when he set out to redevelop the former royal hunting ground and farmlands of Marylebone Park in the early 1800s. Nash's vision was a secluded paradise of wealthy villas hidden among exclusive, private gardens; fortunately for us commonfolk, Parliament intervened in 1811 and guaranteed that the space would remain open to all. Nonetheless, the remaining aspects of Nash's plan set Regent's Park apart from other city spaces; the grand terraces on the park perimeter, the meandering lake, and the **Regent's Canal** (see p. 118) are all part of his legacy. Set within the northern part of the park, near Camden Town, is **London Zoo** (see p. 119); you can get free close-up views of the elephants from the paths around the zoo's southern border.

The exclusive-sounding **Inner Circle** road separates the regal, flower-filled **Queen Mary's Gardens** from the *hoi-polloi* park without. Within the gardens, the **Rose Garden** stands out, while one quadrant is now given over to the **Open-Air Theatre** (see p. 217). Arching around Inner Circle is the **Boating Lake,** though boaters are confined to the central portion. If you're feeling hale, you can rent a rowboat for use on the main lake; kiddies can enjoy themselves on pedalos in the tiny **Children's Boating Lake.** *(Open Apr.-Sept. M-F 10am-5pm, Sa-Su 9am-7pm. Rowboats £3 for 30min., £4 1hr.; under 13 £2, £1; £5 deposit; under 16 with adult only. Pedalos £2 per 30min.; must be 70cm tall at hips.)* Of the 40 **villas** planned by Nash, eight were built, and of these only two remain. After decades housing charities, hospitals, and learned societies, **The Holme** and **St. John's Lodge** have returned to their intended function as private residences for the unimaginably rich. On the northern edge of Inner Circle, the fine, formal **St. John's Lodge Gardens**—entered through an easy-to-miss gate on Inner Circle itself—remain open to the public. The Holme, overlooking the boating lake on the western side of Inner Circle, was designed in 1818 by the 18-year-old prodigy Decimus Burton. Other buildings in the park include the large redbrick complex of **Regent's College,** to the south of Inner Circle, and neo-Georgian **Winfield House,** the residence of the US ambassador, set within the park's western edge.

University College

British Museum

Russell Square

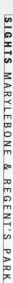

OTHER MARYLEBONE SIGHTS

EDGWARE ROAD. To the west, Marylebone becomes Marylebanon—Edgware Rd. is the center of London's large Lebanese community, though it's popular with Middle Easterners of all nationalities. From Marble Arch to where it meets Marylebone Rd., middle-aged men converse in Arabic over strong coffee in dozens of kebab houses and cafes and veiled ladies swish in and out of numerous jewellers; and English businesses are signposted in Arabic. *(Tube: Marble Arch.)*

LONDON CENTRAL MOSQUE. Near the western boundary of Regent's Park, the golden dome and slim minaret of the London Central Mosque makes an unusual contribution to the local skyline. The land was given to the UK Islamic community in 1944 in recognition for the wartime contributions of Muslims to the British war effort. After rejecting numerous proposals, planning permission was finally given in 1969 to a design by an English Christian, Frederick Gibberd. While it cannot lay claim to any great beauty, especially from within, the interior of the dome is home to an imposing chandelier and some fancy tilework. Remove your shoes before entering the main prayer hall. *(146 Park Rd. ☎ 7724 3363; www.islamicculturalcentre.co.uk. Tube: Baker St. No shorts, miniskirts, or sleeveless tops; women must cover their heads.)*

NEARBY MUSEUMS & GALLERIES

Permanent Collections: ▨ Wallace Collection, p. 147; Sherlock Holmes Museum, p. 148.

BLOOMSBURY

SEE MAP, pp. 344-345

🔊 *NEIGHBORHOOD QUICKFIND: Discover, p. 11; Museums&Galleries, p. 148; Food&Drink, p. 175; Entertainment, p. 217; Shopping, p. 236; Accommodations, p. 293.*

First settled in the 18th century, when its leafy squares were laid out, Bloomsbury acquired its intellectual character in the 19th century as the home of both the British Museum and University College, London's first university. This reputation was bolstered in the early 20th century as Gordon Sq. resounded with the philosophizing, theorizing, and womanizing of the Bloomsbury Group (see below). Though today few people sleep here apart from students and tourists, the high concentration of academic and artistic institutions ensure that the cerebral atmosphere remains.

ACADEMIA

🔊 *Tube: Warren St., Goodge St., and Tottenham Court Rd. stations serve the northern, central, and southern ends of Gower St. respectively. Numerous buses make the one-way trip north-south down Gower St., returning along Tottenham Court Rd.*

The strip of land along **Gower St.** and immediately to its west is London's academic heartland. The eastern side of Gower St. is lined with world-renowned institutions such as UCL (see below), and the Royal Academy of Dramatic Art (RADA; see p. 217). On the other side of UCL from Gower St., **Gordon Square** was home to many of the luminaries of the **Bloomsbury Group,** an early 20th-century coterie of intellectuals including Virginia Woolf, John Maynard Keynes, Lytton Strachey, and Bertrand Russell. Further down Gower St., handsome **Bedford Square** is the only Bloomsbury square to retain all its original Georgian buildings.

UNIVERSITY COLLEGE LONDON. Established in 1828 to provide an education to those excluded from Oxford and Cambridge, UCL was the first in Britain to admit Catholics and Jews. Fifty years later, it became the first to allow women to sit for degrees. The college founder, **Jeremy Bentham,** has occupied the South Cloister since 1850: his will stated that his body should be made available for dissection before being embalmed, dressed, and displayed for posterity. Unfortunately, the doctor proved unable to preserve his head, so a wax model was used: the official line is that the original is kept in the college vaults, but student lore holds that it was stolen by rascals from rival King's College. *(Main entrance on Gower St. South Cloister entrance through the courtyard.)*

SENATE HOUSE. The mere sight of this massive building—home to the University of London central administration—is enough to dishearten even the most determined student activist. Appropriately enough for such a Stalinist construct, during WWII it housed the BBC propaganda unit. George Orwell, who was employed at this so-called "Ministry of Information," used his experience there as the model for the Ministry of Truth in *1984*. *(At the southern end of Malet St. Tube: Goodge St. or Russell Sq.)*

ST. PANCRAS AND EUSTON ROAD

⁊ Tube: *King's Cross/St. Pancras unless otherwise specified.*

Until recently barely considered part of Bloomsbury at all, the opening of the British Library in 1998 has lent an academic sheen to what is still a gritty neighborhood.

▨ BRITISH LIBRARY. Castigated during its long construction by traditionalists for being too modern and by modernists for being too traditional, since its 1998 opening the new British Library building has won plaudits from visitors and regular users alike for its stunning interior. The heart of the library is underground, with space for 12 million books on 200mi. of shelving; the above-ground brick building is home to the reading rooms, an engrossing museum (see p. 148), and the **King's Library.** Displayed in a glass cube towards the rear of the building, the 65,000 volumes were collected by George III and bequeathed to the nation by his less bookish son, George IV, in 1823: mobile shelves ensure that all the books remain accessible to library users. Various works of art are scattered around the building and the forecourt, the most impressive being Eduardo Paolozzi's monumental statue of Newton after William Blake: the union of art and science represents the library's purpose as the repository of all knowledge. *(96 Euston Rd. ☎ 7412 7332; www.bl.uk. Tours of public areas M, W, F 3pm and Sa 10:30am and 3pm; £5, concs. £3.50. Tours including reading rooms Tu 6:30pm and Su 11:30am and 3pm; £6, conc. £4.50. Reservations recommended for all tours. Open M and W-F 9:30am-6pm, Tu 9:30am-8pm, Sa 9:30am-5pm, Su 11am-5pm. Free.)*

ST. PANCRAS OLD CHURCH. The oldest parish in Britain, the first church on this site was reputedly founded by Roman legionaries in 314, although the present building dates from the 13th century. Since at least the 17th century it has been known as a desolate spot, and following a Satanist attack in 1985 has been hard to get into except for services; if you do get a peek, don't miss the 6th-century altar stone. The recently restored **churchyard** is where Mary Godwin (author of *Frankenstein*) met Percy Bysshe Shelley in 1813 and insisted they make love on her mother's grave. Also in the churchyard is Sir John Soanes's mausoleum and the **Hardy Tree,** a monument devised by the young Thomas Hardy with hundreds of gravestones radiating out from a weeping ash. *(St. Pancras Rd. www.stpancrasoldchurch.org.uk. Prayer services M-Th 9am and 5:30pm; Mass Su-M 9:30am, Tu 7pm, Sa 10am.)*

ST. PANCRAS PARISH CHURCH. The new parishioners of fashionable 19th-century Bloomsbury soon tired of the dilapidated Old Church, and in 1816 work started on a new one. The design is a replica of the 2500-year-old Erectheon in Athens, with an octagonal tower based on the Acropolis's Tower of the Winds. Together with the abundant use of gold leaf inside, by its completion in 1822 the church had cost £90,000, making it the most expensive London church after St. Paul's Cathedral. *(On the corner of Euston Rd. and Upper Woburn Pl. Tube: Euston.)*

ST. PANCRAS STATION. Given a choice, most visitors would assume that the low, modern concourse on one side of the Midland Rd. and Euston Rd. intersection was a railway station, and the soaring Gothic spires on the other the British Library. In fact, the Victorian extravaganza is the facade of St. Pancras Station, formerly the station's Midland Grand Hotel, considered the most sumptuous in the world at its 1874 opening. Today Sir George Gilbert Scott's building is but a hollow shell awaiting redevelopment as a Marriott. Trains still puff in and out of the 1868 trainshed, an engineering masterpiece in its own right; when built, the single 74m iron span created the largest undivided indoor area ever seen. *(Euston Rd.)*

OTHER BLOOMSBURY SIGHTS

ST. GEORGE'S BLOOMSBURY. The shrapnel-scarred Corinthian portico of this 1730 Hawksmoor church is in desperate need of repair, but the interior is in perfect condition, with an unusual flat ceiling undecorated except for a central plaster rose. Anthony Trollope was baptized before the gilded mahogany altar, which was also

117

the setting of Dickens's *Bloomsbury Christening*. The church's most unusual feature is its stepped spire, based on the ancient Mausoleum of Halikarnassos (much of the original is now in the British Museum); rather than King Mausolus, it's topped by a statue of George I. *(Bloomsbury Way. Tube: Russell Square. Open M-Sa 9:30am-5:30pm.)*

THOMAS CORAM FOUNDATION. In 1747, retired sea captain Thomas Coram established the Foundling Hospital for abandoned children. In order to raise funds, he sought the help of prominent artists and composers including William Hogarth and Frederick Handel, who donated works and other gifts for auction and to the hospital itself. These and other treasures are displayed in the Foundation museum, which is **closed for restoration** until 2003. *(40 Brunswick Sq. ☎ 7841 3600. Tube: Russell Square.)*

CORAM'S FIELDS. Close by the Foundation lie seven acres of old Foundling Hospital grounds that have been preserved as a children's park. Toddlers will delight in the petting zoo and paddling zoo, not to mention the special under-5 toilets; under 12s will relish the hi-tech playgrounds. *(93 Guilford St. ☎ 7837 6138. Open daily 9am-dusk or 5pm, whichever is earlier. No adults admitted without children. Free.)*

NEARBY MUSEUMS AND GALLERIES
Major Collections: British Museum, p. 134.

Other Permanent Collections: ▨ British Library Galleries, p. 148; Percival David Foundation of Chinese Art, p. 149; Pollock's Toy Museum, p. 149.

Exhibition Spaces: Brunei Gallery, p. 150; October Gallery, p. 150.

NORTH LONDON

CAMDEN TOWN

*☷ Sights nearest **Tube: Camden Town** unless otherwise noted. **NEIGHBORHOOD QUICKFIND:** Discover, p. 12; **Museums&Galleries**, p. 150; **Food&Drink**, p. 177; **Nightlife**, p. 196; **Entertainment**, p. 218; **Shopping**, p. 237.*

An island of good, honest tawdriness in an increasingly affluent sea, Camden Town has effortlessly thrown off attempts at gentrification thanks to the ever-growing **Camden Market.** Now London's fourth most popular tourist attraction, on weekends the market presents a variety of life unmatched even by **London Zoo,** a serene jaunt up the Regent's Canal from the market's nerve-centre in Camden Lock.

CAMDEN HIGH STREET AND CAMDEN MARKET
*☷ Tube: Camden Town or Chalk Farm. For more information, see **Shopping**, p. 237.*

You should experience Camden Town on a weekend for the spectacle rather than the merchandise. The stores on **Camden High St.** are most remarkable for their facades, with giant shoes, masks, and other brightly colored papier-mâché objects protruding dangerously from the storefronts. If you actually want to shop, come on a weekday when the stores are open and the crowds are gone. Of the many markets off the High St., the most visually appealing is **Camden Lock Market,** in a series of buildings around an open courtyard facing the canal, while **Stables Market** has the best selection of merchandise. The markets nearest the station, **Camden Market** and **Camden Canal Market,** are the most crowded and tackiest.

REGENT'S CANAL
☷ Location: Access the canal from Camden Lock or at Regent's Park Rd. bridge.

Part of the Grand Union Canal, which in the days before railways was the main artery for bringing goods to London from the north, at Camden Lock, where Camden High St. crosses the canal, the water level makes a steep rise; you'll frequently see narrowboats being raised or lowered through the locks. Heading west along the canal, the post-industrial landscape gives way to well-kept Victorian houses and gardens before emerging into Regent's Park. The canal actually passes through the middle of London Zoo, though the banks are too high to afford a view of any wildlife; various boats carry passengers along the serene waters. The **Jenny Wren** makes the 90min. return trip to Little Venice. *(☎ 7485 4433 or 7485 6210. Call for schedule. £5.50*

FROM
TOWER OF LONDON

TO
EIFFEL TOWER

VIA
A HIGH SPEED ATTRACTION

THE CENTRE OF **LONDON** TO THE CENTRE OF **PARIS** IN JUST 3 HO

eurostar.com   *enjoy your journey* eurost

Sa-Su afternoons, under 14 £3.50; other times £5/£3.)
The **London Waterbus Compay** does the same run,
but also offers a stop at the Zoo. (☎ 7482 2550.
*Apr.-Oct. departures every hour 10am-5pm; Nov.-Mar. Sa-
Su hourly 11am-4pm. Single to Little Venice £4.20, children £2.80; return £5.60/£3.60. Single to Zoo, including admission, £10.50/£8.)*

LONDON ZOO

🖬 **Location:** *Main gate on Outer Circle, Regent's Park.*
Contact: ☎ *7449 6552; www.londonzoo.com.* **Tube:**
*Camden Town plus 12min. walk or short jaunt on bus
#274.* **Open:** *daily 10am-5:30pm, last admission
4:30pm.* **Admission:** *£10, students & seniors £8.50,
ages 2-16 £7, family £30.*

London Zoo has come a long way since first
opening in 1826—the earliest buildings are now
considered too small to house animals, and
instead torture parents with an array of stuffed
toys. Today, thousands of little critters from
around the world run around freely, their guardians trying frantically to keep up, as the animals
look on with indifference from their enclosures.
Chimps huddle in their rope-strung compound,
lions eye the domestic animals of the petting
farm from a very English-looking patch of
savannah, and Hanuman Langur monkeys con-
template another night on Bear Mountain. With
a long and often pioneering history, many of the
buildings are as interesting as the animals they
contain—pick up the free *Animal Architecture* leaflet. If the 5m high doors of the **Giraffe
House** were designed from necessity, the monu-
ment-valley style concrete peaks of **Bear Mountain,** towering over Regent's Park, are a pure
flight of fancy. Everyone's favorite is the **Penguin Pool,** designed by avant-garde firm Tecton
in 1934. If the cool white architecture and clean
lines are straight out of the Bauhaus, the spiral
slide is pure Fisher Price. Penguin feeding
(2:30pm daily) is always popular, as is the elephant washing (3:30pm); other activities take
place throughout the day, and are detailed in the
Daily Events leaflet.

NEARBY MUSEUMS AND GALLERIES

Permanent Collections: The Jewish Museum, Camden, p. 151.

HAMPSTEAD AND HIGHGATE

🖬 *NEIGHBORHOOD QUICKFIND: Discover, p. 12; Muse-
ums&Galleries, p. 150; Food&Drink, p. 178; Entertainment, p. 218; Accommodations, p. 298.*

HAMPSTEAD VILLAGE

🖬 **Tube:** *Hampstead unless otherwise specified.*

Hampstead first caught the attention of well-
heeled Londoners in the 17th century, when it
became fashionable to take the waters at Hamp-

Camden High

Camden Locks and Canals

Abbey Road Studios

DUST TO DUST...

"In affectionate remembrance of English Cricket, which died at the Oval on 29th August, 1882, deeply lamented by a large circle of sorrowing friends and acquaintances, R.I.P. N.B. The body will be cremated and the ashes taken to Australia"

—Sporting Times, 1882

In most sports, every player's dream is to lift a heavy silver urn or receive a gold medal. English cricketers, however, fantasize about getting their hands on a 120-year old lump of charred wood—the Ashes.

It all started in 1882, when the first international Test series resulted in defeat for an over-confident English team against a bunch of upstart Australians. This shocked the English establishment so greatly that the Sporting Times published the now-immortal obituary notice.

The following year, the English captain swore to bring back these metaphorical ashes. His wish took a literal turn when some Australians burned a stump used in one of the games, and presented it to him following the English victory.

Today, the ashes reside permanently in a terracotta urn in the Lord's Museum—despite the fact that England hasn't won since 1986. RIP, indeed.

stead Wells, on the site of **Well Walk** today. In the 1930s, Hampstead found itself at the forefront of a European avant-garde in flight from fascism. Residents such as Aldous Huxley, Piet Mondrian, Barbara Hepworth, and Sigmund Freud lent the area a cachet that grows to this day.

FENTON HOUSE. One of the first houses to be built in Hampstead, Fenton House is best approached along the long gravel avenue from Holly Hill. The first two floors of the house are home to a delicate collection of china, porcelain, and needlework as well as numerous early keyboard instruments. More instruments can be found on the top floor, including an 18th-century "double guitar," proving that Britain's fascination with excessively stringed instruments predates Jimmy Page. (Hampstead Grove. ☎ 7435 3471. Concerts every other Th May-Oct.; £14, students £12.50. Open Mar. Sa-Su 2-5pm; Apr.-Oct. W-F 2-5pm, Sa-Su and holidays 11am-5pm. £4.30, kids £2.15, family £10.50. Joint ticket with 2 Willow Rd. £6.30.)

KEATS HOUSE. In this house, the great Romantic poet John Keats produced some of his finest work, including Ode to a Nightingale, composed under a plum tree in the garden. Here he fell in love with and married his neighbor, Fanny Brawne, and coughed up his first drops of consumptive blood, all in the two years from 1818 to 1820. Inside the house, copies of Keats' poems lie scattered about the rooms, together with Keats memorabilia and biographical displays. (Keats Grove. ☎ 7435 2062; www.keatshouse.org.uk. Rail: Hampstead Heath or Tube: Hampstead. Tours Sa-Su 3pm. Open May-Oct. Tu-Su noon-5pm. £3, students&seniors £1.50, under 16 free.)

TWO WILLOW ROAD. Looking like an unimposing 1950s-style mini-block, Two Willow Road was actually built in 1939 as the avant-garde home of architect Ernö Goldfinger. Ian Fleming hated it so much, he named a James Bond villain after him. From within, the house is a masterpiece of modernist living, designed by Goldfinger down to the last teaspoon. Everything looks as if the family had just popped out to raid Fort Knox—clothes still in their dry-cleaning plastic sheaves and family photos on the mantelpiece sit next to works of art by Bridget Riley, Henry Moore, and Goldfinger's long-put-upon wife, Ursula. Although she bankrolled his projects, Goldfinger summarily took over her studio for his office and replaced the kitchen with a tiny alcove, from which she had to cook for dinner parties of 60. A cold finger, indeed. (Off South End Green, near Rail: Hampstead Heath (Zone 3); 15min. walk from Hampstead Tube (Zone 2). ☎ 7435 6166. Open Apr.-Oct. Th-Sa noon-5pm; 1hr. guided tours every 45min. 12:15-4pm. £4.30, kids £2.15; joint ticket with Fenton House £6.30.)

HAMPSTEAD HEATH

⊞ Tube: *Hampstead or Train: Hampstead Heath.* **Open:** *24hr.* **Be extremely careful after dark.**

Hampstead Heath is one of the last remaining traditional commons in England, open to all since at least 1312 thanks to the pluckiness of local residents (being famous and rich probably helped), who in the 19th century successfully fought off attempts to develop it. Indeed, since Parliament declared in 1871 that the Heath should remain "forever open, un-enclosed, and un-built-upon," it has grown from 336 to 804 acres. On public holidays in spring and summer, **funfairs** are held at South End Green and on the south side of Spaniards Rd.

▩ KENWOOD. Girdled by Hampstead Heath, Kenwood is a picture-perfect example of an English country estate. The Neoclassical house and grounds were laid out by Robert Adams in for the first Earl of Mansfield, and recent restoration has done much to restore both to their 18th-century glory. **Kenwood forest** survives to the south of the house, separated by a pasture ground and lakes with a bandstand where concerts are given in the summer (see p. 218). The main part of **Kenwood House** presents a grandiose cream-stuccoed facade to the pasture, and is home to the impressive **Iveagh Bequest** of Old Masters (see p. 150). *(Road access from Hampstead Ln. ☎8348 1286. Walk from Hampstead or Highgate (both about 20min.) or take bus #210 from Archway or Golders Green Tube. Grounds open Apr.-Oct. daily 8am-8pm, Oct.-Mar. 8am-4pm.)*

▩ HILL GARDEN. Hidden in a small annex of the Heath just behind Jack Straw's Castle pub is this exquisite secret garden. Walking through the woods, you come across a formal garden with a raised collonade standing on arches, like a surreal vision of Italy. From one end of the flower-encrusted walkway, you have an uninterrupted view of northwest London; from here, a staircase leads down to a reflecting pool and the garden proper. *(Open daily 8:30am to 1hr. before sunset.)*

PARLIAMENT HILL. Highgate's portion of the Heath is called Parliament Hill; legend claims that it was from here Guy Fawkes and his accomplices planned to watch their destruction of Parliament in 1605 (see p. 55). It's well worth the hike to the top for a stunning panorama stretching to St. Paul's, Westminster, and beyond. At the foot of the hill, a series of ponds mark the final gasp of the River Westbourne before it vanishes under concrete on its way to the Thames; the brave can swim for free in dark (but fresh) waters of the sex-segregated **bathing ponds.** *(The southeastern part of the Heath. Bus #214 or C2 from Kentish Town Tube, or Rail: Gospel Oak or Hampstead Heath.)*

HIGHGATE VILLAGE

⊞ Bus: *#214 from Tube:Kentish Town, or #210 or 143 from Tube:Archway (both Zone2). Don't take the Tube to "Highgate"—the station is a long way from the village.*

Sitting 424ft. above the Thames at the top of Highgate Hill, Highgate is the second-highest spot in London. Long regarded as a healthy spot to get out of the London air, the village has its share of famous residents; Charles II and his mistress cavorted in 16th-century **Lauderdale House,** while legend has it that Charles's father's nemesis once resided in the 17th-century **Cromwell House** across the street. *(104 The Bank, on a terrace above Highgate High St. Closed to the public.)*

THE GROVE. At the very top of Highgate West Hill, the road splits in three. The left-hand fork leads to a row of 17th-century houses known as **North Grove;** Samuel Taylor Coleridge lived at no. 3, entertaining Carlyle, Emerson, and an ancient mariner or three. Just where the road forks, a gatehouse leads to Witanhurst, the largest private residence in London. The rightmost fork, **South Grove,** runs past the historic Flask pub (see p. 179) to meet up with Highgate High Street at the center of Highgate Village. **No. 16,** occupies the site of Arundel House, where philosopher Francis Bacon died of a chill after an early attempt to refrigerate a chicken.

HIGHGATE CEMETERY. London's first private cemetery is divided in two by Swain's Ln. The older **West Cemetery,** opened in 1839, contains a fascinating array of Victorian tombs, many of them in stunningly bad taste, such as the Egyptian-style catacombs. Famous residents among the 160,000 interred here include George Eliot, Michael Faraday, and the Dickens family. The **East Cemetery,** which can be visited at leisure, is larger, less overgrown, and somewhat better preserved; **Karl Marx** (d. 1883)

HOLY SMOKE

It's a measure of how far the campaign to legalize drugs in Britain has come in recent years that on July 2, 2002, Brixton's police chief announced that his men would no longer arrest people for use and possession of small quantities of cannabis. Coppers didn't even respond when skeptics tested police resolve by lighting up joints on the steps of the police station itself. While officially dope remains illegal—Brixton police still chase dealers—if the scheme is succesful in reducing drug-related crime, it's likely to be extended across London.

Oddly enough, it was the right-wing Conservative Party that first made legalization a mainstream issue—a number of senior figures, including Mrs. Thatcher's former darling Michael Portillo, have openly supported the idea. But even that didn't stop them losing the 2001 election—and Tony Blair's supposedly "liberal" Labour government is firmly opposed to any relaxation of current drugs laws. Still, with many newspapers and public figures calling for the legalization of cannabis—and with opinion polls supporting them—many believe it's only a matter of time before London becomes the new Amsterdam.

is the star of the show. (☎8340 1834; www.highgatecemetery.co.uk. East cemetery: Open Apr.-Nov. M-F 10am-5pm, Sa-Su 11am-5pm; Dec.-Mar. daily 10am-4pm. £2, children free. West Cemetery: Tours M-F noon, 2, and 4pm (3pm Nov.), Sa-Su every hr. 11am-5pm. £3, no kids under 8. Cameras £1 per section.)

NEARBY MUSEUMS AND GALLERIES
Permanent Collections: ▣ Iveagh Bequest, p. 150; Freud Museum, p. 150.

ST. JOHN'S WOOD & MAIDA VALE

🎜 *NEIGHBORHOOD QUICKFIND: Discover p. 12; Museums&Galleries, p. 150; Entertainment, p. 218.*

LORD'S CRICKET GROUND. The most famous cricket ground in the world, Lord's is a must for cricketing enthusiasts. To see the **Lord's Museum,** home to cricket's most famous trophy, the **Ashes Urn** (see *dust to dust...*, p. 120), go to a match or sign up for one of the 100min. tours, which also take in the MCC member's Long Room, the ground and stands, and the media center. On game days, tours after 10am skip the Long Room and media center, though visitors get a discount on tickets for the day's game as compensation; there are no tours during Test matches. *(Enter at Grace Gate, near the intersection of Grove End Rd. and St. John's Wood Rd. ☎7432 1033; www.lords.org/. Tube: St. John's Wood (10min.). Tours daily noon and 2pm, Apr.-Sept. also 10am. £6.50, students & seniors £5, under 16 £4.50; family £19.)*

ABBEY ROAD. Abbey Rd. itself is a long, busy thoroughfare stretching from St. John's Wood to Kilburn, but the only part most people are interested in is the famous **zebra crossing** right at its start, where it merges with Grove End Rd. Naturally, everyone wants their own photo-op crossing the street, much to the annoyance of local drivers, before adding to the graffiti on the almost illegible street sign. Next to the crossing, the **Abbey Road Studios,** where the Beatles made most of their recordings, is closed to the public. *(Tube: St. John's Wood.)*

NEARBY MUSEUMS & GALLERIES
Exhibition Spaces: ▣ Saatchi Gallery, p. 151.

FURTHER NORTH

🎜 *NEIGHBORHOOD QUICKFIND: Discover, p. 12; Museums&Galleries, p. 150; Food&Drink, p. 179; Entertainment, p. 218.*

GOLDERS GREEN
🎜 *Tube: Golders Green.*

This little corner of North London is the center of Britain's Jewish community. **Golders Green Rd.** is the axis around which life revolves; a few blocks down from the station Hebrew signs start to predominate. The main attraction of the area is Golders Green Park, as well as the kosher restaurants along Golders Green Rd. (see p. 179).

GOLDERS GREEN CREMATORIUM. Britain's first crematorium presents a neo-Romanesque facade to the conventional cemetery facing it across Hoop Lane, jealously guarding several acres of gardens from prying eyes. What look from afar to be horticultural labels in the flower beds in fact bear the names of the departed lying beneath each plant, breaking the dust-to-dust cycle to be reincarnated in a blaze of blossoms. This is still the busiest crematorium in the land; luminaries to have gone up in smoke include T.S. Eliot (every day is "Ash Wednesday" now), H.G. Wells, Peter Sellers, Bram Stoker, Mark Bolan, Gustav Holst, Anna Pavlova, and five prime ministers. Sigmund Freud's ashes, in his favorite Greek vase, are locked in the Ernest George Columbarium; ask an attendant to let you in on weekdays. (☎8455 2374. From Tube: Golders Green, turn right twice into Finchley Rd. and follow it under the bridge; Hoop Ln. is on the right (10min.). Grounds open daily, summer 9am-6pm, winter 9am-4pm; Chapel and Hall of Memory daily 9am-5pm. Free.)

◼ SHREE SWAMINARYAN MANDIR

🛈 **Location:** 105-119 Brentfield Rd., Neasden. From Tube: Neasden, turn left and follow the signs (15min.). **Contact:** ☎8965 2651; www.swaminaryan.org. **Notes:** All visitors must cover knees and shoulders, remove their shoes, and refrain from talking or photography within the temple. **Open:** daily 9am-6:30pm; murtis on view 9am-noon and 4-6pm. **Admission:** Understanding Hinduism exhibit £2, seniors and ages 6-16 £1.50; temple free.

Among light industrial estates and endless suburban houses, a fantasy creation of domes and towers rises like an otherworldly vision. The largest Hindu temple outside India, nothing like it has been built in England since the Middle Ages: all 5000 tons of marble and limestone were hand-carved in India. Unless you're particularly interested in the life of the sect's founder and reputed avatar Lord Swaminaryan (who among other feats stood naked on one leg for three months), skip the self-congratulatory "Understanding Hindusim" exhibition and proceed straight up to the temple. Niches around the side hold the shrines of the 11 garishly dressed *murtis*, idols infused with the presence of God.

NEARBY MUSEUMS & GALLERIES
Permanent Collectsion: ◼ Royal Airforce Museum, p. 150.

WEST LONDON

SHEPHERD'S BUSH & HAMMERSMITH

🛈 **Transportation note:** Confusingly, Shepherd's Bush and Hammersmith each have two entirely separate Tube stations. In **Shepherd's Bush**, the Central Line station is at the west end of the Green, while the Hammersmith & City Line is somewhat far west of the Green on Uxbridge Rd.; Tube: Goldhawk Rd. is also convenient. Both **Hammersmith** stations are close to each other, but the Piccadilly/District line is more convenient for the bus station. Both Shepherd's Bush and Hammersmith are in Zone 2. **NEIGHBORHOOD QUICKFIND: Discover,** p. 13; **Food&Drink,** p. 179; **Entertainment,** p. 220; **Accommodations,** p. 299.

BBC TELEVISION CENTRE. North of Shepherd's Bush proper is this vast media complex, its impressive array of satellite dishes visible for miles. The BBC is always on the lookout for people willing to be part of studio audiences (see Entertainment, p. 220); for a more in-depth experience, take a 90min. **backstage tour** of the center. (Wood Ln. ☎0870 603 0304; www.bbc.co.uk. Tube: White City. Tours run M-Sa 10:20am, 1, and 2:40pm. Minimum age 14. Booking required; no tickets sold at the door. £7.95, seniors £6.95, students & ages 14-15 £5.95.)

HAMMERSMITH RIVERSIDE. Though inland Hammersmith is nothing special, press on past the motorway down Hammersmith Bridge Rd. and you'll find a different world, serene and relaxed. The green **Hammersmith Bridge**—the first suspension bridge in London, built in 1824—marks the divide between commercial riverfront development downstream of the bridge and the upstream pedestrian embankment. Immediately next to the bridge, **Lower Mall** is a row of late-Georgian houses and pubs leading into **Furnival Gardens,** a popular spot for sunbathing. A narrow alley at the end of the park marks the beginning of **Upper Mall,** a row of early 18th-century houses including the venerable Dove pub (see p. 179), where *Rule Britannia* was penned, and **Kelmscott House,** where William Morris spent the last 20 years of his life.

FURTHER WEST

CHISWICK

🚇 *TRANSPORTATION: For sights, use Tube: Hammersmith then #190 bus or Tube: Turnham Green and #E3 bus. Zone 2/3.*

CHISWICK HOUSE. Both Chiswick House and its gardens were created by Richard Boyle, the 3rd Lord Burlington (1694-1753) and the first of many Englishmen to fall in love with Italy and want to recreate its charms at home. However, Richard didn't stop at switching malt for balsamic vinegar and shaving parmesan on his rocket; instead, he delved into the study of architecture and, with the help of his friend William Kent, designed this remarkable house. Based on Palladio's Villa La Rotonda in Rome, the cool, airy design, with a spectacular domed central hall, marble floors, and ceiling frescoes by "dear old Kentino," were hugely influential, kick-starting the English aristocracy's obsession with Palladian architecture and drawing criticism from Hogarth for its un-Englishness. The **gardens** were as innovative; laid out by William Kent, they were the first example of the less formal, naturalistic manner that came to be known as the English style —ironically, given their Italian pretentions. *(Between the Great West Rd. and the Great Chertsey Rd. ☎8995 0508; www.english-heritage.org.uk. Open Apr.-Sept. daily 10am-6pm, Oct. daily 10am-5pm, Nov.-Mar. W-Su 10am-4pm. House £3.30, students & seniors £2.50, kids £1.50; gardens free.)*

HOGARTH HOUSE. In contrast to Chiswick House's extravagance is the modest abode of William Hogarth, who saw Lord Burlington as a sycophant who imported foreign trends to England. Hogarth moved here in 1749 to escape the noise and heat of London—he'd be dismayed to see it now overlooks a busy six-lane highway. Inside, the few rooms display numerous editions of Hogarth's prints, including all the *Progresses*, together with explanations of the symbolism behind them. *(Great West Rd., just north of Chiswick House. ☎8994 6757. Open Apr.-Oct. Tu-F 1-5pm, Sa-Su 1-6pm; Nov.-Mar. closes 1hr. earlier. Free.)*

ROYAL BOTANICAL GARDENS, KEW

🚇 *Location: Kew, on the south bank of the Thames. The main entrance and visitors center is at Victoria Gate, nearest the Tube; the "Main Gate," on Kew Green nearer Kew Pier, is smaller and usually less crowded. Contact: ☎8940 5622; www.kew.org. Tube: Kew Gardens (Zone 3). Tours: Start at Victoria Gate visitors center. 1hr. walking tours daily 11am, 2pm; free. "Explorer" hop-on hop-off shuttle makes 35min. rounds of the gardens; first shuttle departs Victoria Gate 11am, last 3:35pm. £2.50, ages 5-15 £1.50. "Discovery" 1hr. buggy tours for mobility impaired M-F 11am and 2pm; free, booking required. Open: Apr.-Aug. M-F 9:30am-6:30pm, Sa-Su 9:30-7:30pm; Sept.-Oct. daily 9:30am-6pm; Nov.-Mar. daily 9:30am-4:15pm. Last admission 30min. before close. Glasshouses close 5:30pm Apr.-Oct., 3:45pm Nov.-Mar. Admission: £6.50, "late entry" (45min. before close) £4.50; students & seniors £4.50; under 16 free with adult.*

Founded in 1759 by Princess Augusta as an addendeum to Kew Palace, the Royal Botanical Gardens have since expanded to swallow the palace grounds entirely, now extending in a 300-acre swathe along the Thames. No ordinary park, Kew is a leading center for plant science, thanks in no small part to its living collection of thousands of flowers, fruits, trees, and vegetables from across the globe.

The three great **conservatories** and their smaller offshoots, housing a staggering variety of plants ill-suited to the English climate, are the highlight of the gardens. Most famous is the steamy Victorian **Palm House.** Inside, among a veritable jungle of tropical plants, is Encephalartos Altensteinii, "The Oldest Pot Plant In The World," which is not at all what it sounds like but interesting nonetheless. Downstairs, a tame aquarium is devoted to algae, coral, and seaweed, though there are plenty of colorful fish swimming among the plants. The **Temperate House** is the largest ornamental glasshouse in the world, with an overwhelming display of useful fauna from the world's warmer regions, including 27 types of eggplant. Brushing up against the ceiling, the 20m-tall, 157-year-old Jubea Chilensis is the world's largest indoor plant. The **Princess of Wales Conservatory,** opened in 1987 by Diana but named for Augusta, has a larger area under glass than any other, thanks to its innovative pyramid-like structure. The interior is divided into 10 different climate zones, from rainforest to desert, including one entirely devoted to orchids. The newest of Kew's indoor attractions is not a greenhouse at all: the **Plants and People** exhibition, across the Pond from the Palm House, investigates the many uses to which plants are put. While much of it is fairly obvious, the petroleum offers a renewable solution to global warming—this high-octane fruit powered the Japanese army in WWII.

Outside the controlled environment of the houses, the gardens are home to a wide variety of cloud-and-rain loving fauna from around the world. Created in 1910, the **Japanese Gateway and Garden** brings eastern formalism to a collection that also includes local specialities such as the **Rose Garden,** the **Lilacs,** the **Azaleas,** and **Rhododendron Dell,** created by Capability Brown. Though the gardens blaze most brightly between March and June, the **Woodland Glade** is renowned for displays of autumn color, while the **Winter Garden** flowers between November and February. Close to the Thames in the northern part of the gardens, **Kew Palace** (closed for renovations) is a modest red-brick affair originally built by a Dutch merchant in 1631. Behind the palace, 17th-century medicinal plants flourish in the **Queen's Garden;** small placards boast their use, from one that "cures bites of mad dogs" to those that "stirreth up bodily lust." Right at the opposite end of the gardens, **Queen's Charlotte's Cottage** is a faux-rustic building given by George III to his wife as a picnic site. Various decorative **follies** are scattered around the gardens; most ridiculous is the 10-storey **Pagoda,** which looks as Chinese as the Tower of London, but must have been more impressive when fire-breathing dragons guarded each floor.

SOUTH LONDON

LAMBETH

🔂 *NEIGHBORHOOD QUICKFIND: Discover, p. 13; Museums&Galleries, p. 151; Nightlife, p. 199.*

Stretching inland from the Thames opposite Parliament, Lambeth is a borough of contrasts. The riverbank is dominated by two ancient institutions: the Archbishop of Canterbury's **Lambeth Palace** (see below) and the current modern incarnation of **St. Thomas's Hospital,** founded in the 13th century near London Bridge and relocated here in the 19th. Inland Lambeth—the childhood home of Charlie Chaplin—has seen little progress since Victorian times, remaining largely poor and deprived, though with pockets of wealth. You might be surprised to find out the the famous **Lambeth Walk** is not an irreverent style of stride, but the name of an unassuming street leading south off Lambeth Rd.

LAMBETH PALACE. Ever since Archbishop Langton decided he needed to be nearer the center of things in 1207, the Archbishops of Canterbury have used Lambeth Palace as their London residence. The palace retains a late-medieval appearance from the outside thanks to the 15th-century gateway and Lollard's tower, where John Wyclif's followers were imprisoned; inside, much is 19th century, though the Great Hall, with a hammerbeam roof, and guard room impress. To the north, **Archbishops Park** stretches along Lambeth Palace Rd. behind high walls, allowing the archbishops to cavort in peace. *(Tube: Lambeth North. Visits by prior arrangement only; contact Lambeth Palace, Lambeth Palace Rd., SE1.)*

NEARBY MUSEUMS & GALLERIES

Permanent Collections: Imperial War Museum, p. 151; Florence Nightingale Museum, p. 152; Museum of Garden History, p. 152.

BRIXTON & DULWICH

🔂 *NEIGHBORHOOD QUICKFIND: Discover, p. 13; Museums&Galleries, p. 151; Food&Drink, p. 180; Nightlife, p. 198; Entertainment, p. 220; Shopping, p. 238; Accommodations, p. 299.*

Initially, Brixton was just another south London railway suburb—indeed, as Electric Ave. and Electric Ln. (the first streets in south London with electric lighting) testify, at one point it was positively prosperous. A poor, working-class area by the turn of the century, Brixton's greatest upheaval came after WWII: starting in 1948, a steady stream of Caribbean immigrants made Brixton the heart of London's West Indian community. Simmering racial tensions erupted with major riots in 1981 and 1985, and Brixton while still has its problems, today the area is undoubtedly on the up. Now a fashionable area for young artists and media professionals looking for a more urban experience, this "new Brixton" of trendy bars, restaurants, and clubs has little in common with the (still very much present) old Brixton of Caribbean market stalls, curry-goat vendors, and reggae stores. Arrive in the morning for a wander around **Brixton Market** (p. 238) to see Afro-Caribbean Brixton in full swing, then return in the evening as young new Brixtonians pile out of work and into the bars. *(Tube:Brixton.)*

A short bus ride or train journey from Brixton, **Dulwich** could hardly offer a greater contrast. South London's snobbiest suburb, home to Margaret Thatcher, Dulwich bumbled along as an unremarkable country village until 1605, when Elizabethan heartthob Edward Alleyn (played by Ben Affleck in *Shakespeare in Love*) bought the local manor. His legacy lives on in the College of God's Gift, established according to his will for the education of 12 poor children. The original **Old College** buildings, including the chapel where Alleyn is buried, still stand close to Dulwich Picture Gallery (see p. 151), though **Dulwich College**, now with 1600 very wealthy pupils, has since moved south to a palatial 19th-century site on College Rd. designed by Charles Barry. The college still profits from its privately-owned stretch of College Rd., south of the Common; its **toll gate** is the last in London. *(Rail:North or West Dulwich.)*

BROCKWELL PARK & LIDO. In many ways an archetypal London park, with tennis courts, playgrounds, and a bowling green, Brockwell Park offers great views of London landmarks. *(Between Tulse Hill & Dulwich Rd.; from Tube: Brixton, turn left, bear left at the fork onto Effra Rd., then turn left again onto Brixton Waterlane, which has an entrance to the park; 15min. Open daily 7:30am-dusk.)* The eastern edge of the park, off Dulwich Rd., holds the popular **Brockwell Lido,** often described as "London's beach." In fact it's a 1930s outdoor swimming pool, but summer "Beach BBQs," draw crowds from across London. *(☎7274 3088. Open late May to mid-Sept. M-Th 6:45-10am and noon-7pm, F 6:45-10am and noon-6pm, Sa-Su noon-6pm. Beach BBQ July-Aug. F 8-11:30pm; £15, kids £8, including food. Morning swim £2, concs. £1.50; afternoons £4, student £3, seniors & kids £2.50.)*

NEARBY MUSEUMS & GALLERIES

Permanent Collections: Dulwich Picture Gallery, p. 151; Horniman Museum, p. 152.

EAST LONDON

WHITECHAPEL & THE EAST END

🔢 *NEIGHBORHOOD QUICKFIND: Discover, p. 14; Museums&Galleries, p. 152; Food&Drink, p. 180; Nightlife, p. 199; Entertainment, p. 221; Shopping, p. 239.*

The boundary between the East End and City of London is as sharp today as it was when Aldgate and Bishopsgate were real gateways in the wall separating the rich and powerful City from the poorer quarters to the east. The oldest part of the East End, in the 17th century **Whitechapel** thronged with Huguenots escaping religious persecution in France; two centuries later, refugees from the pogroms made this the heart of Jewish London. Today, though the streets are still full of bearded men in skullcaps, the wearers are Muslim: Whitechapel is now the home of London's largest Bangladeshi community, as evinced by the minaret of the **East London Mosque**. *(82-92 Whitechapel Rd. Tube: Aldgate East.)* In addition to cockneys and Bangladeshis, the East End is home to an increasing number of artists, drawn by cheap rents. The best reason to visit the East End, though, is for its vibrant **markets** (see Shopping, p. 239), which draw shoppers from all over London looking for saris on Brick Ln., leather jackets on Petticoat Ln., or crafts on Spitalfields.

BEVIS MARKS SYNAGOGUE. The city's oldest standing synagogue was built in 1701, though its congregation goes back to 1656, when Spanish and Portuguese Jews accepted Cromwell's invitation to come to London, ending 367 years of exile. True to its origins, services are still partly conducted in Portuguese. In 1813, an argument with the synagogue led Isaac D'Israeli to have his children baptized, a decision which made it possible for his son Benjamin to enter politics. Though "Bevis Marks" has an agreeably Jewish sound, the name derives from Bury's Mark, a 12th-century monastic house on the site. *(Tube: Aldgate; from Aldgate High St. turn right onto Houndsditch;*

Creechurch Ln. on the left leads to Bevis Marks. ☎ 7626 1274. Organized tours Su-W and F noon; call in advance. Open Su-M, W, and F 11:30am-1pm, Tu 10:30am-4pm. Entrance donation £1.)

CHRIST CHURCH. Now an island of Anglicanism amid a spectrum of other traditions, Christ Church is Nicholas Hawksmoor's largest church, and considered by many to be his masterpiece. Alas, this 1714 building is in a sorry state; derelict since 1957, only now is it slowly being restored to its former glory. While the facade has been cleaned and repaired, work on the grandly proportioned interior has just started. *(Commercial St., opposite Spitalfields market. ☎ 7247 7202. Tube: Liverpool St.)*

SPITALFIELDS MARKET. Originally one of London's main vegetable markets, Spitalfields was threatened with commercial development when the traders moved further east to Leyton. Thanks to strong local opposition, one half of the enormous market hall was saved, and now hosts a thriving array of crafts, antiques, and bric-a-brac along with food stalls and cafes, plus an organic food market on Fridays. *(Commercial St. ☎ 7377 1496. Tube: Liverpool St. For market details, see Shopping, p. 239.)*

BRICK LANE. In Brick Lane, even the street signs are written in Bengali: this is the epicenter of Bangladeshi Britain. Most famous for its vibrant Sunday market and scores of curry houses, Brick Ln. has recently become the unlikely center of the East End's creative renaissance: the former **Truman Brewery**, covering 11 acres on both sides of Brick Lane at no. 91 and 150, is now occupied by design and media consultancies, sleek stores, and a cafe-bar-club trio that together form one of London's hottest nightspots. *(Tube: Shoreditch (open only in rush hour), Aldgate East, or Liverpool St.)*

WHITECHAPEL BELL FOUNDRY. Sole survivor of the metalworking businesses common in the medieval East End, the oldest manufacturing company in Britain sits inconspicuously on Whitechapel Rd. Possibly founded as early as 1420, their most famous (and biggest) commission was the 13.5 tons of Big Ben, in 1858. The foundry runs occasional Saturday tours, when the furnaces are silent; at other times, you can browse a small historical exhibition and gift shop. *(32-34 Whitechapel Rd. ☎ 7247 2599; www.whitechapelbellfoundry.co.uk. Tube: Aldgate East. Tours: Sporadic Sa 10am and 2pm. Advance booking required; min. age 14. £8. Exhibition: Open M-F 9am-5pm. Free.)*

NEARBY MUSEUMS & GALLERIES
Permanent Collections: Museum of Childhood, p. 153.
Exhibition Spaces: Whitechapel Art Gallery, p. 153.

HOXTON & SHOREDITCH

▶ *From **Tube:** Old St., walk down Old St.; the center of the "Shoho scene" spreads either side of Old St. between the junction with Great Eastern St. and Kingsland Rd./Shoreditch High St. **NEIGHBORHOOD QUICKFIND: Discover,** p. 14; **Museums&Galleries,** p. 152; **Food&Drink,** p. 181; **Shopping,** p. 239; **Entertainment,** p. 221; **Nightlife,** p. 199.*

You'd be forgiven, wandering in the morning around the streets of Hoxton (north of Old St.) and Shoreditch (to the south), for wondering what all the fuss is about—this may be London's most fashionable district, but at first glance it looks like a pretty depressing, dirty, and impoverished neighborhood. Indeed, until the early 1990s it was so poor that many of its buildings were derelict. To struggling artists such as Damien Hirst, Sarah Lucas, and Tracey Emin, that translated into a whole lotta space for not much money, and Hoxton became the focus for an underground art scene that soon burst onto the world stage. Eventually word got around that this was the cool place to be, bringing an influx of artists from all over the world, followed by graphic designers, web designers, and ultimately media execs. The upshot is that while **"Shoho,"** as the area has wittily been dubbed, still looks like a deserted slum—especially before lunchtime, when most people are sleeping off last night's party—the artists have been forced further out into Hackney.

NEARBY MUSEUMS & GALLERIES
Permanent Collections: Geffrye Museum, p. 153.
Exhibition Spaces: Lux Gallery, p. 153.
Commercial Galleries: Victoria Miro, p. 153; White Cube^2, p. 153.

DOCKLANDS

🎫 **NEIGHBORHOOD QUICKFIND: Discover,** p. 14; **Food&Drink,** p. 181; **Entertainment,** p. 221; **Shopping,** p. 239.

Countering heritage-obsessed Greenwich across the Thames, brash young Docklands is the largest commercial development in Europe. From the 19th century to the 1960s, this man-made archipelago was the commercial heart of the British Empire, with cargoes from across the world being loaded and unloaded in a never-ending stream of activity. The post-war boom meant that the 1950s saw the docks busier than ever before; yet within thirty years they were empty, killed off by the switch to deep-water container ships that were simply too big to fit. In 1981, the Conservative government founded the London Docklands Development Corporation (LDDC) to redevelop this vast area—itself as big as metropolitan Paris—as a showpiece of unrestrained entrepreneurial development. The result has been called the "architectural embodiment of Thatcherism," a strange mix of hi-tech office buildings and suburban-style housing, all knitted together by the driverless trains of the Docklands Light Railway.

ISLE OF DOGS

Not an island at all, this giant peninsula formed by a curve in the Thames is the heart of Docklands and home to its most famous development, Canary Wharf (see below). To complete the misnomer, it's probably nothing to do with dogs, either, though Henry VIII did keep his royal kennels here; more likely the word is a corruption of the 19th-century dykes built to keep the river at bay. Despite its high profile, the Isle isn't all new developments—the southern part has barely been touched, home to both impoverished housing estates and the green pastures of **Mudchute Park,** with stunning vistas overlooking Greenwich and the Dome. *(DLR: Mudchute.)*

CANARY WHARF. For almost a decade, the pyramid-topped tower of **One Canada Square,** commonly called Canary Wharf, was an iconic sign of Docklands; at 800 ft., it's Britain's tallest building. It's still there, but in the past two years has been joined by a brace of almost equally tall companions—the most visible sign of Dockland's current boom. Under the tower, the vast **Canada Place** and **Cabot Square** malls suck in shoppers from all over London, while the dockside plaza is lined with pricey corporate drinking and eating haunts. *(Tube/DLR: Canary Wharf.)*

GREENWICH

🎫 *All sights are closest to* **DLR: Cutty Sark.** *The* **Greenwich Tourist Information Centre,** *Pepys House, 2 Cutty Sark Gdns. (☎0870 608 2000) offers all the usual services as well as a slick exhibition on local history. Walking tours leave the center daily at 12:15 and 2:15pm. (£4, concs. £3, under 14 free.) Open daily 10am-5pm.* **NEIGHBORHOOD QUICKFIND: Discover,** p. 14; **Museums&Galleries,** p. 152; **Food&Drink,** p. 183; **Shopping,** p. 239; **Entertainment,** p. 221.

Greenwich, on the south bank, first found fame and fortune as the site of the Elizabeth Is favorite palace, Placentia. Home of the Royal Navy until 1998, Greenwich's position as the "home of time" is intimately connected to its maritime heritage—the Royal Observatory, site of the Prime Meridian, was originally founded to produce the accurate star-charts essential to navigation. It's this connection with timekeeping that led to Greenwich being chosen as the site of Britain's most famous white elephant, the **Millennium Dome.** Situated some way from the historic sights in North Greenwich, it's an imposing, brooding presence, clearly visible from much of East London, and, since the much-maligned "Millennium Experience" closed its doors on December 31, 2000, London's largest piece of unsold real estate. If you're planning on spending a day or two sightseeing in Greenwich, consider buying the **Greenwich Passport Ticket,** giving entry to the National Maritime Museum, the Royal Observatory, and the Cutty Sark. *(Available at the Tourist Information Centre (see below) and participating sights. Ticket valid on any 2 days within 1 year of issue. £12, students & seniors £9.60.)*

RIVER TRIPS. Many people choose to enhance their nautical experience by making the 1hr. **boat** trip from Westminster; boats are also a popular way of getting to the Thames Barrier (see p. 131). Note that Travelcard holders get 33% off riverboat fares. **City Cruises** operates from Westminster Pier to Greenwich via the Tower of London. *(☎7930 9033; www.citycruises.com. Apr.-Oct. daily every 40min. 10am-5:40pm; last departure* *from Greenwich 5:35pm. £6, all-day "rover" ticket £7.50; kids £3, £3.75; family rover (2 adults + 3 kids) £19.50.)* **Westminster Passenger Association** boats also head from Westminster Pier for Greenwich, with some boats making a stop at St. Katharine's Docks and the Thames Barrier too. Their "Sail&Rail" ticket combines a one-way boat trip between Westminster and Greenwich with unlimited all-day travel on the DLR. *(☎ 7930 4097; www.wpsa.co.uk. Apr. to early Oct. daily every 3min. 10:30am-5pm daily, last departure from Greenwich 6pm, from Thames Barrier 3:30pm. To Greenwich £6, return £7.50, Sail&Rail £8.30; seniors £4.80, £6, £7; kids £3, £3.75, £4.20; family £15.75, £19.50, £23.)* Note that WPSA doesn't let you board at Greenwich for the Thames Barrier; you'll need to catch a **Campion Launches** service. *(☎ 8305 0300. 25min., 4 departures daily Apr.-Oct. at 11:15am, 12:30, 2, and 3:30pm; last return at 4pm. £3.50, return £5; seniors £3, £4.25; kids £2.25, £3.)*

ROYAL OBSERVATORY GREENWICH

🛈 *Location: At the top of Greenwich Park, a steep climb from the National Maritime Museum; for an easier walk, take The Avenue from the top of King William Walk. Contact: ☎ 8312 6565; www.rog.nmm.ac.uk. Open: Daily 10am-5pm; last admission 4:30pm. Admission: £6, students £4.80, seniors & under 16 free; with National Maritime Museum & Queen's House £10.50, students £8.40, seniors & under 16 free. For Greenwich Passport ticket, see above. Planetarium £2 extra, concs. £1.50.*

Charles II founded the Royal Observatory in 1675 along with the post of Astronomer Royal, and charged both with finding a solution to the vexing problem of determining longitude. Even though longitude was eventually solved without reference to the sky, the connection lives on—the **Prime Meridian** started out as the axis along which the astronomers' telescopes swung. The meridian is marked by an LED strip in the courtyard endlessly tickering Observatory trivia; play the "now I'm west, now I'm east" game for as long as you're amused before ducking into **Flamstead House,** created by Wren "for the Observator's habitation and little for pomp." The **Octagon Room**—a rare surviving Wren interior, with wraparound windows designed to accommodate long telescopes—falls into the latter category, used to entertain curious visitors rather than conduct serious experiments. Take a peek into the telescope displayed there to see how the tradition lives on. Downstairs, **Finding the Longitude** tells the story of how the problem was finally solved by a self-taught clockmaker, John Harrison, together with working models of his four extraordinary timepieces. In 1833, the famous red **Time Ball** on the observatory roof was installed so that ships in the harbor could set their clocks to Greenwich Mean Time; the ball is raised daily at 12:58pm and dropped unspectacularly at 1 o'clock. Next to the Meridian Building's telescope display, climb the **Observatory Dome,** cunningly disguised as a freakishly large onion, to see the 28" telescope, constructed in 1893 and still the 7th largest refracting 'scope in the world. Unfortunately, light pollution led to the abandoning of Greenwich as a scientific observatory in 1954. You can still get a peak at the stars, though, at the regular **Planetarium** shows hosted in the South Building.

QUEEN'S HOUSE

🛈 *At the foot of Greenwich Park, on Trafalgar Rd. For details, see Museums&Galleries, p. 153.*

Now part of the National Maritime Museum (see p. 152), Inigo Jones' Queen's House was England's first Palladian villa. It was commissioned in 1616 by Anne of Denmark, James I's queen, but was not completed until 22 years later, for Charles I's wife Henrietta Maria. Known to the queen as her "house of delights," and celebrated by architects for its purity, the building is not without its quirks. Most obviously is the fact that it's built on either side of a carriageway, with a "bridge room" across the top—the house was formerly the main gateway into the Palace of Placentia, since replaced by the Royal Naval College.

CUTTY SARK

🛈 *Location: King William Walk, by Greenwich Pier. Contact: ☎ 8858 3445; www.cuttysark.org.uk. Open: Daily 10am-5pm, last entry 4:30pm. Admission: £3.50, concessions £2.50, families £8.50.*

The last of the great tea clippers, even landlubbers will appreciate the Cutty Sark's thoroughbred lines—it's no surprise she was the fastest ship of her time, making the round trip from China in only 120 days, laden with 1.3 million pounds of tea. Retired from the sea in 1938, the deck and cabins have been restored to their 19th-century

prime, while the hold houses an exhibition on the ship's history and a fascinating collection of figureheads, from a set of cherubs by Grinling Gibbons to the stern figure of Abraham Lincoln. Kids can also practice knots, experiment with pulleys, and swing in a hammock. Close by the Cutty Sark, visitors can admire the exterior of the **Gypsy Moth,** the cozy 54ft. craft in which 64-year-old Francis Chichester sailed solo around the globe in 1966, covering nearly 30,000 miles. Thought he didn't achieve his goal of matching the Cutty Sark, he set numerous solo-sailing speed records during his 226 days afloat, and was knighted on his return.

ROYAL NAVAL COLLEGE

🛈 Location: *King William Walk.* **Contact:** ☎ *8269 4744; www.greenwichfoundation.org.uk.* **Open:** *M-Sa noon-5pm, Su 12:30-5pm.* **Admission:** *£3, students&seniors £2, under 16 free.*

On the site of Henry VIII's Palace of Placentia—where both he and Elizabeth I were born—the Royal Naval College was founded by William III in 1694 as the Royal Hospital for Seamen, a naval retirement home along the same lines as the army's Royal Hospital in Chelsea (see p. 108). However, the strict regime on offer proved unpopular with former seamen, and in 1873 it was converted into the Royal Naval College. The most recent upheaval came in 1998, when the Navy packed its bags and the newly formed University of Greenwich blew in. Visitors are free to wander the grounds of Christopher Wren's campus. To Mary II's insistence that the new buildings not restrict the view from the Queen's House, Wren responded with two symmetrical wings separated by a colonnaded walkway. Buy a ticket to gain access to the incredible **Painted Hall,** which took Sir James Thornhill 19 years to complete. Ticket holders also have access to the simple **Chapel,** with Benjamin West's painting of a shipwrecked St. Paul, and the bizarre **Crown Jewels of the Millennium** exhibit. The fact that it's held in the university bar should alert you to the fact that the 140 crowns, from the Tsar's to the Shah's, might not be the genuine articles.

OTHER GREENWICH SIGHTS

ST. ALFEGE. Greenwich's parish church stands on the site where Alfege, an early Archbishop of Canterbury, was murdered by Viking raiders on April 19, 1012; no doubt the story made an early impression on another church-burner, Henry VIII, baptized here in 1491. Hawksmoor designed the current incarnation, finished in 1718, though his tower was too ambitious for parishioners' wallets; the current tower is the 13th-century medieval one, though clad in 18th-century stonework. *(Greenwich Church St. www.st-alfege.org. Open daily 10am-4pm. Free.)*

GREENWICH PARK. Another former royal hunting-ground, Greenwich Park is more than a pleasant spot for sunbathing; sights scattered around its hills include the remains of a 1st-century Roman settlement and Saxon tumuli (burial mounds). On the east side of the park is the **Queen Elizabeth Oak,** a rather grand title for a big dead log; for centuries before collapsing a few years ago, the tree marked the spot where Henry VIII frolicked with an 11-fingered Anne Boleyn. The garden in the southeast corner of the park combines English garden and fairy tale, complete with a deer park. The **Children's Boating Pool** gives kids a chance to unleash pent-up seafaring energy accumulated in the nearby museums, while bands oom-pa-pa from the bandstand nearby on summer Saturdays. *(Park open daily 7am-dusk.)*

THAMES BARRIER. Around the next bend in the Thames from Greenwich stands the world's largest movable flood barrier, the reason that London no longer enjoys the exciting high tides of yesteryear. Constructed during the 1970s and (over)hyped as "the eighth wonder of the world," the barrier spans 520m and consists of 10 separate movable steel gates; when raised, the main gates stand as high as a five-story building, though global warming threatens to undermine its effectiveness. A surprisingly intriguing visitors' center has a working model of the barrier, in addition to exhibits explaining its history. *(Take the Campion Launches boat from Greenwich (see p. 128), or take bus 161 or a 45min. walk from Tube: North Greenwich. ☎ 8305 4188. Open M-F 10am-5pm, Sa-Su 10:30am-5:30pm. £3.40, concessions £2, families £7.50.)*

NEARBY MUSEUMS & GALLERIES

Permanent Collections: 🗻 National Maritime Museum, p. 152; Queen's House, p. 153.

Museums & Galleries

Centuries as the capital of an empire upon which the sun never set, together with a decidedly English penchant for collecting, have endowed London with a spectacular set of museums. Art lovers, history buffs, and amateur ethnologists will not know which way to turn when they arrive. And there's even better news for museum lovers—after a decade which saw many museums move from free admission to becoming some of the capital's most expensive attractions, the government now plans to return all major collections to free admission by November 2001. However, note that almost all charge extra for temporary exhibitions—often so popular that tickets must be booked in advance.

MUSEUMS & GALLERIES BY TYPE

ART: PERMANENT COLLECTIONS		ART: EXHIBITION SPACES	
◙ Courtauld Institute	West End	Bankside Gallery	South Bank
◙ Dulwich Picture Gallery	South	Barbican Art Galleries	City
Estorick Collection	North	Brunei Gallery	Bloomsbury
Guildhall Art Gallery	City	Hayward Gallery	South Bank
◙ Iveagh Bequest	North	◙ Institute of Contemporary Art	West End
National Gallery	Major Collections	Jerwood Gallery	South Bank
National Portrait Gallery	West End	Lux Gallery	East
Queen's Gallery	Westminster	October Gallery	Bloomsbury
Queen's House	East	The Photographers' Gallery	West End
◙ Sir John Soane's Museum	Holborn	Royal Academy	West End
Tate Britain	Major Collections	◙ Saatchi Gallery	Northwest
Tate Modern	Major Collections	Serpentine Gallery	Kensington
◙ Wallace Collection	Marylebone	Whitechapel Art Gallery	East

ART: COMMERCIAL GALLERIES	
Annely Juda Fine Art	West End
Anthony D'Offay	West End
Bernard Jacobson	West End
Christie's	West End
Marlborough Fine Arts	West End
Robert Sandelson	West End
Sotheby's	West End
White Cube	West End
White Cube²	East
Victoria Miro	East

APPLIED & DECORATIVE ARTS	
Crafts Council	North London
Design Museum	South Bank
Geffrye Museum	East
Gilbert Collection	West End
Percival Davis Foundation	Bloomsbury
Victoria & Albert	Major Collections

BIOGRAPHICAL	
Dickens House Museum	Holborn
Florence Nightingale Museum	South
Freud Museum	North
Sherlock Holmes Museum	Marylebone

HISTORICAL	
Bank of England Museum	City
British Museum	Major Collections
Cabinet War Rooms	Westminster
Clink Prison Museum	City

HISTORICAL (CONT.)	
Jewish Museum	North
Museum of London	City

SCIENCE & MEDICINE	
Cabinet War Rooms	Westminster
Florence Nightingale Museum	South
Freud Museum	North
Hunterian Museum	Holborn
Natural History Museum	Kensington
St. Bartholomew's Hospital	Clerkenwell
Science Museum	Kensington

MILITARY	
Guard's Museum	Westminster
Imperial War Museum	South
National Army Museum	Chelsea
Royal Airforce Museum	North

OTHER	
British Library Galleries	Bloomsbury
Guildhall Clock Museum	City
London Canal Museum	North
London's Transport Museum	West End
Museum of Garden History	South
Museum of Childhood	East
National Maritme Museum	East
Pollock's Toy Museum	Bloomsbury
Theatre Museum	West End

MAJOR COLLECTIONS

BRITISH MUSEUM

*LOCATION: Great Russell St., **Bloomsbury**. Rear entrance on Montague St. **LOCAL QUICKFIND:** Sights, p. 116; Museums&Galleries, p. 148; Food&Drink, p. 175. **CONTACT:** ☎ 7323 8000; www.thebritishmuseum.ac.uk. **TUBE:** Tottenham Court Rd., Russell Sq., or Holborn. **AUDIOGUIDES:** £2.50. **TOURS:** Start at Great Court info desk; free. **Highlights Tour** (90min.): M-Sa 10:30am and 1pm; Su 11am, 12:30, 1:30, 2:30, and 4pm. Advanced booking recommended. £7, concs. £4. **Focus tour:** (60min.): M-W and Sa 3:15pm; Th-F 3:15, 5:30, and 7pm; Su 4:30pm. £5, concs £3. **OPEN:** Great Court M 9am-6pm, Tu-W and Su 9am-9pm, Th-Sa 9am-11pm. Galleries Sa-W 10am-5:30pm, Th-F 10am-8:30pm. **ADMISSION:** Free; £2 suggested donation. Temporary exhibitions around £7, concs. £3.50.*

The funny thing about the British Museum is that there's almost nothing British in it. Founded in 1753 as the personal collection of Sir Hans Sloane, in 1824 work started on the current Neoclassical building, which took another 30 years to construct. With 50,000 items, the magnificent collection is somewhat undermined by a chaotic layout and poor labelling, especially in the less popular galleries, while staff shortages mean that even famous galleries are frequently and randomly closed to the public.

GREAT COURT. Things are getting better, though. The opening of the **Great Court** in Dec. 2000—the largest covered square in Europe—finally restored to the museum its focal point. For the past 150 years used as the book stacks of the British Library (now transferred to St. Pancras; see p. 117), the courtyard remains dominated by the enormous rotunda of the **Reading Room**. The blue chairs and desks, with ingenious fold-out lecterns, have shouldered the weight of research by Marx, Lenin, and Trotsky as well as almost every major British writer and intellectual.

WESTERN GALLERIES. From the Great Court, a right (as you enter) leads to the Museum's most popular wing. Star of the **Egyptian sculpture** is the **Rosetta Stone**, whose trilingual inscriptions (in Greek, Heterotic, and Hieroglyphic) made the deciphering of ancient Egyptian possible. *(Room 4.)* Just as imposing are the monumental friezes and reliefs of the Assyrian, Hittite, and other ancient **Near-Eastern** civilizations. *(Rooms 6-10, ground floor. The southern end of room 4 leads into room 6.)* Most famous of the massive array of **Greek sculpture** on show are the **Elgin Marbles,** carved under the direction of classical Athens' greatest sculptor, Phidias. *(Room 18.)* Equally impressive (and far less crowded) are the almost perfectly preserved **Bassae Friezes,** in, displaying scenes from the battle between Perseus and the Amazons. *(Room 16, upstairs from 17.)* Other Hellenic highlights include bits and bobs from two of the seven Wonders of the Ancient World, the **Temple of Artemis** at Ephesus and the **Mausoleum of Halikarnassos.** *(Rooms 21-22.)* Upstairs, the **Portland Vase** presides over **Roman** ceramics and housewares. When discovered in 1582 the base had already been broken and replaced. In 1845, it was shattered by a drunken museum-goer; when it was put back together, 37 small chips were left over. Since then, the vase has been beautifully reconstructed twice, with more left-over chips being reincorporated each time—don't touch! *(Room 70.)*

NORTHERN GALLERIES. Revenge of the mummy: just when you thought you'd nailed Ancient Egypt, along come another 8 galleries. Rooms 61-63 contain painted wooden **sarcophagi** and bandaged **mummies** in various states of repairs. *(Rooms 61-68, upper floor.)* More overspill from the West wing continues the Near Eastern theme; musical instruments and board games from the world's first city, **Ur,** show that life's priorites have changed little since. *(Rooms 51-59.)* Opened in March 2001, the **African Galleries** are perhaps the best-presented in the museum. The dramatic lighting and soft sound of chanting create a hushed atmosphere. *(Room 25, lower floor.)* With no South American artefacts at all, **Americas** collection uses gimmickry to disguise its shortfall; the **Mexican** gallery, does its best to imitate a Mayan temple, hot, humid, and dark. *(Rooms 26-27.)* Just off the Montague Pl.

entrance, is a particularly fine collection of **Islamic art.** *(Room 34.)* Immediately above it, Room 33 (the largest in the museum) is dedicated to the art of **China,** the **South Asia,** and **Southeast Asia,** with some particularly fine Hindu sculpture. Upstairs, the highlight of the **Korean** display is a *sarangbang* house built on-site. *(Room 67.)* A teahouse, meanwhile, is the centerpiece of the **Japanese** galleries. *(Rooms 92-94.)*

SOUTH AND EAST GALLERIES. The upper level of the museum's southeast corner is dedicated to ancient and medieval **Europe,** including most of the museum's British artefacts. Room 50 contains the preserved body of **Lindow Man,** an Iron Age Celt apparently sacrificed in a gruesome ritual. The centerpiece of room 41 is treasure excavated from the **Sutton Hoo Burial Ship;** the magnificent inlaid helmet is the most famous example of Anglo-Saxon craftsmanship. Next door, Room 42 is home to the enigmatic **Lewis Chessmen,** an 800-year-old Scandinavian chess set mysteriously abandoned on Scotland's Outer Hebrides. Also in this part of the museum are the frankly dull **Clock Gallery** (Room 44) and **Money Gallery** (Room 68).

NATIONAL GALLERY

⊡ LOCATION: *Main entrance on north side of* **Trafalgar Sq.;** *disabled access at Sainsbury Wing, on Pall Mall East, and Orange St. entrances.* **LOCAL QUICKFIND:** *Sights, p. 79; Museums&Galleries, p. 139; Food&Drink, p. 159.* **CONTACT:** ☎ 7747 2885; www.nationalgallery.org.uk. **TUBE:** *Charing Cross or Leicester Sq.* **AUDIOGUIDES:** *Free; £4 suggested donation.* **TOURS:** *Start at Sainsbury Wing info desk. 1hr. gallery tours daily 11:30am and 2:30pm, W also 6:30pm; free.* **OPEN:** *Th-Tu 10am-6pm; W 10am-9pm, Sainsbury Wing exhibitions to 10pm.* **ADMISSION:** *Free; some temporary exhibitions £6-7, seniors £4-5, students and ages 12-18 £2-3.*

The National Gallery was founded by an Act of Parliament in 1824, with 38 pictures displayed in a townhouse; it grew so rapidly in size and popularity that it was decided to construct a purpose-built gallery in 1838. Since then, numerous additions have been made, the most recent (and controversial) being the massive Sainsbury Wing—Prince Charles described it as "a monstrous carbuncle on the face of a much-loved and elegant friend." If you're pressed for time the **Micro Gallery,** in the Sainsbury Wing, print you out a personalized tour of the paintings you want to see.

SAINSBURY WING. The climate-controlled rooms of the gallery's newest extension house its oldest, most fragile paintings, dating from 1260 to 1510. The most famous of the many devotional **medieval** paintings on display is the *Wilton Diptych*, a 14th-century altarpiece made for (and featuring) Richard II. A stunning **early Renaissance** collection features Botticelli's *Venus and Mars*, an early plea to make love not war, and Piero della Francesca's *Baptism of Christ*. One of the museum's most famous works, the *Leonardo Cartoon* is a detailed preparatory drawing by Leonardo da Vinci for a never-executed painting. Other Leonardos on display include his second *Virgin on the Rocks* (his first attempt is in the Louvre, Paris).

WEST WING. With paintings from 1510 to 1600, the West Wing is dominated by the Italian **High Renaissance** and the first flowering of Flemish art. In room 8, the artistic forces of Rome and Florence fight it out, with versions of the *Madonna and Child* by Raphael and Michelangelo; room 9 focuses on northern Italy, with Titian's enigmatic three-headed *Allegory of Prudence* and Veronese's imposing *Family of Darius before Alexander*. Many of the earlier Flemish works in room 12 are by artists known only by such florid titles as "Master of the Female Half-Length."

NORTH WING. Continuing our journey through time, the North Wing spans the **17th century,** with an exceptional array of Flemish work spread out over 10 rooms. Room 23 boasts no fewer than 17 Rembrandts; the famous *Self Portrait at 63* gazes knowingly at a young artist across the room: his *Self Portrait at 34*. Room 29 is dominated by Rubens's *Samson and Delilah*, along with dozens of his other works. Velàzquez's super-sensuoue *The Toilet of Venus* is at odds with the rest of his mostly religious output on show in room 30.

EAST WING. The East Wing, home to paintings from **1700-1900,** is the most popular in the gallery—unsurprisingly, since it's here that you'll some of the world's best-loved canvases, including Van Gogh's *Sunflowers* and Cézanne's *Bathers* in room 45, and two of Monet's *Waterlilies* in room 43. A reminder that there was art on this side of the channel too, room 34 flies the flag with portraits by Reynolds and Gainsborough, as well as six luminescent Turners, ranging from the stormy realism of *Dutch Boats in a Gale* to the proto-Impressionist blur of *Margate from the Sea*.

TATE BRITAIN

⊡ LOCATION: *Millbank, near Vauxhall Bridge, in* **Westminster.** *Wheelchair access via Clore Wing.* **LOCAL QUICKFIND:** *Sights, p. 106; Museums&Galleries, p. 145; Food&Drink, p. 169.* **CONTACT:** ☎ 7887 8008; www.tate.org.uk. **TUBE:** *Pimlico.* **AUDIOGUIDES:** *£1.* **TOURS:** *1hr. Free.* **Highlights Tour:** *M-F 2:30, 3:30pm, Sa 3pm.* **Turner:** *M-F 11:30am.* **TALKS:** *Frequent evening talks by contemporary artists, usually W or Th; call for details and ticketing. Regular events include:* **Gallery Talks,** *W-Th 1:15pm;* **Painting of the Month,** *M 1:15pm and Sa 2:30pm;* **Friday Lectures,** *F 1pm;* **Slide Lectures,** *Sa 1pm and first 3 Su of month 2:30pm.* **OPEN:** *Daily 10am-5pm.* **ADMISSION:** *Free; special exhibitions £3-5.*

The original Tate opened in 1897 as a showcase for "modern" British art—modern being extended back to 1790 to allow the inclusion of the Turner bequest of 282 oils and 19,000 watercolors. Before long, the remit had expanded further still to include contemporary art from all over the world, as well as British art from the Middle Ages on. Despite numerous expansions, it was clear that the dual role as national museum of both British and modern art was too much for one building; the problem was resolved in 1999 with the relocation of almost all the contemporary art to the new Tate Modern at Bankside (see p. 137). At the same time, the original Tate was rechristened Tate Britain, and rededicated to British art—a tag which also includes foreign artists working in Britain and Brits working abroad. Not content with cosmetic changes, Tate Britain also embarked on a massive new expansion project: the **Tate Centenary Development,** due to be completed in late 2001, will provide six new exhibition galleries. Once the building work is completed, the gallery will be entirely rehung, arranged chronologically with themed subdivisions. The **Clore Gallery** will continue to display the **Turner Bequest;** other painters to feature heavily are William Blake, John Constable, Joshua Reynolds, Dante Gabriel Rossetti, John Hodgkin, Lucien Freud, and David Hockney. Sculptors are less well represented, though Jacob Epstein's *Jacob and the Angel* (1940-41), in the Sackler Octagon, is a favorite with the crowds. Recent BritArt is mostly absent, having been transferred to the Tate Modern. However, the annual **Turner Prize** for contemporary art is still held here. In recent years the prize has gone to less controversial works—after a decade that saw Damien Hirst, Chris Ofili, and Rachel Whiteread take the prize, an apparent backlash started in 1999 when Tracey Emin's unmade bed famously failed to win. The shortlisted works go on show from early November to mid-January every year.

TATE MODERN

⚑ LOCATION: *Bankside,on the* **South Bank;** *main entrance and wheelchair access on Holland St.; secondary entrance on Queen's Walk.* **LOCAL QUICKFIND:** *Sights, p. 100; Museums&Galleries, p. 144; Food&Drink, p. 168.* **CONTACT:** ☎ *7887 8888; www.tate.org.uk.* **TUBE:** *Southwark or Blackfriar's.* **AUDIOGUIDES:** *5 tours including for children and the visually impaired. £1.* **TOURS:** *meet on the gallery concourses; free.* **History/Memory/ Society** *10:30am, level 3;* **Nude/Body/Action** *11:30am, level 3;* **Landscape/Matter/Environment** *2:30pm, level 5;* **Still Life/Object/Real Life** *3:30pm, level 5.* **TALKS:** *M-F 1pm. Meet at concourse on appropriate level; free.* **OPEN:** *Su-Th 10am-6pm, F-Sa 10am-10pm.* **ADMISSION:** *Free; special exhibitions £5-7, concs. £1 off.*

Since opening in May 2000, Tate Modern has been credited with single-handedly reversing the long-term decline in museum-going numbers in Britain. The largest modern art museum in the world, its most striking aspect is the Giles Gilbert Scott's building, formerly the Bankside power station. A conversion by Swiss firm Her-

Tate Britain

Tate Modern

National Gallery

zog and de Meuron has added a seventh floor with wraparound views of north and south London, and turned the old **Turbine Hall** into an immense atrium that doubles as an exhibition space that often overpowers the installations commissioned for it. Of actual gallery space, a full one third—the entirety of level 4—is dedicated to temporary exhibitions. One nice touch is the provision of rest areas around the galleries, with chairs, books, and recorded commentary on various subjects by artists, intellectuals, and celebrities.

For all its popularity, the Tate has been criticized for its controversial curatorial method. By grouping works according to themes such as "Subversive Objects" or "Staging Discord," you might say the Tate has turned itself into a work of conceptual art—as many words are used to explain the logic behind each room's collection as the meaning behind the works themselves. Perhaps mindful of criticism, curators have stealthily begun arranging more works by period and artist, but officially, everything is still categorized according to four major themes: **Still Life/Object/Real Life** and **Landscape/Matter/Environment** on level 3, and **Nude/Action/Body** and **History/Memory/Society** on level 5. Even skeptics must admit that this arrangement throws up some interesting contrasts: successes include the nascent geometry of Cézanne's *Still Life with Water Jug* overlooking the checkerboard tiles of Carl André's *Steel Zinc Plain* in the "Desire for Order" room of the Still Life/Object/Real Life, and the juxtaposition of Monet's indistinct *Waterlilies* with Richard Long's energetic *Waterfall Line*, painted directly onto the gallery wall with mud, in Landscape/Matter/Environment. In other rooms, the purported theme is little more than a smokescreen for some conventional curation: also in Landscape/Matter/Environment, the "Inner Worlds" array of works by Dalí, Miró, Magritte, Ernst, and de Chirico proves only that Surrealism by any other name is no less bizarre. The greatest achievement of the thematic display is that it forces visitors into contact with an exceptionally wide range of art. It's now impossible to see the Tate's more famous pieces, which include Marcel Duchamp's *Large Glass*, Andy Warhol's *Marilyn Diptych*, and Picasso's *Weeping Woman*, without also confronting challenging and invigorating works by little-known contemporary artists.

VICTORIA & ALBERT MUSEUM

⚐ LOCATION: *Main entrance on Cromwell Rd., in* **Kensington**; *wheelchair access on Exhibition Rd.* **LOCAL QUICKFIND:** *Sights, p. 112; Museums&Galleries, p. 146; Food&Drink, p. 172.* **CONTACT:** ☎ *7942 2000; www.vam.ac.uk.uk.* **TUBE:** *South Kensington.* **TOURS:** *Meet at rear of main entrance; free.* **Introductory tours:** *Daily 10:30,11:30am, 1:30, 2:30pm; W also 4:30pm.* **Focus tours:** *Daily 12:30, 1:30pm. Subjects change every 6 weeks.* **TALKS&EVENTS:** *Meet at rear of main entrance.* **Gallery talks:** *Daily 1pm; 45-60min. Free.* **Late View Events:** *Talks, tours, and live music W from 6:30pm; last F of month also fashion shows, debates, and DJs.* **OPEN:** *Th-Tu 10am-5:45pm, W plus last F of month 10am-10pm.* **ADMISSION:** *Free (from Dec. 1, 2001); additional charge for some special exhibitions.*

Founded in 1852 as the Museum of Manufactures to encourage excellence in art and design in the aftermath of the Great Exhibition (in which the British were consternated by apparent French superiority in matters of taste), the original curators were deluged with objects from around the globe. Today, as the largest museum of the decorative (and not so decorative) arts in the world, the V&A rivals the British Museum for the sheer size and diversity of its holdings—as befits an institution dedicated to displaying "the fine and applied arts of all countries, all styles, all periods." Its five *million* square meters of galleries house the best collection of Italian Renaissance sculpture outside Italy, the largest array of Indian art outside India, and a fashion gallery reaching from the 16th century to the latest designer collections. Visitors should be aware that staff shortages can lead to the temporarily closure of less-popular galleries without notice; if you really want to see something in a cordoned-off gallery, insist politely at the main entrance information desk and they'll send someone along to give you a private viewing.

BRITISH GALLERIES. The subject of a £31 million refit, the vast British Galleries should open in November 2001, spread over 3 floors. The curators promise a series of recreated rooms from every period between 1500 and 1900 charting the development of British taste in concert with its growth as an imperial power.

DRESS COLLECTION. The V&A's world-famous costume collection is not meant to be a socially balanced—you'll find no everyday or working-class clothes here—but a dazzling array of the finest *haute couture*. Men's and women's clothes are displayed on identikit white mannequins, with panels describing the major designers of the 20th century. Don't miss the 1960s sunglasses on show in case 5.

EUROPE. The ground-floor European collections, ranging from 4th-century Byzantine tapestry to Alfonse Mucha posters, are staggering in their breadth. If you only see one thing in the museum, make it the **Raphael Gallery,** hung with six massive cartoons (preliminary paintings) for tapestries commissioned by Leo X in 1515 to hang in the Sistine Chapel. The **Sculpture Gallery,** home to Canova's *Three Graces* (1814-17) and voluptuous *Sleeping Nymph* (1820-24), is not to be confused with the **Cast Courts,** a deceptive collection of the world's sculptural greatest hits, from Trajan's Column to Michelangelo's *David*—they're actually startlingly good reproductions.

ASIAN GALLERIES. The V&A's Asian collections are particularly formidable—if the choice of objects occasionally seems to rely on national cliches (Indian temple carvings, Chinese porcelain), it perhaps says more about the way in which the V&A has formed opinion than followed it. The Turkish and Egyptian ceramics of the **Islamic Art** collection are literally overshadowed by the gigantic Ardabil carpet, woven in Iran in 1539 and containing an estimated 30 million knots. In addition to the requisite swords, armor, and paintings, the **Japanese** gallery displays an intriguing array of contemporary ceramic sculpture.

UPPER FLOORS. In contrast to the geographically laid-out ground floor, the upper levels are mostly arranged by material; here you'll find long specialist galleries devoted to everything from musical intruments to stained glass. In the **textile** collection, long cabinets contain pull-out drawers with swatches of thousands of different fabrics. Turnstiles and solid steel doors protect the contents of the the **Jewelry** gallery. Two exceptions to the materially themed galleries are the **Leighton** gallery, with a frescoes by the eponymous Victorian painter, and the large **20th-century** collections. Here, arranged by period and style, are design classics from Salvador Dali's 1936 sofa modelled on Mae West's lips to a pair of 1990s rubber hotpants.

HENRY COLE WING. The 6-level Henry Cole wing is home to the V&A's collection of **British paintings,** including some 350 works by Constable and numerous Turners. Also here is a display of **Rodin** bronzes, donated by the artist in 1914, and the "world's greatest collection" of **miniature portraits,** including Holbein's *Anne of Cleves*. In the library-like **print room,** anyone can ask to see original works from the prodigious collection. The **Frank Lloyd Wright** gallery contains a full-size recreation of the office commissioned by Edgar J. Kauffmann for his Pittsburgh department store in 1935.

MUSEUMS BY NEIGHBORHOOD

THE WEST END

⚑ For the **National Gallery,** see Major Collections, p. 136. **NEIGHBOROOD QUICKFIND: Discover,** p. 2; **Sights,** p. 79; **Food&Drink,** p. 159; **Nightlife,** p. 190; **Entertainment,** p. 209; **Shopping,** p. 226; **Accommodations,** p. 284.

▧ THE COURTAULD INSTITUTE GALLERIES

SEE MAP, p. 330-331

⚑ **Location:** Somerset House, Strand. ☎ 7848 2549.; www.courtauld.ac.uk. **Tube:** Charing Cross or Temple. **Tours:** Tu, Th, and Sa at noon (1hr.); £5.50, concs. £5. **Open:** M-Sa 10am-6pm, Su noon-6pm. **Admission:** £4, UK seniors £3, under 18 free; free to all M 10am-2pm. Joint ticket with Gilbert Collection £7, seniors £5.

In the elegant environs of Somerset House (see p. 87), the Courtauld's small but outstanding collection ranges from early 14th-century Italian religious works to 20th-century abstractions. After the Virgins and elaborately haloed Christs of the early **Renaissance** gallery, on the ground floor, the collection moves upstairs to a fine array of **15th- and 16th-century** works, including Botticelli's *Christ on the Cross* and Peter Brueghel's *Landscape with flight into Egypt*. Scattered around the 1st-floor galleries are plaster casts of famous Greek and Roman sculptures, a reminder of the building's past—many an 18th-century artist spent hours copying such casts in the

Royal Academy's "Antique Academy," (now Room 7). The 2nd floor houses a fabulous array of **Impressionist** and **Post-Impressionist** masterpieces including Manet's *A Bar at the Follies Bergères*, van Gogh's *Self Portrait with Bandaged Ear*, and Cézanne's *The Card Players*. Other artists represented include Monet, Degas, Renoir, and Gauguin. By arranging the pictures chronologically, rather than by artist, the display emphasizes the continuous development of art; Cézanne's late *Winding Road* (1904) is a clear forerunner of Kandinsky's abstract work.

▨ LONDON'S TRANSPORT MUSEUM

⁊1 Location: *Southeast corner of Covent Garden Piazza.* **Contact:** *☎ 7565 7299; www.ltmuseum.co.uk.* **Tube:** *Covent Garden or Charing Cross.* **Open:** *Sa-Th 10am-6pm, F 11am-6pm (last admission 5:15pm).* **Admission:** *£6, students&seniors £4, under 16 free with adult.*

The LTM is one of that rarest of museums—informative *and* fun—and adults too will find themselves engrossed in the history of London's public transportation system. Kids especially will enjoy clambering over the buses, trams, and Tube trains and playing with the many interactive displays, most of which are conveniently located at kiddy-level. Four different Tube simulators allow you to experience how technology has made Underground trains easier and safer to operate, while the "Fast Forward" display explores the future of transport, from sci-fi hovercars to electric miniscooters. The **museum shop** sells hot-ticket "Angel" Tube-logo T-shirts and crop-tops, as well as the famous London Underground posters (£5-10).

NATIONAL PORTRAIT GALLERY

⁊1 Location: *St. Martin's Pl., at the start of Charing Cross Rd.* **Contact:** *☎ 7312 2463; www.npg.org.uk.* **Tube:** *Leicester Sq. or Charing Cross.* **Wheelchairs:** *Enter on Orange St.* **Audioguides:** *Free; £4 suggested donation.* **Lectures:** *Sa-Su 3pm, Tu and Th 1:10pm; free, but popular events require tickets, available from the info desk.* **Evening Events:** *Talks and films Th 9pm; free-£3. Live classical and jazz music every F 6:30pm; free.* **Open:** *M-W and Sa-Su 10am-6pm, Th-F 10am-9pm.* **Admission:** *Free; exhibitions free-£5.*

This artistic *Who's Who* in Britain began in 1856 as "the fulfillment of a patriotic and moral ideal." The museum was recently bolstered by the addition of the sleek Ondaatje Wing in 2000, which greatly increased the space available to displays of patient Englishmen. New facilities include a **Micro Gallery,** with multiple iMacs allowing you to search for pictures by artist or subject and then print out a personalised tour; and a 3rd-floor **restaurant** offering some of the best views in London—although the inflated prices (meals around £15) will limit most visitors to a coffee.

To see the paintings in historical order, take the long escalator from the Ondaatje reception hall to the top-floor Tudor gallery, and work your way around and down to the contemporary works on the ground floor. The size of the collection, however, makes a complete tour of the gallery a long and exhausting prospect, not helped by endless galleries of bewhiskered Victorians. History buffs will enjoy the **second floor,** where the change from the dashing favorites of the Tudor court to the serious gentlemen of the Kit-Kat Club (a group of 18th-century politicians dedicated to crunchy chocolate wafers) illustrates the changing balance between King and Parliament. Among the more interesting of the innumerable Victorian portraits on the **first floor** are Patrick Brontë's cartoonish sketches of his sisters. Also on the first floor, the early 20th-century gallery announces the belated arrival of modern art in Britain with self-portraits by Epstein and Gaudier-Brzeska. The post-war **balcony gallery** illustrates the rise of pop culture with Mike McCartney's snaps of his brother and friends. Contemporary Britain is represented on the **ground floor;** whether Posh Spice and Fatboy Slim will still be on show in 50 years' time is debatable.

OTHER PERMANENT COLLECTIONS

THE GILBERT COLLECTION. In new galleries in the lower level of Somerset House, the Gilbert Collection of Decorative Arts opened in 2000 to widespread acclaim. Make sure to pick up a free audioguide and magnifying glass as you enter—the latter is invaluable for studying the displays of hardstone and micromosaics. Just as intricate are the "Gold Boxes," ornate 18th-century snuff-boxes; pride of place goes to those made for Frederick the Great of Prussia, inlaid with diamonds, emeralds, and rubies. Unrelated to the rest of the collection, the boat resting in the King's Barge House, on the lower level, is a reminder that the Thames once came up to the walls of Somerset House. *(Enter from Somerset House, Strand, or from Victoria Embankment. ☎ 7420 9400;*

www.gilbert-collection.org.uk. Tube: Charing Cross, Embankment, or Temple.1hr. tours held Tu, Th, and Sa 2pm; £5.50, concs. £5, including admission. Open M-Sa 10am-6pm, Su noon-6pm. £4, students & seniors £3, disabled £2, under 18 free; joint admission with Courtauld £7, seniors £3.)

THEATRE MUSEUM. The entrance hall, with a display of giant puppets, is the high point of a rather dry series of displays dealing with the history of London theater and showbiz people. The most interesting galleries are the "Wind in the Willows," which describes what's involved in producing a play; and an impressive selection of opera and ballet costumes, including original Leon Bakst pieces from the *Ballets Russes.* Kids will enjoy the make-up demos (11:30am, 1, 2:30, 3:30, and 4:30pm) and costume workshops (12:30 and 3pm) but there's little else to keep them occupied. *(Russell St. ☎ 7943 4700; www.theatremuseum.org. Tube: Covent Garden. Open Tu-Sa 10am-6pm, last admission 5:30pm. £4.50, students £2.50, over 60 and under 16 free.)*

EXHIBITION SPACES

Museum of London

▨ **Royal Academy,** Burlington House, Piccadilly (☎ 7300 8000; www.royalacademy.org.uk). Tube: Piccadilly Circus or Green Park. Founded in 1768 as both an art school and meeting place for Britain's foremost artists, the Academy rapidly consolidated its position as the mouthpiece of the establishment. Naturally, rebellious young artists scorn it as the deathbed of innovation, only to swoon a few years later at the offer of becoming one of the 80 exalted Academicians who run the place (Gavin Turk was the latest example, in 2001). Exhibitions, whether in the ornate main galleries or the minimalist top-floor Sackler extension, are always of the highest standard. Anyone can submit a piece for inclusion in the **Summer Exhibition** (June-Aug.), held every year since 1769; Academicians pick and choose from the 10,000 artworks submitted yearly. Another annual fixture is the **RA Schools Show** (mid-June), which displays the work of students on Britain's most prestigious art course. Exhibitions for 2002 include **Masters of Edo Style** (Nov. 24, 2001 to Feb. 17, 2002); and **Paris: Capital of the Arts 1900-1968** (Jan. 26-Apr. 12, 2002). Late opening on Fridays brings **free jazz** to the Friends room after 6:30pm, and **candlelit suppers** to the cafe (2 courses £12.75). Open Sa-Th 10am-6pm, F 10am-10pm. Around £7; concs. £1-4 less depending on status.

Antiquities Collection, British Museum

▨ **Institute of Contemporary Arts** (ICA), Nash House, the Mall (☎ 7930 3647; www.ica.org.uk). Tube: Charing Cross or St. James's Park. A grand neoclassical pediment in London's most conservative neighborhood, just down the road from Buckingham Palace, is the last place you'd expect to find Britain's national center for the contemporary arts—but at least it's conveniently located for attacking the establishment. The very cool ICA offers temporary exhibitions of all manner of new art, an avant-garde cinema, a theater, and a

British Museum

groovy late bar that hosts frequent club nights and gigs. Open M noon-11pm, Tu-Sa noon-1am, Su noon-10:30pm; galleries close 7:30pm. "Day membership," giving access to galleries and cafe/bar, £1.50 M-F, £2.50 Sa-Su. Cinema £6.50, before 5pm £4.50; concs. £5.50, £3.50.

EXHIBITION SPACES

The Photographers' Gallery, 5 and 8 Great Newport St. (☎ 7831 1772; www.photo-net.org.uk). Tube: Leicester Sq. London's only public gallery devoted entirely to camerawork (including film and video). Two exhibitions run concurrently at each address, addressing both fine-art and social-documentary photography. The bookshop, at no. 8, has a good selection of photographic monologues. Also frequent talks. Open M-Sa 11am-6pm, Su noon-6pm.

COMMERCIAL GALLERIES & AUCTION HOUSES

Mayfair is the center of London's art market—and despite the genteel aura, it's not all Old Masters and Prince Charles's watercolors. Indeed, **Cork Street,** running parallel to Old Bond St. between Clifford St. and Burlington Gdns., is lined with dozens of **commercial galleries** specializing in British and international contemporary art; nearby roads also have a number of avant-garde galleries. This is the place to pick up on new trends before the museums get in on the act; most exhibitions are of very high quality, and best of all, commercial galleries are always free to browsers.

Annely Juda Fine Art, 23 Dering St. (☎ 7629 7578; www.annelyjudafineart.co.uk). Tube: Bond St. On the 3rd and 4th fl. (use elevator). Specializes in early Russian avant-garde and contemporary Japanese art, though artist list includes names like Anthony Caro and David Hockney. Open M-F 10am-6pm, Sa 10am-1pm. Free.

Anthony D'Offay, 9, 23 (1st fl.), and 24 Dering St. (☎ 7499 4100). Tube: Bond St. One of London's premier galleries for new art, often in non-traditional media. Always thought-provoking. Often runs 2-3 exhibitions concurrently. Open M-F 10am-5:30pm, Sa 10am-1pm. Free.

Bernard Jacobson Gallery, 14a Clifford St.(☎ 7495 8575; www.jacobsongallery.com). Tube: Bond St. or Piccadilly Circus. Small gallery specializing in contemporary British and American art. Open M-F 10am-6pm, Sa 11am-1pm.

Christie's, 8 King St. (☎ 7839 9060; www.christies.com). Tube: Green Park. While not quite as welcoming as Sotheby's (maybe it's the St. James's location), London's other big auctioneer is still open to all, with galleries of soon-to-be-sold furniture, historical documents, and artwork. Open M-F 9am-4:30pm; during sales also Tu to 8pm and Su 2-5pm. Free.

Marlborough Fine Arts, 6 Albermarle St. (☎ 7629 5161; www.marlboroughfineart.com). Tube: Green Park. Spacious gallery representing some of the biggest contemporary artists, including R.B. Kitaj and Frank Auerbach. Open M-F 10am-5:30pm, Sa 10am-12:30pm.

Robert Sandelson, 5 Cork St. (☎ 7439 1001; www.robertsandelson.com). Tube: Bond St. or Picadilly Circus. 2 floors of contemporary works with an experimental edge. Regular artists to show here include Bridget Riley and Micha Klein. Open M-F 10am-6pm, Sa 11am-4pm.

Sotheby's, 34-35 New Bond St. (☎ 7293 5000; www.sothebys.com). Tube: Bond St. Prior to each auction, the items to be sold are displayed for viewing in the many galleries. Anything and everything of value passes through these halls, from postage stamps to Old Masters. Accompanying each sale is a glossy catalog (£5-20); old catalogs sometimes half-price. Open for viewing M-F 9am-4:30pm, and some Su noon-4pm. Free.

White Cube, 44 Duke St. (☎ 7930 5373). Tube: Green Park or Piccadilly Circus. Hidden behind an unassuming residential door; ring the bell and climb 2 flights of stairs to reach this tiny, surreal space with its narrow entrance and walls that hover 1cm above the floor. Regular artists include some of the biggest names in international contemporary art; British artists are usually shown at the White Cube[2] in Hoxton (see p. 153). Open Tu-Sa 10am-6pm. Free.

HOLBORN

⚑ *NEIGHBORHOOD QUICKFIND:* **Discover,** p. 6; **Sights,** p. 88; **Food&Drink,** p. 164; **Nightlife,** p. 194; **Entertainment,** p. 212; **Shopping,** p. 232.

■ **SIR JOHN SOANE'S MUSEUM.** Eccentric architect John Soane let his imagination run free when designing this intriguing museum for his own collection of art and antiquities. His use of perspective in the narrow hallways, coupled with strategically placed mirrors, are delightfully disorienting—the curators have labeled the rooms with compass directions to aid navigation. Idiosyncratic cupolas cast light on a bewildering panoply of ancient carvings; in the Picture Room, multiple Hogarths hang from fold-out panels. Other curiosities include the the massive sarcophagus of Seti I and Soane's own neoclassical proposals for the rebuilding of Parliament. *(13 Lincoln's Inn Fields. Tours Sa 2:30pm, tickets sold from 2pm; £3. Open Tu-Sa 10am-5pm, first Tu of month also 6-9pm. Free; £1 donation requested.)*

DICKENS HOUSE MUSEUM. It was during Dickens's short residence at this house (1837-1839) that he made the transition from successful hack to blockbuster novelist. Only the first-floor drawing room has been restored to its original state; the rest of the four-story house is home to various items looted from places mentioned in his novels, personal correspondance, and the "National Dickens Library," a basement room lined with aging editions of the master's work. *(48 Doughty St. ☎7405 2127; www.dickensmuseum.com. Open M-Sa 10am-5pm; last admission 4:30pm. £4, students&seniors £3, kids £2, families £9.)*

HUNTERIAN MUSEUM. Buried within the grandiose Royal College of Surgeons, this is not one for the squeamish. John Hunter (1728-1793), considered the founder of modern surgery, had a keen interest in the anatomy of all living things and during his lifetime amassed almost 14,000 specimens of flora and fauna. Only 3500 survived the Blitz, but that's more than enough pickled animals than Damien Hirst could ever need. Endless shelves are laden with colorless specimens of human and animal organs, including an array of human foetuses at various stages of development. *(35-43 Lincoln's Inn Fields. ☎7869 6560. Tube: Holborn. Tours W 2pm; free. Open M-F 10am-5pm. Free.)*

CLERKENWELL

🖪 NEIGHBORHOOD QUICKFIND: *Discover, p. 6; Sights, p. 92; Food&Drink, p. 166; Nightlife, p. 194; Entertainment, p. 213; Accommodations, p. 285.*

MUSEUM OF ST. BARTHOLOMEW'S HOSPITAL. Bart's, as the hospital is known, has existed since 1123, when Henry I's courtier Rahere founded both the hospital and nearby St. Bartholomew the Great (see p. 93). The tiny museum tells how

SEE MAP, pp. 334-335

William Harvey discovered the circulation of the blood here in the 17th century. On the Grand Staircase hang two huge Hogarths (the artist was born in nearby Bartholomew Close); for a close-up, you'll have to go on the tour. Also in the hospital grounds is **St. Bartholomew-the-Less**, mostly an 1820s restoration but with a 15th-century tower. *(West Smithfield. ☎7601 8033. Tube: Barbican, Farringdon, or St. Paul's. Tours, including Smithfield area, F 2pm; £4, concs. £3. Open Tu-F 10am-4pm. Free.)*

CITY OF LONDON

🖪 NEIGHBORHOOD QUICKFIND: *Discover, p. 7; Sights, p. 93; Food&Drink, p. 167; Entertainment, p. 213; Accommodations, p. 285.*

🏛 MUSEUM OF LONDON

🖪 Location: *London Wall; enter through the Barbican or from Aldersgate. Wheelchairs use elevator at Aldersgate entrance.* **Contact:** *☎7600 3699; www.museumoflondon.org.uk.* **Tube:** *St. Paul's or Barbican.* **Tours:** *30min. gallery tours Tu 2:30pm; free.* **Events:** *Frequent demonstrations, talks, and guided walks; free-£10.* **Open:** *M-Sa 10am-5:50pm, Su noon-5:50pm; last admission 5:30pm.* **Admission:** *£5, concs. £3, under 17 free; tickets valid 1yr. from date of issue.*

SEE MAP, p. 334-335

Perched in the corner of the Barbican complex (see Sights, p. 97), the Museum of London resembles some latter-day fortress from the outside, entered from Aldersgate via a forbidding black tower in the center of a busy traffic roundabout as impassable as any moat. The engrossing collection traces the history of London from its Roman foundations to the present day, cleverly incorporating bits of architectural history, such as the adjacent ruins of the ancient city walls. The **Roman** galleries are particularly impressive, with a reconstructed dining room built over an original mosaic floor and a first-century oak ladder looks solid enough to climb. Collections from more recent times include the **Cheapside Hoard,** a 17th-century goldsmith's bounty uncovered in 1912. The largest object on display is the **Lord Mayor's State Coach,** built in 1757. Dripping with gold carvings, and with side panels by Cipriani, it's only slightly less magnificent than the Queen's version in Buckingham Palace mews (see Sights, p. 107). New for 2002 is the **World City Gallery,** an expanded and improved look at London from 1789 to 1914.

OTHER PERMANENT COLLECTIONS

BANK OF ENGLAND MUSEUM. Housed within the Bank itself (see p. 98), the museum traces its history from the events leading up to its foundation in 1694 to the present day. Waxworks man a recreation of Sir John Soane's original Stock Office, while a display of banknotes includes a handwritten one from 1697 for the sum of £22—the ease of forgery and the annoyance of exchanging odd sums led to the introduction of standard printed notes soon after. The stack of gold bars displayed in the rotunda turns out to be fake, but an array of genuine bullion lies around it, from Roman ingots to one presented to the Bank by N.M. Rothschild in 1958. *(Bartholomew Ln. ☎ 7601 5545; www.bankofengland.co.uk. Tube: Bank. Open M-F 10am-5pm. Free.)*

GUILDHALL ART GALLERY. A telling example of the Corporation of London's self-importance, this incredibly sumptuous new gallery is devoted to displaying the City's art collection—they seem to have expected millions to flock to see aging portraits of forgotten Lord Mayors. Battle the non-existent crowds to reach the basement galleries, which hold a fine collection of Victorian and Pre-Raphealite art with works by Constable, Leighton, Rossetti, and Millais. *(Guildhall Yard, off Gresham St. ☎ 7332 3700; www.guildhall-art-gallery.org.uk. Open M-Sa 10am-5pm, Su noon-4pm. Free all day F and Sa-Th after 3:30pm; otherwise £2.50, students&seniors £1, kids free.)*

GUILDHALL CLOCK MUSEUM. A tiny museum bearing over 500 years of clocks, watches, chronometers, and sundials, including a watch that belonged to Mary Queen of Scots and the one worn by Sir Edmund Hillary when he climbed Everest. The museum was closed in 2001 for rebuilding and should open in early 2002 with an exhibition on the history of clocks and watches. *(Enter through Guildhall Library on Aldermanbury. ☎ 7606 3030. Tube: St. Paul's, Bank, or Moorgate. Call for hours and admission prices.)*

EXHIBITION SPACES

Barbican Art Galleries (☎ 7638 8891; www.barbican.org.uk), between London Wall, Beech St., Aldersgate, and Moorgate. Tube: Barbican or Moorgate. The Barbican has two important gallery spaces. The **Barbican Gallery** (Level 3) hosts big-name shows, often with a populist twist that recently have veered towards the photographic. Lesser-known international works and craft, often curated as part of complex-wide events, are held in **The Curve,** a semicircular gallery that wraps around the back of the concert hall. Barbican Gallery: Open M-Tu and Th-Sa 10am-6pm, W 10am to 8 or 9pm, Su noon-6pm; £7, concs. £5, under 12 free. The Curve: Open M, W, F-Sa 10am-7:30pm, Tu and Th 10am-6pm, Su noon-7pm; Free.

SOUTH BANK

⚑ For **Tate Modern,** see Major Collections, p. 137. **NEIGHBORHOOD QUICKFIND: Discover,** p. 7; **Sights,** p. 100; **Food&Drink,** p. 168; **Entertainment,** p. 214; **Accommodations,** p. 285.

SEE MAP, p. 336-337

Anchored by the gigantic **Tate Modern** (see p. 137), the South Bank is home to some of London's top public contemporary-art galleries, from established masters at the Hayward to promising newcomers at the Jerwood. In addition to the galleries listed below, there are also frequent exhibitions in the foyer and sculptural displays on the river terrace of the **Royal Festival Hall** (see p. 214). Design aficionados will obviously want to see the Design Museum, but they should not neglect the innovative works on show in the workshops and galleries of **OXO Tower Wharf** (p. 102).

PERMANENT COLLECTIONS

DESIGN MUSEUM. Housed in a classic Art Deco riverfront building, this thoroughly contemporary museum is the brainchild of design maestro Terence Conran. The **Collection Gallery** explores the development of mass-market design with a constantly changing selection of objects; most fun are the dozens of funky chairs that patrons are encouraged to try out. The **Review Gallery** focuses on the future, from innovative current designs to conceptual prototypes, while the **Temporary Gallery** presents exhibitions concentrating on individual designers, movements, and even single products. *(28 Shad Thames, Butler's Wharf. ☎ 7403 6933; www.designmuseum.org. Tube: Tower Hill or London Bridge. Open daily 10am-6pm, last entry 5:15pm. £5.50, students £4.50, ages 5-15 and over 60 £4, family (2 adults + 2 kids) £15.)*

THE CLINK PRISON MUSEUM. Satisfyingly onomatopoeic, the original jail on this site was so notorious that even today English prisoners are said to be "in the clink." At the heart of the Liberty of the Clink (see *the wages of sin*, p. 102), the Clink was the private prison of the Bishop of Winchester from the 13th century until rioters burned it down in 1780. Now a Victorian warehouse occupies the site, but a museum in the basement attempts to chill visitors with tales of medieval punishments, complete with waxwork inmates and torture implements. Just past the museum on Clink St. stand the remains of the Bishops' **Winchester Palace.** *(1 Clink St. Do not pass Go, do not collect £200. Tube: London Bridge. ☎ 7378 1558; www.clink.co.uk. Open daily 10am-6pm. Guided tours £1, on demand. £4, concs. £3, families £9.)*

EXHIBITION SPACES

Hayward Gallery, South Bank Centre (☎ 7960 4242; www.haywardgallery.org.uk). Tube: Waterloo, Embankment, or Temple. Behind the Royal Festival Hall, this stark modernist block, instantly recognizable by its signature roof sculpture, is the South Bank Centre's appropriately high-powered artistic wing. Contemporary art predominates, with occasional forays into the early 20th century. Open Th-M 10am-6pm, Tu-W 10am-8pm. £7, concs. £5, under 12 free.

Bankside Gallery, 48 Hopton St. (☎ 7928 7521). Tube: Blackfriars. Run jointly by the Royal Watercolour Society and the Royal Society of Printmakers, this small gallery mostly displays members' works. The exception is the annual Open Exhibition (mid-July to early Aug.), when anyone can submit watercolors for inclusion. Open Tu 10am-8pm, W-F 10am-5pm, Sa-Su 1-5pm. £3.50, concs. £2; some exhibitions free.

Jerwood Gallery, 171 Union St. (☎ 7654 0171; www.jerwoodspace.co.uk). Tube: Southwark or Borough. Part of the Jerwood Space, primarily a center for performing arts, the Jerwood Gallery gives promising young artists a "leg-up," most famously by hosting the prestigious Jerwood Painting Prize exhibition (Sept.-Oct.). Check what's on before setting out, since they only run six 6-week exhibitions per year. Open M-Sa 10am-6pm, Su noon-6pm. Free.

WESTMINSTER

🔢 *For **Tate Britain,** see Major Collections, p. 136. **NEIGHBORHOOD QUICKFIND: Discover,** p. 8; **Sights,** p. 106; **Food&Drink,** p. 169; **Entertainment,** p. 215; **Shopping,** p. 232; **Accommodations,** p. 286.*

CABINET WAR ROOMS

🔢 *Location: Clive Steps, King Charles St. Contact: ☎ 7930 6961; www.iwm.org.uk/cabinet/index.htm. Tube: Westminster. Open: daily Apr.-Sept. 9:30am-6pm, Oct.-Mar. 10am-6pm; last admission 5:15pm.* SEE MAP, p. 338-339 *Admission: £5.40, students&seniors £3.90, disabled £2.70, under 16 free.*

In 1938, as storm clouds gathered over Europe, work started on converting the coal cellars of the Ministry of Works into the bomb-proof nerve center of a nation at war. For six tense years, Churchill, his cabinet and generals, and dozens of support staff lived and worked in these dank, low-ceilinged quarters; the day after the war ended in 1945 they were abandoned, shut up, and left undisturbed for decades until their reopening in 1981. A Churchillian-voiced audioguide talks you through the 19 rooms on show, supplemented with original recordings and recreations to bring them to life. Highlights include the small room containing the top-secret transatlantic hotline—the official line was that it was Churchill's personal loo, though what the staff thought about their leader's apparent incontinence in times of crisis is unrecorded.

OTHER PERMANENT COLLECTIONS

QUEEN'S GALLERY. The Queen's Gallery will open in spring 2002, displaying works from the richly endowed Royal Collection. Five rooms will also be dedicated to exhibitions of paintings, prints, furniture, decorative arts, and jewelry. *(Buckingham Palace Rd. Tube: St. James's Park. For hours and prices, call Buckingham Palace, ☎ 7839 1377.)*

GUARDS MUSEUM. Right next to Wellington Barracks, this museum charts the history of the bearskin-toting soldiers guarding Buckingham Palace. Kids will jump at the chance to try on a guard's hat, but the rest of the collection of uniforms, medals, and regimental silver will be best appreciated by military enthusiasts. Near the museum looms the bunker-like **Guard's Chapel,** rebuilt after a V1 flying bomb killed and maimed hundreds of guardsmen during the morning service on June 18, 1944. *(Birdcage Walk. ☎ 7930 4466 ext. 3271. Tube: St. James's Park or Victoria. Open daily 10am-4pm; closed for military functions and parades. £2; students, seniors, and under 16 £1.)*

CHELSEA

SEE MAP, p. 346

🚇 TRANSPORTATION: *The only Tube station in Chelsea is Sloane Sq.; from here buses 11, 19, 22, 211, and 319 run down the King's Rd.* **NEIGHBORHOOD QUICKFIND: Discover,** *p. 8;* **Sights,** *p. 108;* **Food&Drink,** *p. 170;* **Entertainment,** *p. 215;* **Shopping,** *p. 232.*

NATIONAL ARMY MUSEUM. Starting somewhat arbitrarily with the battle of Agincourt in 1415, the chronological displays use life-size recreations, videos, dioramas, and masses of memorabilia to bring home the changing but always challenging nature of land warfare through the ages, concentrating particularly on WWI. Naturally, there's a large Waterloo display, complete with the skeleton of Napoleon's favorite horse, Marengo. Overall, the exhibits are engrossing enough to interest the non-enthusiast and entrance aficionados. *(Royal Hospital Rd. ☎ 7730 0717; www.national-army-museum.ac.uk. Open daily 10am-5:30pm. Free.)*

KENSINGTON & EARL'S COURT

SEE MAP, p. 340-341

🚇 *For the* **Victoria & Albert Museum,** *see Major Collections, p. 138.* **NEIGHBORHOOD QUICKFIND: Discover,** *p. 9;* **Sights,** *p. 112;* **Food&Drink,** *p. 172;* **Entertainment,** *p. 216;* **Shopping,** *p. 233;* **Accommodations,** *p. 287.*

South Kensington's Albertopolis (see p. 112) is home to three of London's biggest and best museums: the **Victoria & Albert Museum** (see p. 138), the **Natural History Museum,** and the **Science Museum.** While it's tempting to try and "do" them in a day, to visit more than two is a feat of superhuman stamina. While most visitors take the signposted feeder tunnels from the Tube to the museums, it's really just as quick (and far more pleasant in good weather) to take the overland route—especially since none of the tunnels actually deposit you next to the museum entrances.

🏛 NATURAL HISTORY MUSEUM

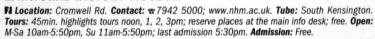

🚇 Location: *Cromwell Rd.* **Contact:** *☎ 7942 5000; www.nhm.ac.uk.* **Tube:** *South Kensington.* **Tours:** *45min. highlights tours noon, 1, 2, 3pm; reserve places at the main info desk; free.* **Open:** *M-Sa 10am-5:50pm, Su 11am-5:50pm; last admission 5:30pm.* **Admission:** *Free.*

Architecturally the most impressive of the South Kensington trio, this cathedral-like Romanesque building has been a favorite with Londoners since 1880. Occupying the main building, the **Life galleries** offer a shrewd insight into the minds of the curators—the relative importance of the displays perfectly mirrors the natural proclivities of school-aged children. In the aftermath of *Jurassic Park*, people expect to see living, breathing creatures and the **Dinosaur** galleries do not disappoint. Indeed, you half expect the alarmingly realistic T-Rex—complete with bad breath—to come thumping down the corridors. The enormous **Human Biology** exhibition keeps adults and children intrigued with an endless succession of interactive and hi-tech displays, not to mention the extremely detailed reproduction gallery. **Mammals** are dealt with more traditionally, with dozens of life-sized models dominated by the massive blue whale overhead. The Kansas board of education would do well to visit the **Origin of Species** display on the first floor, a convincing defence of evolution. Less succesful galleries include **Ecology,** an attempt to foster environmental awareness without any mention of global warming—surely unrelated to BP-Amoco's sponsorship?

If anything, the **Earth Galleries** are even more engrossing, reached via a long escalator that pierces a giant model of the earth on its way to **The Power Within,** an exposition of the awesome forces beneath the earth's surface. A walk-through model of a Japanese supermarket provides a literally earth-shattering recreation of the Kobe earthquake. One same floor, **Restless Surface** explores the gentler action of wind and water in reshaping the world. The story of the Earth itself, from the big bang to the way in which life has shaped the environment, is the subject of **From the Beginning,** on the first floor, while the **Earth's Treasury** presents an enormous array of minerals, from sandstone to diamonds. On the ground floor, **Earth Today and Tomorrow** explores the human impact on the environment.

SCIENCE MUSEUM

Location: Exhibition Rd. **Contact:** ☎ 0870 870 4868; IMAX 0870 870 4771; www.science-museum.org.uk. **Tube:** South Kensington. **IMAX cinema:** Shows every 60-70min., 10:45am-4:25pm M-F. 11am-5:50pm Sa-Su; call for prices and bookings. **Activities:** Daily demonstrations and workshops in the basement galleries and theater. **Open:** Daily 10am-6pm. **Admission:** Free.

Dedicated to the Victorian ideal of Progress (with a capital P), the Science Museum doesn't really live up to its name—the overwhelming focus is on the transformative power of technology rather than the wonders of pure science. Few enough patrons care about the distinction, though—they're too busy ogling the enormous array of planes, trains, and automobiles, with a few rockets thrown in for good measure.

Overall, the museum is an odd mix of state-of-the-art interactive displays, impressive historical artefacts, and some truly mind-numbing galleries (standard weights and measures? light bulbs?) Most impressive is the gigantic **Making of the Modern World** hall, a collection of pioneering contraptions from "Puffing Billy" (1815), the oldest surviving steam locomotive, to the Apollo 10 command module, by way of Crick and Watson's original 1952 wire model of DNA, and hundreds of other genuine artefacts large and small. Nearby, the **Exploration of Space** makes do with mostly replica rockets. The **Flight** gallery on the top floor tells the story of air travel from Victorian attempts at steam-powered flight to Jumbo Jets, helped by a supporting cast of dozens of airplanes and backed up by the hands-on **Flight Lab,** with a literally suck-it-and-see approach to aerodynamics. More fun displays are in the basement: if the **Garden,** for children aged 6 and under, and **Things,** for 7-11s, are of more entertainment than educational value, **Launch Pad** provides an enjoyable introduction to DIY science for adults and teens: communicate across the room using giant sound dishes, try building an arch, or discover the whacky world of angular momentum. The newest part of the museum is the blue-lit **Wellcome Wing,** dominated by the overhead curve of the vast **IMAX** cinema. Here, hi-tech interactive displays explore the workings of the brain in **Who Am I** and let you digitize and distort your head in **Digitopolis.**

EXHIBITION SPACES

Serpentine Gallery, off West Carriage Drive, Kensington Gardens (☎ 7402 6075; www.serpentinegallery.org). Tube: South Kensington, Lancaster Gate, or High St. Kensington. This discrete neoclassical pavilion is the unlikely venue for some of London's top contemporary art shows. Gallery talks most Sa 3pm. Open daily 10am-6pm. Free, £1 donation requested.

MARYLEBONE & REGENT'S PARK

NEIGHBORHOOD QUICKFIND: Discover, p. 11; **Sights,** p. 114; **Entertainment,** p. 217; **Food&Drink,** p. 174; **Accommodations,** p. 292.

THE WALLACE COLLECTION

Location: Hertford House, Manchester Sq. **Contact:** ☎ 7563 9500; www.wallace-colection.com. **Tube:** Bond St. or Marble Arch. 1hr. **Tours:** W and Sa 11:30pm and Su 3pm (1hr.); free. **Talks:** M-F at 1pm and occasional Sa at 11:30pm; free. **Open:** M-Sa 10am-5pm, Su noon-5pm. Talks on are held M-F 1pm. **Free.**

SEE MAP, p. 344-345

Housed in palatial Hertford House, this stunning array of paintings, porcelain, and armor was bequeathed to the nation by the widow of Sir Richard Wallace in 1897. On the **ground floor,** the Front State Room retains its original appearance, with sumptuous furnishings and society portraits. China buffs will swoon at the collection of Sèvres porcelain in the Back State Room next door. Italian and Flemish works dominate the 16th-Century Galleries and Smoking Room, including some fascinating

Royal Academy of Art

National Gallery

British Museum Great Court

relief miniatures and a 1575 pocket sundial. The pride of the ground floor, though, is the four **Armoury Galleries,** crammed with richly decorated weapons and burnished suits of armor. Even Darth Vader would think twice before messing with the mounted Teuton, whose 1475 get-up is one of the only complete surviving war-harnesses. The **1st floor** is home to a world-renowned array of 18th-century French art, announced on the staircase by six large-scale and numerous smaller works by Boucher, including the *Rising* and *Setting of the Sun*, all billowing clouds and trembling pink flesh. More Bouchers occupy the West Room and West Gallery, which also houses Fragonard's *The Swing*, while in the Small Drawing Room is a display of Venice views by Canaletto and Guardi. The **Great Gallery** has a varied collection of 17th-century work, with works by van Dyck, Rembrandt, Rubens, Titian, and Velázquez as well as the collection's most celebrated piece, Frans Hals' *Laughing Cavalier*. In the modern **basement,** the Conservation Gallery has a small display on the manufacture of furniture and armor; you can touch, weigh, and even try on various pieces, including a 16th-century helmet.

OTHER PERMANENT COLLECTIONS

SHERLOCK HOLMES MUSEUM. It takes a master sleuth to deduce that this meticulously recreated home-from-Holmes was never actually the residence of the great detective—only if you shell out 50p for the *Portrait of a Legend* leaflet will you find an admission that Holmes was a fictional character. Or was he? This 19th century house fits so perfectly to Dr. Watson's description of his and Holmes's lodgings, right down to the number of steps on the staircase, that following the premise that, "once you have excluded the impossible, whatever remains, however unlikely, must be the truth," leads you to the inescapable conclusion that this truly was Holmes's home. *(Marked "221b Baker St.;" actually at 239.* ☎ *7935 8866; www.sherlock-holmes.co.uk. Tube: Baker St. Open daily 9:30am-6:30pm. £6, ages 7-16 £4.)*

BLOOMSBURY

SEE MAP, pp. 344-345

🚩 For the **British Museum,** see p. 134. **NEIGHBORHOOD QUICKFIND: Discover,** p. 11; **Sights,** p. 116; **Food&Drink,** p. 175; **Entertainment,** p. 217; **Shopping,** p. 236; **Accommodations,** p. 293.

BRITISH LIBRARY GALLERIES

🚩 For practical information, see **Sights,** p. 117.

Housed within the British Library is an appropriately stunning display of books, manuscripts, and related artefacts from around the world and across the ages. The relatively small size of the exhibition is an advantage, since all the works on display are worthy of attention. Displays are arranged by theme: **Historical documents** include three original copies of the Magna Carta, while scientific collections are illustrated by pages from Leonardo da Vinci's notebook. If the **literature** section is as strong as you'd expect, with a 1420 copy of the *Canterbury Tales*, rival early editions of *Hamlet*, and James Joyce's handwritten draft of *Finnegan's Wake*, the **music collection** is more of a surprise. In addition to handwritten scores from the likes of Mozart and Beethoven, there's a whole cabinet devoted to the Beatles, with the original scrawled lyrics to *I want to hold your hand*. The **Bible display** contains the oldest works in the library, including the 2nd-century *Unknown Gospel*, while the **Sacred Texts** and **Illuminated Manuscripts** cabinets also have their share of richly decorated parchment, including the famous Hebrew *Golden Haggadah* (1320) and the illustrated *Luttrell Psalter*. In the **Printing** display, the *Million Charms of Empress Shotoku* is not an early erotic novel, but a scroll of Buddhist charms printed in 764. By comparison, the first European printed book, the *Gutenberg Bible*, was not produced until 1454. To the rear of the exhibition, the **Turning the Page** computer gallery lets you get a closer look at some of the more famous works. Downstairs, the **Workshop of Sounds and Images** is aimed at a younger audience, with interactive displays charting the history of record-making, from parchment to TV.

Cabinet War Rooms

OTHER PERMANENT COLLECTIONS

PERCIVAL DAVID FOUNDATION OF CHINESE ART.
Next door to Virginia Woolfe's old haunt, this Georgian townhouse rather bullishly touts itself as being home to the finest collection of china outside China, with 1700 ceramic items from the 10th to the 18th century. Temporary exhibitions, often using pieces from the collection to illustrate trends and themes in Chinese art, occupy the ground floor; the 1st floor houses rare Ru, Guan, Sun, Ding, and Celadon wares; and the 2nd floor is a treasure trove of blue-and-white Ming and figuratively painted Qing work. *(53 Gordon Sq. ☎ 7387 3909. Tube: Euston Sq., Euston, or Russell Sq. Open M-F 10:30am-5pm. Free.)*

British Library, Bloomsbury

POLLOCK'S TOY MUSEUM.
A maze of tiny 18th- and 19th-century rooms and passageways congested with antique playthings. Highlights include Eric, the oldest known teddy bear ("born" 1905) and "Saucy Frauleins," who expose their themselves at the tug of a string. One room is devoted to toy theaters, of which the late Mr. Pollock was the leading producer. None of the toys on display can be accessed,

Imperial War Museum

which limits the museum's appeal for children; however, young'uns not totally dependent on computers will enjoy the old-fashioned toy shop by the entrance, with traditional playthings from 10p marbles to £50 hobbyhorses. *(1 Scala St. ☎ 7636 3452; www.pollocks.cwc.net. Tube: Goodge St. Open M-Sa 10am-5pm. £3, under 18 £1.50.)*

EXHIBITION SPACES

Brunei Gallery, Thorhaugh St. (☎ 7898 4915; www.soas.ac.uk/gallery). Tube: Russell Sq. On the campus of the School of Oriental and African Studies, this beautiful space is devoted to well-curated exhibitions of African and Asian art and culture. As its patron is the world's 3rd richest man, the Sultan of Brunei, you'd expect nothing less. Open M-F 10:30am-5pm. Free.

October Gallery, Lundonia House, 24 Old Gloucester St. (☎ 7242 7367; www.theoctobergallery.com). Tube: Russell Sq. A 2-room venue promoting contemporary and traditional art from around the world. At lunchtimes, one room becomes a popular cafe; in better weather art and tables also mix in the small rear garden. Open Tu-Sa 12:30-5:30pm; food to 2:30pm. Free.

NORTH LONDON

🔢 *NEIGHBORHOOD QUICKFIND: **Discover,** p. 12; **Museums&Galleries,** p. 150; **Food&Drink,** p. 176; **Nightlife,** p. 196; **Entertainment,** p. 218; **Shopping,** p. 237; **Accommodations,** p. 298.*

🖼 **THE IVEAGH BEQUEST.** A stout collection bequeathed to the nation by Edward Guinness, Earl of Iveagh, the Kenwood setting (see p. 121) and the magnificent pictures make it one of the finest small galleries in London. Highlights include works by Rembrandt, Vermeer, Turner, and Botticelli. More in keeping with the feel of the house are numerous Georgian society portraits by Reynolds, Gainsborough, and Romney, including multiple renditions of Nelson's paramour, Lady Hamilton. A portrait of the original owner of Kenwood, the Earl of Mansfield, hangs in the beautifully restored library, complete with gilded friezes, frescoed ceiling, and false books. *(Kenwood House, Highgate (Zone 3); for directions, see p. 121. Audioguide £3.50, students&seniors £2.60, kids £1.75; 1hr. tours £3.50/£2.50/£1.50. Open Apr.-Sept. Sa-Tu and Th 10am-6pm, W and F 10:30am-6pm; Oct. closes 5pm; Nov.-Mar. closes 4pm. Free.)*

🖼 **ROYAL AIR FORCE MUSEUM.** This enormous museum contains more military hardware than most small countries. Exhibitions detail every aspect of life for those fighting in and against the RAF, but the real stars are the planes—scores of 'em, from wood-and-cloth biplanes of 1914 to 1980s Harriers. As for the Finest Hour "3-D audio-visual extravaganza," never before in the history of over-hyped attractions have so many waited so long for so little—much more fun is the bumpy flight simulator in the main building. *(Grahame Park Way. ☎ 8205 2266; www.rafmuseum.org.uk/. From Tube: Colindale (Zone 4), turn left and walk about 10min. Open daily 10am-6pm; last admission 5:30pm. £7.50, students £4.90, seniors and under 16 free; half-price after 4:30pm.)*

FREUD MUSEUM. The comfortable home in which Sigmund Freud spent the last year of his life, after fleeing Nazi persecution in Vienna in 1938, could be that of any successful doctor of the period. The central-European furnishings, the infamous couch, and his collection of "old and dirty gods" sit as they did during his life, only now labelled with explanations of each item's psychoanalytic significance. Upstairs hangs Dalí's portrait of Freud and temporary exhibitions of art. The Anna Freud room is dedicated to his daughter, also a psychoanalyst, who lived and practiced in the house until her death in 1979. A keen believer in the therapeutic power of manual work, she would knit and weave clothes for friends while listening to patients—perhaps including the original Freudian slip? *(20 Maresfield Gdns. ☎ 7435 2002; www.freud.org.uk. Tube: Hampstead or Finchley Rd., or Rail: Finchley Rd. & Frognal. Open W-Su noon-5pm; £4, concs. £2, under 12 free. Children over 12 can blame it on their parents.)*

ESTORICK COLLECTION. The Futurists were a revolutionary artistic movement whose aims included destroying old buildings, abolishing museums, celebrating the noise of machinery, and reinventing food (recipes included sausage cooked in black coffee and perfume). Ninety years after their heyday, these bad boys of Italian art are tastefully displayed in an 18th-century Georgian mansion on a peaceful leafy square, filled with the smell of food from the cafe. *(39a Canonbury Sq. ☎ 7704 9522; www.estorickcollection.com. Tube: Highbury & Islington (Zone 2); walk down Canonbury Rd. from the station. Open W-Sa 11am-6pm, Su noon-5pm. £3.50, students&seniors £2.50, under 16 free.)*

THE JEWISH MUSEUM. Actually two complementary museums. The **Jewish Museum, Camden** holds a collection of objects and artwork celebrating the history and achievements of Jews in Britain. Upstairs is devoted to artefacts, with a display of table settings for each Jewish festival; pride of place goes to a magnificent 16th-century Venetian synagogue ark. *(129-131 Albert St. ☎ 7284 1997. Tube: Camden Town (Zone 2). Open M-Th 10am-4pm, Su 10am-5pm; closed Su in Aug. and during Jewish holidays. £3.50, seniors £2.50, students&kids £1.50, family £8.)* The much smaller **Jewish Museum, Finchley** focuses on 19th- and early 20th-century life in London's East End. The small Holocaust Education gallery is particularly moving, telling the story of London-born Auschwitz survivor Leon Greenman; he occasionally pops in to answer questions. *(80 East End Rd. ☎ 8349 1143. Tube: Finchley Central (Zone 4). Take the "Regent's Park Rd." exit from the Tube, turn left into Station Rd., then right into Manor View, which runs into East End Rd. by the museum; 10min. Open M-Th 10:30am-5pm, Su 10:30am-4:30pm; closed Su in Aug. and Jewish holidays. £2, students&seniors £1, kids free.)*

EXHIBITION SPACES

Saatchi Gallery, 98a Boundary Rd. (☎ 7624 8299). From St. John's Wood Tube, head down Grove End Rd., turn right into Abbey Rd.; Boundary Rd. is about a 12min. walk up on the left. A changing array of works from Charles Saatchi's vast collection of contemporary British art. The only permanent piece on display is Richard Wilson's 1987 installation *20:50*, a whole room filled with 2.5ft. of used oil, pierced by a lone walkway. The oil surface is so smooth and reflective, only the overpowering smell convinces you that there's anything there at all. Open Sept.-July Th-Su noon-6pm. £5, concs. £3, under 12 free.

Crafts Council, 44a Pentonville Rd (☎ 7278 7700; www.craftscouncil.org.uk). Fantastic exhibitions on everything from traditional architecture to *haute couture* via many wierd and wacky detours. Reference area upstairs includes a library and photo database. Tiny store sells pricey but beautiful objects—how about a red string necklace with 3 knots for £140? Open Tu-Sa 11am-6pm, Su 2-6pm. Free.

SOUTH LONDON

◪ NEIGHBORHOOD QUICKFIND: Discover, *p. 13;* **Sights,** *p. 125;* **Food&Drink,** *p. 180;* **Nightlife,** *p. 198;* **Entertainment,** *p. 220;* **Shopping,** *p. 238;* **Accommodations,** *p. 299.*

◪ IMPERIAL WAR MUSEUM

◪ Location: *Lambeth Rd., Lambeth.* **Contact:** *☎ 7416 5320, recorded info 0900 160 0140; www.iwm.org.uk.* **Tube:** *Lambeth North or Elephant & Castle.* **Open:** *Daily 10am-6pm.* **Admission:** *£6.50, students £5.50, under 16 & over 60 free; free for all after 4:30pm.*

A pair of massive 15-inch naval guns guard the entrance to the Imperial War Museum; formerly the infamous lunatic asylum known as Bedlam, today it illustrates another type of human madness. Although the array of hardware on show in the **Large Exhibits Hall**—including the tank used by Montgomery at El Alamein—might suggest otherwise, the museum is commendably un-jongiostic. In the basement, the the **Trench Experience** recreates the conditions of WWI right down to the sweet stench, while life on the home front in WWII is the subject of the **Blitz Experience.** On the first floor, the much-touted **Secret War** reveals little about intelligence operations—declassification hasn't proceeded much past WWII. Similarly, little insight into the psychology of war is revealed by the second-floor **art collection,** mostly the work of government war artists. The largest and most impressive display is not directly connected to war: the **Holocaust Exhibition,** spread over two floors, graphically documents Nazi atrocities; a scale model of Auschwitz is accompanied by piped testimony from survivors, while a moving displays tells how parents were gulled into sending their disabled children to "hospitals" where they served as guinea pigs. *(Not recommended for children under 14.)*

◪ DULWICH PICTURE GALLERY

◪ Location: *Gallery Rd., Dulwich.* **Contact:** *☎ 8693 5254; www.dulwichpicturegalery.org.uk.* **Rail:** *North Dulwich or West Dulwich plus well-signed 10min. walk, or* **Tube:** *Brixton and bus P4 to the door.* **Open:** *Tu-F 10am-5pm, Sa-Su 11am-5pm.* **Tours:** *Sa-Su 3pm; free.* **Admission:** *£4, seniors £3, students&kids free; free for everyone F.*

Housing a marvelous array of Old Masters, England's first public gallery is the unlikely legacy of Polish misfortune: in 1790, the King of Poland decided to invest in a national art collection and commissioned two London dealers to buy up the best pictures available. Unfortunately for the dealers (not to mention the Poles), the partition of Poland in 1795 left them with a full-blown, unpaid-for collection in hand; incredibly, rather than selling the works they decided to put them on public display. Sir John Soane agreed to design the building for free, and his quirky style is in full evidence in the domed mausoleum where the benefactors are buried. Elsewhere, the high-ceilinged halls are home to a stunning collection of mostly 17th and 18th-century work. Rubens and van Dyck feature most prominently while other Dutch masterpieces include Rembrandt's *Portrait of a Young Man*, believed to be his son. Italy is represented by Tiepolo, Ricci, and Veronese, France by Poussin and Watteau, with Gainsborough, Reynolds, and Hogarth making up the English section.

OTHER PERMANENT COLLECTIONS

FLORENCE NIGHTINGALE MUSEUM. In the grounds of St. Thomas's Hospital, where Florence Nightingale's first school of nursing opened in 1860. Apparently her unimaginative parents decided to name their children after their place of birth: Florence got lucky, but her sister Parthenope was not so fortunate. The museum goes out of its way to show that nursing was just one of Florence's many talents: she also reformed the army, designed hospitals, and lobbied for the foundation of a public health service in India. *(St. Thomas's Hospital, 2 Lambeth Palace Rd. ☎ 7620 0374; www.florence-nightingale.co.uk. Tube: Waterloo or Westminster. Open M-F 10am-5pm, Sa-Su 11:30am-4:30pm; last entry 1hr. before closing. £4.80, concs. £3.60, family (2 adults + 2 kids) £10.)*

HORNIMAN MUSEUM & GARDENS. This eccentric museum is the legacy of 19th-century tea merchant Frederick Horniman. A flood of lottery money has brought modernisation of the museum and collections without affecting their scope. The new **African Worlds** gallery offers a vast selection of artifacts from past and present African cultures: 16th-century Benin bronzes feature alongside the world's largest *ljele* (Nigerian masquerade costume). The **Natural History** collection is more Victorian, with stuffed animals and skeletons behind glass cases, while the conservation-minded **Living Worlds** aquarium has a small but colorful collection of fish in waterfall tanks cascading down the stairs. Late 2001 sees the opening of a **Music Gallery.** The neighboring hillside **garden** holds a tiny domestic zoo and offers brilliant views of St. Paul's in the distance. *(100 London Rd. ☎8699 1872; www.horniman.ac.uk. Rail: Forest Hill, or #P4 bus from Tube: Brixton. Open M-Sa 10:30am-5:30pm, Su 2-5:30pm. Free.)*

MUSEUM OF GARDEN HISTORY. Housed in a former church, on a site once cultivated by the Tradescents, intrepid 17th-century horticulturalists who scoured the globe for new plants to bring home and cultivate. The Tradescents lie in what is now the museum garden, surrounded by labeled offshoots of their discoveries; also here is the tomb of Captain William Bligh, who after surviving the famous mutiny on the Bounty in 1789 apparently went on to inspire another as governor of New South Wales in 1808. *(Lambeth Palace Rd., at the end of Lambeth Bridge. Tube: Westminster or Lambeth North. ☎7401 8865. Open daily 10:30am-5pm. "Voluntary" charge £2.50, concs. £2.)*

EAST LONDON

🔢 **NEIGHBORHOOD QUICKFIND: Discover,** p. 14; **Sights,** p. 126; **Food&Drink,** p. 180; **Nightlife,** p. 199; **Entertainment,** p. 221; **Shopping,** p. 239.

🏛 NATIONAL MARITIME MUSEUM

🔢 **Location:** Trafalgar Rd., between the Royal Naval College and Greenwich Park. **Contact:** ☎8858 4422; www.nmm.ac.uk. **DLR:** Cutty Sark. **Open:** Daily June to early Sept. 10am-6pm, early Sept. to May 10am-5pm; last entry 30min. before close. **Admission:** £7.50, after 4:30pm £6; students £6, £4.80; seniors&under 16 free. Combined ticket with Queen's House and Royal Observatory £10.50, students £8.40, seniors&under 16 free. For Greenwich Passport ticket, see p. 128.

The NMM's exceptionally broad-ranging displays cover almost every aspect of seafaring history. Child-friendliness is achieved by designing the galleries to resemble a nautical theme park: the **Explorers** section recreates an Antarctic ice-cave and the foredeck of a ship, while in **Rank & Style** naval uniforms are displayed in separate wardrobes. But be careful—once your kid gets into the **All Hands** interactive gallery, complete with steamship and canon-aiming simulators, you'll find it hard to get them out again. Under the glass canopy, the **Future of the Sea** is a stark warning of how man's activities are affecting the maritime environment. Other displays include the

P&O-sponsored **Passengers' Gallery,** a rather one-sided look at passenger liners, and a string of British-oriented rooms, such as **Trade & Empire,** charting the economic benefits to Britain of subjugating 1/4 of the world's population, and **Maritime London.** Pride of the naval displays, naturally, is the **Nelson Room,** which tells the stirring tale of one 12-year-old midshipman's rise through the ranks. Budding Emma Hamiltons will break down at the sight of his blood-stained Trafalgar uniform.

QUEEN'S HOUSE. Next to the National Maritime Museum, the **Queen's House** (see also Sights, p. 129) is now the setting for the Museum's collection of naval portraits, wittily entitled **A Sea of Faces.** Only naval enthusiasts are likely to get excited by the array of forgotten admirals and sea captains, but a visit is worthwhile for the interior of Inigo Jones' marvelous building. *(Details as for NMM. £1, seniors & under 16 free.)*

OTHER PERMANENT COLLECTIONS

MUSEUM OF CHILDHOOD. In the original V&A building (transferred from Kesnington to Bethnal Green in the 1860s), this museum is absurdly popular with families. In order to make the museum more palatable to the thousands of children that infest it daily, the displays of historic toys are interspersed with play areas where kids can try out a rocking horse, put on their own puppet show, play games, and generally exhaust their parents. Upstairs, the galleries tracking childhood through the ages puzzle boys and girls alike with an invitation to try out a replica 15th-century birthing stool. *(Cambridge Heath Rd. ☎8980 2415; www.museumofchildhood.org.uk. Tube: Bethnal Green. Open Sa-Th 10am-5:50pm. Free.)*

GEFFRYE MUSEUM. Set in an elegant terrace of former almshouses founded by 17th-century Lord Mayor Sir Robert Geffrye, this "Museum of English Domestic Interiors" traces the history of interior design through a series of meticulously recreated living rooms. It focuses on the high end of the market, from an Elizabethan noble's parlour to a 1990s yuppie-style loft studio complete with an IKEA kitchen. The 20th-century displays occupy a space-age extension at the rear, which also houses excellent temporary exhibits as well as a Design Centre where local East End designers display their wares. *(Kingsland Rd. ☎7739 9893; www.geffrye-museum.org.uk. Tube: Old St. then bus #243 or 10min. walk along Old St. and left into Kingsland Rd., or Tube: Liverpool St. and bus #149 or 242. Open Tu-Sa 10am-5pm, Su noon-5pm. Free.)*

MAJOR EXHIBITION SPACES

Whitechapel Art Gallery, Whitechapel High St. (☎7377 7888; www.whitechapel.org). Tube: Aldgate East. Long the sole artistic beacon in a culturally and materially impoverished area, now at the forefront of the East End's buzzing art scene. Excellent, often controversial shows of contemporary art on two floors. Open Tu and Th-Su 11am-5pm, W 11am-8pm. Free.

Lux Gallery, 2-4 Hoxton Sq. (☎7684 2785; www.lux.org.uk). Part of the trailblazing Lux complex (see Entertainment, p. 221), Hoxton's only public exhibition space provides relief from the navel-gazing antics of many local galleries with a broad range of international contemporary art, often related to current film screenings. Open Tu-Su noon-7pm. Free.

COMMERCIAL GALLERIES

East London is home to the largest concentration of artists in Europe, centered around the Hoxton and Shoreditch, with outposts in Bethnal Green and Hackney. Dozens of small commercial galleries and one-off shows dot the streets; hard to find and with erratic opening hours, it's best to check what's on and arm yourself with a good map before heading out. The *East London Gallery Guide* and the arty *Shoreditch Map*, available free from most galleries in the area, will help you find what you're looking for, and maybe a few things you weren't.

White Cube², 48 Hoxton Sq. (☎7930 5373; www.whitecube.com). Tube: Old St. At the epicenter of the Hoxton scene, this single-roomed gallery is a much larger sibling to the St. James's original (see p. 142). Jay Jopling has shown almost every major current British artist here, from Anthony Gormley to Tracey Emin. Open Tu-Sa 10am-6pm. Free.

Victoria Miro, 16 Wharf Rd. (☎7336 8109; www.victoria-miro.com). Tube: Old St. Walk north up City Rd. towards Angel, then turn right after the McDonald's; ring the bell for entry. Cavernous former warehouseshowing broad-based exhibitions of top contemporary artists; gallery list includes Chris Ofili, Peter Doig, and Jake & Dinos Chapman. Open Sept.-July Tu-Sa 10am-6pm, Aug. Tu-W and F-Sa noon-6pm. Free.

Food & Drink

Forget stale stereotypes about British food: in terms of quality and choice, London's restaurants offer a gastronomic experience as diverse, stylish, and satisying as you'll find anywhere on the planet—until you see the bill. For it's a sad truth that while the media scream about food being the new rock'n'roll, and chefs and restaurateurs have become household names, pound-for-pound restaurants in London charge what would be exhorbitant prices across the Atlantic or the channel. Any restaurant charging under £10 for a main course is regarded as "cheap"; add drinks and service and you're nudging £15.

TIPS FOR EATING CHEAPLY

That said, it *is* possible to eat cheaply—and eat well—in London. The trick, as always, is knowing where and (just as importantly) when to eat. If your hostel, B&B, or hotel includes a **"Full English Breakfast"** in its prices, you're half-way there—this cholesterol-laden feast of fried meat, eggs, and bread will dissuade you from looking at anything more than a sandwich for lunch. If you're looking to spend that little bit more, lunchtime and early-evening special offers make it possible to dine in style and stay on budget.

SANDWICHES. The budgeteers daytime fallback, and in many parts of central London sandwiches are the only affordable option. Chains such as Prêt-à-Manger and EAT (see p. 158) have brought high-quality prepacked sandwiches to the masses, while hundreds of snack bars offer made-to-order "sarnies" for under £2. Note that, in most cases, if you ask for a ham sandwich, you'll get a slice of ham between two pieces of buttered bread: no salad, no pickle, no mayo, and certainly not "overstuffed" to American specifications.

PUB GRUB. If you want a proper sit down meal without paying through the earth, pubs offer a glimmer of hope. Far more than mere drinking haunts, most pubs offer a range of hot and cold fare during the day and occasionally in the evenings; for around £6 you can lunch on traditional English specials like bangers'n'mash (sausage and mashed potato) or steak and kidney pie. However, "pub grub" may be cheap, but it's not always cheerful—meals may be left under hot lamps for hours or microwaved from frozen. Look for a pub where locals are eating, and keep away from the tourist trail.

EXOTIC TASTES. Many of the best budget meals are found in the amazing variety of **ethnic restaurants. Indian** food is recognised as being Britain's unofficial national cuisine—Prince Charles, when asked to describe the archetypal British meal, showed he shared popular taste and chose the classic Anglo-Indian hybrid chicken tikka masala. **Turkish** restaurants are also experts at cooking up low-budget feasts, while some of the cheapest and tastiest dinners in town are **Chinese.** In the last few years, **Japanese** cuisine has shed its upmarket image with a proliferation of noodle bars offering giant bowls of *ramen* for £5-6. For the best and cheapest ethnic food, head to the source: Whitechapel for Bengali baltis, Islington for Turkish *meze*, Marylebone for Lebanese *shwarma*, and Soho for Cantonese *dim sum*.

GROCERIES AND SUPERMARKETS. Most hostels and student halls have kitchen facilities for residents, and cooking for yourself is almost always cheaper than eating out. The cheapest places to get the ingredients for your own meal in London are often the local markets; for listings of street markets, see Shopping, p. 224. If you like all your food under one roof, London's largest supermarket chains are **Tesco, Safeway,** and **Sainsbury's. Asda, Kwik-Save,** and **Somerfield** are "budget" supermarkets, with a pile-it-high, sell-em-cheap ethos, while **Waitrose** and **Marks & Spencer** (or "Marks & Sparks") are more upmarket and a good source of fancier ingredients. For night owls, the branches of **Hart's** stay open 24 hours. And if you're willing to splurge, the food halls of **Harrods, Harvey Nichols, Selfridges,** and **Fortnum and Mason's** are attractions in their own right.

RESTAURANTS BY TYPE

AFTERNOON TEA
Browns	Mayfair
Fortnum & Mason	Mayfair
▨ The Lanesborough	Knightsbridge
The Orangery	Kensington
The Ritz	Mayfair
▨ St. Martin's Lane Hotel	Soho
Savoy	Trafalgar Sq. & Strand

AMERICAN & CANADIAN
Arkansas Cafe	Whitechapel
Chelsea Bun Diner	Chelsea
▨ Grand Central	Hoxton/Shoreditch
Maple Leaf	Covent Garden
Tinseltown 24hr. Diner	Clerkenwell

BREAKFAST
Al's Cafe Bar	Clerkenwell
Al Fresco	Westminster
Chelsea Bun Diner	Chelsea
Fox & Anchor	Clerkenwell
▨ Grand Central	Hoxton/Shoreditch
Poîlane	Belgravia
Tinseltown 24hr. Diner	Clerkenwell

CAFES
Al's Cafe Bar	Clerkenwell
Bar Italia	Soho
Bluebird	Chelsea
The Blue Room	Soho
Books for Cooks	Notting Hill
Cafe 1001	Whitechapel

CAFES (CONT.)
Cafe Bar & Juice Bar	Brixton
Cafe in the Crypt	Covent Garden
Cafe in the Park	Holborn
Cafe Society	Mayfair
▨ Candid Arts Trust Cafe	Islington
Gloriette	Knightsbridge
Monmouth Coffee House	Covent Garden
Old Compton Cafe	Soho
Pâtisserie Valerie	Soho
Raison d'Être	Kensington
Riverside Studios Cafe	Hammersmith
The Tea & Coffee Plant	Notting Hill
▨ The Troubadour	Earl's Court

CHINESE
C.T.J.	Bloomsbury
Harbour City	Chinatown (Soho)
▨ Jenny Lo's Teahouse	Westminster
▨ Mr Kong	Chinatown (Soho)
▨ New Culture Revolution	
	Chelsea, Camden Town
Oriental Canteen	Kensington
▨ Royal China	Bayswater
Wong Kei	Chinatown (Soho)

DESSERT
Beverly Hills Bakery	Knightsbridge
▨ la Bottega del Gelato	Bayswater
Gloriette	Knightsbridge
Lisboa Patisserie	Notting Hill

DESSERT
Marine Ices — Camden Town
Pâtisserie Valerie — Soho

EASTERN EUROPEAN
L'Autre (Polish) — Mayfair
Na Zdrowie (Polish) — Holborn
Patio (Polish) — Patio
Trojka (Russian) — Camden Town
 Wódka (Polish) — Kensington

ENGLISH
See also Pubs, Gastropubs, and Modern British
Bibo Cibo — Covent Garden
 Bleeding Heart Tavern — Holborn
 George's Portobello Fish Bar — Notting Hill
Goddard's Pie & Mash — Greenwich
 St. John — Clerkenwell
 Stockpot — Chelsea, Knightsbridge

FOOD SHOPS
Green's — Westminster
Monmouth Coffee House — Covent Garden
Neal's Yard Bakery & Tea Room — Covent Garden
 Neal's Yard Dairy — Covent Garden
Poilâne — Belgravia
Sundance — Chelsea
The Tea & Coffee Plant — Notting Hill

FRENCH
Le Crêperie de Hampstead — Hampstead
La Madeleine — Oxford & Regent Sts.
Le Mercurey — Islington
Pâtisserie Valerie — Soho
Raison d'Être — Kensington
 Tartuf — Islington

GAY AND LESBIAN
Balans — Kensington, Soho
King William IV — Hampstead
Old Compton Cafe — Soho
SW9 — Brixton

GASTROPUBS
Duke of Cambridge — Islington
The Eagle — Clerkenwell
Hoxton Sq. Bar & Kitchen — Hoxton/Shoreditch

INDIAN
Aladin — Whitechapel
 Cafe Spice Namaste — City
 Diwana Bhel Poori House — Bloomsbury
Masala Zone — Oxford & Regent Sts.
Nazrul — Whitechapel

INTERNATIONAL
 Giraffe — Marylebone, Hampstead, Islington
World Food Cafe — Covent Garden

ITALIAN
See also Pizza
Cantina del Ponte — South Bank
Carluccio's — Oxford & Regent Sts.
 Da Beppe — Bloomsbury
Marine Ices — Camden Town

JAPANESE
 Itsu — Soho
Noto — City
Noto Sushi — North
Wagamama — Chain
Yo! Sushi — Chain

JEWISH
Blooms — Golders Green
Brick Lane Beigel Bakery — Whitechapel
 Carmelli Bakery — Golders Green
Knosherie — Holborn
Reubens — Marylebone
Solly — Golders Green

JUICES
The Blue Room — Soho
Cafe Bar & Juice Bar — Brixton
Fluid — Notting Hill
Ranoush Juice — Marylebone
Squeeze — Kensington

LATE NIGHT
Bar Italia — Soho
Brick Lane Beigel Bakery — East
Knosherie — Holborn
Old Compton Cafe — Soho
Tinseltown 24hr. Diner — Clerkenwell

LATIN AMERICAN
L'Autre (Mexican) — Mayfair
Cubana (Cuban) — South Bank

MIDDLE EASTERN
Alounak Kebab (Persian) — Bayswater
 Gallipoli (Turkish) — Islington
Gem (Kurdish) — Islington
Manzara (Turkish) — Notting Hill
 Mô (Moroccan) — Oxford & Regent Sts.
 Patogh (Persian) — Marylebone
Ranoush Juice (Lebanese) — Marylebone
Tas (Turkish) — South Bank

MODERN BRITISH
Bluebird — Chelsea
Cafe on Level 7 — South Bank
People's Palace — South Bank
Tiles — Westminster

ORGANIC
Alara Wholefoods — Bloomsbury
Duke of Cambridge — Islington
Green's — Chelsea
Quiet Revolution — Clerkenwell
Sundance — Chelsea

PIZZA
ASK — Chain
Bar Room Bar — Hampstead
ECCo — Westminster, Bloomsbury
Gourmet Pizza Co. — South Bank
Pizza Express — Chain
Strada — Oxford & Regent Sts.
Zizzi — Marylebone

PUBS		SNACKS & SANDWICHES (CONT.)	
See also Gastropubs		The Grain Shop	Notting Hill
Black Friar	City	Green's	Westminster
Blakes	Camden Town	Manzara	Notting Hill
Cittie of Yorke	Holborn	Prêt-à-Manger	Chain
Dog & Duck	Soho	Raison d'Être	Kensington
The Dove	Hammersmith	Woolley's	Holborn
The Flask	Highgate		
Fox & Anchor	Clerkenwell	**SOUTHEAST ASIAN**	
Freedom Brewing Co.	Covent Garden	🗷 busaba eathai (Thai)	Soho
The Grapes	Docklands	Yelo (Thai)	Hoxton/Shoreditch
Grouse & Claret	Belgravia	Makan	Notting Hill
Jeremy Bentham	Bloomsbury	Mandalay (Burmese)	Marylebone
King's Head & Eight Bells	Chelsea	Nusa Dua (Indonesian)	Soho
King William IV	Hampstead		
The Lamb	Bloomsbury	**SPANISH/PORTUGUESE**	
Lamb and Flag	Covent Garden	Goya	Westminster
Maple Leaf	Covent Garden	Lisboa Patisserie	Notting Hill
Princess Louise	Holborn	Navarros	Bloomsbury
Prospect of Whitby	Docklands		
Punch Tavern	Holborn	**VEGETARIAN**	
Red Lion	Westminster	Bah Humbug	Brixton
Scarsdale	Kensington	Cafe Emm	Soho
Sherlock Holmes	Trafalgar Sq. & Strand	C.T.J.	Bloomsbury
Simpson's	City	Futures	City
T.S. Queen Mary	Trafalgar Sq. & Strand	The Gate	Hammersmith
Ye Grapes	Mayfair	The Grain Shop	Notting Hill
🗷 Ye Olde Cheshire Cheese	Holborn	Green's	Westminster
🗷 Ye Olde Mitre Tavern	Holborn	Neal's Yard Bakery & Tea Room	
Yo! Below	Soho		Covent Garden
		Quiet Revolution	Clerkenwell
SNACKS & SANDWICHES		The Place Below	City
See also Cafes		World Food Cafe	Covent Garden
Alara Wholefoods	Bloomsbury		
Al Fresco	Westminster	**WINE BARS**	
Beverly Hills Bakery	Knightsbridge	Gordon's Wine Bar	Trafalgar Sq. & Strand
EAT	Chain	🗷 Odette's Wine Bar	Camden Town
Futures	City	Tiles	Westminster
		🗷 Vats	Bloomsbury

RESTAURANTS BY NEIGHBORHOOD

NOTABLE CHAINS

ASK. A recent pretender to Pizza Express's crown, with a similar emphasis on hip, design-conscious restaurants serving pastas, salads, and thin-crust pizzas for around £5-7. Not quite as dependable as Pizza Express, but getting there. Open daily noon-11:30pm.

EAT (☎ 7222 7200). Despite the cringeworthy name (it stands for "Excellence And Taste"), this coffee bar-sandwich joint combo is a hit with Londoners. A small range of salads, soups, and sushi complements the sandwiches; it's all made fresh daily, preservative free. Food £1.50-3.50; coffees from £1.10. Open M-F 7am-6pm, some Sa 10am-5pm.

Pizza Express (☎ 01895 618 618). For decades a London-based mini-chain famed for crisp, Italian-style pizza and modern design, Pizza Express has recently massively expanded—there are now branches across Europe. While Pizza Express continues to offer reliable, reasonably priced food in attractive surroundings, those with big appetites may find the ever-shrinking pies (now around 8" diameter) unsatisfying. Pizzas and salads £5-8.

Prêt-à-Manger (☎ 7827 8888). These bustling, chrome-adorned sandwich bars are regularly mobbed for their sarnies, baguettes, and salads (£2-3), all made daily on the premises without "obscure" additives and preservatives. Eat-in price 17.5% higher. Most branches open around 7-7:30am, closing 3-4pm in business districts, 6-7pm in tourist areas.

Wagamama (www.wagamama.com). Pioneer of the noodle-bar revolution, Wagamama continues to pull the punters. It's not clear why, though—the transformation from one-location wonder to international chain has brought with it a downward trend in food quality. That said, it's still good value (ramen from £5.60), and good fun. Locations in Bloomsbury, Soho, Marylebone, Camden Town, Kensington, Knightsbridge, and Covent Garden. Generally open M-Sa noon-11pm, Su 12:30-10:30pm. MC, V.

Yo!Sushi (www.yosushi.com). The original Yo!Sushi, at 51 Poland St. (Tube: Oxford Circus), pioneered conveyor-belt sushi and the chain has spread like wildfire. Diners sit at an island bar, picking from a never-ending stream of small plates, color coded by price (£1.50-3.50). There's no doubt that it's fun, but portions are scrawny (a filling meal will come to around £20 each), and there's no knowing how long that raw fish has been circling on the (unrfrigearated) onveyor belt. Open daily noon-midnight. AmEx, MC, V.

THE WEST END

OXFORD STREET & REGENT STREET

◪ NEIGHBORHOOD QUICKFIND: Discover, p. 2; **Sights,** p. 79; **Nightlife,** p. 190; **Entertainment,** p. 209; **Shopping,** p. 226.

Food on Oxford St. itself is as depressing and tourist-oriented as you'd expect, with fast-food chains competing with dodgy-looking kebab and pizza vendors. Fortunately, sidestreets **SEE MAP, p. 330-331** offer better food and better value. Londoners have long kept quiet about **St. Christopher's Place,** reached by an innocuous-looking alleyway opposite Bond St. Tube. This pedestrian *piazza* a stone's throw north of Oxford St. feels like a lost piece of the Mediterranean, ringed by the terrace seating of numerous mid-range restaurants. Less picturesque but just as affordable, **Kingly Street,** between Regent St. and Carnaby St., is popular with local *boutiquiers*.

▨ Mô, 23 Heddon St. (☎ 7434 4040). Tube: Piccadilly Circus or Oxford Circus. A "salad bar, tea room, and bazaar," Mô transports you to Marrakesh. The interior is hung with traditional lanterns and festooned with Moroccan crafts, all for sale—including the carved chairs, floor cushions, and low tables used by diners. Put together a selection of 4 traditional salads, dips, and meats (£6), washed down with a sweet mint tea (£1.50). No reservations, but very popular—arrive early or late. Open M-W 11am-11pm, Th-Sa noon-midnight.

Carluccio's, St. Christopher's Pl. (☎ 7935 5927). Tube: Bond St. Good, no-frills Italian cooking; choose from the more formal basement seating, shared tables on the ground floor, or a *piazza*-style patio. The short menu is simplicity itself: antipasti £3.50-7, main dishes £5-10. Also sandwiches and *calzone* to take away (£3-4) and a deli with Italian hams, gourmet pastas, and olive oils. Open M-F 8am-11pm, Sa 10am-11pm, Su 11am-10pm. AmEx, MC, V.

La Madeleine, 5 Vigo St. (☎ 7734 8353). Tube: Piccadilly Circus. Sit back, sip a perfectly brewed leaf tea (£1.30), and rejoice in a little bit of *temps perdu*. Lunchtime menu includes a daily changing *plat du jour* (£7), omelettes (£6-7) and a 2-course set meal with wine (£10). Open M Sa 8am-7pm. MC, V.

Masala Zone, 9 Marshall St. (☎ 7287 9966). Tube: Oxford Circus. Masala Zone brings Indian catering into the new millennium with a dramatically lit interior and an open kitchen. Subtly spiced, smartly presented food ranges from Anglo-Indian favorites (£5-6) to tapas-style "street food" (£2.50-4). The Ayurvedic Thali draws on traditional Indian medicine to create a diabetic banquet. Open M-F noon-2:30pm and 5:30-11pm, Sa 12:30-3pm and 5:30-11:30pm, Su 12:30-3pm and 6:30-10:30pm. MC, V.

Strada, 15-16 New Burlington St. (☎ 7287 5967). Tube: Oxford Circus. Also at Upper St. and Holborn. The wood-fired oven, hand-spun pizzas (£5-9)—twice the size of most chain pizzeria's offerings—have all the right ingredients to make *la dolce vita,* though pasta portions (£6-12) can seem stingy by comparison. Open M-Sa 11am-11pm, Su 11am-10:30pm. AmEx, MC, V.

MAYFAIR & ST. JAMES'S

◪ NEIGHBORHOOD QUICKFIND: Discover, p. 2; **Sights,** p. 80; **Museums&Galleries,** p. 139; **Entertainment,** p. 209; **Shopping,** p. 228.

One of the most pleasant places to eat and drink is in and around the pedestrian alleys of **Shepherd Market.** Don't forget that Mayfair is within easy reach of the restaurants around Oxford St. and Regent St. (see p. 159) and Soho (p. 161)

the BIG $plurge

Tea Total

Afternoon tea is perhaps the high point of English cuisine. A social ritual as much as a meal, at its best it involves a long afternoon of sandwiches, scones, pastries, tinkling china, and restrained conversation. And even a cup of tea.

The inherent qualities of "tiffin" notwithstanding, the main attraction of afternoon tea today is the chance to lounge in sumptuous surroundings that at any other time would be beyond all but a Sultan's budget. The Ritz is the most famous place to "take tea," but most of London's top hotels have got in on the act. It's a win-win situation: they get to charge over £20 for hot water, dried leaves, and cakes, you get to relax in the kind of luxury you've only ever dreamed about. Note that you'll often need to book in advance, especially for weekends, while many hotels have a strict dress code; see listings for details.

Top places for tea in London include: **Browns**, p. 160; **Fortum and Mason**, p. 160; **The Lanesborough**, p. 171; **The Ritz**, p. 160; **The Savoy**, p. 164; and **The Orangery** of Kensington Palace, p. 172. For a different take on tea, try the Philippe Starck-designed **St. Martin's Lane**, p. 162.

Cafe Society, upstairs at 4-5 Burlington Arcade (☎ 7499 5758). Tube: Piccadilly Circus or Green Park. Enter via the Immaculate House store and climb 2 floors. There's a sense of disbelief in finding this tiny cafe hidden away above the Burlington Arcade, with only 5 tables and one large double bed (with breakfast tray). Large salads (£6.25) and giant sandwiches (£3.50-5) for lunch, while set breakfasts range from the *City* (toast, croissant, cappuccino, and juice; £4) to the *Yacht* (with smoked salmon and caviar; £8). Open M-Sa 9am-5:30pm.

L'Autre, 5b Shepherd St. (☎ 7499 4680). Tube: Hyde Park Corner or Green Park. With a French name, English decor, and a menu mixing Polish and Mexican favorites, you might say this small restaurant is a touch confused. The cozy interior and hearty Polish fare (£8-10) are perfect for a cold winter's day; in summer, sit on the pavement and munch burritos (£7.50). Open M-Sa noon-2:30pm and 5:30-10:30pm, Su 5:30-10:30pm. AmEx, MC, V.

Ye Grapes, Shepherd Market (☎ 7499 1563). Tube: Hyde Park Corner or Green Park. Ye Grapes has a country-pub feel, with a dark, traditional interior lined with hunting trophies. No food, but you can bring your own (11am-4pm) from nearby takeouts (no kebab or curry!), and enjoy it with a pint (from £2.60). Open M-Sa 11am-11pm, Su noon-10:30pm.

AFTERNOON TEA

Brown's, Albemarle St. (☎ 7493 6020). Tube: Green Park. Opened by Byron's butler in 1837, Brown's was London's first luxury hotel, and still oozes old-fashioned charm. Tea is taken in the cosy drawing room, with dark paneling and comfy settees. M-F sittings 3 and 4:45pm (book 1 week ahead for Th-F); Sa-Su tea served 3-4:45pm (no reservations). Set tea £23, with champagne £33. No jeans or trainers. AmEx, MC, V.

Fortnum & Mason, 181 Piccadilly (see Shopping, p. 229). The patio restaurant, overlooking the food hall of the Royal Family's official grocery store, is a popular place to take tea for Londoners, not least because it's half the price of most hotels. "Special" tea, £12, served M-Sa 3-5:45pm. AmEx, MC, V.

The Ritz, Piccadilly (☎ 7493 8181). Tube: Green Park. The most famous place for afternoon tea in the world. Tea is served in the sumptuous Palm Court, complete with gilded fountains. Reserve at least 1 month ahead for one of the weekday sittings, 3 months for weekends; alternatively, skip lunch and arrive at noon for an early tea. No jeans or trainers; jacket and tie preferred for men. Sittings at 3:30 and 5pm daily. Set tea £27. AmEx, MC, V.

SOHO

▥ TRANSPORTATION: All listings are near Piccadilly Circus, Leicester Sq., and Tottenham Court Rd. Tubes. **NEIGHBORHOOD QUICKFIND: Discover,** p. 2; **Sights,** p. 83; **Museums&Galleries,** p. 139; **Nightlife,** p. 191; **Entertainment,** p. 209; **Shopping,** p. 229; **Accommodations,** p. 284.

Soho is one of the best places in London to eat and drink; the incredible array of restaurants, cafes, and bars cater to every taste, budget, and sexuality. Bustling **Chinatown's** main attraction are the dozens of Cantonese restaurants. While **Gerrard Street** is considered Chinatown's heart, restaurants here cater as much to non-Chinese; those on **Lisle Street,** one block south towards Leicester Sq., are often cheaper and more "authentic." **Wardour Street** and the southern side of **Shaftesbury Avenue,** just north of Gerrard St., harbor numerous late-night and 24hr. restaurants that, while hardly culinarily challenging, are an institution for hungry post-clubbers.

busaba eathai, 106-110 Wardour St. (☎7255 8686). Wildly popular eatery from the founder of Wagamama, which (unlike its sibling) has kept quality up and prices down. *Busaba* is a Thai flower, while *eathai...*well, work it out. Locals and students queue for great Thai food (£5-8) at shared square tables in a cozy, wood-paneled room. Open M-Th noon-11pm, F-Sa noon-11:30pm, Su noon-10pm. AmEx, MC, V.

Itsu, 103 Wardour St. (☎7479 4794). The perfection of *kaiten-sushi* (conveyor-belt sushi), providing a genuinely groundbreaking gastronomic experience in a stylish retro-modern interior. A steel monorail delivers (labeled!) fusion delights such as green bean and pesto rolls (£2) and organic salmon tartar (£3) as well as more traditional raw-fish plates. Expect to spend about £15 each. Open M-Th 12:30-11pm, F-Sa 12:30pm-midnight, Su 1-10pm. AmEx, MC, V.

Bar Italia, 22 Frith St. (☎7437 4520). A fixture of the late-night Soho scene, immortalized by *Pulp.* Despite its name, you won't find anything stronger than an espresso here (£1.60), but it's still *the* place for a post-club panini (£3.50-5). The large, loud TV is never turned off—appropriate, since John Logie Baird gave the first-ever demonstration of television upstairs in 1922. Open 24hr. except M 3-7am.

The Blue Room, 3 Bateman St. (☎7437 4827). Away from the hubbub, a cosmopolitan crowd relaxes on the couches of this laid-back hang-out, sipping on smoothies (£2.50-3.25) and munching on sandwiches (£3-4.50) and salads (£3.50-4.50). Take-away prices 10-20% less. Open M-F 8am-10:30pm, Sa 10am-10:30pm, Su noon-10:30pm. Cash only.

Café Emm, 17 Frith St. (☎7437 0723). Cheap, generous portions in an unpretentious bistro setting, with lots of vegetarian dishes. Main courses £5.50-£7.50, from veggie pancakes to rump steak. Open daily noon-2:30pm, Su-Th 5:30-10:30pm, F-Sa 5:30-midnight. MC, V.

Nusa Dua, 11 Dean St. (☎7437 3339). Tube: Tottenham Court Rd. Despite being named after a luxury Balinese resort, this is a popular outlet for affordable Javanese and Singaporean cooking. The downstairs, with exotic fish tanks and Indonesian carvings, is more crowded than the smaller ground floor. Plentiful chicken and vegetarian dishes £5.10, duck and seafood £6.45. Open M-F noon-midnight, Sa-Su 6pm-midnight. MC, V.

Old Compton Café, 34 Old Compton St. (☎7439 3309). *The* gay cafe, though you wouldn't know it from the tourist-filled outside tables (neither do the tourists). Salads and sandwiches £2-5, all-day breakfast £3-4.50. Open 24hr. Cash only.

Pâtisserie Valerie, 44 Old Compton St. (☎7437 3466). Opened in 1926, this continental patisserie has become a London institution. The frills are saved for the renowned cakes; seating is at shared tables in a resolutely unmodernised interior. Cakes and pastries £1.20-3, sandwiches £3.50-5.95. Open M-F 7:30am-8pm, Sa 8am-8pm, Su 9:30am-7pm. **Branches** at 8 Russell St. and 105 Marylebone High St. AmEx, MC, V.

CHINATOWN

Tube: *Leicester Sq.*

Mr Kong, 21 Lisle St. (☎7437 7341). Do people really eat "goose web with fish lips and sea cucumber," or is it just there to convince Westerners of this small restaurant's authenticity? In any case, you won't go wrong with Mr Kong's superb cuisine; less adventurous eaters should try the deep-fried Mongolian lamb (£6.50), like crispy duck only more tender, and served with lettuce. £7 min. for dinner. Open daily noon-3am. AmEx, MC, V.

Harbour City, 46 Gerrard St. (☎7439 7859 or 7287 1526). Gerrard St.'s best and biggest Cantonese restaurant. Extremely popular for keenly priced, menu-ordered *dim sum* (served daily noon-5pm). The giant noodle bowls (£4-6) would satisfy two hungry giants; other dishes run £6-10. Open M-Th noon-11:30pm, F-Sa noon-midnight, Su 11am-11pm. AmEx, MC, V.

Wong Kei, 41-43 Wardour St. (☎7437 3071). Tube: Piccadilly Circus or Leicester Sq. While renovations in 2001 have removed much of the kitsch charm of this Chinatown stalwart, little else

Wagamama

has changed: the waiters remain as famously curt as ever, and prices absolute rock-bottom. Be prepared to share a table. Won-ton noodle soup £2.50, roast duck and rice £3.50. Open daily noon-11:30pm. Cash only.

PUBS

Dog and Duck, 18 Bateman St. (☎ 7494 0697). Tube: Tottenham Ct. Rd. This historic pub occupies the site of the Duke of Monmouth's Soho House, its name a reminder of the area's hunting past. The theme is continued in the original Victorian tiled interior—look out for the dog-and-duck themed tiles lower down opposite the bar, and the matching mosaic underfoot at the Frith St. entrance. Open M-F noon-11pm, Sa 2-11pm, Su 6-10:30pm.

Yo!Below, 52 Poland St., below Yo!Sushi (☎ 7439 3660). Tube: Oxford Circus. Another concept-driven Yo! venture (see p. 159), drinkers sit at tables recessed into the floor, complete with self-service beer taps (£1.30 for a small glass), while staff belt out karaoke, give free massages, and tell fortunes. The geeky clientele thinks it's cool, but execrable music and a palpable lack of atmosphere may leave you feeling unsatisfied. Food specials include beer and bento for £5 noon-5pm. Open daily noon-1am, food to 11pm. AmEx, MC, V.

The Grapes Ale House

COVENT GARDEN

🚇 Tube: Covent Garden. **NEIGHBORHOOD QUICKFIND: Discover,** p. 2; **Sights,** p. 84; **Museums&Galleries,** p. 139; **Nightlife,** p. 193; **Entertainment,** p. 209; **Shopping,** p. 231; **Accommodations,** p. 284.

Despite, or perhaps because of, its trendiness, Covent Garden is not known for its gastronomic delights. The piazza is dominated by unremarkable tourist-oriented cafes and high-priced restaurants catering to the theater and opera crowds, sidestreets by sandwich bars and theme pubs. Salvation comes in the form of **Neal's Yard,** a small open courtyard that over the past three decades has evolved into a wholesome haven of vegetarian, vegan, and organic delights.

Neal's Yard Dairy, 17 Shorts Gdns. (☎ 7240 5700). Enormous selection of mostly British and Irish cheeses, all produced in small farms by traditional methods; massive wheels of stilton and cheddar line the shelves. Also sells organic milks and yoghurts. You'll smell it from a mile off. Open M-Sa 9am-7pm. MC, V.

St. Martin's Lane Hotel, 45 St. Martin's Ln. (☎ 7300 5500). Tube: Leicester Sq. This Philippe Starck-designed hotel is so cool, it doesn't even have a sign outside (it's the white building with the yellow-lit revolving door). Afternoon tea (£16) is a steal compared to other top hotels, with no reservations or dress code necessary. Tea served daily 3-5pm. AmEx, MC, V.

Belgo Centraal, 50 Earlham St. (☎ 7813 2233). All the gimmicks in the world, from the industrial-style lift that lows you to the dining room, to the monk-cowled waiters, can't disguise that Belgo's once-brilliant food

Bar Italia

is spiraling down in quality and up in price. One to avoid. Open M-Sa noon-11:30pm, Su noon-10:30pm. Wheelchair access. AmEx, MC, V.

Bibo Cibo, 59 Endell St. (☎ 7240 3343). Self-consciously cool cafe/bar, with a very contemporary minimalist-luxury interior. Both the downstairs bar and the swanky-looking upstairs restaurant serve the same range of pub fare (sausage and mash £7). Sa night DJs play commercial funk/soul/hiphop. 2-for-1 main courses lunchtimes and selected drinks 5-8pm. Open M-Sa 11:30am-midnight, Su 11:30am-10:30pm. AmEx, MC, V.

Monmouth Coffee House, 27 Monmouth St. (☎7645 3562). Cozy wood-paneled store selling 14 different coffees, roasted on site. Get a bag o' beans to go, or savor a cup in the tiny wood booths of the "sample room," at the back. Fresh filter coffee, made to order, £1.20; espresso £1. Open M-Sa 9am-6:30pm. MC, V (£5 min.)

Neal's Yard Bakery & Tearoom, 6 Neal's Yard (☎7836 5199). A small, open-air counter sells fresh organic breads (loaves from 90p) as well as vegan faves like beanburgers (£2.85 eat-in, £2.20 take-away); take your food up to the rustic tea room if you want to sit. Eat-in minimum £1.50 M-F noon-3pm and Sa noon-close. Open M-Sa 10:30am-4:30pm.

World Food Café, upstairs at 14 Neal's Yard (☎7379 0298). Bright, airy location overlooking Neal's Yard, with shared pine tables and yellow plastic chairs. Order from the open-plan kitchen in the center of the room, pay on your way out. Substantial £6 "light" vegetarian meals range from filled oat pancakes to Greek salads; £8 "platters" include Indian *thalis* and Turkish *meze*. Open M-F 11:30am-4:30pm, Sa 11:30am-5pm. MC, V (£10 min.).

PUBS

Freedom Brewing Co., underneath Thomas Neal's at 41 Earlham St. (☎7240 0606). Tube: Covent Garden. One of London's few micro-breweries, and winner of numerous awards. Pints from £3, sampler gives you a sip of 3 beers for £1.70. Food is standard, if pricey, pub fare: sandwiches £6, main dishes £7-11. Open M-Sa 11am-11pm, Su noon-10:30pm.

Lamb and Flag, 33 Rose St. (☎7497 9504). Once commonly called the "Bucket of Blood" for the violence of the bareknuckle fights held upstairs. The traditional dark-wood interior and no-music policy make it a great place for a quiet pint, though not after 6pm when the two floors (and courtyard) fill with local workers. Food daily noon-3pm. Live jazz upstairs Su from 7:30pm. Open M-Th 11am-11pm, F-Sa 11am-10:45pm, Su noon-10:30pm.

Maple Leaf, 41 Maiden Ln. (☎7240 2843). Start a rousing chorus of "O Canada" as you down Alberta beefburgers (£6.45), *quebecois* poutine (fries with cheese and gravy, £4) and Molson on tap (£2.87). M 6-9pm chicken wings are 20p each. Hockey nights W-Th from 7pm. Open M-F 11am-11pm, Sa noon-11pm, Su noon-10:30pm. AmEx, MC, V.

Old Compton St., Soho

Covent Garden

A Little Vino

TRAFALGAR SQUARE & THE STRAND

NEIGHBORHOOD QUICKFIND: Discover, p. 2; **Sights,** p. 85; **Museums&Galleries,** p. 139; **Nightlife,** p. 194; **Entertainment,** p. 209;.

The Strand shares Covent Garden's culinary shortcomings, being dominated by American chains, tourist traps, and famed, expensive establishments like the old-fashioned *Simpsons in the Strand*. Fortunately, **Craven Passage** and **Villiers Street**, between the Strand and Victoria Embankment, have a number of pleasant bars and pubs serving fairly priced standards. **Trafalgar Square's** eateries are hidden away inside its various historic buildings—**Crivelli's** restaurant, in the National Gallery (see p. 136), combines affordable Italian favorites with a view of the Square, though it can't compete with the National Portrait Gallery's top-floor restaurant, whose vertiginous views are matched by its high prices—save it for a coffee or tea. On a sunny day, few places can match the outdoor **River Terrace** at Somerset House (see p. 87). Again, it's expensive (mains £12-15), but makes the perfect spot for a cool drink.

Cafe in the Crypt, St. Martins-in-the-Fields, Trafalgar Sq. (see p. 86; ☎ 7839 4342). Decent self-service food in a great underground space below the famous church. Don't look down—you might be sitting over an 18th-century gravestone. Hot dishes and salads £6-6.50; get soup and dessert for £4.50. Open M-Sa 10am-8pm, Su noon-8pm.

Gordon's Wine Bar, 47 Villiers St. (☎ 7930 1408). Tube: Embankment or Charing Cross. Main entrance by York Watergate, just behind Victoria Embankment Gardens. While Gordon's has limited terrace seating, its real attraction is the honeycomb of low candlelit vaults, black with smoke and tar. Choose a hot or cold main dish, then pile on as much as you like from the self-serve salad bar for £5-7. Sherry and port are decanted from wood barrels (£3 per glass). Very popular at lunch and early evenings with local workers. Open M-Sa 11am-11pm.

The Savoy, Strand (☎ 7836 4343). Tube: Charing Cross. One of London's most famous and most historic hotels, and second only to the Ritz in popularity for afternoon tea. On Sundays, a band plays hits from the 20s to the 40s as the floor is opened up to dancers. No jeans, shorts, or sneakers; jacket and tie preferrred. Reserve 1-2 days ahead M-F, 2 weeks Sa-Su. Tea daily 3:30-5pm. Set tea £22 M-F, £25 Sa, £28 Su. AmEx, MC, V.

PUBS

Sherlock Holmes, 10 Northumberland St. (☎ 7930 2644). Tube: Charing Cross. In the former Northumberland Hotel, as mentioned in the *Hound of the Baskervilles*. Numerous Holmesian "artefacts" are displayed in the pub, while adjacent to the upstairs restaurant (mains £9-12) is a replica of Holmes's study. Sherlock Holmes Ale £2.30, sandwiches £3-5, hot meals £6. Food served daily noon-10pm. Open M-Sa 11am-11pm, Su noon-10:30pm. MC, V.

T.S. Queen Mary, Victoria Embankment. (☎ 7240 9404). Tube: Embankment or Temple. This 1930s Turbine Steamer is now moored permanently on the banks of the Thames. While the occasionally swaying deck can be disconcerting at first, after a few pints (£2.60), you'll barely notice. On weekends, the ship becomes a floating disco. Open M-Th noon-11pm, F-Sa noon-2am, Su noon-6pm. Cover £5 Th after 10pm, £7 F-Sa after 9pm.

HOLBORN

SEE MAP, pp. 334-335

NEIGHBORHOOD QUICKFIND: Discover, p. 6; **Sights,** p. 88; **Museums&Galleries,** p. 142; **Nightlife,** p. 194; **Entertainment,** p. 212; **Shopping,** p. 232.

In the 18th century, there was one tavern in Holborn for every five homes—and while their number has since decreased, pubs are still your best bet for nourishment in a district unusually devoid of restaurants and snack bars, cheap or otherwise. This situation can be partially attributed to the Inns of Court, which graciously provide dining halls for their numerous members. Fortunately, barristers' respect for tradition and the bottle mean that Holborn is home to some of London's most ancient pubs, cosy enclaves of smoke-blackened wood, comfort food, and hand-pulled ales. If pub grub you'd rather snub, head for the maze of passageways between Holborn station and Lincoln's Inn Fields, home to a number of affordable eateries.

Bleeding Heart Tavern, corner of Greville St. and Bleeding Heart Yard (☎ 7404 0333). This two-level establishment is split between the light, laid-back upstairs pub with some bril-

FOOD & DRINK RESTAURANTS BY NEIGHBORHOOD

liant beers (Adnams £2.40) and the cosy restaurant below, whose thick tablecloths, fresh roses, and candles make a romantic backdrop to hearty and delicious English fayre, such as thick slabs of spit-roasted pork with crackling (£8). Get 2 courses for £10 5-7:30pm. If you want to splurge, the pricier **Bleeding Heart Bistro** (☎7242 8238) and much pricier **Bleeding Heart Restaurant** (☎7242 2056), both around the corner in Bleeding Heart Yard, rank among London's finest French restaurants. If you're curious, the name derives from the 1626 murder of Elizabeth Hatton by her jilted lover, the Spanish ambassador; the body was found in the yard, her heart "still pumping." Tavern open M-F 11am-11pm. AmEx, MC, V.

Cafe in the Park, Lincoln's Inn Fields (☎7404 1414). Tube: Holborn. In the southwestern part of Lincoln's Inn Fields, diners congregate underneath the marquis or in the gardens to a background of Caribbean music. Chicken and steak sizzles on the outdoor grill (£1-3 per piece). Sandwiches and salads £1.50-3. Open daily May-Sept. 11am-9pm, food 11am-3pm.

The Knosherie, 12-13 Greville St. (☎7242 1590). Tube: Farringdon or Chancery Ln. Near the jewellers of Hatton Garden, this friendly "kosher-style" eatery serves classic deli food and English dishes in a pink-and-gold interior. Specializes in hot salt beef (corned beef to Americans), from £2.90. Open daily 24hrs. AmEx, MC, V.

Na Zdrowie, 11 Little Turnstile (☎7831 9679). Tube: Holborn. The bright minimalist ethos of this small den fortunately doesn't extend to the menu—there are 45 vodkas on offer for around £2 a shot. Fantastically popular in the evening, at quieter times patrons tuck into the sandwiches (£2-2.50) and hearty Polish fare (£4-5). Open M-F noon-9pm, Sa 6-9pm. MC, V.

Woolley's, 33 Theobald's Rd.; rear entrance on Lamb's Conduit Passage (☎7405 3028). Tube: Holborn. Narrow take-out joint in two parts: salads (£1.35-3.50) and jacket potatoes (£1.40-2.50) are dished out from the Theobald's Rd. side, whilst Lamb's Conduit supplies freshly made sandwiches (£1.20-3). Open M-F 7:30am-3:30pm.

PUBS

Ye Olde Cheshire Cheese, Wine Office Ct. by 145 Fleet St. (☎7353 6170). Tube: Blackfriars or St. Paul's. Dark labyrinth of oak-panelled rooms on three floors, dating from 1667 and one-time haunt of Johnson, Dickens, Mark Twain, and Theodore Roosevelt. Drink in the small front bar; munch on sandwiches (£4-5) in the Cheshire bar at the back; tuck into meaty traditional dishes in the Chophouse (main courses £7-10); sup on daily hot specials (£4.25) in the downstairs cellar bar; or savor fancier cuisine in the 2nd-floor Johnson Room (£7-12). Food served M-F noon-9:30pm, Sa noon-2:30pm and 6-9:30pm, Su noon-2:30pm. Open M-F 11:30am-11pm, Sa 11:30am-3pm and 5:30-11pm, Su noon-3pm. AmEx, MC, V.

Enjoy a Cold Pint

Enjoy Some Fine Liquor

Enjoy the Beautiful Weather

Ye Olde Mitre Tavern, 1 Ely Court, between Ely Place and Hatton Garden (☎ 7405 4751). Tube: Chancery Lane. Down an obscure alley, this classic pub fully merits its name—it was built in 1546 by the Bishop of Ely. With oak beams and spun glass, the pint-sized front room is perfect for nestling up to a warm bitter (£1.80); the rear room offers slightly more space. No hot meals, but bar snacks served to 9:30pm. Open M-F 11am-11pm.

Cittie of Yorke, 22 High Holborn (☎ 7242 7670). Tube: Chancery Lane or Holborn. Look for the gleaming brass sign. Founded in 1430, the current Victorian building harks back with an enormous vaulted wooden roof enclosing what is claimed to be the longest bar in the world. The snug enclosed booths were specially designed for lawyers needing to discuss business in private. Also smaller front room and cellar bar. Food £5, burgers from £2. Open M-Sa 11:30am-11pm; food until 9:30pm. AmEx, MC, V.

Princess Louise, 208 High Holborn (☎ 7405 8816). Tube: Holborn. Last redecorated in 1891, this pub has an ornate tiled interior with a stunning ceiling. The quieter, plainer upstairs room is primarily for diners (pub grub £4-5), but you can get sandwiches downstairs (£2-3). Food M-Sa noon-2:30pm. Open M-F 11am-11pm, Sa noon-11pm. AmEx, MC, V.

The Punch Tavern, 99 Fleet St. (☎ 7353 6658). Tube: Blackfriars. This big, skylit pub occupies the old site of the Punch and Judy show—decor includes a funky collection of wooden puppets. Popular enough for lunch that some people reserve tables; dishes such as salmon fishcakes or scampi are £5.50, jacket potatoes £3. Open M-F 11am-11pm. AmEx, MC, V.

CLERKENWELL

SEE MAP, pp. 334-335

🔏 NEIGHBORHOOD QUICKFIND: Discover, p. 6; **Sights,** p. 92; **Museums&Galleries,** p. 143; **Nightlife,** p. 194; **Entertainment,** p. 213; **Accommodations,** p. 285.

There's no shortage of fine dining in Clerkenwell—and even the best restaurants offer some affordable sustenance. For something light, frequent one of the many sandwich bars south of Farringdon station and on Charterhouse St.; there are also cheap snack bars, pubs, and Chinese takeaways on West Smithfield, just south of the market. For a proper sit-down meal, your best bet is **Exmouth Market,** a pedestrian street north of Clerkenwell Rd. blanketed on both sides with all manner of eateries, from pie'n'mash to *Moro,* one of London's trendiest (and priciest) restaurants.

🍴 St. John, 26 St. John St. (☎ 7251 0848). Tube: Farringdon. St. John has stormed the London restaurant scene, winning countless prizes for its eccentric English cuisine—they call it "nose to tail eating," and certainly few body parts are wasted. Prices in the posh restaurant are high (mains £14) but you can enjoy similar bounty (in smaller quantities) in the airy, warehouse-style bar: fantastic lamb sandwich £5, roast bone-marrow salad £6, brawn (pig's feet and cow's head stew...yum) £5.50. A bakery at the back of the bar churns out delicious fresh loaves for £1.50. Bar open M-F 11am-11pm, Sa 6-11pm. MC, V.

🍴 Quiet Revolution, 41 Old St. (☎ 7253 5556). Tube: Barbican. "100% organic cafe" in a streamlined space with shared tables and plywood furnishings, plus a bamboo-strewn terrace. Big soup selection £4-5, hot dishes around £6, combo lunch (soup, salad, and smoothie) £8. Take-away £1 cheaper. Open M-F 9am-11pm, Sa-Su 10am-9pm. MC, V.

Al's Café Bar, 11-13 Exmouth Market (☎ 7837 4821). Tube: Angel or Farringdon. This stylish cafe/bar (with an attached club) is a favorite hangout for journalists from the nearby *Guardian* newspaper. £6 lunch specials (M-F noon-6pm) include 6oz. rump steak; otherwise salads are £5-6, main courses £6.50-9. All-day breakfast £5.50. Open M-F 8am-2am, Sa-Su 10am-midnight. Last orders 1hr. before close. MC, V (£10 min.).

The Eagle, 159 Farringdon Rd. (☎ 7837 1353). Tube: Farringdon. The original gastropub, the Eagle kicked off the whole stripped-wood, mismatched-furniture craze that has turned hundreds of pubs from cosy boozers into poseur hangouts overflowing with arugula and shaved parmesan. Unsurprisingly, it's always packed. Main dishes £10. Open M-F 12:30-2:30 and 6:30-10:30pm, Sa 12:30-3:30 and 6:30-10:30pm, Su 12:30-3:30pm. Cash only.

Fox & Anchor, 115 Charterhouse St. (☎ 7253 5075). Tube: Farringdon. As one of the only places in London where you can get a beer with your breakfast (£7), it does a roaring trade in the mornings—reservations are recommended, especially Th-F, though these days market custom comes second to power-breakfasting businessmen. It's also a gay-friendly pub, though straight punters predominate. Open M-Th 7am-7pm, F 7am-11pm; may close early.

Tinseltown 24-Hour Diner, 44-46 St. John St. (☎7689 2424) Tube: Farringdon. A cavernous underground haven for pre- and post-clubbers, Tinseltown's hours are more commendable than its food, which ranges from burgers (£5.50) to curries (£6). Still, there's nothing like a full-on shake with added chocolate bar (£3.50) after a hard night's dancing, except maybe a Full Monty breakfast (£3.50-5). Open 24hr.

CITY OF LONDON

🡶 NEIGHBORHOOD QUICK-FIND: Discover, p. 7; **Sights,** p. 93; **Museums&Galleries,** p. 143; **Entertainment,** p. 213; **Accommodations,** p. 285.

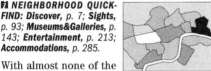

With almost none of the City's 300,000-strong **SEE MAP, p. 334-335** workforce sticking around for supper, and with hardly any residents, it's not surprising that the vast majority of City eateries open only for weekday lunch. Even at lunchtime, the choice is limited: since the City hums entirely to the beat of financiers and their support staff, it more-or-less comes down to either a hurriedly-grabbed sandwich, or a millionaire's banquet. If it's the former you're after, there's no shortage of choices, with sandwich bars on every corner (it helps to get off the main roads)—long queues will form outside the better establishments between noon and 1:30pm on weekdays. For something slightly different, the alleyways of **Leadenhall Market,** just south of Leadenhall, pack in numerous mid-range chain restaurants, cafes, and pubs, including a Pizza Express (see Notable Chains, p. 158). Protected by the glass roof of Horace Jones's Victorian market hall, you can sit out on the cobbles even when it's pelting down outside.

Drink & Dine

🡶 Futures, 8 Botolph Alley, between Botolph Ln. and Lovat St. (☎7623 4529). Tube: Monument. Suits besiege this tiny take-away, dishing out a daily-changing variety of vegetarian soups (£2-3), salads (£3), and hot dishes (£4). Open M-F 7:30-10am and 11:30am-3pm. **Branch** in Exchange Sq. (behind Liverpool St).

Old Spitalfields Market

🡶 Cafe Spice Namaste, 16 Prescot St.(☎7488 9242). Tube: Tower Hill or DLR: Tower Gateway. The standard bearer for a new breed of Indian restaurants. Bright, carnivalesque decoration brings an exotic feel to this old Victorian warehouse, as does the extensive menu of Goan and Parsee specialities. Meat dishes are on the pricey side (£10-12), but vegetarian meals are a bargain (£6-8). Open M-F noon-3pm and 6:15-10:30pm, Sa 6:30-10pm. AmEx, MC, V.

Black Friar, 174 Queen Victoria St. (☎7236 5650). Tube: Blackfriars. The Black Friar's claim to be "London's most unique pub" rests upon its art-deco imitation of the 12th-century Dominican friary that once occupied this spot. Immensely popular with the post-work crowd. Food served 11:30am-2:30pm. Open M-F 11:30am-11pm, Sa noon-5pm, Su noon-4:30pm.

At Docklands

PUB REVOLUTION

London, like much else in life, is far more fun after a few beers. In recognition of this phenomenon, the social institution that is the English pub was created centuries ago, coddling tipplers of all affiliations with dark-wood paneling, velvet stools, and brass accents. However, Britain's style obsession of recent has not left even this bastion of tradition untouched: in a bid to create a more "youthful" vibe, hundreds of pubs have stripped out their tobacco-encrusted carpets and chintzy floral wallpaper and joined the stampede towards stripped-wood floors, modern art, and (for inexplicable reasons) Thai food.

However, while these modernized pubs may have purists choking on their bitter, at least they're still locally run, for locals; the appearance may have changed, but the tradition lives on. More worrying by far is the inexorable expansion of uniform **chain pubs**; while most English pubs are owned by big breweries, traditionally the publican was left to his own devices. Now, though, scarcely a high street in Britain is without a giant, characterless **All Bar One, Pitcher & Piano,** or **Slug & Lettuce** branded boozer—Britain's oldest pub, Drury Lane's White Heart (est. 1201), was recently turned into an outpost of **It's A Scream.**

Noto, 7 Bread St. (☎ 7329 8056). Tube: St. Paul's or Mansion House. Japanese businessmen flock to this tiny, low-key noodle joint, set back from the road. Sit at the bar, order ramen or curries (£6-8), slurp it down, pay at the cashier. Life's great when you're a salaryman. Open M-F 11:30am-9pm. Cash only. Upscale **branch** at 2-3 Bassishaw Highwalk (☎ 7256 9433; Tube: Moorgate).

The Place Below, St. Mary-le-Bow, Cheapside. (☎ 7329 0789) Tube: St. Paul's, Mansion House, or Bank. In the 11th-century crypt of St. Mary-le-Bow church, vegetarian dishes provide salvation for the weary traveler. In the summer, they also set up tables outside. Salads and hot dishes £7.50-6.50, sandwiches £5; take-away £1-2 less (and there are plenty of benches in the churchyard). Open M-F 7:30am-4pm, with lunch 11:30am-2:30pm MC, V.

Simpson's, Ball Court, off 38½ Cornhill (☎ 7626 9985). Tube: Bank. "Established 1757" says the sign on the alley leading to this pub; indeed, it remains so traditional a man stands in the door to greet you. Different rooms divide the classes: quaffers populate the basement wine bar (sandwiches £2-4), drinkers the standing-only ground-floor bar, and diners the ground-floor and upstairs restaurants, with long wood tables and benches (traditional main dishes £6-7). Open M-F 11:30am-3pm (last orders).

SOUTH BANK

◨ NEIGHBORHOOD QUICK-FIND: Discover, p. 7; **Sights,** p. 100; **Museums&Galleries,** p. 144; **Entertainment,** p. 214; **Accommodations,** p. 285.

SEE MAP, p. 336-337 Until recently, no one would dream of going to the South Bank to eat—the choice was between overpriced restaurants in the big cultural complexes and the greasy spoons of Borough High St. But the rapid development of the area into a major cultural destination, not to mention increasing yuppification, have made this one of London's top spots for eating out—and the views are unbeatable. In addition to the places listed below, check out the **National Film Theatre** cafe under Waterloo Bridge (see p. 214) and the numerous pavement eateries of **Gabriel's Wharf,** between the National Theatre and the OXO Tower. Those who prefer to roll their own couldn't do better than ▨**Borough Market,** where stalls lay out such gourmet delights as unpasteurized cheeses, fresh breads, and cured meats. (Off Borough High St. Tube: London Bridge. Open F noon-6pm, Sa 6am-4pm.)

▨ **Cantina del Ponte,** 36c Shad Thames, Butler's Wharf (☎ 7403 5403). Tube: Tower Hill or London Bridge. Amazing riverside location by Tower Bridge. If the weather's poor, a model of the bridge inside will remind you what you're missing. Given the quality of the Italian-style food (especially the desserts), the set menu is a bargain at £10 for 2 courses, £12 for 3 (available M-F noon-3pm 6-7:30pm); otherwise pizzas are £7-8, regular mains £12-15. Live Italian music Tu and Th evenings. Open M-Sa noon-3pm and 6-10:45pm, Su noon-3pm and 6-9:45pm. MC, V.

■ **Tas,** 72 Borough High St. (☎ 7403 7200; Tube: London Bridge) and 33 The Cut (☎ 7928 2111; Tube: Waterloo). Dynamic duo of stylish and unfeasibly affordable Turkish restaurants. Generous and tasty stews and baked dishes—many vegetarian—outshine the respectable kebabs. Main courses £6-8; set menus include 2 courses for £7 and mezes (selection of starters) £7-10. Live music from 7:30pm. Fan-Tas-tic. Evening reservations essential. Open M-Sa 12:30-11:30pm, Su 12:30-10:30pm. AmEx, MC, V.

■ **People's Palace,** Royal Festival Hall (☎ 7928 9999). Despite the Stalinist name, this is the swankiest of the Festival Hall's many eateries. Its chief virtue is the fantastic location on the second floor of the Hall, with vast windows overlooking the river; the Mediterranean-style food is top-notch too. While dinner is pricey (mains £15+), at lunchtime main courses, such as confit of duck or roast salmon, are all £8. Perfect for when you want to impress someone. Open daily noon-3pm and 5:30-11pm. MC, V.

Café on Level 7, Tate Modern, Bankside (☎ 7887 8888). Tube: Southwark or Blackfriar's. On the top floor of Tate Modern (see Museums&Galleries, p. 137), windows on both sides give great perspectives of the City and south London, while specially commissioned murals cover the end walls. Slick and stylish, with artistically presented modern British food: baked aubergine £7.75, braised ham hock £8. Sandwiches served in the afternoon (£3-5). The "East Room", at the other end of the building, serves snacks all day, with the same great view. Open Su-Th 10am-5:30pm (last order), F-Sa 10am-9:30pm. AmEx, MC, V.

Cubana, 48 Lower Marsh. (☎ 7928 8778). Tube: Waterloo. Look for the giant salsa dancer squashing Uncle Sam. Hardly revolutionary, but immensely popular nonetheless: generous tapas (£3.50-5) and main courses (£7-10) take second place to the spiky cocktails (£5, 2-pint jug £15). At lunch, get 2 tapas for £5, a 2-course meal for £6, and 3 courses for £8. Reservations recommended. Salsa with live band F-Sa nights. Open M-F noon-midnight, Sa 6pm-midnight, Su 3:30-8:30pm. AmEx, MC, V.

Gourmet Pizza Co., Gabriel's Wharf, 56 Upper Ground (☎ 7928 3188). Tube: Southwark or Waterloo. On the embankment, this adventurous pizzeria offers the best-value riverside dining in town. Pizzas £6-9. Open M-Sa noon-11pm. AmEx, MC,V.

WESTMINSTER

🖪 *NEIGHBORHOOD QUICKFIND: Discover, p. 8; Sights, p. 106; Museums&Galleries, p. 145; Entertainment, p. 215; Shopping, p. 232; Accommodations, p. 286.*

SEE MAP, p. 338-339

With one of London's highest concentrations of office workers, from tens of thousands of poorly paid clerks and civil servants to ministers, Lords, and business leaders, Westminster has no shortage of restaurants at every price range—at least for a weekday lunch. In the evenings, sandwich bars shut up and restaurants raise their prices, while many places shut entirely over weekends. **Strutton Ground,** a short pedestrian road between Victoria and Great Peter St., is particularly rich in budget pickings, from sandwich and salad bars to Chinese buffets. South of Victoria, **Tachbrook Street** also has a number of cheap eats, as well as a tiny but superior food market. (Market M-Sa 9am-5pm.)

■ **Jenny Lo's Teahouse,** 14 Eccleston St. (☎ 7259 0399). Tube: Victoria. Long before noodle bars hit the big time, Jenny Lo was offering stripped-down Chinese fare at communal tables. The modern interior bustles on weekdays, but with seating on 2 floors, you won't have to wait long to sample cha shao (pork noodle soup; £5.00) or sichuan aubergine (£5.75). Teas, blended in-house, are served in attractive hand-turned stoneware (from 85p). Open M-F 11:30am-3pm and 6-10pm; Sa noon-3pm and 6-10pm. £5 min. Cash only.

Al Fresco, 77 Wilton Rd. (☎ 7333 8298). Tube: Victoria. The warm yellow interior banishes rainclouds and transports you to a Mediterranean resort—maybe Ibiza, judging by the number of English 20-somethings. Focaccia sandwiches, from £2.70 (30p eat-in supplement), share the menu with baked potatoes (from £3.50), English breakfasts (from £3.25), and exotic fruit milkshakes (£1.95). Open M-Sa 8am-6pm, Su 9am-6pm. AmEx, MC, V.

PUB REVOLUTION II: REVENGE OF THE GASTROPUBS

If you walk into an ordinary looking pub looking for some cheap, traditional pub grub, only to find that the menu starts at £12 and includes dishes like "seared yellowfin tuna with chanterelle mushrooms and shaved parmesan," you've been gastropubbed.

Around 10 years afo, a couple of eager punters came up with the idea of serving restaurant-quality food in a laid-back pub atmosphere. The result, in 1991, was **The Eagle,** in Clerkenwell (see p. 166). To many people's surprise, it was (and is) a runaway success; there seems to be no end of people willing to queue (gastropubs rarely take reservations) and pay prices that equal those of genuinely swanky restaurants for food they have to order at the bar and eat at shared tables.

While it's easy to laugh, gastropubs are one of the fastest growing areas of the London restaurant scene—as much thanks to the usually excellent food as to their current trendiness. And for all their inherent contradictions, they do perform an invaluable community service by keeping yuppies and media whores off the streets.

ECCo (Express Coffee Company), 40 Strutton Ground (☎7233 0557). Tube: Victoria or St. James's Park. The same great deals as the Bloomsbury original (see p. 175), including made-to-order 11" pizzas for £3. Open M-F 7am-7:30pm, Sa-Su 7am-4pm.

Goya, 34 Lupus St. (☎7976 5309). Tube: Pimlico. Corner tapas bar, with serious bow-tied Spanish waiters serving snacks and drinks to a chattering crowd of smartly turned-out locals on the outside tables. Interior seating is limited, but mirrors and large windows give it a spacious feel. Generous tapas mostly £4-5; 3 per person is more than plenty. Sangria £2.50; note alcohol is only served with food. Open daily noon-11:30pm. MC, V.

Greens, 11-13 Strutton Ground (☎7222 4588). Tube: Victoria or St. James's Park. Organic health-food store selling a wide range of vegetarian meals to take away, from serve-yourself salads to hot stews and curries, all £2-3. Open M-F 7am-6pm. AmEx, MC, V.

Red Lion, 48 Parliament St. (☎7930 5826). Tube: Westminster. *The* politicians' hangout, where the Chancellor's press secretary was infamously overheard leaking information in 1998. TVs carrying the Parliament cable channel allow MPs to listen to the debates over a warm pint, while a "division bell" alerts them to drink up when a vote is about to be taken. Despite the distinguished clientele, the food (sandwiches £3, hot dishes £6) is decidedly ordinary. Open M-Sa 11am-11pm, Su noon-7pm; food served daily noon-3pm. MC, V.

Tiles, 36 Buckingham Palace Rd. (☎7834 7761). Tube: Victoria. Within spitting distance of Buckingham Palace. Small round tables grace the blue-and-white tiled floor, and large mirrors add to the airy atmosphere. Modern British cooking includes duck confit salad (£5.45 starter, £7.95 main) and penne with mushrooms and spinach (£6.95). 50 wines from £2.50 per glass. Open M-F noon-11pm, food served noon-2:30pm and 6-10pm. AmEx, MC, V.

CHELSEA

SEE MAP, p. 346

◪ TRANSPORTATION: The only Tube station in Chelsea is Sloane Sq.; from here buses 11, 19, 22, 211, and 319 run down the King's Rd. **NEIGHBORHOOD QUICKFIND: Discover,** *p. 8;* **Sights,** *p. 108;* **Museums&Galleries,** *p. 146;* **Entertainment,** *p. 215;* **Shopping,** *p. 232.*

As with everything else in Chelsea, it's all happening on the **King's Road.** While restaurants can be found scattered along the length of this busy thoroughfare, affordable eateries are concentrated most highly between Sydney St. and the World's End kink. Here you'll find pubs, pancake houses, noodle bars, American-themed diners, and pizzerias, as well as some fancier joints for those with romance on their minds.

New Culture Revolution, 305 King's Rd. (☎7352 9281). Cheap Chinese with flair. See Camden Town, p. 177.

Bluebird, 350 King's Rd. (☎7559 1222). An auto-shop turned gastronomic pit-stop, this designer food emporium includes a flashy, dateworthy restaurant upstairs, a forecourt cafe with seafood, juice, and crepe bars, and a gourmet supermarket. Cafe food includes crepes £3-5, burgers and steaks £6-7; restaurant mains £12.50 including rump of lamb or corn-fed chicken. Cafe open M-Sa 8am-11pm, Su noon-6pm; restaurant M-F noon-3pm and 6-11pm, Sa 11am-3:30pm and 6-11pm, Su 11am-3:30pm and 6-10pm; store M-W 9am-8pm, Th-Sa 9am-9pm, Su 11am-5pm. AmEx, MC, V.

Chelsea Bun Diner, 9a Limerston St. (☎7352 3635). Wannabe American diner with a West Coast twist. "Overfilled" sandwiches (£1.60-3.20) and breakfasts (from £3.50) served until 6pm; the Ultimate Breakfast (£8.50) includes 3 eggs, 3 pancakes, bacon, sausage, burger, hash browns and french toast. Pasta, chicken, burgers, and omelettes £6-8. Minimum £3.50 per person lunch, £5.50 dinner. Open M-Sa 7am-midnight, Su 9am-7pm. MC, V.

King's Head and Eight Bells, 50 Cheyne Walk (☎7352 1820). Henry VIII occasionally dropped in here with his erstwhile friend Thomas More. Today people are more likely to lose their heads trying the yard-of-ale challenge—glug down the contents of the 3ft. long, 2.5-pint capacity tube in under 2 minutes without spilling a drop, and it's on the house. Sandwiches and jacket potatoes £3-4, main meals £6-7. Open M-Sa 11am-11pm, Su noon-10:30pm.

Pizza Express, 152 King's Rd. (☎7351 5031). See Notable Chains, p. 158. Perhaps the most impressive of Pizza Express's locations, in the former home of dancer Princess Astafieva. A triumphal archway supported by caryatids and topped by a bronze chariot separates the large courtyard from the sidewalk, while interior seating is on three atmospheric floors, including a jazz club. Open daily 11:30am-midnight.

Stockpot, 273 King's Rd. (☎7486 9185). Another outpost of this unfeasably cheap, reasonably tasty minichain. See p. 171.

Sundance, 250 King's Rd., entrance on Sydney St. (☎7351 2929). Around an open courtyard, this "organic megamarket" offers soup-, juice-, and noodle-bars, a sit-down restaurant, plus a butcher's, grocery store, and walk-in reflexology clinic. Stores open M-Sa 9am-8pm, food stalls noon-3pm.

KNIGHTSBRIDGE & BELGRAVIA

▶ NEIGHBORHOOD QUICKFIND: Discover, p. 9; **Sights,** p. 109; **Shopping,** p. 233; **Accommodations,** p. 171.

Knightsbridge is not, at first glance, promising territory for affordable eats—one look at the prices in Harrod's many restaurants is enough to make you lose your appetite. But cast your net a little wider, and you'll haul in the benefits. **Beauchamp** (BEE-cham) **Place,** off the Old Brompton Rd., is lined

SEE MAP, p. 338-339

with all manner of restaurants and cafes at all price ranges, and there are more bargains to be found in other side streets. **Belgravia** is a tougher nut to crack; there's little chance of finding a sit-down meal for under £15 each. Explore the mews behind **Grosvenor Pl.** for hidden pubs, or take advantage of the gourmet delis and specialty food stores on **Elizabeth St.** to assemble a picnic fit for a prince—the only problem, given that most of the area's parks are resident-only, is finding a place to eat it.

KNIGHTSBRIDGE

Stockpot, 6 Basil St. (☎7589 8627). Tube: Knightsbridge. Many worse restaurants get away with charging twice the prices of this supercheap stalwart. No-frills pinewood interior is the setting for bargains like beef stroganoff (£3.65) and grilled lamb cutlets (£4.30). 2-course set menu £3.90. Open M-Sa 7:30am-11pm, Su noon-10:30pm.

The Lanesborough, Hyde Park Corner (☎7259 5599). Tube: Hyde Park Corner. The sheer opulence of the Regency interior out-ritzes The Ritz—who would have thoght that 10 years ago this was a hospital? Afternoon tea is served in the Conservatory, a large glass-ceilinged room modelled on the Prince Regent's oriental-fantasy Brighton Pavilion: heavy silk furnishings, palm fronds, painted vases, and mannequin mandarins. Moreover, there's no dress code, and if you don't want a full tea, you can order a la carte (scones with jam and clotted cream £6.50). Set tea £22.50, champagne tea £26.50. Min. charge £9.50 per person.

Beverly Hills Bakery, 3 Egerton Terrace (☎ 7584 4401). Tube: South Kensington or Knightsbirdge. Tiny cafe-cum-bakery, with only 3 tables. The absence of Matt Dillon is offset by the all-natural goodies, baked on-site. Sandwiches £2-3, generous smoothies £2.50, American muffins £1.20. Eat-in prices around 20% higher. Open M-Sa 7:30am-6pm, Su 8:30am-5pm.

Gloriette, 128 Brompton Rd. (☎ 7589 4750). Tube: Knightsbridge. Venerable *pâtisserie* that recently started serving hot meals too. Leaf teas £2 per pot, delicious cakes and pastries £2.60-3.30, sandwiches £5-7. More substantial fare includes veal goulash (£7.50) and 2-course set meals (£8). Open M-F 7am-9pm, Sa 7am-8pm, Su 9am-6pm. MC, V.

BELGRAVIA

Grouse & Claret, Little Chester St. (☎ 7235 3438). Tube: Hyde Park Corner or Victoria. Traditional-style (though newish) pub on a quiet Belgravia mews, with lots of frosted-glass booths and polished wood. Food in the two bars includes freshly-carved hot gammon sandwiches (£3.15) and dinners (£6); the classier upstairs "Claret Room" offers classic English cooking such as Cotswold duck and steak & kidney pud. Open M-Sa 11am-11pm. MC, V.

Poilâne, 46 Elizabeth St. (☎ 7808 4910). Tube: Victoria or Sloane Sq. Paris's most famous *boulangerie* now brings its freshly baked delights to Belgravia; the loaves are pricey (£2-3), but *pain au chocolat* is a snip at 85p. Open M-F 7:30am-7:30pm, Sa 7:30am-6pm. MC, V.

KENSINGTON & EARL'S COURT

SEE MAP, p. 340-341

🔟 *NEIGHBORHOOD QUICKFIND: Discover, p. 9; Sights, p. 112; Museums&Galleries, p. 146; Entertainment, p. 216; Shopping, p. 233; Accommodations, p. 287.*

Kensington proper is not known for food, budget or otherwise; the most attractive spot is **Kensington Court,** a short pedestrian street lined with budget and mid-range pavement cafes and restaurants always popular on warm summer evenings. Things are much better in **South Kensington;** the area around the station positively overflows with cafes, sandwich bars, and cheap restaurants. On **Bute Street,** just opposite the Institut Francais's *lycée* (high school), you're as likely to hear French spoken as English in the sidewalk cafes, *pâtisseries,* and continental delis that provide some delicious budget eats. Nor is **Earl's Court** short of cafes and restaurants; both Earl's Court Rd. and Old Brompton Rd. have a good variety of affordable places to eat, though they tend to be scruffier than their posher northern and eastern neighbors.

🖼 **Wódka,** 12 St. Alban's Grove (☎ 7937 6513). Tube: Gloucester Rd. Proving that Polish food isn't all pierogi, Wódka (VOOT-ka) brings a dash of modernism to classics from braised rabbit (£12) to venison (£13.50). Set lunch £11 for two courses, but it's worth the splurge for a romantic evening. Pass over the pricey wines for one of the many flavored *wódki* (£2.50-3 a shot). Open M-F 12:30-2:30pm and 7-11:15pm, Sa-Su 7-11:15pm. AmEx, MC, V.

🖼 **The Troubador,** 265 Old Brompton Rd. (☎ 7370 1434). Tube: Earl's Court. Cosy old-fashioned interior festooned with curios and a shady rear garden play host to a laid back but fairly smart crowd. Sandwich platters with salad and crisps, £4-5, pasta £5-7, hot specials £7-10. Also poetry and folk-music nights (see p. 216). Open daily 9am-midnight. MC, V.

Balans, 187 Kensington High St. (☎ 7376 0115). Tube: High St. Kensington. Thoroughly mixed outpost of this growing gay-oriented cafe-bar chain (other branches include Soho, Chelsea, and Miami), popular with families at lunchtime. The bright designer interior makes it a nice spot for a drink; the Asian-Mediterranean fusion food (£6-10) is more hit-and-miss. 2-for-1 cocktails (£5) 4-7pm. Open daily 8pm-1am. MC, V.

The Orangery, Kensington Palace (☎ 7938 1406). Tube: High St. Kensington or Queensway. Built for Queen Anne's dinner parties, this airy Neoclassical building is now a popular setting for light lunches (£7-8) and afternoon teas (from £8). Open daily 10am-6pm. MC, V.

Oriental Canteen, 2a Exhibition Rd. (☎ 7581 8831). Tube: South Kensington. Perfect for filling up between museums, this tiny glass-fronted diner offers enormous portions at hard-to-beat prices. The short menu sticks to Chinese favorites. Roast duck and rice £4, Singapore noodles £3.50. Open daily noon-9:30pm. Cash only.

Raison d'Être, 18 Bute St. (☎ 7584 5008). Tube: South Kensington. Catering to the local French community, this stylish cafe offers a bewildering range of filled *baguettes* (£2.20-5) as well as a few *salades composées* (£3.50-4.70), all freshly made to order. Open M-F 8am-6pm, Sa 9:30am-4pm. Cash only.

The Scarsdale, 23a Edwardes Sq. (☎7937 1811). Tube: High St. Kensington. Allegedly built by a French speculator to house Napoleonic officers following the inevitable conquest of Britain, it's now a picture-perfect pub, welcoming the crowds to a sea of flowers outside and the fireplace and hanging lanterns within. Mains £10-13 (served noon-3pm and 6-10pm), salads and sandwiches £5-7, served all day. Open M-Sa noon-11pm, Su noon-10:30pm. MC, V.

Squeeze, 27 Kensington High St. (☎7376 9786). Tube: High St. Kensington. Generous smoothies and juices (£2.50-3.50) in a cheery interior: couches, brightly colored chairs, and a giant fruit mural. Open M-F 8am-8pm, Sa 9am-8pm, Su 10am-8pm; winter closes 7pm.

NOTTING HILL

⏺ *NEIGHBORHOOD QUICKFIND: Discover, p. 10; Sights, p. 113; Nightlife, p. 195; Entertainment, p. 216; Shopping, p. 234.*

Food in Notting Hill basically comes down to a choice between numerous overpriced, overhyped, and by far overtrendy media enclaves—many doubling as bars, such as Bridget Jones's favorite 192 and the Damien Hirst-designed Pharmacy (see Nightlife, p. 195)—and the dirt cheap and gen-

SEE MAP, p. 342

erally excellent cafes and takeouts serving the market crowds around Portobello Rd. For the widest variety of food, hunt around at the southern end of the general market and under the Westway.

🖾 **George's Portobello Fish Bar,** 329 Portobello Rd. (☎8969 7895). Tube: Ladbroke Grove. George opened up here in 1961, and while the shop has gone through various incarnations (it's currently disguised as a 50s-style diner), the fish and chips is still as good as ever. Choose your piece from the recently-fried fillets on display or ask them to rustle up a new one (£4-5), add a generous helping of chunky chips (£1), and wolf it down outside (no inside seating). Kebabs and burgers too. Open Su-F 11am-midnight, Sa 11am-9pm. Cash only.

Books for Cooks, 4 Blenheim Crescent (☎7221 1992). Tube: Ladbroke Grove. At lunchtime, chef-owner Eric and his crew of culinary pros "test" recipes from new titles, much to the enjoyment of customers (though the tables can make book-browsing a trifle tricky). There's no telling what will be on offer, but you can rely on the cakes (£2). Food available M-Sa 10am-2:30pm or so. Bookstore open M-Sa 10am-6pm. Daily cookery workshops held in upstairs demo kitchen (£25; reservations essential). MC, V, AmEx.

Fluid, 13 Elgin Crescent (☎7229 4871). Tube: Ladbroke Grove. Also at Vogue House, Hanover Sq. (☎7499 9052; Tube: Oxford Circus). Ultra-minimalist juice bar—just 5 chairs, 4 stools, no tables, a motorcycle mural, and a great fruity smell. Single juices from £1.90, smoothies from £2.75. Open M-F 8:30am-6pm, Sa 9am-6pm, Su 10am-6pm.

The Grain Shop, 269a Portobello Rd. (☎7229 5571). Tube: Ladbroke Grove. The main attraction here are the generous home-made takeaway bakes and salads; mix as many dishes as you like to make up a small (£2.25), medium (£3.45), or gut-busting large (£4.60) box. Even on non-market days, the fast-moving line stretches out of the shop and down Portobello Rd. Organic breads baked on-site (£1-2). Open M-Sa 9:30am-6pm. MC, V.

Lisboa Patisserie, 57 Golborne Rd. (☎8968 5242). Tube: Ladbroke Grove. Tiny Iberian bakery-cum-cafe, packed with nicotine-infused Portuguese and Moroccan men intent on their coffee. Fantastic selection of cakes and pastries, 45p and up—don't miss the Portuguese custard pie. Glass of coffee 75p. Open daily 8am-8pm. Cash only.

Makan, 270 Portobello Rd. (☎8960 5169). Tube: Ladbroke Grove. One of a number of barebones eateries snuggling under the Westway. Ignore the menu and head straight to the counter to choose from the dozens of curries on display—don't be afraid to mix part-portions different dishes. Generous eat-in plates (£4-6) cost 80p-£1 more than their smaller takeaway brethren. Open M-Sa 11:30am-6:30pm. Cash only.

Manzara, 24 Pembridge Rd. (☎7727 3062). Tube: Notting Hill Gate. In addition to the standard kebabs, this Turkish takeaway specializes in *pide,* pizza-like pastries rolled and filled with all manner of delicacies (£4 takeaway, £6 eat-in). Open daily 7am-midnight. Cash only.

The Tea and Coffee Plant, 170 Portobello Rd. (☎7221 8137). Tube: Ladbroke Grove. There's an overpowering smell of coffee from the ever-trundling bean-roaster at the back of this tiny shop, which sells a wide range of fairly traded and organic caffeine-based infusions. Chew a bean before committing to a kilo (£14), or sip on a fresh espresso (75p). Mail order available. Open Tu-Th 10:30am-6:30pm, F-Sa 9:15am-6pm.

BAYSWATER

SEE MAP, p. 342

⚑ NEIGHBORHOOD QUICKFIND: Discover p. 10; **Entertainment,** p. 217; **Shopping,** p. 236; **Accommodations,** p. 289.

Cheap and central, Bayswater was an immigrant magnet in the years after WWII, and as such served a pioneering role in developing Britain's tastebuds. The **Standard Tandoori,** on Westbourne Grove, was one of London's first Indian restaurants, while houmus, kebabs, and other Middle Eastern delights were also introduced to Londoners through Bayswater's large Arab population. Today, **Westbourne Grove** continues to offer a wide range of food; for those of a less adventurous disposition, **Whiteley's** mall (see p. 236) has a good selection of quality chain restaurants.

☒ Royal China, 13 Queensway (☎7221 2535) Tube: Bayswater or Queensway. Royal China's lacquered, swan-themed walls give it a glitzy flavor that thankfully isn't mirrored in the prices. Renowned for London's best *dim sum* (£2-3 per dish; count on 3-4 dishes each), ordered from a menu rather than a trolley—which means that not only is the food freshly made, but you actually know what you're getting. Set meals start from £7-10. *Dim sum* served M-Sa noon-5pm, Su 11am-5pm; on weekends, arrive early or expect to wait 30-45min. Open M-Th noon-11pm, F-Sa noon-11:30pm, Su 11am-10pm. AmEx, MC, V.

☒ La Bottega del Gelato, 127 Bayswater Rd. (☎7243 2443). Tube: Queensway. Now in his 70s, Quinto Barbieri still gets up at 4:30am every morning to make the best *gelati* this side of the Rubicon. Right opposite Hyde Park, it's perfect for a post-prandial stroll. Scoops from £1.30. Open daily 10am-7pm, later in summer. Cash only.

Alounak Kebab, 44 Westbourne Grove (☎7229 0416). Tube: Bayswater or Royal Oak. With decor ranging from a golden rococo fountain to a silver pendulum clock, Alounak's decor is hard to define; the food, however, is thoroughly Persian. Slow grilled kebabs (from £5.60) are served with mouthwateringly fluffy saffron rice or fresh *taboon* bread, baked to order in the traditional clay oven by the door; for a more authentic Persian experience, try one of the daily changing specials (£7). 10% service extra. Open daily noon-midnight. MC, V.

MARYLEBONE & REGENT'S PARK

SEE MAP, p. 344-345

⚑ NEIGHBORHOOD QUICKFIND: Discover, p. 11; **Sights,** p. 114; **Museums&Galleries,** p. 148; **Entertainment,** p. 217; **Accommodations,** p. 292.

Long regarded as something of a food wilderness, Marylebone is staging a fightback with numerous fashionable restaurants and modern sandwich bars opening up around **Marylebone High St.** Nevertheless, the Middle Eastern oasis of Edgware Rd. aside, this is not a place to go searching for great meal deals.

☒ Patogh, 8 Crawford Pl. (☎7262 4015). Tube: Edgware Rd. *Patogh* is Persian for "meeting place," and this certainly is a focal point for London's Iranian community. The generous portions are out of proportion with the tiny space; order a *kebab-e-koobideh* (minced-lamb kebab) with bread to receive a delicious 12" flatbread strewn with grilled meat, herbs, and *torshi* (Iranian pickles). Open daily noon-midnight. Cash only.

☒ Mandalay, 444 Edgware Rd. (☎7258 3696). About 7min. walk north from Edgware Rd. Tube. Looks ordinary, tastes extraordinary; this down-to-earth Burmese restaurant has a wall plastered with awards and accolades. Lunch specials are good value (curry and rice £3.70, 3 courses £5.90), but be sure to ask for the full menu, which includes a page of explanation of Burmese cuisine. No smoking. Open M-Sa noon-2:30pm and 6-10:30pm. AmEx, MC, V.

☒ Giraffe, 6-8 Blandford St. (☎7935 2333). Tube: Bond St. or Baker St. Second branch of the deservedly popular world-food micro chain, with the same winning combination of delicious eats (mains around £8), modern decor, and great music. See Hampstead, p. 178.

Ranoush Juice, 43 Edgware Rd. (☎ 7723 5929). Tube: Marble Arch. The cheapest arm of the Maroush Edgware Rd. restaurant empire, this upscale kebab house is commonly regarded as the best Lebanese joint on the Edgware Rd.—and that's up against some stiff competition. Fortunately, you don't need a sultan's ransom to enjoy kebabs (£2.50-4). The thick, sweet juices (£1.50) may not be to everyone's taste, and despite the piles of fruit on the counter are rarely squeezed to order. Open daily 9:30am-3am. Cash only.

Reubens, 79 Baker St. (☎7486 0035). Tube: Baker St. One of the only kosher eateries in central London, Reubens does double service as an eat-in deli and a pricey basement restaurant. The hot salt beef is carved before your eyes (sandwich £6, platter £9). Open Su-Th 11:30am-10pm, F 11:30am to 2hr. before shabbat. Cash only in deli.

Zizzi, 34 Paddington St. (☎7224 1450). Tube: Baker St. Take a hint from the large wood-fired oven dominating the open-plan kitchen at this smart, popular Italian restaurant, and pass over the solid but uninspired pasta dishes (£6-7) for deliciously crunchy, hand-thrown pizzas (£5-7.50)—watch the show-off staff spin your pie to within a millimeter of perfection. In summer, the windows come off and tables spill outside; even so, bookings are recommended F-Sa. Open Su-Th 11am-11pm, F-Sa 11am-11:30pm. AmEx, MC, V.

BLOOMSBURY

⁊ NEIGHBORHOOD QUICKFIND: Discover, p. 11; **Sights,** p. 116; **Museums&Galleries,** p. 148; **Entertainment,** p. 217; **Shopping,** p. 236; **Accommodations,** p. 293.

SEE MAP, pp. 344-345

At the heart of London's student community, Bloomsbury is overflowing with top-notch budget food. Running parallel to Tottenham Court Rd., **Charlotte Street** (Tube: Goodge St.) has for decades been one of London's best-known foodie streets, with a range of fashionable restaurants at all price ranges. A string of extremely cheap Indian vegetarian eateries and sweet shops lines **Drummond St.,** near Euston, while on the other side of Bloomsbury, bordering Holborn, **Sicilian Ave.** has some great sandwich and snack shops on an attractive pedestrian street.

▨ Da Beppe, 116 Tottenham Court Rd. (☎7387 6324). Tube: Warren St. Simply put, probably the best Italian restaurant in London. Beppe himself keeps the patrons coming back for more with positively Texan-sized platters of authentic Italian delicacies. Choose from 34 pastas and risottos (£6.50-8.50), 20 pizzas (£5-8.50), and numerous specialty meats (£8.50-10). Open M-Sa noon-3pm and daily 6-11pm. AmEx, MC, V.

▨ Diwana Bhel Poori House, 121-123 Drummond St. (☎7387 5556). Tube: Warren St. or Euston. No frills or frippery here—just great, cheap south Indian vegetarian food. Why bother with the £5.10 lunch buffet (daily noon-2:30pm) when £4.85 will get you a *Paneer Dosa* (rice pancake filled with potato and cheese) that's more than enough. Outside buffet hours, the *Thali* set meals offer great value (£4-6). Open daily noon-11:30pm. AmEx, MC, V.

▨ Vats, 51 Lamb's Conduit St. (☎7242 8963). Tube: Russell Square. Small front conceals a long romantic space. Friendly staff are happy to let you taste before you commit (at least for wines available by the glass). Food is pricey (starters £5-6, mains £9-16) but delicious. Long wine list leans towards Bordeaux, with "good ordinary claret" £3.50 per glass or £14 per bottle; Burgundy from £16. Open M-Sa noon-11:30pm. AmEx, MC, V.

Alara Wholefoods, 58-60 Marchmont St. (☎7837 1172). Tube: Russell Sq. In addition to the market, an in-store kitchen offers self-service salads and bakes for about £3.50 per lb.; eat them standing at the indoor counter, sit on the patio, or get it to go. Open M-F 9:30am-6pm, Sa 10am-6pm. MC, V.

C.T.J., 339 Euston Rd. (☎7387 5450). Tube: Warren St. All day vegetarian Chinese buffet, including *faux*-meaty delights such as pseudo duck with hoisin sauce and sweet-and-sour soya, as well as deep-fried vegetables, noodles, and rice, all for £5. Quality (and temperature) vary according to the dish and the time of day, but there's no denying that it's great value. Open daily noon-10pm. Cash only.

ECCo (Express Coffee Co.), 46 Goodge St. (☎7580 9250). 11" thin-crust pizzas, made to order, cost an incredible £3; sandwiches and baguettes, on in-store baked bread, cost from £1, and rolls from 50p. Buy any hot drink before noon and get a delicious fresh-baked croissant for free. Pizzas available from noon on. Open daily 7am-11pm. Cash only.

Navarro's, 67 Charlotte St. (☎7637 7713). Tube: Goodge St. Bustling *tapas* restaurant, with traditional tiles and handpainted tables. It's not a place for lounging, though—the chairs could have been devised by the Inquisition as atonement for such pleasures as sautéed octo-

175

DOGS & DUCKS

Pubs are an aspect of London that is impossible to miss—there's a place to tipple on virtually every street corner. With titles like "The Dog & Duck," pub names, however, appear to be mysteriously unrelated to the offerings inside. That's not usually the case. Pub names with the word "bell" in them often referred to nearby church or monastery ringers; Christian religious icons such as lambs and doves soon found their way onto pub signs, then into the names themselves. Even the unlikely name "The Bull" has a religious derivative, "bull" being a corruption of the Latin word for monastery.

Pubs also tried to align themselves with nobility; some, like the "King William IV" pub, are named after individual royal figures. It was often too impractical, however, to constantly shift names with the political tides, so many pubs adopted general terms associated with the monarchy, such as "The Crown" and "The King's Head." To align themselves with noble families, pubs often took the names of the creatures that appeared on a family coat-of-arms; the lion was a popular example of this phenomenon.

pus (£5) or meatballs in wine sauce (£4). 2-3 *tapas* per person is plenty, especially if you want to leave room for unusual desserts such as cheese and quince preserve (£3). Open M-F noon-3pm and 6-10pm, Sa 6-10pm. AmEx, MC, V.

Wagamama, 4A Streatham St. (☎ 7323 9223). Tube: Tottenham Ct. Rd. See p. 158. Original branch of the noodle empire, convenient for British Museum-goers.

PUBS

The Jeremy Bentham, 31 University St. (☎ 7387 3033). Tube: Goodge St. Two floors packed with students from nearby University College London (after whose founder it is named). In better weather, the crowd spills onto the patio and pavement at front. Pints from £2.20, with well-regarded pies from £4.25 and sandwiches and burgers from £3. Open M-Sa 11am-11pm, Su noon-10:30pm.

The Lamb, 94 Lamb's Conduit St. (☎ 7405 0713). Tube: Russell Sq. Popular with doctors from the many nearby hospitals, this old-fashioned pub is also a celebrity hangout—regulars include Peter O'Toole, and fading daguerreotypes of past thespian tipplers line the walls. The swivelling "snob screens" around the bar originally provided privacy for "respectable" men meeting with ladies of ill-repute. Food served daily noon-2:30pm and M-Sa 6-9pm. Open M-Sa 11am-11pm, Su noon-10:30pm. MC, V.

NORTH LONDON

ISLINGTON

🚇 *Tube: Angel unless otherwise noted. NEIGHBORHOOD QUICKFIND: Discover, p. 12; Sights, p. 118; Museums&Galleries, p. 149; Nightlife, p. 196; Entertainment, p. 218; Shopping, p. 237; Accommodations, p. 298.*

There are over 100 restaurants on **Upper Street** alone, and an estimated 200 within the immediate vicinity. Naturally, all the big chains are out in force, but they face tough competition. Off Upper St., at Islington Green, **Essex Rd.** still preserves some of the old Islington feel, with cheaper, more downmarket eateries, although it too is rapidly yuppifying. For a real taste of the old days, head to **Chapel Market,** just off Upper St. opposite Angel Tube, where a traditional working-class meal can be had for under £2. For the truly adventurous, **M. Manze,** near the fish stall, will give you a ladleful of hot eels smothered in green gravy, with a dollop of mash, for £2.60. One taste of this authentic London fayre will suffice to explain how Indian food gained such rapid acceptance in England.

🔾 **Tartuf**, 88 Upper St. (☎ 7288 0954). Have a fantastic cutlery-free experience with Alsatian *tartes flambées* (£5-6), a cross between a crepe and a pizza, only much tastier. In true French fashion Eric, the garrulous owner, has resisted offers to franchise—it's his high standards and personal touch that make this such a sterling find. Before 3pm get one savory and one sweet *tarte* for £4.90; for £9.80 each, a table can have an all-you-can-eat pigfest. Open M-F noon-3pm and 5-11:30pm, Sa-Su noon-11:30pm. MC, V.

▨ **Gallipoli,** 102 Upper St., and **Gallipoli Again,** 120 Upper St. (☎7359 0630). Patterned wall tiles, hanging lamps, and Anatolian pop provide the authentic background to such Turkish delights as "Iskender Kebap," grilled lamb served with yoghurt and marinated pita bread (£6.95). There's also an exceptional range of appetizers (most £2.75): the meze (£6) combination is large enough for three. Reserve F-Sa. Open M-Th 10am-11pm, F-Sa 10am-midnight, Su 11am-10:30pm. MC, V.

▨ **Giraffe,** 29-31 Essex Rd. (☎7359 5999). The same succesful formula as the Hampstead original (see p. 178). Open M-F 8a-11:30pm, Sa 9am-11:30pm, Su 9am-11pm. AmEx, MC, V.

▨ **Candid Arts Trust Cafe,** 3 Torrens St. (☎7837 4237). Behind Angel Tube, opposite the Blue Angel pub; it's the door beneath the horse sculpture; go up 2 floors to reach the cafe. Lush antique furniture and serene, sexually-provocative paintings form the perfect background for serious discussions and romantic overtures. Sandwiches £2.50, other dishes £4-6. Open M-Sa noon-10pm, Su noon-5pm. Cash only.

Duke of Cambridge, 30 St. Peter's St. (☎7359 3066). The 100% organic menu of this friendly gastropub includes a vegan soup (£4.50) and vegetarian options. Mains £7.50-12. Open M 5pm-11:30pm, Tu-F noon-11pm, Sa noon-11pm, and Su noon-10:30pm; dinner daily 6:30-10:30pm, lunch Tu-F 12:30-3pm and Sa-Su 12:30-3:30pm. AmEx, MC, V.

Gem, 265 Upper St. (☎7359 0405). About half-way between Angel and Highbury & Islington Tubes. A diamond for the price of a bauble, Kurdish specialties help Gem stand out from the run of Anatolian eateries nearby. Everyone gets a freshly made Kurdish pastry, made on the griddle by the entrance. Plenty of vegetarian choices. Fantastic value set meals; £7 for a 4-course lunch, £9 for a 5-course dinner. Reserve F-Sa night. Open daily noon-midnight. MC, V.

Le Mercury, 140a Upper St. (☎7354 4088). Pseudo-French food at pseudo-French prices, which translates into a great deal by London standards. £6 gets you a main course of pork medallions, duck *à l'orange*, or entrecote, though paying extra for vegetables (£2) undermines the low prices. Reserve for evenings. Open M-Sa noon-1am, Su noon-11:30pm. MC, V.

CAMDEN TOWN

▨ **Tube:** Camden Town unless otherwise noted. **NEIGHBORHOOD QUICKFIND: Discover,** p. 12; **Sights,** p. 118; **Museums&Galleries,** p. 149; **Food&Drink,** p. 177; **Nightlife,** p. 196; **Entertainment,** p. 218; **Shopping,** p. 237.

On weekends, **Camden High St.** fills with the odor of cheap sausages and fried onions—though there's no shortage of good food to be found in the markets. **Camden Lock** and **Camden Canal** markets combine a fair selection of stands with some canalside seating, but the widest range of world food is found in **Stables Market.** Outside the market, Camden has no shortage of restaurants, many of which can be found on Camden High St.; **Parkway,** running from the Tube towards Regent's Park, is home to several noodle bars and old stalwarts. Away from the hubub towards posh Primrose Hill, a number of good mid-priced restaurants cater to more refined tastes on **Regent's Park Rd.**

▨ **New Culture Revolution,** 43 Parkway (☎7267 2700). Budgeteer, kowtow to the NCR! Prophetically named—when this small restaurant opened in 1994, serving simple steaming bowls of noodles in a modern, functional setting, East Asian food in London was associated with greasy takeaways or stodgy Chinatown brasseries. Noodles, dumplings, and north-Chinese food, including lots of fish and vegetables, all under £6. Open M-Th noon-3:30pm and 5:30-11pm, F noon-11pm, Sa-Su 1-11pm. AmEx, MC, V.

▨ **Odette's Wine Bar,** 130 Regent's Park Rd. (☎7586 5486). Tube: Chalk Farm. Odette's Restaurant, upstairs, is one of London's best restaurants, with prices to match—but the wine bar in the basement offers its own culinary delights at far lower prices. Few places are as romantic as a table in one of the snug alcoves; the infernally slow service will give you plenty of time to gaze into you partner's eyes. Most starters £5-7, mains £8-10. Naturally, an exceptional range of wines, including many half bottles. Open M-Sa 5:30-10:30pm. V, MC.

Marine Ices, 8 Haverstock Hill (☎7482 9003). Tube: Chalk Farm. The Mansi family have been in charge here since 1930, and now supply their superb *gelati* to 1500 restaurants in and around London. Get it at the source for £1.20 for a single scoop, £2.40 for a sit-down

FLAKES & SMARTIES

British food has character (of one sort or another), and the traditional snack menu is a unique hodgepodge of sweets, crisps, and squashes. Favorite **chocolate bars** include Flake (a stick of flaky chocolate often stuck into an ice cream cone), Crunchie (honeycombed magic), and the classic Dairy Milk. Other favorites include Fruit & Nut, Lunch Break, and Aero Bars. **Sweets** come in many forms—the fizzy Refreshers, the chewy Wine Gums, or frosted Fruit Pastilles. **Crisps** (potato chips to the Yanks) are not just salted, but come in a range of flavors, including prawn cocktail, cheese & onion, chicken, bacon, and salt & vinegar. All this sugar and salt can be washed down with Lilt, a pineapple and grapefruit flavored **fizzy drink** (soda), or a drinkbox-ful of Ribena, a super-sweet blackcurrant manna from heaven. This latter beverage belongs to a family of drinks known as **squashes,** fruit-based syrups watered down to drink. But the food that expatriate Britons miss most is **Marmite,** a yeast extract which is spread on bread or toast. If you weren't fed Marmite as a baby, you'll never appreciate it; most babies don't either.

sundae. The family-friendly restaurant offers solid Italian standards at very reasonable prices (pastas, pizzas, and meats £6-8). *Gelateria* open M-Sa 10:30am-11pm, Su 11am-10pm; restaurant M-F noon-3pm and 6-11pm, Sa noon-11pm, Su noon-10pm. V, MC.

Trojka, 101 Regent's Park Rd. (☎7483 3765). Ostensibly a Russian tea room, the three-horse trap of its name could be taken to refer to the Russian, Ukrainian, and Polish influences tugging on the menu. If your budget doesn't stretch to the sevruga caviar *blinis* (£49), Danish caviar makes an affordable substitute (£3.70 starter, £6.50 main). *Pelmeni* (pierogi; £6) are perfect for a light supper. F-Sa nights £1 supplement for violin renditions of "Eastern European" kitsch classics. Open daily 9am-10:30pm. MC, V.

WKD, 18 Kentish Town Rd. (☎7267 1869). See Nightlife, p. 198.

HAMPSTEAD AND HIGHGATE

⚐ Tube: Hampstead unless otherwise noted. **NEIGHBORHOOD QUICKFIND: Discover,** p. 12; **Sights,** p. 119; **Museums&Galleries,** p. 149; **Food&Drink,** p. 178; **Entertainment,** p. 218; **Accommodations,** p. 298.

Mid- to upper-range restaurants crowd among the shops on **Hampstead High Street;** for more budget-friendly fare, head up **Heath Street.** At the bottom of the hill, pleasant cafes and smart restaurants set up outside tables on the broad pavements around **Belsize Park. Highgate** is rather short on eating opportunities—there's a Pizza Express in the village at 28 Highgate High St., but otherwise it's mostly pubs.

▨ Le Crêperie de Hampstead, 77 Hampstead High St. Totally authentic French crêpes (only much better), prepared before your eyes in the tiniest van imaginable. Mushroom garlic cream £3, Banana Butterscotch Cream Dream £2.40. 35p gets you gooey Belgian chocolate (plain, milk, or white) instead of sticky syrup. Lemon and sugar £1.65. Open M-Th 11:45am-11pm, F-Su 11:45am-11:30pm. Cash only.

▨ Giraffe, 46 Rosslyn Hill (☎7435 0343). A contemporary giraffe theme, an eclectic international menu, and toe-tapping music make Giraffe a treat. Superb salads—try the sushi rice, avocado, and daikon (£4.30). Main courses run from Louisiana fishcakes (£8.25) to Toulouse sausages (£7.95). "Giraffe Time" gives you 2 courses for £6.50 and 2-for-1 drinks M-F 5-7pm. Open M-F 8a-11:30pm, Sa 9am-11:30pm, Su 9am-11pm. AmEx, MC, V.

Bar Room Bar, 48 Rossyln Hill (☎7435 0808). There's a New York feel to this self-consciously hip but laid-back bar and art gallery. Ponder the bizarre teacup chandelier, or head out to the heated rear garden. DJs spin Th-Su nights. Pizzas £5-7; two-for-one special Tu 7-11pm. Or settle for a bowl of jelly beans (£1.50) and a cocktail (£4). "Meet the artist" gallery openings first W of every month. Open M-Sa 11am-11pm, Su noon-10:30pm. MC, V.

PUBS

The Flask, 77 Highgate West Hill. (☎8348 7346). Bus #214 from Kentish Town or #210 from Archway. Built in 1663, the low-ceilinged, labrynthine interior is perfect for long winter evenings, while summer drinkers regularly spill over from the beer garden onto the green in front. The menu mixes Olde English (sausage and mash, £5.75) with modern British (Chorizo melt £4.50). Open M-Sa 11am-11pm, Su noon-10:30pm; food served M-F noon-3pm and 6-10pm, Sa noon-4pm and 7-10pm, Su noon-4pm only. MC, V.

King William IV (KW4), 77 Hampstead High St. (☎ 7435 5647). The rainbow flag fluttering outside the well-kept 18th-century facade gives it away—this is one of London's most popular gay pubs. Sandwiches (£2.50) and more innovative fare (orange pork chops,£5.25) is served daily noon-5pm, with traditional roast Su (£5.50). Weekly ladies night (call for dates). Open M-Sa 11am-11pm, Su noon-10:30pm.

FURTHER NORTH

🚇 Tube: Golders Green (Zone 2) unless otherwise noted. **NEIGHBORHOOD QUICKFIND: Discover,** p. 12; **Sights,** p. 122; **Museums&Galleries,** p. 149; **Entertainment,** p. 218.

🍽 Carmelli Bakery, 128 Golders Green Rd. (☎8455 2074). Carmelli's golden, egg-glazed *challah* (£1.20-1.70) is considered the best in London; the bagels and sinfully good pastries (£1.50) aren't far behind. Packed Friday afternoons, as every Jewish mother in London scrambles to get bread for *shabbat;* popular enough at other times to warrant frequent 24hr. opening. Open M-W 6am-1am, then continously from 6am Th to about 1hr. before sunset on F, and again from nightfall Sa all through Su to 1am M morning.

🍽 Noto Sushi, Oriental City, 399 Edgware Rd. (☎8200 1189, answered in Japanese). Tube: Colindale (Zone 4). Turn right onto Colindale Av. and right again on Edgware Rd. In the food hall of a giant East Asian-flavored mall, Noto's sushi is considered the best in London. Most sushi £1.20-1.50; M-Th lunchtime get all-you-can-eat in 1hr. for £15—but you'll have to pay full price for anything left uneaten at the end. Prepacked takeaway boxes offer a filling lunch for £3-5. Takeaway open M-Sa 10am-8pm, Su to 7pm; restaurant 11am-7pm, Su 6pm. MC, V. **Branch** in Harrods, at double the price.

Blooms, 130 Golders Green Rd. (☎8455 1338). Gloomy waiters in white dinner jackets and black bow ties have been an essential a part of the Blooms experience since 1920. Vegetarians will blanche at the thought of such hearty central European favorites as gefilte fish (£3.50), chopped liver (£4.80), and lokshen soup (£2.90). Open Su-Th noon-10:30pm, F 11am to 2 or 3pm.

Solly's, 148 Golders Green Rd. (☎8455 0004). Moroccan lamps hang low over the counter, chock full of mediterranean dips and salads; more trinkets hang from the wooden beams of the rear dining rooms. On Sa evenings, a long line waits patiently for grilled aubergines (£3) and kebabs (£4). Open Su-Th noon-11pm, F noon to mid-afternoon, Sa nightfall-1am.

WEST LONDON

🚇 NEIGHBORHOOD QUICKFIND: Discover, p. 13; **Sights,** p. 123; **Entertainment,** p. 220; **Accommodations,** p. 299.

Not traditionally an area renowned for its restaurants or its pubs, **Shepherd's Bush** offers the most variety on Goldhawk Rd. (Tube: Goldhawk Rd.), with a wealth of cheap ethnic eateries. **Hammersmith** is famous for the riverside pubs alond the Upper and Lower Malls, west of the bridge. During the annual boat race between Oxford and Cambridge universities (late Mar./early Apr.), thousands gather here to drink and watch the rowers speed by at the race's half-way point.

The Dove, 19 Upper Mall (☎8748 5405). Tube: Hammersmith. One of the cosier Hammersmith riverside pubs, with a private terrace overlooking the Thames. Licensed in the 16th century, Charles II was known to drop in; *Rule Britannia* was written in one of the upstairs rooms. The current pub is 18th-century, with a traditional interior and traditional pub grub (£5-6) as well as filled baguettes (£3.50). Open M-Sa 11am-11pm, Su noon-10:30pm; food served M-F noon-2pm and 6:30-9:15pm, Sa noon-2:30 and 6:30-9:15pm, Su noon-2:45pm. MC, V.

The Gate, 51 Queen Caroline St. (☎8748 6932). Tube: Hammersmith. Go through the garden gate and up the external stairs on the right. Considered one of London's top vegetarian restaurants, with prices to match: teriyake aubergine, wild mushroom fricassee, or Thai red curry £9-10. Still, if you want to splash out on a meat-free meal, this is the place. Reserve for evenings. Open M-F noon-3pm and 6-11pm, Sa 6-11pm. AmEx, MC, V.

Patio, 5 Goldhawk Rd. (☎ 8743 5194). Tube: Goldhawk Rd. A facade so unassuming as to be almost invisible conceals a baroque splendor of red tablecloths, blue glasses, and gold-edged mirrors. The menu betrays little of its origins—dishes are prosaically named in English—but the hearty portions (and the staff's accents) give Patio away as thoroughly Polish. "Light meals," e.g. filled pancakes, run £4-6; meat and fish mains £7-9. The 3-course special (£11.90 including vodka) will satisfy the largest appetites. Open noon-3pm and 6pm-midnight. AmEx, DC, MC, V.

Riverside Studios Cafe, in Riverside Studios, Hammersmith (see p. 220; ☎ 8237 1057). Funky cafe-bar in the center of this mini-cultural complex, with a riverside terrace accessed via a long and narrow corridor. Interesting menu: try grilled squid salad (£6.50), chanterelle risotto (£6.20), or lamb burgers (£5). Open M-F 10:30am-11pm, Sa 12:30-11pm, Sa 12:30-9pm; food M-F noon-9pm, Sa-Su 12:30-9pm. MC, V (£5 min.).

SOUTH LONDON

⚑ NEIGHBORHOOD QUICKFIND: Discover, p. 13; **Sights,** p. 125; **Museums&Galleries,** p. 151; **Nightlife,** p. 198; **Entertainment,** p. 220; **Shopping,** p. 238; **Accommodations,** p. 299.

With its ethnic mix coupled with an increasing number of affluent 20- to 30-somethings with money to burn, **Brixton** is rapidly establishing itself as a dining destination. Though newer openings tend to be trendy and increasingly expensive, there are still a number of of cheap restaurants serving African and West Indian cuisine: come during the market (see p. 238) to feast on traditional delights like curry goat.

Bah Humbug, in the crypt of St. Matthew's Church, Brixton Hill (☎ 7738 3184). Crucifixes keep vampires at bay, as does the exclusively vegetarian and fish menu. Prices in the main dining room are high (mains £7-10), but a £7 "munch menu" applies in the lounge area and outside terrace. Su brunch (£4.50, 11am-2pm). Evening reservations essential (not lounge). Open M-Sa 5pm-midnight, Su 11am-midnight MC, V.

Café Bar and Juice Bar, 407 Coldharbour Ln. (☎ 7738 4141). Laid back staff dish out huge portions of Caribbean food: the "soul food special" (£5.50) is a feast of plantain, stewed yams, and salad on 2 plates. Open Su-Th 10am-midnight, F-Sa 10am-1am. AmEx, MC, V.

Fujiyama, 7 Vining St. (☎ 7737 2369). Warm wooden tables and red walls form the backdrop to all your favorite ramen, udon, and soba, plus curries and rice dishes (£5-7). Open Su-Th noon-11pm, F and Sa noon-midnight. AmEx, MC, V.

SW9, 11 Dorrell Pl. (☎ 7738 3116). Tube: Brixton. A stylish celebration of diversity. Gay and straight, black and white congregate at the purple tables. Breakfasts £5-6, meals £6-7.50 (to 10pm). Open Su-W 9:30am-11pm, Th 9:30am-11:30pm, F-Sa 9:30am-1am. MC, V.

EAST LONDON

WHITECHAPEL & THE EAST END

⚑ Tube: Shoreditch (open rush hour and Su morning), or a 10min. walk from Tube: Aldgate East or Tube: Liverpool St. **NEIGHBORHOOD QUICKFIND: Discover,** p. 14; **Sights,** p. 126; **Museums&Galleries,** p. 152; **Nightlife,** p. 199; **Entertainment,** p. 221; **Shopping,** p. 239.

Mention Whitechapel and food to a Londoner, and they'll immediately reply "Brick Lane," "curry," and "bagels." While that's a fairly accurate summing up of the situation—for dirt-cheap Bangladeshi food and Jewish bakeries, **Brick Lane** can't be beat—it ignores the burgeoning popularity of **Spitalfields Market** (see Sights, p. 127). Here, the Edwardian market hall has a number of international food stalls offering daytime market browsers everything from pad thai to crepes; there's even a dedicated seating area. Most food stalls open only for lunch and close Saturday.

Aladin, 132 Brick Ln. (☎ 7247 8210). One of Brick Lane's more popular Balti joints—even the Prince of Wales has been here. Still, don't expect the red-carpet treatment; the diner-style interior's pretty basic, but who cares when you can get a Camilla Parker Bowl of curry for £3-4. BYOB. Open daily 11:30am-11:30pm. Cash only.

Arkansas Café, Old Spitalfields Market (☎ 7377 6999). Arkansan former antique-dealer Bubba now spends his days lovingly tending his oak-fired pits at this indoor-outdoor BBQ shack. The beef is all hormone-free US meat, chickens free-range from France. No fries—instead, settle for salad and sweetcorn with your burger (£4.50) or wild boar sausage (£6.50). Open M-F noon-2:30pm, Su noon-4pm. £5 min. per head. MC, V.

Brick Lane Beigel Bakery, 159 Brick Ln. (☎ 7729 0616). One of the last remaining Jewish businesses in what was once the heartland of Jewish London. Beigel, bagel, schmeigel, schmagel—who cares how you spell it, at 12p each it's not worth arguing. Also platzels, filled beigels, cholla, and pastries, all under £1. Open 24hr.

Café 1001, Dray Walk, off Brick Ln. (☎ 7247 9679). Superchilled hipster hangout in the Truman Brewery complex, with old sofas lined with older rugs, plus outside benches. Cold food runs from parma ham and mozzarella sandwiches (£3.30), to smoked-chicken salad (£4.80). Smoothies £2.50. Officially open M-F 8am-11pm, Sa-Su 10am-11pm, with food served to 6pm, but often closes around 10pm.

Nazrul, 130 Brick Ln. (☎ 7247 2505). Next to Aladin, Nazrul offers a more "traditional" interior—starched tablecloths and dark wallpaper—and similar prices, with big servings of balti from £3.10. Open M-Th noon-3pm and 5:30pm-midnight, F-Sa noon-3pm and 5:30pm-1am, Su noon-midnight. Cash only.

HOXTON & SHOREDITCH

🔢 *NEIGHBORHOOD QUICKFIND: Discover, p. 14; Sights, p. 127; Museums&Galleries, p. 152; Nightlife, p. 199; Entertainment, p. 221; Shopping, p. 239.*

As the tone of "Shoho" shifts from can't-afford-to-eat artists to can't-be-bothered-to-cook media types, a number of pricey eateries have appeared, such as the acclaimed **Real Greek,** in Hoxton Market (behind the Old St. Holiday Inn). For an affordable meal, though, your best bet remains the bar food in trendy drinking haunts.

🔲 **Grand Central,** 93 Great Eastern St. (☎ 7613 4228). Tube: Old St. You could spend all day here: start with waffles and maple syrup for breakfast (£3.40, served to noon), move on to an open-faced hot salt-beef sandwich (corned beef to Americans; £5.25) for lunch, wild salmon hash (£6.50) for dinner, then relax with one of 26 different bourbons (£1.90-2.40) as the nighttime crowds pile in to hear DJs play the latest electronica, soul, hip-hop, house, and R&B. Open M-F 7:30am-midnight, Sa 10am-midnight, Su noon-10:30pm. MC, V.

Hoxton Square Bar & Kitchen, 2-4 Hoxton Sq. (☎ 7613 0709). This long, dark space, with raw gray concrete walls and 1970s-style swivel chairs, is London's first gastrobar. Packed with spikey-haired drinkers every evening, they also cook up mediterranean-style fare in the open-plan kitchen (mains £7-9, sandwiches £5-6, served all day). Open M-Sa noon-midnight, Su noon-10:30pm. MC, V.

Yelo, 8-9 Hoxton Sq. (☎ 7729 4629). Tube: Old St. Affordable and stylish, this Thai restaurant offers noodles, curries, rice dishes and salads for £4-5. Small bowl of rice £1.50 extra. Eat out overlooking the square in summer, then head next-door to the basement Yelo Bar for cocktails (£2.50-6). Open M-Th noon-3pm and 6-11pm, F noon-3pm and 6-11:30pm, Sa 2-11:30pm, Su 2-10:30pm.

DOCKLANDS

🔢 *NEIGHBORHOOD QUICKFIND: Discover, p. 14; Sights, p. 128; Food&Drink, p. 180; Entertainment, p. 221; Shopping, p. 239.*

While Docklands has yet to appear on the gastronomic map, inn-keepers have long taken advantage of its riverside charms—the oldest buildings around are the pubs along the banks of the Thames. Most have a terrace built on piles over the river, making them the perfect spot from which to watch the world float by.

The Grapes, 76 Narrow St. (☎ 7987 4396). DLR: Westferry. The Grapes was cast as "The Six Jolly Porters" in Dickens' *Our Mutual Friend.* Known for seafood, served at the bar (pint of prawns £4.75, dressed crab £7) and in the upstairs restaurant (mains £11+). Open M-F noon-3pm and 5:30-11pm, Sa 7-11pm, Su noon-3pm and 7-10pm. Food served M-Sa noon-3pm and 7-9pm, Su noon-3pm. MC, V.

Prospect of Whitby, 57 Wapping Wall (☎ 7481 1095). Tube: Wapping. Built in 1520, stone floors and a pewter bar pale beside the river views. Mains courses £5-7, sarnies £3-4. Food M-Sa noon-2:30pm and 6-9pm, Su noon-3pm and 6-9pm. Open M-F 11:30am-11pm, Su noon-10:30pm. AmEx, MC, V.

Visit **StudentUniverse.com** for real deals on student travel anywhere.

 StudentUniverse.com

Real Travel Deals

800.272.9676

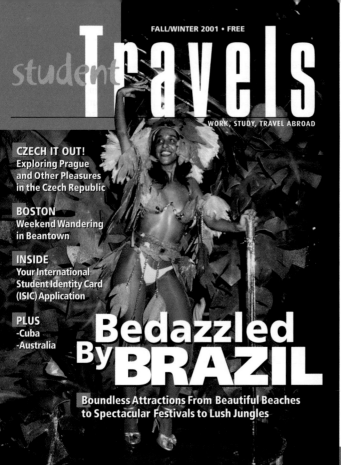

GREENWICH

▶ *NEIGHBORHOOD QUICKFIND: Discover, p. 14; Sights, p. 128; Museums&Galleries, p. 152; Food&Drink, p. 183; Entertainment, p. 221.*

There's no shortage of places to eat in Greenwich, but many have a distinct touristy feel—this is one of the few places in London where visitors outnumber locals. Ignore the dodgy snack and fish'n'chips bars along Greenwich Church St. and instead head along Nelson Rd. or duck into the market.

Goddard's Pie & Mash, 45 Greenwich Church St. DLR: Cutty Sark. Saved from closure by a local campaign, Goddard's has been serving the good folk of Greenwich since 1890. All the original London working-class favorites are dished up on the wooden benches: Pies 90p (take-away), eat-in lunch special pie or pasty with mash £1.90, fruit pie and ice-cream 95p. Open M-W 10am-6:30pm, F-Sa 10am-9:30pm. Cash only.

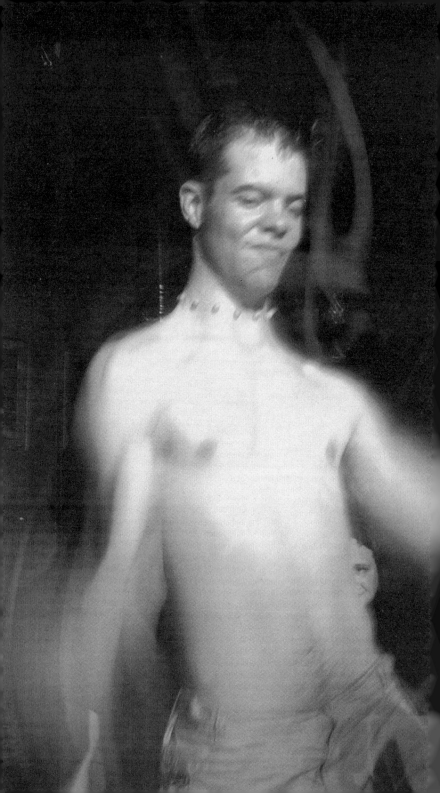

Nightlife

NIGHTLIFE BY TYPE

BARS

In London these days, drinking is the new dancing, and bars are the new nightclubs. An explosion of club-bars has invaded the previously forgotten zone between pubs and clubs, offering seriously stylish surroundings and top-flight DJs together with plentiful lounging space and a wide selection of Bourbon whiskey (the current "in" drink). Often incorporating both restaurants and dancefloors, the new breed of bars are designed as one-stop nightspots, combining all you need for an evening's entertainment under one roof. Usually, club-bars are open from noon or early evening, allowing you to skip the cover charge (if there is one) by arriving early and staying put as the scene shifts around you. On the other hand, they tend to close earlier than clubs, usually between midnight and 2am, so you'll need to move on to a "real" nightclub for serious nighttime action.

NIGHTCLUBS

Every major DJ in the world either lives in London or makes frequent visits to the city. While the US may have introduced house music to the world, the UK has taken the lead in developing and experimenting with new types of dance music, and club culture in London is all pervasive—to believe the hype, 18- to 30-year-old Londoners live to party. Such is the variety and fast-changing nature of London nightlife that even weekly publications have trouble keeping up—even *Time Out*, the Londoner's clubbing bible, only lists about half the club happenings in London on any given night.

BARS

192	Notting Hill
AKA	Holborn
Blakes	North
Cafe Kick	Clerkenwell
Cantaloupe	East
⬛ Filthy MacNasty's	North
⬛ Freud	Covent Garden
Fridge Bar	South
Gate	Notting Hill
Grand Central	East
Liquid Bar	East
Living Room	South
Match EC1	Clerkenwell
Pharmacy	Notting Hill
Point 101	Soho
Satay Bar	South
Shoreditch Electricity Showrooms	East
The Social	Oxford & Regent Sts.
Soshomatch	East
Spot	Covent Garden
Vibe Bar	East
Vinyl Addiction	North

GAY

79CXR	Soho
Admiral Duncan	Soho
BarCode	Soho
Bar Fusion	North
Black Cap	North
The Box	Covent Garden
Brief Encounter	Covent Garden
Candy Bar	Soho
Comptons of Soho	Soho
First Out	Soho
The Fridge	South
G-A-Y	Soho
Heaven	Trafalgar Sq.
Ku Bar	Soho

GAY (CONT.)

SW9	South
Vespa Lounge	Soho

NIGHTCLUBS

333	East
93 Feet East	East
Africa Centre	Covent Garden
Bar Rumba	Soho
Bagley's Studios	North
Brixton Academy	South
Bug Bar	South
Camden Palace	North
Cargo	East
Dogstar	South
The End	Holborn
Electric Ballroom	North
⬛ Fabric	Clerkenwell
Fluid	Clerkenwell
The Fridge	South
Heaven	Trafalgar Sq.
Herbal	East
Hanover Grand	Oxford & Regent Sts.
Jazz Cafe	North
Madame Jojo's	Soho
Mass	South
Ministry of Sound	South
⬛ Notting Hill Arts Club	Notting Hill
OneFour Four	Soho
Propaganda	Oxford & Regent Sts.
⬛ Scala	North
Sound	Soho
⬛ Soshomatch	East
The Syndrome	Soho
Turnmills	Clerkenwell
Subterania	Notting Hill
Velvet Room	Soho
WKD	North

DRESS. London clubs often fall into one of two categories: those for dancing, and those for posing. In the former, dress codes are generally relaxed; it's not uncommon to find clubbers dressed in nothing fancier than jeans, a stylish T-shirt, and trainers (sneakers), although women are usually expected to make more of an effort and pulling on a pair of "proper" shoes never hurts your chances. At posers' clubs, however, dress is crucial, and what's expected depends very much on the scene. If you're not sure what to wear, call up the club beforehand (although answers like "New York super-funk glam" aren't always that helpful); otherwise, black and slinky is generally safe. The exception to the easy categorisation are theme nights, especially retro clubs—at *Carwash* (see p. 189), you're unlikely to get in unless you look like an extra from *Saturday Night Fever*. If a bouncer tells you it's "members and regulars only," he thinks you're not up to scratch; however, persistence can pay off, especially when accompanied by a good sob story—like how it's your best friend's birthday and she's already inside.

PLANNING. Planning is important for the discriminating clubber. Look before you leap, and especially before you drink. Avoid the bright glitzy clubs in Leicester Square (e.g. Equinox and Hippodrome), in which no Londoner would be seen dead—they're crowded with out-of-town English youth looking to get lucky. Instead, comb through the listings in *Time Out* and the *Guide* supplement to the *Guardian* newspaper on Saturdays; *Time Out* also prints the weekly "TOP" club pass (look in the clubbing section), which gives you discounts on entry to many of the week's shenanigans. For popular clubs, it's worth learning the names of the DJs (not to mention the type of music) just to prove to the bouncer that you're part of the scene. Working out how to get home afterwards is crucial; remember that the Tube and regular buses stop shortly after midnight, and after 1am black cabs are like gold dust. If there's no convenient night bus home, ask the club in advance if they can order a minicab (unlicensed taxicab) for you on the night; otherwise, order your own (see p. 315 for phone numbers). Although it's technically illegal for minicabs to ply for hire, whispered calls of "taxi, taxi" or honking horns signal their presence outside clubs and in nightlife-heavy neighborhoods—however, you've no guarantee that the driver is reputable or even insured. If you have no other option, agree on a price before you get in, and never ride alone.

SELECTED CLUB NIGHTS

London clubbing revolves around promoters and the nights they organise rather than the bricks-and-mortar clubs themselves. This gives London clubbing both its incredible range and its infuriating ephemeralness, as promoters arrange one-off events, move regular nights between clubs, or just get married and find a "proper" job. While some locations have a music policy that favors one genre of clubbing over another—the Ministry of Sound is solidly house-based, for example—in most clubs what's on one night has nothing to do with what's on the next. Below is a selection of particular club nights that we think are something special; however, it's inevitable that some will move to different clubs or different nights, shift from weekly to monthly or vice versa, or simple fold altogether. Always call ahead to check the details still hold, and don't forget that these listings barely scrape the surface of what's on offer.

MONTHLY		FRIDAY	
Ammo City	Cargo	Deep Funk	Madame Jojos
■ Big Beat Boutique meets Bugged Out		Escape from Samsare	The Fridge
	Fabric	Full Tilt	Electric Ballroom
Milk'n'2 Sugars	The End	G-A-Y Camp Attack	G-A-Y (London Astoria)
Rollerdisco	Bagley's Studios	Popstarz	Scala
		Rotation	Subterania
MONDAY		School Disco	Hanover Grand
G-A-Y Pink Punder	G-A-Y (Mean Fiddler)	There	Heaven
THIS!	Bar Rumba		
		SATURDAY	
TUESDAY		Blow Up!	Syndrome
Feet First	Camden Palace	■ Carwash	Sound
		Factor 25	Hanover Grand
WEDNESDAY		G-A-Y	G-A-Y (London Astoria)
Fresh'n'Funky	Hanover Grand	Funkin' Pussy	Africa Centre
■ Swerve	Velvet Rooms	Love Muscle	Fridge
		Saturday Night	Electric Ballroom
THURSDAY			
■ Anohka	93 Feet East		
G-A-Y Music Factory	G-A-Y (Mean Fiddler)		

GAY NIGHTS

G-A-Y, see Soho, p. 193.

Factor 25, Sa at the Hanover Grand (see p. 190). In one of London's smartest clubs, a night for glamorous boys who like to dress up. Bouncy house and funky beats keep the crowd grinding away. 10:30pm-5am. £12.

Love Muscle, every other Sa at the Fridge (see p. 199). As big and brash as they come, led by Yvette and her stage troupe of shimmying bronzed boys. "Hot and steamy fun"—their words. 10pm-6am, followed by after party at Fridge Bar (see p. 198; £6). 10pm-6am. £13.

Popstarz, F at Scala (see p. 197). A long running gay/mixed extravaganza. Covers the whole musical spectrum: the Rubbish Room is devoted to the most embarrassing hits of the 80s, the Love Lounge hosts 70s funk and disco, indie lives in Common Room, while house stays home in the Big Beat Bar. 10pm-5am. £8, free with flyer before 11pm.

There, F at Heaven. See **House and Garage,** below.

on the cheap

Like many things in London, clubbing is an expensive pastime. Cover charges at major clubs run £10-15, and you'll probably spend as much again on drinks—cocktails range £5-10, with even a beer setting you back £3-5. Add in a taxi home, and an evening's entertainment can easily set you back £50.

However, there are ways of limiting the damage. Firstly, **arrive early**—cover charges rise after 10 or 11pm. However, since most clubs don't get busy until midnight, it's easy to lose the savings in extra drinks until the dancefloor fills up.

Secondly, bring a **club flyer** along. Usually available in dance-music shops, presenting a flyer can often save you pounds on the door. Alternatively, if you're a student try showing an **ISIC card**—most clubs only give discounts to NUS (National Union of Students) card holders, but it's worth a try.

Thirdly, avoid weekends and instead opt for **midweek clubbing**, when cover charges are lower—though there are fewer options, London has enough students, slackers, and devoted party people to pack a few clubs even Su-W.

Alternatively, skip nightclubs altogether and head to a **club-bar.** Increasingly popular, these have smaller dancefloors (and more couches), but still attract top DJs for covers that vary from free to £5.

188

FUNK AND JAZZ

Swerve, W at Velvet Room (see p. 192), occasional extra nights elsewhere (☎7471 4777). It's always *carnivale* here, as ace resident Fabio lays big beats over samba sounds to creat toe-tapping, funky drum'n'bass. True to its roots, Swerve draws a racially mixed crowd of industry regulars and serious movers. 10pm-2:30am. £8, students £4.

Deep Funk, F at Madame Jojo's (see p. 191). Funkier than an evening with James Brown, plumbing the depths of 60s and 70s forgotten 45s. Most of the laid-back student crowd are content to sit back and watch the amazing feats of the dedicated movers and shakers dominating the sunken floor—or are they just scared of being shown up? Things get churning around 11:30pm. 10pm-3am. £8; £5 before 11pm.

THIS! (That's How It iS), M at Bar Rumba (see p. 191). It's been a while since the Bar Rumba's Saturday heyday, but on a Monday you won't do better than THIS! Jazzy sounds swing uptempo through the evening, from Miles Davis to seriously dancy jazz-funk—hell, you could listen all night to this, and most people do, though there's no shortage of freestylers bopping and swerving on the 'floor. 10pm-3am. £5.

HIPHOP

Fresh'n'Funky, W at the Hanover Grand (see p. 190). All the brothas in the house get down to the Grand for a stomping midweek hiphop party. Judging from the ultra-high security, the gangsta theme extends beyond the dress code. In any case, this is not meant to be a relaxing night out—come here to strut your stuff. 10pm-4am; start queuing early. £7, £5 before 11pm.

Funkin' Pussy, Sa at the Africa Centre (see p. 193). The line starts early for this unpretentious night of US hiphop in a converted community centre. Head-spinning breakdancers at the back and polished hip-hop pros on stage don't faze the laid back crowd of B-boys, funk-deprived students, and lost Australians. 10:30pm-3am. £8, 1st 50 people £4.

Rotation, F at Subterania (see p. 196). Long-running night with a West London crowd of glamorous brothas and pale imitations shaking it to the mildy commercial hip-hop/soul/reggae/rap sounds of DJ Femi Fem. Gets busy around midnight. DC fairly relaxed, but girls may feel out-of-place in anything but the tightest, shortest dresses. 10pm-3am. £8, £5 before 11pm.

HOUSE AND GARAGE

Ammo City, various nights including monthlies at Cargo (see p. 201) and Mass (see p. 199). A self-described "lifestyle community," Ammo City organizes avant-garde club nights, gigs, and events for London's underground beautiful people posse. Check www.ammocity.com for the latest happenings.

Escape From Samsara, F at the Fridge. Is everyone raving mad, or are they just in a trance? Massive night out, with a midnight stage show and stilt walkers moving among the fluorescent hangings. Around the dancefloor, stalls sell essentials like glo-sticks (£2.5

each) and king-size Rizlas (£1), plus anything else that fluoresces under UV. DC fairly relaxed, but the brighter, tighter, and spanglier the better. 10pm-6am. £14, £9 before 11pm, free to first 30 with drum or digeridoo. If you're still not satisfied, escape to the Fridge Bar after party (see p. 198; £6).

Milk'n'Two Sugars (MN2S), last F of month at The End (see p. 194; ☎8767 9925). It takes a long time—and thorough body search—to get into this popular night. Inside, there's no stopping the crowd of serious House addicts pumping to deep Chicago soundz. Selective entry keeps the dancefloors heaving but not overcrowded: dress to glow and show. 10pm-5am. £15; £10 before midnight, £3 after 3am.

There, F at Heaven (see p. 194). There's room for everyone at this totally mixed straight/gay/lesbian danceathon on five floors. All manner of house, prog, trance and dance play to relaxed crowd just out for a good time. Currently the hottest item in the East Asian fashion underground. 10:30pm-6am; £10.

Riverboat Action

INDIE & ALTERNATIVE

Full Tilt, F at the Electric Ballroom (see p. 198). London's oldest and best-known alternative night; goths from across the city flock to this festival of leather, ripped lace, and pierced flesh. 10:30pm-3am. £5.

Feet First, Tu at Camden Palace (see p. 197). 15-year-old indie/alternative/rock midweeker, with a mix of leather-clad goths and T-shirted students thrashing wildly to heavy guitar sounds. 30min. gig at 12:30am—Pulp, Blur, and Feeder all played here before hitting the big time. Selected beer £1 per bottle, £2 per pint. 10pm-2:30am. £5.

RETRO

🎞 **Carwash,** Sa at Sound (see p. 191; ☎7403 8585; www.carwash.co.uk). London's top retro night is a celebration of disco, heavy on the funk and light on the cheese. The main floor swings to unadultered 70s favorites, with a glammed-up crowd pulling all the classic disco moves, while the ground-floor bar becomes the Psychadelic Shack, with funky eclectic breaks and beats from the 50s to the present. Strict DC, especially for guys with no dolls: pull out your best frilly glam-rock shirt. Entry includes the disco-house night at neighboring **Delirium,** whose looser DC makes it a favorite with Carwash rejects. 10pm-4:30am. £12, £5 after 2am. Delirium alone £10.

Bar Rumba

Blow Up!, Sa at Syndrome (see p. 192; www.blowup.co.uk). Surely Austin Power's favorite night out, a crazy mix of 60s-70s pop, funk, and psychedelia draw London's Mod community like a like a Beatle to a flame. The flavor shifts to northern soul after the midnight live set. 10pm-5am. £10, £8 before 11:30pm, £3 after 3am.

Rollerdisco, last Sa of month at Bagleys Studios (see p. 197). Taking hot'n'sweaty to a whole new level, this claims to be Europe's largest disco on wheels. Regular and inline skaters perform endless circles around the three dancefloors to a background of pumping

Compton's of Soho, Old Compton St.

NIGHT SCHOOL

In the past year, Londoners have grown used to seeing groups of youngsters, still dressed in school uniform, queuing up for 18+ nightlcubs and cavorting with each other in ways their mothers certainly wouldn't approve of. Rather than calling the police, though, more and more people are joining in: we're not talking about an epidemic of teenage delinquency, but rather the newest (and craziest) craze in London clubbing—**School Disco.**

Since starting in a small restaurant in 1999, the original School Disco has moved and expanded as it's grown in popularity, now running two nights a week spawning a host of imitators. Londoners, it seems, can't wait to pull on those itchy polyester skirts, trousers, ties, and jackets most were only too glad to dump a few years before, before dancing to cheesy 80s chart hits and getting down to serious business in the snogging room. So if you never found out why high school was meant to be "the best days of your life," now's your chance to make up (and make out).

School Disco (☎8699 9983; www.schooldisco.com) is held F at the **Hanover Grand** (see p. 190) and Sa at **Po Na Na Hammersmith**, 242 Shepherd's Bush Rd. (Tube: Hammersmith). Both 10pm-3am, £10. Strict "school uniform" dress code: check the website for details and a list of school outfitters.

house and occasional retro faves; the overall standard of skating is hardly intimidating, though the Starlight Express cast frequently turn up and railroad everyone into submission. If you forget your wheels, you can rent a pair of skates for £5. 2-8pm. £15.

Saturday Night, Sa at the Electric Ballroom (see p. 198). As in Fever, of course. A Travoltingly popular celebration of the decade style forgot. While plenty get kitted up in afro wigs and floral-print polyester, *this* 70s show belongs to the disco pros who take the stage at midnight. The music on the main floor reaches from the late 60s to the early 80s, with some later party anthems; upstairs 70s tunes are remixed into 00s dance tracks. 10:30pm-3am. £10.

School Disco, see sidebar, p. 190.

TECHNO & BREAKBEATS

🎟 **Anokha** (www.anokha.co.uk), Th at 93 Feet East (see p. 200). Unique midweeker by Talvin Singh, mixing a world-dance sensation from Hammond-organ funk to tribal chants over thumping tabla rhythms for a completely diverse crowd of new-agers, Shoho artists, and relaxed Indian youth. A musical chicken tikka masala, only much, much tastier. 9pm-3am. £7.

🎟 **Big Beat Boutique meets Bugged Out!,** normally first F of the month at Fabric (see p. 195). For advance tickets, call ☎7344 4444. Cynics might say that nights like these are the result of a culture in which no one can sing and no one can dance. *Let's Go* says stop whining and get yourself down to this mammoth monthly. With beats from the likes of Jon Carter, James Holroyd, and the mighty Chemical Brothers themselves, you're in line for some serious trance action. Unless you neglect to buy tickets in advance, in which case you'll just be in line until dawn. 10pm-5am; start queuing *early*, even if you're on the guest list. £15.

NIGHTLIFE BY NEIGHBORHOOD

THE WEST END

SEE MAP, p. 330-331

OXFORD ST. & REGENT ST.

🔎 **NEIGHBORHOOD QUICK-FIND: Discover,** p. 2; **Sights,** p. 79; **Food&Drink,** p. 159; **Entertainment,** p. 209; **Shopping,** p. 226.

Hanover Grand, 6 Hanover St. (☎7499 7977). Tube: Oxford Circus. Grand is the name of the game: plush velvet couchers, red curtains on the balcony bar, an imposing staircase and impeccably well-dressed clientele. Less grand, but welcome, is the snack bar by the cloakroom (ice cream or hot dog, £1.50). W *Fresh'n'Funky* (see p. 188); F *School Disco* (see *Night School* sidebar); Sa *True* garage (£15). Dress up. Open W 10pm-4am, F-Sa 10:30pm-4:30am.

Propaganda, 201 Wardour St. (☎ 7434 3820; www.propagandabar.co.uk). Tube: Oxford Circus or Tottenham Court Rd. Ultra-plush club-bar; once you've settled into the long white couch opposite the glowing bar, you won't want to get up; with waitress service, you won't need to; when you see the bill (shots £6), you won't be able to. If you dare, join the fashionable set on the pop-art dancefloor, or slink into the adjoining restaurant (snacks £3-6, mains £7-10), served all night. Frequently closed for private functions, but regular nights include: M movies (5pm-midnight; free); Th *Spin* soul and funk (9pm-3am; £8, free before 10pm); and F *Sintillate* US house, R&B, hip-hop, and disco (9pm-3am; £15, £10 before 10pm).

The Social, 5 Little Portland St. (☎ 7636 4992; www.thesocial.com). Tube: Oxford Circus. DJ-driven bar in the narrow space under the Little Portland St. pavement—glass tiles overhead let in the moonlight (though they're unfortunately too small and opaque to offer interesting views of passing pedestrians). A media-crowd favorite, with too many packed into the tiny "dancefloor" to do anything but yell at each other. Cocktails £4.80, shooters £3. DJs nightly from 7pm. Open M-Sa noon-midnight, Su 5-10:30pm. No cover.

SOHO

◨ NEIGHBORHOOD QUICKFIND: Discover, *p. 2;* **Sights,** *p. 83;* **Museums&Galleries,** *p. 139;* **Food&Drink,** *p. 160;* **Entertainment,** *p. 209;* **Shopping,** *p. 229;* **Accommodations,** *p. 284.*

DRINKING

Point 101, 101 New Oxford St. (☎ 7379 3112). Tube: Tottenham Court Rd. Underneath the signature Centrepoint office tower, 101 has an appropriately 1970s look, with low steam-moulded plywood chairs and tables, and long vinyl booths in the balcony bar (accessed via a separate door). Unfortunately, the 70s theme extends to the stodgy food; fortunately, it stops short at the nightly DJ'd music, which tends towards jazz, latin, and soul. On weekdays the space can seem intimidatingly large; on weekends it's far too small. Open M-Th 8am-2am, F-Sa 8am-2:30am, Su 8am-11:30pm. AmEx, MC, V.

DANCING

Bar Rumba, 35 Shaftesbury Ave. (☎ 7287 2715; www.barrumba.co.uk). Tube: Piccadilly Circus. The only place to be four years ago, now suffering from the fickleness of club fashion but still with some great nights in its long, single-dancefloor basement space. The sound system goes for high fidelity over volume. M *This!* (see p. 188) starts off the week with a bang; Tu *Rumba Pa'ti* brings serious Latin dancers (10pm-3am, £3; dance class 6:30-8:30pm, £6); W *Space* goes disco-house (10pm-3am, £5, £3 before 11pm); Th *Movement* drum'n'bass (8:30pm-3am; £6, £3 before 10pm); F *Night People* eclectica, from disco to hip-hop (9pm-4am; £10, £6 before 11pm); Sa *Garage City* (9pm-6am; £12, £7 before 11pm); Su *Bubbling Over* soul, swing, and funk (8pm-1am; £5, £3 before 10pm).

Madame Jojo's, 8-10 Brewer St. (☎ 7734 3040). Tube: Piccadilly Circus. Intimate red-hued club, with a smallish sunken dancefloor inviting grand entrances down the blue-lit staircase. W alternates *Mixamatosis* hip-hop, jungle, funk, and reggae (10pm-2am; £5) with *Muqueca* Latin and Brazilian tunes (10pm-3am; £5); 2nd Th of the month brings *Supersession* R'n'B, boogaloo, and funk (9pm-3am; £5, £3 before 11pm); 3rd Th *Carbon Imprints* hip-hop and funk (9:30pm-3am; £6, £4 before 11pm); 4th Th *Hustlin* hip-hop and jazzy breaks (9pm-3am; £5, £3 before 11pm); F *Deep Funk* says it all (see p. 188); Sa *Showtime* drag cabaret followed by *Groove Sanctuary* nu-jazz and soulful house (10:30pm-3am; £8); Su *Soda* morning recovery US house and funky disco (9am-3pm; £10) followed by *Tropicalzimo* total eclecticism from jazz and funk to house and techno (9pm-2am; £5, £3 before 11pm).

One Four Four, 144 Charing Cross Rd., down the alleyway (☎ 7692 9964). Tube: Tottenham Court Rd. Warehouse-style venue: 3 storeys, 4 dancefloors, with not a penny spent on the decor—seating is on park benches and old sofas, and the vibe is screw-fashion-let's-have-fun. W *Nemesis* nu-metal and trad rock (11pm-3:30am; £6); F *Elements* wildly popular tech-house, rave, and funk (10:30pm-6am, £12).

Sound, 10 Wardour St. (☎ 7287 1010). Tube: Leicester Sq. or Piccadilly Circus. A cheesy Leicester Sq. location can't keep this swinger down. A real labyrinth of a club, with the large, loud main room and balcony bar on the 1st and 2nd floors, the (sometimes separate, sometimes included) Sound Bar on the ground floor, and a basement restaurant and semi-separate club with its own entrance through the Swiss Centre on Leicester Sq. Th *Bliss* R&B, soul, and UK garage (10pm-3am; £8, £5 before 11pm); F *Funk* pure R&B (10pm-4am; £12, £10 before 11:30pm); Sa ▨ *Carwash* retro-funk (see p. 189). Also frequent live gigs.

LATE NIGHT ROW

Everyone bemoans the early closing time of 11pm imposed on pubs UK-wide as a major style-cramper. In the last few years, there has been discussion of changing these laws, instituted during WWI to keep essential workers from staying out too late, though now clearly unnnecessary. However, Westminster City Council recently instituted a ban in Covent Garden on the ever-proliferating way around these rules, the **late license.** Only those bars and pubs that currently possess them will be allowed to stay open past the standard closing times, and therefore will become even more crowded. In addition, at least on the record, no venue in Covent Garden is allowed to remain open past 1am, although the enforcement of this will likely be spotty. Soho—the traditional center of London's nightlife scene—is also coming under increasing pressure, with a number of clubs being closed down for minor licence violations in the past few years. (The most famous casualty was Leicester Square's 7-storey Home megaclub, crippled less than a year after opening when its license was restricted to midnight.) While Westminster claims these measures are being enacted on behalf of local residents, many club and bar owners are simply pulling out altogether and moving to the more liberal climes of East London, where the Hoxton scene is booming as a result.

The Syndrome, 54 Berwick St. (☎ 7437 6830). Tube: Tottenham Court Rd. One long room, with a bar at either end and unusually high couches around the red and blue walls. Sa retro *Blow Up!* for the Powers that be (the Austin Powers, that is; see p. 192).

Velvet Room, 143 Charing Cross Rd. (☎ 7734 4687). Tube: Tottenham Court Rd. Small, showing its age, and packed even midweek—if people don't come for the single small dancefloor or dated bubble-tube decor, they must be here for the music. Velveteers aren't here to preen: this crowd knows its DJs. M *Off the Hook* brings R'n'B and hiphop to a gay audience (10pm-3am; £5); Tu *Syndicate* garage (10:30pm-3am; £7); W is ▨ *Swerve,* with Brazilian beatz from fantastic Fabio (see p. 188); Th *Ultimate Bass* has funky techno from Carl Cox (10pm-3am; £6, £4 before 11:30pm), F *House and Trance* (10pm-4:30am; £10, £7 before 11pm, £5 after 2:30am); Sa finishes the week with *Big and Clever* house (10pm-4am; £10, £8 before 11pm).

GAY & LESBIAN

79CXR, 79 Charing Cross Rd. (☎ 7734 0769). Tube: Leicester Sq. Snuck under a brick colonnade, this split-level gay bar is mostly notable for its late hours. Open M 1pm-2am, Tu-Sa 1pm-3am, Su 1-10:30pm.

Admiral Duncan, 54 Old Compton St. (☎ 7437 5300). Tube: Leicester Sq. or Piccadilly Circus. Always a popular hangout, now forever noted as a defiant symbol against intolerance. Strong security is the only reminder of the 1999 bombing; today this narrow standing-room pub throbs to a laid-back male crowd. Open M-Sa 11am-11pm, Su noon-10:30pm.

BarCode, 3-4 Archer St. (☎ 7734 3342). Tube: Piccadilly Circus. On a dark alley in the seedier side of Soho is this bustling, cruisy men's bar. The only thing better groomed than the clientele is the designer interior. F-Sa the action shifts to the downstairs dancefloor. Open daily noon-11pm.

Candy Bar, 23-24 Bateman St., on the corner of Greek St. (☎ 7437 1977). Tube: Tottenham Ct. Rd. The UK's first full-time lesbian den, with a groovy bar and a basement dancefloor. DJs W-Su. Tu *Loose* striptease; W funk, soul, and disco; Th R&B and garage; F uplifting house; Sa house, funk, and soul; Su pop, retro, and indie. Gay men admitted as guests. Open M-Tu 5pm-1am, W-F 5pm-3am, Sa 3pm-3am, Su 5-11pm. F-Sa £5 after 9pm.

Comptons of Soho, 53 Old Compton St. (☎ 7479 7461). Tube: Leicester Sq. or Piccadilly Circus. Soho's "official" gay pub is always busy with a no-nonsense male crowd of all ages. Horseshoe bar encourages the exchange of meaningful glances, while upstairs (opens 6pm) offers a more mellow scene with pool table. Open M-Sa 11am-11pm, Su noon-10:30pm. MC, V.

First Out, 52 St. Giles High St. (☎ 7240 8042). Tube: Tottenham Court Rd. Skip the ground floor cafe serving so-so veggie standards (lasagne £4.25) and head down to the funky-but-friendly basement bar. Predominantly lesbian, but plenty of gay men too except F, when the women-only *Girl Friday* takes over. Open M-Sa 10am-11pm, Su 11am-10:30pm. Cash only.

G·A·Y (☎0906 100 0160; www.g-a-y.co.uk). M and Th at the Mean Fiddler, 165 Charing Cross Rd., F-Sa at the Astoria (see p. 211). Tube: Tottenham Court Rd. London's biggest gay and lesbian night, four nights a week. Frequently besieged by teenage girls on weekend nights—bands to have played include the Spice Girls and Boyzone—but the majority-gay door policy keeps the atmosphere camp. M *Pink Pounder* 90s classics with 70s-80s faves in the bar (10:30pm-4am; £1 with flyer or ad, available at most gay bars, students free); Th *Music Factory* house, dance, and a little pop (11pm-4am; £1 with flyer or ad, students free); F *Camp Attack* attitude-free 70s and 80s cheese (11pm-4am; £3); Sa *G·A·Y* big night out, rocking the capacity crowd with commercial-dance DJs, and live pop performances. (10:30pm-5am; £10).

Ku Bar, 75 Charing Cross Rd. (☎7437 4303; www.ku-bar.co.uk). Tube: Leicester Sq. Don't be fooled by the naked-lady mosaic; this fashionable hangout is definitely gay, attracting well-dressed, younger men and those that love them. Drinks deals include cocktail pitchers £7 before 9pm, Carlsberg £1 per bottle all day M-F. Get your tickets to *G.A.Y.* (see p. 193) here and skip the queue. Pints from £2.70. Open M-Sa 12:30-11pm, Su 12:30-10:30pm.

Vespa Lounge, St. Giles Circus (☎7836 8956). Tube: Tottenham Court Rd. Above the Conservatory restaurant, at the foot of Centrepoint tower. Relaxed lesbian lounge bar with blue walls, comfy seats, pool table. Thai food supplied by downstairs restaurant. "Laughing Cows" comedy night first Su of month (£5-8), plus occasional theme nights. Gay men welcome as guests. Open M-Sa 6-11pm, Su 6-10:30pm.

COVENT GARDEN

🔽 *NEIGHBORHOOD QUICKFIND: Discover, p. 2; Sights, p. 84; Museums&Galleries, p. 139; Food&Drink, p. 162; Entertainment, p. 209; Shopping, p. 231; Accommodations, p. 284.*

As with restaurants, Covent Garden's popularity with tourists means easy money for bars and clubs, which in turn translates into high prices and low quality. An exception (sort of) to this rule is in the many Commonwealth expat hangouts in the streets near the piazza, which can provide a good night out—provided you're Canadian, Australian, South African, or Kiwi. Otherwise, while on a warm evening the Piazza makes a great place for a long drink, it won't be long before you're heading down to Soho.

DRINKING

Freud, 198 Shaftesbury Ave. (☎7240 9933). Invigorate your psyche in this offbeat underground hipster hangout. Sand-blasted wall occasionally echo to live music (including from the didgeridoo-playing waiters). Cheap cocktails (from £3.40) beat an hour on the couch. Light meals 11am-4:30pm (£3.50-6). Open M-Sa 11am-11pm, Su noon-10:30pm. MC, V.

Spot, 29 Maiden Ln. (☎7379 5900). Frequent live acts, from singers to standup, at this 3-floor club-bar; dance in the velvet-trimmed basement, drink in the coolly bright bar, lounge in the wood-paneled Oval Room. Dance music F-Sa, songs acts Su. Open daily noon-1am. £5 cover F-Su after 9pm. AmEx, MC, V.

DANCING

Africa Centre, 38 King St. (☎7836 1973). Tube: Covent Garden. A community centre by day, this is antithesis of a designer club, with a bar reminiscent of a school canteen and a warehouse-like dancefloor. It attracts a racially diverse crowd for carefree nights. F *Limpopo Club* follows a live African band with music from across the continent (10pm-3am; £8, £7 in advance); Sa *Funkin' Pussy* is the place to be for hiphop and breakdancing (see p. 188).

GAY

The Box, 32-34 Monmouth St. (☎7240 5828). Recently renovated, this spacious gay/mixed bar-brasserie is popular with a stylish media/fashion crowd. Daily changing food specials (main courses around £9). They're very proud of their Ally McBeal-style unisex toilets. Also sells club tix. Open M-Sa 11am-11pm, Su 7-10:30pm. MC, V.

Brief Encounter, 42 St. Martin's Ln. (☎7557 9851). Despite being beneath Ian Schrager's ultra-hip St. Martin's Lane hotel (see p. 162), this is not a pretty-boy hangout. Small, dark, no-nonsense space, popular with an older gay crowd. DJs play from 8pm M-Sa. £2 pints daily 3-6pm. Open M-Sa 3-11pm, Su 5-10:30pm.

TRAFALGAR SQUARE & THE STRAND

⚑ NEIGHBORHOOD QUICKFIND: Discover, p. 2; **Sights,** p. 85; **Museums&Galleries,** p. 139; **Food&Drink,** p. 164; **Nightlife,** p. 194; **Entertainment,** p. 209.

With the exception of Heaven (below), the only significant late-night action happens on Dec. 31, when thousands of inebriated Britons and tourists gather in Trafalgar Sq. to ring in the new year with indiscrimate kissing and a mad rush for the night buses.

Heaven, The Arches, Craven Terrace (☎ 7930 2020; www.heaven-london.com). Tube: Charing Cross or Embankment. Though running regulr mixed nights, "the world's most famous gay disco" dispels any doubts about its orientation with ubiquitous racks of *boyz* magazine. Labyrinthine interior rewards explorers—try every unguarded door to discover the fantastically lit main floor, the upstairs second room, a third bar-cum-dancefloor, a coffeebar, and an elusive red-themed chill-out room. M mixed *Popcorn* with chart-toppers, 70s-80s disco hits, commercial house, and £1.50 drinks (10:30pm-3am; £4); W gay *Fruit Machine* house, garage, soul, and swing (10:30pm-3am; £6, £4 before 11:30pm); F mixed *There* hard house and trance (see p. 189); Sa gay/lesbian *Heaven* dance, trance, house, and disco (10pm-5:30am; £12).

HOLBORN

SEE MAP, pp. 334-335

⚑ NEIGHBORHOOD QUICKFIND: Discover, p. 6; **Sights,** p. 88; **Museums&Galleries,** p. 142; **Food&Drink,** p. 164; **Entertainment,** p. 212; **Shopping,** p. 232.

AKA, 18 West Central St. (☎ 7419 9199; www.akalondon.com), next to The End (see below). Tube: Tottenham Ct. Rd. or Holborn. Leans toward the bar side of club-bar. There's nowhere like the candlelit island lounge, high above the main action, for people watching. Cocktails £6-7. Free movies projected on the back wall M 7:30pm; it's "members only," but you can join at the door. Tu *Armaghetto* live jazz, funk, and soul (£4); W alternates between "hiphopfunkacidbreakselectrodubfunkyhouseplease" and tech-house; F rocks to 21st-century soul (£5). Open Su-F 6pm-3am, food to 1am. Dress nicely!

The End, 16A West Central St. (☎ 7419 9199; www.the-end.co.uk). Tube: Tottenham Court Rd. or Holborn. With speaker walls capable of some earth-shattering bass on 2 dancefloors, The End is best known as a house-and-garage hotspot. Stylish toilets to match the Ritz, and—yes!—a drinking fountain are signs of an unusual attention to detail. M *Trash* glam rock to cutting edge (10pm-3am; £4); Th *Atelier* gay-friendly festival of funky house (9pm-4am; £7, £5 before 11pm); Sa *As One* joins up with AKA to provide 3 floors and 4 bars of futuristic dance (10pm-6am; £15 in advance); Su *Riot* all-day celebration of hard house (2pm-midnight; £7, £5 before 5pm). F one-offs and monthlies, including Milk'n'2 Sugars (see p. 189).

CLERKENWELL

SEE MAP, pp. 334-335

⚑ NEIGHBORHOOD QUICKFIND: Discover, p. 6; **Sights,** p. 92; **Museums&Galleries,** p. 143; **Food&Drink,** p. 166; **Entertainment,** p. 213; **Accommodations,** p. 285.

If London's fashionable epicenter has shifted east to Hoxton, so much the better for Clerkenwell—less posing, more partying! Most nightspots are found around Charterhouse St. and St. John's St., with a lower concentration on Clerkenwell Rd. Be aware that this isn't the most pleasant area to walk at night: while it hasn't got a particularly dangerous reputation, the streets tend to be narrow, winding, and dark, so you may feel uncomfortable walking by yourself.

DRINKING

Cafe Kick, 43 Exmouth Market (☎ 7837 8077; www.cafekick.co.uk). Tube: Farringdon or Angel. Dedicated to the twin goals of drinking and football (soccer), this is a place most men would call heaven. There's a jovial, Latin American feel to this cafe-bar, dominated by multiple foosball tables (50p per game). Open M-Sa noon-11pm, Su noon-10:15pm.

Match EC1, 45-47 Clerkenwell Rd. (☎ 7250 4002; www.matchbar.com). One of a microchain of four, this Match stays on the bar side of club/bar, with an emphasis on cocktails—(£5.75-

6.50). Lounge on the sofas, eat in one of the snug booths (main courses £6.50-11), or crush into the sunken bar. Open M-Sa 11am-midnight. AmEx, MC, V.

DANCING

⬛ Fabric, 77a Charterhouse St. (☎73368898; www.fabriclondon.co.uk). Tube: Farringdon. Bigger than a B52 and 100 times as loud. When they powerup the underfoot subwoofer (the main dancefloor is one giant speaker), lights dim across London. 3 dancefloors, chill-out beds, multiple bars, and unisex toilets crammed with up to 2500 dance-crazed Londoners. Yow. Various monthlies F (9:30pm-5am; £10-15), Sa *Fabric Live* (9:30pm-7am; £12).

Fluid, 40 Charterhouse St. (☎7253 3444). Tube: Farringdon. Just down the road from Fabric, the perfect antidote to megaclub madness. Sushi bar by day, by night Fluid becomes an intimate nightclub. With a Tokyo cityscape at one end and a glowing bar at the other, the basement dancefloor is too small for serious dancing; instead, chill upstairs on the faboo leather couches under the soft glare of *manga* projections. *Killimanjaro* deep'n'funky house F, *Neutral* "quirky party grooves" Sa. Restaurant open M-F noon-3pm and 6-9pm; club Th-F 9pm-2am and Sa 10pm-4am. Generally free before 10pm (Sa 11pm), then £3.

Turnmills, 63 Clerkenwell Rd. (☎7250 3409; www.turnmills.co.uk). Tube: Farringdon. Clubbing Tomb Raider style: enter through a Spanish restaurant into a subterranean labyrinth of themed zones, from post-industrial jungle to French bistro. The glammed-up, affluent 20s-30s crowd is more intent on eyeing up than getting down. Th *Club A&V* VJ-led night of live music, drum'n'bass, and breaks (9pm-4am, £6); F *The Gallery* top-rated house with art show (10:30pm-7:30am, £10); 1st Sa of month *London Calling* "love groove dance party" (10pm-4am, £12), other Sa *Headstart* deep house, alt house, and nu-eclectic (10pm-4am; £8, £5 before 11pm). After 4am Sa, things turn gay for *Trade's* dance marathon (to Su 1pm, £15).

Heaven

Pharmacy

NOTTING HILL

⁊ NEIGHBORHOOD QUICK-FIND: Discover, p. 10; **Sights,** p. 113; **Food&Drink,** p. 173; **Entertainment,** p. 216; **Shopping,** p. 234.

SEE MAP, p. 342

Notting Hill nightlife today is dominated by pretentious bars filled with even more pretentious types intent on flaunting their wealth and good looks. Fortunately, these "Notting Hillbillies" are too concerned about their beauty sleep to be into real clubbing, which allows the few serious nightspots to remain some of the best in the city.

DRINKING

192, 192 Kensington Park Rd. (☎7229 0482). Tube: Ladbroke Grove. Despite 192's popularity amongst

Spinning Beats

area media execs leading to its repeated mention in the *Bridget Jones* books, the plush red couches are alarmingly reminiscent of an Angus Steakhouse. Wide range of reasonable wines (£3-6 per glass), smaller selection of pricey food (£10-13) Bar open M-Sa noon-11pm, Su noon-10:30pm. Open M-Sa 12:30-11:30pm, Su 12:30-11pm. AmEx, MC, V.

Gate, 87 Notting Hill Gate (☎7727 9007; www.gaterestaurant.co.uk). Tube: Notting Hill Gate. Stylish bar-club-restaurant with a contemporary 60s feel. At 10pm, there's an exodus from the restaurant (rosemary skewered lamb £12) to the laid-back bar (cocktails £6-7) as the DJs start spinning: Th hiphop and R&B, F-Sa deep house. Restaurant open M-Sa 6-10:45pm, Su 6-10pm; bar M-Sa 5pm-1am, Su 5pm-midnight. No cover. MC, V.

Pharmacy, 150 Notting Hill Gate (☎7221 2442). Tube: Notting Hill Gate. The talk of the town when it first opened, this Damien Hirst-designed joint is just *so* 1997, darling. Clinical environment of bright lights and pill-laden medicine cabinets—though there'd be an outcry if drug companies charged this much for cocktails (£6-7). Fortunately, Hirst's influence stopped at the menu—the steak (£8.50) is formaldehyde-free. The upstairs restaurant is one of the priciest in London (mains £16-18). Bar open M-Th noon-3pm and 5:30pm-1am, F noon-3pm and 5:30pm-2am, Sa noon-2am, Su noon-midnight. AmEx, MC, V.

DANCING

🌑 **Notting Hill Arts Club,** 21 Notting Hill Gate (☎7460 4459). Tube: Notting Hill Gate. Why do club promoters spend millions on on giant venues, mind-melting sound systems, and flashy decor, when this no-frills basement—with turntables on folding tables, one dancefloor, and no decoration beyond projections and art left over from daytime exhibitions—is consistently the coolest nightspot in the city, if not the world? A friendly, laid-back crowd, from rock stars to rastafarians, sips absinthe (£5.50) and grooves to a range of eclectic music. Tu *Bemsha!* live Latin beats and jazz impro (6pm-1am; £5, free before 8pm); W *Poptones presents...* live new signings with dance favorites; Th alternates *Soleal* afro-latin beats, hiphop, and jazz with *Future World Funk* global beatfest (6pm-1am; £5, free before 8pm); F *Inspiration Information* black music from jazz to hiphop (6pm-2am; £6, free before 8pm, £5 8-10pm); Sa daytime *Rough Trade Sessions* live music from new and established acts (4-8pm); free); Sa evenings a number of one-offs and monthly nights; Su acclaimed *Lazy Dog* journey from deep house to soul (4-11pm; £5, free before 6pm).

Subterania, 12 Acklam Rd. (☎8960 4590). Tube: Ladbroke Grove. Tucked underneath the Westway motorway at the point where rastafarian meets trustafarian, Subterania is smallish but well-designed: posers man the first-floor balcony, while a hole in the wall separating the bar area from the circular dancefloor directs the exchange of meaningful glances. The whole building shakes to the bass—or was that a 16-wheeler passing overhead? W *Roddigans Reggae* (10pm-2am; £6, £5 before 11pm); F *Rotation* leaps from hip-hop to soul (see p. 188); Sa *Solid* garage, R'n'B, and disco house (10pm-3am; £8, £5 before midnight).

NORTH LONDON

🗺 **NEIGHBORHOOD QUICKFIND: Discover,** *p. 12;* **Sights,** *p. 118;* **Museums&Galleries,** *p. 150;* **Food&Drink,** *p. 176;* **Nightlife,** *p. 196;* **Entertainment,** *p. 218;* **Shopping,** *p. 237;* **Accommodations,** *p. 298.*

Nightlife in **Islington** mostly means bar-hopping; with Clerkenwell's superclubs just short jaunt away, there's precious little booty shaking going on—although the seedy area on the Islington side of King's Cross has developed a few superclubs of its own. Famous as a proving ground for new bands, and with swarms of young people blanketing the area every weekend, it comes as a surprise that **Camden Town's** late-night scene is limited to a handful couple of clubs and club-bars. For whatever reason, though, the local council is loathe to hand out late licences; the burgeoning bar scene is abruptly cut short at 11pm, which helps explain why it's more of a hit with local professionals than the pierced youth of Camden.

DRINKING

🌑 **Filthy MacNasty's Whisky Café,** 68 Amwell St. (☎7837 6067). Tube: Angel. This small, friendly Irish pub is frequented by a galaxy of stars—Shane MacGowan and U2 regularly stop by, while Johnny Depp, Kate Moss, and Ewan McGregor are known to drop in. Actually two bars with separate entrances, linked by the passage marked "toilets." Live rock'n'roll 8:30pm, Su 3 and 8:30pm; **Vox'n'Roll,** Tu-W 8:30pm, is one of London's top literary ev nings, with readings by well-known authors. Wide range of whiskies around £2. Open M-Sa 11am-11pm, Su noon-10:30pm.

Blakes, 31 Jamestown Rd. (☎ 7482 2959). Tube: Camden Town. A slightly posy crowd detracts little from this stripped-down modern pub/bar. Mirrors and loud abstract paintings adorn the tall walls, though it's more entertaining to watch the expert staff spin the cocktail shaker. Popular with couples and serious-looking 20- to 30-somethings. Cocktails £4.50-£5.50, including a great whiskey sour; bar food (around £5) served until 10:30pm. Open M-Sa 11am-11pm, Su noon-10:30pm.

Vinyl Addiction, 6 Inverness St. (☎ 7681 7898). Tube: Camden Town. The first bar in London with its own decks, DJs play mostly dance music in a narrow space dominated by the concrete counter—although licensing laws mean that dancing is technically forbidden. A relaxed spot for a coffee or lunch in the day, with an open kitchen at the rear (ciabatta sandwiches from £3), at night it bursts with a youthful crowd. Pint of bitter £2.60; absinthe £5. DJs nightly and from 3pm Sa-Su. Open M-Sa 11:30am-11:30pm, Su 11:30am-10:30pm. Food served until 10pm.

DANCING

🔲 **Scala,** 275 Pentonville Rd. (☎ 7833 2022, tickets 7771 2000; www.scala-london.co.uk). Tube: Kings Cross. Brilliant nights in a seedy area guaranteed to scare out-of-towners—what more could a Londoner ask for? The huge main floor embraces its cinematic past: DJs spin from the projectionist's box, ramped balconies provide a multi-level dance experience, and a giant screen pulsates with mood-enhancing visuals as 3m-high pyramids of speakers detonate the bass. Room 2 is larger than most clubs' room 1s, while for a more intimate experience the tiny floor by the entrance provides hot'n'sweaty relief. F *Popstarz* is a long-running night of gay/mixed eclectica (see p. 187); Sa were in flux at press time but tend to be house-dominated; every other Su *Latin 8* provides 6 straight hours of hip-swinging salsa with a free dance workshop 8:30-9:30pm (8pm-2am; £8). Dress up.

Bagleys Studios, King's Cross Freight Depot, off York Way (☎ 7278 2777; www.bagleys.net). Tube: King's Cross. Walk up York Way (to the right of King's Cross station), turn left just before the canal, then right through some dodgy-looking iron gates, and follow the road left and down (10min.). Prostitutes and drug dealers frequent this area after dark; **travel in large groups or take a taxi** (Bagleys can arrange taxis home). A former movie studio, Bagley's is London's biggest club venue, with a 3000 capacity on up to five cavernous dancefloors. Last F of month *One Love* garage and drum'n'bass; Sa *Freedom* massive house, hard house, and garage night (10:30pm-7am; £14); last Sa of month daytime *Rollerdisco* (see p. 189).

Camden Palace, 1a Camden High St., NW1 (☎ 7387 0428) Tube: Mornington Crescent. A favorite with students, foreign and British alike. In a converted Victo-

Electric Ballrom

Jazz Cafe

The Fridge

rian theater, ornate plasterwork and all, with multiple balconies overlooking the huge single dancefloor. The entire building shakes when they turn up the bass. Completely off the fashion-scene radar, but good for a fun night out. F *Peach* house/trance (10pm-6am; £12, £9 before 11pm); Tu *Feet First* Indie night (seep. 189).

Electric Ballroom, 184 Camde n High St. (☎7485 9006; www.electricballroom.ndi-rect.co.uk). Tube: Camden Town. No one can remember the last time the Ballroom was fashionable, but no-one here cares--they're just out for a good time. Perhaps wisely, instead of investing in the latest sound systems and stylish decor, the management has installed free Sega Dreamcast machines, as well as foosball and pinball, which has the effect of leaving the dancefloor to the ladies. F *Full Tilt* (see p. 189) and Sa *Saturday Night* (see p. 190) attract a regular crowd of Goths and John Travolta-wannabes respectively.

Jazz Café, Camden Town. See Entertainment, p. 218.

WKD, 18 Kentish Town Rd. (☎7267 1869). Tube: Camden Town. The trinity of "Wisdom Knowledge Destiny" meets that of "cafe-music-club." Two category-defying but self-consciously cool floors host funky flavored live music and DJs at night; by day it's an improbable Thai restaurant (main dishes around £4). Not even the palm-reading chef, fresh from 15 years in a Buddhist temple, can predict what the constantly changing line-up will bring next month. M straight jazz; W *Funky Monkey* hip-hop and house; Sa 70s-80s grooves, soul, and funk; every other Su jazz-funk. Food served noon-10pm. Open M-Th noon-2am, F-Sa noon-3am, Su noon-1am. Cover £3-7.

GAY

Bar Fusion, 45 Essex Rd. (☎7688 2882). Tube: Angel. Predominantly gay and lesbian on weekdays, but about 50% straight F-Sa evenings, when things get raucous—get up on the sinuous bar and dance! DJs play house and garage Th-Su from 8pm, and there's a pool table at the back. The photo mural of girls getting on down was unfortunately not taken here. Open M-F 3:30pm-midnight, Sa-Su 1pm-midnight. AmEx, MC, V (£5 min.)

The Black Cap, 171 Camden High St. (☎7428 2721). Tube: Camden Town. North London's most popular gay bar and cabaret draws an eclectic male and female crowd. Upstairs is a friendly pub that could pass for any London local; downstairs live shows start at 12:30am every Tu-Sa night and 10:30pm Su. Cover £2, F-Sa £3; M nights drinks £1 plus £1 cover. Open M-Th noon-2am, F-Sa noon-3am, Su noon-midnight. Food served daily noon-3pm.

SOUTH LONDON

🔝 *NEIGHBORHOOD QUICKFIND: Discover, p. 13; Sights, p. 125; Museums&Galleries, p. 151; Food&Drink, p. 180; Entertainment, p. 220; Shopping, p. 238; Accommodations, p. 299.*

Nightlife is at the forefront of Brixton's renaissance, with an ever-increasing number of bars and clubs catering to London's largest concentration of under-40s. As is the fashion these days, lounging takes priority over dancing, though the proliferation of dancefloor-enabled bars signals a welcome shift back to booty-shaking. While many nightspots targeted at the increasing number of white "new Brixtonians" are little different from their Hoxton or Clerkenwell brethren, there are still plenty of places where black, white, straight, and gay come together to party without pretension. Outside Brixton, south London's undisputed megaclub is the **Ministry of Sound,** now one of the biggest players in the world club scene. Even so, its Elephant & Castle location offers little in the way of pre-club diversions—though what with the length of the queue, you probably wouldn't have time for them anyway.

DRINKING

Fridge Bar, Town Hall Parade, Brixton Hill (☎7326 5100; www.). Tube: Brixton. Next to the Fridge nightclub (see above). Stylish Brixtonites from both sides of the fence mingle in this narrow bar, occasionally nipping downstairs to the small, striped dancefloor. Pull up a stool and meditate on the geometric pastel designs. DJs spin from 9:30pm every night: M roots and reggae, Tu tropical sounds from mambo to jungle, W ghetto-tech house, F-Sa hip-hop, and Su 70s-90s faves. Sa-Su mornings, after-parties continue the previous night's fun from the Fridge club (see p. 199). Open M-Th 6pm-2:30am, F 6pm-4am, Sa 5:30am-noon and 6pm-4am, Su 5:30am-noon and 6pm-2am. M-Th free; F-Su £5-8 after 9pm; after-parties £6.

Satay Bar, 447-450 Coldharbour Ln. (☎7326 5001). Tube: Brixton. Sharing space with an Indonesian restaurant (nasi goreng £4.75), this is one of Brixton's more relaxed bars, with all strata of local society mixing beneath Balinese masks and modern art. During Happy Hour (Su-Th 5-7pm), cocktails are £2.75, with £8 jugs. DJs spin Sa. Open M-Th noon-3pm and 6-11pm, F noon-3pm and 6pm-1:30am, Sa 1pm-1:30am, Su 1-11pm. AmEx, MC, V.

Living Room, 443 Coldharbour Ln. (☎ 7326 4040). Tube: Brixton. Standing room, more like: this popular newcomer to the Brixton party scene is regularly packed even on weekday nights. The upstairs dancefloor has club pretentions, but it's ultimately a DJ-driven drinking den for 20-something new Brixtonians homesick for the sofabars of north London. Open Su-Th noon-2am, F-Sa noon-4am; music starts pumping 9pm nightly. No cover.

DANCING

🎵 **Bug Bar,** Crypt, St. Matthew's Church (☎ 7738 3184; www.bugbar.co.uk). The antithesis of most self-labeled "cool" nightspots, the Bug's super laid-back, friendly crowd gives this whitewashed former church crypt a genuine vibe. You'll be dancing in the aisles—the single dancefloor is nowhere near big enough to contain all the chilled-out movers and shakers. W live acts, from poetry slams to breakbeats (7pm-1am; £3-4, free before 8pm); Th *Sessions* funk, jazz, and R&B (7pm-1am; free); F *Chew the Fat* rare beats and breaks (7pm-3am; £6, £4 9-11pm, free before 9pm); Sa various one-offs, from hip-hop to jazz (7pm-3am; £6, £4 9-11pm, free before 9pm); Su *Simply Boogie* garage, R&B, funk, hip-hop, and "boogie classics" (7pm-2am; free).

Brixton Academy, see Entertainment, p. 220. Massive venue that flattens out the auditorium for occasional F-Sa club nights, sometimes open to 6am. Call for dates and details.

The Dogstar, 389 Coldharbour Ln. (☎ 7733 7515; www.dogstarbar.co.uk). Tube: Brixton. Dogstar was one of the first nightspots to cash in on Brixton's new-found popularity as a bohemian hang-out for aspiring media-types. At 9pm, the tables are cleared from the dance-floor and the projectors above the bar are switched on to complete the metamorphosis from bar to club. M *Nubient* ambient chill-out session; Tu *Bullitt* hip-hop; W *Rude* deep'n'dirty house; Th *DFX* drum'n'bass; F *-Sa* varied house-oriented nights; Su *Negligée* ironically played 60s-80s pop. Open Su-Th noon-2am, F-Sa noon-4am. Su-Th free; F £5, £4 10-11pm, free before 10pm; Sa £7, £5 10-11pm, free before 10pm.

The Fridge, Town Hall Parade, Brixton Hill, SW2 (☎ 7326 5100; www.fridge.co.uk). Tube: Brixton. Turn left from the station and bear right at the fork onto Brixton Hill; it's opposite the church. The giant split-level dancefloor and the stepped wraparound balcony bar give it away as a former cinema. Hard benches in the "restaurant" (burgers £3.25) dissuade loungers, though there's plenty of seating upstairs. F *Escape from Samsara* total trance (see p. 188); Sa usually gay nights, including *Love Muscle* every other week (p. 187). After parties get going Sa-Su mornings from 5:30am at the Fridge Bar (see below).

Mass, St. Matthew's Church, Brixton Hill (☎ 7737 1016; www.massclub.co.uk), upstairs from the Bug Bar. Tube: Brixton. Cimb what feels like more spiral stairs than a Tube station emergency exit to reach two funkily-decorated rooms that fill quickly with a happy crowd intent on dancing the night away. Constantly changing line-up heavy on the house, trance, and drum'n'bass; penultimate F of the month is *Torture Garden* fantasy fetish night, with a strict dress code. Open F 10pm-5am, Sa 9pm-6am. £10-16; sometimes less before 10:30pm.

Ministry of Sound, 103 Gaunt St. (☎ 7378 6528; www.ministryofsound.co.uk). Tube: Elephant and Castle. Take the exit for South Bank University. The granddaddy of all serious clubbing, still hauling in the crowds—arrive early or queue all night. Emphasis on dancing rather than decor, with a massive main room, smaller second dancefloor, and overhead balcony bar (often VIP only). Dress code generally casual, but famously unsmiling doorstaff make it sensible to err on the side of smartness (*no* sports shoes!). F *Smoove* garage and R&B (10:30pm-6am; £12); Sa *Rulin* US and vocal house (midnight-9am; £15).

GAY

SW9, 11 Dorrell Pl., Brixton. Mixed cafe-bar; see Food&Drink, p. 180.

The Fridge (see above). Recently voted London's best gay club for their Sa night stomper.

EAST LONDON

As the self-proclaimed capital of the London scene—and there aren't too many dissenters—**Shoreditch** and **Hoxton**, or "Shoho" as their trendier elements prefer to call it, is now London's main nighttime destination outside Soho. However, the scene here is quite different from the West End—in Shoho, dancing takes definite second place to lounging, and in some bars and clubs the navel-gazing crowds aren't as friendly as you might like. Of course, fashion was always about exclusivity, so you can hardly complain if locals glower at you for crashing the party—instead, get a spiky blue haircut, dress up to the nines in art-student chic, and pout right back.

DRINKING

Grand Central, 93 Great Eastern St. See Food&Drink, p. 181.

Soshomatch, 2 Tabernacle St. (☎ 7920 0701; www.matchbar.com). Tube: Moorgate or Old St. A 2-floor bar/restaurant that converts into a stylish club Th-Sa, Soshomatch is perfect for those seeking to combine a DJ-driven atmosphere with acres of comfy leather couches. The young, relaxed crowd is stylish but without that Hoxton pretention. Th *Love is...* swings from rare groove to jazz and disco to house (10pm-2am; free); F *Ripped* world-influenced cutting-edge house (10pm-2am; £5, free before 10pm); Sa *Mind Fluid* brain-melting nu-jazz to tribal voices to house (6pm-2am; £5, free before 9pm). Open M-W 11am-midnight, Th-Sa 11am-2am. AmEx, MC, V.

Cantaloupe, 35-42 Charlotte Rd. (☎ 7613 4411; www.cantaloupeco.uk). Tube: Old St. Archetypal we're-so-hip Shoho hangout, with chairs made from wood off-cuts, red walls, and a long curved bar at the back. Plop down at one of the long tables and talk football with local artists. Small dishes of Mediterranean food to share £3-4, cocktails £4.50. Open M-F 11am-midnight, Sa noon-midnight, Su noon-11:30pm. AmEx, MC, V.

Liquid Bar, 8 Pitfield St. (☎ 7729 0082). Tube: Old St. Split level "organic bar," serving only organic wine, beer, and food (though non-organic spirits are also available). Admire the changing contemporary art shows on the walls from the low, low couches, engage battle at the foosball table, or writhe away on the tiny downstairs dancefloor. Watch your step on the unexpectedly steep staircase. DJs every night from 7pm or so, concentrating on hip-hop, breaks, and very deep house. Open Tu-Su 4:30-11:30pm.

Shoreditch Electricity Showrooms, 39a Hoxton Sq. (☎ 7739 6934). Tube: Old St. If you wanted to know where the super-cool go, this is the answer. Massive windows make it great for posing, while giant photomurals peer down from the walls and hanging (plastic) flowers cascade over the bar. DJs shake the downstairs floor with various musical eclectica F-Sa from 9pm (free). Bottled beer £2.70-3. Food served 1-3:45pm, e.g. crispy squid (£5) or merguez sausages (£7.25). Open Tu-W noon-11pm, Th noon-midnight, F-Sa noon-1am, Su noon-10:30pm. AmEx, MC, V.

Vibe Bar, 91-95 Brick Ln. (☎ 7247 3479; www.vibe-bar.co.uk). Tube: Aldgate East or Liverpool St. One of the Truman Brewery's two nightspots, this young, fun clubby bar, with an interior straight out of a style mag, has DJs from 7:30pm M-F and 6pm Sa-Su; in summer, the fun extends outside with a second DJ working the shady courtyard. Musics tends towards soul/jazz/funk. Plop on a comfy sofa, tackle a game at a Playstation or check your email for free when you buy a drink. If you're hungry, pub-like food specials run £4-5 (M-F noon-3pm and 6-8pm), with summer barbecues at weekends (F 6pm-9:30pm, Sa 5pm-9:30pm, Su noon-6pm). Open Su-Th noon-11pm, F-Sa noon-1am. Free, sometimes £1-2 after 6pm.

DANCING

Soshomatch, see Drinking, above.

93 Feet East, 150 Brick Lane (☎ 7247 3293; www.93feeteast.com). Tube: Aldgate East or Liverpool St. Past the endless rows of balti houses, in a former brewery, 93 benefits from East London's danger-cool image while being far enough from Shoho to be off the wannabe radar. Each of the three rooms has a different feel: the stark, barn-like main floor is primarily a dance space, the sofa-strewn upstairs room combines dancing and lounging, while the hard-to-find third room (go back to the club entrance and follow the "bar" sign) is a candle-lit chill-out space, with curved wooden benches topped with bean-bag cushions perfect for intimate encounters. W *Rumbamumba* salsas to a live Latin band (7-11pm, £5, students £3); Th *Anokha* hosts Talvin Singh's acclaimed world dance mixes (see p. 190); fortnightly F *Haywire* techno and Euro-house (9pm-3am; £8, £7 students and before 11pm) alternates with *Mr Scruff*'s "Keep it unreal" (10pm-3am; free); Sa brings anything from house to ska (normally 9pm-2am; £5-10).

333, 333 Old St. (☎ 7739 5949). Tube: Old St. Once the definitive Shoho hangout, the 333 is becoming a victim of its own hipness—is all the club a stage, and all the people merely posers? Nevertheless, the crowds (clad in more Diesel than an Alaskan seal after the Exxon Valdez) happily line up to cram into this large 3-floor venue, famously likened to a "Brixton squat." The oddly shaped main room, complete with airline seating, literally bounces to the beat of the dancefloor; the unornamented basement has the feel of a sweaty student venue; and the heaving upstairs is visibly a former pub, despite the wraparound Manhattan mural. Get out the thick-rimmed specs, dye your hair, and arrive early. F monthlies include *Menage à Trois,* with 3 promoters on 3 floors taking you from basement techno-trance to first-floor funkadelia (10pm-5am; £10, £5 before 11pm); Sa *Revolver* brings eclectic funky dance on the main floor, while in true Warhol fashion anyone can get 15min. of fame upstairs—BYO music (10pm-5am, £10, £5 before 11pm).

Cargo, Kingsland Viaduct, 83 Rivington St. (☎ 7739 3440; www.cargo-london.com). Tube: Old Street. Despite the superclub trimmings—two enormous arched rooms, fab acoustics, movie projectors, and an intimate candle-lit lounge—Cargo is crippled by a 1am license. Consequently, it feels more like a pre-club hangout for Beautiful People than a dance club. On the plus side, you can start early; the place is kicking by 9:30pm. Strong Latin line up includes Tu *Cubanito* and deep Latin house F at *Barrio,* both mixing DJs and live music. Onsite restaurant serves world food day and night (£2-5). Open M-F noon-1am, Sa 6pm-1am, Su noon-midnight; sets from 8pm M-Sa, 6pm Su. Normally £3-7.

Herbal, 12-14 Kingsland Rd. (☎ 7613 4462; www.herbaluk.com). Tube: Old Street. Slightly away from the main Shoho drag, Herbal is one of the few area clubs to retain a relaxed, friendly feel unfazed by the neighborhood's rapid climb/decline into the fashionable limelight—maybe because the lighting is too low to offer any posable possibilities. The smaller red-on-red upstairs room has a brighter bar feel with a more relaxed tempo, while the loft-like main floor tempts with wood-block benches and exposed brickwork. Overall, Herbal will appear more to loungers than serious booty-shakers, though there's always plenty of motion on the narrow dancefloor. Wide range of varying one-offs and monthlies, never over £5. Fixtures include: W *turntable anarchy* (£2); Th *PM Scientists* deep house (£3) alternating with the *Groove Armada* funkfest (£5); 2nd F of the month Talvin Singh's drum'n'bass *Carpet* (£3, free before 11pm); Sa monthlies include *Voodoo* hiphop (1st and 3rd; £5, £3 before 10pm), interspersed with *Stumble* deep house (2nd; £5) and *Warm Leatherette* punk, disco, and electronica (4th; £5). All nights run 7:30pm-2am.

Entertainment

When a man is tired of London, he is tired of life; for there is in London all that life can afford.
  —Samuel Johnson, 1777

On any given day or night in London, you can choose from the widest range of entertainment a city can offer. The West End is perhaps the world's theater capital, supplemented by an adventurous "fringe" and a justly famous National Theatre, while new bands spring eternal from the fountain of London's many music venues. Dance, film, comedy, sports, and countless more happenings will leave you amazed at the variety of listings.

ENTERTAINMENT BY TYPE

CINEMA	
Barbican Cinema	City
BFI London IMAX	South Bank
Curzon Soho	West End
Electric Cinema	Notting Hill
Empire	West End
Gate Cinema	Notting Hill
ICA	West End
Lux	East
National Film Theatre	South Bank
Odeon	Chain
Odeon Leicester Sq.	West End
Prince Charles	West End
Pullman Everyman	Hampstead
Renoir	Bloomsbury
The Ritzy	South
Riverside Studios	West
Tricycle Cinema	Northwest
COMEDY	
Canal Cafe Theatre	Northwest
Chuckle Club	Holborn
Comedy Cafe	East
Comedy Store	West End
Donwstairs at the King's Head	Further North
Hackney Empire	East

DANCE

See also Opera & Ballet

Peacock Theatre	Holborn
The Place	Bloomsbury
Sadler's Wells	Clerkenwell

MUSIC: CLASSICAL

Barbican Hall	City
City of London Festival	City
Music on a Summer Evening	Highgate
The Proms	Kensington
Purcell Room	South Bank
Queen Elizabeth Hall	South Bank
Royal Albert Hall	Kensington
Royal Festival Hall	South Bank
St. John's Smith Square	Westminster
St. Martin-in-the-Fields	West End
Wigmore Hall	Marylebone

MUSIC: FOLK & WORLD

Cargo	East
Cecil Sharpe House	North
Hammersmith Irish Centre	West
Spitz	East
The Swan	South
The Troubadour	Earl's Court

MUSIC: JAZZ

100 Club	West End
606 Club	Chelsea
Jazz Cafe	Camden Town
Pizza Express Jazz Club	West End
Ronnie Scotts	West End

MUSIC: ROCK & POP

Borderline	West End
Brixton Academt	South
Cargo	East
Dublin Castle	Camde Town
Forum	Camden Town
The Garage	Islington
London Arena	East
London Apollo	West
London Astoria (LA1)	West End
Sheperd's Bush Empire	West
The Water Rats	Bloomsbury

OPERA AND BALLET

English National Opera	West End
Holland Park Opera	Kensington
Royal Opera House	West End

PUPPETRY

The Barge Theatre	Northwest
Little Angel Theatre	Islington

THEATER: "WEST END"

Adelphi	West End
Apollo Victoria	Westminster
Arts	West End
Barbican Theatre	City
Fortune	West End
Her Majesty's	West End
Gielgud	West End
London Apollo	West
London Palladium	West End
Lyceum	West End
National Theatre	South Bank
New London	West End
Old Vic	South Bank
Open-Air Theatre	Regent's Park
Palace	West End
Phoenix	West End
Player's Theatre	West End
Prince Edward	West End
Prince of Wales	West End
Queen's	West End
Royal Court	Chelsea
St. Martin's	West End
Savoy	West End
Shakespeare's Globe	South Bank
Strand	West End
Theatre Royal Drury Lane	West End
Victoria Palace	Westminster
Whitehall	West End
Wyndhams	West End

THEATER: "OFF-WEST END"

Almeida	Islington
Battersea Arts Centre	South
Donmar Warehouse	West End
Hampstead Theatre	Hampstead
Lyric Theatre	West
RADA	Bloomsbury
Riverside Studios	West
Soho Theatre	West End
Tricycle Theatre	Northwest
Young Vic	South Bank

THEATER: FRINGE

Bush Theatre	West
Etcetera Theatre	Camden Town
The Gate	Notting Hill
The King's Head	Islington
New End Theatre	Hampstead
The Old Red Lion	Islington

OTHER

BBC Television Centre	West
Cycle rickshaws	West End
Earl's Court Exhibition Centre	Earl's Court
First Bowl (ice skating)	Bayswater
Queens Skate Shop	Bayswater

THEATER

The stage for a national dramatic tradition over 500 years old, London theaters maintain unrivaled breadth of choice. Knowing what's on is easy enough: pick up the week's *Time Out*, look through the newspapers' weekend sections, or check out www.officiallondontheatre.co.uk. Knowing what to pick, however, is tougher. For many people, a visit to London isn't complete with going to see a big musical, for others it requires a trip to the National Theatre or Royal Shakespeare Company; in both cases, you're unlikely to be disappointed. Of the enormous variety in between, much is inevitably dross. At a **West End** theater (a term referring to all the major stages, whether or not they're actually in the West End), you can expect a professional, if mainstream production, top-quality performers, and (usually) comfortable seats. **Off-West End** theaters usually present more challenging work, while remaining every bit as professional as their West End brethren; indeed some, such as the Almeida and the Donmar Warehouse, can attract big-name Hollywood stars the West End can only dream of. The **Fringe** is refers to the scores of smaller, less commercial theaters, often just a room in a pub basement with a few benches and a team of dedicated amateurs. With so many fringe productions, few even get reviewed by newspapers and magazines; it's hit-or-miss whether you stumble across the next Tom Stoppard, but even if it turns out to be a flop, you're rarely more than £5 the worse for it.

LONG-RUNNING SHOWS

London's West End is dominated by shows that run for years, if not decades; below we have listed both plays that have already proved their staying power, plus recent arrivals that look set to settle down for the long haul. Despite what the ever-increasing number of ticket peddlers would have you believe, you'll almost always get the best deal by going to the theatre directly—phone bookings (and virtually all transactions through an agent) will attract a supplementary fee of £1-3 per ticket. The one exception is the **Leicester Square Half-Price Ticket Booth** (see p. 211), which is run by the theaters themselves and releases (genuine!) half-price tickets on the day of the show. **Ticket touts** who hawk tickets outside theaters charge sky-high prices for tickets of dubious authenticity; moreover, selling (and by extension buying) tickets from an unauthorised source is a crime.

All You Need Is Love, Queens Theatre, Shaftesbury Ave. (☎ 7494 5040). Tube: Piccadilly Circus. Apparently, God does have an inordinate fondness for Beatles. M-F 7:45pm, plus Th 3pm, Sa 5, 8pm. £13-35, student&senior standby £15 1hr. before curtain.

Art, Wyndhams Theatre, Charing Cross Rd. (☎ 7369 1736). Tube: Leicester Sq. Critically acclaimed comedy that became a surprise West End hit, now in its 6th year. Tu-Sa 8:15pm plus W 3pm, Sa-Su 5pm. £10-33, students&seniors £10-15 (except Sa night).

Blood Brothers, Phoenix Theatre, Charing Cross Rd. (☎ 7369 1733). Tube: Leicester Sq. Willy Russell's musical about identical twins growing up apart. M-Sa 7:45pm plus Th 3pm, Sa 4pm. £12-35, student&senior standby £15 1hr. before curtain.

The Blues Brothers, Whitehall Theatre, Whitehall (☎ 7369 1735). Tube: Charing Cross. Don't forget your hat and Ray-Bans. M-Th 8:15pm, F-Sa 6 and 8:45pm. £15-33.

Buddy, Strand Theatre, Aldwych (☎ 7930 8800). Tube: Covent Garden or Holborn. This retelling of the bespectacled singer's life will soon be older than its protagonist. M-Th 8pm, F-Sa 5:30 and 8:30pm. £10-35, F matinee half-price; students and seniors £10.50 30min. before curtain.

Cats, New London Theatre, Drury Lane (☎ 7405 0072). Tube: Covent Garden. London's longest-ever running musical. Miaow. M-Sa 7:30pm plus Tu and Sa 3pm. £12.50-32.50.

Chicago, The Adelphi, Strand (book through TicketMaster, ☎ 7316 4709). Tube: Charing Cross. Backstage backstabbing and leggy blonds are the twin attractions of this mega-hit musical. M-Sa 8pm plus F 5pm. £16-36.

Closer to Heaven, Arts Theatre, 6-7 Gt. Newport St. (☎ 7836 3334). Tube: Leicester Sq. Yes, it's a musical by the Pet Shop Boys, about being a pop star. M-Sa 8pm plus Sa 4pm. £20-30.

The Complete Works of William Shakespeare (Abridged) and **The Complete History of America (Abridged),** Criterion Theatre, Piccadilly Circus (☎ 7413 1437). Tube: Piccadilly Circus. An *abridged* history of America lasting 2hr.? Who are they kidding? *Shakespeare* W-Sa 8pm plus Th 3pm, Sa 5pm, Su 4pm; *America* Tu 8pm. £8-30.

Fame—The Musical, Victoria Palace, Victoria St. (☎ 7834 1317). Tube: Victoria. As opposed to *Fame—The Breakfast Cereal*. M-Th 7:30pm, F 5:30, 8:30pm, Sa 3pm. £10-33, F matinee half-price; student&senior standby £12.50 M-F 1hr. before curtain.

The Graduate, Gielgud Theatre, Shaftesbury Ave. (☎ 7494 5065). Tube: Piccadilly Circus. A succession of big-name Mrs. Robinsons continues to seduce audiences. M-Sa 8pm plus Th and Sa 3pm. £9-33.

in the know

Take Your Seats

Americans can easily be confused by the terminology used in English theaters and concerts. First, seating terminology: **Stalls** are what Americans call orchestra seats, and are nearest the stage. The **dress circle** is the first tier of balcony above the stalls, often with better views of the stage; both stalls and dress circle are usually the most expensive seats. Above the dress circle comes the **upper circle,** while the cheapest seats at the top of the theater are **slips** or in the **balcony.** Patrons usually refer to them as **the gods,** a reference to their closeness to heaven.

The **interval** is the time for gin or the loo; within seconds the entire theater empties into the appropriately named **crush bar.** Instead of joining the undignified scramble, you can order interval drinks before the show and find them waiting for you—usually on an unguarded side table marked with your name. Fortunately, London theatergoers do not seem to be of the drink-snatching variety.

The King and I, London Palladium, Argyll St. (☎7494 5020). Tube: Oxford Circus. Rodgers and Hammerstein do orientalism. M-Sa 7:30pm plus W and Sa 2:30pm. £15-37.50.

Lady Salsa, Talk of London, part of the New London Theatre, Drury Lane (☎7314 2929). Tube: Covent Garden. Starring 76-year-old legend Hilda Oates, in a musical eulogy to the Cuban revolution. To at least early 2002. M-Th 8pm, F-Sa 7 and 10pm. £15-25, student&senior standby £12.50 1hr. before curtain.

The Lion King, Lyceum Theatre, Wellington St. (☎0870 243 9000). Tube: Charing Cross. Thoughtful experimental drama about a lion cub called Simba. Tu-Sa 7:30pm plus W and Sa 2pm, Su 3pm. £15-35.

Mamma Mia!, Prince Edward Theatre, Old Compton St. (☎7447 5400). Tube: Leicester Sq. Has the musical genre finally met its Waterloo? M-Th and Sa 7:30pm, F 5 and 8:30pm, Sa 3pm. £15-35.

Les Miserables, Palace Theatre, Shaftesbury Ave., entrance on Charing Cross Rd. (☎7434 0909). Tube: Leicester Sq. Actors call them "the glums." Not a patch on the book, but a helluva lot shorter. M-Sa 7:30pm plus Th and Sa 2:30pm. £7-33.

The Mousetrap, St. Martin's Theatre, West St. (☎7836 1443). Tube: Leicester Sq. By Agatha Christie. After half a century on the stage, is there anyone left in London who doesn't know whodunnit in the world's longest-running play? M-Sa 8pm plus Tu 2:45pm, and Sa 5pm. £11-25.

My Fair Lady, at the Theatre Royal Drury Lane, entrance on Catharine St. (☎7494 5000). Tube: Covent Garden. Book early, or your tears will be too late. M-Sa 7:30pm plus W and Sa 2:30pm. £8-38.

Phantom of the Opera, Her Majesty's Theatre, Haymarket (☎7494 5400). A fizzy orange drink. Or is that the Fanta of the opera? Shows M-Sa 7:45pm plus W and Sa 3pm. Box office M-Sa 10am-8pm. £11-33.

Starlight Express, Apollo Victoria, 17 Wilton Rd. (☎0870 400 0870). Tube: Victoria. The show must roll on. M-Sa 7:45pm plus Tu, Sa 3pm. £12.50-30.

The Witches of Eastwick, Prince of Wales Theatre, Coventry St. (☎7839 5971). Tube: Leicester Sq. You'll either be bewitched or turned to stone (possibly both). M-Sa 7:45pm plus W and Sa 3pm. £15-38.

The Woman in Black, Fortune Theatre, Russell St. (☎7836 2238). Tube: Covent Garden. Proving that good writing is scarier than any amount of cinematic gore. M-Sa 8pm plus Tu 3pm and Sa 4pm. £10-29; student&senior standby £10 1hr. before curtain.

FILM

London's film scene offers everything. The heart of the celluloid monster is **Leicester Square** (p. 209), where the latest releases premiere a day before hitting the chains around the city, while the dominant mainstream cinema chain is **Odeon** (☎0870 5050 007; www.odeon.co.uk). Tickets to West End cinemas cost £8-10; weekday screenings before 5pm are usually cheaper. The annual **London Film Festival** (www.lff.org.uk), held in November, takes place at the National Film Theatre (see p. 214). While Hollywood shows are released much later in London than in the US, film buffs will be pleased at the large number of repertory cinemas screening classics and obscure arthouse works. Newspapers and *Time Out* carry listings and reviews of other commercial and independent films; try the *Guardian's* Guide section in their Saturday edition, or their website at www.filmunlimited.co.uk. Also worth perusing are the ICA (p. 141) and NFT (p. 214) monthly schedules, available on-site. Most cinemas have bars and cafés.

COMEDY

Capital of a nation famed for its sense of humor, London takes its comedy seriously. On any given night of the week, you'll find at least 10 comedy clubs in operation; **stand-up** is the mainstay, but **improvisation** is also hot. Most clubs and nights only run once a week or once a month, with a different line-up every time—check listings in *Time Out* or a newspaper to keep up to speed. However, as comedy goes more mainstream, there's an increasing number of purpose-built, full-time comedy venues, of which the **Comedy Store** (p. 210) is the most famous.

Summertime comedy seekers should note that London empties of comedians in **August,** when most head to Edinburgh to take part in the annual festival (and hopefully win an award); on the other hand, **July** is full of feverish comic activity as performers test out new material prior to heading north.

MUSIC

ROCK & POP

Birthplace of the Rolling Stones, the Sex Pistols, Madness, and the Chemical Brothers, home to Madonna and Paul McCartney, London is a town steeped in rock'n'roll history. Every major band and singer in the world has played at least one of its major venues; dates for the biggest acts are usually booked months in advance and often sell out within days of tickets being released, so you need to start planning well before arriving in London to have a chance of bagging a place.

Stadium-filling acts are only the tip of the giant iceberg of London's music scene. Every night in dozens of pubs and smaller venues, hopeful bands play to a devoted crowd of followers and friends, hoping the record-company scout is somewhere in the audience. Naturally, some venues have a better reputation as a solid source of talent than others; the **Water Rats** (p. 218) and the **Dublin Castle** (p. 218) are both pubs with good records of welcoming talented new acts.

Royal Opera House

Globe Theatre

Electric Co.

on the cheap

Cheap Theater

Contrary to public belief, going to the theater in London doesn't have to break the bank—as long as you follow the rules. Buying directly from the **box office** is almost always cheapest; there may be a £1-2 fee if you pay by credit card. For big-name shows, try to get tickets in advance; otherwise, you can queue up at the Half-Price Ticket Booth (p. 211). The cheapest seats in most theaters cost about £10, progressing upward to £40 for good stall seats, although **previews** and **matinees** cost a few pounds less. If a show is sold out, **returns** may be sold (at full price) just before curtain.

While some theaters offer discount student and senior rates for advance bookings, more common are **standbys** (rush tickets to Americans; usually under £10), unsold tickets released to qualifying patrons shortly before curtain; arrive 2hr. beforehand and bring ID. If you are travelling with friends, try asking about group discounts (usually for groups of 10 or more).

Day seats (which may provide only a restricted view) are sold at a reduced price to the public from 9 or 10am only on the day of the performance, but to snag one you'll need to queue up a lot earlier than that.

CLASSICAL

Home to four world-class orchestras, three major concert halls, two opera houses, four ballet companies, and more chamber ensembles than Simon Rattle could shake his baton at, London is ground zero for serious music—and there's no need to break the bank. Every evening for two months over the summer, queues snake around the Royal Albert Hall for the **Proms** (p. 216), the world's largest festival of classical music; others brave the elements to enjoy some outdoor **Music on a Summer Evening** (p. 218) on Hampstead Heath. And the serious opera buffs who populate "the Gods" (so called because the seats are so far from the stage, you may as well be in heaven) in the **Royal Opera House** (p. 211) and the **Coliseum** (p. 210) wouldn't dream of descending to rub shoulders with the wealthy posers below. Beyond the major concert halls, smaller venues offer music of all periods and standards—almost every church in central London has a regular concert program, often for free. To hear some of the world's top choirs, head to Westminster Abbey (p. 77) or St. Paul's Cathedral (p. 71) for Evensong—as a double bonus, you'll also get into the cathedral for free.

JAZZ, FOLK, & WORLD

London's jazz scene is small but serious; this ain't Chicago, but hallowed clubs like **Ronnie Scotts** (p. 211) pull in big-name performers from across the world. For the most part, the scene is low-key and home-grown, with performances taking place in various bars and pubs around town, often in the suburbs. The **Pizza Express** chain of restaurants (p. 158) often features jazz in its larger and swankier branches, in addition to operating a full-time jazz club (p. 211).

Folk (which in London usually means **Irish**) and **world** music keep an even lower profile, though big-name acts make occasional appearances at major concert venues—the **South Bank Centre** (p. 214) runs a strong and varied program in its three halls. In general, folk and world outings are restricted to pubs and community centers. The **Swan Stockwell** (p. 221) and the **Hammersmith Irish Centre** (p. 220) are two of the best-known venues for Celtic music, while the **Africa Centre** (see Nightlife, p. 193) has a weekly music spot.

SPECTATOR SPORTS

> Many evils arise which God forbid
> —Edward II, banning football in
> London in 1314

Britain may not produce the best sportsmen in the world—it's been over 60 years since a local won Wimbledon, 35 since the English team lifted the football World Cup, and almost 20 since they last won the Ashes in cricket—but they count among the world's most enthusiastic spectators. While this has occasionally been less than positive (football hooliganism comes to mind), for the most part watching sports is an essential part of English social cohesion.

FOOTBALL. Whether or not football (the term "soccer" is an abbreviation of Association Football) was invented here—the Italians also lay claim to it—there's no doubt that the sport in its current form is an English creation. During the season (late August to May), over half a million people attend professional matches every Saturday, dressed with fierce loyalty in team colors. Though violence at stadiums have dogged the game for years, the atmosphere has become tamer now that stadiums sell seats rather than standing spaces and with the increasing (though still tiny) number of women attending matches. The big three London teams are **Arsenal,** Highbury Stadium, Avenell Rd. (☎7704 4000; Tube: Arsenal), **Chelsea,** Stamford Bridge, Fulham Rd. (☎7386 7799; Tube: Fulham Broadway) and **Tottenham Hotspur,** White Hart Lane (☎8365 5000; BR: White Hart Lane).

RUGBY. Rugby was allegedly created when an inspired (or confused) Rugby School student picked up a regular football and ran it into the goal. Never as popular in London as it is in the north, locals still turn out loyally to support England, even if they have little idea who their local team is. The most significant contests, including the springtime **Six Nations Championship** (featuring England, Scotland, Wales, Ireland, France, and Italy) are played at **Twickenham** (☎8831 6666; Rail: Twickenham).

CRICKET. For non-Commonwealth visitors who have no understanding of the game, cricket can seem baffling—matches amble on for days and often end in draws. But who cares? The sun is (hopefully) shining, the beer is warm, and there's little enough action that you can read the newspaper and still not miss anything. In a bid to attract younger viewers, one-day matches have been introduced, with risk-taking players dressed in gaudy colors, but purists complain that it's just not cricket. Every summer a touring nation plays England in a series of matches around the country, always including one at **Lord's** (see Sights, p. 122) and often another at the **Oval,** in south London (☎7582 7764; Tube: Oval).

TENNIS. Every year, for two weeks in late June and early July, tennis buffs all over the world focus their attention on **Wimbledon.** Reserve months ahead or arrive by 6am (gates open 10:30am) to secure one of the 500 Centre and no. 1 court tickets sold every morning; otherwise, you'll have to settle for a "grounds" tickets to the outer courts. No center court tickets are sold during the last four days. On the first Saturday of the championships, 2000 extra Centre Court tickets are put up for sale at the "bargain" price of £30. (All England Lawn Tennis Club. ☎8971 2473. Tube: Southfields or Rail: Wimbledon. Grounds £7-12, after 5pm £5-7; show courts £17-50.)

ENTERTAINMENT BY NEIGHBORHOOD

THE WEST END

⓪ NEIGHBORHOOD QUICKFIND: *Discover,* p. 2; *Sights,* p. 79; *Museums&Galleries,* p. 139; *Food&Drink,* p. 159; *Nightlife,* p. 190; *Shopping,* p. 226; *Accommodations,* p. 284.

The West End is London's entertainment nexus—so dominant is the West End that the term "West End Theatre" has come to refer to any major mainstream London **theater,** whether or not it lies within the West End. **Shaftesbury Avenue** in Soho, **Drury**

SEE MAP, p. 330-331

Lane and the **Aldwych** in Covent Garden, and the **Strand** have been synonymous with the London stage for centuries. **Leicester Square,** home of the **Half-Price Ticket Booth,** is an essential stop for the London theatergoer on a budget. Also in Leicester Sq. are London's largest first-run **cinemas.** Lest you fear that the West End is all about mainstream entertainment, don't fret: just as West End theaters need not be in the West End, so Off-West End and fringe theaters can sit happily just yards away from *Mamma Mia!* and *Beautiful Game;* similarly, art-house and repertory films play a stone's throw from Leicester Sq. and Piccadilly Circus.

the BIG $plurge

Gone For A Song

Germanophiles and Italophiles might protest that the phrase English opera is an oxymoron: what opera written in a language as cacophonous as English could possibly match the grandeur of a Puccini libretto? Well, they might dirty their tight black jeans when they learn English opera has a rich history beginning in the 18th century. In 1728 **John Gay** satirized English society in the *Beggar's Opera*, written a good half-century before opera galvanized the Continent. Today, anyone expecting stuffy productions of 19th-century works is in for a shock. While Puccini and Verdi continue to be staples of the scene, Operas provide some of the most avantgarde stagings in London. Nudity, profanity, and screeching chords? Welcome to British opera.

Opera is an art form best experienced in style. Grandest of all London theaters, the **Royal Opera** (see p. 211) will thrill your eyes and ears. Recently reopened after major renovations, this venerable venue is home to some of Europe's finest opera and ballet. A night at the **English National Opera** in the London Coliseum (also on p. 210) is equally enchanting—and it's in English. Standby tickets for both cost from £12.

CINEMA

Curzon Soho, 93-107 Shaftesbury Ave. (☎7439 4805, bookings ☎0871 871 0022). Tube: Leicester Sq. *Time Out* readers voted it London's best cinema in 2001. Independent and international films, plus Su classic and repertory double bills. Frequent talks and Q&A sessions from big-name indie directors. Tu-Su £8; £5 all day M, Tu-Th before 5pm, and Su matinees and double bills; students and seniors £5 Tu-Th; under 15 always £4.

The Empire, Leicester Sq., north side (☎0870 010 2030). London's most famous first-run movie theater, and the cinema of choice for premieres. Book ahead for weekends and evening shows. Screen 1 is the biggy; the other two are nothing special. Screen 1 £9.50, M-F before 5pm £6, seniors £5.50, under 15 £5; Screen 2 £8.50, M-F before 5pm £5.50, seniors and under 15 £5; Screen 3 £7.50, £5, £5.

ICA Cinema, Nash House. See p. 141.

Odeon Leicester Sq., on the east side of Leicester Sq. (☎0870 505 0007). Tube: Leicester Sq. Europe's largest "cinema screen" (not counting IMAXes and planetaria) goes some way to justifying the sky-high prices. Don't confuse it with the other Odeon on the south side of the square (near the Half-Price Ticket Booth). Stalls and rear circle £10, front circle £11; M-F before 5pm and under 15 from £6.

The Prince Charles, Leicester Pl. (☎7957 4009 or 7420 0000; www.princecharlescinema.com). Tube: Leicester Sq. Just off blockbuster-ridden Leicester Sq., the Prince Charles couldn't offer more of a contrast: the *Sing-a-long-a-Sound-of-Music*, where Von Trappists dress as everything from nuns to "Ray, a drop of golden sun" (F 7:30pm, Su 2pm; £12.50, kids £8), and the live-troupe accompanied *Rocky Horror Picture Show* (F 11:45pm; £6, students £3) are both London institutions. Otherwise the fare is second-run Hollywood and recent independents. £3.50, M-F before 5pm £1.75, M evenings £2.

COMEDY

Comedy Store, 1a Oxendon St., SW1 (Tickets from TicketMaster, ☎7344 0234; www.thecomedystore.co.uk). Tube: Piccadilly Circus. The UK's top comedy club sowed the seeds that gave rise to *Ab Fab*, *Whose Line is it Anyway*, and *Blackadder*, while Robin Williams did frequent impromptu acts in the 1980s. Tu *Cutting Edge* (contemporary satire), W and Su Comedy Store Players improvisation, Th-Sa standup. Bar at back sells food before shows and during interval (burger £5.60). Shows Tu-Su 8pm plus midnight Sa. Book ahead. Over 18s only. £12-15, students & seniors £8.

MUSIC: CLASSICAL, OPERA, & BALLET

English National Opera, at the Coliseum, St. Martin's Lane (☎7632 8300; www.eno.org). Tube: Charing Cross or Leicester Sq. In London's largest theater. Known for both innovative productions of the classics and contemporary and avant-garde work. All works sung in English. £6-60; under 18 half-price with adult. Day seats for the dress-circle (£29) and balcony (£3) released M-F 10am (12:30pm by phone); max. 2 per person. Standbys from 3hr. before curtain; students £12.50, seniors £18, Sa also available to general public for £28. If all seats have been sold, standing places are available for £3.

Royal Opera House, Bow St. (☎ 7304 4000). Tube: Covent Garden. Known simply as "Covent Garden" to afficionados, the Royal Opera House is also home to the **Royal Ballet.** Productions tend to be conservative but lavish, just like the wealthy patrons. Prices for the best seats regularly top £100, but standing room and restricted-view seating in the upper balconies can be had for under £5. Student, senior, and under-18 standby 4hr. before curtain £12.50-15. 67 day seats £10-40 from 10am on day of performance. .

St. Martin-in-the-Fields, Trafalgar Sq. (see p. 86; box office ☎ 7839 8362). Frequent concerts and recitals are given in this ornate 18th-century church, home to the acclaimed Academy of St. Martin-in-the-Fields. Free lunchtime concerts most M-Tu and F 1:05pm. Candlelit evening concerts Th-Sa 7:30pm; reserved seating £10-20, unreserved places £6-8.

MUSIC: JAZZ

100 Club, 100 Oxford St. (☎ 7636 0933). Tube: Tottenham Court Rd. Hidden behind a battered doorway, the 100 Club is primarily a jazz venue with frequent excursions into indie rock. Punk burst onto the scene at a legendary gig here in 1976, when the Sex Pistols, the Clash, and Siouxsie & the Banshees all shared the stage in one evening. Regular nights include jazz dance parties F, swing jazz Sa, rhythm and blues Su, "Stompin" swing dance M. Free sessions F at lunch. Open Su-Th 7:30pm-midnight, F-Sa 7:30pm-2am. Cover usually £6-10.

Pizza Express Jazz Club, 10 Dean St. (☎ 7439 8722; www.pizzaexpress.co.uk). Tube: Tottenham Court Rd. Underneath a branch of the popular chain (see p. 158), diners tuck into their pizzas while feasting their ears on music. Atmospheric lighting and a laid-back atmosphere make for a great date spot. Table reservations recommended, especially F-Sa. Doors normally open 7:45pm, with music 9-11:30pm; some F-Sa have 2 shows, with doors opening at 6 and 10pm. Cover (£12-20) added to the food bill. MC, V.

Ronnie Scott's, 47 Frith St. (☎ 7439 0747; www.ronniescotts.co.uk). Tube: Tottenham Court Rd. or Piccadilly Circus. This intimate venue is London's oldest and most famous jazz club. Two bands alternate two sets every night M-Sa, the support starting at 9:30pm and the headline act around 11pm; Su brings lesser-known bands from 8:30pm. Table reservations essential for big-name acts, though there's limited unreserved standing room at the bar—if it's sold out, try coming back at the end of the main act's first set, around midnight. Ask for a nonsmoking table to be right by the stage. Food £5-14, cocktails £7-8. Box office open M-Sa 11am-6pm. Club open M-Sa 8:30pm-3am, Su 7:30-11:30pm. £15 M-Th, £20 F-Sa, £8-12 Su; students £9 M-W. AmEx, MC, V.

MUSIC: ROCK & POP

London Astoria (LA1), 157 Charing Cross Rd. (☎ 7344 0044; www.londonastoria.com). Tube: Tottenham Court Rd. Originally a pickle factory, the Astoria was a strip club and music hall before turning to full-time rock venue in the late 1980s. 2000 capacity. F-Sa hosts the popular G-A-Y clubnight (see p. 193). £10-20.

Borderline, Orange Yard, off Manette St. (☎ 7734 2095; www.borderline.co.uk). Tube: Tottenham Court Rd. Basement space that's still trading off its secret REM gig years ago, now used for lesser-known groups with a strong folk-rock flavor. Music M-Sa from 8pm. Box office open M-F 1-7:30pm. £5-10 in advance, students £5.

THEATER

Half-Price Ticket Booth, on the south side of Leicester Sq. (look for the long lines). Tube: Leicester Sq. Run jointly by London theaters, the HPTB is the only place where you can be sure your half-price tickets are genuine. The catch is that you have to buy them on the day of the performance, in person and in cash, on a strict first-come, first-served basis; there's no choice in seating, with the most expensive tickets sold first; and there's no way of knowing in advance what shows will have tickets available that day. Even so, it's phenomenally popular—come early and be prepared to wait, especially Sa. Noticeboards display what's going on the day; as with the queues, left is for evening performances, right for matinees. £2 booking fee per ticket. Max. 4 tickets per person. Open M-Sa 10am-7pm, Su noon-2:30pm.

Donmar Warehouse, 41 Earlham St. (☎ 7369 1732; www.donmar-warehouse.com). Tube: Covent Garden. Serious contemporary theatre. With productions starring the likes of Nicole Kidman and Colin Firth, the Donmar rarely has difficulty filling its 251 seats. £14-35; student, senior, and under 18 standby £12 30min. before curtain.

Player's Theatre, The Arches, Craven Passage (☎ 7839 1134; www.playerstheatre.co.uk). Tube: Charing Cross. A patch of ground beneath Charing Cross train station that is forever England (circa 1890), the Players offer a rare outlet for Victorian music-hall and variety acts. It's all rather dated, but then, that's the whole point. Shows Tu-Su 8:15pm plus Th 2pm. £15.

Savoy Theatre, Strand (☎ 7836 8888; www.doylycarte.org.uk). Tube: Charing Cross. Recently restored to the magnificence of its Art-Deco heyday, the original home of the D'Oyly Carte Opera Company once again swings to the sounds of Gilbert and Sullivan. £12-35.

Soho Theatre, 21 Dean St. (☎ 7478 0100; www.sohotheatre.com). Tube: Tottenham Court Rd. Modern fringe theater focusing on works by new writers, often from the associated writers' center. Also frequent stand-up comedy. Plays £5 M; Tu-Th £14, students and seniors £10; F-Sa £15, £12.50. Online prices Tu-Sa £12, students and seniors £8. Comedy £6-10.

Long-running shows, see p. 205.

The Adelphi, Strand. *Chicago.*

Arts Theatre, 6-7 Gt. Newport St. *Closer to Heaven.*

Criterion Theatre, Piccadilly Circus. *The Complete Works of William Shakespeare (Abridged)* and *The Complete History of America (Abridged),*

Fortune Theatre, Russell St. *The Woman in Black.*

Her Majesty's Theatre, Haymarket. *Phantom of the Opera.*

Gielgud Theatre, Shaftesbury Ave. *The Graduate.*

London Palladium, Argyll St. *The King and I.*

Lyceum Theatre, Wellington St. Disney's *The Lion King.*

New London Theatre, *Cats.* Also *Lady Salsa* at the **Talk of London.**

Palace Theatre, Shaftesbury Ave. *Les Miserables.*

Queen's Theatre, Shaftesbury Ave. *All You Need Is Love.*

Phoenix Theatre, Charing Cross Rd. *Blood Brothers.*

Prince Edward Theatre, Old Compton St. *Mamma Mia!*

Prince of Wales Theatre, Coventry St. *The Witches of Eastwick.*

St. Martin's Theatre, West St. *The Mousetrap.*

Strand Theatre, Aldwych. *Buddy.*

Theatre Royal Drury Lane, Catharine St. *My Fair Lady.*

Whitehall Theatre, Whitehall. *The Blues Brothers.*

Wyndham's Theatre, Charing Cross Rd. *Art.*

OTHER

Cycle rickshaws (☎ 7437 5696; www.londonpedicabs.com) bring a much-needed touch of Bangkok to an area now largely denuded of strip joints and sex shops. What could be more romantic than a 3am post-club ride home with your new-found love? The stars twinkle, the seat bounces suggestively, and the exhausted driver pants in time with the rhythmically whirring pedals...Rickshaws congregate at various points around the West End, but the most popular pick-up spot is the corner of Frith St. and Old Compton St. (Tube: Piccadilly Circus or Leicester Sq.), Su-Th 5pm-1am, F-Sa 5pm-4am. Short spins around Soho £2.50-3 per person; longer trips £5 per person per mi. Cash only.

HOLBORN

🛈 *NEIGHBORHOOD QUICKFIND:* **Discover,** *p. 6;* **Sights,** *p. 88;* **Museums&Galleries,** *p. 142;* **Food&Drink,** *p. 164;* **Nightlife,** *p. 194;* **Shopping,** *p. 232.*

SEE MAP, pp. 334-335

Chuckle Club, at the Three Tuns Bar, Houghton St. (☎ 7476 1672). Tube: Holborn. Eerily reminiscent of a 1960s British holiday camp, this is not one of those "comedy is hip" clubs. A regularly changing lineup of at least 3 headline acts and numerous tryouts guarantees a few belly laughs among the chuckles. Expect quality heckling from the student-heavy audience. Show Sa 8:30pm: doors open 7:45pm, queue earlier. £8, students £6.

Peacock Theatre, Portugal St. (☎ 7863 8222; www.sadlerswell.com). Tube: Holborn. The (almost) West End outpost of Sadler's Wells (see Clerkenwell, below), London's leading dance venue. Program leans towards contemporary dance and popular dance-troupe shows. Box office open M-Sa 10am-6:30pm, to 8:30pm on performance days. Some wheelchair accessible seats. £8-30; cheaper rates apply M-Th and Sa matinee. Student, senior, and under-16 standbys from 1hr. before performance.

CLERKENWELL

7 *NEIGHBORHOOD QUICKFIND: Discover, p. 6; Sights, p. 92; Museums&Galleries, p. 143; Food&Drink, p. 166; Nightlife, p. 194; Accommodations, p. 285.*

Sadler's Wells, Rosebery Ave. (☎ 7863 8000; www.sadlerswells.com). Tube: Angel. Recently rebuilt as a hulking steel-and-glass megalith, historic Sadler's Wells remains London's premier dance space, with everything from classical ballet to contemporary tap,

SEE MAP, pp. 334-335

plus occasional operas. 10/10 for transportation: Sadlers Wells Express (SWX) bus to Waterloo via Farringdon and Victoria leaves 8min. after the end of each evening show (£1.50, £1 with period Travelcard); those arriving by regular bus can have their fare refunded (and get cash for the journey home!) at the box office. Tickets £8.50-40; student, senior, and under 16 standbys £8.50-15 1hr. before curtain (cash only). Box office open M-Sa 9am-8:30pm.

CITY OF LONDON

7 *NEIGHBORHOOD QUICKFIND: Discover, p. 7; Sights, p. 93; Museums&Galleries, p. 143; Food&Drink, p. 167; Accommodations, p. 285.*

With 39 churches, the City is not short of venues for lunchtime concerts or choral evensong; see separate church listings under Sights, p. 67, for details. Less well-known as venues are the 24 **livery halls**—occasional concerts provide the only opportunity for most people to see inside these bastions of

SEE MAP, p. 334-335

tradition. Contact the **City Music Society** (☎ 7628 6228) or the **City of London Information Centre** (☎ 7606 3030) for information. In June and July, the **City of London Festival** (see below) provides another occasion to get into places like the Mansion House and Middle Temple Hall. The City's primary entertainment venue, though, is the massive **Barbican** arts complex.

Barbican Centre, Barbican; main entrance on Silk St. (general box office ☎ 7638 8891; cinema hotline ☎ 7382 7000; www.barbican.org.uk). Tube: Barbican or Moorgate. See also Sights, p. 97, and Museums&Galleries, p. 144. Equally famous for the quality of its offerings and the impossibility of its layout, the Barbican is a one-stop cultural powerhouse.

Barbican Theatre: A futuristic auditorium seating 1166 in steeply raked, forward-leaning balconies. From Oct. 2001 to May 2002, the **Royal Shakespeare Company** will be spending its last season in residence at the Barbican, after which the theater will be given over to touring companies and short-run shows. Also frequent one-off and short-run **contemporary dance** performances. Prices vary considerably with seat, day, and production; £6-30, cheapest M-F evening and Sa matinee. Student and senior standbys from 9am day of performance.

The Pit: Intimate 200-seater theater used primarily for new and experimental productions. £10-15 depending on production.

Barbican Hall: Recently refurbished, the Barbican Hall is one of Europe's leading concert halls, with excellent acoustics and a nightly performance program. The resident **London Symphony Orchestra** plays over 80 concerts a year; the hall also hosts concerts by international orchestras, jazz artists,and world musicians. Tickets £6-35.

Barbican Cinema: 2 smallish screens, offering a mix of the latest blockbusters with art-house, international, and classic movies. £6.50, seniors & students £5, under 15 £4, family £16.

City of London Festival (box office ☎ 7638 8891; www.colf.org). From late June to mid-July, the City explodes with activities, many in otherwise forbidden spaces: concerts and operas play in livery halls, banks open up their art collections, and walks take you into the City's hidden corners. Pick up the festival guide at the Barbican (see above) or tourist information centres. Booking for ticketed events starts May 1st; tickets sold through the Barbican box office.

SOUTH BANK

🖪 NEIGHBORHOOD QUICKFIND: Discover, p. 7; **Sights,** p. 100; **Museums&Galleries,** p. 144; **Food&Drink,** p. 168; **Accommodations,** p. 285.

When it comes to highbrow entertainment, the South Bank is hard to beat; it offers the most concentrated array of theater, music, and serious film in Britain, if not the world. If you're in the mood for something more lighthearted, try out the massive BFI IMAX cinema, or relax to the free jazz that often fills

SEE MAP, p. 336-337

various foyers. Organized by the community developers responsible for much of the South Bank's vitality, the **Coin Street Festival** (☎ 7401 2255) runs from May to September. A sporadic succession of independent events, the festival celebrates ethnic diversity, modern design, and world music in and around Gabriel's Wharf and OXO Tower Wharf (see p. 102), finishing off in mid-September with the **Mayor's Thames Festival** all along the South Bank.

CINEMA

National Film Theatre (NFT), on the south bank, right underneath Waterloo Bridge (☎ 7928 3232; www.bfi.org.uk). Tube: Waterloo, Embankment, or Temple. One of the world's leading cinemas, with a mind-boggling array of films. 6 different movies hit the 3 screens every evening, starting around 6pm. The cafe spreading under the bridge belies the zero-tolerance food and drink policy in the auditoria. Annual membership (£16, concs. £11) gives £1 off movies, priority booking, and a free ticket when you join. All films £6.85, concessions £5.25.

BFI London IMAX Cinema (☎ 7902 1234; www.bfi.org.uk/imax/), at the south end of Waterloo bridge, accessed via underground walkways from the South Bank. Tube: Waterloo. At the center of a busy traffic intersection, this stunning glass drum houses the UK's biggest screen. Shows start every 65-70min.; last show 8pm Su-Th, 9:30pm F-Sa. £6.95, students & seniors £5.95, kids £4.95; extra film £4.20.

MUSIC: CLASSICAL, WORLD, & JAZZ

South Bank Centre, on the south bank of the Thames between Hungerford and Waterloo bridges (☎ 7960 4242; www.rfh.org.uk). Tube: Waterloo or Embankment. All manner of "serious" music is on the program at this megaplex of concert halls and performance spaces, though not much goes on during August. Tickets for all events can be purchased from the Royal Festival Hall box office (open daily 10am-9pm; phones M-Sa 9am-9pm, Su 9:30am-9pm); Queen Elizabeth Hall and Purcell Room box offices open 45min. before performance. Some discounts for students, seniors, and under-18; standbys may also be released 2hr. before performance (check on ☎ 7921 0973).

Royal Festival Hall: 2500-seat concert hall with the best acoustics in London. Some of the cheapest seats are the choir benches, which put you right behind the orchestra. The two resident orchestras, the **Philharmonia** and the **London Philharmonic,** predominate, but big-name jazz, latin, and world-music groups also visit; the hall converts to a theater when dance and ballet troupes drop by. Classical concerts £6-30; others around £10-30.

Queen Elizabeth Hall: Mid-sized venue used for smaller musical ensembles; more varied program than the Festival Hall. World-class jazz soloists and Indian DJs share the space with choirs and classics; also occasional literary evenings. Around £10-20.

Purcell Room: Intimate hall for chamber music, soloists, and small groups, with the usual varied South Bank repertoire. Around £10.

Free events: Free lunchtime and afternoon music often fills the cavernous Festival Hall foyer (a.k.a. "Level 2 Terrace") and the Queen Elizabeth Hall foyer, while dance demos and workshops often take to the Festival Hall "ballroom" (the large sunken space at the rear of level 2).

THEATER

National Theatre, just downriver of Waterloo bridge (info ☎ 7452 3400, box office ☎ 7452 3000; www.nationaltheatre.org.uk). Tube: Waterloo, Embankment, or Temple. Since opening under the direction of Laurence Olivier in 1963, the National has been at the forefront of British theater. Popular musicals and hit plays, which often transfer to the West End, subsidize more experimental works. The **Olivier** stage seats 1160 in a fan-shaped open-stage layout, the **Lyttelton** is a proscenium theater with 890 seats; while the 300-seat **Cottesloe** offers flexible staging for experimental dramas. Box office open M-Sa 10am-8pm. Complicated pricing scheme: Olivier/Lyttelton £10-32, Cottesloe £13-24; day seats, from 10am on day of performance, Olivier/Lyttelton £10, Cottesloe £13; standby (2hr. before curtain) £15 all theaters; standing places, only available if all seats sold, £6. Numerous concessions include: matinees £15 for seniors, £10 under 18s; M-Th evenings £15 for under 25s; disabled £8-15; student standbys from 45min. before curtain £8.

Shakespeare's Globe Theatre, 21 New Globe Walk (☎ 7401 9919; www.shakespearesglobe.org). Tube: Southwark or London Bridge. This may be a faithful reproduction of the original 16th-century playhouse where Shakespeare himself performed, but productions are anything but stuck in the past. Choose between the three covered tiers of hard, backless wooden benches (cushions £1 extra) or stand through a performance as a "groundling." If you can, go for the latter: it costs less, allows a historical communion with the Elizabethan peasantry, and puts you much closer to the stage. However, groundlings should prepare for the possibility of rain: the show *will* go on, and umbrellas are prohibited. For tours of the Globe, see Sights, p. 102. Wheelchair access in yard only. Performances mid-May to late Sept. Tu-Sa 7:30pm, Su 6:30pm; from June also Tu-Sa 2pm, Su 1pm. Box office open M-Sa 10am-6pm, 8pm on performance days. Seats £11-27, concs. £9-23; yard (i.e. standing) £5.

Old Vic, Waterloo Rd. (☎ 7928 2651; www.oldvictheatre.com). Tube: Waterloo. Still in its original 1818 hall (the oldest theater building in London), the Old Vic is one of London's most historic and most beautiful theaters. These days, it hosts touring companies playing everything from Shakespeare to pantomime. Prices and schedule set by visiting companies.

Young Vic, 66 The Cut (☎ 7928 6363; www.youngvic.org). Tube: Waterloo. Close to the Old Vic but completely independent, the Young Vic is in pointed contrast to its older cousin: the building is a plain breezeblock affair, and the theater itself—with only 8 rows of seats surrounding the flat stage—can be unnervingly intimate. One of London's top off-West End companies, with a (soft) focus on younger writers and younger viewers. Box office open M-Sa 10am-8pm. £10-12, seniors £8-10, students & kids £5-7.

WESTMINSTER

▣ *NEIGHBORHOOD QUICKFIND: Discover, p. 8; Sights, p. 106; Museums&Galleries, p. 145; Food&Drink, p. 169; Shopping, p. 232; Accommodations, p. 286.*

Long-running shows, see p. 205.

  Apollo Victoria, Wilton Rd. *Starlight Express.*

  Victoria Palace, Victoria St. *Fame—The Musical.*

SEE MAP, p. 338-339

St. John's Smith Square, Smith Sq. (☎ 7222 1061). Tube: Westminster or St. James's Park. A former church (see p. 108), now a full-time concert venue with a program weighted towards chamber and early music. Concerts daily Sept. to mid-July, once or twice a week mid-July to Aug. Performances generally start 7:30pm. Tickets £5-15, depending on seat and concert; student & senior discounts sometimes available.

CHELSEA

▣ *TRANSPORTATION: The only Tube station in Chelsea is Sloane Sq.; from here buses 11, 19, 22, 211, and 319 run down the King's Rd. NEIGHBORHOOD QUICKFIND: Discover, p. 8; Sights, p. 108; Museums&Galleries, p. 146; Food&Drink, p. 170; Shopping, p. 232.*

▨ **Royal Court Theatre,** Sloane Sq. (☎ 7565 5000; www.royalcourttheatre.com). Called "the most impoartant theater in Europe" by the *New York Times,* this venerable stage is dedicated to challeng-

SEE MAP, p. 346

ing new writing and innovative interpretations of classics. Experimental work usually runs in the intimate Upstairs auditorium. Main auditorium £5-25; concessions £9 in advance, £5 on the day; standing places 10p 1hr. before curtain. Upstairs £5-15, concessions £9. M all seats £5, both auditoria.

606 Club, 90 Lot's Rd. (☎ 7352 5953; www.606club.co.uk). Hard to find; look for the brick arch with a light bulb opposite the power station, and ring the doorbell by the metal grille door to be let downstairs. The intrepid will be rewarded with some of the best British and European jazz in a friendly, cosy venue. Note that alcohol is served only with the pricey meals (£11-16), and only diners can reserve tables. On the plus side, the music charge is voluntary, and inexpensive. M-W doors 7:30pm, 1st band 8-10:30pm, 2nd 10:45pm-1am; Th doors 8pm, music 9:30pm-1:30am; F-Sa doors 8pm, music 10pm-2am; Su (vocalists) doors 8pm, music 9pm-midnight. Optional music charge added to final bill; £5 Su-Th, £6 F-Sa.

KENSINGTON & EARL'S COURT

🔖 *NEIGHBORHOOD QUICKFIND: Discover*, p. 9; *Sights*, p. 112; *Museums&Galleries*, p. 146; *Food&Drink*, p. 172; *Shopping*, p. 233; *Accommodations*, p. 287.

MUSIC: CLASSICAL, OPERA, & FOLK

SEE MAP, p. 340-341

🎵 **The Proms** (www.bbc.co.uk/proms/), at the Royal Albert Hall (see below). This summer season of classical music has been held every year since 1895, with concerts every night from mid-July to mid-September. "Promenade" refers to the tradition of selling dirt-cheap standing tickets, and it's the presence of up to 1000 dedicated prommers, that gives the concerts their unique atmosphere (that and the lack of air conditioning). Seats for popular concerts can sell out months in advance, while lines for standing places often start mid-afternoon. The **arena,** immediately in front of the orchestra, tends to be more popular; the **gallery** has more space, but you need binoculars to see the musicians. The famous **Last Night** is an unabashedly jingoistic celebration complete with Union Jack-painted faces, flag-waving, and mass sing-a-longs of Rule Britannia. Regarded with horror by "serious" music lovers, it's so popular that you have to have attended at least five other concerts before they'll let you take part in a lottery for tickets. Tickets go on sale in mid-May (£5-30); standing places sold from 90min. before the concert (£3). Season ticket £140 arena, £110 gallery; half-season £80, £60. If you don't get in, all concerts are transmitted live on BBC Radio 3 (91.3FM), and the Last Night broadcast on a big screen in Hyde Park.

Holland Park Opera, Holland Park (☎ 7602 7856). Tube: High St. Kensington or Holland Park. Open-air opera in the grounds of a Jacobean mansion, with a generally conservative program tailored to its generally conservative patrons. No need to fear the rain—it's all done under a stretched white canopy. Performances mid-June to early Aug. Tu-Sa 7:30pm, occasional matinees Sa 2:30pm. Box office open from mid-May M-Sa 10am-6pm or 30min. before curtain. £28, concessions £22.50 F evening and Sa matinees only.

The Troubadour, 265 Old Brompton Rd. See Food&Drink, p. 172. Acoustic entertainment served up in the basement of this warm cafe. Bob Dylan and Paul Simon played here early in their careers. Lots of variety: M attracts poets, F offers jazz, Sa folk bands. Entertainment starts 8:30pm. £4-8.

GENERAL VENUES

Earl's Court Exhibition Centre, Warwick Rd. (☎ 7385 1200; www.eco.co.uk). Tube: Earl's Court (follow signs for Exhibition Centre exit). London's main venue for trade fairs and mega expos, from the London Car Show to the Great British Beer Festival. Also occasional rock concerts—Madonna, U2, and Janet Jackson played here in 2001.

Royal Albert Hall, Kensington Gore (see p. 113 for details). 5300-seat Victorian megavenue holding anything from trade fairs to pop concerts. From mid-July to mid-September, the hall rocks to the sound of the **Proms** (see above).

NOTTING HILL

🔖 *NEIGHBORHOOD QUICKFIND: Discover*, p. 10; *Sights*, p. 113; *Food&Drink*, p. 173; *Nightlife*, p. 195; *Shopping*, p. 234.

SEE MAP, p. 342

Electric Cinema, 191 Portobello Rd. (info ☎ 7727 9958, tickets ☎ 7229 8688). Tube: Ladbroke Grove. London's oldest purpose-built cinema (built 1910) has recently reopened after a 15-year hiatus, restored to its original baroque splendor. For that extra special experience, go for a luxury armchair or 2-seat sofa. Independent and international films, with late-night blockbuster reruns Sa 11pm, and classics, recent raves, and double bills Su 2pm. Features £6.50 M-F, £7.50 Sa-Su, students&seniors £4 M-F before 6pm and kids all day; luxury seats £7.50 M-F, £8.50 Sa-Su; 2-seat sofa £16, £18. Double bills and late shows £5.50.

The Gate, 11 Pembridge Rd. (box office ☎ 7229 0706). Tube: Notting Hill Gate. In a tiny room above the Prince Albert pub, the Gate bills itself as the "home of international drama"— they often premier new foreign works (in English translation) even before they've been given in their home countries. Performances M-Sa 7:30pm. Box office open for phone bookings M-Sa 10am-6:30pm, in person from 7pm. £12, concessions £6.

Gate Cinema, 87 Notting Hill Gate (☎ 7727 4043). Tube: Notting Hill Gate. Opened in 1911 the Gate's rather dour exterior is a result of post-war reconstruction. Fortunately, the auditorium remains a beautiful piece of Victoriana. Art-house and "discerning" Hollywood flicks. £6.50, first show M-F £3.50, students&seniors £3 M-F before 6pm and F-Sa after 11pm.

BAYSWATER

🖪 NEIGHBORHOOD QUICKFIND: Discover p. 10; **Food&Drink,** p. 174; **Shopping,** p. 236; **Accommodations,** p. 289

SEE MAP, p. 342

Bayswater's location on the edge of Hyde Park and Kensington Gardens make it an obvious destination for lazy summer days. Indoor pursuits are harder to come by; the **UCI cinema** in Whiteley's (see p. 236) was London's first multiplex.

Firstbowl, 17 Queensway (☎ 7229 0172). Tube: Queensway or Bayswater. Central London's only ice rink, with 12 lanes of 10-pin bowling, video-game arcade, and bar thrown in. Bowling open M-Sa 10am-11:30pm, Su 10am-11pm; £4.50 per game (kids £3.50 before 6pm), plus £1 shoe hire. Ice rink sessions daily 10am-2pm, 2-5pm, and 5-7pm, plus M-Th 8-11pm and Su 8-10pm; £5 per session plus £1 skate hire. Ice disco F-Sa 7:30-11pm, £6.50.

Queens Skate Shop, 35 Queensway (☎ 7727 4669). Minutes from the broad boulevards of Hyde Park, this specialist store rents out blades by the day. Open daily 11am-7pm. Rentals £10 per day, Tu evening special (6:30pm Tu to 6:30pm W) £5. Passport or £100 cash deposit. MC, V (£12 minimum).

MARYLEBONE & REGENT'S PARK

🖪 NEIGHBORHOOD QUICKFIND: Discover, p. 11; **Sights,** p. 114; **Museums&Galleries,** p. 147; **Food&Drink,** p. 174; **Accommodations,** p. 292.

SEE MAP, p. 344-345

Open-Air Theatre, Inner Circle, Regents Park (☎ 7486 2431; www.open-air-theatre.org.uk). Tube: Baker St. Bring blankets and waterproofs to this open-air stage—performances take place rain or shine. Program runs early June to early Sept., and always includes 2 Shakespeares, a musical, and a children's performance. Barbecue before evening shows. Performances M-Sa 8pm with matinees 2:30pm Th and Sa May-June and Sept. and daily Aug. £8.50-23; family £12 per person for best available seat, min. 4 people with at least 1 under 16; student&senior standby £8 from 1hr. before curtain.

Wigmore Hall, 36 Wigmore St. (☎ 7935 2141; www.wigmore-hall.org.uk). Tube: Oxford Circus. London's premier chamber-music venue, in a beautiful setting with excellent acoustics; occasional jazz recitals. Seats are neither raked nor staggered; shorter patrons will spend the evening contemplating the ornate mural above the stage. Box office open M-Sa 10am-8:30pm, Su 10:30am-5pm Nov. to mid-Mar., mid-Mar. to Oct. 10:30am-8pm. Phone bookings close 90-120min. earlier; £1 supplement. Concerts most nights 7:30pm; £8-20, student&senior standby £8-10 1hr. before start (cash only). Daytime concerts Su 11:30am (£9) and M 1pm (£8, seniors £6).

BLOOMSBURY

🖪 NEIGHBORHOOD QUICKFIND: Discover, p. 11; **Sights,** p. 116; **Museums&Galleries,** p. 148; **Food&Drink,** p. 175; **Shopping,** p. 236; **Accommodations,** p. 293.

SEE MAP, pp. 344-345

The Place, 17 Duke's Rd. (☎ 7387 0031; www.theplace.org.uk). Tube: Euston or King's Cross/St. Pancras. Reopening in autumn 2001 after a complete refit, The Place is Britain's top venue for contemporary dance. Seasons run Jan.-June, and Sept.-Nov. Over 100 companies participate in the "Resolution" festival (Jan.-Feb.), with 3 new works per night. Performances £10, concessions £8.

RADA (Royal Academy of the Dramatic Arts), 62-64 Gower St., entrance on Malet St. (☎ 7636 7076; www.rada.org). Britain's most famous drama school has 3 on-site theaters, with productions throughout the academic year—catch the next Ken Branagh or Ralph Fiennes before they hit the big time. Also regular Foyer events, with plays, music, and readings M-Th at 7 or 7:30pm (free-£3) and open-mic nights F 7pm (free). Box office open M-F 10am-5pm.

Renoir, Brunswick Sq. (☎ 7837 8402). Tube: Russell Sq. As its name suggests, this independent movie house—hidden within the concrete bowels of the bleak Brunswick Centre housing estate—has a strong emphasis on European and especially French cinema. Bar/cafe from 30min. before each screening. £6.50; 1st performance of the day £4.50, concessions £3.

The Water Rats, 328 Grays Inn Rd. (☎ 7837 7269). Tube: King's Cross/St. Pancras. A pub-café by day, a stomping venue for top new talent by night. Oasis were signed here after performing their first London gig. Open for coffee M-F 8am-noon, surprisingly good lunches (£4-6) M-F noon-2pm, and music M-Sa 8pm-midnight (cover £5, students £4).

NORTH LONDON

◪ NEIGHBORHOOD QUICKFIND: *Discover,* p. 12; *Sights,* p. 118; *Museums&Galleries,* p. 150; *Food&Drink,* p. 176; *Nightlife,* p. 196; *Shopping,* p. 237; *Accommodations,* p. 298.

CINEMA

Pullman Everyman, 5 Holly Bush Vale (☎ 7431 1777; www.everymancinema.com). Tube: Hampstead. One of London's oldest movie theatres, this 1930s picture house has recently been revamped. Lean back on the leather sofas of the "luxury" balcony, or snuggle into one of the love seats in the stalls. Mostly new independent films. Kiddy faves every Sa morning (£5). Cafe open M-F 5:30-10pm, Sa 10am-10pm, Su noon-10pm; bar F-Su only. Stalls £6.80 Tu-Su, £5 M, concessions £5 Su-F; luxury seats £12.

Tricycle Cinema, see Tricycle Theatre (below) for details; entrance on Buckley Rd. Large-screen luxury cinema specialising in independent and foreign films. Singles night and a gay/lesbian "introductions" evening the 1st Th and 3rd Tu of the month respectively, both including pre-movie champagne and post-movie bar. (£12, concessions £9.) Family films M 1pm (£4, concessions £3). Supercheap matinees Th 2:30pm, £2.50. Regular features £6.50, £4 M and Tu-F before 5pm; concessions £1 less M-F before 8pm and Sa-Su before 5pm.

COMEDY

Canal Cafe Theatre, above the Bridgehouse pub, Delamere Terrace (☎ 7289 6054). Tube: Warwick Ave. (Zone 2). Walk up Warwick Ave., turn right and walk along the canal; it's at the far end of the bridge to your left. One of the few comedy venues to specialize in sketch, as opposed to stand-up, comedy. Despite the name, don't count on the upstairs bar being open. Weekly changing shows W-Sa 7:30pm (£5, concs. £4). *Newsrevue,* Th-Sa 9:30pm and Su 9pm, is London's longest-running comedy sketch show, presenting an irreverent weekly take on current events since 1970. (£6, concs. £5.) First-timers must purchase £1 membership.

Downstairs at the King's Head, 2 Crouch End Hill (☎ 8340 1023). Bus #W7 from Finsbury Park or #41 from Archway (Zone 3). One of the oldest comedy clubs in the city in a cosy space under a pub. Try-outs every Th give up to 16 new acts their 15min. of fame (£4, concs. £3); Sa-Su "comedy cabarets" mix 5 diverse acts, from stand-up to songs to ventriloquism (£6, concs. £5). Shows starts 8:30pm, doors open 7:30pm.

MUSIC: CLASSICAL, FOLK, & JAZZ

Jazz Café, 5 Parkway (☎ 7916 6060; tickets ☎ 7344 0044; www.jazzcafe.co.uk). Tube: Camden Town. With a crowded front bar and balcony restaurant overlooking the large dancefloor and stage, this would be a popular nightspot even without the top line-up of jazz, soul, funk, and Latin performers (tickets £10-16). Jazzy club nights follow the show F-Sa (£8-9) and every other Su (free). Bring your horn to the jam session Su noon-4pm (£1). Open M-Th 7pm-1am, F-Sa 7pm-2am, Su 7pm-midnight. V, MC.

Cecil Sharpe House, 2 Regent's Park Rd. (☎ 7485 2206). Run by English Folk Dance and Song Society, in practice a home to traditions from around the world. Celtic ceilidhs, Balkan kolas, and Caribbean quadrilles stomp in the main hall Th-Su 7:30-11pm (£5-8); with numerous daytime and evening classes from clog dancing to fiddle playing (around £3).

Music on a Summer Evening, in Kenwood, Highgate (see p. 121; ☎ 7413 1443). Popular classics and lakeside fireworks held July-Sept. Aficionados will shrink from the amplified sound system. If a view of the orchestra isn't important, stay outside the enclosure and listen for free—the music is audible for miles around. Deckchairs £17-20; concessions £15-17.50 "Promenade" (no seat—bring a groundsheet or risk a wet bum) £14.50/£12.50.

MUSIC: ROCK & POP

🎵 **Filthy MacNasty's Whisky Café,** 68 Amwell St. Tube: Angel. Famous for rock and poetry nights. See **Nightlife,** p. 196.

Dublin Castle, 94 Parkway (☎8806 2668). It's Madness in the back room every Tu, with a Blur of record execs and talent scouts on the lookout for the next big thing at *Club Fandango*. During the day, the room becomes a kickboxing club—look out for former European Champion, Keith Wilson. Three bands nightly 8:45-11pm; doors 8:30pm. £5, £4 students.

Forum, 9-11 Highgate Rd. (☎7284 1001, box office ☎7344 0044; www.meanfiddler.com). Tube: Kentish Town. Turn right out of tube station and cross the road. Lavish Art Deco theater turned top venue, with great sound and good views, that attracts some of the biggest bands: Van Morrison, Bjork, Oasis, Jamiroquai, and many others have played this 2000-capacity space. When no gigs are on, a cheesy 60s-80s disco takes over Sa (10pm-2am; £8).

The Garage, 20-22 Highbury Corner (☎8963 0940, box office ☎7344 0044; www.thegarage.co.uk). Tube: Highbury and Islington. Indie venue attracting big-name bags, but some patrons complain about its sound system. Lesser acts play the upstairs room. Music 8-11:30pm, followed by an indie clubnight to 2am F-Sa (included in gig ticket, else £6). £5-15.

THEATER

🎭 **The Almeida,** Almeida St. (☎7359 4404; www.almeida.co.uk). Tube: Angel or Highbury & Islington. During renovations (until May 2002), productions will be held in a disused coach depot at Omega Pl., off Caledonian Rd. The top fringe theater in London, if not the world; Hollywood stars, including Kevin Spacey and Nicole Kidman, queue up to prove their acting cred here. Ken Stott stars in Brian Friel's *Faith Healer* from Nov. 22 2001 to Jan. 19 2002; Oliver Ford Davies will be King Lear in early 2002. Box office open 9:30am-curtain. Shows M-Sa 7:30pm, with matinee Sa 3pm. £6-27.50; students and seniors £7-11.

The Barge Theatre, moored in Little Venice by Blomfield Rd. (☎7249 6876). Tube: Warwick Avenue. Kids have thrilled for years to puppet and shadow-puppet shows beneath the bright awnings of this Little Venice institution, while occasional adult-oriented shows are a reminder of the long and ribald history of puppetry as a serious performance art. Children's shows most weekends and daily during holidays at 3pm; call for program. £6.50, concessions £6.

Etcetera Theatre, upstairs at the Oxford Arms, 265 Camden High St. (☎7482 4857). Five rows of seating leading straight onto a good-sized stage, with two plays per night. Experimental stuff, mostly new writers and unsolicited scripts, though local mega-dramatist Alan Bennet *(The Madness of King George III)* has premiered a couple of pieces here. Box office opens 30min. before the show. Shows M-Sa 7:30 and 9:30pm, Su 6:30 and 8:30pm. £8, concessions £5; includes 1yr. membership giving £1.50 off future tickets.

Hampstead Theatre, 98 Avenue Rd. (☎7722 9301). Tube: Swiss Cottage. Small theatre dedicated to new writing. Works are selected from hundreds of unsolicited scripts submitted by budding unknowns from around the UK. Acting alumni include John Malkovich. Shows M-Sa 8pm and Sa 3pm. Tickets £10 M and 3pm Sa, £15 Tu-F, £17 Sa 8pm. Limited student tickets (£7) available in advance for 8pm shows; more for matinees, plus standbys.

The King's Head, 115 Upper St. (☎7226 1916). Tube: Angel or Highbury & Islington. London's first pub theatre, and still one of the best. Mostly new writing, produced in-house or by touring companies. Succesful productions often transfer to the West End. Alums include Hugh Grant, Gary Oldman, and *Ab Fab's* Joanna Lumley. Shows 8pm M-Sa and 3:30pm Sa-Su; tickets £12-14, students and seniors M-Th and matinees £9.50.

Little Angel Theatre, 14 Dagmar Passage, off Cross St. (☎7226 1787; www.littleangeltheatre.com). Tube: Angel or Highbury & Islington. Kids have thrilled to puppet shows here since 1961; the puppets are made in the adjoining workshop. Morning shows generally for ages 3+, afternoons for 4+, with occasional adult evening productions. Performances held 11am and 3pm Sa-Su and daily during school vacations. Reservations essential. £5-6.

New End Theatre, 27 New End, NW3 (☎7794 0022). Tube: Hampstead. Thought-provoking new work produced to a high standard by local and touring companies. £8-16, concessions £6-14. Box office open M-F 10am-8pm, Sa-Su 1-8pm.

The Old Red Lion, 418 St. John St. (☎7837 7816). Tube: Angel. New writing and adaptations in an L-shaped auditorium. Performances Tu-Su 7:45/8pm (£10, Su and Tu-Th students and seniors £8), poetry or comedy M (£5/£4); occasional lunchtime runs daily 1:15pm (£5).

Tricycle, 269 Kilburn High Rd., NW6 (☎7328 1000; www.tricycle.co.uk). Tube: Kilburn or Rail: Brondesbury Park. A real three-in-one, with cinema (see above), art gallery, and a theater known for new minority playwrights. Performances M-F 8pm, Sa 4 and 8:15pm. Box office open M-Sa 10am-9pm, Su 3:30-9pm. £6.50-30; concs. £2 less Th-F, pay-what-you-can M and 4pm Sa; students £5 W. Also 1hr. kid's shows every Sa 11:30am and 2pm (£4).

WEST LONDON

🔁 *NEIGHBORHOOD QUICKFIND: Discover, p. 13; Sights, p. 123; Food&Drink, p. 179; Accommodations, p. 299.*

BBC Television Centre, Wood Lane (see Sights, p. 123). Tube: White City. The BBC records over 600 shows with live studio audiences every year. Book 5 weeks ahead, though less-popular shows often have tickets available nearer the time. Minimum age limits apply to all shows. Apply by phone at ☎ 8576 1227, fax 8576 8802, email tv.ticket.unit.@bbc.co.uk, or write to: BBC Audience Services, Room 301 Design Building, Television Centre, Wood Lane, London W12 7RJ. Free.

Bush Theatre, Shepherd's Bush Green (☎ 7610 4224; www.bushtheatre.co.uk). Tube: Shepherd's Bush. Above a branch of O'Neill's. Well-known for innovative plays by new writers, both commissioned and from unsolicited manuscripts. Telephone booking M-Sa 10am-6pm. Box office open M-Sa from 6:30pm. Usually £10, students £5.

Hammersmith Irish Centre, Black's Rd. (info ☎ 8563 8232, tickets ☎ 8741 3211; www.lbhf.gov.uk/irishcentre). Tube: Hammersmith. Run by the local council, this claims to be London's foremost Irish cultural center. The large hall hosts Irish bands, trad sessions, and ceilidhs as well as comedians and literary readings. Performances F-Sa 8:15am. Free-£10.

London Apollo, Queen Caroline St. (Book via Ticketmaster on ☎ 7344 4444 24hr.; www.london-apollo.co.uk). Tube: Hammersmith. In the shadow of the Hammersmith Flyover, this venue hosts diverse musical and theatrical diversions, from the Chinese state circus to the Naked Chef to pop bands. 2002 sees *Riverdance* (mid-May to June). Box office open M-Sa 10am-6pm or 15min. after curtain, performance Su from 4pm. £7-30, depending on show.

Lyric Theatre, King St. (☎ 8741 2311; www.lyric.co.uk). Tube: Hammersmith. Behind a concrete facade is this ornate 1895 theater, with a history of presenting classy, controversial productions. Above the main theatre, the small **Lyric Studio** is geared towards experimental drama. Box office open M-Sa 10am-6pm, to curtain on performance nights. Main stage £5-20 depending on production, Studio £10, M all tickets £5; concessions £5-7.50.

Riverside Studios, Crisp Rd. (☎ 8237 1111; www.riversidestudios.co.uk). Tube: Hammersmith. From the Tube, take Queen Caroline St. under the motorway and follow it right past the Apollo (15min.) to the Thames. Former movie studio, now a highbrow cultural haven. The 2 **theaters** offer international work as well as home-grown fringe productions and comedy. The **cinema** plays international art-house, with the occasional classic and frequent double bills. Box office M-F 9am-9pm, Sa-Su noon-9pm. Plays £10-14, concs. £7-10; films £5.50, £4.50.

Shepherd's Bush Empire, Shepherd's Bush Green (bookings on Ticketweb, ☎ 7771 2000; www.shepherds-bush-empire.co.uk). Tube: Shepherds Bush. Turn-of-the-century theater once famous for hosting BBC gameshows, now a surprisingly intimate music venue (capacity 2000). Almost everyone who's anyone in music has played here, especially Bjorn Again. Currently not that busy, with about 50 bands per year. £10-20.

SOUTH LONDON

🔁 *NEIGHBORHOOD QUICKFIND: Discover, p. 13; Sights, p. 125; Museums&Galleries, p. 151; Food&Drink, p. 180; Nightlife, p. 198; Shopping, p. 238; Accommodations, p. 299.*

Battersea Arts Centre (BAC), Old Town Hall, 176 Lavender Hill (☎ 7223 2223). Tube: Clapham or Rail: Clapham Junction. One of London's top off-West End venues, best known for experimental theater but also hosting comedy, opera, and "mainstream" (radical corruptions of Shakespeare and other canonical texts) works on its main and two studio spaces. In Oct holds British Festival of Visual Theatre. Tickets £10-13, concs. £6.50; Tu "pay what you can."

Brixton Academy, 211 Stockwell Rd. (bookings on Ticketweb, ☎ 7771 2000; www.brixton academy.co.uk). Tube: Brixton. Beautiful 1929 Art Deco ex-theater; sloping floor ensures even those at the back have a chance to see the band. Broad policy covers all the bases from the Pogues to Senegalese stars. 4300 capacity. Also occasional club nights. Box office open only on performance evenings. £10-15, sometimes up to £30. Cash only on the door.

The Ritzy, Brixton Oval, Coldharbour Ln., SW2 (☎ 7737 2121, bookings ☎ 7733 2229). Tube: Brixton. Classy picture house combining the mainstream and the esoteric on 5 screens. Regular features include "world cinema matinee" daily 2pm (£2), kids films Sa 10:30am (£2, kids £1), and Su double bills. £6.50, all day M and Tu-F before 6pm £4; students & seniors £3 all day M-Th and F-Su before 6pm; under 16 £2.50 before 6pm.

The Swan, 215 Clapham Rd. (☎ 7978 9778; www.theswanstockwell.com) Tube: Stockwell. Opposite the Tube. Large, dark pub with music every night; some F-Su a second band plays upstairs. M traditional Irish; Tu "Celtic jazz;" W antipodean night; Th-Su Irish rock. Music starts 9:30pm. Open M-W 5-11:30pm, Th 5pm-2am, F 5pm-3am, Sa 7pm-3am, Su 7pm-2am. Free M-Th; F £5, £2.50 before 9pm; Sa £6, £3 before 9pm; Su £4, free before 10pm.

EAST LONDON

7 *NEIGHBORHOOD QUICKFIND: Discover, p. 14; Sights, p. 126; Museums&Galleries, p. 152; Food&Drink, p. 180; Nightlife, p. 199; Shopping, p. 239.*

⬛ Comedy Cafe, 66 Rivington St. (☎ 7739 5706; www.comedycafe.co.uk). Health warning: prolonged exposure may lead to uncontrollable laughter. Skip the food (burgers £7) and save up your cash for beers (£2.50-3). Be prepared to run up a substantial bar bill, but at least you'll be laughing all the way to the ATM. Reserve F-Sa. Doors 7pm, show 9pm, dancing to 2am. W free try-out night, Th £3, F £10, Sa £12.

Cargo, Kingsland Viaduct, 83 Rivington St. See Nightlife, p. 201. Club-bar that triples as a venue, with diverse live acts intermixed with club DJs most nights, starting 8pm. £3-8.

Greenwich and Docklands International Festival (☎ 8305 1818, bookings ☎ 8858 7755; www.festival.org/).10 days in early July bring international musicians, dancers, and theatrical troupes to outdoor stages and alternative venues all over East London, culminating in a fireworks spectacular. Individual events free-£20.

Hackney Empire, 291 Mare St. (☎ 8985 2424; www.hackneyempire.co.uk). Rail: Hackney Central or Tube: Bethnal Green then bus #D6, 106, or 253. An unlikely location for such an ornate theater, but it's pulled in the stars over the years. Charlie Chaplin performed here early in his career, and it's still primarily a comedy venue, with the occasional musical, opera, and drama. Comedy usually £8-10, other shows £10-15.

London Arena, Limeharbour (☎ 7538 1212 or 08705 121212 24hr.; www.londonarena.co.uk). Tube: Crossharbour. Giant shedlike space that since 1998 has established itself as London's leading megavenue for commercial pop. Guns'n'Roses kick off here in December 2001, followed by S Club 7 in February '02. At other times, the arena serves as the base of the **London Knights** hockey team. Box office open M-F 9am-8pm, Sa 10am-6pm. £10-25.

Lux Cinema, 2-4 Hoxton Sq. (☎ 7684 0200). Tube: Old St. While most of Hoxton's trendy spots revel in post-industrial squalor, this center for celluloid and digital arts is the place to go for something obscure and peculiar, though frequent themed runs keep past and recent classics on the back burner too. Shows usually W-Su evenings. £6, concessions £4.

Spitz, 109 Commercial St. (☎ 7392 9032; www.spitz.co.uk). Above a restaurant in Spitalfields market, this venue hosts an eclectic range of live music, from klezmer, jazz, and world music to indie pop and rap. All profits go to help Bosnian and Kosovan children. Music most Tu-Sa 8pm; £5-8.

Shopping

From its earliest days, London has been a trading city, its wealth and power built upon almost two millennia of commerce. Today even more so than at the Empire's height, London's economy is truly international—and thanks to the outward-looking and fundementally eclectic nature of Londoners' diverse tastes, the range of goods on offer is unmatched anywhere in the world. From Harrods' proud boast to supply "all things to all people," to African crafts on sale in Brixton market, you could shop for lifetime.

SHOPPING BY TYPE

ACCESSORIES	
@work	East
Butler & Wilson	Oxford & Regent Sts.
Willma	Notting Hill

ALCOHOL	
The Beer Shop	East
▨ Gerry's	Soho

BOOKS: NEW	
Blackwell's	Soho
Books for Cooks	Notting HIll
Foyle's	Soho
Gay's the Word	Bloomsbury
Hatchard's	Mayfair

BOOKS: NEW (CONT.)	
Mega City Comics	North
Silver Moon Women's Bookshop	Soho
Stanford's	Covent Garden
The Travel Bookstore	Notting Hill
Unsworths	Bloomsbury
Waterstone's	Mayfair, Bloomsbury
Zwemmer's	Soho

BOOKS: USED	
Bookmongers	South
Mega City Comics	North
Sotheran's	Mayfair
Music & Video Exchange	Notting Hill

CLOTHES: BOTH SEXES

Browns Labels for Less	Oxford & Regent Sts.
Central Park	Kensington
Cinch	Oxford & Regent Sts.
Cyberdog	Covent Garden, North
Diesel	Covent Garden
Diesel StyleLab	Covent Garden
FCUK	Notable chain
Harvey Nichols	Knightsbridge
The Laden Showrooms	East
Muji	Chain
Paul Smith	Covent Garden
Pauric Sweeney	East
Proibito Sale Shop	Oxford & Regent Sts.
Sox-Kamen Designs	Chelsea
Ted Baker	Oxford & Regent Sts.
Urban Outfitters	Kensington
U TH	Mayfair
Zara	Oxford & Regent Sts.

CLOTHES: VINTAGE

Annie's	North
Delta of Venus	Bloomsbury
Dolly Diamond	Notting Hill
Laurence Corner	Bloomsbury
Music & Video Exchange	Notting Hill
One of a Kind	Notting Hill
Pandora	Knightsbridge

CLOTHES: MEN

Dupe Clothes	Covent Garden
Oscar Milo	Mayfair
Paul Smith Sale Shop	Mayfair
Top Man	Chain

CLOTHES: WOMEN

Antoine et Lilli	Notting Hill
Hoxton Boutique	East
Jigsaw	Chain
Karen Millen	Chain
Lotus Leaf	Oxford & Regent Sts.
Mango	Oxford & Regent Sts.
Miss Sixty	Covent Garden
Oasis	Chain
Season	Bayswater
Teaze	Notting Hill
Therapy	Oxford & Regent Sts.
Topshop/Miss Selfridge	Chain
Willma	Notting Hill
World's End	Chelsea

CLOTHING: SPORTSWEAR

Nike Town	Oxford & Regent Sts.
Lillywhite's	Oxford & Regent Sts.

COSMETICS

Lush	Chain
Neal's Yard Remedies	Covent Garden
Pengaligons	Covent Garden

DEPARTMENT STORES

Fortnum & Mason	Mayfair
Harvey Nichols	Knightsbridge

DEPARTMENT STORES (CONT.)

Harrods	Knightsbridge
John Lewis	Oxford & Regent Sts.
Fortnum & Mason	Mayfair
Liberty	Oxford & Regent Sts.
Marks & Spencer	Oxford & Regent Sts.
Selfridges	Oxford & Regent Sts.

GIFTS & MISCELLANY

L. Cornelissen & Son	Bloomsbury
James Smith & Son	Bloomsbury
Purves & Purves	Bloomsbury
Twinings	Holborn

MARKETS

Bermondsey Market	South
Brick Lane	East
Brixton Market	South
Camden Passage	North
Camden Markets	North
Chapel Market	North
Greenwich Markets	East
Jubilee Market Hall	Covent Garden
Petticoat Lane	East
Portobello Market	Notting Hill
Spitalfields	East

MUSIC: MEGASTORES

HMV	Oxford & Regent Sts.
Tower Records	Mayfair
Virgin Megastore	Oxford & Regent Sts.

MUSIC: USED & SPECIALIST

Black Market	Soho
Carbon Music	Knightsbridge
Daddy Kool	Soho
Honest Jon's	Notting Hill
Intoxica!	Notting Hill
Music & Video Exchange	Notting Hill
Out on the Floor	North
Ray's Jazz Shop	Covent Garden
Rough Trade	Notting Hill
Red Records	South
Reckless Records	Soho
Sister Ray	Soho
Uptown Records	Soho
Vinyl Addiction	North

MUSIC: EQUIPMENT

Music & Video Exchange	Notting Hill
Turnkey	West End

SHOES

Buffalo	Covent Garden
Dr. Marten's	Covent Garden
Office	Covent Garden
Shellys	Chain
Sukie's	Chelsea
Swear	Covent Garden

TOYS & HOBBY

Hamleys	West End
The Kite Store	Covent Garden
London Doll House Co.	Covent Garden

SHOPPING BY NEIGHBORHOOD

NOTABLE CHAINS

As in almost any prosperous city, London retailing is dominated by own-label chains. Fortunately, local shoppers are picky enough that buying from a chain doesn't mean abandoning the flair and quirky styling Londoners are famed for: to be successful, stores must have an eagle eye for trends and change lines often enough to keep punters coming back—sometimes bringing out new clothes every few days. Most chain stores have a flagship on or near Oxford St., often with a second flagship in Covent Garden. These two locations are also preferred by international brands such as Levi's and Nike, though in these cases, you're paying London prices for the same lines you get at home.

Lush (01202 668 545; www.lush.co.uk). 5 London locations: 123 King's Rd. (Tube: Sloane Sq.); Covent Garden Piazza (Tube: Covent Garden); 40 Carnaby St. (Tube: Oxford Circus); Quadrant Arcade, 80-82 Regent St. (Tube: Piccadilly Circus); and the concourse of Victoria Station (Tube: Victoria). All-natural cosmetics that look good enough to eat; soap is hand-cut from blocks masquerading as cakes and cheeses (£3-5), facial masks scooped from guacamole-like tubs. Vegan cosmetics are marked with a green dot.

Karen Millen (☎01622 664 032; www.karenmillen.co.uk). 5 central London locations: 262-264 Regents St. (Tube: Oxford Circus); 22-23 James St. (Tube: Covent Garden); 33 Kings Rd. (Tube: Sloane Sq.); 46 South Molton St. (Tube: Bond St.); and Kensington High St. (Tube: High St. Kensington). Show-stopping formalwear; best known for richly embroidered brocade suits and evening gowns, but plenty of shiny, shimmering dresses and separates as well. Regent St. open M-W and F-Sa 10am-6:30pm, Th 10am-7pm, Su noon-6pm. MC, V.

FCUK (www.frenchconnection.com). Flagship at 396 Oxford St. (☎7529 7766; Tube: Bond St.). With stores in 21 countries, the shop formerly known as French Connection needs no introduction. Open M-W and F-Sa 10am-8pm, Th 10am-9pm, Su noon-6pm. AmEx, MC, V.

Jigsaw (☎8392 5678; www.jigsaw-online.com). 13 London locations: flagship at 126-127 New Bond St. (Tube: Bond St.) The essence of Britishness, distilled into quality mid-priced womenswear. Restrained, classic cuts that prize elegance over fad-based fashions. Bond St. store open M-W and F-Sa 10am-6:30pm, Th 10am-7:30pm, Su noon-6pm. AmEx, MC, V.

Muji (www.muji.co.jp). 7 London locations: 41 Carnaby St. (☎7287 7323; Tube: Oxford Circus); 135 Long Acre (Tube: Covent Garden); 157 Kensington High St. (Tube: High St. Kensington); 118 King's Rd. (Tube: Sloane Sq.); 6-17 Tottenham Ct. Rd. (Tube: Tottenham Ct. Rd.); and Whiteleys Shopping Centre (Tube: Bayswater). Minimalist lifestyle stores, with a clean Zen take on everything from clothes to kitchenware. Carnaby St. open M-W and Sa 10am-7pm, Th 10am-8:30pm, F 10am-8pm, Su noon-6pm. AmEx, MC, V.

Oasis (www.oasis-stores.com). Dozens of branches: flagship at 292 Regent St. (☎7323 5978; Tube: Oxford Circus). Smartly priced range of colorful, sexy clothes for work and play, plus shoes and accessories, that's a favorite with students and 20-somethings. Regent St. store open M-W and F-Sa 10am-7pm, Th 10am-8pm, Su noon-6pm. AmEx, MC, V.

Shellys, 266-270 Regent St., on Oxford Circus (☎7287 0939). Tube: Oxford Circus. Smaller stores at: 159 Oxford St., 19-21 Foubert's Pl., and 44-45 Carnaby St. (all Tube: Oxford Circus); 40 Kensington High St. (Tube: High St. Kensington); 14-18 Neal St. (Tube: Covent Garden); and 124b King's Rd. (Tube: Sloane Sq.). The Topshop of shoes, with a good selection of reasonably priced, reasonably funky footwear. Women's selection better than men's. Regent St. store open M-W and F-Sa 10am-7pm, Th 10am-8pm, Su noon-6pm. AmEx, MC, V.

Topshop/Top Man/Miss Selfridge. Dozens of locations; flagship at 214 Oxford St (☎7927 0000; Tube: Oxford Circus). Cheap fashions for young people—over-25s will feel middle-aged. The flagship store brings them all under one roof, though Topshop dominates with an enormous range of strappy shoes and skimpy clubwear over 3 floors. Miss Selfridge, on the ground floor, has an even younger, girlier feel; Top Man is all shiny Ts, cargo pants, and polyester suits, with free foosball. 10% student discount. Open M-W and F-Sa 9am-8pm, Th 9am-9pm, Su noon-6pm. AmEx, MC, V.

THE WEST END

OXFORD STREET & REGENT STREET

☛ NEIGHBORHOOD QUICKFIND: Discover, p. 2; **Sights,** p. 79; **Food&Drink,** p. 159; **Nightlife,** p. 190; **Entertainment,** p. 209.

SEE MAP, p. 330-331

Most tourists are likely to be disappointed by **Oxford Street.** In many ways, it's just the standard British high street writ large: here you'll find the flagships of all the mainstream British chains, from Marks & Spencer to FCUK, mixed with a lot of dross and stale pizzas. If Londoners still flock to Oxford St., it's for the many **department stores** that line its northern edge between Oxford Circus and Marble Arch, and for the fashionable boutiques of pedestrian **South Molton Street,** stretching south into Mayfair from Bond St. Tube. East of Oxford Circus, and especially near Tottenham Court Rd., things are much more downmarket, with budget chains and dodgy "sale shops," although the presence of Virgin and HMV **music megastores** provide distractions.

Regent Street is altogether a more refined affair, despite the presence of a Disney Store. Inevitably, there are plenty of shops aimed at tourists (of the big-spending variety), but it's also home to venerable shops such as Aquascutum and Liberty, not to mention the toyshop of the gods, Hamley's. **Oxford Circus,** where Regent St. and Oxford St. cross, is home to mega-flagships of international brands such as Nike and Benetton. Behind Regent St., **Carnaby Street** has finally got over its post-60s hangover and has a decent selection of youth fashions from famous-but-still-credible brands such as Diesel, though pickier types will find more interesting and obscure designer pickings in nearby **Foubert's Place** and **Newburgh Street.**

DEPARTMENT STORES

Liberty, 210-220 Regent St.; main entrance on Gt. Marlborough St. (☎7734 1234; www.liberty.co.uk). Tube: Oxford Circus. Liberty's focus on top-quality design and handicrafts makes it more like an gigantic boutique than a full-blown department store. The galleried Tudor building (actually built in 1922) is home to the world-famous Liberty prints, used for everything from brollies to shirts. Enormous hat department, a whole hall of scarves, and small but perfectly formed cosmetics department. Lots of contemporary designer clothes. Open M-W 10am-6:30pm, Th 10am-7pm, F-Sa 10am-7pm, Su noon-6pm. AmEx, MC, V.

Hamley's, 188-189 Regent St. (☎7734 3161). Tube: Oxford Circus. Seven floors filled with every conceivable toy and game; dozens of strategically placed product demonstrations are guaranteed to turn mummy's darling into a snarling, toy-demanding menace. The Bear Factory lets you choose your animal, give it a voice, and have it stuffed and sewn while you wait (from £15). 4th floor has enough model cars, planes, and trains for even the most die-cast enthusiast. Free use of game consoles in basement. Open M-F 10am-8pm, Sa 9:30am-8pm, Su noon-6pm. AmEx, MC, V.

John Lewis, Oxford St. (☎7629 7711). Tube: Oxford Circus. A socialist department store, run by the workers—yes, that check-out girl is a partner. Somewhat dowdy clothes, but great for houseware and electronics, with the best haberdashery department in London. Their "Never Knowingly Undersold" policy means they'll refund you the difference if you find the same item cheaper elsewhere. Open M-W and F-Sa 9:30am-6pm, Th 10am-8pm. AmEx, MC, V.

Marks & Spencer (www.marks-and-spencer.co.uk). Hundreds of stores: flagship at 458 Oxford St. (☎7935 7954; Tube: Bond St. or Marble Arch). Universally known as M&S or Marks and Sparks, this icon has fallen on hard times, as label-conscious consumers eschew its solid but unexciting in-house clothes. The high-class supermarket is still going strong: millions rely on its gourmet microwave meals, pre-washed salads, and fresh sandwiches. Open M-W and F-Sa 10am-6:30pm. AmEx, MC, V.

Selfridges, 400 Oxford St. (☎7629 1234; www.selfridges.co.uk). Tube: Bond St. The total department store—tourists may flock to Harrods, but Londoners will plump for Selfridges every time.Fashion departments are not cheap, but cover the gamut from traditional tweeds to space-age clubwear, and the vast cosmetics department features every conceivable makeup brand from Bobbi Brown to Miss Mascara. With 14 cafes and restaurants, a hair salon, a bureau de change, and even a hotel, shopaholics need never leave. Massive January and July sales. Open M-W 10am-7pm, Th-F 10am-8pm, Sa 9:30am-7pm, Su noon-6pm. AmEx, MC, V.

ACCESSORIES

Butler and Wilson (B&W), 20 South Molton St. (☎ 7409 2955; www.butlerandwilson.com). Tube: Bond St. A magpie's paradise. Literally brilliant range of glittering costume and not-so-costume jewelry, including lots of ornate chokers, tiaras, pendants, and body chains. Also Indian-style beaded handbags, tops, sandals, and hairbands. Open M-W and F-Sa 10am-6pm, Th 10am-7pm, Su noon-6pm. AmEx, MC, V.

CLOTHES: GENERAL

Cinch, 5 Newburgh St. (☎ 7287 4941). Tube: Oxford Circus. Cinch specializes in classic Levi's cuts from the 40s to the 70s, with a mixture of both repro and original gear (pick up an unworn pair of 1960s 505s for £850). Other retro gear includes genuine 70s T-shirt transfer stickers (£10), stacking dodecahedral lampshades (£30), contemporary art, and some vinyl. Open M-Sa 8am-11pm, Su noon-6pm. MC, V.

Mango, 106-112 Regent St. (☎ 7240 6099). Tube: Piccadilly Circus. Right next to Zara, another UK foothold for a Spanish fashion empire. Mango's all-female range is just as well cut and keenly priced as its neighbor, but with a slightly harder edge. Also at 225-235 Oxford St. (Tube: Oxford Circus) and 8-12 Neal St. (Tube: Covent Garden). Regent St. store open M-W and F-Sa 10am-7pm, Th 10am-8pm, Su noon-6pm. MC, V.

Ted Baker, 5-7 Foubert's Pl. (☎ 7437 5619). Tube: Oxford Circus. Also at 1-4 Langley Ct., Covent Garden (☎ 7497 8862; Tube: Covent Garden). Mid-priced modern classics for men and women at work or at play, from one of Britain's best-known and most influential names. Open M-W and F-Sa 10:30am-7pm, Th 10:30am-7:30pm, Su 11am-5pm.

Therapy, under House of Fraser on Oxford St. (☎ 7529 4700). All the clubwear from all the major labels, from Diesel and DKNY to budget high-street names like Morgan and Warehouse, under one roof, plus a juice bar. A must for girls who want to have fun. Open M-Tu 10am-7pm, W-F 10am-9pm, Sa 9:30am-7pm, Su noon-6pm. AmEx, MC, V.

Zara, 118 Regent St. (☎ 7534 9500). Tube: Piccadilly Circus. Also at 242-248 Oxford St. (☎ 7318 2700; Tube: Oxford Circus); and 48-52 Kensington High St. (☎ 7368 4680; Tube: High St. Kensington). Stylish Spanish brand that has taken Europe by storm with its sleek, competitively priced clothes. Menswear is especially popular. Prices labeled in 27 currencies reveal that Londoners pay about 10% more than Parisians, and 30% less than New Yorkers. Regents St. store open M-W and F-Sa 10am-7pm, Th 10am-8pm, Su noon-6pm. MC, V.

CLOTHES: SALES SHOPS

Proibito Sale Shop, 9 Gees Court, St. Christopher's Pl. (☎ 7409 2769) and 42 South Molton St. (☎ 7491 3244). Tube: Bond St. for both. Casual-, club-, and jeanswear from top designer names for up to 70% off—get a pair of Valentino jeans for only £35. Also stocks Guess?, Moschino, D&G, and Versace, for both guys and dolls. Open M-W 10am-6:30pm, Th 10am-7:30pm, F-Sa 10am-7pm, Su noon-6pm. AmEx, MC, V.

Browns Labels for Less, 50 South Molton St. (☎ 7514 0052). Tube: Bond St. Remainders from the Browns fashion mini-empire that's slowly taking over South Molton St. The range is small, especially for menswear, but reductions are unbelievable: D&G hipsters dropped from £180 to £30. Open M-W and F-Sa 10am-6:30pm, Th 10am-7pm. AmEx, MC, V.

Lotus Leaf, 5 Guys Ct. Tube: Bond St. Small sale shop selling stylish, colorful women's clothes at knock-down prices—most items under £10, including Elle and Morgan separates; posher Fenn Wright Mason items for £50. Open M-Sa 10am-7pm, Su 11am-5pm. Cash only.

CLOTHES: SPORTSWEAR

Nike Town, 236 Oxford St. (☎ 7612 0800). Tube: Oxford Circus. Less a store than a mega marketing exercise; in addition to a mind-boggling array of swoosh-emblazoned sportswear, there are museum-style displays on the past and future of running shoes, free 15min. sports-injury checkups (2nd fl.), and telescope-style machines running 3D Nike commercials. Open M-W 10am-7pm, Th-Sa 10am-8pm, Su noon-6pm. AmEx, MC, V.

Lillywhite's, 24-36 Lower Regent St. (☎ 7915 4000). Tube: Piccadilly Circus. An 8-floor sporting goods mecca, selling everything from polo mallets to Polo™ shirts. With slow lifts and no escalators, only the sportiest will ever make to the top floor. Open M-Sa 10am-8pm, Su noon-6pm. AmEx, MC, V.

MUSIC

Virgin Megastore, 14-16 Oxford St., W1 (☎ 7631 1234). Tube: Tottenham Court Rd. With 4 floors, fully deserves its name (well, the second half). Covers the entire musical spectrum,

on the cheap

Sale Crazy

Twice a year, in January and July, London goes sale crazy. Prices are slashed in almost every shop and crowds take full advantage of extended opening hours. Real pros scout out what's on offer in the days leading up to the sale—staff can normally tell you what will be reduced and by how much—and then turn up early on the first day of the sale to ensure success (there are often queues outside Harrods). Some department stores will even (unofficially) sell items at their sale prices a day or two before the sale officially starts—it can't help to ask. On the other hand, if you're willing to cope with a reduced choice, it pays to wait—in the last days of the sales prices are slashed even further, often up to 80%. One word of warning, though: if a bargain looks too good to be true, it probably is. Many more expensive shops order lower-quality merchandise especially for the sales that they wouldn't dream of offering their regular customers.

including books, zines, and posters, plus lots of DVDs, videos, and computer games in the basement—join the line for the free PS2 consoles. "Virgin Space" internet cafe on ground and 1st floors has plenty of terminals, all with webcam; £4 per hour includes soft drink. Open M-Sa 9:30am-10pm, Su noon-6pm. AmEx, MC, V.

HMV, 150 Oxford St., W1 (☎7631 3423; www.hmv.co.uk). Tube: Oxford Circus. Three massive floors, with an exceptional range of new vinyl on the ground floor, especially dance music. The games department, on level 1, has fewer free consoles than Virgin, but they're not as busy. Open M-Sa 9am-8pm, Su noon-6pm. AmEx, DC, MC, V.

MAYFAIR & ST. JAMES'S

⚡ NEIGHBORHOOD QUICKFIND: Discover, *p. 2;* **Sights,** *p. 80;* **Museums&Galleries,** *p. 139;* **Food&Drink,** *p. 159;* **Entertainment,** *p. 209.*

Nowhere is Mayfair's aristocratic pedigree more evident than in the scores of high-priced boutiques, many bearing Royal Warrants to indicate their status as official palace suppliers. **Bond Street** is the location of choice for the biggest designer names. Its southern end (called Old Bond St.) is equally renowned for its jewellers and silversmiths. Less mainstream designers set up shop on **Conduit Street,** which marks the point at which Old Bond St. meets New Bond St.; here you'll find the likes of Vivienne Westwood, Alexander McQueen, and Yohji Yamamoto. **Savile Row,** which runs south off Conduit St., and **Jermyn Street,** one block south of Piccadilly, are the home of old-fashioned elegance, where tailors measure up millionaires for handmade bespoke suits whose understated style belies their four-figure price-tags. Near Piccadilly, a number of Regency and Victorian **arcades** are lined with exquisite boutiques whose wares seem not to have changed in a hundred years.

BOOKS AND MUSIC

Hatchard's, 187 Piccadilly (☎7439 9921; www.hatchards.co.uk). Tube: Green Park. A close reading of the Royal Warrants displayed will confirm suspicions aroused by the black bookshelves that London's oldest bookshop (est. 1797) is now an undercover branch of Waterstone's. Still, as you'd expect from Prince Charles's official bookseller, there's a strong (pro-)royalty dept. Open M and W-Sa 9am-6pm, Tu 9:30am-6pm, Su noon-6pm. AmEx, MC, V.

Sotheran's of Sackville Street, 2-5 Sackville St. (☎7439 6151). Tube: Piccadilly Circus. Founded in 1761 in York, Sotheran's moved to London in 1815. Dickens frequented these silent stacks, and the firm handled the sale of his library after his death in 1870. While the hushed atmosphere and locked shelves give an impression of exclusivity, there are plenty of affordable books, and the staff are charming. Open M-F 9:30am-6pm, Sa 10am-4pm. AmEx, MC, V.

Tower Records, 1 Piccadilly Circus (☎ 7439 2500; www.tower.co.uk). Tube: Piccadilly Circus. London's first music megastore, with an exit direct from the Tube station to make shopping even easier. Internet access on every floor (£1.50 per 20min.), books, DVDs, video games, and the odd CD. The basement stage often features live bands, webcast around the world. Open M and Sa 8:30am-midnight, Tu-F 9am-midnight, Su noon-6pm. AmEx, MC, V.

Waterstone's, 203-206 Piccadilly (☎ 7851 2400; www.waterstones.co.uk). Tube: Piccadilly Circus. The 8 floors house Europe's largest bookshop. In addition to the prerequisite cafe, there's a swanky basement restaurant and a 4th-floor internet station that charges by the minute (from 50p for 5min.). The top floor is dedicated to events, including book signings by big-name authors (£2-4). Open M-Sa 10am-11pm, Su noon-6pm. AmEx, MC, V.

CLOTHES

🎨 **Oscar Milo,** 19 Avery Row (☎ 7495 5846). Tube: Bond St. Fantastic menswear boutique: these clothes may not be cheap (separates and shoes around £90), but are a bargain for what you get: beautifully cut trousers and shirts, and seriously smooth footwear will make you look (and feel) like a million pounds. Open M-W and F-Sa 10am-6pm, Th 10am-7pm. AmEx, MC, V.

Paul Smith Sale Shop, 23 Avery Row. Tube: Bond St. Smallish range of last-season and clearance items, plus some made-for-sale-shop stuff (mostly suits), from the acknowledged master of modern British menswear. The best deals are still pricey (dress shirts reduced from £225 to £95), but there are more affordable bargains, too: £60 shirts for £35, £65 jeans for £40. Open M-W and F-Sa 10am-6pm, Th 10am-7pm. AmEx, MC, V.

UTH, 27-29 Brook St. (☎ 7499 2521). Tube: Bond St. Also at 9-10 Floral St. (Tube: Covent Garden). Formerly Jigsaw Menswear, Uth offers seriously smart clothes whose sober colors belie an often funky cut. Most separates around £70. Open M-Sa 10:30am-7pm, Su noon-6pm. MC, V.

DEPARTMENT STORES

Fortnum & Mason, 181 Piccadilly (☎ 7734 8040; www.fortnumandmason.com). Tube: Green Park or Piccadilly Circus. Founded in 1707, Fortnum's is famed for its sumptuous food hall, with liveried clerks, chandeliers, and fountains. Don't come here to do the weekly grocery shopping, though—prices aside, the focus is very much on gifts and luxury items, especially chocolates, preserves, and teas. Few tourists make it to the upper floors that complete London's smallest, snootiest department store. Open M-Sa 10am-6:30pm. AmEx, MC, V.

SOHO

🔊 *NEIGHBORHOOD QUICKFIND: Discover, p. 2; Sights, p. 83; Museums&Galleries, p. 139; Food&Drink, p. 160; Nightlife, p. 191; Entertainment, p. 209; Accommodations, p. 284.*

Fortnum & Mason

Portobello Market

Brixton Market

Despite Soho's eternal trendiness, it's never been much of a shopping destination—between all the bars and cafes, there's precious little space left for boutiques. The main exception to this rule in central Soho are the record stores of **D'Arblay** and **Berwick Streets,** unsurprising given the area's position at the heart of the British media industry. On the eastern fringe of Soho, the many musical instrument and equipment shops of **Denmark Street** have led it to be dubbed London's "Tin Pan Alley". The major artery of **Charing Cross Road,** meanwhile, has long been London's bookshop central.

BOOKS

Blackwells, 100 Charing Cross Rd. (☎ 7292 5100; www.bookshop.blackwell.co.uk). Tube: Tottenham Ct. Rd. or Leicester Sq. The London flagship of Oxford's top academic bookshop, with everything on one enormous floor. Go for the postmodern theory, stay for the huge selection of fiction. Open M-Sa 9:30am-8:30pm, Su noon-6pm. AmEx, MC, V.

Foyles, 113-119 Charing Cross Rd. (☎ 7437 5660; www.foyles.co.uk). Tube: Tottenham Ct. Rd. or Leicester Sq. Foyles corrects the often unequal fight between book and book-buyer: finding the title you want is a game of stealth and patience played out over 5 floors crammed with famously impenetrable shelves. Even so, with every book you'll ever want somewhere in the building, it's the place to go when all else fails. There's also a strong sheet music department, and a small art gallery—but no cafe! Open M-Sa 9:30am-7:30pm, Su noon-6pm. AmEx, MC, V.

Silver Moon Women's Bookshop, 64-68 Charing Cross Rd. (☎ 7836 7906; www.silvermoonbookshop.co.uk). Tube: Leicester Sq. The largest women's bookshop in Europe, with an exhaustive selection of books by, for, and about women. Lesbian department downstairs is Britain's biggest. Open M-F 9:30am-7:30pm, Sa 10am-6:30pm, Su noon-6pm. AmEx, MC, V.

Zwemmers, 24 Litchfield St. (☎ 7240 4158; www.zwemmer.com). Tube: Leicester Sq. A multi-store art book empire, headquartered at Litchfield St. The store here, just east of Charing Cross Rd., specializes in books on art, and has a small **art gallery** upstairs. Across the street at 80 Charing Cross Rd., the focus is on media (mainly film and photography); 72 Charing Cross Rd. covers design. All three open M-F 10am-6:30pm, Sa 10am-6pm. AmEx, MC, V.

LIQUOR

🏷 **Gerry's,** 74 Old Compton St. (☎ 7734 2053). Tube: Piccadilly Circus or Leicester Sq. Gerry's stocks a staggering selection of hard liquor, in all sizes from miniatures to magnums. With 30 different tequilas, 100+ vodkas (including cannabis flavor, £10), and an incendiary Bulgarian absinthe that's 83% alcohol by volume (half-bottle £20), you could get drunk just looking. Open M-F 9am-6:30pm, Sa 9am-5:30pm. Cash only.

MUSIC: EQUIPMENT

Turnkey, 114-116 Charing Cross Rd. (☎ 7419 9999; www.turnkey.uk.com). Tube: Tottenham Court Rd. A must for the creative dance DJ. Basement copystations allow you to burn hundreds of grooves, riffs, and loops straight onto CD or ZIP disks. Upstairs, play to your heart's content on dozens of dedicated analysers, processors, and PCs. You'll also find turntables, a massive range of guitars, and keyboards. Open M-Sa 10am-6pm. AmEx, MC, V.

MUSIC: RECORDED

Black Market, 25 D'Arblay St. (☎ 7437 0478; www.blackmarket.co.uk). Tube: Oxford Circus. Metal-clad walls and massive speakers characterize this all-vinyl dance emporium. House and garage upstairs, phenomenal drum & bass section below. Also sells club tix and own-label merchandise, with bags £25-40, T-shirts and hats £15-35. Open M-Sa 11am-7pm.

Daddy Kool, 12 Berwick St. (☎ 7437 3535; www.daddykoolrecords.com). Tube: Oxford Circus or Piccadilly Circus. The basement has probably Soho's best reggae colection, with loads of obscure 7" and LPs; upstairs has reggae CDs along with rock, pop, hip-hop, soul, dance, country, and easy listening on vinyl and CD, plus classic posters and a case of Beatles memorabilia. Open M-F 10:30am-7pm, Sa 10am-6pm. MC, V.

Reckless Records, 26 and 30 Berwick St. (☎ 7437 3362 and 7437 4271; www.reckless.co.uk). Tube: Tottenham Court Rd. or Oxford Circus. #30 is the DJs' favorite exchange shop, with bucketfuls of used vinyl and CDs covering house, funk, disco, and soul; #26 has everything else from rock to classical, with rarities and zines downstairs. Open daily 10am-7pm. AmEx, MC, V.

Sister Ray, 94 Berwick St. (☎ 7287 8385). Tube: Oxford Circus, Piccadilly Circus, or Tottenham Court Rd. Rare outlet for indie and alternative music on both vinyl and CD; lots of goth, metal, and punk. Also decent dance selection, with ambient, trance, techno, and beats. Open M-Sa 9:30am-8pm, Su 11am-5pm. MC, V.

WorldPhone. Worldwide.

MCI^{SM} gives you the freedom of worldwide communications whenever you're away from home. It's easy to call to and from over 70 countries with your MCI Calling Card:

1. Dial the WorldPhone® access number of the country you're calling from.
2. Dial or give the operator your MCI Calling Card number.
3. Dial or give the number you're calling.

- London   0800-89-0222 BT
              0500-89-0222 CWC

Sign up today!
Ask your local operator to place a collect call
(reverse charge) to MCI in the U.S. at:

1-712-943-6839

For additional access codes or to sign up, visit us at www.mci.com/worldphone.

www.mci.com/worldphone

It's Your World...

Uptown Records, 3 D'Arblay St. (☎ 7434 3639; www.uptownrecords.uk.com). Tube: Oxford Circus. Ever wondered what top DJs do in the daytime? You'll find lots of them working in this small all-vinyl store, advising shoppers on the latest house, garage, and hip-hop happenings. Open M-W and F-Sa 10:30am-7pm, Th 10:30am-8pm. AmEx, MC, V.

COVENT GARDEN

🔼 *TRANSPORTATION: All listings are nearest Tube: Covent Garden unless otherwise noted.* **NEIGH-BORHOOD QUICKFIND: Discover**, *p. 2;* **Sights**, *p. 84;* **Museums&Galleries**, *p. 139;* **Food&Drink**, *p. 162;* **Nightlife**, *p. 193;* **Entertainment**, *p. 209;* **Accommodations**, *p. 284.*

Once the hottest proving ground for new designers, Covent Garden is increasingly mainstream—almost every chain with an eye on the youth market has a second flagship in the area, in addition to their main stores around Oxford and Regent St. The **piazza** itself is now dominated by mid-priced chains posing as small boutiq̇es, though there are still enough quirky shops left to make it worth a wander. Just north of the piazza, **Floral Street** is now firmly established as the smoothest, smartest street in the area, with top designer names like Paul Smith next to up-and-coming brands like Uth (see p. 229). Ever popular, **Neal Street** led the regeneration of Covent Garden back in the 90s but today is uncannily indistinguishable from Carnaby St. (see p. 226). Still a top destination for funky footwear and mid-priced club clobber, the fashion focus has shifted to nearby streets such as **Shorts Gardens** to the east for svelte menswear and **Earlham** and **Monmouth Streets** to the west for a corresponding selection of women's clothing.

BOOKS AND MUSIC

Ray's Jazz Shop, 180 Shaftesbury Ave. (☎ 7240 3969). Tube: Covent Garden or Holborn. At the confluence of Shaftesbury Ave. and Monmouth St. Lots of 2nd-hand vinyl (£5) and new CDs (£10-15); head downstairs for blues, roots, and gospel. Also some latin, folk, and world. Open M-Sa 10am-6:30pm, Su 2-5:30pm. MC, V.

Stanfords, 12-14 Long Acre (☎ 7836 1321; www.stanfords.co.uk). The self-proclaimed best map store in the world, and we believe them. With a staggering range of hiking maps, city maps, road maps, flight maps, star maps, wall maps, and globes, you need never be lost again. Also a massive selection of travel books (including the full range of *Let's Go*) and some hiking accessories. Open M and W-F 9am-7:30pm, Tu 9:30am-7:30pm, Sa 10am-7pm, Su noon-6pm. MC, V.

CLOTHES

🔲 **Diesel StyleLab,** 12 Floral St. (☎ 7836 4970; www.dieselstylelab.com). This new label does much to recapture the original anarchic spirit that first propelled Diesel to fame. Fantastically funky patterns, unusual materials, and offbeat cuts at regular Diesel prices—expensive, but worth it. Open M-Sa 11am-7pm, Su noon-6pm. AmEx, MC, V.

🔲 **Cyberdog,** 9 Earlham St. (☎ 7836 7855; www.cyberdog.co.uk). Tube: Leicester Sq. See listing for main store in Camden Town, p. 238; this branch has a smaller, more wearable selection. Open M-Sa 11am-7pm, Su 1-6:30pm. AmEx, MC, V.

Diesel, 43 Earlham St. (☎ 7497 5543; www.diesel.com). Cult Italian brand that almost single-handedly rehabilitated polyester. Unfortunately, as Diesel cashes in on its fame by churning out increasingly mainstream clothes, it's rapidly losing the offbeat touch that justified its high prices. Open M-W and F-Sa 10am-7pm, Th 10am-8pm, Su noon-6pm. AmEx, MC, V.

Dupe Clothes Manchester England, 42 Shorts Gdns. (☎ 7836 5920). Tube: Covent Garden. On a short street packed with trendy menswear boutiques, Dupe stands out for its quirky cutting and attention to detail. These clothes may not be cheap (shirts £80, pants £100), but they'll guarantee a second look. Open M-Sa 10am-7pm, Su noon-6pm. MC, V.

Miss Sixty, 39 Neal St. (☎ 7836 3789; www.misssixty.com). The newest Italian streetwise clothing craze. Bright, patterned, and skin-hugging female fashions in a laid-back and sexy style. Open M-W and F-Sa 10am-6:30pm, Th 10am-7:30pm, Su noon-6pm. AmEx, MC, V.

Paul Smith, 40-44 Floral St., WC2 (☎ 7379 7133; www.paulsmith.co.uk). Meandering two-storey shop selling the full range of beautiful, unaffordable clothes and accessories from the man who put British fashion back on the map. The (marginally) cheaper Paul Smith Jeans and R. Newbold ranges can be found around the corner at 9-11 Langley Court. Open M-W and F-Sa 10:30am-6:30pm, Th 10:30am-7pm, Su 1-5pm. AmEx, MC, V, your right arm.

COSMETICS AND TOILETRIES

Neal's Yard Remedies, 15 Neal's Yard (☎7627 1949). Jars behind the counter hold every concievable herb, from basil and mint to bladderwrack and pilewart, while on the shelves cobalt-blue bottles hold essential oils, soaps, and lotions. Gift boxes from £10. Open M-Sa 10am-7pm, Su 11am-5pm. AmEx, MC, V.

Penhaligon's, 41 Wellington St. (☎7836 2150; www.penhaligons.co.uk). Branches on Bond St. and Piccadilly Circus. Founded by a former palace barber, this is still where the royals get their aftershave. Churchill never left home without a dab of *Blenheim Bouquet*—get a miniature set including this and three other colognes for £22. Also feminine fragrances, scented candles, and masculine accessories. Open M-Sa 10am-6pm, Su noon-5pm. AmEx, MC, V.

FOOTWEAR

Buffalo, 47-49 Neal St. (☎7379 1051). In the mid-1990s, no art student would be seen without a pair of Buffalo's signature high-soled shoes. Today, a more mainstream crowd stampedes this ever-popular store, but there's no denying that as shoe fashions advance beyond chunky sneakers, Buffalo looks increasingly stuck in the mud. Open M-Sa 10:30am-7pm, Su 2-6pm. AmEx, MC, V.

Dr. Marten's Dept. Store, 1-4 King St. (☎7497 1460). Tourist-packed 5-tiered megastore, with baby docs, papa docs, and the classic yellow-stitched boots. Also branded clothes and bags. Open M-W and F-Sa 10am-7pm, Th 10:30am-8pm, Su noon-6pm. AmEx, MC, V.

Office, 57 Neal St. (☎7379 1896). The largest outlet of London's foremost fashion footwear retailer. Office's range is not only ultra-stylish, it's also perfectly wearable. Most women's shoes run £20-50, men's £60-130. The **sale shop** at 61 St. Martin's Ln. (☎7497 0390; Tube: Leicester Sq.) has a more limited, more conventional selection, though there are some good deals to be found. Neal St. store open M-W and F-Sa 10am-7pm, Th 10am-8pm, Su noon-6pm. Sale shop open M-Sa 10am-7pm, Su noon-6pm. MC, V.

Swear, 61 Neal St. (☎7240 5313; www.swear-online.com). This hipper-than-thou footwear boutique takes the high-soled sneaker to new levels, literally and aesthetically. Skateboarder wannabes can get ready-worn sneakers (£50); footwear fetishists will swoon at the rubber-taloned trainers (£95). Open M-Sa 11am-7pm, Su 2-6pm. AmEx, MC, V.

MARKETS

Jubilee Market Hall, south side of Covent Garden Piazza. Large covered market, purportedly antique on M, general Tu-F, and arts and crafts Sa-Su, but in reality an everyday mix of clothes and souvenirs. Open daily 10am-7pm.

HOLBORN

SEE MAP, pp. 334-335

◪ NEIGHBORHOOD QUICKFIND: Discover, *p. 6;* **Sights,** *p. 88;* **Museums&Galleries,** *p. 142;* **Food&Drink,** *p. 164;* **Nightlife,** *p. 194;* **Entertainment,** *p. 212.*

With Covent Garden so close—and with barristers not renowned for their sense of dress—it's hardly surprising that Holborn is not a top shopping destination. **High Holborn** is a busy road with a fair selection of common high-street chains, while **Fleet Street** has a few shops serving lawyers who just spilled port down their shirtfronts.

Twining's, 216 Strand (☎7353 3511). Tube: Temple. Twining's remains the oldest family-run business in Britain to remain on the same premises (since 1706). Proportionately, it's also London's narrowest shop. A tiny museum in the back traces the tea's lineage, past rows of Earl Grey (£1.45 per 125g), Prince of Wales (£1.50 per 100g), and other noble blends. This may be as close as you get to royalty. Open M-F 9:30am-4:45pm. AmEx, MC, V.

CHELSEA

SEE MAP, p. 346

◪ TRANSPORTATION: *The only Tube station in Chelsea is Sloane Sq.; from here buses 11, 19, 22, 211, and 319 run down the King's Rd.* **NEIGHBORHOOD QUICKFIND: Discover,** *p. 8;* **Sights,** *p. 108;* **Museums&Galleries,** *p. 146;* **Food&Drink,** *p. 170;* **Entertainment,** *p. 215.*

No serious shopper can come to London and ignore Chelsea. If **Sloane Square** is well, too Sloaney (the English equivalent of US Preppy), the **King's Road** is all things to all shoppers. The western end of the street, where it comes out of Sloane Sq., is home to a few mid-priced chains as well as the massive **Peter Jones** department store (a branch of John Lewis, p. 226), but as a whole the King's Rd. is remarkable for its incredible range of one-off boutiques at all price ranges, which bring it a vitality and diversity lost in the megachain-dominated streets of other London shopping meccas.

World's End, 430 King's Rd. (☎ 7352 6551). The fountain of cool, this boutique's past incarnations include SEX, Malcom McLaren and Vivienne Westwood's proto-punk store that gave birth to the Sex Pistols. Westwood still runs the sloping-floored boutique, though the clothes are now as unaffordable as they are unwearable. Open M-Sa 10am-6pm. AmEx, MC, V.

Sox-Kamen Designs, 394 King's Rd. (☎ 7795 1830). Small boutique selling own-designed clothes at high-street prices. On the smarter side of casual, with luxurious materials and sleek cuts. Skirts and shirts from £40. Open M-Sa 10:30am-6:30pm, Su noon-4pm. MC, V.

Sukie's, 285 King's Rd. (☎ 7352 3431). Brilliant selection of funky-but-formal footwear, in classic styles but with unusual colors, materials, and textures. For groovers and shakers of both sexes. Open M-Sa 10am-7pm, Su 1-6pm. MC, V.

KNIGHTSBRIDGE & BELGRAVIA

◪ NEIGHBORHOOD QUICKFIND: Discover, p. 9; **Sights,** p. 109; **Food&Drink,** p. 171; **Accommodations,** p. 287.

Knightsbridge's main shopping arteries are the **Old Brompton Road,** with representatives of most mid- and upmarket chains between Harvey Nichols and Harrods, and ultra-exclusive **Sloane Street,** which rivals Bond Street for designer boutiques. All in all, this is a district that favors gold cards and big budgets—Armani, Chanel, Dior, Gucci, Hermes, Kenzo, Versace, and Yves St. Laurent are among its storefronts.

SEE MAP, p. 338-339

Pandora, 16-22 Cheval Pl. (☎ 7589 5289). Tube: Knightsbridge. The Harvey Nick's of second-hand clothes, Pandora is a dress agency, reselling clothes on behalf of wealthy women whose appetites exceed their closet space. The big-name designer garments are all "seasonally correct," under 2 years old, and often barely worn. Open M-Sa 9am-6pm. MC, V.

Harrods, 87-135 Old Brompton Rd. (☎ 7730 1234; www.harrods.com). Tube: Knightsbridge. Big things have small beginnings; in 1849 Mr. Harrod opened a small grocery store, and by 1901 had done well enough to construct the terracotta behemoth that now bears his name. Huge and bewildering, the only thing bigger than the store itself is the mark-up on the goods—it's no wonder that only tourists and oil sheikhs actually shop here (you even have to pay £1 to use the bathrooms). Open M-Sa 10am-7pm. AmEx, MC, V, your soul.

Harvey Nichols, 109-125 Knightsbridge (☎ 7235 5000). Tube: Knightsbridge. Imagine Bond St., Rue St. Honore, and Fifth Avenue all rolled up into one store. Five of its 8 floors are devoted to the sleekest, sharpest fashion, from the biggest names to the hippest contemporary unknowns. 5th-floor food hall is home to a swanky restaurant, a branch of Yo!Sushi (see p. 159) and the chic 5th Floor Cafe, while there's a juice bar on the main floor and a Wagamama in the basement (see p. 158). Open M-Tu and Sa 10am-7pm, W-F 10am-8pm, Su noon-6pm. AmEx, MC, V.

KENSINGTON & EARL'S COURT

◪ NEIGHBORHOOD QUICKFIND: Discover, p. 9; **Sights,** p. 112; **Museums&Galleries,** p. 146; **Food&Drink,** p. 172; **Entertainment,** p. 216; **Accommodations,** p. 287.

Many people prefer **Kensington High Street** to Oxford St., and it's easy to see why: it offers just as wide a range of mid-priced UK and international chains as its West End rival in a much more compact and less crowded area. Karen Millen, Monsoon, Next, Diesel, Zara, Office...if you've heard of it, it's probably here. On the other hand, there are no sidestreets lined with trendy one-off boutiques, and **Barkers,** the only department store, is on the small side—if you're looking for anything other than mainstream clothes, go elsewhere. **Kensington Church Street** provides a mildly alternative, if pricey, shopping experience, with arty antiques, handicrafts, and specialist stores.

SEE MAP, p. 340-341

on the cheap

Market Economy

Unlike in Paris, Milan, and New York, London's fashion scene has always been a bottom-up affair, starting out in the street before percolating through to the catwalks. For your best bet of seeing where fashion is going, you need to hit the **markets**—trends are born in **Camden Market** (p. 237) and **Portobello Market** (p. 234), the two biggest destinations for fashionistas on a budget. It's not just clothes you'll find here, either: antiques, books, music, shoes, and almost anything you'll ever need (and many you won't) are up for sale in the streets, and bargaining is part of the fun. However, some traders will to try take advantage of foreigners; to make sure you know the difference between a bargain and a rip-off, check up high-street prices before hitting the markets—and make sure you like what you buy, since the chance of getting a refund from a market trader is virtually nil.

Central Park, 19-21 Kensington Church St. (☎7937 3672). Tube: High St. Kensington. Dramatic discounts on men's and women's designer casuals, with FCUK, Nicole Farhi, and Ralph Lauren at 30-50% off. Also trendy own-label womenswear, with skirts and tops for £10. Open M-Sa 10am-6:30pm, Su 11am-5pm. MC, V; 50p surcharge for purchases under £10.

Urban Outfitters, 36-38 Kensington High St. (☎7761 1001). Tube: High St. Kensington. 6-level deconstructed megastore, with raw concrete columns still bearing the scars of previous incarnations. Clothes, accessories, and housewares for the young, hip, and plastic-obsessed. **Carbon Music,** on the lower ground floor, has an eclectic selection of vinyl and CDs with numerous variable-speed decks. Open M-W and F-Sa 10am-7pm, Th 10am-8pm, Su noon-6pm. AmEx, MC, V.

NOTTING HILL

SEE MAP, p. 342

▶ NEIGHBORHOOD QUICK-FIND: Discover, p. 10; **Sights,** p. 113; **Food&Drink,** p. 173; **Nightlife,** p. 195; **Entertainment,** p. 216.

The best reason to visit Notting Hill is the world-renowned **Portobello Market,** which brings an influx of color and vivacity to an otherwise gentrified area. In fact, Portobello Rd. is home to a number of distinct markets, occupying different parts of the street and operating on different days: Saturdays, when all come together in a mile-long row of stalls, is the best day to visit. The **antiques market** is what most people associate with Portobello Rd.; it stretches north from Chepstow Villas to Elgin Crescent. Here, stalls face off against the tables set up by specialist stores; most of what's on display outside is cheapish bric-a-brac, little of it truly rare or very old. True enthusiasts will find that missing piece from their collection in the myriad booths of the numerous indoor market halls. (Sa 7am-5pm. Tube: Notting Hill Gate.) Further north, from Elgin Crescent to Lancaster Rd., is the **general market,** with food, flowers, and household essentials. A number of gourmet stalls selling continental breads and organic produce show up on Saturdays. (M-W 8am-6pm, Th 9am-1pm, F-Sa 7am-7pm. Tube: Westbourne Park or Ladbroke Grove.) North of Lancaster Rd., with arms stretching along the Westway, is the **clothes market,** with a wide selection of second-hand clothes, New Age bangles, and cheap clubwear, oddly interspersed with dodgy-looking used electricals. (F-Sa 8am-3pm. Tube: Ladbroke Grove.) Finally, north of the Westway the **Golborne Rd. market** has a dowdier, local air, though along Golborne Rd. itself the Moroccan influence makes itself felt with stalls selling gourmet olives, steaming couscous, and Berber handicrafts. (M-Sa 9am-5pm; busiest Sa. Tube: Ladbroke Grove.)

BOOKS

The Travel Bookshop, 13-15 Blenheim Crescent (☎7229 5260; www.thetravelbookshop.co.uk). The specialist bookshop featured in *Notting Hill*, today besieged by Grantophiles in search of instant karma. Open M-Sa 10am-6pm, Su 11am-4pm. MC, V.

Books For Cooks, 4 Blenheim Crescent. See Food&Drink, p. 173.

Music and Video Exchange, see Music, above.

CLOTHES & ACCESSORIES

One of a Kind, 253 Portobello Rd. (entrance on Lancaster Rd.; ☎ 7792 5284; www.1kind.com). Tube: Ladbroke Grove. Ring the bell to gain access to this wonderland of vintage designerwear. Clothes, shoes, and accessories line every available inch of wallspace, with more hanging from the ceiling. Shoes start at £30, clothes around £45, and rise rapidly into the stratosphere—some of the pieces on the display are literally priceless. Open M-F 11am-6pm, Sa 10:30am-6:30pm, Su noon-5pm. AmEx, MC, V.

Antoine et Lilli, 32 Uxbridge St. (☎7792 9922; www.antoineetlilli.com). Tube: Notting Hill Gate. Having already captivated *parisiennes* with their particular style of ethnically influenced, colorful femininity, Antoine et Lilli have begun a stealth operation in London with this tiny Notting Hill boutique. New stock arrives weekly, keeping the small selection of all-natural clothes, jewelry, and cosmetics fresh and perfectly *à la mode*. Open M-Sa 10am-7pm, Su 2-6pm. AmEx, MC, V.

Willma, 339 Portobello Rd. (☎8960 7296). Fluorescent cases present an exclusive range of accessories and clothes sourced from up-and-coming designers around the world, mostly one-offs. Not cheap, but nor is it all bank-breaking: tops from £20, novelty knickers from £10. Get out the gold card for the bags and purses (£100+). Open Tu-Sa 11am-6pm. MC, V.

Dolly Diamond, 51 Pembridge Rd. (☎ 7792 2479). Tube: Notting Hill Gate. Jackie Onassis or Audrey Hepburn? Choose your look from among Dolly's great selection of classic 50s-70s clothes, along with some elegant 20s-40s evening gowns. Dresses £40-120, leather jackets £40-80, ball gowns £75+. Smaller selection of men's formalwear upstairs. Open M-F 10:30am-6:30pm, Sa 9:30am-6:30pm, Su 11am-5pm. "Cash preferred."

Teaze, 47 Pembridge Rd. (☎7727 8358). Tube: Notting Hill Gate. Everything you need for a sweaty night out. Wide range of anti-slogan T-shirts with sexual overtones, as in the *Kickers* knock-off: "Knickers—not worn since 1994"; novelty lingerie, with themes from Che Guevara to Catholicism; and last but not least, tubs of liquid latex (£13) for the true skin-tight look. Open M-Sa 10:30am-6:30pm, Su noon-5pm. AmEx, MC, V.

MUSIC

Rough Trade, 130 Talbot Rd. (☎7229 8541). Tube: Ladbroke Grove. Branch at 16 Neal's Yard (☎7240 0105; Tube: Covent Garden), under Slam City Skates. Choosing from the wide selection of music made easier by the small, opinionated reviews tacked to most CDs and records. Open M-Sa 10am-6:30pm, Su 1-5pm. AmEx, MC, V.

Honest Jon's, 276-278 Portobello Rd., W10 (☎8969 9822). Tube: Ladbroke Grove. Still funky after all these years. 276 holds an impressive jazz, latin, and world-music collection, 278 a wide selection of reggae, hip-hop, house, and garage on both vinyl and CD, as well as soul and funk holdings. Open M-Sa 10am-6pm, Su 11am-5pm. AmEx, MC, V.

Intoxica!, 231 Portobello Rd. (☎7229 8010; www.intoxica.co.uk). Tube: Ladbroke Grove. All vinyl. Enviable stock of surf-rock, rockabilly, soundtracks, and other exotica. Downstairs jazz, blues, and 60s soul reign. Many pricey 60s originals (£20-50), as well as new and recent indie and hiphop. Open M-Sa 10:30am-6:30pm, Su noon-4pm. AmEx, MC, V.

Music and Video Exchange (☎7221 1444; www.mveshops.co.uk). Tube: Notting Hill Gate. A used-goods mini-empire, spreading like kudzu. On Notting Hill Gate, no. 38 is the chain's main record store, 40 has singles (vinyl & CD), 42 specializes in dance music, and 34 in classical music; videos and DVDs are hawked from 34, and musical instruments, hi-fi, and mixing equipment from 56. On Pembridge Rd. no. 14 stocks books and a wide range of old comics and magazines; 16 focuses on computers, especially games (hardware and software); 20 and 30-34 have clothes, shoes, and accessories; and 28 stocks super-cheap remainders from other stores. Stores are open daily 10am-8pm. AmEx, MC, V.

VINTAGE DEALS

Always keeping one eye on the past, Londoners were into **vintage clothes** long before the fashion world finally caught up with it in 2001—after all, why shell out for the latest retro gear when you can have an authentic vintage item for a tenth of the price? And if you baulk at the idea of used clothing, don't despair—some specialist stores have unworn "new" clothes that never got sold the first time around.

While most stores mainstays are 1970s and 1980s gear, making flared jeans, flower-power dresses, and glam-rock frocks a bargain, there are also good deals to be found on more recent items. Dress agencies such as **Pandora** sell recent-season numbers on behalf of wealthy women who've simply run out of closet space (or don't like wearing the same dress twice).

Of course, with clothes as with wine, great vintages demand high prices. As a rule, the older it is, the more it costs—you won't find a 1930s dress for under a few hundred pounds. But some of the rarest clothes aren't that old. **One of a Kind**, in Notting Hill (p. 235), carries a few *haute couture* dresses created by top designers for celebrity clients which are literally priceless—the owner refuses to sell them.

BAYSWATER

⚑ NEIGHBORHOOD QUICK-FIND: Discover p. 10; **Food&Drink,** p. 174; **Entertainment,** p. 217; **Accommodations,** p. 289.

SEE MAP, p. 342

As with eating, shopping in Bayswater is largely confined to two streets. **Queensway** has an uninspiring range of tourist tittle-tattle, electronics stores, and high-street chains. **Westbourne Grove,** on the other hand, has a number of trendy boutiques, especially near Notting Hill.

Season, 100 Westbourne Grove (☎ 7584 9333). Tube: Bayswater or Royal Oak. Small but exquisite collection of one-offs from designers around the world are united by their femininity, with lots of beadwork and sequins. T-shirts from £30, tops from £40, dresses £200 and up. Open M-W and F-Sa 10:30am-6pm, Th 10:30am-8pm, Su noon-6pm. AmEx, MC, V.

Whiteleys Shopping Centre, Queensway (☎ 7229 8844; www.whiteleys.com). Tube: Bayswater. Housed in a former department store, Whiteleys is a cut above the average mall. There's a good selection of stylish cheap- and mid-range clothes stores, including Oasis, H&M, Karen Millen, Jigsaw, Muji, and Gap. On the 2nd floor is a **UCI** multiplex cinema, while the 4th floor houses an small contemporary **art gallery.** Shops open M-Sa 10am-8pm, Su noon-6pm.

BLOOMSBURY

⚑ NEIGHBORHOOD QUICK-FIND: Discover, p. 11; **Sights,** p. 116; **Museums&Galleries,** p. 148; **Food&Drink,** p. 175; **Entertainment,** p. 217; **Accommodations,** p. 293.

SEE MAP, pp. 344-345

As home to the British Library, the British Museum, and most of London's academic institutions, Bloomsbury's other main commodity is **books;** the streets around the British Museum in particular are crammed with specialist and cut-price bookshops, while the Waterstones on Gower St. (see below) is one of London's largest. If you're after **electronics** equipment, head to **Tottenham Court Rd.** Don't be afraid to haggle with the salesmen, especially if you're paying cash or have seen the item cheaper elsewhere.

BOOKS

Gay's the Word, 66 Marchmont St. (☎ 7278 7654; www.gaystheword.co.uk). Tube: Russell Sq. One of only 2 specialist gay and lesbian bookshops in the UK. Also well-endowed with erotic postcards, serious movies, and free magazines. Noticeboard with accommodations listings. Open M-Sa 10am-6:30pm, Su 2-6pm. AmEx, MC, V.

Unsworths, 12 Bloomsbury St. (☎7436 9836; www.unsworths.com). Tube: Tottenham Court Rd. Up to 90% off publishers' prices on a wide range of literature and academic books, many US-sourced, with an emphasis on the humanities. Used and antiquarian books downstairs. Open M-Sa 10am-8pm, Su noon-8pm. AmEx, MC, V.

Waterstones, 82 Gower St. (☎7636 1577). Tube: Goodge St. Cafe, hundreds of magazines, cheap remainders and frequent signings are additional attractions of this five-floor behemoth. Open M and W-F 9:30am-8pm, Tu 10am-8pm, Sa 9:30am-7pm, Su 11am-5pm. MC, V.

CLOTHING

▨ **Delta of Venus,** 151 Drummond St. (☎7387 3037; www.deltaofvenus.co.uk). Tube: Warren St., Euston, or Euston Sq. A small but unbeatable array of vintage clothes spanning the 1960s to the early 1980s. Dresses £18-40, shirts £10-18; rummage box £3 per item. New limited-edition screen print T-shirts (£24). Posters (£10). Open M-Sa 11am-7pm. MC, V.

Laurence Corner, 62-64 Hampstead Rd. (☎7813 1010). Tube: Warren St., Euston, or Euston Sq. Primarily an army surplus shop, with racks of fatigues and old uniforms at knock-down prices, but with a decent selection of used clothing, both military and civilian: from gas masks (£30) and shiny-buttoned greatcoats (from £20), to lurid space-age outfits worn by Millennium Dome performers (from £20). Open M-Sa 9:30am-6pm. AmEx, MC, V.

GIFTS AND MISCELLANY

▨ **L. Cornelissen & Son,** 105 Great Russell St. (☎7636 1045). Tube: Tottenham Court Rd. With its original 1855 interior, Cornelissen's looks more like an apothecary's than an art store. Jars of raw pigment, crystals, and lumps of evil-smelling "dragon's blood" reach to the ceilings, while mahogany drawers hide a fantastic array of brushes, nibs, paints, and crayons. Open M-F 9:30am-5:30pm, Sa 9:30am-5pm. MC, V.

▨ **Purves and Purves,** 220-224 Tottenham Court Rd. (☎7580 8223). A temple to modern living, Purves is *the* shop for design aficionados. Affordable items include funky fridge magnets (£3), and "fle-sexi" flexible salt- and pepper-shakers (£18). Open M, W and F-Sa 9:30am-6pm, Tu 10am-6pm, Th 9:30am-7:30pm, and Su 11:30am-5:30pm. MC, V.

James Smith & Son, 53 New Oxford St. (☎7836 4731; www.james-smith.co.uk). Tube: Tottenham Court Rd. No complaints about the weather from the Smith family—they've been in the umbrella business since 1830. Signature handmade gentlemen's brollies (from £50) come in any color, so long as it's black. They also sell a variety of colorful ladies' and cheaper mass-produced models. Open M-F 9:30am-5:30pm, Su 10am-5:30pm. AmEx, MC, V.

Paperchase, 213 Tottenham Court Rd. (☎7467 6200; www.paperchase.co.uk). Tube: Goodge St. Unbeatable selection of cards and giftwrap on the ground floor; pens, frames, and more giftwrap on the first; art and graphics supplies on the second, including paper by the sheet in all types, colors, textures, patterns, weights, and sizes, and yet more giftwrap. Open M-W and F-Sa 9:30am-7pm, Th 9:30am-8pm, Su noon-6pm. MC, V.

NORTH LONDON

⚑ *NEIGHBORHOOD QUICKFIND: Discover, p. 12; Sights, p. 118; Museums&Galleries, p. 150; Food&Drink, p. 176; Nightlife, p. 196; Entertainment, p. 218; Accommodations, p. 298.*

In **Camden Town,** you find hundreds of identical stores flogging the same chunky shoes and leather trousers they've been selling for years and thousands of stalls hawking the same trinkets. If you're here to shop, arrive early and have a game plan—amid the dross there are genuine bargains and incredible avant-garde items to be found, but you need to dig deep.

MARKETS

Camden Markets, off Camden High St. and Chalk Farm Rd. Tube: Camden Town.

Stables Market, nearest Chalk Farm and the best of the bunch. The railway arches hold some of the most outrageous club- and fetish-wear ever made, plus a good selection of vintage clothes. The horse hospital, overlooking Chalk Farm Rd., is home to antiques and collectibles. A free map of the market is available at the main entrance. Most of the shops open daily.

Camden Lock Market, from the railway bridge to the canal, was the original market. Arranged around a food-filled courtyard on the Regent's Canal, the mostly indoor shops sell pricier items such as carpets, and household goods. Most stalls operate F or Sa-Su only.

Camden Canal Market, down the tunnel opposite Camden Lock, starts out promisingly with jewelry and watches, then degenerates rapidly into sub-par club clothes and tourist trinkets. The canalside location makes it a good spot for a bite to eat, though. Open F-Su.

The Camden Markets, the nearest to Camden Tube, and correspondingly the most crowded and least innovative. Jeans, sweaters, and designer fakes at average prices. Open F-Su.

Inverness Street Market, off Camden High St. opposite the Tube, is a daily fruit'n'veg market unconnected to the madness surrounding it. Open daily.

Camden Passage Market, Islington High St. Tube: Angel. Turn right from the tube; it's the alleyway that starts behind "The Mall" antiques gallery on Upper St. Not to be confused with Camden Market (see above). *The* place for antiques; smaller items may dip into the realm of the affordable, especially old prints and drawings. Shops vastly outnumber stalls; both tend to open only W and Sa, 8:30am-6pm.

Annie's, 10 Camden Passage (☎7359 0796). *Vogue, Elle,* and *Marie Claire* regularly use these beautiful vintage frocks in their photo shoots. 1920s dresses are the priciest (£200-500); accessories are more affordable (hats £30). Open M-Tu and Th-F 11am-6pm, W and Sa 8am-6pm. AmEx, MC, V.

Chapel Market, Chapel Market. Tube: Angel. None of your arty-farty bourgeois crap here—this living reminder of Islington's recent past is an honest-to-god cockney street market. Everything from fruit-and-veg and fresh bread to washing powder, but predominantly cheap'n'cheerful clothes. No-frills budget eateries line the road behind the market stalls. Open M-Sa 9am to mid-afternoon.

MUSIC: USED & SPECIALTY.

Out on the Floor, 10 Inverness St. (☎7267 5989). Tube: Camden Town. Used records and CDs, specialising in 60s-70s rock, soul, and funk. Open daily 10am-6pm. MC, V.

Vinyl Addiction, 6 Inverness St. (☎7482 1230). Tube: Camden Town. Underneath the bar of the same name (see p. 197), this tiny store is a mecca for DJs and anyone looking for the latest in dance music. Open M-Sa 11am-7:30pm, Su noon-7pm.

OTHER

Cyberdog/Cybercity, arch 14, Stables Market (☎7482 2842). Tube: Camden Town. Unbelievable, unwearable club clothes for superior lifeforms. Alien gods and goddesses will want to try on the fluorescent body-armor or steel corsets with rubber breast hoses. Open M-F 11am-6pm, Sa-Su 10am-7pm. AmEx, MC, V.

Mega City Comics, 18 Inverness St. (☎7485 9320). Tube: Camden Town. Plastic-wrapped comics in mint condition, from collector's items to the latest foreign imports, start at 50p. Mostly American stuff, but covers the range from Tintin to erotic Manga; also animated videos and DVDs. Open M-W and Sa-Su 10am-6pm, Th-F 10am-7pm. MC, V (£10 min.).

SOUTH LONDON

🔢 *NEIGHBORHOOD QUICKFIND: Discover,* p. 13; *Sights,* p. 125; *Museums&Galleries,* p. 151; *Food&Drink,* p. 180; *Nightlife,* p. 198; *Entertainment,* p. 220; *Accommodations,* p. 299.

If you're looking for the fruits of West Indian cultures, **Brixton** is the place to be. For the best selection, come to the bustling market (see below), laden with Caribbean and African foods, clothes, and crafts.

Brixton Market, along Electric Ave., Pope's Rd., and Brixton Station Rd., as well as inside markets in Granville Arcade and Market Row. Tube: Brixton. Nowhere is Brixton's ethnic heritage more evident than here; giant snails slime in tubs next to salt cod, and African crafts. Open M-Tu and Th-Sa 8:30am-5pm, W 8:30am-1pm.

Bookmongers, 439 Coldharbour Ln., SW9 (☎7738 4225). Tube: Brixton. Fabulous second-hand bookstore with good-condition hardbacks at half the cover price and a big selection of paperbacks for just 50p at the back. Open M-Sa 10:30am-6:30pm. MC, V.

Red Records, 500 Brixton Rd., SW2 (☎7274 4476). Tube: Brixton. "Black Music Specialists" reads the sign, and so they are. Impressive collection of reggae, hip-hop, soul, garage, and jazz on new & used vinyl, CD, and tape. Open M-Sa 9:30am-8pm. AmEx, MC, V.

Bermondsey Market (a.k.a. New Caledonian), Bermondsey Sq. Tube: Bermondsey. Antiques sold here turn up in Camden Passage or Portobello the next day, suitably marked up—you have to start early (5am) to grab the good stuff. Open F 5am-2pm.

EAST LONDON

⛿ NEIGHBORHOOD QUICKFIND: Discover, p. 14; **Sights,** p. 126; **Museums&Galleries,** p. 152; **Food&Drink,** p. 180; **Nightlife,** p. 199; **Entertainment,** p. 221.

In East London, the **street-market** tradition is alive and well, helped along by large immigrant communities; the South Asian-dominated Brick Lane and Petticoat Lane are justly famous. In **Hoxton, Shoreditch,** and especially the stretch of **Brick Lane** just north of the Truman Brewery (see p. 127), independent young designers have opened up boutiques frequented by local artists and arty pretenders. Predictably, corporate-oriented **Docklands** has gone in the opposite direction, with the huge Cabot Place and adjacent Canada Place shopping malls offering the full range of British and international clothing chains and mainstream designer stores.

ALCOHOL

The Beer Shop, 14 Pitfield St. (☎7739 3701). Tube: Old St. 600 beers from around the world line the walls of this store, whose hoppy smell comes from the all-organic brewery next-door ("Eco Warrior" ale £2.25 per 0.5L). Home-brewing equipment, bottles and glasses, and a decent array of organic wines and ciders. Open M-F 11am-7pm, Sa 10am-4pm. MC, V.

CLOTHING & ACCESSORIES

Hoxton Boutique, 2 Hoxton St. (☎7684 2083; www.hoxtonboutique.co.uk). Tube: Old St. If you fear you're not funky enough for Soho, drop in here first. Jane Murrow (who used to work with Nicole Farhi) and Alison Whalley turn on the offbeat style for Shoreditch lasses. Most items £50-100. Open Tu-F 11am-7pm, Sa 11am-6pm, Su noon-5pm. MC, V.

Pauric Sweeney, 25a Pitfield St. (☎7253 5150). Tube: Old St. Ring for entry. Tiny, supercool clothing boutique. All manner of showy, funky partywear, from £30 accessories to a £600 made-to-measure leather dress. Open M-Sa 10:30am-7:30pm. AmEx, MC, V.

The Laden Showroom, 103 Brick Ln. (☎7247 2431; www.laden.co.uk). Tube: Aldgate East or Liverpool St. Up-to-the-minute casual and clubwear for up-and-coming artists, by up-and-coming London-based designers. Both new and recently used items, most under £30, all dripping with irony. Open M-Sa noon-6pm, Su 10am-6pm. AmEx, MC, V.

@work, 156 Brick Ln. (☎7377 0597; www.artworkgallery.com). Contemporary applied arts boutique, specializing in unique, offbeat jewelry, often made from unusual materials: necklaces from bottle-caps, perspex rings, and fishing-line earrings. £10 and up.

MARKETS

Brick Lane. Tube: Shoreditch or Aldgate East. At the heart of Whitechapel's sizeable Bangladeshi community, Brick Ln. hosts a large weekly market with a South Asian flair (food, rugs, spices, bolts of fabric, strains of sitar) in addition to its perennial supply of curry houses, colorful textile shops, and grocers. Open Su 8am-2pm.

Greenwich Markets. Numerous weekend markets converge on Greenwich, which on Sundays is blanketed with stalls and shoppers seeking the ultimate bargain.

Crafts Market, in the block surrounded by King William Walk, Greenwich Church St., College Approach, and Romney Rd. DLR: Cutty Sark. Antiques and collectibles Th, arts & crafts F-Su. Open Th-Su 10am-6pm.

Village Market, on Stockwell St. DLR: Cutty Sark. Food court, clothes, and bric-a-brac. Indoor stalls open F-Sa 10am-5pm, Su 10am-6pm; outdoor market Sa 7am-6pm, Su 7am-5pm.

Antiques Market, Greenwich High Rd. Rail: Greenwich. Mostly 20th century stuff; busiest in the summer. Open Sa-Su 9am-5pm.

Petticoat Lane. Tube: Liverpool St., Aldgate, or Aldgate East. Streets of stalls, mostly cheap clothing and household appliances, with lots of leather jackets around Aldgate East. The real action begins at about 9:30am. Open Su 9am-2pm; starts shutting down around noon.

Spitalfields. Tube: Shoreditch or Liverpool St. Formerly one of London's main wholesale vegetable markets, which has since relocated to Docklands; now a new-agey crafts market with a wide range of food stalls, plus an organic food market twice a week. Crafts market M-F 11am-3:30pm, Su 10am-5pm; organic market F and Su 10am-5pm.

Daytripping

For all the capital's many and varied charms, even the most die-hard London-lover feels the need to get out of the city occasionally. With Britain's comprehensive (if occasionally creaking) transportation network capable of spiriting you anywhere in the country in under a day, there's no excuse for staying cooped up in London for weeks on end when the historic and bucolic charms of England await at your doorstep. But first, a word of explanation about the organization of this chapter. **Short daytrips near London** covers sights and towns that are close (and small) enough to be easily covered in a day; you can leave after breakfast and return in time for dinner without breaking a sweat. If you're pressed for time, **Overnight Trips** could be done as long, full-day trips, but their distance and/or size makes it worth staying over. Most of the sights listed as being **"Near"** overnight trip destinations also make excellent short daytrips direct from London. All the trips are listed in order of increasing travel time by train from London.

SHORT DAYTRIPS NEAR LONDON

RICHMOND

Richmond is the point where London ends and the countryside begins, a leafy suburb along a the Thames that, while accessible by Tube, is a town in its own right. Edward III built the first royal palace here in 1358, but a major fire in 1497 literally took the Sheen off the area—that's what it was called until 1501, when Henry VII named the rebuilt palace (later destroyed by Cromwell) after his earldom in Yorkshire. For a fantastic view of the upper Thames valley, climb the steep incline of **Richmond Hill;** so many artists set up their easels on the 17th-century terrace that Parliament has declared it a protected site.

Daytrips from London

N

North Sea

English Channel

Strait of Dover

CHANNEL TUNNEL

FRANCE

Calais
Boulogne

20 miles
20 kilometers
0

Harwich
Ipswich
Bury St. Edmunds
Colchester
Southend
Rochester
Chelmsford
Saffron Walden
Anglesey Abbey
Cambridge
Bedford
Luton
Watford
Northampton
High Wycombe
Reading
Oxford
Woodstock
Bladon
Blenheim Castle
Warwick
Warwick Castle
Alcester
Stratford-upon-Avon
Worcester
Cheltenham
Gloucester
Bristol
Cheddar Gorge
Wells
Glastonbury
Bath
Lacock
Avebury
Stonehenge
Salisbury
Winchester
Southampton
Portsmouth
Isle of Wight
Bournemouth
Weymouth
Windsor
Guildford
Crawley
Chichester
Arundel
Little-hampton
Amberley
Worthing
Brighton
Newhaven
Lewes
Eastbourne
Pevensey
Battle
Hastings
Rye
Royal Tunbridge Wells
Maidstone
Leeds Castle
Canterbury
Chilham Castle
Folkestone
Dover
Deal
Sandwich
Ramsgate
Broadstairs
Margate
Romney Marsh
South Downs
SOUTH DOWNS WAY
River Thames

LONDON

M1
M11
M25
M40
M4
M3
M23
M2
M20
M50
M5

A11
A12
A120
A127
A10
A45
A6
A428
A41
A34
A420
A40
A49
A46
A36
A303
A30
A31
A35
A33
A27
A32
A24
A23
A22
A21
A259
A20
A28
A2
A257
A25
A4
A43
A5
A6

RICHMOND PARK. The largest city park in Europe, Richmond's 2500 acres were first enclosed by Charles I, who in 1637 generously built a wall around other people's property. The park still shelters some 800 deer. Heading right along the footpath from Richmond Gate will bring you to **Henry VIII's Mound,** actually a bronze-age barrow. Look through a small hole cut into the foliage at the top of the mound for a glimpse of St. Paul's in the distance. Bertrand Russell grew up in **Pembroke Lodge,** an 18th-century conversion job by Sir John Soane that's now a popular cafe. Deeper into the park, the **Isabella Plantation** bursts with color in the spring, while fans of *Billy Elliot* will recognize **White Lodge,** built by George II in 1727, as the home of the Royal Ballet School's youth section. *(Main gate at the top of Richmond Hill. Park Office ☎(020) 8948 3209. Bus # 371 from Richmond (70p). Open daily Mar.-Sept. 7am-dusk, Oct.-Feb. 7:30am-dusk. **Health warning:** Tick-borne Lyme disease is a risk in the park; wear long trousers.)*

HAM HOUSE. Some way downriver of Richmond, Ham House sits among resplendent gardens. William Murray received the house as a reward for being Charles I's "whipping boy"—he took the punishment whenever the future king misbehaved. Today, the house has been returned to the height of its glory, filled with 17th-century portraits, furniture, and tapestries. The exquisite **Cherry Garden** is actually a diamond array of lavender, santolina, and hedges with not a cherry tree in sight. *(At the bottom of Sandy Ln., Ham. ☎(020) 8892 9620. #65 or 371 from Richmond station, or walk 30min. along the Thames. A tiny ferry crosses the river from Marble Hill, Twickenham, Sa-Su 10am-6:30pm or dusk, Feb.-Oct. also M-F 10am-6pm; 50p, kids 30p. House open Apr.-Oct. Sa-W 1-5pm, gardens year-round Sa-W 11am-6pm or dusk. £6, kids £3, family £15; gardens only £2, £1, £5.)*

OTHER SIGHTS. On the top floor of the old Victorian town hall, the **Museum of Richmond** has a small array of interesting exhibits on the history of Richmond. *(Whittaker Ave. ☎8332 1141; www.museumofrichmond.com. Open Tu-Sa 11am-5pm; May-Sept. also Su 1-4pm. £2, students & seniors £1, kids free.)* Across the river from Ham House, **Marble Hill** was built in 1724 by Henrietta Howard, using an allowance from her former lover, George II. The house has been restored its mid-18th century condition, including many original artworks. *(Marble Hill Park, Richmond Rd. ☎(020) 8892 5115. Bus #33, 90, H22, R68, R70, or 290 from Richmond; alternatively, a ferry crosses from Ham House, Richmond (see above). Open Apr.-Sept. daily 10am-6pm, Oct. daily 10am-5pm, Nov.-Mar. W-Su 10am-4pm. £3.30, students & seniors £2.50, kids £1.70.)* Only James Gibbs's richly decorated Octagon Room survives of 18th-century **Orleans House.** Louis Philippe, Duc d'Orleans, rode out the French Revolution here before making king in 1830. The adjoining stables now house exhibitions of local art. *(Riverside, Twickenham. Transportation as for Marble Hill. ☎8892 0221. House open Apr.-Sept. Tu-Sa 1-5:30pm, Su 2-5:30pm; Oct.-Mar. closes 4:30pm; grounds daily 9am-dusk. Free.)*

PRACTICALITIES

GETTING THERE. At the end of the District line, the quickest route to **Richmond** is by **Tube** or **Silverlink train** (Zone 4). For a more leisurely, scenic journey, **boats** make the 2hr. cruise upriver from Westminster. *(Westminster Passenger Association, Westminster Pier. ☎(020) 7930 2062; www.wpsa.co.uk. Tube: Westminster. Departures Mid-Apr. to Sept. daily 10:30am, 11:15am, and noon, returning 4, 5, and 6pm. Tides may affect schedules; call to confirm. £7, return £11; ages 5-15 £3, £5; 33% discount with Travelcard.)*

ORIENTATION & PRACTICAL INFORMATION. From **Richmond** station, turn left onto The Quadrant, which becomes George St. and then Hill St. Turning right from Hill St. onto Bridge Rd. takes you across Richmond Bridge into **Twickenham,** while bearing left onto Hill Rise leads to Richmond Hill and Richmond Park. Running from Hill St. to the river, Whittaker Ave. is home to the **Tourist Information Centre,** where you can pick up a free map. *(Old Town Hall, Whittaker Ave. ☎(020) 8940 9125; www.richmond.gov.uk. Open May-Sept. M-Sa 10am-5pm, Su 10:30am-1:30pm; Oct.-Apr. M-Sa 10am-5pm.)*

HATFIELD HOUSE

Built for the Bishop of Ely in 1497, Hatfield was acquired by Henry VIII as a residence for the royal children. Elizabeth I is most associated with Hatfield; it was here that she turned from prisoner to Queen on the death of her sister, Mary I. Keep an eye out for Liz's fanciful, 22 ft. long family tree, tracing her lineage to Adam and Eve via Noah, Julius Caesar, and King Arthur. All that remains of Elizabeth's palace is the

Great Hall; the rest was razed to make way for the magnificent mansion that dominates the estate today, which, in a final homage to Elizabeth, was designed in the shape of an 'E' by chief minister to James I and first Earl of Salisbury Sir Robert Cecil. (☎(01707) 262823. House open late Mar. to late Sept. Tu-F 10am-4pm, Sa-Su 1-4:30pm. Grounds open late Mar. to late Sept. Tu-Su 11am-6pm. £6.60, kids £3.30. Grounds only £4, children £3. Prices rise for "Connoisseurs Friday," when tours are longer and more gardens are open: £10, grounds only £6.)

GETTING THERE. Trains arrive from **King's Cross.** (20min., every 30min.) **National Express buses** arrive from **Victoria Coach Station.** (☎(08705) 808080 1hr., every hour. £8.)

HAMPTON COURT

Although a monarch hasn't lived here for 250 years, Hampton Court exudes regal charm. Cardinal Wolsey built the first palace here in 1514, showing the young Henry VIII how to act the part of a splendid and powerful ruler—a lesson Henry learned all too well, confiscating it in 1528, and embarking on a massive building program. In 1689, William III and Mary II employed Christopher Wren to bring Hampton Court up to date, but less than 50 years later George II abandoned the palace for good. The **palace** is divided into six 45-60min. routes, all starting at **Clock Court,** where you can pick up a program of the day's events and an audioguide; in addition, costumed guides roam the palace, regaling visitors with tales of times gone by. In **Henry VIII's State Apartments,** only the massive Great Hall and exquisite Chapel Royal hint at the magnificence of Henry's court. Below, the **Tudor Kitchens** offer insight into how Henry ate himself to a 54" waist. Predating Henry's additions, the 16th-century **Wolsey Rooms** are complemented by Renaissance masterpieces, including a boyish self-portrait by Raphael. As so often, Wren's work steals the show; in this case with the **King's Apartments,** restored following a 1986 fire to their original appearance under William III. Mary II's death postponed the completion of the **Queen's Apartments** until 1734; here, the restrained Georgian interiors contrast with flamboyancy of Queen Anne. Last and least, the **Georgian Rooms** were created by William Kent for George II's family. Scarcely less impressive are the **gardens.** Palace tickets are required for entry to the **South Gardens,** of which the first is the ornate **Privy Garden,** built for the private enjoyment of William III. Nearby, the giant **Great Vine** is the world's oldest, planted in 1768. Secreted away in the neighboring Lower Orangery is Mantegna's series **The Triumphs of Caesar** (1484-1505). One of the most important works of the Italian Renaissance, it's displayed in semi-darkness to protect the fragile colors. The rest of the gardens are open to all; the **Home Park** stretches beyond the cone-cut yews of the **East Front Gardens.** North of the palace, the **Wilderness,** a pseudo-natural area earmarked for picnickers, holds the ever-popular **Maze,** planted in 1714. Its small size belies its devilish design; "solve" it by getting to the middle and back. (☎ (020) 8781 9500; www.hrp.org.uk. Open mid-Mar. to late Oct. M 10:15am-6pm, Tu-Su 9:30am-6pm; late Oct. to mid-Mar. closes 4:30pm; last admission 45min. before closing. Palace & gardens £10.80, students & seniors £8.30, kids £7.20, family (2 adults + 3 kids) £32.20; Maze only £2.90, kids £1.90; gardens (excl. south gardens) free. Free admission for worshippers at Chapel Royal services, held Su 11am and 3:30pm.)

GETTING THERE. The fastest way is to take the **train** to Hampton Court from Waterloo; the Palace is 5min. walk. (32min., every 30min. Day return £4; reductions with Travelcard.) More relaxing, scenic, and slower, are **boats** from Westminster. It's a long trip (3.5-4hr.); to leave time to see the Palace take it one-way and return by train, or board at Kew (see p. 124) or Richmond (p. 241) instead. (Westminster Passenger Association, Westminster Pier. ☎7930 2062; www.wpsa.co.uk. Tube: Westminster. Departures Mid-Apr. to Sept. daily 10:30, 11:15am, and noon, returning 3, 4, and 5pm. Tides may affect schedules; call to confirm. £10, return £14; ages 5-15 £4, £7; 33% discount with Travelcard.)

WINDSOR AND ETON

The town of Windsor and its attached village of Eton are completely overshadowed by two bastions of the British class system, Windsor Castle and Eton College. Windsor itself is filled with specialty shops, tea houses, and pubs, which for all their charm pale beside the fortress high above the Thames.

WINDSOR CASTLE. built by William the Conqueror in the 1070s and 1080s as a fortress rather than a residence, Windsor is the largest inhabited castle in the world, still used as a residence by the Royal Family. The castle's main attractions are found in the **Upper Ward.** Stand in the left queue as you enter to detour past **Queen Mary's Doll House,** an exact replica of a grand home down to tiny books in its library handwritten by their original authors. The **state apartments**, used for official entertainment, are decorated with works by Holbein, Rubens, Rembrandt, Van Dyck, and Queen Victoria herself. A stroll to the **Lower Ward** brings you to the 15th-century **St. George's Chapel,** with delicate vaulting and exquisite stained glass. The site of Edward and Sophie's wedding, 10 sovereigns lie here, including George V, Edward IV, Charles I, and Henrys VI and VIII. (☎(01753) 831 118. *As a "working castle," large areas may be closed at short notice. Audioguide £3.50. Open Apr.-Oct. daily 10am-5:30pm, last entry 4pm; Nov.-Mar. 10am-4pm, last entry 3pm. £11, seniors £9, under 17 £5.50, family £27.50.)*

ETON COLLEGE. Founded by Henry VI in 1440 as a school for paupers, Eton is England's pre-eminent public (i.e. private) school. Pupils still wear tailcoats to every class and raise one finger in greeting to any teacher they pass (this is also common in some state-run schools, but with less respectful connotations). For all its air of privilege, Eton has shaped some notable dissidents, including Aldous Huxley and George Orwell; it seems unlikely that Prince Harry will join their ranks. *(Across Windsor Bridge, and along Eton High St. ☎(01753) 671 177. Tours daily 2:15pm and 3:15pm; £4, under 16 £3.10. Open daily July-Aug. and late Mar. to mid-Apr. 10:30am-4:30pm; mid.-Apr. to June and Sept. to late Mar. 2-4:30pm. £3, kids £2.25.)*

PRACTICALITIES

GETTING THERE. Windsor has two train stations, both in walking distance of the castle. Trains to **Windsor & Eton Central** arrive from both **Victoria** and **Paddington** stations via **Slough**, while those to **Windsor & Eton Riverside** come direct from **Waterloo.** (☎08457 484 950. *All services 50min., 2 per hr. Day return £6.90).*

ORIENTATION & PRACTICAL INFORMATION. Windsor village slopes downhill in an elegant crescent from the foot of its castle. **High St.,** which becomes **Thames St.** at the statue of Queen Victoria and continues downhill to the Thames, spans the top of the hill; the main shopping area, **Peascod St.,** meets High St. at the statue. The **Tourist Information Centre,** near Queen Victoria, sells local maps, guides, and tickets to Legoland. *(24 High St. ☎ (01753) 743 900; www.windsor.gov.uk. Open May-June daily 10am-5pm; July-Aug. M-F 9:30am-6pm, Sa 10am-5:30pm, Su 10am-5pm; Sept. M-Sa 10am-5pm, Su 10am-4pm; Oct.-Apr. Su-F 10am-4pm, Sa 10am-5pm.)*

Pond Gardens, Hampton Court

East Front Gardens, Hampton Court

Musician in Fountain Court, Hampton Court

OVERNIGHT TRIPS

BRIGHTON

The undisputed home of the dirty weekend, Brighton sparkles with a risqué, tawdry luster. Back in 1784, the future George IV sidled into town for some hanky-panky. Having staged a fake wedding with a certain "Mrs. Jones" (Maria Fitzherbert), he headed off to the farmhouse known today as the Royal Pavilion, and the royal rumpus began. Kemp Town (jokingly called Camp Town), among other areas of Brighton, has a thriving gay population, while the immense student crowd, augmented by flocks of foreign youth purportedly learning English, feeds Brighton's decadent clubbing scene. Lovingly known as "London-by-the-Sea," Brighton's open demeanor and youthful spirit make for a memorable sojourn for adventurous travelers.

SIGHTS. In 1750, when Dr. Richard Russell wrote a treatise on the merits of drinking seawater and bathing in brine; thus began the transformation of sleepy Brighthelmstone into a fashionable town with a hedonistic bent, led by the most decadent layabout of them all, the Prince Regent (soon to be George IV). **The Royal Pavilion** is the epitome of Brighton gaudiness; the prince enlisted John Nash to turn an ordinary farmhouse into the Oriental/Indian/Gothic/Georgian palace visible today. (☎(01273) 290 900. Open June-Sept. daily 10am-6pm; Oct.-May 10am-5pm. £5.20, students & seniors £3.75, kids £3.20.) The Pavilion's gaudiness permeates to the beachfront, where the **Palace Pier** has slot machines and video games galore, with a rollercoaster thrown in for good measure. Farther along, the now decrepit **West Pier** lies abandoned out in the sea. Full-scale renovation was set to begin in the spring of 1999, but the abrupt collapse of part of the pier put a wrinkle in the plans. Even though Brighton was the original seaside resort, don't expect too much from the **beach**—the weather can be nippy even in June and July, and the closest thing to sand is fist-sized brown rocks. On sunny days, visitors have to fight for a patch of rock. Inland, fishermen's cottages once thrived in **the Lanes**, a jumble of 17th-century streets south of North St. constituting the heart of Old Brighton. Those looking for fresher shopping opportunities should head towards **North Laines**, off Trafalgar St., where alternative merchandise and colorful cafes still dominate.

NIGHTLIFE. Even Londoners come clubbing in Brighton. For the latest happenings, check *The Punter*, a local monthly, and *What's On*, a poster-sized flysheet. Gay and lesbian venues are found in the *Gay Times* ($2.50) and *Capital Gay* (free). Most clubs are open M-Sa 10pm-2am. **Zap Club,** a cavernous space under the arches of old World War II, is place to be for hard-core grinding to rave and house music. (King's Rd. Arches. ☎(01273) 202 407.) **Event II** is among the most technically armed, crammed with the down-from-London crowd looking for wild thrills. (West St. ☎(01273) 732627.) Gay clubbers flock to zany **Zanzibar**. (129 St. James's St. ☎(01273) 622 100.)

PRACTICALITIES

GETTING THERE. Travelers to Brighton by **train** have two options. **Connex** trains from **Victoria** are faster, but **Thameslink** commuter services are more frequent and may be more convenient, with stops at **King's Cross, Farringdon, City Thameslink,** and **London Bridge.** (Queens Rd. ☎08457 484 950. Connex: 50min., every 30min. Thameslink: 60-80min., every 15min. £10.50). **National Express buses** stop at Pool Valley, at the southern angle of Old Steine; buy tickets from **One Stop Travel.** (16 Old Steine. ☎(01273) 700 406; National Express ☎(08705) 808080. 2hr., 15 per day. £8.)

ORIENTATION & PRACTICAL INFORMATION. Queen's Rd. connects the train station to the English Channel, becoming **West St.** at the intersection with **Western St.** Funky stores and restaurants cluster around **Trafalgar St.** The narrow streets of **the Lanes**, left off Prince Albert St., provide an anarchic setting for Brighton's nightlife. **Old Steine**, a road and a square, runs in front of the Royal Pavilion, while **King's Rd.** runs along the waterfront. The **Tourist Information Centre** runs **walking tours** June-Aug. (10 Bartholomew Sq. ☎0906 711 2255; www.visitbrighton.com. Walking tours £3. Open M-Tu and Th-F 9am-5pm, W and Sa 10am-5pm; Mar.-Oct. also Su 10am-4pm.)

ACCOMMODATIONS. Frequent conventions make rooms scarce—book early or consult the TIC upon arrival. Many mid-range B&Bs line **Madeira Pl.;** shabbier B&Bs and hotels collect west of **West Pier** and in Kemp Town east of **Palace Pier.** The TIC also keeps a list of guest houses owned and operated by gays or lesbians. ▓**Baggies Backpackers** has live jazz, spontaneous parties, murals, and spacious mixed- and single-sex dorms, plus some doubles. *(33 Oriental Pl. ☎(01273) 733 740. Key deposit £5. Dorms £11, doubles £27.)* Lively ▓**Brighton Backpackers Hostel** has a great location with many rooms overlooking the ocean, innovative artwork, and a parakeet-keeping, guitar-playing manager. Four- to 8-bed mixed- and single-sex dorms. *(75-76 Middle St. ☎(01273) 777717; fax (01273) 887 778. No reservations. Dorms £11, doubles £25.)* **Cavalaire Guest House** has comfortable rooms ideal for a lazy weekend in town. *(34 Upper Rock Gdns. ☎(01273) 696 899; fax (01273) 600 504. Singles £25; doubles £42-55.)*

CAMBRIDGE

Cambridge was a typical market town until the 13th century, when an academic schism sent Oxford's refugees to the banks of the Cam. In contrast to metropolitan Oxford, Cambridge is feistily determined to retain its pastoral academic robes; as a town it's smaller, quieter, and arguably more beautiful. Visitors can enter most colleges from 9am to 5:30pm, though virtually all close during the exam period from May to mid-June.

KING'S PARADE TO ST. JOHN'S ST. Founded twice—by Queen Margaret of Anjou in 1448 and again by Elizabeth Woodville in 1465—**Queens' College** has the only unaltered Tudor court in Cambridge. The Mathematical Bridge was built in 1749 without a single bolt or nail, but a meddling Victorian took apart the bridge to see how it worked and the inevitable occurred—he couldn't put it back together without using iron rivets every half-inch. *(Silver St. ☎(01223) 335 511. College open Mar.-Oct. daily 10am-4.30pm. Closed during exams. £1.)* The most famous colleges are found along the east side of the Cam between Magdalene Bridge and Silver St. Founded, along with Eton, by Henry VI, **King's College** features most heavily on postcards thanks to its soaring chapel, perhaps the finest piece of Gothic architecture in the world. *(King's Parade. ☎(01223) 331 100. Chapel and grounds open M-Sa 9:30am-4:30pm, Su 9:30am-2:30pm. Evensong 5:30pm most nights. Contact TIC for tours. £3.50, concs. £2.50, under 12 free.)* Behind King's chapel, the white stone facade of **Senate House** is where graduation ceremonies are held. *(Closed to visitors.)* Just opposite, you can climb the tower of **Great St. Mary's,** the university's official church, for a view of the greens and the colleges. Pray that the 12 bells don't ring while you're ascending. *(Tower open M-Sa 9:30am-5pm, Su 12:30-5pm. £1.85, children 60p, families £4.20.)* Founded by Henry VIII, **Trinity College** is the largest and wealthiest college. Isaac Newton heads a list of alumni including Byron, Tennyson, Nabokov, Russell, Wittgenstein, and Nehru. The pride of the college is Christopher Wren's Library, whose treasures include A.A. Milne's handwritten manuscript of *Winnie the Pooh* and Newton's own *Principia*. *(Trinity St. ☎(01223) 338 400. Chapel and courts open daily 10am-5pm. Library open M-F noon-2pm, Sa 10:30am-12:30pm. Easter-Oct. £1.75, otherwise free.)* Next to Trinity, arch-rival **St. John's College** was established in 1511 by Henry VIII's mother. The Bridge of Sighs connects the older part of the college to the neo-Gothic extravagance of New Court. The oldest complete building in Cambridge, School of Pythagoras' 12th-century pile of wood and stone hides in the college gardens. *(St. John's St. ☎(01223) 338 600. Open daily 10am-4:45pm. £2, students & seniors £1.20, families £4.)*

OTHER MAJOR COLLEGES. Founded as "God's-house" in 1448 and renamed in 1505, **Christ's** has since won fame for its association with John Milton and Charles Darwin—his rooms were on G staircase in First Court. *(St. Andrews St. ☎(01223) 334 900. Gardens open in summer M-F 9:30am-noon; term-time M-F 9:30am-4:30pm. Free.)* Occupying a 15th-century Benedictine hostel, **Magdalene College** (MAUD-lin), sometime home of C.S. Lewis, is renowned for its traditionalism—the college dining hall is still entirely candlelit. The **Pepys Library** in the second court houses the inveterate diarist's journals. *(Magdalene St. ☎(01223) 332 100. Library open Easter-Aug. 11:30am-12:30pm and 2:30-3:30pm; Sept.-Easter M-Sa 11:30am-12.30pm. Free.)* **Peterhouse,** Trumpington St., is the oldest and smallest college, founded in 1294. *(☎(01223) 338 200. Call for opening hours.)* **Corpus Christi,** founded in 1352 by the townspeople, contains the

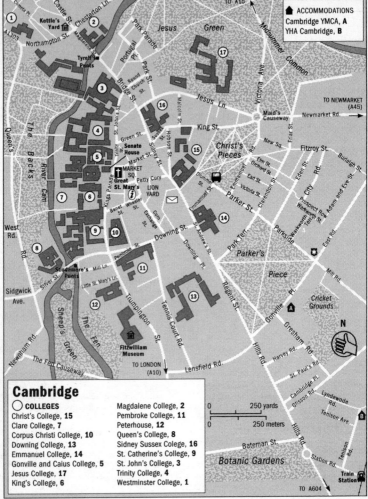

Cambridge

○ **COLLEGES**

Christ's College, **15**	Magdalene College, **2**
Clare College, **7**	Pembroke College, **11**
Corpus Christi College, **10**	Peterhouse, **12**
Downing College, **13**	Queen's College, **8**
Emmanuel College, **14**	Sidney Sussex Colege, **16**
Gonville and Caius College, **5**	St. Catherine's College, **9**
Jesus College, **17**	St. John's College, **3**
King's College, **6**	Trinity College, **4**
	Westminster College, **1**

dreariest and oldest court in Cambridge, though its library maintains the snazziest collection of Anglo-Saxon manuscripts in England, among them the *Anglo-Saxon Chronicle*. Alums include Sir Francis Drake and Christopher Marlowe. *(Trumpington St. ☎(01223) 338 000.)*

OTHER SIGHTS. The **Fitzwilliam Museum** has aa fine array of Impressionists and some Blake drawings and woodcuts, along with ancient statuary, medieval armor, and far-eastern porcelain. *(Trumpington St. ☎(01223) 332 900. Tours Sa 2:30pm; £3. Open Tu-Sa 10am-5pm, Su 2:15-5pm. Free, suggested donation £3.)* The former house of Tate curator Jim Ede, ◪**Kettle's Yard** hardly resembles a museum at all; the early 20th-century art is displayed as Ede left it, among a homely atmosphere of beds, books, and trinkets. Adjacent to the house, a modern gallery shows contemporary art. *(☎(01223) 352 124. House open Apr.-Sept. Tu-Sa 1:30-4:30pm, Su 2-4:30pm; Oct.-Mar. Tu-Su 2-4pm. Gallery open year-round Tu-Su 11:30am-5pm. Free.)* The **Round Church,** where Bridge St. meets St. John's St., is one of five surviving circular churches in England, first built in 1130 on the pattern of the Church of the Holy Sepulchre in Jerusalem. *(☎311602. Free.)* On warm days, Cambridge takes to the river on **punts,** traditional flat-bottomed boats propelled by a pole. Numerous outfits will equip you with boat and pole for £8-10 per hour, with a £40-50 deposit.

PRACTICALITIES

GETTING THERE. Trains arrive every 30min. from **King's Cross** (50min.) and **Liverpool St.** (85min.); beware that the station is a good 30min. walk from the center (head to the end of Station Rd., turn right, and keep going), and city buses (85p) are rare after 6pm and on Sundays. *(Station Rd. ☎08457 484 950. Day return £14.50.)* **Buses** are much slower, but drop you right in the center; **National Express** arrives from **Victoria Coach Station.** *(Drummer St. ☎08705 808 080. 2hr., 17 per day, from £8.)*

ORIENTATION & PRACTICAL INFORMATION. Cambridge has two main avenues, both suffering from multiple personality disorder. The main shopping street starts at **Magdalene Bridge** and becomes **Bridge St., Sidney St., St. Andrew's St., Regent St.,** and finally **Hills Rd.** as it nears the train station. The other street—starting out from Bridge St. as **St. John's St.,** then **Trinity St., King's Parade,** and **Trumpington St.**—is the academic thoroughfare, parallel to the river but separated from it by colleges. The **Tourist Information Centre,** a block south of Market Sq., runs 2hr. walking tours. *(Wheeler St. ☎(01223) 322 640, accommodations hotline ☎(01223) 457 581; www.tourism-cambridge.com. Walking tour £7, kids £4; call for times. Open Apr.-Oct. M-F 10am-5:30pm, Sa 10am-5pm, Su 11am-4pm; Nov.-Mar. M-F 10am-5:30pm, Sa 10am-5pm.)*

ACCOMMODATIONS. Hostel & B&B reservations are essential in summer. Pick up a guide from the TIC (50p), or check the comprehensive list in the window after it closes. At **YHA Cambridge,** the staff fosters a relaxed, welcoming atmosphere, although more showers wouldn't hurt. *(97 Tenison Rd. ☎(01223) 354 601; fax 312780. Breakfast £3.50. Crowded Mar.-Oct.; in summer, call weeks ahead. 3- to 4-bed dorms £15.10, under 18 £11.40.)* Welcoming both men and women, **Cambridge YMCA** has a good location between the train station and town center. *(Gonville Pl. ☎(01223) 356 998; fax 312749. Breakfast included. Singles £23; shared room (usually twins) £18.50.)*

OXFORD

Oxford had been a center of learning for a century before Henry II founded the university in 1167. Though tourists now outnumber scholars, Oxford has irrepressible grandeur, and there are pockets of sweet quiet, most famously the perfectly maintained quadrangles ("quads") of the university's 39 colleges. Most colleges are free to enter, though some charge admission in high season; however opening hours for visitors are restricted, especially April to early June as students prepare for exams.

ASHMOLEAN MUSEUM. Opened in 1683, the Ashmolean was Britain's first public gallery, and now plays host to familiar favorites including Leonardo, Monet, Manet, Van Gogh, Michelangelo, Rodin, and Matisse. Renovated galleries also house ancient Islamic, Greek, and Far Eastern art. *(Beaumont St. From Carfax, head up Commarket St., which becomes Magdalen St.; Beaumont St. is on the left. ☎(01865) 278 000. Open Tu-Sa 10am-5pm, Su 2-5pm, later in summer. Free.)*

MAJOR COLLEGES. Christ Church, grand enough for Charles I to make it his capital during the Civil War, is centered around Tom Quad, named for the bell which has rung at 9:05pm (the original student curfew) every evening since 1682. The college's art gallery includes works by Tintoretto and Vermeer, with Leonardo and Michelangelo occasionally coming out of hiding. *(Down St. Aldates St. from Carfax; for gallery only, enter at Canterbury Gate off Oriel St. ☎(01865) 276 492. College open M-Sa 9:30am-5:30pm, Su 11:30am-5:30pm; gallery Apr.-Sept. M-Sa 10:30am-1pm and 2-5:30pm, Su 2-5:30pm; Oct.-Mar. closes 4:30pm. £2.50, concs. £1.50, family £6.; gallery £1, students & seniors 50p.)* **Merton College** has Oxford's oldest quad, the 14th-century Mob Quad, and an equally ancient library holding the first printed Welsh Bible. *(Merton St. ☎276310. Open M-F 2-4pm, Sa-Su 10am-4pm. Closed around Easter and Christmas and on some Saturdays. Free.)* **University College** dates from 1249 and vies with Merton for the title of oldest college; misbehaving alums include Shelley, expelled for his pamphlet *The Necessity of Atheism,* and a non-inhaling Bill Clinton. *(High St. ☎(01865) 276 619.)* Around since 1341, **Queen's College** was rebuilt by Wren and Hawksmoor in orange, white, and gold. A trumpet call summons students to dinner. *(High St. ☎(01865) 279 121. Closed except to authorized tours.)* **Magdalen College** (MAUD-lin), with flower-laced quads and a private deer park, is considered Oxford's handsomest, and was a natural choice for budding

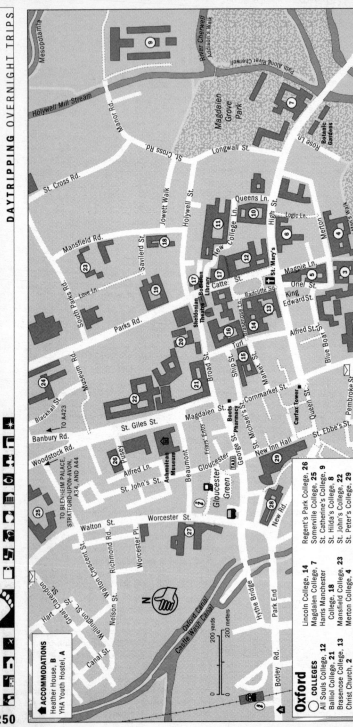

▲ ACCOMMODATIONS
Heather House, **B**
YHA Youth Hostel, **A**

Oxford
○ **COLLEGES**
All Souls College, **12**
Balliol College, **21**
Brasenose College, **13**
Christ Church, **2**
Corpus Christi College, **3**
Exeter College, **16**
Hertford College, **17**
Jesus College, **15**

Lincoln College, **14**
Magdalen College, **7**
Harris Manchester
College, **18**
Mansfield College, **23**
Merton College, **4**
New College, **11**
Nuffild College, **28**
Oriel College, **5**
Pembroke College, **1**
The Queen's College, **10**

Regent's Park College, **26**
Somerville College, **25**
St. Catherine's College, **9**
St. Hilda's College, **8**
St. John's College, **22**
St. Peter's College, **29**
Trinity College, **20**
University College, **6**
Wadham College, **19**
Worcester College, **27**

aesthete Oscar Wilde. *(On High St. near the River Cherwell. ☎(01865) 276 000. Open July-Sept. M-F noon-6pm, Sa-Su 2-6pm; Oct.-June 2-5pm. Apr.-Sept. £2, concessions £1; Oct.-Mar. free.)* Founded in 1555, **Trinity College** has a splendid Baroque chapel, with a limewood altarpiece, cedar lattices, and cherubim everywhere. *(Broad St. ☎(01865) 279 900. Open daily 10:30am-noon and 2-4pm. £2, concessions £1.)* Founding in 1379, **New College** is actually one of Oxford's oldest. Every three years, the city mayor inspect the state of the old city wall, which passed through the croquet lawn. "Spoonerisms" are named for former warden William Spooner, who once rebuked a student that he had "tasted the whole worm." *(New College Ln. ☎(01865) 279 555. Open daily Easter-Oct. 11am-5pm; Nov.-Easter 2-4pm, use the Holywell St. Gate. £1.50.)*

OTHER SIGHTS. The **Bodleian** was endowed in 1602 and is Oxford's principal library. No one has ever been allowed to take out even one of its five million volumes. Only scholars may enter the reading rooms; student ID may suffice, but an academic letter of introduction is recommended. *(Catte St. Take High St. and turn left on Catte. ☎(01865) 277 224. Tours start at the Divinity School, across the street; in summer M-F 4 per day, Sa-Su 2 per day; in winter 2 per day. £3.50. Open M-F 9am-6pm, Sa 9am-1pm; 2-day reader ticket £3.)* A teenage Christopher Wren knocked off the Roman-style **Sheldonian Theatre**, now the site of graduation ceremonies; its cupola affords an inspiring view. The stone heads on the fence behind the theater are a 20th-century study of beards. *(Broad St. ☎(01865) 277 299. Open M-Sa 10am-12:30pm and 2-4:30pm. £1.50, children £1.)* A hike up the medieval **Carfax Tower's** 99 spiral stairs gives a fantastic view of the city, plus a peep into the bell-ringing chamber. *(Corner of Queen St. and Cornmarket St. ☎(01865) 792 653. Open Apr.-Oct. daily 10am-5:30pm; Nov.-Mar. 10am-3:30pm. £1.20, under 16 60p.)* Haul yourself past the rural banks of the rivers Thames (called Isis in Oxford) and Cherwell on a traditional **punt.** Magdalen Bridge Boat Co. rents from March to November. *(Magdalen Bridge. ☎(01865) 202 643. M-F £9 per hr., Sa-Su £10 per hr., deposit £20 plus ID. Open daily 10am-9pm.)*

PRACTICALITIES

GETTING THERE. The railway station, a 10min. walk from the historic center, is served by **Thames Trains** from **Paddington**. *(Botley Rd., down Park End. Station ☎(01865) 794 422, trains (08457) 484 950. 1hr., 2-4 per hr., day return £14.80.)* The **bus station** is more central. **Stagecoach Oxford** and **Oxford CityLink** operate frequent bus services to **Victoria Coach Station.** *(Gloucester Green. Stagecoach ☎(01865) 772 250; CityLink ☎(01865) 785 400. Both 1½hr., 1-6 buses per hr. Next-day return £7.50, concs. £6.50.)*

Ashmolean Museum, Oxford

Pembroke College, Oxford

St. Johns College

ORIENTATION & PRACTICAL INFORMATION. While Oxford is a fair-sized town, the historic center is easily walkable. The easiest way to orient yourself is to locate the colossal **Carfax Tower,** from which most colleges lie to the east. The **Tourist Information Centre,** beside the bus station, sells a £1 street map and guide with a valuable index. *(The Old School, Gloucester Green. ☎(01865) 726 871; fax (01865) 240261). Open M-Sa 9:30am-5pm; Easter-Oct. also Su 10am-3:30pm.)*

ACCOMMODATIONS. Book at least a week ahead June-Sept. The superbly located **YHA Youth Hostel** is an immediate right from the station onto Botley Rd. *(2a Botley Rd. ☎(01865) 762 997; fax 769402. Breakfast included. 4- to 6-bed dorms £18, students £17, under 18 £13.50.)* **Heather House** has sparkling rooms and exceptionally helpful staff. *(192 Iffley Rd. ☎/fax (01865) 249 757. Walk 20min. or take the "Rose Hill" bus from the bus or train station or Carfax Tower (70p). Singles £30 1st night, £27 after; doubles with bath £58, £54.)*

NEAR OXFORD: BLENHEIM

The largest private home in England, Blenheim (BLEN-em) was built in appreciation of the Duke of Marlborough's victory over Louis XIV at the eponymous battle in 1704. The 11th Duke now calls the palace home, though he has to pay the Crown a rent of one French Franc every year (or 0.152449 Euros from January 2002). Another scion of the family, **Winston Churchill** spent his early years here; his baby curls are on display, while his mortal remains rest in the nearby village churchyard of Bladon. **Capability Brown** designed the 2100 acres of fantastic gardens. *(☎(01993) 811 091. Open daily mid-Mar. to Oct. 10:30am-5:30pm, last entry 4:45pm; grounds year-round 9am-9pm. £9, students & seniors £7, kids £4.50.)*

GETTING THERE. The palace is in **Woodstock,** 8 mi. north of Oxford; take the **Stagecoach Express** *(☎(01865) 772 250. 20min., return £3.50.)*

CANTERBURY

Flung somewhere between the cathedral and the open road, the soul of Canterbury is as flighty as the city's itinerant visitors. Archbishop Thomas à Becket met his demise in Canterbury Cathedral after an irate Henry II asked, "Will no one rid me of this troublesome priest?" and a few of his henchmen took the hint. In the near millennium since, the site has become the focus of many pilgrimages dedicated to the "the hooly blisful martir." Geoffrey Chaucer saw enough irony in pilgrim flocks to capture them in his *Canterbury Tales.*

■ **CANTERBURY CATHEDRAL.** The focal point of English Christianity since St. Augustine consecrated it in the 6th century, Canterbury Cathedral became the nation's primary pilgrimage destination following the 1170 murder of Archbishop (now Saint) Thomas à Becket. The murder site is closed off by a rail—a kind of permanent police line—around the Altar of the Sword's Point. In the adjacent **Trinity Chapel,** a solitary candle marks where Becket's body lay until 1538, when Henry VIII burned his remains and destroyed the shrine to show how he dealt with bishops who crossed the king. In a structure plagued by fire and rebuilt time and again, the 12th-century **crypt** remains intact. The **Corona Tower,** 105 steps above the easternmost apse, is recently renovated. *(☎(01227) 762 862. Cathedral open Easter-Sept. M-Sa 9am-6:30pm, Su 12:30-2:30pm and 4:30-5:30pm; Oct.-Easter M-Sa 9am-5pm, Su 12:30-2:30pm and 4:30-5:30pm; Precincts daily 7am-9pm. £3.50, concs. £2.50; photography permit £2.)*

OTHER SIGHTS. Inevitably, someone would come up with an attraction called **The Canterbury Tales.** Let the gap-toothed Wife of Bath and her waxen companions entertain you with abbreviated versions of the tales. *(St. Margaret's St. ☎(01227) 479 227. Open July-Aug. daily 9am-5.30pm; Mar.-June and Sept.-Oct. 9:30am-5:30pm; Nov.-Feb. Su 10am-4:30pm, Sa 9:30am-5:30pm. £5.90, concs. £4.90, family £18.50.)* Soaring arches, crumbling walls, and silent altars are all that remain of **St. Augustine's Abbey,** founded in AD 598. Don't miss St. Augustine's humble tomb under a pile of rocks. *(Outside the city wall near the cathedral. ☎(01227) 767 345. Open Apr.-Oct. daily 10am-6pm; Nov.-Ma 10am-4pm. £2.60, students and seniors £2, kids £1.30.)* Just around the corner from St. Augustine's on North Holmes St. stands the **Church of St. Martin.** King Ethelbert married the Christian Princess Bertha here in AD 562, paving the way for England's con version to Christianity. Joseph Conrad lies in an underground heart of darkness. (☎(01227) 459 482. Open M-Su 9am-5pm. Free.) The **Canterbury Heritage Museum** spans Canterbury's history from its earliest days to beloved children's-book character Rupert Bear, the creation of local artist Mary Tourtel. (Stour St. ☎(01227) 452 747. Open June-Oct. M-Sa 10:30am-5pm, Su 1:30-5pm; Nov.-May M-Sa 10:30am-5pm. £1.90, concs. £1.20.) England's first Franciscan friary, **Greyfriars** was built over the River Stour in 1267 by Franciscan monks who arrived in the country in 1224, two years before Francis of Assisi died. A small museum and chapel are found inside the simple building. (Stour St. Open summer M-F 2-4pm. Free.) The **Roman Museum**, Butchery Ln., houses hairpins, building fragments, and other artifacts from Roman Canterbury in a hands-on exhibit. (☎(01227) 785 575. Open June-Oct. M-Sa 10am-5pm, Su 1:30-5pm; Nov.-May M-Sa 10am-5pm. Last admission 4pm. £2.50, concs. £1.60.) Near the city walls to the southwest lie the massive remnants of **Canterbury Castle,** built for the Conqueror himself.

Catte Street, Oxford

PRACTICALITIES

GETTING THERE. Canterbury has two **train** stations. **Connex South** runs to **Canterbury East** from **Victoria.** (Station Rd. East, off Castle St. ☎(08457) 484950. 1½hr.; 2 per hr.; £15.70, day return £16.10.) Connex also serves **Canterbury West** from **Charing Cross** and **Waterloo.** (Station Rd. West, off St. Dunstan's St. 1½hr.; every hr. Phone & prices as above.) Open M-Sa 8:15am-5:15pm. **National Express** buses arrive at St. George's Ln. from **Victoria Coach Station.** (☎08705 808080. 2hr., every hr. £6-8.)

ORIENTATION AND PRACTICAL INFORMATION. Canterbury is roughly circular, as defined by the eroding city wall. An unbroken street crosses the city from northwest to southeast, changing names from **St. Peter's St.** to **High St.** to **The Parade** to **St. George's St.** The **tourist information centre** gives out a free mini-guide. (34 St. Margaret's St. ☎(01227) 766 567, bed booking hotline ☎(01227) 780 063. Open M-Sa 9:30am-5:30pm, Su 10am-4pm.)

Royal Blenheim, Oxford

ACCOMMODATIONS. Reserved ahead in summer, or arrive mid-morning to grab recently vacated rooms. B&Bs are concentrated around the lanes stemming from High St., with quite a few scattered near West Station. Oh-so-wittily named, **Kipps, A Place to Sleep** is a 5-10min. walk from the city center, with a variety of accommodations and terrific kitchen. (40 Nunnery Fields. ☎(01227) 786 121; fax (01227) 766 992. Towels £1. Key deposit £10. Dorms £11-13; singles £15; doubles £28.) **YHA Canterbury** is ¾ mi. from East Station and ½ mi. southeast of the bus station; book at least 1 week ahead in summer. (54 New Dover Rd. ☎(01227) 462 911; fax 470752. Reception 7:30-10am

Sheldonian Theatre, Oxford

and 1-11pm. Dorms £11, under 18 £7.90.) Gloriously central, **The Tudor House** was built in the 16th century; front rooms have a view of the cathedral. *(6 Best Ln., off High St.* ☎*(01227) 765 650. Singles £18; doubles £36, with bath £44; family rooms £50.)*

NEAR CANTERBURY: LEEDS CASTLE

Billed as "the Loveliest Castle in the World," Leeds Castle was built immediately after the Norman Conquest. Henry VIII made it a lavish dwelling whose 500 acres of woodlands and gardens still host unusual waterfowl, including black swans. The ground floor is an ideal example of a royal Tudor residence, in sharp contrast to the more modern and stylish second floor. Outside, lose yourself in a **maze** of 2400 yew trees; the sculpted grounds, vivid gardens, and forests, meanwhile, are almost a maze in themselves. *(*☎*(01622) 765400 or (0870) 600 8880. Castle open Mar.-Oct. daily 11am-7:30pm; Nov.-Feb. 10:15am-5:30pm. Grounds open Mar.-Oct. daily 10am-7pm; Nov.-Feb. 10am-5pm. Last admission 2hr. before close. Castle and grounds £10, students & seniors £8.50, kids £6.50, families £29. Grounds only £8.50, students & seniors £7, kids £5.20, families £24.)*

GETTING THERE. Leeds Castle is 3 mi. southwest of Canterbury on the A20 London-Folkestone road near Maidstone. Take the train to **Bearsted** from **Canterbury West** or **London Victoria;** a shuttlebus runs to the castle ($3.20).

BATH

A visit to the elegant spa town of Bath remains *de rigueur*, even if it is now more of a museum—or perhaps a museum's gift shop—than a resort. Romans built an elaborate complex of baths to house the curative waters at the town they called *Aquae Sulis,* and the excavated remains of that complex draw in visitors today. Queen Anne's visit to the hot springs here in 1701 reestablished the city's prominence, making it a meeting place for 18th-century artists, politicians, and intellectuals.

ROMAN BATHS. Bath flourished for nearly 400 years as a Roman spa city, but it was not until 1880 that sewer diggers inadvertently uncovered the first glimpse of advanced Roman engineering. Underneath the baths, the **museum** makes up for the entrance price with its display on Roman building design, including central heating and internal plumbing. Penny-pinching travelers can view one of the baths in the complex for free by entering through the **Pump Room.** *(Stall St.* ☎*(01225) 477 759. Open Apr.-July and Sept. daily 9am-6pm; Aug. 9am-6pm and 8-10pm; Oct.-Mar. 9:30am-5pm; last admission 30min. before close. £7.50, seniors & students £6.50, kids £4.20, family £18.50. Joint ticket with Museum of Costume £9.50, seniors & students £8.50, kids £5.50, family £25.)*

BATH ABBEY. An anomaly among the city's Roman and 18th-century Georgian sights, the 15th-century abbey still towers over its neighbors. The abbey saw the crowning of Edgar, "first king of all England," in AD 973. The whimsical west facade sports angels climbing ladders up to heaven and two angels climbing down. *(Next to the Baths.* ☎*(01225) 477 752. Open M-Sa 9am-4:30pm, Su 1-2:30pm and 4:30-5:30pm. Free suggested donation £1.50.)* Below the abbey, the **Heritage Vaults** detail the abbey's history and its importance to Bath. *(*☎*(01225) 422 462. Open M-Sa 10am-4pm; last admission 3:30pm. £2, students & seniors £1, kids free.)*

OTHER SIGHTS. The **Museum of Costume** hosts a dazzling, albeit motionless, parade of 400 years of catwalk fashions, with everything from silver tissue garments to Queen Victoria's "generously cut" wedding gown. *(Bennett St.* ☎*(01225) 477 752. Open daily 10am-5pm. £4.20, seniors £3.75, kids £3. Also joint ticket with Roman Baths; see above.)* The museum is in the basement of the **Assembly Rooms,** which staged fashionable events in the 18th century. *(*☎*477789. Open daily 10am-5pm. Free.)* The **Jane Austen Centre** organizes Austen's references to Bath (a "dismal sight"), and invites dilettantes to experience the city as it was in 1806. Tours of the sights in her novels run three days per week according to demand. *(40 Gay St.* ☎*(01225) 443 000. Open Apr.-Sept. M-Sa 10am-5:30pm, Su 10:30am-5:30pm; Oct.-Mar. M-Sa 10am-5pm, Su 10:30am-5pm. £4, students & seniors £3, kids £2, family £10. Tours £3.50, students & seniors £2.50, kids £2, family £8.)* Walk up Gay St. to **The Circus,** which has attracted illustrious residents for two centuries. Blue plaques mark the houses of Gainsborough, Pitt the Elder, and Dr. Livingstone. Proceed from there up Brock St. to **Royal Crescent,** a half-moon of Georgian

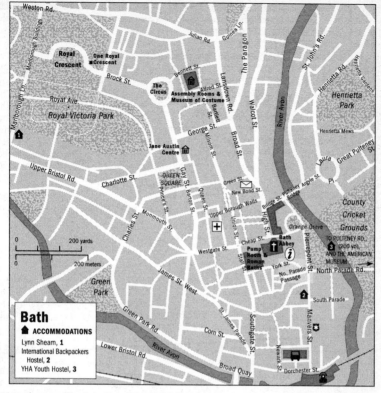

Bath

⌂ ACCOMMODATIONS

Lynn Sheam, **1**
International Backpackers Hostel, **2**
YHA Youth Hostel, **3**

townhouses. The interior of **One Royal Crescent** has been painstakingly restored to a near-perfect replica of a 1770 townhouse, authentic to the last teacup. (*1 Royal Cresc.* ☎428126. *Open mid-Feb. to Oct. Tu-Su 10:30am-5pm; Nov. Tu-Su 10:30am-4pm. £4, concs. £3.50, family £10.*) **The American Museum** will appeal to Homesick Yankees and those who want to visit the States vicariously but haven't yet found a McDonald's, with a series of furnished rooms transplanted from historically significant homes. (*Claverton Manor. Climb Bathwick Hill, or take bus #18. ☎(01225) 460 503. Museum open late Mar. to Oct. Tu-Su 2-5pm. Gardens open late Mar. to Oct. Tu-F 1-6pm, Sa-Su noon-6pm; also M in Aug. House, grounds, and galleries £5.50, students & seniors £5, kids £3. Grounds, Folk Art, and New Galleries only £3, kids £2.*)

PRACTICALITIES

GETTING THERE. Trains from **Paddington** are the fastest way to get to Bath, but those from **Waterloo** are much cheaper. (*Railway Pl., at the south end of Manvers St. ☎08457 484 950. Paddington: 1½hr., 2 per hr., £34. Waterloo: 2¼hr., 4 per day, £21.*) Yet slower and cheaper are **National Express buses** from **Victoria Coach Station.** (*☎08705 808 080. 3hr., 9 per day. £11.50.*)

ORIENTATION & PRACTICAL INFORMATION. Beautiful **Pulteney Bridge** and **North Parade Bridge** span the River Avon, which bends around the city. The **Roman Baths,** the **Pump Room,** and **Bath Abbey** cluster in the city center, while the **Royal Crescent** and **The Circus** lie to the northwest. The **Tourist Information Centre** offers the usual services. (*Abbey Chambers. ☎(01225) 477 101. Open May-Sept. M-Sa 9:30am-6pm, Su 10am-4pm; Oct.-Apr. M-Sa 9:30am-5pm, Su 10am-4pm.*)

ACCOMMODATIONS. B&Bs cluster on **Pulteney Rd.** and **Pulteney Gdns.** From the stations, walk up Manvers St., which becomes Pierrepont St., right onto North Parade Rd., and past the cricket ground to Pulteney Rd. For a more relaxed (and more expensive) setting, continue past Pulteney Gdns. (or take the footpath from behind the train station) to **Widcombe Hill. YHA Bath Youth Hostel** is in a secluded Italianate mansion overlooking the city. In summer reserve a week in advance. *(Bathwick Hill. ☎(01225) 465 674; fax (012225) 482 947. From North Parade Rd., turn left onto Pulteney Rd., right onto Bathwick Hill, and then 20min. up a steep footpath, or take Badgerline "University" bus #18 (6 per hr. until midnight; return £1) from the bus station or the Orange Grove roundabout. Dorms £11, under 18 £7.75.)* In contrast, **International Backpackers Hostel** has an extremely convenient location, up the street from the stations and 3 blocks below the baths. Each room and bed is identified by a music genre and artist ("I'm sleeping in Rap"). *(13 Pierrepont St. (☎446787; fax 446305; info@backpackers-uk.demon.co.uk). Breakfast £1. Dorms £12.)* **Lynn Shearn** has friendly proprietors and inviting rooms, complete with boardgames and hairdryers. *(Prior House, 3 Marlborough Ln. ☎(01225) 313 587; fax (01225) 443 543. Take bus #14 from the station to Hinton Garage or make the 12min. walk; look for 2 black signs. No smoking. Doubles from £40, with bath £45.)*

SALISBURY & STONEHENGE

Salisbury's fame comes from two remarkable historic monuments: its cathedral, with the highest spire in England, and the mysterious monoliths of nearby Stonehenge. Both draw druids, occultists, and new-age hippies, who assert that Salisbury is at the center of Britain's network of "ley lines," mysterious configurations of ancient monuments believed to have magical powers.

SALISBURY CATHEDRAL. Salisbury Cathedral rises from its grassy close to a neck-breaking height of 404 ft. Built in just 38 years, starting in 1320, the cathedral has a singular and weighty design. The bases of the marble pillars bend inward under the strain of 6400 tons of limestone—if a pillar rings when you knock on it, you should probably move away. Nearly 700 years have left the cathedral in need of structural and surface repair, and scaffolding shrouds parts of the outer walls where the stone is disintegrating. The chapel houses the oldest functioning mechanical clock, a strange collection of wheels and ropes that has ticked 500 million times over the last 600 years. Much to King John's chagrin, the best-preserved of four surviving copies of the *Magna Carta* rests in the Chapter House. *(33 The Close. ☎(01722) 555 120. Cathedral open June-Aug. M-Sa 7:15am-8:15pm, Su 7:15am-6:15pm; Sept.-May daily 7:15am-6:15pm; Chapter House June-Aug. M-Sa 9:30am-7:45pm, Su 9:30am-5:30pm; Sept.-May daily 9:30am-5:30pm. Suggested donation £3.50, students & seniors £2.50, kids £2, family £8.)*

STONEHENGE. A ring of submerged colossi amid swaying grass and indifferent sheep, Stonehenge stands unperturbed by whipping winds. The present stones—22 ft. high—comprise the fifth temple constructed on the site. The first probably consisted of an arch and circular earthwork furrowed in 3050 BC, and was in use for about 500 years. Its relics are the **Aubrey Holes** (white patches in the earth) and the **Heel Stone** (the rough block standing outside the circle). The present shape, once a complete circle, dates from about 1500 BC. The monument is still more impressive considering that its stones, weighing up to 45 tons, were hauled all the way from Wales and were erected by an tedious process of rope-and-log leverage—legend holds that the stones were magically transported here by Merlin. In 300 BC, Celts arrived from the Continent and claimed Stonehenge as their shrine; today, Druids are permitted to enter Stonehenge on midsummer to perform ceremonial exercises. *(☎(01980) 624 715. Open June-Aug. daily 9am-7pm; mid-Mar. to May and Sept. to mid-Oct. 9:30am-6pm; mid-Oct. to mid-Mar. 9:30am-4pm. £4.20, students & seniors £3.20, kids £2.50, family £10.60.)* Getting to Stonehenge from Salisbury doesn't require much effort—as long as you don't have a 45-ton rock in tow. **Wilts and Dorset bus** #3 runs from Salisbury station. *(☎(01722) 336 855. 40min., return $5.25.)* For the same price as a Salisbury-Stonehenge return, an **Explorer** ticket allows you to travel all day on any bus, including those stopping by **Avebury**, Stonehenge's less-crowded cousin. The most scenic **walking** or **cycling** route from Salisbury is the **Woodford Valley Route.** Go north on Castle Rd., bear left just before Victoria Park onto Stratford Rd., and follow the road over the bridge through Lower, Middle, and Upper Woodford. After about 9 mi., turn left onto the A303 for the last mile. If Stonehenge isn't enough rock for you, keep your eyes peeled to your right in Wilsford for Sting's Jacobean mansion.

PRACTICALITIES

GETTING THERE. **Trains** arrive from **Waterloo** every 30min. *(South Western Rd., across the Avon. ☎08457 484 950. 1½hr. £22-30.)* **National Express buses** make the trip from **Victoria Coach Station;** the tourist center sells tickets. *(8 Endless St. Bus station ☎(01722) 336 855; National Express ☎08705 808 080. 2¾hr., 4 per day. Return £13.10.)*

ORIENTATION & PRACTICAL INFORMATION. That all roads in Salisbury seem to lead to its cathedral gates is no accident—the streetplan was charted by Bishop Poore in the 13th century. The **Tourist Information Centre** is in the Guildhall, Market Sq., and runs 1½hr. **city tours.** *(Fish Row. ☎(01722) 334 956; www.visitsalisbury.com. Tours Apr.-Oct. 11am and 8pm; £2.50, children £1. Open June-Sept. M-Sa 9:30am-6pm, Su 10:30am-4:30pm; Oct.-Apr. M-Sa 9:30am-5pm; May M-Sa 9:30am-5pm, Su 10:30am-4:30pm.)*

ACCOMMODATIONS. Salisbury's proximity to Stonehenge breeds B&Bs but also "No Vacancy" signs. **YHA Salisbury Youth hostel** is tucked into a cedar grove; reservations are essential in summer. *(Milford Hill House, Milford Hill. ☎(01722) 327 572; fax (01722) 330 446. Lockout 10am-1pm. Curfew 11:30pm. Dorms £11, under 18 £7.60; annex £10, under 18 £6.90.)* **Matt and Tiggy's** is a welcoming 450-year-old house with warped floors and ceiling beams, with an overflow house nearby. Mellow, hostel-style, 2- to 4-person rooms. *(51 Salt Ln, just up from the bus station. ☎(01722) 327 443. Breakfast £2.50. Sheets £1. 2- to 4-bed dorms £11-12.)* Nearby, **Mrs. Taaffe** has cosy rooms with TV. *(34 Salt Ln. ☎(01722) 326 141. Singles £16; doubles £32.)*

STRATFORD-UPON-AVON

Shakespeare lived here. Admittedly, he got out as soon as he could, but even so millions make the pilgrimage here every year, showing their dedication by purchasing "Will Power" T-shirts, dining on faux-Tudor fast food, and dutifully traipsing through all the many sights vaguely connected to the Bard and his extended family. Yet for all that Stratford has milked its one cow beyond the morally reasonable, it remains deserving of a visit for the grace of the weeping Avon and the excellence of the Royal Shakespeare Company's theatrical productions.

SHAKESPEAREAN SIGHTS. Two combination tickets are available for Will-seekers. The **Heritage Trail** ticket covers the "official" Shakespeare sights in town—the Birthplace, Hall's Croft, and Nash's House and New Place. *(£8.50, students & seniors £7.50, kids £4.20.)* For fanatics, the **Combination Ticket** throws in the more distant Anne Hathaway's Cottage and Mary Arden's House. *(£12, students and seniors £11, kids £6.)* The least crowded way to pay homage is to visit the Bard's tiny grave in **Holy Trinity Church,** though groups still pack the arched door at peak hours. *(Trinity St. £1, students & kids 50p.)* **Shakespeare's Birthplace** is now half period recreation and half life-and-work exhibition. *(Henley St. ☎(01789) 204 016. Open Mar. 20-Oct. 19 M-Sa 9am-5pm, Su 9:30am-5pm; Oct. 20-Mar. 19 M-Sa 9:30am-4pm, Su 10am-4pm. £6, students & seniors £5.50, kids £2.50, family £15.)* **Hall's Croft** follows the work of Dr. John Hall, who aside from being Shakespeare's son-in-law was one of the first doctors to keep detailed records of his patients. *(Old Town. Open Mar. 20-Oct. 19 M-Sa 9:30am-5pm, Su 10am-5pm; Oct. 20-Mar. 19 M-Sa 10am-4pm, Su 10:30am-4pm. £3.50, students & seniors £3, kids £1.70, family £8.50.)* The first husband of Shakespeare's granddaughter Elizabeth, Thomas Nash has only a tenuous connection to the bard, but a ticket to **Nash's House** also gets you a peak at what little remains of **New Place,** Stratford's hippest home when Shakespeare bought it in 1597. *(Chapel St. Open Mar. 20-Oct. 19 M-Sa 9:30am-5pm, Su 10am-5pm; Oct. 20-Mar. 19 M-Sa 10am-4pm, Su 10:30am-4pm. £3.50, students & seniors £3, ids £1.70, family £8.50.)* Will's wife's birthplace, **Anne Hathaway's Cottage** is 1mi. north of Stratford along ill-marked footpaths. This is the thatched cottage on all the posters; if you've seen the birthplace, there's little need to go inside. *(☎(01789) 292 100. Open Mar.-Oct. daily 9am-5pm; Nov.-Feb. 9:30am-4:30pm. £4.50, students & seniors £4, kids £2.)* Three miles further along the paths, **Mary Arden's House** was restored in the style a Victorian entrepreneur determined to be precisely that of Shakespeare's mother. *(☎(01789) 293 455. Open Mar.-Oct. M-Sa 9:30am-5pm, Su 10am-5pm; Nov.-Feb. M-Sa 10am-4pm, Su 10:30am-4pm. £5.50, students & seniors £5, kids £2.50, family £13.50.)*

Stratford-upon-Avon

Stratford-upon-Avon

♠ **ACCOMMODATIONS**
Clodagh's B&B, **3**
Backpackers Hostel, **1**
YHA Stratford, **2**

THE PLAY'S THE THING. One of the world's finest repertory companies, the acclaimed **Royal Shakespeare Company** is what makes Stratford more than a exploitative tourist trap—and they even perform plays by other dramaturges. However, only the Bard's work graces the stage at the towering **Royal Shakespeare Theatre,** Waterside. Renaissance and restoration plays are given at the neighboring **Swan Theatre,** built to resemble a 16th-century playhouse, while the **Other Place,** on Southern Ln., is an black-box theater for more experimental work. If you don't manage to get tickets in advance, join the queue for the main box office, in the Royal Shakespeare Theatre foyer, about 20min. before opening for same-day sales. A happy few get returns and standing-room tickets for evening shows; queue 1-2hr. before curtain. The RSC also conducts **backstage tours** that cram camera-happy groups into the wooden "O"s of the RST and the Swan. (*Tours:* ☎412602. *Daily 1:30 and 5:30pm, and after performances. £4, students & seniors £3. Box office:* ☎(01789) 403 403, 24hr. info ☎(01789) 403 404; www.rsc.org.uk. Open M-Sa 9am-8pm. RST tickets £5-40, Swan £5-36, Other Place £10-20. Standing places £5 (RST & Swan only). Same-day tickets ½ price for under 25s, some at £8-12 for students & seniors—be ready to pounce.*)

PRACTICALITIES

GETTING THERE. Thames Trains serve Stratford's rail station from **Paddington.** (*Station Rd., off Alcester Rd.* ☎08457 484 950. 2¼hr., 7-10 per day. Return £22.50.) **National Express buses** stop at Riverside Car Park, off Bridgeway Rd. near the Leisure Centre; buy tickets at the tourist centre. (☎08705 808 080. 3hr., 3-4 per day. £11)

ORIENTATION & PRACTICAL INFORMATION. Stratford's center is barely half a mile across, with the train station at its western edge; to get to the **Tourist Information Centre** from the station, turn left into Alcester Rd. which becomes Greenhill St., Wood St., Bridge St., and finally Bridgefoot. (☎(01789) 293 127; bed booking hotline ☎(01789) 415 061. Open Apr.-Oct. M-Sa 9am-6pm, Su 11am-5pm; Nov.-Mar. M-Sa 9am-5pm.)

ACCOMMODATIONS. Be sure to make reservations well ahead in summer, especially for single rooms. **B&Bs** in the £15-26 range line Grove Rd., Evesham Pl., and Evesham Rd.; if that fails, try Shipston Rd. and Banbury Rd. across the river, a 15-20min. walk from the station. **Stratford Backpackers** is one for more sociable pilgrims, with a superb central location. *(33 Greenhill St. ☎/fax (01789) 263 838. Photo ID required. Dorms £12 1st night, £11 after.)* **YHA Stratford** is 2 mi. from town, but makes up with attractive grounds, a 200-year-old building, and friendly staff. *(Hemmingford House, Wellesbourne Rd., Alveston. ☎(01789) 297 093. Follow the B4086 road for 35min., or take the hourly #X18 bus from Bridge St. (£1.70). Midnight lockout. Breakfast included. 2- to 15-bed dorms £15.50, under 18 £11.50.)* For more privacy, **Clodagh's B&B** is one of Stratford's best values, with superb shared showers and internet access. *(34 Banbury Rd. ☎(01789) 269 714. Singles £16.50, doubles £33.)*

NEAR STRATFORD: WARWICK CASTLE

Many historians, architects, and fire-breathing dragons regard Warwick Castle as England's finest medieval fortress. Climb the 530 steps to the top of the towers and see the countryside unfold like a fairytale kingdom of hobbits and elves. The dungeons are filled with life-size wax figures of soldiers preparing for battle, while "knights" and "craftsmen" talk about their trades. *(☎(01926) 495 421, 24hr. recording ☎(01926) 406 600. Open Apr.-Oct. daily 10am-6pm; Nov.-Mar. 10am-5pm. Lockers £1. Mid-May to early Sept. £11.50, students £8.60, seniors £8.20, kids £6.75, family £30; Mar. to early May and early Sept. to mid-Feb. around £1 cheaper.)*

GETTING THERE. Trains come from **Stratford** and **London Marylebone.** *(Stratford: 20 min., 1 per hr., £2.50. Marylebone: 2½hr., 2 per hr., £24.50, day return £19.50.)* **National Express buses** make the journey from **Stratford** and **Victoria Coach Station.** *(Stratford: 4 per day, 15min., day return £2. London: 3 per day, 3hr. Day return £12.50.)*

Planning Your Trip

A CITY FOR ALL SEASONS

In a city as perennially popular with tourists as London, it's essential to plan your trip in advance—a week or two in the low season, up to two months ahead for the summer, Easter, and Christmas periods. Travelling in the low season can also save you money, and will give you more room to enjoy the city—though with 8 million "locals," tourists are rarely in a majority outside visitor attractions.

WEATHER. Summers tend to be mild though hot days visit London occasionally. It's just as rainy during the summer as it is the rest of the year. On a positive note, it doesn't get terribly cold in the winter; prepare for blustery wind and rain, not snow. London, by the way, isn't very foggy—the "pea soupers" of city lore were banished by clean-air legislation in the 1960s, which turned the city into a smoke-free zone.

Most temperatures in the UK are quoted using the Celsius scale, though many older people still prefer Fahrenheit. To convert from °C to °F multiply by 9/5 and add 32. To convert from °F to °C subtract 32 and multiply by 5/9.

AVG. TEMP. (LOW/HIGH), PRECIPITATION											
JANUARY			**APRIL**			**JULY**			**OCTOBER**		
°C	°F	mm	°C	°F	mm	°C	°F	mm	°C	°F	mm
6/2	43/36	54	13/6	55/43	37	22/14	72/57	59	14/8	57/46	57

Moooooore Room.

Real American Airlines deals
for students and faculty,
online at StudentUniverse.
Earn AAdvantage miles and
enjoy *more room throughout
Coach only on American*.

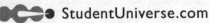 StudentUniverse.com

featuring
American Airlines

800.272.9676

TOURIST OFFICES

🔲 *Tourist information tailored to visitors from specific countries can be found at www.visitbritain.com. For **tourist information offices in London**, see the Service Directory, p. 317.*

London is represented abroad by the **British Tourist Authority** (BTA), and in the UK by the **London Tourist Board.** BTA offices abroad supply advance tickets to major attractions and travel passes as well as information on how to get to Britain, where to stay, and what to do. They also sell the **Great British Heritage Pass,** which gives entrance to almost 600 sights around Britain. (7 days £35, 15 days £46, 1 month £60.) BTA offices are found in:

Australia, Level 16, Gateway, 1 Macquarie Pl., Sydney NSW 2000 (☎(02) 9377 4400; fax 9377 4499). Open M-F 9am-5pm.

Canada, Air Transaat Building, Pearson Airport, Mississauga, Ontario L4V 1T1 (☎1-888-VISIT UK or (905) 405-1720; fax 405-1835). Open M-F 9am-5pm; phones M-F 10am-6pm.

Ireland, Britain Travel Centre, 18-19 College Green, Dublin 2 (☎(01) 670 8000; fax 670 8244). Open M, W-Th 9am-5:30pm, Tu 10am-5:30pm, F 9am-5pm, Sa 10am-2pm.

New Zealand, Level 17, New Zealand House, 151 Queen St., Auckland 1 (☎(09) 303 1446; fax 377 6965). Open M-F 9am-5pm.

South Africa, Lancaster Gate, Hyde Park Ln., Hyde Lane, Hyde Park, Johannesburg; mailing address PO Box 41896, Craighall 2024 (☎(011) 325 0342; fax 325 0344).

United States, 551 Fifth Ave., 7th Floor, New York, NY 10176 (☎1-888-462-2748). Open M-F 9am-6pm. Also 625 N. Michigan Ave., 10th floor, Chicago, IL 60611. Open M-F 9am-5pm.

ESSENTIAL INFORMATION

PUBLIC HOLIDAYS

During public holidays, commonly called bank holidays, London switches to a Sunday timetable: shops open limited hours, transportation is less frequent, and bars and restaurants close early. The exceptions are Christmas, when the entire city closes down, and New Year's Day and Good Friday, when many shops and restaurants remain closed. Holidays are always scheduled for Mondays, except for New Year, Christmas, and Boxing Day, which always fall on the same dates, and (obviously) Good Friday. Below is a list of the holidays and their dates for 2002; this only applies to England and Wales, as Scotland and Northern Ireland have their own holiday calendars.

New Year: January 1.

Good Friday: March 29.

Easter Monday: April 1.

May Day: May 6.

Spring: May 26.

August: August 26.

Christmas: December 25.

Boxing Day: December 26.

DOCUMENTS AND FORMALITIES

EMBASSIES & CONSULATES

BRITISH CONSULAR SERVICES ABROAD

🔲 *For up-to-date information on entry requirements and British consular services, check the Foreign Office (www.fco.gov.uk). For **foreign consular services in London,** see the Service Directory, p. 313.*

In general, while there may be numerous British consulates in a country, only a limited number will offer full consular services, including visa and work permit issuance. Forms are usually available from all consulates; ask the main consulate, embassy, or High Commission to find the nearest British diplomatic mission.

Australia, British High Commission, Consular Section, Level 10, SAP House, Akuna and Bunda Sts., Canberra ACT 2601 (☎01902 941 555; fax (02) 6257 5857; bhc.consular@uk.emb.gov.au; www.uk.emb.gov.au). Open M-F 8am-2pm.

Canada, British High Commission, Immigration Section, 80 Elgin Street, Ottawa, Ontario K1P 5K7; entrance on Queen St. (☎(613) 237-2008; fax 232-2533; www.britain-in-canada.org). Open M-F 9am-noon; phones M-F 10am-3pm.

Ireland, British Embassy, 29 Merrion Rd., Dublin 4 (☎(01) 205 3822=; fax 205 3890; www.britishembassy.ie). Open M-F 9:30am-noon; phones M-F 8:30-9:30am and 2-3pm.

New Zealand, British High Commission, Immigration Section, 44 Hill St., Wellington 1; mailing address P.O. Box 1812, Wellington (☎(04) 495 0889; fax 471 1974; www.brithigh-comm.org.nz). Open 9am-2pm; phones 9:30am-noon and 2-3:30pm.

South Africa, British High Commission, Visa Section, Liberty Life Place, Block B, 1st Floor, Glyn St., Hatfield, Pretoria 0083; mailing address PO Box 13611, Hatfield 0028 (☎(012) 483-1400; fax 483-1433; www.britain.org.za). Open M-F 8:15am-noon.

United States, British Embassy, 19 Observatory Circle NW, Washington D.C. 20008 (☎(202) 588-7800; fax 588-7850; www.britainusa.com). Open daily 8-11:30am. Visa services also offered at the following Consulates General:

> **Northeast:** 845 Third Ave., New York, NY 10022 (☎(212) 745 0200). Open M-F 9am-noon.

> **Midwest:** The Wrigley Building, 400 North Michigan Ave., Suite 1300, Chicago, IL 60611 (☎(312) 346 1810; fax 464 0661). Open M-F 9am-12:30pm.

> **West:** 11766 Wilshire Blvd., Suite 400, Los Angeles, CA 90025 (☎(310) 477-3322; fax 575-1450). Open M-F 8:30-11:30am.

PASSPORTS AND VISAS

ENTRY REQUIREMENTS. Citizens of European Union countries need only a valid national identity card to enter the UK; citizens of all other countries must be in possession of a valid passport and, if necessary, visa (see below). Note that while the Common Travel Area has abolished regular checks on travel between the UK and Ireland, travelers may still be required to produce the necessary documentation on arrival. Britain does not allow entrance if the holder's passport expires in under six months; returning home with an expired passport is illegal, and may result in a fine.

VISAS. European Union citizens do not need a visa to enter the UK. Citizens of Australia, Canada, New Zealand, South Africa, and the USA do not require visas for visits of under six months; for a complete list of countries with visa-free travel to the UK, check http://visa.fco.gov.uk/. Tourist visas cost £35, and can be obtained from the British consulates listed on p. 263. A visa or relevant permit is required by all non-EU citizens intending to **work** or **study** in the UK, or who intend to stay longer than 6 months for whatever reason. EU citizens staying over 3 months must apply for a residence permit after their arrival in the UK. For details of long-term visas and work, study, and residence permits, see **Living in London,** p. 301.

PHOTOCOPIES. Be sure to photocopy the page of your passport with your photo, passport number, and other identifying information, as well as visas, travel insurance policies, plane tickets, and traveler's check numbers. Carry one set of copies in a safe place, apart from the originals, and leave another set at home. Consulates also recommend that you carry an expired passport or an official copy of your birth certificate in a part of your baggage separate from other documents.

LOST PASSPORTS. If you lose your passport, immediately notify local police and your nearest national embassy or consulate. To expedite its replacement, you will need to know all information previously recorded and show ID and proof of citizenship. In some cases, a replacement may take weeks to process, and may be valid only for a limited time. Any visas in your old passport will be irretrievably lost. In an emergency, ask for temporary traveling papers that will permit you to re-enter your home country. Your passport is a public document belonging to your nation's government. You may have to surrender it to a foreign government official, but if you don't get it back in a reasonable amount of time, inform your nearest consulate.

IDENTIFICATION

When you travel, carry two or more forms of identification with you, including at least one photo ID; a passport combined with a driver's license or birth certificate usually suffices. To combat theft or loss, never carry all your IDs together.

For more information on the forms of identification listed below, contact the the **International Student Travel Confederation (ISTC),** Herengracht 479, 1017 BS Amsterdam, Netherlands (☎ +31 20 421 2800; fax 421 2810; istcinfo@istc.org; www.istc.org).

STUDENT, TEACHER, & YOUTH IDENTIFICATION. The **International Student Identity Card (ISIC),** the most widely accepted form of student ID, provides discounts on sights, accommodations, food, and transport. All cardholders have access to a 24hr. helpline for medical, legal, and financial emergencies (in North America call 877-370-ISIC, elsewhere call US collect +1 715-345-0505), and US-issued cardholders are also eligible for insurance benefits (see **Insurance,** p. 269). Many budget and student travel agencies issue ISICs; see p. 271 for details. The card is valid from September of one year to December of the next. Cards cost US$22 in the USA, significantly less in other countries (£6 in the UK), though holders of non-US issued cards are not eligible for insurance benefits. Applicants must be in further education, and be aged 13 or over. The **International Teacher Identity Card (ITIC)** offers similar benefits to teachers and academics for the same price. This one-year **International Youth Travel Card (IYTC;** formerly the GO 25 Card) offers travelers under 26 many of the same benefits as the ISIC. Most organizations that sell the ISIC also sell the IYTC (US$22).

MONEY

🔊 For inormation about getting, using, and saving money while in London, including tips on **budgeting,** **exchanging moneys,** and using **cash** and **credit cards** abroad, see Once in London, p. 45.

ℹ ESSENTIAL INFORMATION

PIN CUSHION

To use a cash or credit card to withdraw money from a cash machine (ATM) in Europe, you must have a four-digit Personal Identification Number (PIN). If your PIN is longer than four digits, ask your bank whether you can just use the first four, or whether you'll need a new one. Credit cards don't usually come with PINs, so if you intend to hit up ATMs in Europe with a credit card to get cash advances, call your credit card company before leaving to request one.

People with alphabetic, rather than numerical, PINs may also be thrown off by the lack of letters on European cash machines. The corresponding numbers to use are:

1=QZ
2=ABC
3=DEF
4=GHI
5=JKL
6=MNO
7=PRS
8=TUV9=WXY

Note that if you mistakenly punch the wrong code into the machine three times, it will swallow your card for good.

CURRENCY & EXCHANGE

THE POUND (£)		
AUS$1 = £0.36		£1 = AUS$2.75
CDN$1 = £0.45		£1 = CDN$2.22
IR£1 = £0.80		£1 = IR£1.25
NZ$1 = £0.30		£1 = NZ$3.33
ZAR1 = £0.084		£1 = ZAR11.90
US$1 = £0.69		£1 = US$1.44
EUR€1 = £0.63		£1 = EUR€1.58

The rates above were valid in August 2001; check newspapers or the *Let's Go* online currency converter (www.letsgo.com) for the latest exchange rates.

While there are no hard-and-fast rules, exchanging money in London is generally competitive with—and for North Americans, often cheaper than—exchanging it at home. However, you'll get the best rate by using a cash (ATM) card to withdraw money from your home account while in London, though a service charge ($1-5) may be applied per transaction. It's advisable to have enough ready cash in pounds to last your first few days, especially if arriving over a weekend or public holiday.

Money From Home In Minutes.

If you're stuck for cash on your travels, don't panic. Millions o
people trust Western Union to transfer money in minutes to over 18
countries and over 95,000 locations worldwide. Our record of safet
and reliability is second to none. You can even send money by phon
without leaving home by using a credit card. For more informatio
call Western Union: USA 1-800-325-6000, Canada 1-800-235-000

www.westernunion.com

WESTERN UNION | MONEY TRANSFER

The fastest way to send money worldwide.

TRAVELER'S CHECKS

🛈 *For advice on using traveler's checks in London, see p. 45. For traveler's check **refund hotline** numbers, see the Service Directory, p. 312.*

Traveler's checks are one of the safest and least troublesome means of carrying funds. Check issuers (**American Express, Thomas Cook,** and **Visa** are the most recognized) provide refunds for lost and stolen checks, and often additional services such as emergency message services and stolen credit-card assistance. Checks are issued in a range of major currencies; typically you will pay a 1-2% commission on checks bought (or cashed) in local currencies, while for those bought/cashed in foreign currencies, you'll lose on the exchange rate (though rates are often better than for cash), and may still have to pay commission. If you intend to use traveler's checks to pay for goods and services in London, be sure to buy pound-denominated checks, as very few establishments will accept foreign-denominated traveler's checks. Otherwise, you may find it better to buy checks in your home currency and take advantage of special traveler's-check exchange rates offered by British banks.

While traveling, keep check receipts and a record of which checks you've cashed separate from the checks themselves, and leave a list of check numbers with someone at home. Never countersign checks before you cash them, and always bring your passport as ID. If your checks are lost or stolen, contact your issuer's refund center to be reimbursed; they may require a police report verifying the loss or theft. Ask about toll-free refund hotlines and the location of refund centers when purchasing checks, and always carry emergency cash.

American Express: Call 800 25 19 02 in Australia; in New Zealand 0800 441 068; in the UK 0800 521 313; in the US and Canada 800-221-7282. Elsewhere call US collect +1 801-964-6665; www.aexp.com. 1-4% commission at AmEx offices and banks.

Citicorp: In the US and Canada call 800-645-6556; elsewhere call US collect +1 813-623-1709 (both 24hr.). 1-2% commission.

Thomas Cook MasterCard: In the US and Canada call 800-223-7373; in the UK call 0800 62 21 01; elsewhere call UK collect +44 1733 31 89 50. 2% commission. Thomas Cook offices, common in London, cash checks commission-free.

Visa: In the US call 800-227-6811; in the UK, 0800 89 50 78; elsewhere call UK collect +44 20 7937 8091. Call for the location of their nearest office.

CASH (ATM) AND CREDIT CARDS

🛈 *For info on **using cards** in London, including **cash advances,** see Once in London, p. 45.*

CREDIT CARDS. Where they are accepted, credit cards often offer superior exchange rates—up to 5% better than the retail rate used by banks and other currency exchange establishments. Credit cards may also offer services such as insurance or emergency help, and are sometimes required to reserve hotel rooms or rental cars. **MasterCard** and **Visa** are the most welcomed; **American Express** cards are less frequently accepted, **Diners Club** rarely, and **Discover** never. Credit cards are also useful for **cash advances,** which allow you to withdraw local currency from associated banks and ATMs abroad. If you intend to use your credit card extensively in London, alert your card issuer before leaving; otherwise, automated systems could block your card for "suspicious activity." If you will also be making cash advances through cash machines in London, you will need to ask your card issuer for a 4-digit PIN.

CASH (ATM) CARDS. Cash machines are common in London, and you should have no trouble accessing your home bank account from any British cash machine. ATMs get the same wholesale exchange rate as credit cards, but there is often a limit on the amount of money you can withdraw per day (around US$500), and typically also a charge of US$1-5 per withdrawal made by the issuing bank. Before you leave, memorize your PIN in numeric form since British cash machines do not have letters on their keys; also, if your PIN is longer than four digits, ask your bank whether you need a new number.

BUDGETING

It's a good idea to work out a daily budget and stick to it. Based on the estimates below, you could get away with spending £35 (US$50) a day, sharing a cheap B&B room, buying food in supermarkets, only hitting the free sights, and staying home at night, but £50 is a more reasonable minimum if you want to fully experience London.

Accommodations: count on spending at least £15 per person night in a dorm or a shared hotel room. For **longer stays** (over a week), you should be able to negotiate a discount.

Food: by shopping in supermarkets and eating frugally, you could get away with spending £8 per day; at restaurants you're unlikely to spend less than £15, even if you're careful.

Admissions charges range from nothing for many major museums to over £10 for popular attractions, so ask yourself if you really need to see that animated wax model of Elvis.

Entertainment & Nightlife can really add up: club covers are rarely under £10, and a pint of beer is about £3. Theater and concert tickets range from £5 for student standbys at off-West End locations to £20+ for cheaper tickets to a well-known show.

Transport: At a bare minimum, 2 bus rides a day will cost £2; for any serious sightseeing you should invest in a Travelcard (see p. 33), at least £4 a day or £15.90 a week.

CUSTOMS

Upon entering the UK, you must declare certain items from abroad and pay a duty on the value of those articles that exceeds the allowance established by the EU customs service. Note that goods and gifts purchased at **duty-free** shops abroad are not exempt from duty or sales tax at your point of return and thus must be declared as well; "duty-free" merely means that you need not pay a tax in the country of purchase. Upon returning home, you must similarly declare all articles acquired abroad and pay a duty on the value of articles in excess of your home country's allowance. In order to expedite your return, make a list of any valuables brought from home and register them with customs before traveling abroad. Also be sure to keep receipts for all goods acquired abroad. Upon entering Britain, you must declare certain items from abroad and pay a duty on the value of those articles that exceed the allowance established by the UK's customs service. It's wise to make a list, including serial numbers, of any valuables you carry from home (especially those made abroad); registering this list with customs before your departure and having an official stamp will avoid import duty charges and ensure an easy passage on your return.

HEALTH

◪ For advice on obtaining **urgent treatment** in the UK, see Once in London, p. 46. For how to obtain **long-term care**, see Living in London, p. 309. For listings of **clinics, emergency rooms** and **late-night chemists** (pharmacies), see the Service Directory, p. 311.

Common sense is the simplest prescription for good health. Drink lots of fluids, wear sturdy, broken-in shoes, and don't over-exert yourself. In your **passport,** write the names of any people you wish to be contacted in case of a medical emergency, and list any allergies or medical conditions of which you want doctors to be aware. Matching a prescription to a foreign equivalent is not always easy, safe, or possible. Carry up-to-date, legible prescriptions or a statement from your doctor stating the medication's trade name, manufacturer, chemical name, and dosage. While traveling, be sure to keep all medication with you in your carry-on luggage.

FIRST-AID KIT. For a basic first-aid kit, pack bandages, pain reliever, antiseptic cream, a thermometer, a Swiss Army knife, tweezers, moleskin, decongestant, diarrhea and stomach medication, antihistamines, sunscreen, burn ointment, and a syringe for emergencies (get an explanatory letter from your doctor).

PRE-EXISTING CONDITIONS. Those with medical conditions may want to obtain a Medic Alert ID tag (first year US$35, annually thereafter US$20), which identifies the condition and gives a 24hr. collect-call number. Contact the Medic Alert Foundation, 2323 Colorado Ave, Turlock, CA 95382, USA (☎1-888-633-4298; www.medicalert.org). **Diabetics** can contact **Diabetes UK** (☎0800 013 4443) or the **American Diabetes Association**, 1701 North Beauregard St., Alexandria, VA 22311 (☎1-800-232-3472 www.diabetes.org), to receive copies of the article "Travel and Diabetes" and a diabetic ID card. Those down under can contact **Diabetes Australia,** Churchill House, 1st fl., 218 Northbourne Ave., Braddon, ACT 2612 (☎ (02) 6230 1155).

IMMUNIZATIONS. Travelers over two years old should be sure the following vaccines are up to date: MMR (measles, mumps, and rubella); DTaP or Td (diptheria, tetanus, and pertussis), OPV (polio), HbCV (haemophilus influenza B), and HBV (hepatitus B).

HEALTH & TRAVEL INSURANCE

Falling ill or having an accident abroad can be extremely expensive—costs can easily run into hundreds of thousands of pounds. For your personal and financial well-being, therefore, it's important to make sure that you have adequate **medical coverage** for your trip. **UK residents, EU citizens** in posession of a valid E111 form (available from post offices before you depart), citizens of some **Commonwealth** countries, full-time **students** at UK institutions, and those **working** (legally) in the UK are eligible for free medical treatment through the National Health Service (see p. 309). Most private **US medical insurance** policies will cover costs incurred abroad, though be sure to check with your provider; you may be required to pay up-front for treatment and then claim the amount back later. **US Medicare** does *not* cover foreign travel. **Canadians** are protected by their home province's health insurance plan for up to 90 days after leaving the country; check with the provincial Ministry of Health or Health Plan Headquarters for details. If you're unsure whether you have sufficient coverage for your trip to London, consider purchasing **travel insurance,** which normally also covers property loss, trip cancellation/interruption, and emergency evacuation. Expect to pay around US$50 per week for full coverage.

US-issued **ISIC** and **ITIC** (see p. 264) provide minimal insurance benefits, including US$100 per day of in-hospital sickness for up to 60 days, US$3000 of accident-related medical reimbursement, and US$25,000 for emergency medical transport; that may sound like a lot, but won't get you far in London. Cardholders also have access to a toll-free 24hr. helpline for medical, legal, and financial emergencies overseas (US and Canada cardholders US collect +1 713-267-2525). Most **American Express** and **Visa** and **Mastercard Gold** or **Platinum** cards grant automatic car-rental insurance (collision and theft, but not liability) and in-transit flight accident coverage on purchases made with the card.

INSURANCE PROVIDERS. Council and **STA** (see p. 271) offer a range of plans that can supplement your basic coverage. Other insurance providers in the US and Canada include: **Access America** (☎ 800-284-8300); **Berkely Group/Carefree Travel Insurance** (☎ 800-323-3149; www.berkely.com); **Globalcare Travel Insurance** (☎ 800-821-2488; www.globalcare-cocco.com); and **Travel Assistance International** (☎ 800-821-2828; www.worldwide-assistance.com). Providers in the **UK** include **Campus Travel** (☎ 01865 25 80 00) and **Columbus Travel Insurance** (☎ 020 7375 0011). In **Australia,** try **CIC Insurance** (☎ 9202 8000).

ⓘ ESSENTIAL
INFORMATION

EU CUSTOMS

The 15 countries of the European Union (Austria, Belgium, Denmark, Finland, France, Germany, Greece, Ireland, Italy, Luxembourg, Netherlands, Portugal, Spain, Sweden, and the UK) form a single market for trade purposes.

This means that there are no customs controls at internal EU borders (i.e., you can take the blue customs channel at the airport), and travelers are free to transport whatever legal substances they like as long as it is for their own personal (non-commercial) use—which is officially interpreted to mean up to 800 cigarettes, 10L of spirits, 90L of wine (60L of sparkling wine), and 110L of beer. While it's perfectly legal to bring larger quantities, you'll need a pretty convincing explanation of how you intend to get through it all yourself!

You should also be aware that duty-free was abolished on June 30, 1999 for travel between EU member states; however, travelers between the EU and the rest of the world still get a duty-free allowance when passing through customs.

PLANNING YOUR TRIP HEALTH

GETTING THERE

BY PLANE

When it comes to airfares, a little effort can save you a bundle. If your plans are flexible enough to deal with the restrictions, courier fares are the cheapest. Tickets bought from consolidators and standby seating are also good deals, but last-minute specials, airfare wars, and charter flights often beat these fares. The key is to hunt around, to be flexible, and to ask persistently about discounts. Only those traveling on expense accounts should ever pay full price for a ticket.

AIRFARES

Airfares to London peak between June and mid-September, and again from early December to New Year. Fares are almost always much higher for trips that do not include a Saturday night. "Open return" tickets are normally pricier than fixing a return date when buying the ticket—check if you can change the date once you've booked. Round-trip flights are the cheapest; "open-jaw" (arriving in and departing from different cities) tickets tend to be pricier. On commercial airlines, patching one-way flights together is the most expensive way to travel; however many "budget" airlines charge independently for each segment. Depending on route and season, **fares** for roundtrip flights to London range: US$200-600 from the eastern USA and Canada, US$300-800 from the west; AUS$1300-1800 from Australia; NZ$2000-3500 from New Zealand; and ZAR4000-6000 from South Africa.

BUDGET & STUDENT TRAVEL AGENCIES

Travelers holding **ISIC, ITIC,** or **IYTC** cards (see p. 264) qualify for discount fares from student travel agencies. Most flights from budget agencies are on major airlines, but in peak season some may sell seats on less reliable chartered aircraft. A major advantage of student tickets over similarly-priced bucket-shop deals is that dates of travel can normally be changed for a small fee (US$20-40). Most of the following agencies have London offices; these are listed in the **Service Directory,** p. 311.

Council Travel (www.counciltravel.com). Countless US offices, including branches in Atlanta, Boston, Chicago, L.A., New York, San Francisco, Seattle, and Washington, D.C. Check the website or call 800-2-COUNCIL (226-8624) for the office nearest you.

STA Travel (www.statravel.com). The largest student and youth travel organization, with over 250 offices worldwide, including on or near most major campuses in the Australia, New Zealand, South Africa, the US, and the UK. Check the website for a listing of all their offices,

ℹ ESSENTIAL INFORMATION

INTERNET FLIGHT PLANNING

The Internet is one of the best places to look for travel bargains—it's fast and convenient, and you can spend hours exploring options without driving your travel agent insane.

Many airline sites offer special last-minute deals on their web pages, though these are often only available to those on their frequent-flier programs. For links to practically every airline in the world, see www.travelpage.com.

Trad-style travel agents: These sites do the manual legwork compiling deals, then contact you.

www.bestfares.com
www.onetravel.com
www.lowestfare.com
www.travelzoo.com

Student deals:

www.statravel.com
www.counciltravel.com
www.studentuniverse.com

Full travel services: Book your entire trip from airport pickup to restaurants.

msn.expedia.com
www.travelocity.com

Auction sites:

www.priceline.com. You name your price, but are obliged to buy any ticket that meets it. Be prepared for antisocial hours and odd routes.

www.skyauction.com. Bid on both last-minute and advance-purchase tickets.

Just one last note—to protect yourself, make sure that the site you use has a secure server before handing over any credit card details. Happy hunting!

or call the following numbers: Australia 1300 360 960; Canada and US 1-800-781-4040; New Zealand 0800 874 773; in South Africa call the Cape Town office at (021) 418 6570.

Student Universe (US ☎ 1-800-272-9676; www.studentuniverse.com). Internet-based student travel agency; for flights starting outside the US, call the number above. They don't require an ISIC card, so that's US$22 saved straight off.

Travel CUTS (Canadian Universities Travel Services), 187 College St., Toronto, ON M5T 1P7 (☎ 416-979-2406; fax 979-8167; www.travelcuts.com). 60 offices across Canada.

usit (www.usitworld.com). The international arm of Council Travel (see above), with offices on and near campuses in 18 countries worldwide. "Gateway" offices in major cities also offer services for arriving travelers, including discounted accommodations, tours, and theater tickets. Check the website for a listing of branches, or call the following reservation numbers: Ireland ☎ (01) 602 16 00; New Zealand ☎ 0800 874 823; South Africa ☎ 0860 000 111. usit is represented in Australia by **Student UNI Travel** (☎ (02) 9232 8444; www.sut.com.au).

DIRECT AIRLINE BOOKING

COMMERCIAL AIRLINES

The commercial airlines' lowest regular offer is the **APEX** (Advance Purchase Excursion) fare. Generally, reservations must be made 7-21 days ahead of departure, with seven- to 14-day minimum-stay and up to 90-day maximum-stay restrictions. These fares carry hefty cancellation and change penalties (fees rise in summer). Book peak-season APEX fares early; by May you will have a hard time getting your desired departure date. While major commercial carriers offer the most convenient flights, they won't come cheaply unless you can grab a last-minute or internet-only promotion. Some smaller commercial carriers offer cheaper rates for trans-Atlantic flights, though normally between a restricted set of destinations and involving an interchange. These include:

Icelandair: US ☎ 1-800-223-5500; www.icelandair.com. Stopovers in Iceland for no extra cost on most transatlantic flights. New York to London May-Sept. US$500-730; Oct.-May US$390-$450. For last-minute offers, subscribe to their email Lucky Fares.

Finnair: US ☎ 1-800-950-5000; www.us.finnair.com. Cheap round-trips from San Francisco, New York, and Toronto to Helsinki; connections throughout Europe.

Martinair: US ☎ 1-800-627-8462; www.martinair-usa.com. California or Florida to Amsterdam, then connect throughout Europe. Mid-June to mid-Aug. US$880; mid-Aug. to mid-June US$730.

EUROPEAN DISCOUNT AIRLINES

Travelers from Ireland and the continent can take advantage of the numerous no-frills budget airlines criss-crossing Europe. By only taking direct bookings, flying between lesser-known airports and cutting back on free drinks, food, and sometimes baggage allowances, this new breed of carrier offer regular services at prices that are often lower than trains and ferries, let alone commercial airlines.

buzz: UK ☎ 0870 240 70 70; www.buzzaway.com.

easyJet: UK ☎ 0870 600 00 00; www.easyjet.com.

go: UK ☎ 0845 605 43 21, elsewhere call UK +44 1279 66 63 88; www.go-fly.com.

Ryanair: Ireland ☎ 01 812 12 12, UK 0870 156 95 69; www.ryanair.ie.

CHEAP ALTERNATIVES

AIR COURIER FLIGHTS

Those who travel light should consider courier flights. Couriers help transport cargo on international flights by using their checked luggage space for freight. Generally, couriers must be over 21, travel with carry-ons only, and must deal with complex flight restrictions; flights are usually round-trip only, with short fixed-length stays (usually one week) and a limit of a one ticket per issue. You'll also have to pay an annual membership fee to the broker of $50-60. Most courier companies operate only out of major North American hubs. In summer, the most popular destinations usually require an advance reservation of about two weeks (you can usually book up to two months ahead). Super-discounted fares are common for "last-minute" flights (3-14 days ahead). Prices quoted below are round-trip to Europe.

Air Courier Association, 15000 W. 6th Ave. #203, Golden, CO 80401 (☎ 800-282-1202; www.aircourier.org). 10 departure cities in the US and Canada. US$150-360. Membership US$64.

International Association of Air Travel Couriers (IAATC), 220 South Dixie Highway #3, PO Box 1349, Lake Worth, FL 33460 (☎ (561) 582-8320; fax 582-1581; www.courier.org). From 9 North American cities. Membership US$45-50.

Global Courier Travel, PO Box 3051, Nederland, CO 80466 (www.globalcouriertravel.com). Searchable online database. Six departure points in the US and Canada, plus Sydney, Auckland, and Dublin. Membership US$40, 2 people US$55.

PACKING

Pack lightly: set out everything you think you'll need, then pack half of it and twice the money. For a long stay in London, you might prefer a **suitcase** to a conspicuous backpack.

Bring a small **daypack** for carrying things around, but don't go overboard—there's no need to carry any more than you would on a day out in your home city (OK, maybe a camera and *Let's Go*). If your hostel or hotel has a safe, leave your valuables there; otherwise keep your passport, and other valuables with you in a purse, neck pouch, or money belt. Bring a combination lock for your bag or for hostel lockers. Don't forget a sweater (even in summer), an alarm clock, and an umbrella or raincoat. Pack lightly!

FILM & CAMERAS

Film in London costs around £3.50 for a roll of 24 exposures. If you're not a serious photographer, you can save the hassle of bringing a proper camera and just purchase **disposable cameras** in London. Try to buy film at chemists (such as Boots) and supermarkets to avoid tourist rip-off prices.

CURRENT & ADAPTERS

In London, electric current is 240 volts AC, enough to fry any 110V North American appliance. Americans and Canadians should buy an adapter (which changes the shape of the plug) and a converter (which changes the voltage). European, South African, and New Zealand 220V and Australian 250V applliances will work fine on 240V; just bring an adapter.

Worldwide Courier Association (☎800-780-4359, ext. 441; www.massiveweb.com). From New York, San Francisco, L.A., and Chicago to London US$259-299. Membership US$58.

STANDBY FLIGHTS

Traveling standby requires considerable flexibility. Companies dealing in standby flights sell vouchers rather than tickets, along with the promise to get to (or near) your destination within a certain window of time (typically 1-5 days). You call in before your specific window of time to hear your flight options and the probability that you will be able to board each flight. You can then decide which flights to try to make, show up at the appropriate airport at the appropriate time, present your voucher, and board if space is available. Vouchers can usually be bought for both one-way and round-trip travel. You will receive a monetary refund only if every available flight within your date range is full; if you opt not to take an available flight, you can only get credit toward future travel. Carefully read agreements with as tricky fine print can leave you in the lurch. To check on a company's service record in the US, call the Better Business Bureau (☎(212) 533-6200). It is difficult to receive refunds, and clients' vouchers will not be honored when an airline fails to receive payment in time. One established standby company in the US is **Whole Earth Travel,** 325 W. 38th St., New York, NY 10018 (☎1-800-326-2009; fax (212) 864-5489; www.4standby.com) and Los Angeles, CA (☎888-247-4482), which offers one-way flights to Europe from the Northeast (US$169), West Coast and Northwest (US$249), Midwest (US$219), and Southeast (US$199).

TICKET CONSOLIDATORS

Ticket consolidators, or "bucket shops," buy unsold tickets in bulk airlines and sell them at discounted rates. The best place to look is in the Sunday travel section of any major newspaper, where many bucket shops place tiny ads. Call quickly, as availability is typically extremely limited. Not all bucket shops are reliable, so insist on a receipt that gives full details of restrictions, refunds, and tickets, and pay by credit card (2-5% fee) so you can stop payment if you never receive tickets. For more, see www.travel-library.com/air-travel/consolidators.html.

CHARTER FLIGHTS

Charters are flights a tour operator contracts with an airline to fly extra loads of passengers during peak season. Charter flights fly less frequently than major airlines, make refunds particularly difficult, and are almost always fully booked. Schedules and itineraries may also change or be cancelled at the last moment (as late as 48 hours before the trip, and without a full refund), and check-in, boarding, and baggage claim are often much slower. **Discount clubs** and **fare brokers** offer members savings on last-minute charter and tour deals. Study contracts closely; you don't want to end up with an unwanted overnight layover. One company is **Travelers Advantage,** Trumbull, CT, USA. (☎203-365-2000; www.travelersadvantage.com. US$60 annual fee includes discounts and cheap flight directories.)

BY CHANNEL TUNNEL

Traversing 27 mi. under the sea, the Chunnel is undoubtedly the fastest, most convenient, and least scenic route from the continent to Britain.

Eurostar, Eurostar House, Waterloo Station, London SE1 8SE (UK ☎0990 18 61 86; US ☎800-387-6782; elsewhere call UK +44 1233 61 75 75; www.eurostar.com). 10-28 trains per day to London from Paris (3hr., US$75-159) and Brussels (3hr., 50min., US$75-159). Tickets are available by phone, online, or from most European rail stations.

Eurolines, 52 Grosvenor Gardens, London SW1 (☎1582 400 694; www.eurolines.co.uk or www.eurolines.com) offers bus-chunnel combos. Unlimited 30-day (£229, under 26 and over 60 £199) or 60-day (£279/249) travel between 30 major European cities in 16 countries.

Eurotunnel (UK ☎08000 96 99 92; www.eurotunnel.co.uk) shuttles cars between Kent and Nord-Pas-de-Calais. Return fares for car and occupants range £219-299. Same-day return £110-150, 5-day return £139-195. Book online or via phone.

BY BOAT

The following fares listed are one-way for adult foot passengers unless otherwise noted. Though standard return fares are in most cases simply twice the one-way fare, fixed-period returns (usually within five days) are almost invariably cheaper. Ferries run year-round unless otherwise noted. **Bikes** are usually free, although you may have to pay up to £10 extra in high-season. For a **camper/trailer** supplement, you will have to add anywhere from £20-140 to the "with car" fare. A directory of ferries in this region can be found at www.seaview.co.uk/ferries.html.

Hoverspeed: UK ☎08702 40 80 70; France ☎03 21 46 14 54; www.hoverspeed.co.uk. Fast catamaran and hovercraft service to Dover from Calais (35-55min., every hr., £24) and Ostend, Belgium (2hr., 5-7 per day, £28); also Folkestone-Boulogne (55min., 3-4 per day, £24) and Newhaven-Dieppe (2¼-4¼hr., 1-3 per day, £28).

Irish Ferries: Ireland ☎01890 31 31 31; UK ☎08705 17 17 17; www.irishferries.ie. Rosslare-Pembroke (3¾hr.) and Dublin-Holyhead (2-3hr., return IR£20-60).

P&O Stena: UK ☎0870 600 0611; from Europe +44 1304 864 003; www.posl.com. Dover-Calais (1¼hr., every 30min.-1hr.; £24).

SeaFrance: UK ☎08705 71 17 11; France ☎03 21 46 80 00; www.seafrance.co.uk. Dover-Calais (1½hr., 15 per day, UK£15).

Stena Line: UK ☎01233 64 68 26; www.stenaline.co.uk. Fishguard-Rosslare (1-3½hr., £22-30); Holyhead-Dublin (4hr., £18-20); Holyhead-Dún Laoghaire (1-3½hr., £20-28); Stranraer-Belfast (1¾-3¼hr., £18-24; Mar.-Jan.).

SPECIFIC CONCERNS

WOMEN TRAVELERS

⚡ *Resources for women in London are listed in the Service Directory, p. 317.*

Even in a city as cosmopolitan and liberal as London, women traveling alone have extra safety concerns; the key is to be prepared, and not to act unduly rashly. In particular, just because you're on vacation, that doesn't mean you should do anything you wouldn't do at home. Most hostels offer women-only rooms or will make one up on request; you should also be sure in any hostel or hotel that your door locks properly from the inside. If a hostel has communal showers, check them out before booking. By choosing centrally located accommodations, you'll help avoid solitary late-night treks and Tube rides. Look as if you know where you're going and approach older women or couples for directions if you're lost or uncomfortable; always carry extra money for a phone call, bus, or taxi just in case, and memorize or write down the number of a local taxi firm before going out.

Generally, the less you look like a tourist, the better off you'll be. Wearing a conspicuous **wedding ring** may help prevent unwanted overtures; even a mention of a husband waiting back at the hotel may be enough to discount your potentially vulnerable, unattached appearance. Your best answer to verbal harassment is no answer at all; feigning deafness, sitting motionless, and staring straight ahead at nothing in particular will do a world of good that reactions usually don't achieve. The extremely persistent can sometimes be dissuaded by a firm, loud, and very public "Go away!" Don't hesitate to seek out a police officer or a passerby if you are being harassed. Memorize the emergency numbers in places you visit, and consider carrying a whistle or airhorn on your keychain. A self-defense course will not only prepare you for a potential attack, but will raise your level of awareness of your surroundings as well as your confidence.

TRAVELING ALONE

There are many benefits to traveling alone, including independence and greater interaction with locals. On the other hand, any solo traveler is a more vulnerable target of harassment and street theft. Lone travelers need to be well-organized and look confident at all times. Try not to stand out as a tourist, and be especially careful in deserted or very crowded areas. If questioned, never admit that you are traveling alone. Maintain regular contact with someone at home who knows your itinerary. For more tips, read *Traveling Solo* by Eleanor Berman (Globe Pequot Press; US$17) or subscribe to **Connecting: Solo Travel Network,** 689 Park Rd., Unit 6, Gibsons, BC V0N 1V7 (☎(604) 886-9099; www.cstn.org; membership US$28). Several services link solo travelers with companions who have similar travel habits and interests; contact the **Travel Companion Exchange,** P.O. Box 833, Amityville, NY 11701 (☎(631) 454-0880; www.whytravelalone.com; US$48).

OLDER TRAVELERS

▶ *Age Concern offers practical advice and information for the elderly in Britain. (☎8765 7200.)*

Travelers aged 60 or over can take advantage of discounts on museums, movies, theaters, and concerts at many locations in London; look for rates marked "concessions," "concs," or "OAP" (Old Age Pensioner). Even if you don't see a discount listed, it doesn't hurt to ask. Older travelers should be aware that London is not a friendly city for the mobility-impaired; unless you have a love of stairs, travel on the Tube at your peril. See **Travelers with disabilities,** below, and the paragraph on disabled acces to transportation in **Once in London,** p. 34, for more information.

No Problem! Worldwise Tips for Mature Adventurers, by Janice Kenyon (Orca Book Publishers; US$16) and *Unbelievably Good Deals and Great Adventures That You Absolutely Can't Get Unless You're Over 50*, by J. Rattner Heilman (NTC/Contemporary Publishing; US$13) are good resources for mature travelers. The following organizations offer trips targeted at an older audience.

Elderhostel, 11 Ave. de Lafayette, Boston, MA 02111 (☎877-426-8056; www.elderhostel.org). 1- to 4-week "educational adventures" in London on varied subjects for those 55+.

The Mature Traveler, P.O. Box 15791, Sacramento, CA 95852 (☎800-460-6676). Deals, discounts, and travel packages for the 50+ traveler. Subscription $30.

GAY AND LESBIAN TRAVELERS

▶ *For gay and lesbian **resources** in London, see the Service Directory, p. 314.*

Soho, particularly around Old Compton St., is London's gay nexus, though gay bars and pubs can be found throughout the city; *Let's Go* has included numerous rainbow-toting cafes, bars, and nightclubs in neighborhood listings. *Boyz* (www.boyz.co.uk) is the main gay listings and lifestyle magazine for London (free from gay bars and clubs), while www.gingerbeer.co.uk offers the lesbian lowdown.

RESOURCES

Gay's the Word, 66 Marchmont St., London. The UK's largest gay bookshop. See p. 236.

Giovanni's Room, 1145 Pine St., Philadelphia, PA 19107 (☎215-923-2960; www.queerbooks.com). An international lesbian/feminist and gay bookstore with mail-order service.

Out and About (www.planetout.com) offers a bi-weekly newsletter addressing travel concerns and a comprehensive site addressing gay travel concerns.

FURTHER READING

Spartacus International Gay Guide 2001-2002. Bruno Gmunder Verlag (US$33).

Damron's Accommodations and *The Women's Traveller.* Damron Travel Guides (US$14-19).

Ferrari Guides' Gay Travel A to Z, Ferrari Guides' Men's Travel in Your Pocket, and *Ferrari Guides' Inn Places.* Ferrari Publications (US$16-20). Purchase online at www.ferrariguides.com.

TRAVELERS WITH DISABILITIES

▶ *Resources for disabled travelers in London are listed in the Service Directory, p. 313. For information on accessibility on **public transportation**, see Once in London, p. 34.*

London makes few concessions to disabled travelers. The Tube is almost entirely out-of-bounds to those who cannot handle steps, buses and taxis are rarely wheelchair enabled, and few hostels, B&Bs, and cheap (and not-so-cheap) hotels have lifts. Though refurbishment has rendered some theaters and concert halls accessible, the vast majority remain without wheelchair bays or elevators. Those with disabilities should always inform airlines and hotels of their needs when making reservations, both to determine what facilities are available and to give them time to prepare. Call ahead to restaurants, museums, and other establishments to find out about accessibility.

Britain has strict quarantine regulations on animals entering the country to avoid rabies; **guide dogs** (seeing-eye dogs) fall under the new PETS regulations; pets coming from EU countries, Australia and New Zealand can avoid quarantine by being microchipped, vaccinated, bloodtested, and certified against tapeworm and ticks before entering the UK. All other animals will be quarantined for six months. Call the PETS helpline at 0870 0241 1710 or consult www.maff.gov.uk/animalh/quarantine.

The London Tourist Board's *London For All* leaflet, available at London Visitor's Centres (see p. 317), includes information on accessibility in London. *Access in London*, by Gordon Couch (Quiller Press; $12) is an in-depth guide to accommodations, transport, and accessibility in London.

USEFUL ORGANIZATIONS

Mobility International USA (MIUSA), P.O. Box 10767, Eugene, OR 97440 (☎(541) 343-1284, voice and TDD; www.miusa.org). Sells *A World of Options: A Guide to International Educational Exchange, Community Service, and Travel for Persons with Disabilities* (US$35).

Society for the Advancement of Travel for the Handicapped (SATH), 347 Fifth Ave., #610, New York, NY 10016 (☎212-447-7284; www.sath.org). An advocacy group that publishes free online travel information and the travel magazine *OPEN WORLD* (US$18, free for members). Annual membership US$45, students and seniors US$30.

Directions Unlimited, 123 Green Ln., Bedford Hills, NY 10507 (☎1-800-533-5343). Books individual and group vacations for the physically disabled.

TRAVELERS WITH CHILDREN

⚐ *For information on child and family discounts on* **transportation** *in London, see p. 33. For* **children's** **activity** *hotlines, see the Service Directory, p. 312.*

Family vacations require that you slow your pace and plan ahead. If you decide to stay in a B&B or small hotel, call ahead and make sure it's child-friendly. If you rent a car, make sure the rental company provides a car seat for younger children. **Be sure that your child carry ID** in case of an emergency or in case he or she gets lost.

Many museums, shows, and tourist attractions offer discounts for children, often at the same "concession" rate as students and seniors, as well as "family" tickets (normally for two adults and two children, not necessarily related). Most large museums in London also offer special activity packs and tours for children. B&Bs and hotels typically offer discounts for children sharing an adult's room, while restaurants will often be willing to prepare specail child-sized portions. Infants under two generally fly for 10% of the adult fare on international flights when sitting on an adult's lap, while those aged 2-11 get a seat for 75% of the adult fare.

ⓘ ESSENTIAL INFORMATION

SENDING MAIL TO LONDON

Airmail provides a rapid and affordable service for letters and small parcels. Current delivery times and rates to London are as follows (correct as of 2001):

Australia: 4-5 days. AUS$1.50 for up to 50g.

Canada: 3-5 days. CA$1.05 for up to 20g.

Ireland: 2-3 days. IR£0.30 for up to 35g.

New Zealand: 7 days. NZ$2 for up to 200g (max size 120mm.235mm.10mm).

South Africa: 7 days. ZAR3 for up to 50g.

US: 3-5 days. US$0.80 for up to 1oz.

For information on **addressing mail** for Britain, and on **sending mail within and from Britain,** see Once in London, p. 39.

LONDON CALLING

To call London from abroad, first, dial the international dialing prefix (in Australia, 0011; Canada or the US, 011; the Republic of Ireland or New Zealand 00; South Africa, 09); second, dial the country code for the UK, (44); third, dial the London city code less the leading zero (20); and last, the local 8-digit number.

For information on **calling within and from London,** see Once in London, p. 40.

The London Tourist Board publishes the pamphlet *Where to Take Children*, filled with child-friendly sights, restaurants, and services, and available at London Visitor's Centres. For general info on holidaying with children, consult one of the following books:

Backpacking with Babies and Small Children, Goldie Silverman. Wilderness Press (US$10).

Take Your Kids to Europe, Cynthia W. Harriman. Cardogan Books (US$18).

How to take Great Trips with Your Kids, Jane Portnoy. Harvard Common (US $10).

Have Kid, Will Travel: 101 Survival Strategies for Vacationing With Babies and Young Children, Claire and Lucille Tristram. Andrews McMeel Publishing (US$9).

Adventuring with Children: An Inspirational Guide to World Travel and the Outdoors, Nan Jeffrey. Avalon House Publishing (US$15).

Trouble Free Travel with Children, Vicki Lansky. Book Peddlers (US$9).

DIETARY CONCERNS

In a country battered by foot-and-mouth disease and besieged by mad cows, it's not surprising that one in five Britons aged under 25 are vegetarian. Almost all restaurants offer a range of vegetarian dishes. South Indian **bhel poori** and **Thai-Chinese Buddhist** buffets are increasingly popular with budgetarians of all dietary persuasions for their cheap, filling, and wholesome fare, including plenty for vegans.

Bhel poori and Buddhist restaurants are also a boon to **kosher** travelers, since they offer religiously exacting standards and a complete absence of meat products. Jews with a taste for meat, or who prefer to eat in rabbinically certified establishments, will spend most of their mealtimes in the enclaves of North London, particularly **Golders Green** (see p. 122). For more information, check out the *Jewish Travel Guide*, by Michael Zaidner (Vallentine Mitchell; US$17). Travelers who keep **halal** will have little trouble eating well in London, as long as they have a good appetite for North Indian, Turkish, and middle-eastern food. **Marylebone** and **Bayswater** have the highest concentration of Lebanese restaurants and Islington the most Turkish. While Indian restaurants are fairly ubiquitous (though not all are *halal*), the **East End** is known for its large Bangladeshi community.

ADDITIONAL INFORMATION

USEFUL PUBLICATIONS

London A-Z, Geographers Map Co. (£6). The world's best map, for the world's best city.

Time Out magazine has detailed listings for entertainment, nightlife, and exhibitions in London. On sale every W; £2.20.

The Guardian newspaper on Sa contains *The Guide*, a pocket-sized entertainment, nightlife, and events supplement, also with TV and radio listings. 50p.

WORLD WIDE WEB

For tips and website listings for buying airline tickets on the web, see p. 271.

Almost every aspect of budget travel is accessible via the web. Within 10min. at the keyboard, you can buy airline tickets, make a reservation at a hostel, and get hot tips from other travelers who have just returned from London. Listed here are some budget travel sites to start off your surfing; other relevant web sites are listed throughout the book. Because website turnover is high, use search engines (such as www.google.com) to strike out on your own.

THE ART OF BUDGET TRAVEL

How to See the World: www.artoftravel.com. Travel tips, from cheap flights to self defense to interacting with local culture.

Rec. Travel Library: www.travel-library.com. A fantastic set of links for general information and personal travelogues.

Backpacker's Ultimate Guide: www.bugeurope.com. Tips on packing, transport, and where to go. Also country-specific travel info.

Backpack Europe: www.backpackeurope.com. Helpful tips, a bulletin board, and links.

INFORMATION ON LONDON

London Tourist Board: www.londontouristboard.com. Information for visitors, including addresses of London Visitor Centers.

LondonTown: www.londontown.com. Tourist information, special offers, maps, listings, and resources for travelers with special needs.

Visit Britain: www.visitbritain.com. The British Tourist Associationwebsite. Lots of useful information about visiting Britain and London.

This Is London: www.thisislondon.co.uk. Run by the Evening Standard newspaper, with news, reviews, and listings for a local audience, including jobs, classifieds, and long-term accommodations.

Transport For London: www.londontransport.co.uk. Comprehensive information on public transportation in London, including ticket prices and current service reports.

London Theatre Guide: www.londontheatre.co.uk. Reviews, listings, tickets, chatrooms, and theater seating plans.

CIA World Factbook: www.odci.gov/cia/publications/factbook/index.html. Tons of vital statistics on Britain's geography, government, economy, and people.

PlanetRider: www.planetrider.com. A subjective list of links to London's "best" cultural and tourist-oriented websites.

AND OUR PERSONAL FAVORITE...

Let's Go: www.letsgo.com. Our constantly expanding website features photos and streaming video, online ordering of all our titles, info about our books, a travel forum buzzing with stories and tips, and links that will help you find everything you ever wanted to know about London.

Accommodations

Sorry folks, but this isn't going to be pretty. Just as real estate prices make Londoners clutch their heads and scream, hotels and hostels are incredibly expensive. The further bad news is that high prices are not often a sign of quality, with grotty or, at best, achingly kitsch interiors, surly staff, and draconian payment procedures being the norms. For information on how to find **Long-term accommodations,** see Living in London, p. 307.

ACCOMMODATIONS TIPS

PLAN AHEAD. No matter where you plan to stay, it is essential to plan ahead, especially in summer. In a pinch, **tourist offices** can help you find a room (see **Service Directory,** p. 317), while private hostels will usually grant you a patch of floorspace if all else fails. When reserving in advance, it's worth the price of a phone call or fax to **confirm a booking.** Almost all accommodations require a **deposit** to secure the reservation; the proprietor should specify the amount (usually one night's stay) and advise on the best way to make payment (usually by credit card). Be sure to check the **cancellation policy** before handing over the deposit; most require 24hr. notice, but some are entirely non-refundable.

DISCOUNTS. Most B&Bs offer discounted rates for **long-term** stays (over a week), though not all advertize the fact—be sure to ask, and insist, if necessary—while most private hostels offer super-cheap weekly rates for guests staying over a month. Another good source of discounts is travelling in the **low season,** generally consider to be October through March, excepting Christmas (although September, April, and May are slow enough that you may be able to wrangle a few pounds' discount); again, B&B and hostel owners may be open to a little gentle persuasion. If you're brave enough to arrive in London without prearranged accommodation and lucky enough to find a hotel with a vacancy in the afternoon or early evening, you're in a strong bargaining position—if you don't take the room, it will most likely go empty.

PAYMENT. It's perfectly normal (though not defensible) for accommodations in London to demand full payment on arrival—that way, you can't just up and leave if you don't like the room or find somewhere nicer. For this reason, always insist on being shown the room before handing over any money; that way, you'll only lose your one-night deposit should the room turn out to be unacceptable.

The vast majority of accommodations accept payment by either cash, credit card, or sterling travelers cheques—note that almost nowhere will accept travelers checks made out in foreign currency, and those that do use horrendous exchange rates to make the conversion. A number of lower-end accommodations don't take credit cards, so be sure to find out before checking in; those that do often levy a 3-5% surcharge for those paying by plastic. Conversely, you may be able to negotiate a small reduction for cash payments (but don't count on it).

TYPES OF ACCOMMODATION

HOSTELS

Hostels offer travelers a bed in a shared dormitory, and are a great way of meeting fellow travelers; if you're traveling alone, a hostel is almost certainly your cheapest option. Shared dorms can hold anything from 3 to 20 beds, typically on a sliding price scale with smaller rooms being more expensive. Hostels in London are either run by the **Youth Hostel Association** (YHA), an affiliate of Hostelling International (HI), or are independent **private hostels;** the difference is explained below.

YHA/HI HOSTELS

YHA hostels (www.yha.org.uk) are invariably more expensive than private ones, but are generally better kept, with well-maintained bathrooms, more facilities, and knowledgable staff; reductions for under 18s make them popular with families. On the other hand, they tend to be more institutional-feeling, and draw a less bohemian crowd. While bedding is included in the price at all London hostels, towels are not; some hostels offers towels for sale, otherwise you must supply your own. All hostel rooms are equipped with large lockers that require your own padlock (available for purchase at hostels; £3). Most YHA hostels operate cheap cafeterias for dinner, and can supply a picnic lunch; all have laundry facilities and well-equipped kitchens.

MEMBERSHIP. To take full advantage of YHA hostels, you need to be a member of the YHA or another HI-affiliated hostelling association, such as the American Youth Hostels (AYH). Non-members can stay in YHA hostels, but must purchase a "Welcome Stamp" for the first six nights (£2.10), after which you become a full member; you can also purchase membership straight away. In addition to being able to stay at YHA hostels, HI members are eligible for a range of discounts on sights and activities in London. *(Adults, 1-parent families, and groups £12.50; under 18 £6.25; family £25.)*

RESERVATIONS. YHA hostels in London are invariably oversubscribed; in the summer, beds fill up months in advance, and sometimes hostels have not been able to accommodate every written request for reservations, let alone walk-ins. However, hostels occasionally hold a few beds free until a few days before, and in a large hostel there's a good chance that someone will fail to show up or check-out early—it's always worth asking. If you want to risk it without reservations, turn up as early as possible and expect to queue; otherwise, directly with the hostel in question, or the central YHA or HI system. *(☎ 7373 3400; lonres@yha.org.uk; www.yha.org.uk. Telephone bookings taken M-Sa 9am-5pm.)*

PRIVATE HOSTELS

Private hostels vary widely in price and quality, but as a rule are cheaper and have a more "fun" feel than their YHA equivalents—with a few exceptions, they also have fewer facilities and a less family-friendly atmosphere (many have a minimum age of 16 or 18). On the other hand, a lack of formal rules and the general laissez-faire attitude means that those who value privacy, quiet, and tidiness should think again about staying at a private hostel—though a few are as well-run as any YHA equivalent. As with YHA hostels, prices generally include sheets but not towels, and most have kitchens (in various states of repair).

RESIDENCE HALLS

Over summer vacation, many of London's universities and college turn their student residences into vast budget hotels, offering B&B-style accommodation at hostel prices. Most residence halls have student-priced bars, TV lounges, and games rooms with pool, ping-pong, and/or foosball tables. The downside is that rooms tend to be fairly ascetic—standard student digs—and shared bathrooms rather institutional; additionally, the bulk of accommodation is single rooms, with the occasional twin and triple, so they're not ideal for couples or large groups. All halls have shared "pantries" (small kitchens), but they're mostly designed for students to hear tins of baked beans in; kitchenware, crockery, and cutlery are rarely supplied.

Given their low prices, great locations, and good facilities, it's not surprising that residence halls fill extremely rapidly; it's often necessary to book months in advance. Moreover, many halls don't take walk-ins, so some form of advance booking is required, even if just the night before. Many of London's colleges run a **central accommodations office:**

University College London Residential Services, 24-36 Bidborough St., (☎ 7554 7780; fax 7554 7781). Tube: King's Cross/St. Pancras. Runs 8 halls, mostly around Bloomsbury. Rooms available Apr and mid-June to mid-Sept. Office open M-F 9am-5pm.

King's Campus Vacation Bureau, 127 Stamford St., SE1 (☎ 7928 3777; fax 7928 5777; vac.bureau@kcl.ac.uk; www.kcl.ac.uk). Tube: Waterloo. Accommodations at the halls of King's College London, mostly located on the South Bank.

B&BS AND HOTELS

Bed and Breakfasts—or B&Bs—are smallish hotels, usually in a converted townhouse, run by a family or a proprietor. The term "B&B" encompasses accommodations of wildly varying quality and personality, often with little relation to price. Some are nothing more than budget hotels that serve breakfast, with small, dreary, and bare rooms. Others (often on the same street as their nightmarish doubles) are unexpected oases of comfort, beautifully decorated and with excellent facilities. A **basic room** means that you share the use of a shower and toilet in the hall. A room **with bath** contains a private shower or bath and a toilet, and tends to cost £10-20 more. Be aware, however, that in-room showers are often awkward prefab units jammed into a corner. **Family room** in B&B lingo generally means a quad or quint with at least one double bed and some single beds. Most B&Bs serve **English breakfasts**—eggs, bacon, toast, fried bread, baked beans, tomato (baked or stewed), and tea or coffee. **Continental breakfast** means some form of bread, cereal, and hot drink.

Apart from B&Bs, a few **hotels** descend into the realms of the affordable—or at least, overlap in price with London's ridiculously expensive B&Bs. In general, these fall into two catefories. The first is once-grand hotels that never modernised. On the one hand, you've got lifts, bars, restaurants, and sometimes even bell-hops; on the other, it can be like a trip back in time to the 1970s, with aging decor, dodgy plumbing, and a radio pre-set to stations that haven't broadcast for 20 years. The second category are the increasingly numerous and ultra-modern **chain hotels,** which offer large well-equipped rooms. The downside to these, aside from a lack of character, is that they're only economic for travelers in groups of two or more, since they usually charge a flat rate per room; additionally, breakfast is rarely included in the prices. Advance booking is strongly recommended.

ACCOMMODATIONS BY PRICE

UNDER £20			
Dean Court Hotel	Bayswater	International Student House	Marylebone
✷ The Generator	Bloomsbury	Pickwick Hall International Backpackers	Bloomsbury
Hyde Park Hostel	Bayswater	Quest Hotel	Bayswater
Hyde Park Inn	Bayswater	✷ YHA Hampstead Heath	North

£20-30	
▨ Arosfa Hotel	Bloomsbury
Carr-Saunders Hall	Bloomsbury
City University Finsbury Residence	Clerkenwell
Commonwealth Hall	Bloomsbury
Garden Court Hotel	Bayswater
George Hotel	Bloomsbury
Georgian House Hotel	Westminster
▨ High Holborn Residence	West End
Hotel Orlando	West
▨ Hyde Park Rooms Hotel	Bayswater
▨ Indian YMCA	Bloomsbury
▨ Kandara Guesthouse	North
Langland Hotel	Bloomsbury
Lord Jim Hotel	Earl's Court
LSE Bankside House	South Bank
Mowbray Court Hotel	Earl's Court
Oxford Hotel	Earl's Court
Passfield Hall	Bloomsbury
Roseberry Hall	Clerkenwell
▨ Star Hotel	North
Wellington Hall	Westminster
Windsor Guest House	West
YHA City of London	City
YHA Holland House	Kensington
YHA Oxford St.	West End
YHA Rotherhithe	East
YHA St. Pancras International	Bloomsbury

£30-40	
Abbey House Hotel	Kensington
▨ Admiral Hotel	Bayswater
Alexander Hotel	Westminster
Barry House Hotel	Bayswater
Cardiff Hotel	Bayswater
Edward Lear Hotel	Marylebone
Hadleigh Hotel	Marylebone
▨ Hampstead Village Guest House	North
Hotel Ibis Euston	Bloomsbury
James & Cartref House	Belgravia
▨ Jenkins Hotel	Bloomsbury
Melbourne House	Westminster
Mitre House Hotel	Bayswater
▨ Morgan House	Belgravia
▨ Luna Simone Hotel	Westminster
Ruskin Hotel	Bloomsbury
Seven Dial's Hotel	West End
▨ Travel Inn County Hall	South Bank
▨ Vicarage Private Hotel	Kensington

OVER £40	
Beaver Hotel	Earl's Court
▨ Crescent Hotel	Bloomsbury
Kensington Gardens Hotel	Bayswater
Number 7 Guesthouse	South
Royal National Hotel	Bloomsbury
▨ Swiss House Hotel	Kensington

Prices given refer to **cost per person** in the cheapest typical accommodation: a shared dorm in a hostel, a single room in a residence hall, or a double in a B&B or hotel.

ACCOMMODATIONS BY NEIGHBORHOOD

THE WEST END

SEE MAP, p. 330-331

▨ **NEIGHBORHOOD QUICKFIND: Discover,** p. 2; **Sights,** p. 79; **Museums&Galleries,** p. 139; **Food&Drink,** p. 159; **Nightlife,** p. 190; **Entertainment,** p. 209; **Shopping,** p. 226.

Accommodations in this area are scarce at any budget—unless you book months in advance, you won't find a bed here. If you want to be close to the Soho action, don't forget that many Bloomsbury accommodations are but a short walk away.

▨ **High Holborn Residence,** 178 High Holborn, WC1V 7AA (☎7379 5589; fax 7379 5640; www.lse.ac.uk/vacations). Tube: Holborn or Tottenham Court Rd. Comfortable, modern residence well located for Covent Garden exploits. Accommodation is in "flats" of 4-5 rooms, each with phone, sharing well-equipped kitchen and bathroom; ensuite rooms much larger. Some rooms wheelchair-enabled. Elevator, laundry, bar, TV room, and games room. Continental breakfast included. Open mid-June to late Sept. Singles £28-35; twins £47-57, with bath £57-67; triples with bath £67-77. Rates highest in July, lowest mid-Aug. to Sept. MC, V.

YHA Oxford Street, 14-18 Noel St. (☎7734 1618; fax 7734 1657; oxfordst@yha.org.uk). Tube: Oxford Circus. Small, sparse hostel, with limited facilities but an unbeatable location for Soho nightlife. One 2-bed "dorm" has a double bed. Windowless lounge with TV and internet terminal and stuffy bathrooms contrast with large, light, and well-equipped kitchen. Linen included. Towels £3.50. Prepacked continental breakfast £3.30. Reserve at least 1 month ahead. 3- to 4-bed dorms £21.50, under 18s £17.50; 2-bed dorms £23.50.

Outlet, 32 Old Compton St. (☎7287 4244; fax 7734 2249; homes@outlet.co.uk; www.outlet4homes.com). Tube: Piccadilly Circus or Leicester Sq. Shared apartments around Old Compton St. for gays and lesbians, plus complete flats for all. See website for pics. Office open M-F 10am-7pm, Sa noon-5pm. Up to 30% discount for long stays. Studio apartments from £80, 1-bedroom from £100, 2-bedroom from £120, 3-bedroom from £150. Shared accommodation (gay/lesbian only) from £45 doubles, £65 with private bathroom. Also manages long-term apartments. MC, V.

Seven Dials Hotel, 7 Monmouth St., WC2H 9DA (☎7240 0823; fax 7681 0792). Tube: Covent Garden or Holborn. The fantastic location of this tiny B&B compensates for the occasionally quirky accommodation. Rooms are pleasantly furnished if smaller than average; those at the front are brighter, with triple glazing to keep out the noise. All have TV, phone, kettle, and sink; most have ceiling fan. English breakfast included. Reserve well ahead; 72hr. cancellation policy. Singles £65, with shower £75, with bath £85; doubles £75, with shower £85; with bath £95; twin with bath £100; triple with bath £115. AmEx, MC, V.

CLERKENWELL

SEE MAP, pp. 334-335

⚑ *NEIGHBORHOOD QUICKFIND: Discover, p. 6; Sights, p. 92; Museums&Galleries, p. 143; Food&Drink, p. 166; Nightlife, p. 194; Entertainment, p. 213.*

City University Finsbury Residences, 15 Bastwick St., EC1Y 3PE (☎7040 8035; fax 7040 8563; www.city.ac.uk/ems). Tube: Barbican. Don't judge a building by its cover—this might be a grim 1970s tower block, but the inside is freshly renovated, and it's in walking distance of City sights, Islington restaurants, and Clerkenwell nightlife. Standard singles in the main building; Peartree Court, next door, has apartments for 3-6. English breakfast included. Rooms available late June to mid-September. £21; Peartree Court £25 per person. MC, V.

Rosebery Hall, 90 Rosebery Ave., EC1R 4TY (☎7278 3251; fax 7278 2068). Tube: Angel. Exit left from the Tube, cross the road, and take the second right into Roseberry Ave (10min.) Modern student residence in two buildings arranged around a sunken garden. Rooms are plain but modern, with phone, sink, and standard narrow beds. "Economy twins" are just singles with an extra bed. Rooms in the newer block are more spacious, with handicap-enabled bathrooms. TV lounge, laundry, and bar. Open Easter and mid-June to mid-Sept. Reserve 6 weeks ahead for July with 1 night or 25% deposit; £10 cancellation fee. English breakfast included. Singles £26-31; twins £46, economy £36, with bath £57; triples £55. MC, V.

CITY OF LONDON

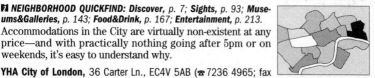

SEE MAP, p. 334-335

⚑ *NEIGHBORHOOD QUICKFIND: Discover, p. 7; Sights, p. 93; Museums&Galleries, p. 143; Food&Drink, p. 167; Entertainment, p. 213.*

Accommodations in the City are virtually non-existent at any price—and with practically nothing going after 5pm or on weekends, it's easy to understand why.

YHA City of London, 36 Carter Ln., EC4V 5AB (☎7236 4965; fax 7236 7681). Tube: St. Paul's. Housed in the beautifully frescoed former buildings of St. Paul's Choir School, within spitting distance of the cathedral. The interior is standard hostel, though: ageing interlocking bunks, vinyl and formica canteen and lounges. Single-sex dorms all have sinks and lockers. Secure luggage storage, currency exchange, laundry, and internet access. English breakfast and linens included. Towels £3.50. Reception 7am-11pm. Private room rates: single £27.80, under 18 £23.70; double £51, £41 if includes one child under 16; triple £72, £61; quad £94, £82; quint £118, £102; sextuple £138, £123. Dorms (prices per person): 3-4 bed £24.70, under 18 £21; 5-8 beds £23.50, £19.90; 10-15 beds £21.15, £18.90. MC, V.

SOUTH BANK

SEE MAP, p. 336-337

⚑ *NEIGHBORHOOD QUICKFIND: Discover, p. 7; Sights, p. 100; Museums&Galleries, p. 144; Food&Drink, p. 168; Entertainment, p. 214.*

Though the South Bank possesses some of the best views in London, its budget hotels don't—still, where else in London could you roll out of bed and be breakfasting by the Thames in under five minutes? While it's not the best place for night owls, it's perfect for culture vultures, and with the City, West End, and Westminster a bridge away, you'd be hard pressed to find a more convenient base for sightseeing.

Travel Inn County Hall, Belvedere Rd., SE1 7PB (☎0870 238 3300; fax 7902 1619; www.travelinn.co.uk). Tube: Westminster or Waterloo. Though it's in County Hall (see p. 101), don't expect any grand views from this budget chain—the river front is hogged by a Marriott. On the other hand, you're seconds from the South Bank and Westminster. All 313 rooms are clean and modern, with bathroom, kettle, and TV. Facilities include elevator, restaurant, and bar. Prices by the room, making it a great deal for families. Reserve at least 1 month ahead; cancel by 4pm on day of arrival. Continental breakfast £5, English £6, kids £3.50. Doubles/ singles and family rooms (2 adults + 2 kids) £74.95. AmEx, MC, V.

LSE Bankside House, 24 Sumner St., SE1 9JA (☎7633 9877; fax 7574 6730; www.lse.ac.uk/vacations). Tube: Southwark or London Bridge. Another of the London School of Economics' well-kept student halls, facing the back of the Tate Modern. Over 500 rooms, all with phone. Facilities include elevator, laundry, TV lounge, games room, and bar. Open July 6-Sept. 28, 2002. English breakfast included. Singles £28, with bath £41; twins with bath £55.50; triples with bath £81; quads with bath £93. Some rates higher without reservations: singles £35, with bath £60; twins with bath £70. MC, V.

WESTMINSTER

SEE MAP, p. 338-339

🎯 NEIGHBORHOOD QUICKFIND: Discover, p. 8; **Sights,** p. 106; **Museums&Galleries,** p. 145; **Food&Drink,** p. 169; **Entertainment,** p. 215; **Shopping,** p. 232.

Pimlico, south of Victoria station, is a gridlike district of towering late Georgian and early Victorian terraces that are home to dozens of B&Bs—among them some of London's best. However, virtually none have elevators, so if stairs are a problem be sure to request a ground-floor room. While Pimlico itself has little to offer the visitor, Westminster Abbey, Parliament, and Buckingham Palace are minutes away, and Victoria's fantastic transportation links put all of London within easy reach.

RESIDENCE HALLS

Wellington Hall, 71 Vincent Sq. SW1P 2PA (☎7834 4740; fax 7233 7709; reservations ☎7928 3777). Tube: Victoria. A beautiful Edwardian building overlooking Westminster School's playing fields. Smallish rooms have sink; ask for one overlooking the square rather than the busy road at the back. What the bathrooms lack in privacy, the breakfast room makes up for in mock-Tudor magnificence. TV lounge, pool table, laundry, and bar. Open Easter and mid-June to mid-Sept. English breakfast included. Singles £27.50; twins £42.

B&BS

Luna Simone Hotel, 47/49 Belgrave Rd. (☎7834 5897; fax 7828 2474; www.lunasimonehotel.com). Tube: Victoria or Pimlico. Stuccoed Victorian facade conceals ultra-modern yellow and blue rooms with TV, phone, kettle, and hairdryer. Sparkling bathrooms compare favorably with hotels triple the price, while the breakfast room could be mistaken for a hip noodle bar. On the downside, some singles are cramped. English breakfast included. Reserve 2 weeks ahead; 48hr. cancellation policy. Singles £40, low season (Nov.-Easter) £35, with bath £35/45; doubles £80/60, with bath £65/50; triples with bath £100/80. 10% discount for stays over 7 nights in low season. MC, V.

Alexander Hotel, 13 Belgrave Rd., SW1V 1RB (☎7834 9738; fax 7630 9630; www.alexanderhotel.co.uk). Tube: Victoria. Recently renovated rooms, eclectically furnished with quality fittings, dark-tiled bathrooms, and satellite TV. A halbard-wielding suit of armor keeps order in the breakfast room. Prices vary according to demand. Singles £35-65, doubles £65, triples from £85, quads and quints £100-120. MC, V.

Georgian House Hotel, 35 St. George's Drive, SW1V 4DG (☎7834 1438; fax 7976 6085; www.georgianhousehotel.co.uk). Tube: Victoria. Rooms are large and well equipped, with TV, phone, hairdryer, kettle, and matching furniture. Top-floor "student" rooms, available to all, are smaller with fewer fittings. Rooms in the annex, on Cambridge St., have bath but no phone. English breakfast included. Reserve 1 month ahead for Sa-Su and student rooms. Singles £36, student £26, with bath £49, annex £43; doubles £42, £48, £66, £56; triples £63, £69, £82, £72; quads with bath £90, student £70, annex £82; quints with bath £96. MC, V.

Melbourne House, 79 Belgrave Rd. (☎7828 3516; fax 7828 7120; www.melbournehousehotel.co.uk). Tube: Pimlico. An extraordinarily clean, well-kept establishment. Non-smoking rooms all have TV, phone, and kettle; their pride and joy is the superb basement double, with triangular bathtub large enough for two. Continental breakfast included. Reserve 2 weeks ahead; 48hr. cancellation policy. Singles £30, with bath £55; doubles with bath £75; triples with bath £95; quad with bath £110. MC, V (payment on arrival; cash preferred).

Surtees Hotel, 94 Warwick Way, SW1 (☎7834 7163/7394; fax 7460 8747; www.surtees-hotel.co.uk). Tube: Victoria. Window ledges and a front yard overflowing with flowers welcome guests to this friendly B&B. Larger rooms range from a bunk-bed quad to the giant 6-bed, two-room basement suite. Doubles and triples are on the small side but bright and nicely decorated. English breakfast included. Singles £30, with bath £50; doubles £55, £65; triples £70, £80; quad £80, £90; family suite with bath £100. AmEx, MC, V.

KNIGHTSBRIDGE & BELGRAVIA

◪ NEIGHBORHOOD QUICKFIND: Discover, p. 9; **Sights,** p. 109; **Food&Drink,** p. 171; **Shopping,** p. 233.

Belgravia's accommodation is concentrated on **Ebury St.,** a fairly busy road of Georgian terraces that's as close to Victoria and Sloane Sq. as it is to Belgravia proper. Not that that's a disadvantage—on the contrary, with Westminster's sights and Chelsea's shops within walking distance, you'd be hard pressed to do better. Many B&Bs here are in such demand that prices and quality often seem out of step.

SEE MAP, p. 338-339

▧ Morgan House, 120 Ebury St., SW1W 9QQ (☎7730 2384, fax 7730 8442; www.morgan-house.co.uk). Tube: Victoria or Sloane Sq. Charming staff welcome guests to 11 beautifully kept if small rooms, with TVs, kettles, phones for incoming calls, and occasionally fireplaces. English breakfast included. Reserve 2-3 months ahead, especially for the 3 ensuite rooms. Singles £42, with bath £65; doubles £62, £80; quad with bath £120. MC, V.

James and Cartref House, 108 and 129 Ebury St., SW1 9QD (☎7730 7338/6176; fax 7730 7338; www.jamesandcartref.co.uk). Tube: Victoria. Really two separate B&Bs on opposite sides of Ebury St., under the same family's ownership. The James looks in better shape, with well-kept rooms and hallways and a bright breakfast room overlooking the garden; the Cartref feels older, though with more ensuite rooms and an ornate dining room with fireplace. All rooms come with TV, kettle, hairdryer, and fan. English breakfast included. Reserve with 1 night deposit; 10% non-refundable, rest refundable on 2 weeks' notice. Singles £50, with bath £60; doubles £68, £82; triples £90, £105; family room (1 double and 2 bunks for kids under 12) with bath £130. MC, V.

KENSINGTON & EARL'S COURT

◪ NEIGHBORHOOD QUICKFIND: Discover, p. 9; **Sights,** p. 112; **Museums&Galleries,** p. 146; **Food&Drink,** p. 172; **Entertainment,** p. 216; **Shopping,** p. 233.

Surprisingly for such a chi-chi neighborhood, Kensington is not entirely devoid of affordable accommodations—then again, it's a big place and a "Kensington" address doesn't necessarily put you within walking distance of the main sights and shops. Decidedly less chi-chi **Earl's Court** remains deservedly popular with backpackers and budget travelers, with good transportation and local amenities compensating for the slightly out-of-the-way location.

SEE MAP, p. 340-341

KENSINGTON

YHA Holland House, Holland Walk, W8 7QU (☎7937 0748; fax 7376 0667; holland-house@yha.org.uk). Tube: High St. Kensington or Holland Park. On the edge of Holland Park, accommodation is split between a 17th-century mansion and a less attractive 1970s unit; dorms in both are similar, with 12-20 interlocking bunks. Caters mostly to groups. Facilities include lockers, laundry, TV room, luggage storage, and kitchen. Breakfast included. Book 1 month ahead in summer. £20.50, under 18 £18.50. AmEx, MC, V.

▧ Vicarage Private Hotel, 10 Vicarage Gate, W8 4AG (☎7229 4030; fax 7792 5989; www.londonvicaragehotel.com). Tube: High St. Kensington. Beautifully kept Victorian house with ornate hallways, TV lounge, and superbly appointed rooms: cast-iron beds, solid wood furnishings, and luxuriant drapes, all with kettle and hairdryer, ensuite rooms also with TV.

Welcome to

Abbey House

Hospitality, Quality & Genuine Value in the Heart of London.

If you are planning a trip to England and looking for a B&B in London Abbey House is the place to stay. Situated in a quiet garden square adjacent to Kensington Palace, this elegant Victorian house retains many of its original features including the marble entrance hall and wrought iron staircase. Once the home of a Bishop and a member of Parliament it now provides well maintained quality accommodation for the budget traveller who will be well looked after by its owners the Nayachs.

Write or call for a free colour brochure.

Recommended by more travel guides than any other B&B.

ABBEY HOUSE HOTEL

11 Vicarage Gate, Kensington, London W8 4AG

Reservations: 020-7727 2594
Fax: 020-7727 1873

www.AbbeyHouseKensington.com

Bathrooms new and spotless. English breakfast included. Reserve months ahead with 1 night's deposit; US$ personal checks accepted for deposit with at least 2 months notice. Singles £45; doubles £74, with bath £98; triples £90; quads £98. No credit cards.

Swiss House Hotel, 171 Old Brompton Rd., SW5 A11 (☎7373 2769; fax 7373 4983; www.swiss-hh.demon.co.uk). Tube: Gloucester Rd. or South Kensington. Beautiful B&B, from the plant-filled hall to the large rooms with wood floors and canopied beds. All rooms have TV, phone, fan, and bathroom. Book 2-3 months ahead for summer. Continental breakfast included; English breakfast £6. Singles £68, with shower only £48; doubles £85-99; triples £114; quads £128. 5% discount for stays over 7 nights and cash payments. AmEx, MC, V.

Abbey House Hotel, 11 Vicarage Gate, W8 4AG (☎7727 2594; fax 7727 1873; www.abbey-housekensington.com). Tube: High St. Kensington. Spacious, pastel rooms with TV, desk, sink, and matching furniture. Very helpful staff. 5 bathrooms between 16 rooms. 24hr. free tea, coffee, and ice room. English breakfast included. Singles £45, doubles £74, triples £90, quads £100. Winter discounts available. No credit cards.

EARL'S COURT

All listings nearest Tube: Earl's Court.

YHA Earl's Court, 38 Bolton Gdns., SW5 0AQ (☎7373 7083; fax 7835 2034). Tube: Earl's Court. Rambling Victorian townhouse that's more casual than most YHAs. Ongoing refurbishment is replacing interlocking triple-deckers with proper bunks and adding dozens of modern bathrooms. The 3- to 16-bed dorms, with lockers and sink, are all single sex. Garden, kitchen, laundry, 2 TV lounges, internet access, and luggage storage. Reserve 1 month ahead with full payment; £5 cancellation charge. Linen included. Prepacked continental breakfast £3.30. Dorms £18.50, under 18s £16.50; twins £51, including breakfast. AmEx, MC, V.

Beaver Hotel, 57-59 Philbeach Gdns. (☎7373 4553; fax 7373 4555). From the talking elevator to separate smoking and non-smoking TV lounges, the Beaver displays unusual attention to detail. Rooms range from basic basics with phone and washbasin to 2 new plush ensuite doubles with matching curtains and bedspreads, TV and hairdryer; bathrooms are spotless, many with bathtub. English breakfast included. Singles £40, with bath £60; doubles with bath £85; triples with bath £99. Car parking £8. AmEx, MC, V.

Mowbray Court Hotel, 28-32 Penywern Rd. (☎7373 8285/7370 3690; fax 7370 5693; www.m-c-hotel.mcmail.com). Large B&B making a claim for hotel status with elevator and bar. Rooms vary from smallish to enormous, the slightly dated feel compensated by facilities including TV, trouser press, hairdryer, and phone. Single beds are unusually wide, bathrooms unusually nice. Continental breakfast included. Reserve well ahead for larger rooms; 24hr. cancellation policy. Singles £45, with bath £52; doubles £56, £67; triples £69, £80; quads £84, £95; quints £100, 110; sextuples £115, £125. Discounts for long stays. AmEx, MC, V.

Oxford Hotel, 24 Penywern Rd., SW5 9SU (☎7370 1161; fax 7373 8256; oxfordhotel@btinternet.com). Rooms are a decent size, but minimally furnished: most have a bed, a TV, a clothes rail, and maybe a chair. Check the mattresses before you commit; those in the annex down the road tend to be better. Continental breakfast included. Reserve 2-3 weeks ahead for June. Singles with shower only £35, with bath £49; doubles £55, £65; triples £66, £76; quads £83, £89; quints £100, £110. 10-15% reduction for stays over 1 week. AmEx, MC, V.

Philbeach Hotel, 30-31 Philbeach Gdns. (☎7244 6884; fax 7244 0149; www.philbeachhotel.freeserve.co.uk). London's largest gay and lesbian B&B. The reception and TV lounge promise 3-star luxury, but rooms vary considerably: "budget singles" are extremely basic, while one ensuite double features a cast-iron bedframe, writing desk, and full bay window. Standard rooms have TV, phone, kettle, and sink. Continental breakfast. Budget singles £35, regular £50, with bath £60; doubles £60, with bath £69; triples £75, £100. AmEx, MC, V.

BAYSWATER

NEIGHBORHOOD QUICKFIND: Discover p. 10; Food&Drink, p. 174; Entertainment, p. 217; Shopping, p. 236.

Bayswater is London's B&B central—it seems as though every sidestreet is lined with converted Victorian houses offering rooms to all takers. Roads around **Queensway,** such as **Inverness Terrace, Queensborough Terrace,** and **Leinster Square** are home to a number of basic backpacker hostels. On the other side of

SEE MAP, p. 342

If you are on a budget, but still have high standards, come to the

Euro Hotel

And here's why...

The hotel dates from 1807

- Clean comfortable rooms with TV, tea & coffee and telephone
- Superb all-you-can-eat full English breakfast
- A quiet and safe neighborhood
- A short walk from Central London's attractions, nightlife, and shopping
- Special rates for children
- Discount for long stays
- Prices from £51 to £120 per room

Everyone gets a friendly welcome at the Euro Hotel. Visitors from every country of the world return time and again because of its friendly staff, its fantastic location, and its reasonable prices. If you are travelling outside the peak season, be sure to ask for a special price!

The breakfast parlor overlooks the garden

EURO HOTEL
53 Cartwright Gardens
London WC1H 9EL
Tel: 011 44 207 387 4321
Fax: 011 44 207 383 5044

email: reception@ eurohotel.co.uk

Visit our web site at www.eurohotel.co.uk

Bayswater, the area around **Paddington** is convenient for travelers arriving from Heathrow: **Sussex Gardens** has a high concentration of dependable accommodations.

A word of warning for the elderly, infirm, and those with small children: almost all the B&Bs are in converted 5- or 6-storey townhouses, almost invariably with **very steep staircases**. Either go for one of the very few with elevators (described in listings) or ask for a room on a lower floor.

HOSTELS

▨ **Hyde Park Hostel,** 2-6 Inverness Terr., W2 3HY (☎ 7229 5101; fax 7229 3170; www.astorhostels.com). Tube: Queensway or Bayswater. Space-filling configuration of bunks in 12-bed women's and 18-bed mixed dorms leaves little room, and foam-pad mattresses could be chunkier, but smaller rooms are more spacious and bathrooms a cut above average. Internet access, hip late-bar with DJs and bands Th-Sa, cafeteria, kitchen, laundry, pool/TV lounge, secure luggage room. Continental breakfast and linen included. Ages 16-35 only. Reserve 2 weeks ahead for summer; 24hr. cancellation policy. Online booking with 10% non-refundable deposit. 12-bed dorms £10-12; 10-beds £12.50-14; 8-beds £14-15.50; 6-beds £15-16.50; 4-beds £16-17.50; quads £16-17.50; twins £20-22.50 per person. MC, V.

Hyde Park Inn, 48-50 Inverness Terr., W2 3JA (☎ 7229 0000; fax 7229 8886; www.hyde-parkinn.com). Very cheap and fairly cheerful. Smaller dorms are more spacious than the 10-bed room. Internet, laundry, kitchen, lockers (£1 per day), luggage store (£1.50 per bag per day). Continental breakfast included. £10 deposit for linen and keys. 10-bed dorms £9-11, 8-bed £11-12, 6-bed £12-14, 4-bed £14.50-17, 3-bed £15.50-19, double/twins £18-21, singles £29-32. MC, V (2.5% surcharge).

Dean Court Hotel, 57 Inverness Terr., W2 (☎ 7229 2961; fax 7727 1190). Tube: Bayswater. A hybrid B&B/hostel, with many of the advantages of both. Sleep soundly in real beds (no bunks!). Only 3 showers and 1 bath for 70 beds, though. All rooms have sink; 24hr. kitchen and TV lounge access. Call 2 days ahead for dorms (no deposit); longer for hotel rooms (24hr. cancellation policy). Linen and English breakfast included; towels included only for hotel rooms. Dorms £17, doubles £48, twins £49, triples £70, quads £80. AmEx, MC, V.

Quest Hotel, 45 Queensborough Terr., W2 3SY (☎ 7229 7782; fax 7727 8106; www.astor-hostels.com). Tube: Bayswater or Queensway. Another in the Astor chain, but much smaller and not as well kept as the Hyde Park Hostel (see above). Dorms are all mixed sex, and most have bathrooms; those that don't could be 2 floors from a shower. No-smoking policy only enforced on request. No lockers; leave valuables at reception. Kitchen. Continental breakfast and linen included. Book months ahead for the 2 twins, 2-3 weeks for dorms in summer. 4- to 8-bed dorms £15-16; twins £20 per person. MC, V.

HOTELS AND BED & BREAKFASTS

▨ **Admiral Hotel,** 143 Sussex Gdns., W2 2RY (☎ 7723 7309; fax 7723 8731; www.admiral143.demon.co.uk). Tube: Paddington. Beautifully kept family-run B&B, all non-smoking. 19 rooms with bathroom, TV, and kettle, decorated in summer colors with autumnal bedspreads. Haters of prefab cabins should request a rooms with a "real" bathroom. Call 10-14 days ahead in summer; 4-day cancellation policy. Singles £48, low season (Oct.-Mar.) £40; doubles £70, low season £55; triples £75-90; quads £88-100; quints £92-115. MC, V.

▨ **Hyde Park Rooms Hotel,** 137 Sussex Gdns. W2 2RX (☎ 7723 0225; fax 7723 0965). Tube: Paddington. That rarest of species—a B&B run by a Londoner. White rooms with fluorescent-colored bedspreads all have sink and TV, and most benefit from solid wood furniture with tall wardrobes. The one quad is lit only by skylight, but makes it up in size. Timer-less electric-bar heating requires active temperature control. Reserve 2 weeks ahead in summer. 24hr. cancellation policy. Singles £30, with bath £40; doubles £40-45; with bath £50-55; triples and quad £20 per person, with bath £24. AmEx, MC, V (5% surcharge).

Barry House Hotel, 12 Sussex Pl., W2 2TP (☎ 7723 7340; fax 7723 9775; hotel@barry-house.co.uk; www.barryhouse.co.uk). Tube: Paddington. Very bright if slightly tight rooms with phone, TV, kettle, and hairdryer. Almost all have tiny (but not prefab) ensuite bathrooms, with 2 bathrooms between the 3 bathless singles. Reserve 6 weeks ahead in summer; 4-day cancellation policy. Singles £38, Jan.-Feb. £32; singles with bath £50, £48; doubles £78, £65; triples £92, £75; quads £114, £99; quints £125, £109. AmEx, MC, V (3% surcharge).

Cardiff Hotel, 5-9 Norfolk Sq., W2 1RU (☎ 7723 9068; fax 7402 2342; stay@cardiff-hotel.com; www.cardiff-hotel.com). Tube: Paddington. All rooms have cream fleur-de-lys wallpaper, TV, kettle, and phone; most have new wood furnishings, including desk; and the majority are reasonably sized and bright. Singles can be a little cramped, as are most ensuite bathrooms, but they are all almost clinically clean. English breakfast included. 48hr. cancellation policy. Singles with shower only £45, with bath £55-69; doubles with bath £79, triples with bath £90; quads with bath £99; quints with bath £120. MC, V.

Garden Court Hotel, 30-31 Kensington Gdns. Sq., W2 4BG (☎7229 2553; fax 7727 2749; www.gardencourthotel.co.uk). Tube: Bayswater or Queensway. The snazzy reception feels like a 3-star Tuscan resort—but rooms are solidly English B&B: varying widely in size, but all decorated to a high standard and equipped with sink, TV, hairdryer, and phone. Guests have access to the patio garden. Reserve at least 1 week ahead in summer; strict 14-day cancellation policy. English breakfast included. Singles £39, with bath £58; doubles £58, £88; triples £72, £99; family quad (2 double beds) £82, £120. MC, V.

Kensington Gardens Hotel, 9 Kensington Gdns. Sq., W2 4BH (☎7221 7790; fax 7792 8612; www.kensingtongardenshotel.co.uk). Tube: Bayswater or Queensway. A tall, narrow Victorian townhouse with numerous period details. It's worth the climb up the steep stairs to reach the well-appointed rooms with kettle, TV, phone, minibar, fan and hairdryer on demand, and even a welcome bowl of snacks and nibbles. All rooms have pleasant ensuite bathrooms; the 4 shower-only singles share 3 hall toilets. Continental breakfast included; English breakfast £5.50. Singles £58-62, doubles £85, triple £105. MC, V.

Mitre House Hotel, 178-184 Sussex Gdns., W2 1TU (☎7723 8040; fax 7402 5695; reservations@mitrehousehotel.com; www.mitrehousehotel.com). Tube: Paddington. 70 rooms, an elevator, bar, lounge, and breakfast room with windows mark this out as a hotel among the throngs of B&Bs surrounding it. Rooms vary widely in size and brightness; ask for one at the front, or best of all on the corner. All rooms have satellite TV, phone, and decent ensuite bathrooms, many with bathtub. Confusing nomenclature: "Family rooms" are 2-room suites (triple and double) with a shared bathroom, while "Junior suites" are large, single-room doubles, with lounge area and jacuzzi. English breakfast included. 48hr. cancellation policy. Singles £70, doubles £80, triples £90, family £100, junior suite £110. AmEx, MC, V.

MARYLEBONE & REGENT'S PARK

⊞ NEIGHBORHOOD QUICKFIND: Discover, p. 11; **Sights,** p. 114; **Museums&Galleries,** p. 147; **Entertainment,** p. 217; **Food&Drink,** p. 174.

SEE MAP, p. 344-345

Marylebone's West End-fringe location means that while it's not short on accommodations, these are usually far beyond the price range of anyone but those on corporate expense accounts. While there are a number of B&Bs, don't expect facilities or rooms to be up to, say, Bloomsbury standards: here, you're paying to be in walking distance of Oxford St. Though little happens after dark, the number of buses trundling past Marble Arch mean you're never more than a short night-bus ride away from Soho.

HOSTELS

International Student House, 229 Great Portland St., W1B 1SH (☎7631 8300; fax 7631 8315; accom@ish.org.uk; www.ish.org.uk). Tube: Great Portland St. A thriving international metropolis in a great location near Regent's Park and minutes from Oxford Circus. Most rooms similar size, varying primarily in the number of beds—singles seem huge, bunk-bedded quads less so—and have desk, sink, phone, and fridge. Spartan 8- to 10-bed dorms have sink and lockers. Facilities include 3 bars (open to 3am F-Sa), nightclub/venue, cheap cafeteria, fitness center (£3 per day), cinema, and laundry; guests get 15min. free internet, then £2 per hr. Continental breakfast included except for dorms (£2); English breakfast £3. £10 key deposit. Reception M-F 7:45am-10:30pm, Sa-Su 8:30am-10:30pm. Reserve min. 1 month ahead. Singles £31, with bath £33; twins £45, with bath £51; triples £60; quads £70; dorms £10 per person. Weekly rates (Sept.-May): single £188, twin £280. MC, V.

BED AND BREAKFASTS

Edward Lear Hotel, 28-30 Seymour St., W1H 5WD (☎7402 5401; fax 7706 3766; edwardlear@aol.com; www.edlear.com). Tube: Marble Arch. This was once the home of Ed Lear, though no owls nor pussies are here. The rooms may be basic, but you just have to face it: for the location it's really not dear. Be wary of rooms with just showers: you may find the cubicle towers right next to the bed: choose one with bath instead, unless you like integral showers. All rooms have phone, kettle, TV; in the lounge you can email free. Plus there's breakfast included, and so we concluded: this hotel gets three out of three. Singles £49, with shower only £58; doubles £70, with shower only £82, with bath and WC £93; triples £83, with shower only £92, with bath and WC £105; family quad with bath only £100, with bath and WC £110. MC, V.

Hadleigh Hotel, 24 Upper Berkeley St., W1H 7PF (☎ 7262 4084). Tube: Marble Arch. The fraying carpets in the hallway don't inspire confidence, but rooms are pleasant, spacious, and equipped to executive standard: in addition to sparkling bathrooms, TVs, and kettles, all have extra in-room sink, minibar, and even iron with fold-out board. Continental breakfast £2.50. Call 1 week ahead. Singles £59-64, doubles £69-77, triples £87, 2-bedroom apartment £138. AmEx, MC, V.

BLOOMSBURY

⊓ *NEIGHBORHOOD QUICKFIND: Discover, p. 11; Sights, p. 116; Museums&Galleries, p. 148; Food&Drink, p. 175; Entertainment, p. 217; Shopping, p. 236.*

Bloomsbury's quiet squares and Georgian terraces, once home to luminaries such as Charles Darwin and Bertrand Russell, are now home to an endless assortment of accommodations of every size, shape, and variety—from dodgy places near King's Cross charging by the hour to London's

SEE MAP, pp. 344-345

self-appointed "coolest" hotel (the pricey myhotel, on Bedford Sq.), to its largest (the Royal National, with over 1300 rooms). While every area has its share of good and bad places to stay, be warned that the vicinity of King's Cross is renowned as a hotbed of prostitution and drug-dealing at night. Night-livers should note that the southern part of Bloomsbury, around the British Museum, is within easy walking distance of the West End action.

HOSTELS

▨ **The Generator,** Compton Pl. (off 37 Tavistock Pl.), WC1H 9SD (☎ 7388 7666; fax 7388 7644; www.lhdr.demon.co.uk). Sleep in cell-like units with bare walls and metal bunks, relax in the "Turbine," complete with video games and pool tables, receive nutrition at the "Fuel

Stop," or interface with the 'net in the "Talking Head" quiet area. The bar, open M-Sa 6pm-2am and Su 6pm-12:30am, has a free jukebox and big-screen TV, with beers and shots £1 during happy hour (6-9pm). 8-bed basement dorms have lockers and share cavernous military-style bathrooms; upper floors have smaller rooms and slightly more privacy. Staff are strict about rules (including no noise in the dorms after 9pm), but with 800 beds, that's a necessity. Reserve for weekends. Dorms £15; 7- to 8-bed rooms £19 Nov.-Feb., Mar.-Oct. £21.50; 3- to 6-bed rooms £20, £22.50; twins (per person) £23, £26.50; singles £36.50, £41; prices jump 20%+ over New Year. Discounts possible for long stays. MC, V.

Indian YMCA, 41 Fitzroy Sq., W1T 6AQ (☎7387 0411; fax 7383 4735; www.indianymca.org). Tube: Warren St. or Great Portland St. Fantastic location by one of London's most attractive Georgian squares. Rooms are standard student-dorm affairs, with desk and phone, and shared bathrooms have an institutional feel, but with prices this low including both continental breakfast and an Indian vegetarian dinner, who needs charm? Delux rooms are larger and feature TV, fridge, and kettle. £1 temporary membership and 50p reservation fee payable on arrival. Reservations essential. Dorms £20, singles £33, doubles £46, with bath £52; deluxe doubles with bath £75. AmEx, MC, V.

YHA St. Pancras International, 79-81 Euston Rd., NW1 2QS (☎7388 9998; fax 7388 6766; stpancras@yha.org.uk). Tube: King's Cross/St. Pancras. Away from the seediest part of King's Cross, opposite the British Library. Triple glazing and comfortable wooden bunks provide a sound night's sleep. Most of the dorms have ensuite bathrooms and a/c; all have lockers. Lounge with video games and internet access. Linen and English breakfast included. Dinner 6-9pm (£4.90). Kitchen and laundry. 10-day max. stay. Dorms £23.50, under 18 £19.90; twins £51; twins/doubles with bath £56; quads with bath £103. AmEx, MC, V.

Pickwick Hall International Backpackers, 7 Bedford Pl., WC1B 5JE (☎7323 4958). Tube: Tottenham Court Rd. or Russell Sq. Aside from the single 8-bedder, most accommodation is in 2- to 3-bed single-sex "dorms," comparable to B&B rooms. Rules include no smoking, no food in the dorms, and no men on the top floor. TV lounge and kitchen open 7:30am-11:30pm. Laundry room. Continental breakfast and linen included. Reception approx. 8-10am. Call 2-3 days ahead. Dorms £15 per person; singles £25, doubles £40, triples £54. £75 weekly dorm rate for stays over 1 month. AmEx, MC, V.

Ashlee House, 261-265 Gray's Inn Rd., WC1X 8QT (☎7833 9400; fax 7833 6777; info@ashleehouse.co.uk; www.ashleehouse.co.uk). Tube: King's Cross/St. Pancras. Clean, luridly painted rooms crammed with blue steel bunks. King's Cross location convenient but not the pleasantest (or safest) in London. Non-smoking rooms all have washbasins; skylit 16-

bed dorms (2 single-sex and one mixed) are unlocked, while smaller rooms have key-code access. No lockers, but secure luggage room. All but 2 showers have hot water only 5:30am-noon and 6pm-midnight. Linen and breakfast included. Towels £1. Kitchen/TV room, laundry, internet access. 2-week max stay. 16-bed dorms £15, Oct.-Apr. £13; 8- to 10-bed dorms £17, £15; 4- to 6-bed £19, £17; twin £24, £22 per person; single £36, £34. Credit-card machine on order--call to check status.

Astor Museum Inn & Hostel, 27 Montague St. (☎ 7580 5360; fax 7636 7948; museuminn@aol.com; www.astorhostels.com). Tube: Russell Sq. A party hostel doing its best to disturb the peace of this quiet street neighboring the British Museum. The 1st-floor 10-bed dorm, with Georgian plasterwork and balcony, is by far the best room. Laid-back staff don't seem too keen on cleaning, though. 3- to 10-bed co-ed dorms have locking doors but no lockers. Ages 18-35 only. Continental breakfast and linen included. Internet access, kitchen, and TV lounge. Book 2 weeks ahead. £5 key deposit. Dorms £15-18 May-Aug., Sept.-Apr. £14-£17; doubles £22, £20 per person. Off-season weekly dorm rate £75. MC, V (£40 min.).

RESIDENCE HALLS

Carr-Saunders Hall, 18-24 Fitzroy St., W1T 4BN (☎ 7580 6338; fax 7580 4718; www.lse.ac.uk/vacations). Tube: Warren St. Large hall shows its age in places, but rooms are larger than in most student halls and have sink and phone. TV lounge, games room, and elevator to all floors, including panoramic roof terrace, used for breakfast. Reserve 6-8 weeks ahead for July-Aug. Open Easter and mid-June to mid-Sept. English breakfast included. Singles £27 summer, £23.50 Easter; twins £45, £37, with bath £50, £42. MC, V.

Commonwealth Hall, 1-11 Cartwright Gardens, WC1H 9EB (☎ 7685 3500; debbie.hanks@commonwealthhall.lon.ac.uk). Tube: Russell Sq. Post-war block housing 400 basic, slightly worn student singles, with phone but no sink; still, it's unbeatable value. Kitchen on each floor, elevators, bar, cafeteria, tennis and squash courts. Open Easter and mid-June to mid-Sept. Reserve 2 months ahead for July-Aug.; no walk-ins. English breakfast included. Singles £22, half-board £26; students half-board £19. MC, V.

Passfield Hall, 1-7 Endsleigh Pl., WC1H 0PW (☎ 7387 3584; fax 7387 0419; www.lse.ac.uk/vacations). Tube: Euston or Euston Sq. Three converted Georgian blocks arranged around a garden courtyard. Singles are fairly small, but with sink, phone, and fan; twins and triples are much bigger. Unisex bathrooms and kitchen on each floor. TV lounge, games room, and laundry. Open Easter and mid-June to mid-Sept. Book 2 weeks ahead. English breakfast included. Singles £25, twins £46, triples £60. MC, V.

BED AND BREAKFASTS

▨ **Jenkins Hotel,** 45 Cartwright Gdns., WC1H 9EH (☎ 7387 2067; fax 7383 3139; www.jenkinshotel.demon.co.uk). Non-smoking rooms with large windows, floral curtains and antique-style furniture, have a bright, summery feel whatever the weather. Georgie and Tiggy, the hyper-friendly resident labradors, preside over the lower floors, cheerfully getting in the way. All rooms have TV, kettle, phone, fridge, hairdryer, and safe. The only quibble is the tiny prefab bathrooms in some of the rooms. English breakfast included. Reserve 3 months ahead. Singles £52, with bath £72; doubles with bath £85; triples with bath £105. MC, V.

▨ **Crescent Hotel,** 49-50 Cartwright Gdns. (☎ 7387 1515; fax 7383 2054; www.crescenthotelsoflondon.com). Tube: Russell Sq. A real family-run atmosphere, with artistically decorated rooms (some with their original fireplaces) and antiques in the hallways. All rooms have TV, kettle, and phone. Bathrobes lent out with £30 deposit; racquets and balls are available for use in the tennis courts in front of the hotel. Reserve 3 weeks ahead for weekends. Singles £43, with shower only £48, with bath £70; doubles with bath £82; triples with bath £93; quads with bath £105. More for one night stays; discounts for over a week. MC, V.

▨ **Arosfa Hotel,** 83 Gower St., WC1E 6HJ (☎/fax 7636 2115). Tube: Warren St. or Goodge St. The Iberian owners ensure that this small, non-smoking B&B lives up to its Welsh name (meaning "place to rest"). Rooms vary in size—newly installed prefab bathrooms make for some unusual shapes—but charm with framed mirrors and prints; all have TV and sinks. Guests have access to rear garden. English breakfast included. Reserve 1-2 months ahead with 1 night non-refundable deposit. Singles £37; doubles £50, with bath £66; triples £68, £79; quad with bath £92. MC, V (2% surcharge).

George Hotel, 58-60 Cartwright Gdns., WC1H 9EL (☎ 7387 8777; fax 7387 8666; ghotel@aol.com; www.georgehotel.com). Tube: Russell Sq. Meticulous rooms with satellite TV, kettle, phone, and sink, plus hairdryers and irons on request. The forward-facing 1st-floor

rooms are the best, with high ceilings and tall windows; basement and rear rooms are darker. The lounge (with internet terminal) and dining room are both delightful. Reserve 3 months ahead for summer; 48hr. cancellation policy. Singles £50, with shower only £65, with shower and WC £75; doubles £69.50, £77, £90; triples £83, £91.50, £105; basic quads £95. 10% discount for stays over 7 days (Nov.-Jun. only) and internet bookings. MC, V.

The Langland Hotel, 29-31 Gower St., WC1E 6HG (☎7636 5801; fax 7580 2227; langland-hotel@lineone.net; www.langlandhotel.com). Tube: Goodge St. Family atmosphere, wood-framed beds, solid furniture, and plenty of spacious, sparkling bathrooms (cleaned twice daily) help this B&B stand out from its neighbors. All rooms have TV, kettle, and fan. Comfy satellite-TV lounge. Singles £40, with bath £55; doubles £50, £75; triples £70, £90; quads £90, £110; quint (no bath) £100. AmEx, MC, V.

Mentone Hotel, 54-56 Cartwright Gdns., WC1H 9EL (☎7387 3927; fax 7388 4671; www.mentonehotel.com). Tube: Russell Sq. Bright rooms are furnished in a variety of styles, from Louis XIV to the present day, all spotlessly clean with TV, phone, and kettle. English breakfast included. Reserve 2 weeks ahead. Singles £42, with bath £60; doubles £82, triples £93, quad (2 double beds) £102. AmEx, MC, V.

Ruskin Hotel, 23-24 Montague St., WC1B 5BH (☎7636 7388; fax 7323 1662). Tube: Holborn or Russell Sq. Overlooking the east wing of the British Museum, the Ruskin lives up to its name and location with arty decor including a replica Greek frieze above the staircase and a original countryside scene of Camden Town circa 1801 in the spacious lounge. The 1st-floor rooms are spacious, spotless, and, in a word, pink. All rooms have phone, kettle, and hairdryer. Elderly and infirm travelers will appreciate the elevator. English breakfast included. Singles £47; doubles £67, with bath £84; triples £82, £92. AmEx, MC, V.

HOTELS

Hotel Ibis Euston, 3 Cardington St., NW1 2LW (☎ 7304 7712, fax 7388 0001; H0921@accor-hotels.com; www.ibishotel.com). Tube: Euston. Predominantly French staff preside over 350 spacious, modern rooms of this European hotel chain, with cable TV, a/c, phone, desk, and bathroom. "15min. guarantee" promises to resolve any complaint within 15min. or your stay is free. 24hr. snack bar. Restaurant serves 2-course dinner (£8) 6-10:30pm. Breakfast £4.50, served 4am-noon. Doubles and twins £70. MC, V.

Royal National Hotel, Bedford Way, WC1H 0DG (☎7637 2488; reservations ☎7278 7871, fax 7837 4653). London's largest hotel, with 1335 rooms, the Royal National occupies

almost an entire block, with two lobbies and corridors that vanish into the horizon. No doubt considered the epitome of style back in the 1960s, today it offers a certain dated charm, with steel push-button wall radios and formica furniture. All rooms have satellite TV and bathroom. Continental breakfast included. Singles £66, doubles £84, triples £101. MC, V.

NORTH LONDON

⚑ NEIGHBORHOOD QUICKFIND: Discover, p. 12; **Sights**, p. 118; **Museums&Galleries**, p. 150; **Food&Drink**, p. 176; **Nightlife**, p. 196; **Entertainment**, p. 218; **Shopping**, p. 237.

⌂ YHA Hampstead Heath, 4 Wellgarth Rd., NW11 7HR (☎8458 9054; fax 8209 0546; hampstead@yha.org.uk). From Golders Green Tube (Zone 3), turn left into North End Rd.; Wellgarth Rd. is about a 10min. walk up on the left. An out-of-the-way location is the main disadvantage of this manorial hostel, which offers a large garden, email, and common rooms. 24hr. reception, laundry, lockers, currency exchange, and self-service restaurant (dinner 5-8pm, snacks M-F noon-8pm). Linen and breakfast included. 4- to 6-bed dorms £19.90; doubles £46, families (at least one child under 18) £36; triples £67, £53; quads £82, £51; quints £101, £88; sextuples £121, £102. AmEx, MC, V.

⌂ Hampstead Village Guest House, 2 Kemplay Rd., NW3 1SY (☎7435 8679; fax 7794 0254; info@hampsteadguesthouse.com; www.hampsteadguesthouse.com). Tube: Hampstead. Eight rooms in a well maintained Victorian house in the heart of Hampstead village. All rooms have TV, fridge, phone, iron, and kettle. The studio apartment, in a converted garage, sleeps 5 and has a small kitchen. Reservations essential. English breakfast £7. Singles £48-54, with bath £66; doubles £72/84; studio £90 for 1 person, £120 for 2, £138 for 3, £150 for 4, or £162 for 5. MC, V.

⌂ Kandara Guesthouse, 68 Ockendon Rd., N1 3NW (☎7226 5721; fax 7226 3379; admin@kandara.co.uk; www.kandara.co.uk). Bus #38, 56, 73, or 341 from Tube: Angel, or a 15min. walk from Highbury & Islington Tube (Zone 2). If nobody answers at no. 68, try the owner's house at no. 65. Far from the Tube—but with so many buses to the West End (including 2 night buses), it's a blessing in disguise. A simply beautiful B&B, sparkling clean, tastefully decorated, and pleasantly spacious. Five bathrooms between 11 rooms keep queues to a minimum. Online booking. Reserve 2 weeks ahead. Breakfast included. Singles £39-45, doubles £49-59, triples £58-68; price for single quad on application. MC, V.

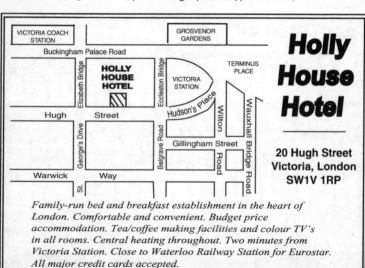

Holly House Hotel

20 Hugh Street
Victoria, London
SW1V 1RP

Family-run bed and breakfast establishment in the heart of London. Comfortable and convenient. Budget price accommodation. Tea/coffee making facilities and colour TV's in all rooms. Central heating throughout. Two minutes from Victoria Station. Close to Waterloo Railway Station for Eurostar. All major credit cards accepted.

Tel: 020-7834-5671 Fax: 020-7233-5154
Email: hhhotel@ukgateway.net Web: www.hollyhousehotel.co.uk

Jurys Inn, 60 Pentonville Rd., N1 9LA (☎ 7282 5500; fax 7282 5511; www.jurys.com). Steps from Angel tube, this businesslike hotel offers three-star luxury for B&B prices—at least if you're in a group of 3. Naturally, ensuite bathroom, TVs, kettle, a/c, and hairdryer are standard. 3rd and 4th floors are for smokers; 1st and 2nd are not. Breakfast £8. Room-only rates for up to 3 adults, or 2 adults and 2 kids, £89 per night; weekend rates can drop to £79 with breakfast, and room-only internet rates can go as low as £70. AmEx, MC, V.

WEST LONDON

7 *NEIGHBORHOOD QUICKFIND: **Discover**, p. 13; **Sights**, p. 123; **Food&Drink**, p. 179; **Entertainment**, p. 220.*

Reasonably central, with good transport links, Shepherd's Bush is a popular with budget travelers (especially Australians). Most B&Bs line **Shepherd's Bush Rd.**

Star Hotel, 97-99 Shepherd's Bush Rd., W6 7LP (☎ 7603 2755; fax 7603 0948). Tube: Goldhawk Rd. or Hammersmith. Rooms are relatively spacious and generally light; all have TV, kettle, and large bathroom while phones should be installed by 2002; refurbished rooms have solid wood furniture and granite bathroom floors. English breakfast included. Book 1 month ahead July-Aug; 72hr. cancellation policy. Singles £35-40, doubles £48-58, triples £66-75, quads £84-92; lower apply rates for longer stays. MC, V (3% surcharge).

Dalmacia Hotel, 71 Shepherd's Bush Rd., W6 (☎ 7603 2887; fax 7602 9226; dalmacia@virginbiz.net; www.cityscan.co.uk/sites/3247). Tube: Goldhawk Rd. All rooms have satellite TV, phone, hairdryer, and bath. Nirvana stayed here before they became famous. Email and drink machine in the lobby. Singles £39; doubles £69; triples £89. AmEx, MC, V.

Hotel Orlando, 83 Shepherd's Bush Rd. W6 7LR (☎/fax 7603 4890; www.hotelorlando.co.uk). Tube: Goldhawk Rd. Rooms are decently sized, with the furniture gradually being upgraded to all-pine. All rooms have TV, phone, computer hook-up, and sparkling modern bathrooms. English breakfast included. 72hr. cancellation policy. Singles £40; doubles £52; triples £70; family (1 double + 2 single beds) £88. AmEx, MC, V.

Windsor Guest House, 43 Shepherd's Bush Rd., W6 7LU (☎/fax 7603 2116; neven@windsorghs.freeserve.co.uk). Tube: Goldhawk Rd. Small family-run B&B catering to a mixture of tourists and workmen. Rooms aren't terribly large, but are well-kept and have TV; bathrooms are clean and modern. Breakfast served in airy conservatory looking onto the small garden. Reserve 1 month ahead in summer. Full English breakfast included. Singles with shower only £25, with shower & WC £30; doubles £40, 50; triples £65, 70. No credit cards.

SOUTH LONDON

7 *NEIGHBORHOOD QUICKFIND: **Discover**, p. 13; **Sights**, p. 125; **Museums&Galleries**, p. 151; **Food&Drink**, p. 180; **Nightlife**, p. 198; **Entertainment**, p. 220; **Shopping**, p. 238.*

Number 7 Guesthouse, 7 Josephine Ave., SW2 2JU (☎ 8674 1880; fax 8671 6032; www.no7.com). Tube: Brixton. Go left from the Tube, then fork left onto Effra Rd. (past the church), turn right into Brixton Waterlane and left into Josephine Av. For gays and lesbians only. "Budget singles" are smallish, with sparkling bathroom, TV, fridge, and phone. Standard rooms are a step up in size, with hardwood floors, "deluxe" are larger or with private terrace, and one-room "suites" add A/C and a sitting area. Continental breakfast included. Reserve with 2-night deposit; 48hr. cancellation with loss of £20. Budget single £69; standard double £89, deluxe £99, suite £99-109; triple £129; quad £139. AmEx, MC, V.

Living in London

Nowhere is the old adage about the grass being greener more true than in London. Just as millions of Londoners dream about moving to somewhere less crowded, less noisy, and less rainy, so do vast numbers of foreigners fantasize about being part of the London scene. The truth, naturally, is somewhere in the middle—separate hot-and-cold taps, archaic licensing hours, and sky-high prices are the price you pay for sharing a city with the world's best theaters, clubs, art, and fashion.

Settling into a new city is a stressful experience. Nowhere is as lonely as a city of 7 million strangers and no friends, where everyone knows where they're going except for you. There's also a million things to do: open a bank account, find a place to live, get a telephone—sometimes it can seem overwhelming. Yet just a month later, you'll be calling London "home," and wondering how you ever lived elsewhere.

PRE-DEPARTURE FORMALITIES

◸ The **Foreign & Commonwealth Office's (FCO)** Joint Entry Clearance Unit (JECU; http://visa.fco.gov.uk) has info on visa and work permit requirements and downloadable application forms. Information is also available from the **Home Office Immigration and Nationality Directorate** (www.ind.homeoffice.gov.uk). The **Immigration Advisory Service,** County House, 190 Great Dover St., London SE1 4YB (☎7357 6917; fax 7378 0665; www.vois.org.uk/ias/) is an independent charity that provides free advice and assistance to people applying for UK visas.

For stays over six months, or any stay involving work or study, chances are you'll need some kind of visa or work permit. For a long vacation, a **long-stay visa** will suffice; you'll need to prove you have the means to support yourself without working or recourse to social services during your stay. For **work** and **study** visas, see below. Note that it is **almost impossible to change visa status while in the UK;** you should ensure you have the appropriate visa status when you arrive, or you will have to return home and re-apply for a visa. For information on exact requirements, contact your local British Consulate.

WORK PERMITS AND VISA REQUIREMENTS

EU CITIZENS. Citizens of European Union countries and their families have an unrestricted right to work in the UK. However, for longer stays there are still some formalities to complete. If you will be **working** in the UK for over 3 months, you must apply for a **residence permit** by completing form EEC1, available from police stations, within 6 months of arriving. To **study** in the UK you will be required to prove that you are able to support yourself without recourse to British social services. Note that EU citizens studying for a first degree in the UK pay the same tuition as UK citizens, but are not eligible for maintenance awards.

COMMONWEALTH CITIZENS. Commonwealth citizens aged 17-27 inclusive are eligible for a **working holidaymaker visa,** allowing them to stay and work in the UK for up to 2 years provided that employment is "incidental to a holiday." Essentially, this means that no more than half your stay can be spent in full-time work. (See FCO form INF 5 for details.) Those aged 17 or over and who have at least one **UK-born grandparent** (including Ireland if born before 31 March 1922) are eligible for a **UK Ancestry Visa,** which gives the right to reside and work in the UK for an initial period of 4 years. (See FCO form INF 7 for details.)

US STUDENTS. In general, US citizens require a work permit (see below) to work in the UK. However, US citizens aged 18 or over studying full-time for a degree at a US or Canadian university are eligible for a **Blue Card Permit,** administered by the British and North American Universities Club (BUNAC), allowing them to work for up to 6 months. BUNAC also offers limited assistance in finding housing and employment in the UK, and organizes regular social events. You will need to enter the UK within one semester of graduation, and have at least US$1000 on entry. (PO Box 430, Southbury, CT 06488. ☎ 1 800 GO-BUNAC; info@bunacusa.org; www.bunac.org.uk/.)

STUDENTS AT UK INSTITUTIONS. Full-time students in UK educational institutions have a limited right to part-time and vacation work. See below for details.

WORK PERMITS AND WORK VISAS. If you do not fall into one of the above categories, you will need a **work permit** in order to work in the UK. If you would require a visa to travel to the UK in any case, you will also require a **work visa.** You must already have a job set up in the UK before obtaining a work permit, which can only be applied for through your employer. Work permits are issued by the **Department for Education and Employment** (www.workpermits.gov.uk).

STUDENT VISAS

Non-EU nationals intending to study in the UK must generally have been accepted on a course by a qualifying British educational institution before applying for student status. **Non-visa nationals** (foreigners who do not require visas to enter the UK as visitors) are permitted to enter the country as tourists and then apply for student status once they have been admitted to a course of study. If they have already been accepted on a course, they may apply for student status when entering the UK. To do this, you will need to show a letter of admittance from the school, university, or college, and proof of adequate financial support to cover tuition and maintenance, to the immigration officer at the port of entry. **Visa nationals** are required to obtain a student visa from their local British Consulate before entering the country; to do so, they must provide proof of admittance to a course of study and financial support.

WORKING ON A STUDENT VISA. Non-EU students may work up to 20hr. per week during term-time, and full-time in vacation. However, longer hours may be authorized if deemed a necessary part of the course of study (e.g. as part of medical school training). EU citizens enjoy the same working rights as British citizens.

FINDING WORK

◪ *Information on visa requirements for working in the UK is given on p. 302.*

With unemployment in the UK at its lowest level for decades, there's never been a better time to find work in London. **Casual work,** such as bartending, babysitting, and waiting tables is the easiest to find, though it remains poorly paid. Unscrupulous employers will often take on foreigners without work permits for lower wages; be warned that as an illegal employee your right of redress against any malpractice by your employer will be severely limited. Assuming you are working legally, you will enjoy the protection of UK labor laws. Be warned that you'll pay 23% tax and 10% National Insurance on all but the lowest-paid jobs.

YOUR RIGHTS. The **minimum wage** varies with age and length of employment. 18-21 year olds and those receiving accredited training within six months of starting a new job may not be paid less than £3.20 per hr.; otherwise the rate is £4.10 (£4.20 from Oct. 2002). **Full-time workers** may not be forced to work over 48hr. per week, 13hr. per day, or six days per week. They are also entitled to 4 weeks' paid vacation per year. **Part-time workers** are now entitled to many of the benefits an employer accords full-time employees, including paid vacation on a pro-rated basis. For more information, including details of **maternity leave** and **anti-discrimination laws,** the **Tailored Interactive Guide on Employment Rights** (TIGER; www.tiger.gov.uk) offers comprehensive information on employment law in the UK.

OPTIONS FOR WORK

AU PAIRS/CHILDCARE. Au pairs are typically young women aged 18-25 who perform childcare and light housework for a family in return for board, lodging, and a small amount of pocket money (around £40 per week). Typically they work 25-40hr. per week with one or two nights off. People with childcare qualifications can find much more lucrative work as a live-in nanny, making up to £250 per week in addition to food and lodging.

HOTEL/CATERING WORK. There's no shortage of jobs in London waiting tables, tending bars, or less glamorous behind-the-scenes roles in kitchen and cleaning positions. What these all have in common is that they are poorly paid (typically minimum wage—as little as £3.20 per hr.—or even less for illegal employees) with antisocial hours. And don't expect to boost that much with tips: bartenders are not tipped in the UK, and many restaurants have "service included" in their prices—money which may or may not find its way into your pay.

SECRETARIAL WORK. If you can type like a demon, then **temping** can be a good way to pay the bills. Temps are temporary secretaries on short-term placements (from as little as a day to a few weeks); you'll need to register with a temping agency who'll match available positions to your skills. **Tate,** 7 Hanover Sq., W1S 1HQ (☎7408 0424; fax 7493 8790; info@tate.co.uk; www.tate.co.uk), can arrange secretarial placements and provide support for foreigners in London.

INTERNSHIPS. Finding an internship in London is not difficult—finding a paid one is. Interning has its perks (just ask Monica Lewinsky) but you rarely get paid, and British photocopiers are no different from anywhere else in the world. If you are interested in interning, use college career offices and the internet to investigate options. London's position as a financial hub means that there are hundreds of overpaid summer positions in banks and consultancies, but competition is fierce: applications must normally be completed by February for work starting in June. There is a smaller number of (normally unpaid) internship positions in media and publishing companies, though duties will typically be limited to menial tasks.

VOLUNTEERING. Volunteer jobs are fairly easy to secure. However, if you receive room and board in exchange for your labor, you are "employed" and must get a work visa. You can sometimes avoid the high application fees charged by organizations by contacting the individual workcamps directly. **Volunteers for Peace,** 43 Tiffany Rd., Belmont, VT 05730, is a non-profit organization that arranges placements in London work camps of 10-15 people for 2-3 weeks. Complete and up-to-date listings are published in their International Workcamp Directory, US$15. (☎(802) 259 2759; fax 259-2922; vfp@vfp.org; www.vfp.org/. Registration fee US$200.)

WORK PLACEMENT PROGRAMS

A number of organizations arrange work exchanges in the UK for foreigners. These are great if you need to arrange work in advance for visa reasons, or if you know exactly what you want to do. Be careful, though—you might find yourself paying hefty placement fees for a poorly paid job that you could have found yourself.

Accord Cultural Exchange, 750 La Playa, San Francisco, CA 94121, USA (☎(415) 386-6203); fax 386-0240; leftbank@hotmail.com; www.cognitext.com/accord). Hefty US$750 to arrange au-pair and guest-teacher positions, $1200 unpaid internships. $40 application fee.

interExchange, 161 Sixth Ave, New York, NY 10013 (☎(212) 924-0446; fax 924-0575; www.interexchange.org). US students only. Pay US$950 to get paid $5-6 per hr. in a London hotel, room and board not included. $1250 for an unpaid internship. Fees include BUNAC Blue Card work permit (see **US Students,** p. 302).

Childcare International, Trafalgar House, Grenville Pl., London NW7 3SA (☎8906 3116; fax 8906 3461; office@childint.co.uk; www.childint.co.uk). Arranges childcare placements for mostly Commonwealth and European applicants. Au pairs work 25-30hr. per week, receive full board, lodging, and £40 per week spending allowance. Those with prior childcare experience can work as mothers' helps, 40-50hr. per week in return for board, lodging, and £100 per week. Qualified nannies can make £230 per week. No application fee.

International Exchange Programs (IEP), 196 Albert Rd., South Melbourne, Victoria 3205, Australia (☎(03) 9690 5890), and P.O. Box 1786, Shortland St., Auckland, New Zealand (☎(09) 366 6255; www.iepnz.co.nz). Helps Aussies and Kiwis on a working holidaymaker visa (see p. 302) find work, lodging, and friends. AU$300/NZ$340 fee.

FINDING WORK: FURTHER READING

International Jobs: Where they Are, How to Get Them, Kocher and Segal. Perseus (US$17).

How to Get a Job in Europe, Sanborn and Matherly. Surrey Books (US$22).

Work Abroad: The Complete Guide To Finding A Job Overseas, by Hubbs, Griffiths, and Nolting. Transitions Abroad (US$16).

Summer Jobs: Britain. Vacation-Work (US$17). Lists roughly 30,000 jobs in the UK.

Overseas Summer Jobs 2001, David Woodworth Vacation-Work (US$17).

Directory of Jobs and Careers Abroad, Roberts and Packer. Vacation-Work . (US$17).

International Directory of Voluntary Work, Whetter and Pybus. Vacation-Work (US$16).

The Au Pair and Nanny's Guide to Working Abroad, Griffith and Legg. Vacation-Work (US$17).

STUDYING IN LONDON

▶ *For information on visa requirements for students, see **Student Visas,** p. 302.*

With dozens of institutions, from the sprawling colleges of the University of London and the vast collections of the British Library to the Vidal Sassoon Academy and thousands of part-time courses, you can study almost any subject under the sun in London at any level. Combined with London's other attractions, it not surprising that every year tens of thousands of international students choose to make London their academic home-away-from-home. Even if you didn't come to London to work, taking evening courses—whether in mediaeval architecture, italian cookery, or jazz dance—can be a great way to broaden your horizons and meet similarly minded people. For a comprehensive list of part-time and evening classes, the annual **Floodlight** directory lists over 40,000 courses in Greater London. (www.floodlight.co.uk. Available from all good newsagents. £3.75.)

STUDY ABROAD PROGRAMS

It's not difficult to spend a summer, term, or year studying in London under the auspices of a well-established program. Thousands of students join study-abroad schemes in London every year; if you want the convenience of an all-inclusive package and don't mind the price, they can be ideal—if you actually want to find out what it's like to be a student in London (and maybe make some English friends), they're not so great. Most universities have a study-abroad office that can recommend approved programs.

American Institute for Foreign Study, River Plaza, 9 West Broad St., Stamford, CT 06902 (☎1-800-727-AIFS; www.aifs.com). Organizes all-inclusive study packages at the US-accredited American International University in London and summer art courses at Chelsea and Central St. Martin's art colleges.

Arcadia University (formerly Beaver College) **Center for Education Abroad,** 450 S. Easton Rd., Glenside, PA 19038-3295 (☎ 1-800-232-8379; fax (215) 572-2174; cea@beaver.edu; www.beaver.edu/cea). A range of programs at 9 London universities, combining tailored-for-Americans courses with regular British offerings. Applicants for summer programs must have completed 2 semesters at an accredited university, or 3 for semester abroad programs.

Central College Abroad, Office of International Education, Pella, IA 50219 (☎ 1-800-831-3629; fax (641) 628-5375; studyabroad@central.edu; www.studyabroad.com/central/). A little bit of Iowa in the center of London. Mostly runs its own courses, though applicants can take up to 2 courses at London universities and an unpaid internship.

Council International Study Programs, 633 Third Ave., 20th Floor, New York, NY 10017 (general inquiries ☎ 1-800-40-STUDY; studyinfo@ciee.org). For London specific info, contact Amy MacLeod, UK program advisor (☎ (212) 822 2733; amcleod@ciee.org).

FURTHER READING

www.studyabroad.com

Academic Year Abroad 2001/2002 (US$46) and *Vacation Study Abroad 2001/2002* (US$43), Sarah J. Steen. Institute of International Education Books.

Peterson's Study Abroad and *Peterson's Summer Study Abroad.* Peterson's (both US$30).

ARRANGING IT YOURSELF

Alternatively, go it alone: London is overflowing with universities, art and music schools, and specialist institutions, many of which offer programs for international students. One problem with such an approach is that it might prove difficult to transfer academic credit from London universities to foreign schools—check first—but you'll often save money and have a superior social and academic experience.

ACADEMIC INSTITUTIONS

Between themselves, the University of London and the London Institute encompass the vast majority of London's universities and colleges, though there are also numerous independent specialist institutions. Many offer **special programs** for international students on exchange visits and semesters abroad in addition to **summer schools.**

Enrolling on a **degree course** can present problems to those raised in a different system. UK universities will want to see evidence that you have attained the same educational standard as British 18 year-olds, either by passing the British A-level exams or a recognized equivalent, such as the International Baccalaureate; EU school-leaving credentials are generally admissible. Americans may have problems, since SAT scores and high-school diplomas are not normally accepted; frequently, students must have completed a year of college in the US before being considered equivalent to European school leavers. The **British Council** (see p. 306) can often arrange for people to take British exams in their home countries.

Fees on degree programs for non-EU student depend on the subject and school, from around £8500 per year for humanities to £18,000 for medicine; EU residents pay the same as UK students, currently £1050 per year for all subjects. All foreign students need to show they have access to at least £8250 per year for **living expenses.**

Universities and Colleges Admissions Services (UCAS), PO Box 28, Cheltenham, Gloucestershire, GL52 3ZA (☎ (01242) 22 77 88; enq@ucas.ac.uk; www.ucas.ac.uk). The centralized admissions service for all undergraduate degree courses in the UK. Also provides impartial information to international students on applying to UK universities.

EducationUK (www.educationuk.org), a slick website run by the British Council (see below) to explain the British education system and persuade international students to buy British.

The University of London (www.lon.ac.uk) is an umbrella organization uniting the vast majority all of London's academic institutions, with 17 constituent universities and colleges.

The London Institute, 65 Davies St., W1K 5DA (☎ 7514 6000; fax 7514 6175; www.linst.ac.uk) runs 5 of London's best-known art and design schools, including Central St. Martins College, Chelsea College of Art, and the London College of Fashion.

University College London, Gower St., WC1E 6BT (☎7679 2000; www.ucl.ac.uk) is the biggest of UoL's schools (and one of the UK's top universities), with a complete academic curriculum. Special programs are offered for international **affiliate students** on short-term educational visits and exchanges; affiliates must normally have completed 2 years of university at time of admission to UCL.

SUMMER AND SHORT VOCATIONAL PROGRAMS

Many of London's elite **art, music,** and **drama** academies supplement their income by offering part-time and summer courses to motivated amateurs. Typically there are no admissions requirements (though some courses fill up quickly); the flipside is that you will rarely receive any recognition other than a certificate of attendance for the work you put in. Always check whether you'll be taught by the same master artists as teach the colleges' regular offerings—often the famous name hides the fact that a course is being taught by a part-time teacher they wouldn't dream of subjecting degree-seeking students to. Numerous private-run **vocational schools** also run short courses that are wildly popular with an international crowd.

Royal Academy of the Dramatic Arts (RADA), 62-64 Gower St., WC1E 6ED (☎7636 7076; fax 7323 3865; www.rada.org). The alma mater of Ralph Fiennes, Kenneth Branagh, and Anthony Hopkins offers intensive summer courses in acting, set design, and scriptwriting. Applicants must be at least 18; no prior experience required.

Slade School of Fine Art, part of University College London (see above for address; ☎7679 7772; slade.summer@ucl.ac.uk; www.ucl.ac.uk/slade). Offers a range of general and specialized art courses over the summer, lasting 1-10 weeks. The 2-month Alternative Foundation offers a complete introduction to drawing, painting, sculpting, and printing.

Central St. Martins College of Art and Design, Southampton Row, WC1B 4AP (☎7514 7015; fax 7514 7016; shortcourse@csm.linst.ac.uk; www.csm.linst.ac.uk), offers dozens of evening courses throughout the year as well as a comprehensive summer program covering all aspects of fine art, graphic design, fashion, and film.

Courtauld Institute, Somerset House, Strand WC2R 0RN (☎7848 2413; fax 7848 2416; development@coutauld.ac.uk; www.courtauld.ac.uk) offers 12 week-long summer courses in art history. Courses include gallery visits, focusing on the Courtauld's own impressive collections (see **Museums,** p. 139).

Vidal Sassoon Academy, 56-59 Davies Mews, W1Y 1AS (☎7318 5205; www.vsassoon.com). As many students come here for the scene as for the teaching. 9-month diploma course for beginners £10,000; shorter advanced courses from £1000.

London School of Journalism, 22 Upbrook Mews, W2 3HG (☎7706 3790; fax 7706 3780; learn@lsjournalism.com; www.lsj.org) offers 3-month full-time and 6-month part-time diploma courses (from £2650) as well as a 4-week intensive summer school (£1295). All courses are recognized by the National Union of Journalists, entitling students to NUJ membership.

THE BRITISH COUNCIL

The British Council is the arm of the government charged with promoting education opportunities in Britain, among other responsibilities. Its offices are an invaluable source of information for those intending to study in Britain at a secondary school or university level, or for those enrolling in language classes in Britain. They also offer the opportunity to take British exams for university admission. For branches in countries not listed here, call the London office or check *www.britishcouncil.org/*.

London Office: 10 Spring Gdns, London SW1A 2BN (☎7389 4383; inquiries ☎(0161) 957 7755; general.enquiries@britcoun.org).

Australia: PO Box 88, Edgecliff NSW 2027 (☎016 301 204; fax (02) 9327 4868; enquiries@britishcouncil.org.au; www.bc.org.au).

Canada: 80 Elgin St., Ottawa, Ontario K1P 5K7 (☎(613) 237-1530; ottawa.enquiries@ca.brisihcouncil.org; www.ca.britishcouncil.org).

Ireland: Newmount House, 22/24 Lower Mount St., Dublin 2 (☎(01) 676 4088 or 676 6943; fax 676 6945; www.britishcouncil.org/ireland).

New Zealand: 44 Hill St., PO Box 1812, Wellington 6001 and 151 Queen St., Private Bag 92014, Auckland 1001 (both ☎(04) 472 6049; www.britishcouncil.org.nz).

South Africa: 76 Juta St., Braamfontein, Johannesburg 2001; send mail to PO Box 30637, Braamfontein, 2017 (☎(011) 403 3316; fax 339 7806; johannesburg.enquiries@britishcouncil.org.za; www.britishcouncil.org/southafrica). Also offices in Cape Town and Durban.

United States: British Embassy, 3100 Massachusetts Ave. N.W., Washington, D.C. 20008 (☎1-800-488-2235 or (202) 588-6500; fax 588-7918; www.britishcouncil-usa.org).

FINDING SOMEWHERE TO LIVE

There's a good reason that every year a long-ignored, distant suburb is "outed" as the Next Big Thing in London living—inexorably rising property prices are pushing the urban hip further and further from the center of town. It's the same old story: struggling artists move to a long-depressed borough, then a few years later it's "discovered" by the style magazines and the next thing you know it's all bankers, Starbucks, and BMWs. The people who made it hip, meanwhile, have long since been forced to move to a more distant zone. This year's hapless neighborhood is Hoxton; next on the list looks to be Bethnal Green. Luckily, London is large enough that there are still enough terminally uncool neighborhoods where you might actually be able to afford to live; if you're lucky, you might pick just at the start of the upswing.

St. James's Park

COST

Take a deep breath. If you want to live alone, you'll most probably end up in a **bedsit,** a single room, typically in a converted townhouse, typically miniscule, and typically with a shared kitchen and bathroom. For this privilege, you won't get away paying less than £60 per week in the most distant, depressed suburb; count on at least £100 for anywhere within striking distance of the center. You won't save money by being sociable, either: **flatshares** (shared apartments) cost £60-80 per week in the suburbs, £100-150 in a more fashionable area. **Short-term** housing is pricier and harder to find; it's almost impossible to rent for under a month. When deciding how much you can afford, don't forget to figure in **transport costs;** if you work in the center, living in the suburbs could add £30-50 to your monthly Travelcard cost; if you work outside Zone 1, you'll save if you don't have to go through Zone 1 to get there.

Hyde Park Roller-bladers

COUNCIL TAX. Local taxes are another factor that shouldn't be ignored when choosing a place to live. In England, council tax is levied on each "dwelling", with the amount owed being set by

Helpful Hints

the local council and dependent on the market price of the dwelling. A dwelling is defined as any self-contained living unit—so a house converted into independent flat counts as numerous dwellings, but a house converted into bedsits that share kitchen and bathroom facilities counts as only one dwelling. Who is liable to pay the tax is a complicated matter: in rented flats it's generally the tenant, though if the landlord lives on the premises, he or she is normally liable. In any case, who is responsible for paying the tax should be clearly worked out before moving into any flat. If everyone in the dwelling is a full-time student, or earns less than a certain amount, it may be exempt from council tax; however this is not an automatic exemption and must be applied for. If your dwelling is liable for council tax, expect to pay around £600 per year for a small flat.

TENANTS' RIGHTS

🔢 *For free advice on housing rights, or if you have a dispute with your landlord, go to your local* **Citizens' Advice Bureau (CAB),** *or check www.nacab.org.uk.*

All tenants have certain rights: for example, the landlord is responsible for keeping the accommodation in habitable condition and paying for necessary repairs; it's also illegal for landlords to threaten or harass tenants, or to cut off utilities for late rent payment. Asserting your rights is another matter: few tenants can afford a court dispute with a landlord, and some may even face eviction. It's best to get advice from your local CAB (see above) before demanding action. Note that terms set out in the **tenancy agreement** (lease) cannot override rights laid out by law. Oral agreements have the force of law, but are hard to enforce; it's best to get a signed document.

RESOURCES

🔢 *For a listing of accommodations agencies in London, see the Service Directory, p. 311.*

Do-it-yourselfers willing to put in some time and footwork should rush to the newsagent the morning that London's **small-ads papers** are published, and immediately begin calling. **Loot** is published daily, as is the **Evening Standard** (which, despite its name, can be bought in the morning). Both have the best listings for short rentals (1-2 month). Other sources of vacancies are **Time Out** (published Tu) and **NME** (Th). Bulletin boards in **newsagents** frequently list available rooms, as do the classified sections of major and local newspapers. Beware of ads placed by **letting agencies;** they may try to sell you something more expensive when you call.Though they save a lot of legwork, agencies generally charge 1-2 weeks' rent as a fee, and it's in their interest to find high-priced accommodations. There are few laws regulating letting agencies, and tales of unscrupulous practices are common—make sure to only deal with agencies that are members of the **National Approved Letting Scheme (NALS),** which must adhere to a strict set of standards. Always thoroughly read the contract before signing anything—you might find yourself responsible for repairs that are normally the landlord's responsibility. Note that agencies may legally charge you only once you rent a room through them—don't pay just to register, or to get a list of rooms available. Many London boroughs run **information offices,** which often have listings of reliable local agencies.

BANKING IN LONDON

While you might assume that you'll need a British bank account if you'll be in London for any length of time, unless you're going to be paid in the UK, or are going to have to write checks (e.g. to your landlord), you might find it's not necessary. If you have a credit card that you can arrange to pay while you're abroad (you can normally have the balance paid automatically from your home bank account), use it everywhere you can and your cash needs will drop dramatically—you can even use the credit card to get cash in the UK, though it is normally cheaper to use a regular cash (ATM) card. Since you'll probably be charged a service fee per withdrawal, it's cheaper to make a few large withdrawals than many small ones. Remember to check that your PIN will work in the UK before you leave home. See **Once in London: Money,** p. 44, and **Planning Your Trip: Money,** p. 265, for more information on accessing funds from home while in London.

OPENING AN ACCOUNT

If you'll be working in London, or studying for more than a semester, chances are you'll need a UK bank account. A number of international banks have London branches geared towards expat communities; check with them to see if you can open a UK-based bank account from home. Note that a sterling account is not the same as a UK account: many banks around the world will open an account that quotes your balance in pounds, but for it to be of any use in Britain, the bank needs to be part of the UK check clearing system. **Citibank's** London branch, 335-336 Strand, WC2R (☎0800 008 800; www.citibank.com), is happy to open a London-based account for US residents before they arrive.

If you're obliged to wait until you arrive in London to open an account, you'll find things easier with a letter of introduction from your home bank manager to say that you're a customer in good standing. You'll also need to bring your passport, and a letter from your employer or your university confirming your status in the UK. You may also be asked to bring proof of address, such as a utility bill or lease. Anyone working with a regular income, or enrolled in a course at a British university, should have little trouble opening an account. **Study-abroad** students are screened more rigorously; check with your university bursar's office if they can recommend a bank used to dealing with study-abroad students. The standard account is called a **current account,** and will include a checkbook, a cash card, and a nominal rate of interest.

GETTING MEDICAL CARE

▶ For information on obtaining **urgent care** in the UK, see Once in London, p. 46. For listings of **clinics, emergency rooms,** and **late-night pharmacies,** see the Service Directory, p. 311.

In Britain, the state-run **National Health Service (NHS)** encompasses the majority of health-care providers. Brits are strongly attached to the NHS—after all, it gives them something to complain about. While it's true that waiting lists are longer and comfort levels lower than in pricey private hospitals, going private doesn't mean better doctors: almost all of Britain's top doctors do both NHS and private work. Citizens of the **EU,** most **Commonwealth** citizens, all **full-time students,** (legal) **employees,** and all **UK residents** are eligible for free care on the NHS; note that visits to **opticians** and **dentists** are not covered by the NHS. Others will need to pay up-front; it's a good idea to prepare for the worst with private health insurance. **BUPA,** Cedar House, Chertsey Lane, Staines TW18 3DY (☎0800 600 500; membership@bupa.com; www.bupa.co.uk) is the UK's largest private medical insurance provider. Note that **US insurance** plans' foreign coverage (if they have any) rarely cover extended foreign trips, or non-emergency procedures abroad.

PRIMARY CARE. Your first step is to register with a local **General Practitioner** (GP). Your GP is your first port of call for all non-emergency complaints; you cannot make an appointment with a hospital specialist without a referral from a GP. Most GPs are employed by the NHS, though many will also treat private patients; NHS GPs will also refer you to a private specialist if you ask them. To **register** with a GP, you will be asked to supply your NHS membership number; if you don't have one yet, you'll need to supply proof of eligibility; proof of residence in the local area is also required. Chemists and local community centers can supply you with a list of local doctors, but word-of-mouth is the best way to find a reliable physician. Most London doctors keep a few **surgery hours** per week, during which they offer walk-in service (well, walk-in-sit-down-wait-two-hours); at other times, you'll need to make an appointment. If you are too ill to go to the surgery, some GPs will make **home visits.**

PRESCRIPTIONS. The NHS has a flat-fee system of **prescriptions;** all drugs prescribed by NHS physicians cost £6 (free for seniors, children under 16 or under 18 in full-time education, and the unemployed). For many generic drugs this fee is higher than the ordinary cost of the drug; in this case, you can ask your doctor to write you a private prescription (though they may refuse: overcharging for cheap drugs helps the NHS to subsidize expensive ones). Note that a number of common medicines prescribed by doctors, such as antihistamines, are also available without prescription at chemists—check with the pharmacist before paying the prescription price.

Service Directory

ACCOMMODATION AGENCIES

Jenny Jones, 40 South Molton St. (☎ 7493 4801; fax 7495 2912). Tube: Bond St. No fee. Some 3 month rentals, most 6 months min. Open M 2-5pm, Tu-Th 9:30am-1:30pm and 2:30-5pm, F 9:30am-1pm.

Outlet. Short- and long-term apartments for gays and lesbians. See p. 284.

University of London Accommodations Office, Senate House, Room B, Malet St., (☎ 7862 8880; fax 7862 8084; www.lon.ac.uk/accom). Tube: Russell Sq. Keeps a list of summer room and apartment vacancies. Other services only available to University of London students. Student ID required. Open M-F 9:30am-5:30pm.

AIRPORTS

See **Once in London,** p. 27.

BANKS

See **Living in London,** p. 308.

BICYCLE & SCOOTER RENTAL

Bikepark, 63 New King's Rd. (☎ 7731 7012). Tube: Fulham Broadway. Open M-F 8:30am-7pm, Sa 9am-6pm. £12 1st day, £6 2nd, £4 per day thereafter. £200 credit-card deposit.

London Bicycle Tour Company, Gabriel's Wharf (☎ 7928 6838; www.londonbicycle.com). Tube: Blackfriars or Waterloo. Open daily 10am-6pm Apr.-Oct.; call ahead Nov.-Mar. Bikes and blades £2.50 per hr. up to £12 1st day, £6 per day thereafter. Credit-card deposit required. AmEx, MC, V.

Scootabout, 1-3 Leeke St. (7833 4607). Tube: King's Cross. Moped and scooter rentals. Riders must have already had some experience. Book at least 1 week ahead. Over 21 only; rates depend on age and include insurance cover. 50cc bikes £15-£20 per day, from £95 per week; 2-day min. Credit-card deposit. Helmets occasionally available (£2); enquire when booking. MC, V.

BUDGET TRAVEL AGENCIES

usit (☎ 0870 240 1010; www.usitcampus.co.uk). Many locations: largest at 52 Grosvener Gardens (Tube: Victoria; open M-F 9am-6pm, Sa-Su 10am-5pm).

Council Travel, 28A Poland St. (☎7437 7767). Tube: Oxford Circus. Open M-Tu and Th-F 9:30am-5:30, W 10:30am-5:30pm, Sa 9:30am-4:30pm.

CTS Travel, 44 Goodge St. (☎7636 0031/ 0032; www.ctstravel.co.uk). Tube: Goodge St. Open M and W-F 10am-6pm, Tu 11am-6pm, Sa 11am-4pm.

Flightbookers, 177 Tottenham Court Rd. (☎7757 2504; www.ebookers.com). Tube: Warren St. Cheap flights for non-students. M-F 9am-7pm, Sa 9am-6pm, Su 10am-5pm.

STA Travel (☎0870 1600 599; www. statravel.co.uk). 14 London branches; largest at 85 Shaftesbury Ave. (☎7432 7474; Tube: Piccadilly Circus; open M-W and F 11am-7pm, Th 11am-8pm, Sa 11am-5pm.)

Travel CUTS, 295A Regent St., W1R (☎7255 1944). Tube: Oxford Circus. Open M-W and F 9am-6pm, Th 9am-7pm, Sa 11am-4pm.

BUSES

See **Transportation,** p. 317.

CALLING CARDS

See *Telephone Services,* p. 317.

CAR RENTAL

Foreigners aged over 17 may drive in the UK for up to one year if in posession of a valid driving licence (some exceptions apply).

Budget (☎08701 56 56 56; www.budget.co.uk). Locations includeg Russell Court, Woburn Pl. (Tube: Russell Sq.) Min. age 25.

easyRentACar.com (www.easyrentacar.com). Internet-only rentals. 3 central London locations. Min. age 21. From £7 per day plus £5 preparation fee.

Europcar (0870 607 5000; www.europcar.com). 5 London locations, including 30 Woburn Pl. (Tube: Euston). Min. age 23.

Wheelchair Travel. See **Disability Resources,** p. 313.

CHEMISTS

Most chemists keep standard store hours (approx. M-Sa 9:30am-5:30pm); one "duty" chemist in each neighborhood will additionally open on Sunday, though hours may be limited. Late-night and 24hr. chemists are extremely rare; two are given below.

Bliss, 5-6 Marble Arch (☎7723 6116). Tube: Marble Arch. Open daily 9am-midnight.

Zafash Pharmacy, 233 Old Brompton Rd. (☎7373 2798). Tube: Earls Court. Open 24hr.

CHILDREN

To find out about children's activities in London, call:

Kidsline: ☎7222 8070. Open July-Aug. 9am-4pm, Sept.-June 4-6pm.

What's on for Children: ☎0891 505 456. Charged at 50p per min.

Places for Children to Go: ☎0891 505 460. Charged at 50p per min.

CLINICS

See also **Hospitals,** p. 314.

Audre Lorde Clinic, Ambrose King Centre, Royal London Hospital, Whitechapel (☎7377 7312; Tube: Whitechapel. Women's health clinic. Staffed entirely by women.

Bernhard Clinic, Charing Cross Hospital, Fulham Palace Rd. (☎8846 1576). Tube: Baron's Court or Hammersmith. NHS-run Women's health clinic. By appointment.

Jefferiss Centre for Sexual Health, St. Mary's Hospital, Praed St. (☎7725 6619). Tube: Paddington. Free and confidential sexual health services and supplies, including free condoms and dental dams, and STD and HIV tests and counseling. Open for walk-ins M 8:45am-5pm, Tu and F 8:45am-6pm, W 11:45am-6pm, Th 8am-1pm.

COMMUNITY & CULTURAL CENTERS

See **Gay & Lesbian Services,** p. 314; **Minority Resources,** p. 316; and **Religious Resources,** p. 316.

CONSULATES

See **Embassies & Consulates,** p. 312.

CRISIS LINES

See **Helplines,** p. 314.

CURRENCY EXCHANGE

See also **Banks,** p. 311.

American Express (www.americanexpress.com). For **traveler's check refunds,** call 0800 52 13 13 toll-free 24hr. 17 London locations including:

102-104 Victoria St. (☎7630 6365). Tube: Victoria. Open M-F 9am-5pm.

8 Kensington High St. (☎7761 7905). Tube: High St. Kensington. Open M-Sa 9am-5:30pm.

Paddington Station (☎7706 7127). Tube: Paddington. Open M-F 7:30am-7:30pm, Sa 8am-6pm, Su 9am-6pm.

30-31 Haymarket (☎ 7484 9610). Tube: Piccadilly Circus. Open M-F 8:30am-7pm, Sa 9am-6:30pm, Su 10am-5pm.

Terminal 4, Heathrow (☎8754 7057). Tube: Heathrow Terminal 4. Open daily 7am-7pm.

Thomas Cook (☎08705 666 222, 24hr.; www.thomascook.com). 44 currency-exchange bureaux in London; call to locate one. Cashes Thomas Cook Mastercard traveler's checks commission free. For **traveler's check refunds,** call 0800 622 101.

Travelex (www.travelex.co.uk). 10 London locations, including at the Tower of London, Selfridges, Victoria Station, and the Royal National Hotel.

DENTAL CARE

Dental Emergency Care Service (☎7955 2186). Refers callers to the nearest open dental surgery. Open M-F 8:45am-3:30pm.

Dental Accident & Emergency, Guy's & St. Thomas's Hospital, Guy's Tower, St. Thomas St. (☎7955 4317). Tube: London Bridge. Free walk-in treatment for dental emergencies. Adults treated M-F 9am-5pm (last admission 3:30pm), children M-F 9am-noon and 2-4pm. Sa-Su and holidays use paying services at **Emergency Dental Clinic.** Open Sa-Su and holidays 9am-6pm.

King's Dental Institute, Guy's Campus, St. Thomas St. (☎7955 4204). Tube: London Bridge. Walk-in emergency service. Adults seen M-F from 9am until daily patient quota filled; children M-F 9am-5pm. Emergency Dental Clinic open daily 6-11pm, Sa-Su and holidays also 9:15-11:45am.

Whitecross Dental Care (☎7490 9000; www.whitecross.co.uk). Nationwide network of dental practices, with 17 London clinics including: 79-80 High Holborn (☎7242 0088; Tube: Holborn); 47-49 Victoria St. (☎7233 2323; Tube: Victoria); 26 Paddington St. (☎7224 2727; Tube: Baker St.); and 51 Kentish Town Rd. (☎7284 1110; Tube: Camden Town). Call for other locations. Initial consultation £17.50.

Eastman Dental Hospital, 256 Gray's Inn Rd., (☎7915 100; fax 7915 1012). Tube: Russell Sq., Chancery Ln. or King's Cross. Leading specialist hospital. By appointment only.

DISABILITY RESOURCES

Artsline, 54 Charlton St., NW1 1HS (☎7388 2227; www.artsline.org.uk). Diability access information service for London arts and entertainment. Open M-F 9:30am-5:30pm.

Direct Mobility Hire, 8 Cheapside, North Circular Rd. N13 5Ed (☎8807 9830; www.directmobility.co.uk). Short-term rentals of wheelchairs, mobility scooters, walking aids, chairs, beds, and bathing aids. Minimum rental 1 week. Delivery/pick-up anywhere in London within 24hr.

RADAR (Royal Association for Disability and Rehabilitation), 12 City Forum, 250 City Rd., London EC1V 8AF (☎7250 3222; www.radar.org.uk). Network of 500 charities offering advocacy, information, and support for the handicapped. Also administers the nationwide disabled-toilet key scheme, which gives access to disabled toilets around the UK. Call for details.

London Disability Arts Forum, 34 Osnaburgh St. (☎7916 5484; www.dircon.co.uk). Organizes the annual Disability Film Festival and publishes the **DAIL** (Disability Arts in London) listings magazine, also available in brail and on audiocassette.

Tripscope: ☎08457 585 641, from abroad +44 20 8580 7021; www.justmobility.co.uk/tripscope. Advice on accessible transportation and routes in Britain.

Wheelchair Travel, 1 Johnston Green, Guildford, Surrey GU2 6XS (☎01483 233 640; www.wheelchair-travel.co.uk). Rents hand-controlled and accessible cars (from £40 per day), lift-enabled minivans (from £70 per day). Delivery to anywhere in UK (extra charge). Meet & greet service from £110.

EMBASSIES & CONSULATES

Australia: Australia House, Strand (☎7379 4334; www.australia.org.uk). Tube: Temple. Open M-F 9am-5pm; consular services available 9:30am-3:30pm. In an **emergency,** dial 0500 890 165 toll-free to contact the Foreign Affairs Dept.'s Consulate Officer in Canberra.

Canada: MacDonald House, 1 Grosvenor Sq. (☎7258 6600; www.dfait-maeci.gc.ca/london). Tube: Bond St. Open 8:30am-5pm.

Ireland: 17 Grosvenor Pl. (☎7235 2171). Tube: Hyde Park Corner. Consular services at **Montpelier House,** 106 Brompton Rd. (☎7225 7700). Tube: Knightsbridge. Open M-F 9:30am-4:30pm.

New Zealand: New Zealand House, 80 Haymarket (☎7930 8422; www.newzealandhc.org.uk). Tube: Leicester Sq. Consular section open M-F 10am-noon and 2-4pm.

South Africa: South Africa House, Trafalgar Sq. (☎ 7451 7299; www.southafrica-house.com). Tube: Charing Cross. Consular services nearby at **14 Whitehall** (☎ 7925 8900). Open M-F 8:45am-12:45pm.

United States: 24 Grosvenor Sq. (☎ 7499 9900; www.embassy.org.uk). Tube: Bond St. Open M-F 8:30am-12:30pm and 2-5pm. Phones answered 24hr.

EMERGENCY SERVICES

In an emergency, dial **999** from any fixed phone or **112** from a mobile to reach ambulance, police, and fire services. See also **Crisis & Help Lines,** p. 312; **Hospitals,** p. 314; and **Police,** p. 316.

FINANCIAL SERVICES

See **Banks,** p. 311, and **Currency Exchange,** p. 312.

GAY & LESBIAN RESOURCES

Freedom Cars. Gay & lesbian taxi service. See Minicabs, p. 315.

gingerbeer.co.uk. Lesbian web portal for London, with listings of clubs, bars, restaurants, and community resources.

London Lesbian & Gay Switchboard: ☎ 7837 7324; www.llgs.org.uk. Helpline and information resource. 24hr.

GAY to Z (www.gaytoz.com). Online and printed directory of gay resources and gay-friendly businesses in Britain. Available at gay bookstores, or send £3 (overseas US$10) to: GAY to Z Directories Limited, 41 Cooks Rd., London, SE17 3NG.

Gay's the Word. The largest gay and lesbian bookshop in the UK. See p. 236.

Outlet. Finds accommodations for gays and lesbians. See p. 284.

Silver Moon Women's Bookstore. Large selection of lesbian titles. See p. 230.

HEALTH & FITNESS

*London has hundreds of fitness clubs, ranging from council-run gyms to lavish private clubs. Use Yellow Pages (under "Leisure Centres") to find one near you, or call **Sportsline** (☎ 7222 8000). Don't pay any fees until you've seen all the club facilities and know exactly what you get for your money.*

Chelsea Sports Centre, Chelsea Manor St. (☎ 7352 6985). Tube: Sloane Sq. or South Kensington. Pool, solarium, gym, tennis, ping-pong, volleyball, basketball, football, and badminton. Numerous classes. Open M-

F 7am-10pm, Sa 8am-6:30pm, Su and holidays 8am-10pm. Call for prices.

Kensington Sports Centre, Walmer Rd. (☎ 7727 9747). Tube: Ladbroke Grove. In Notting Hill, despite the name. Pool, sauna, weights, badminton, and squash, plus aerobics, self-defence, and scuba-diving classes. Hours as for Chelsea Sports Centre.

Barbican YMCA, 2 Fann St. (☎ 7628 0697). Tube: Barbican. Weights, Nautilus machines, treadmills and bikes. Non-members £5 per session. Membership £55 per year, £27 for 3 months, plus £3.50 per use, £35 unlimited use per month. Open M-F 7am-9:30pm, Sa-Su 10am-6pm.

Queen Mother Sports Centre, 223 Vauxhall Bridge Rd. (☎ 7630 5522). Tube: Victoria. 1-hr. induction course (non-members £28) required for use of weights (non-members £6.30). Pool open M-Tu 6:30am-8pm, W-F 6:30am-7:30pm, Sa-Su 8am-5:30pm; non-members £2.25 per use, members £1.70. Membership £39 per year. Open M-F 6:30am-10pm, Sa 8am-8pm.

HELPLINES

London Women's Aid: ☎ 0870 599 5443. 24hr. support for victims of domestic violence.

Rape Crisis Centre: ☎ 7837 1600.

Samaritans: ☎ 08457 90 90 90. 24hr. emotional support for depression and suicide.

Victim Support: ☎ 0845 303 0900. Emotional help and legal advice for victims of crime. Open M-F 9am-9pm, Sa-Su 9am-7pm.

HOSPITALS

For urgent care, go to one of the 24hr. **Accident & Emergency** departments listed below. For non-urgent care, or to see a specialist, you will need a referral from your primary care doctor. See also **Clinics,** p. 312, and **Emergency Services,** p. 314.

Charing Cross, Fulham Palace Rd., entrance on St. Dunstan's Rd. (☎ 8846 1234). Tube: Baron's Court or Hammersmith.

Chelsea and Westminster, 369 Fulham Rd. (☎ 8746 8000). Tube: Fulham Broadway then #14 or #211 bus.

Royal London Hospital, Whitechapel Rd. (☎ 7377 7000). Tube: Whitechapel.

Royal Free, Pond St. (☎ 7794 0500). Tube: Belsize Park or Rail: Hampstead Heath.

St. Mary's, Praed St. (☎ 7725 6666). Tube: Paddington.

St. Thomas's, Lambeth Palace Rd. (☎ 7928 9292). Tube: Waterloo.

University College Hospital, Grafton Way (☎ 7387 9300). Tube: Warren St.

Whittington, Highgate Hill (☎ 7272 3070). Tube: Archway.

HOTLINES

See **Helplines,** p. 314.

INTERNET ACCESS

Most large department stores, bookstores, and music stores offer internet access.

easyEverything (☎ 7907 7800; www.easyeverything.com). 5 locations, each with hundreds of terminals: 9-16 Tottenham Court Rd. (Tube: Tottenham Court Rd.); 7 Strand (Tube: Charing Cross); 358 Oxford St. (Tube: Bond St.); 9-13 Wilson Rd(Tube: Victoria); 160-166 Kensington High St. (Tube: High St. Kensington). Prices vary with demand, from £1 per hr.; min. charge £2. Open 24hr.

Virgin Megastore, Oxford St. See p. 227.

BT Multi.phones, installed in Tube and rail stations throughout London. Internet-enabled payphones with touch-screen control.

Internet Exchange, at 3 locations: 37 Covent Garden Market (☎ 7836 8636; Tube: Covent Garden); 47-49 Queensway (☎ 7792 5790; Tube: Bayswater); 125-127 Baker St. (☎ 7224 5402; Tube: Baker St.). Open M-F 7:30am-10:30pm, Sa 8:30am-10:30pm, Su9:30am-10:30pm. 3-7p per minute, £7.50 per day.

Cyberia, 39 Whitfield St., W1 (☎ 7681 4200; www.cyberiacafe.net). Tube: Goodge St. Open M-F 9am-9pm, Sa 11am-7pm, Su 11am-6pm. From 50p.

LEGAL RESOURCES

Embassies may provide legal advice and services to citizens under arrest.

Release: ☎ 7729 9904. 24hr. Advice and information regarding the law and drugs.

Community Legal Service (www.justask.org.uk). Government-run online advice service and directory of legal advisors.

Citizen's Advice Bureaux (☎ www.nacab.org.uk). Independent nationwide network of offices giving free advice on legal and consumer issues. London bureaux include 140 Ladbroke Grove (☎8960 3322; Tube: Ladbroke Grove); 32 Ludgate Hill (☎ 7236 1156; Tube: Blackfriars), 135 Upper St. (☎7359 06139; Tube: Angel or Highbury & Islington). Opening hours very limited and appointments often necessary; call ahead.

Liberty, 21 Tabard St., SE1 4LAX (☎ 7403 3888; www.liberty-human-rights.org.uk). Dedicated to the advancement and protection of civil and human rights. Can provide legal representation for serious human rights cases. Legal advice line (☎7378 8659) answered M and Th 6-8pm, W 12:30-2:30pm.

Police Complaints Authority, 10 Great George St., SW1P 3AE (☎7273 6450; www.pca.gov.uk). For reporting police misconduct. Be sure to note the offending officer's number (worn on the shoulder).

Victim Support. See **Crisis Lines,** p. 312.

LOST PROPERTY

See also **Police,** p. 316.

Transport for London Lost Property Office, 200 Baker St., NW1 5RT (fax 7918 1028). Items left on public transport are first held 48hr. at the bus garage or the Tube station where they were found, then forwarded to the above address. To reclaim an item, write or fax with a Lost Property Enquiry form, available from Tube stations, or go in person. Open M-F 9:30am-2pm. Fee on reclamation.

Public Carriage Office, 15 Penton St. (☎7833 0996). Tube: Angel. For articles left in licensed taxicabs (balck cabs). Open M-F 9am-4pm.

MAIL SERVICES

See **Postal Services,** p. 316.

MEDICAL SERVICES

See **Hospitals,** p. 314; **Clinics,** p. 312; and **Dental Care,** p. 313.

MINICABS

See also **Taxis,** p. 317.

Teksi (☎8455 9999, 7267 0267, 7284 2222, 7419 2222, 7219 4444, 7482 1111, 7495 7000, 7586 2222, 7794 2222, or 7916 5555; www.teksi.com). 24hr. pick-up anywhere in London. Cash rates: £4 first 2mi. (£6 first 3mi. in West End and City), £1.20 additional mi. Airport rates: Heathrow £21, Gatwick £38, Stansted/Luton £35, plus parking and waiting at £10 per hr. V, MC; higher rates, give card no. when you call.

Freedom Cars, 52 Wardour St. (☎7734 1313). Soho-based cab service specializing in gays and lesbians. Pick-up anywhere in London. 24hr. Airport to West End: Heathrow £25.50, Gatwick £36, Stansted/Luton £40 plus parking. Cash only.

Lady Cabs (☎7264 3501). Not limited to women passengers, but will provide a female driver on request. Pick-up in North London only. Open M-Th 8am-midnight, F 8a-1am, Sa 9am-2am, Su 10am-midnight. Cash only.

Ladybirds (☎ 8776 1495). Cabs for women in South London. Pick-up within 6mi. of Croydon. Open Su-Th 7am-midnight, F-Sa to 1:30am. Gatwick £18, Heathrow £23-£26. Cash only.

MINORITY RESOURCES

See also **Gay & Lesbian Services,** p. 314, and **Religious Resources,** p. 316.

Africa Centre, 38 King St. (☎7836 1973; www.africacentre.org.uk). Tube: Covent Garden. Pan-African cultural centre, with a full program of events. Also runs regular nightclub evenings; see p. 193.

Black Cultural Archives, 378 Coldharbour Ln. (☎7738 4591). Tube: Brixton. Artistic and cultural resource. Archives open M-F 10am-4pm by appointment only.

BLINK (www.blink.co.uk). Web resource for the UK's Black and Asian communities, from art and culture to human rights.

Liberty. Human rights advocacy group. See Legal Resources, p. 315.

PHARMACIES

See **Chemists,** p. 312.

POLICE

In an **emergency,** dial 999 from any land phone, or 112 from a mobile phone.

London is covered by two police forces: the **City of London Police** (☎7601 2222; www.cityoflondon.police.uk) for the City, and the **Metropolitan Police** (☎7230 1212; www.met.police.uk) for the rest. For **general inquiries,** write to: New Scotland Yard, Broadway, London SW1H 0BG. In the event of police misconduct, contact the **Police Complaints Authority** (see Legal Resources, p. 315) The following **police stations** are open 24hr.

Albany St.: 60 Albany St. (☎7388 1212). Tube: Great Portland St.

Islington: 2 Tolpuddle St. (☎7704 1212). Tube: Angel.

West End Central: 27 Savile Row (☎7437 1212). Tube: Oxford Circus or Piccadilly Circus.

Charing Cross: Agar St. (☎7240 1212). Tube: Charing Cross.

Bishopsgate: 182 Bishopsgate (☎7601 2606). Tube: Liverpool St.

Marylebone: 1-9 Seymour St. (☎7486 1212). Tube: Marble Arch.

Paddington Green: 2-4 Harrow Rd. (☎7402 1212). Tube: Edgware Rd.

Southwark: 323 Borough High St. (☎7378 1212). Tube: Borough.

POSTAL SERVICES

For information on **Royal Mail** services, see **Once in London,** p. 39.

FedEx (☎0800 123 800). Cheapest express service is International Priority. 500g envelope £25-35 depending on destination.

RELIGIOUS RESOURCES

Buddhist: Buddhapadipa Temple, Calonne Rd., Wimbledon Parkside (☎8946 1357). Tube: Wimbledon Park. The first Buddhist temple in the UK, since 1965.

Anglican/Episcopal: The vast majority of churches in London; there's almost always one within walking distance. **London Diocese,** London Diocesan House, 36 Causton St. (☎7932 1100; www.london.anglican.org) for London north of the Thames. **Southwark Diocese,** 4 Chapel Ct., Borough High St. (☎7403 8686; www.dswark.org) for south London.

Muslim: London Central Mosque, 146 Park Rd. (☎ 7724 3363; www.islamicculturalcentre.co.uk). Tube: Baker St. Also houses the **Islamic cultural centre.**

Jewish: Orthodox, Central Synagogue, Great Portland St. (☎7580 1355; www.brijnet.org/centralsyn). Tube: Great Portland St. or Oxford Circus. Can also advise on kosher restaurants and hotels. **Reform:** West London Synagogue, 33 Seymour Pl. (☎7723 4404; www.wls.org.uk). Tube: Marble Arch.

Orthodox Christian: Greek, Archdiocese of Thyateira and Great Britain, Thyateira House, 5 Craven Hill, W2 3EN (☎7723 4787; www.nostos.com/church). **Russian,** Diocese of Sourozh, Cathedral of the Dormitian and All Saints, 67 Ennismore Gdns. (☎7584 0096; www.sourozh.org). Tube: Knightsbridge or South Kensington.

Hindu: Shree Swaminarayan Mandir, 105-119 Brentfield Rd. (☎8965 2651). Tube: Neasden. Also **cultural center.** See Sights, p. 123.

Roman Catholic: Westminster Diocese, Central Area, 79 St. Charles Sq., W10 6EB (☎8960 4029; www.westminsterdiocese.org.uk).

SPORTS CLUBS

See **Health & Fitness,** p. 314.

TAXIS

The listings below refer to licensed taxicabs ("black cabs"). All operate throughout London and charge the same rates (see **Once in London**, p. 36). For **Minicabs,** see p. 315.

Computer Cabs: ☎ 7286 0286.

Datacab: ☎ 7727 7200.

Dial-a-Cab: ☎ 7253 5000.

Mountview Taxis: ☎ 7272 0272.

TELEPHONE SERVICES

For information on making calls in Britain and useful numbers, see **Once in London,** p. 41.

Calling card access numbers: If calling from a British Telecom phone, use 0800; if using Cable & Wireless, use 0500.

AT&T: 0800/0500 69 00 11

Canada Direct: 0800/0500 890 016

MCI Worldcom: 0800/0500 890 222

Telecom NZ Direct: 0800/0500 890 064

Sprint: 0800/0500 890 877

Telkom South Africa: 0800 890 027

Telstra Australia: 0800 890 061

TICKETS

Ticketmaster (☎ 7344 4444; www.ticketmaster.co.uk) is the UK's largest telephone ticketing agency. Tickets to almost every event, show, mainstream movie theater, and major nightclub in the country. Ask about the booking fee before committing: you may get a better deal booking directly.

Half-Price Ticket Booth, Leicester Sq. Half-price theater tickets on the day. See p. 211.

TOURS

See **Sights,** p. 67.

TOURIST INFORMATION

Britain Visitor Centre (www.visitbritain.com), 1 Regent St. Tube: Oxford Circus. Run by the British Tourist Association. Open M 9:30am-6:30pm, Tu-F 9am-6:30pm, Sa-Su 10am-4pm.

London Visitor Centres (www.londontouristboard.com). Run by the London Tourist Board:

Heathrow Terminals 1,2,3: In the Tube station. Open Oct- Aug. daily 8am-6pm; Sept. M-Sa 9am-7pm and Su 8am-6pm.

Liverpool Street: In the Tube station. Open June-Sept. M-Sa 8am-7pm, Su 8am-6pm; Oct.-May daily 8am-6pm.

Victoria Station: Station forecourt. Open Easter-Sept. M-Sa 8am-8pm, Su 8am-6pm; Oct.-Easter daily 8am-6pm.

Waterloo International: Arrivals hall. Open daily 8:30am-10:30pm.

TRANSPORT INFORMATION

For information on transportation, see **Once in London,** p. 33. For listings, see also **Bicycle & Scooter Rental,** p. 311; **Car Rental,** p. 312; **Minicabs,** p. 315; and **Taxis,** p. 317.

Transport for London (info ☎ 7222 1234; www.londontransport.co.uk) operates the following information centers. All are located in Tube stations unless otherwise indicated.

Euston: Station concourse. Open M-Sa 7:15am-6pm, Su 8:30am-5pm.

Greenwich: Cutty Sark Gdns. Open daily 10am-5pm.

Heathrow Airport: Terminal 1: Arrivals hall. Open M-Sa 7:15am-10pm, 8:15am-10pm Su. **Terminal 2:** Arrivals hall. Open M-Sa 7:15am-5pm, Su 8:15am-5pm. **Terminals 1,2,3:** Tube station. Open M-Sa 6:30am-7pm, Su 7:15am-7p. **Terminal 4:** Arrivals hall. Open M-Sa 6am-3pm, Su 7:15am-3pm.

King's Cross: Open M-Sa 8am-6pm, Su 8:30am-5pm.

Liverpool Street: Open M-F 8a-6pm, Sa-Su 8:45am-5:30pm.

Oxford Circus: Open M-Sa 8:45am-6pm, Su 10am-3pm.

Paddington: Open M-Sa 7:15am-8:30pm, Su 8:15am-8:30pm.

Piccadilly Circus: Open daily 8:45am-6pm.

St. James's Park: Shopping center. Open M-F 8:15am-5:15pm.

Victoria Station: Mainline station. Open M-Sa 7:45am-7pm, Su 8:45am-7pm.

Waterloo International: At the London Visitor Centre. Open daily 8:30am-10:30pm.

WOMEN'S RESOURCES

See also **Clinics,** p. 312, and **Helplines,** p. 314.

Audre Lord Clinic and **Bernard Clinic.** Health clinics staffed by women. See Clinics, p. 312.

Family Planning Association: 2-12 Pentonville Rd. (☎ 0845 310 1334) Tube: Angel. Informational services: contraception, pregnancy test, and abortion referral.

Lady Cabs and **Ladybirds.** Taxi services for women. See Minicabs, p. 315.

Welcome to London
Hyde Park Rooms Hotel

Nice Central Location

**3 minute walk from
Paddington, Heathrow Express**

Full English Breakfast

Clean, Comfortable and Friendly
From:

Single: £30.00
Double: £45.00
Famil: £60.00

137 Sussex Gardens
Hyde Park W2 2RX

Tel 0207 723 0225 • 0207 723 0965

Index

A

A Night to Remember 54
Abbey Road 12, 122
academic institutions 305
accident & emergency depts. 314
Accommodations 281–299
   agencies 311
   B&Bs & hotels 283
   Bayswater 289–292
   Bloomsbury 293–298
   By Neighborhood 284–299
   By Price 283
   City of London 285
   Clerkenwell 285
   hostels 282
   Kensington & Earl's Court 287–289
   Knightsbridge & Belgravia 287
   Marylebone & Regent's Park 292
   North London 298
   residence halls 283
   South Bank 285
   South London 299
   tips 281
   Types 282–283
   West End 284
   West London 299
   Westminster 286
Adam, Robert 57, 110
Adams, John 83
Adams, John Quincy 99
Airbus 30, 31
airfares 271
airlines 271
airplanes 271
airports 27, 311
Albert Hall 113
Albert Memorial 113
Albertopolis 112
alcohol 48
Alfred the Great 52
All Hallows by the Tower 99
All Saints 64
All Souls Langham Place 80
All You Need Is Love 205
Almeida 219
alternative club nights 189
American Express 267, 312
Amis, Martin 64
Andrews, Julie 65
Angles 52

Anglican churches 316
anglo-american glossary 46
Annely Juda Fine Art 142
Anthony D'Offay gallery 142
apartments 307
Apsley House 110
Arsenal 65, 209
Art 205
Arts and Crafts movement 58
the Ashes 120
Asians 63
ASK Pizza 158
Aspects of London 14
Astronomer Royal 129
ATM cards 45, 267
au pairs 303
Augustine 52
Austen, Jane 254

B

B&Bs 283
Bacon, Francis 64, 90, 121
Bank of England 98
Bank to the Tower 98
banks 45
   accounts 308
Bankside Gallery 145
Banqueting House 106
Barbican
   Barbican Centre 213
Barnes, Julian 64
Barry, Charles 58, 70
bars 185
Bath 254–256
Battle of Cable Street 60
Bayswater
   Accommodations 289–292
   Discover 10
   Entertainment 217
   Food & Drink 174
   Shopping 236
BBC 43, 60
   Television Centre 123
Beatles 61, 63
Beau Brummel 58
Becket, Thomas à 252
bed and breakfasts 283
bedsits 307
Beefcake Wellington 110
Beefeaters 73
Belgrave Square 109
Belgravia *see* Knightsbridge & Belgravia

Bell, Clive & Vanessa 60
Bentham, Jeremy 116
Bermondsey Market 238
Bernard Jacobson Gallery 142
Bevis Marks Synagogue 126
bicycles 37
   rental 311
   tours 68
Big Ben 71
birth control 317
Black Death 53
Blair, Tony 62
Blake, William 58, 73, 81, 83
Blenheim 252
blitz 60
Blood Brothers 205
Bloody Mary 55
Bloomsbury
   Accommodations 293–298
   Discover 11
   Entertainment 217
   Food & Drink 175–176
   Museums & Galleries 148
   Shopping 236–237
   Sights 116–118
Bloomsbury Group 60
Blue Card Permit 302
blue plaques 32
Blues Brothers 205
Blur 64
boat tours 68
boats 36, 275
Boleyn, Anne 76
Booker Prize 64
Borough 100
Borough Market 168
Boswell, James 57
Boudicca 51
bowling 217
Boyle, Richard 124
Branagh, Kenneth 65
breakbeats 190
Brick Lane 127, 180, 239
Bridge of Sighs 247
Bridget Jones 64, 173
Brighton 246
Britain Visitor Centre 317
British Council 306
British embassies 263
British Library 117
British Library Galleries 148
British Museum 134–135
Brixton 13, 125
   Food & Drink 180

Brixton Academy 220
Brixton Market 238
broadcasting 43
Broadcasting House 80
Brockwell Park 126
Brompton Oratory 111
Brunei Gallery 149
bucket shops 274
Buckingham Palace 68
Buddhist temple 316
Buddy 205
budget travel agencies 271
budget travel agencies 311
budgeting 268
Burbage, James 55
bureaux de change 45
Burlington Arcade 81
Burlington House 81
bus stations 32
bus tours 67
buses 35
Butler's Wharf 105
Byron, Lord 58, 82

C

Cabinet War Rooms 145
calling card numbers 317
calling cards 42
Cambridge 247–249
Camden Lock Market 237
Camden markets 237
Camden Passage Market 238
Camden Town 12, 118
   Food & Drink 177
Canary Wharf 128
cannabis 122
Canterbury 252–254
Canterbury Tales 149, 252
Canute 52, 97
car rental 312
Carfax Tower, Oxford 251
Carlton House Terrace 82
Carlyle, Thomas 109
Carlyle's House 109
Carnaby Street 79, 226
cash cards 45, 267
casualty depts. 314
cathedrals
   Southwark 103
   St. Paul's 71–??
   Westminster 107
Catholic churches 316
Cats 205
Caxton, William 54

319

Maps

INSIDE

✚ Hospital	✈ Airport	● Sight	⸺ Pedestrian Zone
✪ Police	🚌 Bus Station	🏛 Museum	
✉ Post Office	🚂 Train Station	🛍 Shopping	Park
🛈 Tourist Office	⊖ Tube Station	✇ Entertainment	
💲 Bank	⚓ Ferry Landing	🍴 Food	Water
⚑ Embassy/Consulate	🕇 Church	🍺 Pub or Bar	
▪ Site or Point of Interest	✡ Synagogue	★ Nightlife	
☎ Telephone Office	☪ Mosque	⌂ Hotel/Hostel	The Let's Go thumb always points **NORTH**.
⛺ Camping	💻 Internet Cafe		

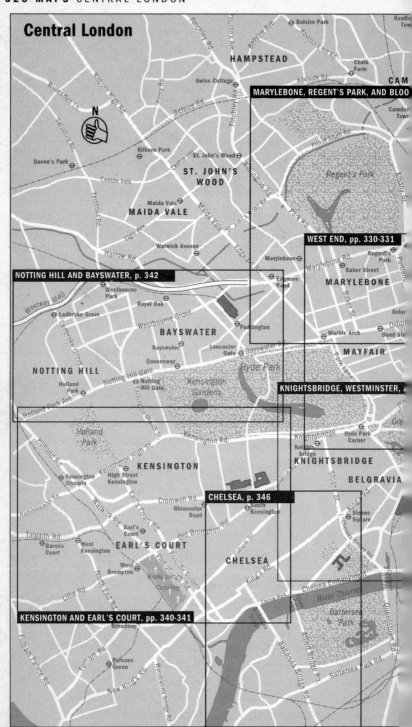

Central London

MARYLEBONE, REGENT'S PARK, AND BLOO

WEST END, pp. 330-331

NOTTING HILL AND BAYSWATER, p. 342

KNIGHTSBRIDGE, WESTMINSTER,

CHELSEA, p. 346

KENSINGTON AND EARL'S COURT, pp. 340-341

HAMPSTEAD

CAM

Regent's Park

ST. JOHN'S WOOD

MAIDA VALE

MARYLEBONE

MAYFAIR

BAYSWATER

Hyde Park

NOTTING HILL

Kensington Gardens

Holland Park

KENSINGTON

KNIGHTSBRIDGE

BELGRAVIA

EARL'S COURT

CHELSEA

River Thames

Battersea Park

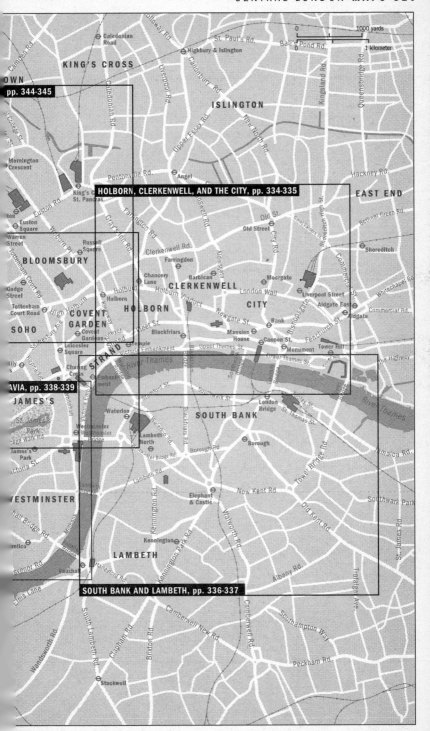

West End

● ⓘ SIGHTS

The Albany, **55**	D4
Burlington Arcade, **21**	C4
Burlington House, **17**	C5
Carnaby Street, **41**	C3
Charing Cross, **74**	E5
Cleopatra's Needle, **85**	F4
Grosvenor Square, **10**	B4
Marble Arch, **1**	A4
Queen's Chapel, **67**	D5
Royal Arcade, **20**	C4
Royal Institution, **22**	C4
Royal Opera Arcade, **64**	D5
Savile Rd., **24**	C4
Savoy, **83**	F4
Shepherd Market, **12**	C5
Somerset House, **87**	F4
St. George's Church, **35**	C4

St. James's Church, **58**	D4
St. James's Palace, **68**	D6
St. Martin-in-the-Fields, **75**	E4
St. Mary-le-Strand, **89**	F4
Trafalgar Square, **72**	E5
Victoria Embankment Gardens, **84**	F4

🏛 MUSEUMS

Annely Juda Fine Art, **45**	C3
Anthony D'Offay, **44**	C3
Bernard Jacobson, **27**	C4
Christie's, **66**	D5
Courtauld Institute, **88**	F4
Faraday Museum, **23**	C4
Gilbert Collection, **90**	F4
ICA, **69**	D5
Marborough Fine Arts, **16**	C5
National Gallery, **70**	E4

National Portrait Gallery, **71**	E4
Robert Sandelson, **26**	C4
Royal Academy, **18**	C4
Sotheby's, **32**	C4

★ NIGHTLIFE

AKA, **81**	E3
The End, **80**	E3
The Hanover Grand, **43**	C3
Heaven, **76**	E5

🍺 PUBS AND BARS

The Coach and Horses, **28**	C4
Point 101, **79**	E3
Sherlock Holmes, **73**	E5
T.S. Queen Mary, **86**	F4
Ye Grapes, **13**	C5

MARYLEBONE

MAYFAIR

Hyde Park

The Serpentine

Green Park

KNIGHTSBRIDGE

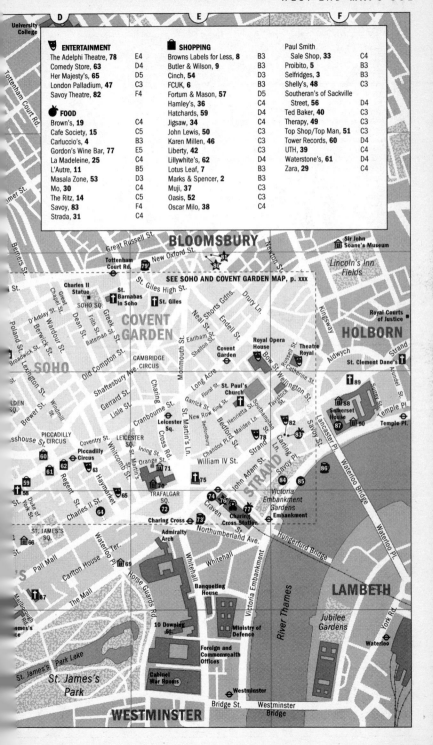

🎭 ENTERTAINMENT

The Adelphi Theatre, **78**	E4
Comedy Store, **63**	D4
Her Majesty's, **65**	D5
London Palladium, **47**	C3
Savoy Theatre, **82**	F4

🍎 FOOD

Brown's, **19**	C4
Cafe Society, **15**	C5
Carluccio's, **4**	B3
Gordon's Wine Bar, **77**	E5
La Madeleine, **25**	D3
L'Autre, **11**	B5
Masala Zone, **53**	D3
Mo, **30**	C4
The Ritz, **14**	C5
Savoy, **83**	F4
Strada, **31**	C4

🛍 SHOPPING

Browns Labels for Less, **8**	B3
Butler & Wilson, **9**	B3
Cinch, **54**	D3
FCUK, **6**	B3
Fortum & Mason, **57**	D5
Hamley's, **36**	C4
Hatchards, **59**	D4
Jigsaw, **34**	C4
John Lewis, **50**	C3
Karen Millen, **46**	C3
Liberty, **42**	C3
Lillywhite's, **62**	D4
Lotus Leaf, **7**	B3
Marks & Spencer, **2**	B3
Muji, **37**	C3
Oasis, **52**	C3
Oscar Milo, **38**	C4

Paul Smith	
Sale Shop, **33**	C4
Proibito, **5**	B3
Selfridges, **3**	B3
Shelly's, **48**	C3
Southeran's of Sackville	
Street, **56**	D4
Ted Baker, **40**	C3
Therapy, **49**	C3
Top Shop/Top Man, **51**	C3
Tower Records, **60**	D4
UTH, **39**	C3
Waterstone's, **61**	D4
Zara, **29**	C4

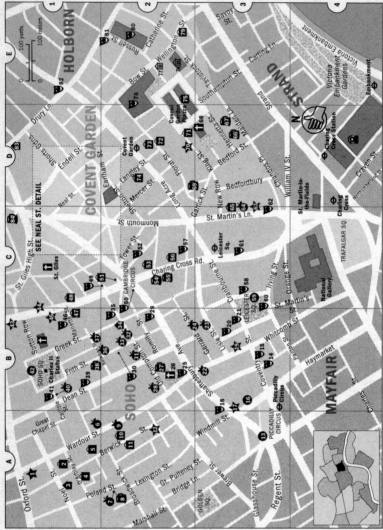

Soho and Covent Garden

SEE SHOPPING, ACCOMMODATIONS,
NIGHTLIFE, FOOD, PUBS, BARS, AND
ENTERTAINMENT LEGEND, p. 333.

SIGHTS

Leicester Square, **59**	C3
Madame Tussaud's Rock Circus, **16**	B3
Piccadilly Circus, **13**	A3
Royal Opera House, **76**	E2
Seven Dials, **104**	NS
Soho Square, **42**	B1
St. Anne's Church, **26**	B2
St. Paul's Church, **68**	D3
Theatre Royal, Drury Lane, **80**	E2

MUSEUMS

London's Transport Museum, **78**	E2
Theatre Museum, **77**	E2

Neal St.

(GRID REFERENCE = NS)

Soho and Covent Garden

SEE MAP, p, 332
SEE SIGHTS AND MUSEUMS LEGEND, p. 332

(NS = NEAL ST. DETAIL)

🛍 SHOPPING

Black Market, **4**	A1
Blackwell's, **51**	C2
Buffalo Boots, **87**	NS
Clog It, **89**	NS
Cyberdog, **103**	NS
Daddy Kool, **10**	A2
Diesel, **92**	NS
Diesel StyleLab, **72**	D2
Dr. Marten's, **71**	D2
Dupe, **91**	NS
Foyles, **47**	B1
Gerry's, **28**	B2
London Doll House Co., **75**	E2
Miss Sixty, **97**	NS
Neal St. East, **74**	D2
Neal's Yard Stores, **96**	NS
Office, **90**	NS
Office Sale Shop, **65**	D3
Paul Smith, **73**	D2
Penhaligon's, **79**	E2
Ray's Jazz Shop, **100**	NS
Reckless Records, **5**	A1
Silver Moon Women's Bookshop, **56**	C2
Sister Ray, **11**	A2
Swear, **86**	NS
Thomas Neal 's, **94**	NS
Turnkey, **48**	C1
Uptown Records, **2**	A1
Zwemmers, **53**	C2

🛏 ACCOMMODATIONS

High Holborn Residences, **83**	D1
Outlet, **34**	B2
Seven Dials Hotel, **99**	NS
YHA Oxford St., **3**	A1

⭐ NIGHTLIFE

Africa Centre, **70**	D2
The Astoria, **43**	B1
Bar Rumba, **17**	B3
The Box, **105**	NS
Brief Encounter, **63**	D3
Madame Jojo's, **12**	A2
One Four Four, **44**	B1
Propaganda, **1**	A1
Sound, **19**	B3
Velvet Room, **45**	B1

🍎 FOOD

bibo cibo, **88**	NS
Bar Italia, **33**	B2
Blue Room, **37**	B1
Busaba Eathai, **6**	A1
Cafe Emm, **36**	B2
Gerry's, **28**	B2
Harbor City, **24**	B3
Itsu, **9**	A2
Monmouth Coffee House, **101**	NS
Mr. Kong, **23**	B3
Neal's Yard Bakery & Tearoom, **98**	NS
Neal's Yard Dairy, **102**	NS
Nusa Dua, **40**	B1
Old Compton Cafe, **32**	B2
Patisserie Valerie, **31**	B2
St. Martin's Lane, **64**	D3
Wong Kei, **22**	B3
World Food Cafe, **95**	NS
Yo! Sushi, **7**	A2

🍺 PUBS AND BARS

79 CXR, **54**	C2

Comptons of Soho, **27**	B2
The Dog and Duck, **38**	B1
Freedom Brewing Co., **93**	NS
Freud, **85**	NS
Ku Bar, **55**	C2
Lamb and Flag, **69**	D3
Maple Leaf, **67**	D3
Point 101, **84**	C1
Spot, **66**	D3
Yo! Below, **8**	A2

♣ ENTERTAINMENT

Arts Theatre, **57**	C2
Borderline, **46**	B1
Curzon Soho, **29**	B2
Comedy Store, **14**	B3
Empire, **21**	B3
English National Opera, **62**	C3
Fortune Theatre, **81**	E2
Gielgud Theatre, **18**	B3
Half-Price Ticket Booth, **60**	C3
New London Theatre, **82**	E1
Odeon Leicester Sq., **58**	C3
Palace Theatre, **50**	C2
Pheonix Theatre, **49**	C2
Pizza Express Jazz Club, **41**	B1
Prince Charles Cinema, **20**	B3
Prince Edward Theatre, **35**	B2
Prince of Wales Theatre, **15**	B3
Queen's Theatre, **25**	B2
Ronnie Scott's, **30**	B2
Royal Opera House, **76**	E2
Soho Theatre, **39**	B1
St. Martin's Theatre, **52**	C2
Theatre Royal, Dury Lane, **80**	E2
Wyndham's Theatre, **61**	C3

Holborn, Clerkenwell, and The City

SEE MAP, pp. 334-335
SEE SIGHTS LEGEND, p. 335

🏛 MUSEUMS

Bank of England Museum, **84**	E4
Barbican Galleries, **80**	D3
Dickens' House, **2**	A2
Guildhall Art Gallery, **73**	D4
Guildhall Clock Museum, **74**	D4
Hunterian Museum, **11**	A4
Museum of London, **76**	D4
Museum of St. Bartholomew's, **55**	C4
Sir John Soane's Museum, **8**	A4

♣ ENTERTAINMENT

Barbican Hall, **81**	D3
Barbican Theatre, **78**	D3
Peacock Theatre, **12**	A5
Sadler's Wells, **40**	B1
Strand Theatre, **16**	A5

🛍 SHOPPING

Twinings, **20**	B5

🍎 FOOD

Al's Cafe Bar, **37**	B2
Bleeding Heart Tavern, **31**	B3
Cafe in the Park, **10**	A4
Cafe Spice Namaster, **101**	F5
Futures!, **94**	E6
The Knosherie, **30**	B3
Leadenhall Market, **91**	E5
Noto, **70**	D5
The Place Below, **68**	D5
Quiet Revolution, **44**	C2
St. John, **49**	C3
Tinseltown 24-Hour Diner, **17**	C3
Woolley's Salad Shop and Sandwich Bar, **4**	A3

🛏 ACCOMMODATIONS

Finsbury Residences, **42**	C2
Roseberry Hall, **39**	B1
YHA City, **60**	C5

🍺 PUBS AND BARS

The Black Friar, **62**	C5
Cittie of Yorke, **6**	A3
The Eagle, **36**	B2
Filthy MacNasty's Whiskey Cafe, **41**	B1
Fox & Anchor, **50**	C3
Simpson's, **88**	E5
Vats, **3**	A3
Water Rats, **1**	A1
Ye Olde Cheshire Cheese, **24**	B4
Ye Olde Mitre Tavern, **28**	B3

⭐ NIGHTLIFE

Cafe Kick, **38**	B1
Fabric, **52**	C3
Fluid, **51**	C3
Match EC1, **45**	C2
Na Zdrowie, **7**	A4
Turnmills, **32**	B3

D   E   F

olborn, Clerkenwell, and The City

SEE MUSEUMS, ENTERTAINMENT, FOOD, ACCOMMODATIONS, PUBS, BARS, AND NIGHTLIFE LEGEND, p. 333

🛈 SIGHTS

Hallows-by-the-	Mansion House, **87**	E5
ower, **98**	F6	Marx Memorial Library, **33**	B2
k of England, **85**	E4	Middle Temple
rbican Centre, **79**	D3	Gardens, **17**	B5
arterhouse, **48**	C3	Middle Temple Hall, **18**	B5
rkenwell Green, **34**	B2	The Monument, **93**	E5
rkenwell Visitors'		Old Bailey, **57**	C4
entre, **35**	B2	Prince Henry's Room, **21**	B5
City of London		Priory of St. John, **43**	C2
nformation Centre, **61**	C5	Royal Courts of Justice, **13**	A5
College of Arms, **63**	C5	Royal Exchange, **87**	E5
dsmiths' Hall, **71**	D4	Samuel Johnson's
y's Inn, **5**	A3	House, **25**	B4
ldhall, **75**	D4	Smithfield Market, **53**	C3
coln's Inn, **9**	A4	Staple Inn, **27**	B4
d's of London, **90**	E5	St. Bartholomew
don Stone, **92**	E5	the Great, **54**	C3
		St. Bride's, **23**	B5

St. Clement Dane's, **14**	A5
St. Dunstan-in-the-East, **99**	E6
St. Dunstan-in-the-West, **26**	B5
St. Etheldreda's, **29**	B3
St. Giles Cripplegate, **77**	D3
St. James Garlickhythe, **64**	D5
St. John's Gate, **46**	C3
St. Lawrence Jewry, **72**	D4
St. Magnus the Martyr, **95**	E6
St. Margaret Lothbury, **82**	E4
St. Mary Aldermary, **64**	D5
St. Mary le Bow, **69**	D5
St. Martin-within-Ludgate, **58**	C5
St. Mary Woolnoth, **89**	E5
Stock Exchange, **83**	E4
St. Olave's, **100**	F5
St. Paul's Cathedral, **59**	C5
St. Sepulchre-	
without-Newgate, **54**	C4
St. Stephen Wallbrook, **67**	D5
Temple Church, **22**	B5
Temple of Mithras, **66**	D5
Tower Bridge Experience, **96**	F6
Tower of London, **97**	F6
Wig and Pen Club, **19**	B5

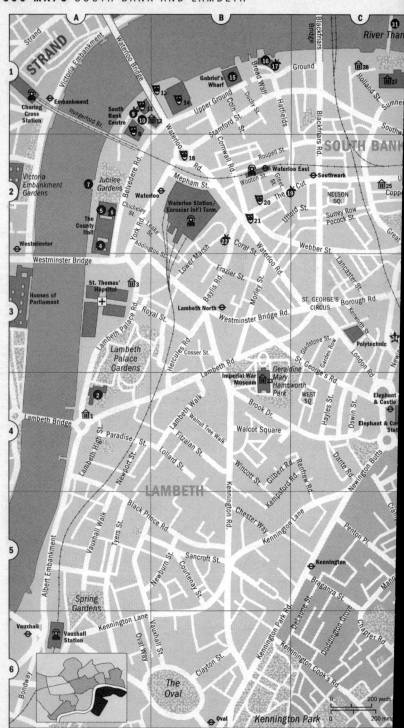

South Bank and Lambeth

● 🛈 SIGHTS

Butler's Wharf, **43**	F2
Dali Universe, **5**	A2
Gabriel's Wharf, **15**	B1
Golden Hinde, **35**	D1
HMS Belfast, **41**	E1
Hay's Galleria, **40**	E1
Lambeth Palace, **2**	A4
London Aquarium, **4**	A2
London Dungeon, **39**	E1
London Eye, **7**	A2
Millenium Bridge, **31**	C1
Old Operating Theatre, **37**	D2
OXO Tower, **16**	B1
Rose Theatre, **32**	D1
South Bank Centre, **10**	A1
Southwark Cathedral, **36**	D1
Shakespeare's Globe Theatre, **30**	C1
Vinopolis, **33**	D1
Winston Churchill's Britain at War, **38**	E2

★ NIGHTLIFE

Ministry of Sound, **24**	C3

🏠 ACCOMMODATIONS

LSE Bankside House, **26**	C1
Travel Inn County Hall, **6**	A2

🏛 MUSEUMS

Bankside Gallery, **28**	C1
Clink Prison Museum, **34**	D1
Design Museum, **44**	F2
Florence Nightingale Museum, **3**	A3
Hayward Gallery, **12**	A1
Imperial War Museum, **23**	B4
Jerwood Space, **25**	C2
Museum of Garden History, **1**	A4
Tate Modern, **27**	C1

🎭 ENTERTAINMENT

BFI IMAX, **18**	B2
National Film Theatre, **13**	B1
National Theatre, **14**	B1
Old Vic, **21**	B2
Queen Elizabeth Hall, **11**	A1
Royal Festival Hall, **8**	A1
Shakespeare's Globe Theatre, **29**	C1
Young Vic, **20**	B2

🍴 FOOD

Cantina del Ponte, **42**	F2
Cubana, **22**	B2
Gourmet Pizza Co., **17**	B1
People's Palace, **9**	A1
Tas, **19**	B2

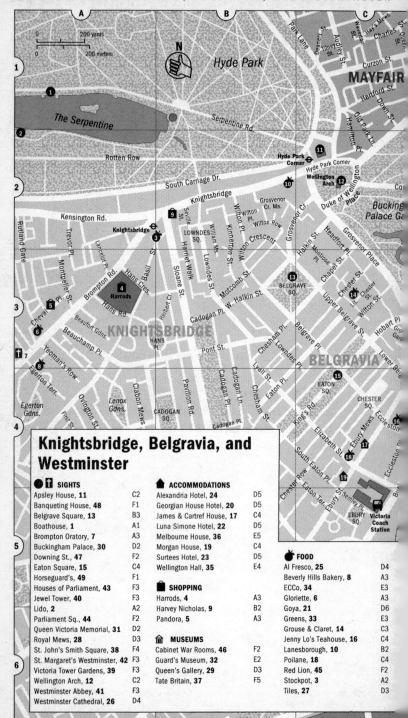

Knightsbridge, Belgravia, and Westminster

● 🛈 SIGHTS

Apsley House, **11**	C2
Banqueting House, **48**	F1
Belgrave Square, **13**	B3
Boathouse, **1**	A1
Brompton Oratory, **7**	A3
Buckingham Palace, **30**	D2
Downing St., **47**	F2
Eaton Square, **15**	C4
Horseguard's, **49**	F1
Houses of Parliament, **43**	F3
Jewel Tower, **40**	F3
Lido, **2**	A2
Parliament Sq., **44**	F2
Queen Victoria Memorial, **31**	D2
Royal Mews, **28**	D3
St. John's Smith Square, **38**	F4
St. Margaret's Westminster, **42**	F3
Victoria Tower Gardens, **39**	F3
Wellington Arch, **12**	C2
Westminster Abbey, **41**	F3
Westminster Cathedral, **26**	D4

🏠 ACCOMMODATIONS

Alexandria Hotel, **24**	D5
Georgian House Hotel, **20**	D5
James & Cartref House, **17**	C4
Luna Simone Hotel, **22**	D5
Melbourne House, **36**	E5
Morgan House, **19**	C4
Surtees Hotel, **23**	D5
Wellington Hall, **35**	E4

🛍 SHOPPING

Harrods, **4**	A3
Harvey Nicholas, **9**	B2
Pandora, **5**	A3

🏛 MUSEUMS

Cabinet War Rooms, **46**	F2
Guard's Museum, **32**	E2
Queen's Gallery, **29**	D3
Tate Britain, **37**	F5

🍎 FOOD

Al Fresco, **25**	D4
Beverly Hills Bakery, **8**	A3
ECCo, **34**	E3
Gloriette, **6**	A3
Goya, **21**	D6
Greens, **33**	E3
Grouse & Claret, **14**	C3
Jenny Lo's Teahouse, **16**	C4
Lanesborough, **10**	B2
Poilane, **18**	C4
Red Lion, **45**	F2
Stockpot, **3**	A2
Tiles, **27**	D3

KNIGHTSBRIDGE, BELGRAVIA, AND WESTMINSTER

Berkeley St.
Jermyn St.
Duke St.
King St.
ST. JAMES'S SQ.
Pall Mall
Waterloo Pl.
Pall Mall East
Cockspur St.
Charing Cross
Northumberland Ave.
Admiralty Arch
Whitehall
Whitehall Pl.

Green Park
St. James's St.
Carlton House Ter.
Horse Guards' Rd.
Horse Guards' Ave.

Queens Walk
ST. JAMES'S
Cleveland Row
The Mall
Horseguard's Parade
49
Horse Guards'
48
Victoria Embankment

Green Park
Stable Yard Rd.
St. James's Palace
47 Downing St.
Richmond Ter.
Cannon Row

31
St. James's Park Lake
Cabinet War Rooms
46 King Charles St.
45
Westminster
Westminster Bridge

30
St. James's Park
Bridge St.
44
PARLIAMENT SQ.
Big Ben
43
Houses of Parliament

29
Birdcage Walk
32
Old Queen St.
Great George St.
42
St. Margaret St.

Buckingham Gate
Queen Anne's Gate
Dartmouth St.
Tothill St.
Broad Sanctuary
41
Westminster Abbey
40 Jewel Tower
Abingdon St.

Palace St.
Wilfred St.
Castle Ln.
Wellington Barracks
Petty France St.
St. James's Park
Caxton St.
Broadway
New Scotland Yard
Great Smith St.
Gt. College St.
39

Bressenden Pl.
Stag Pl.
Victoria St.
Howick Pl.
33
Old Pye St.
Great Peter St.
Sutton Ground
Monck St.
Marsham St.
Tufton St.

Victoria
Ashley Pl.
Ambrosden Ave.
34
Medway St.
38 SMITH SQ.

26
Westminster Cathedral
Carlisle Pl.
Francis St.
Greencoat Pl.
Rochester Row
Greycoat St.
Horseferry Rd.
Lambeth Bridge

Wilton Rd.
Gillingham St.
Willow Pl.
Vincent Sq.
Maunsel St.
WESTMINSTER
Page St.

Guildhouse St.
Longmoore St.
25
Westminster School Fields
Vincent St.
Hide Place
Vincent St.

24
Warwick Way
35
Vincent Sq.
Chapter St.
Regency St.
Douglas St.
Erasmus St.
John Islip St.
Tate Britain
37
Millbank

23
Tachbrook St.
Herrick St.
Atterbury St.

WARWICK SQ.
22
Belgrave Rd.
Moreton St.
Causton St.

Sussex St.
Denbigh St.
36
Rampayne St.
Pimlico
River Thames

Gloucester St.
Charlwood St.
Chichester St.
ST. GEORGE'S SQ.
Aylesford St.
Vauxhall Bridge

21
Lupus St.
DOLPHIN SQ.
Grosvenor Rd.
Albert Embankment

Churchill Gardens Rd.
Claverton St.

Kensington and Earl's Court

● SIGHTS

Albert Memorial, **24**	E1
Kensington Palace, **14**	D1
Leighton House, **3**	B2
Royal Albert Hall, **23**	E2

🏛 MUSEUMS

Natural History Museum, **21**	E3
Science Museum, **22**	F2
Serpentine Gallery, **25**	E1
Victoria & Albert Museum, **26**	F3

🛍 SHOPPING

Central Park, **10**	C1
Urban Outfitters, **15**	D1

🎭 ENTERTAINMENT

Holland Park Open Air Theatre, **2**	B2

🍎 FOOD

Balans, **9**	C2
The Orangery, **13**	D1
Oriental Canteen, **27**	F3
Raison d'Etre, **20**	E3
Scarsdale, **8**	C3
Squeeze, **16**	D1
The Troubador, **19**	D4

🏠 ACCOMMODATIONS

Abbey House Hotel, **12**	C1
Beaver Hotel, **4**	B4
Mowbray Court Hotel, **6**	C4
Oxford Hotel, **7**	C4
Philbeach Hotel, **5**	C4
Swiss House Hotel, **17**	D4
Vicarage Private House, **11**	C1
YHA Holland House, **1**	B1
YHA Earl's Court, **18**	D4

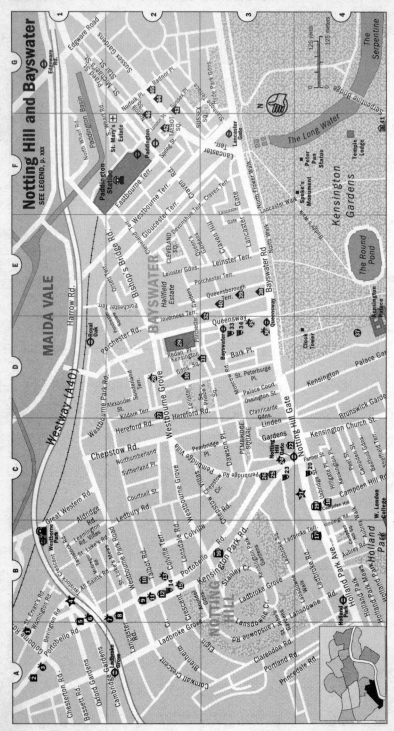

Notting Hill and Bayswater

SEE LEGEND, p. xxx

MAIDA VALE

BAYSWATER

NOTTING HILL

Westway (A40)

Kensington Gardens

The Serpentine

The Long Water

The Round Pond

Kensington Palace

Paddington Station

Notting Hill and Bayswater SEE MAP, p. 342

🔵 SIGHTS
Diana Fountain, **37**	D4

⭐ NIGHTLIFE
Notting Hill Arts Club, **21**	C4
Subterania, **4**	B1

🖼 SHOPPING
Antoine et Lilli, **18**	C4
Dolly Diamond, **26**	C3
Honest Jon's, **5**	B1
Intoxica, **9**	B2
Music and Video Exchange, **22**	C3
One of a Kind, **8**	B2
Rough Trade, **10**	B2
Season, **27**	D2
Teaze, **25**	C3
The Travel Bookshop, **12**	B2
Whiteleys, **29**	D2
Wilma, **2**	A1

🎭 ENTERTAINMENT
Electric Cinema, **14**	B2
First Bowl, **34**	D3
Gate Cinema, **20**	C4
The Gate, **23**	C3
Queens Skate Shop, **33**	D3

🍎 FOOD
Alounak Kebab, **28**	D2
Books for Cooks, **11**	B2
Fluid, **15**	B2
George's Portobello Fish Bar, **3**	A1
The Grain Shop, **7**	B2
La Bottega del Gelato, **36**	D3
Lisboa Patisserie, **1**	A1
Makan, **6**	B1
Manzara, **24**	C3
Royal China, **35**	D3
The Tea and Coffee Plant, **13**	B2

🍺 PUBS
192, **16**	B3
Gate, **19**	C4
Pharmacy, **17**	B4

🏛 MUSEUMS
Serpentine Gallery, **41**	F4

🏠 ACCOMMODATIONS
Admiral Hotel, **44**	G2
Barry House Hotel, **43**	G2
Cardiff Hotel, **46**	F2
Dean Court Hotel, **32**	D3
Garden Court Hotel, **30**	D2
Hyde Park Hostel, **38**	E3
Hyde Park Inn, **40**	E3
Hyde Park Rooms Hotel, **45**	G2
Kensington Gardens Hotel, **31**	D3
Mitre House Hotel, **42**	F2
Quest Hotel, **39**	E3

Marylebone, Regent's Park, and Bloomsbury SEE MAP, pp. 344-345

🔵🏛 SIGHTS
All Souls Langham Place, **26**	D5
Avenue Gardens, **20**	C3
Boating Lake, **14**	B3
British Library, **44**	E3
Broadcasting House, **24**	C5
Camden Tourist Information Centre, **45**	E3
Coram's Fields, **80**	F4
English Gardens, **19**	C3
Fitzroy Square, **34**	D4
London Central Mosque, **1**	A3
London Planetarium, **11**	B4
London Zoo, **18**	B2
Madame Tussaud's, **12**	B4
Queen Mary's Gardens, **13**	B4
Regent's Park, **17**	B3
RIBA, **22**	C5
Senate House, **65**	E5
St. George's Bloomsbury, **76**	E5
St. John's Lodge, **16**	B3
St Pancras Parish Church, **48**	E3
St. Pancras Station, **43**	E3
Thomas Coram Foundation, **81**	F4
University College London, **37**	D4

🖼 SHOPPING
Delta of Venus, **38**	D4
Gay's the World, **56**	E4
James Smith & Sons, **77**	E6
L. Cornelissen, **73**	E5
Lawrence Corner, **39**	D4
Paperchase, **28**	D5
Purves & Purves, **67**	E5
Unsworth, **72**	E5
Waterstone's, **61**	E4

🏛 MUSEUMS
British Museum, **71**	E5
Brunei Gallery, **62**	E4
October Gallery, **78**	F5
Percival David Foundation, **58**	E4
Pollock's Toy Museum, **29**	D5
Sherlock Holmes Museum, **10**	B4
Wallace Collection, **7**	B5

⭐ NIGHTLIFE
Bagleys Studio, **42**	E2
Scala, **84**	F3

🍎 FOOD
Alara Wholefoods, **57**	E4
CTJ, **36**	D4
Da Beppe, **33**	D4
Diwana Bhel Poori House, **40**	D4
ECCo, **27**	D5
Giraffe, **23**	C5
Jeremy Bentham, **35**	D4
Mandalay, **2**	A5
Navarro's, **30**	D5
Patogh, **3**	A5
Pizza Express, **74**	E5
Ranoush, **4**	B6
Reubens, **8**	B5
Vats, **79**	F4
Wagamama, **75**	E5
Zizzi, **9**	B5

🏠 ACCOMMODATIONS
Arosfa Hotel, **64**	E5
Ashlee House, **83**	F3
Astor's Museum Inn, **70**	E5
Carr-Sanders Hall, **31**	D5
Commonwealth Hall, **50**	E3
Crescent Hotel, **51**	E4
Edward Lear Hotel, **5**	B6
The Generator, **54**	E4
George Hotel, **53**	E4
Hadleigh Hotel, **6**	B6
Hotel Ibis Euston, **41**	D3
Indian YMCA, **32**	D4
International Student House, **21**	C4
Jenkins Hotel, **49**	E3
The Langland Hotel, **66**	E5
Mentone Hotel, **52**	E4
Passfield Hall, **55**	E4
Pickwick Hall International Backpackers, **69**	E5
Royal National Hotel, **59**	E4
Ruskin Hotel, **68**	E5
YHA St. Pancras International, **46**	E3

🎭 ENTERTAINMENT
Open Air Theatre, **15**	B3
The Place, **47**	E3
RADA, **63**	E5
Renoir, **60**	F4
Water Rats, **82**	F3
Wigmore Hall, **25**	C6

Marylebone, Regent's Park, and Bloomsbury

SEE LEGEND, p. xxx

0 — 200 yards
0 — 200 meters

Primrose Hill

Gloucester Ave
Fitzroy Rd
Regent's Park Rd.
Gloucester Cr
Oval Rd
Parkway
Can
To
Delance
Park Village
Morning

Acacia Rd.
Townshend Rd.
Avenue Rd.
St. Edmund's Terr.
St. John's Wood Terr.
Allitsen Rd.
Chalbert Rd.
Prince Albert Rd.
Grand Union Canal

London Zoo **18**

REGENT'S PARK

Broad Walk
Outer Circle
Albany St.
Cumb
Chester Rd.
Redhill

Public Gardens

Wellington Rd.

St. John's Wood Rd.

Lodge Rd.

London Central Mosque **1**

Outer Circle

Boating Lake **14**

Inner Circle **16**
15
Queen Mary's Gardens
13
17

19
20
M

Park Rd.

Rossmore Rd.

Clarence Gate

Glentworth St.

10

11 **12**

PARK SQ.

Regent's Park **21**
Pos
Park Crescent

Church St.
Bradley St.
Lisson St.
Lisson Grove

Marylebone Station

DORSET SQ.

Baker St.

Marylebone

MELCOMBE SQ.

Marylebone Rd.

2

Edgware Rd.
Chapel St.
York St.
Crawford St.
Shouldham St.
Old Marylebone Rd.
Upper Montagu St.
Gloucester Pl.
Baker St.
Chiltern St.
Paddington St.

Devonshire St.
Beaumont St.
Wimpole St.
Weymouth St.
Portland Pl.

9

8 Dorset St.
Manchester St.
New Cavendish St.
Harley St.

MARYLEBONE
23
Marylebone High St.
Welbeck St.
Queen Anne St.

Montagu Pl.
MONTAGU SQ.
Blandford St.

Praed St.

Seymour St.
Brown St.
BRYANSTON SQ.
George St.

MANCHESTER SQ.
7

Wigmore St.
25
CAVEN SQ.

Sussex Gardens

CAMBRIDGE SQ.
OXFORD SQ.

Hyde Park Cr.
Kendal St.
Connaught St.
CONNAUGHT SQ.

6
Upper Berkeley St.
PORTMAN SQ.
Seymour St.
5
Orchard St.
Duke St.
James's St.

MAYFAIR

GLOUCESTER SQ.
HYDE PARK SQ.
Hyde Park St.
Albion St.

4
Marble Arch
Oxford St.
North Audley St.

Bayswater Rd.

Bond St.
Davies St.
New Bond St.
Brook St.

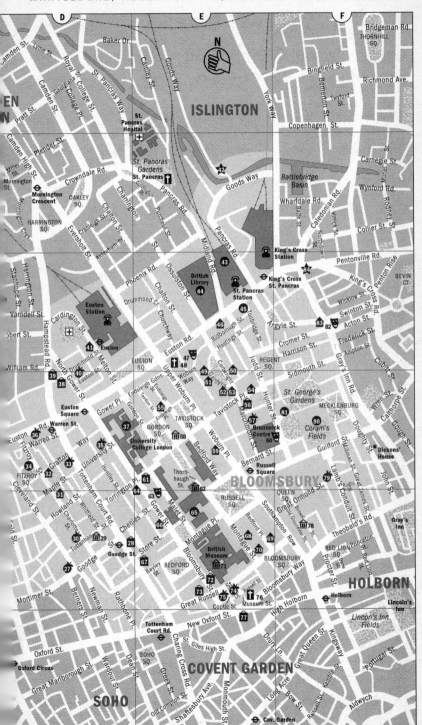

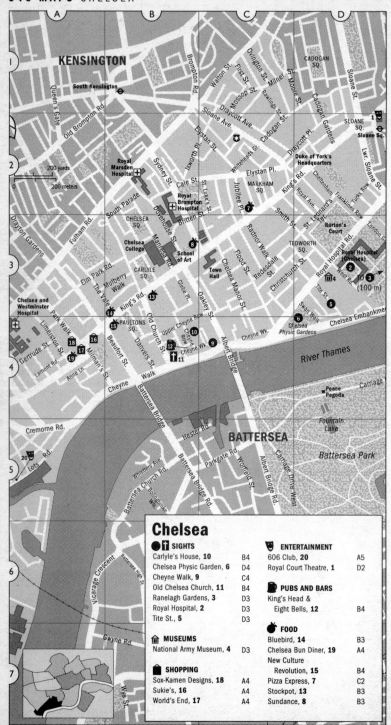

Chelsea

● 🛈 SIGHTS

Carlyle's House, **10**	B4
Chelsea Physic Garden, **6**	D4
Cheyne Walk, **9**	C4
Old Chelsea Church, **11**	B4
Ranelagh Gardens, **3**	D3
Royal Hospital, **2**	D3
Tite St., **5**	D3

🏛 MUSEUMS

National Army Museum, **4**	D3

🛍 SHOPPING

Sox-Kamen Designs, **18**	A4
Sukie's, **16**	A4
World's End, **17**	A4

🎭 ENTERTAINMENT

606 Club, **20**	A5
Royal Court Theatre, **1**	D2

🍺 PUBS AND BARS

King's Head & Eight Bells, **12**	B4

🍴 FOOD

Bluebird, **14**	B3
Chelsea Bun Diner, **19**	A4
New Culture Revolution, **15**	B4
Pizza Express, **7**	C2
Stockpot, **13**	B3
Sundance, **8**	B3

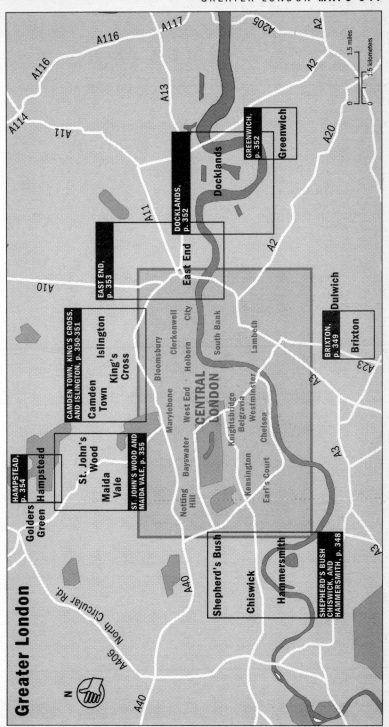

Greater London

N

GREENWICH, p. 352

Greenwich

DOCKLANDS, p. 352

Docklands

EAST END, p. 353

East End

CAMDEN TOWN, KING'S CROSS, AND ISLINGTON, p. 350-351

Islington

Camden Town

King's Cross

Clerkenwell

City

Bloomsbury

Holborn

South Bank

BRIXTON, p. 349

Brixton

Dulwich

Lambeth

HAMPSTEAD, p. 354

Hampstead

Golders Green

ST. JOHN'S WOOD AND MAIDA VALE, p. 355

St. John's Wood

Maida Vale

Marylebone

West End

CENTRAL LONDON

Knightsbridge

Belgravia

Westminster

Bayswater

Notting Hill

Kensington

Earl's Court

Chelsea

North Circular Rd.

Shepherd's Bush

Chiswick

Hammersmith

SHEPHERD'S BUSH, CHISWICK, AND HAMMERSMITH, p. 348

1.5 miles

1.5 kilometers

0

A117
A116
A116
A114
A11
A205
A2
A2
A13
A20
A11
A10
A2
A3
A23
A3
A40
A406
A40

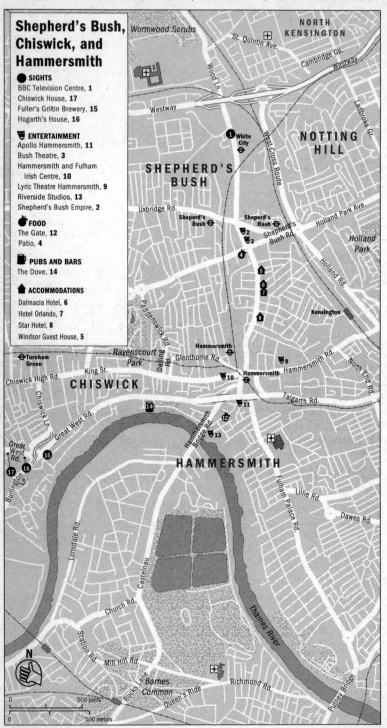

Shepherd's Bush, Chiswick, and Hammersmith

● SIGHTS
BBC Television Centre, **1**
Chiswick House, **17**
Fuller's Griltin Brewery, **15**
Hogarth's House, **16**

● ENTERTAINMENT
Apollo Hammersmith, **11**
Bush Theatre, **3**
Hammersmith and Fulham
  Irish Centre, **10**
Lyric Theatre Hammersmith, **9**
Riverside Studios, **13**
Shepherd's Bush Empire, **2**

● FOOD
The Gate, **12**
Patio, **4**

● PUBS AND BARS
The Dove, **14**

● ACCOMMODATIONS
Dalmacia Hotel, **6**
Hotel Orlando, **7**
Star Hotel, **8**
Windsor Guest House, **5**

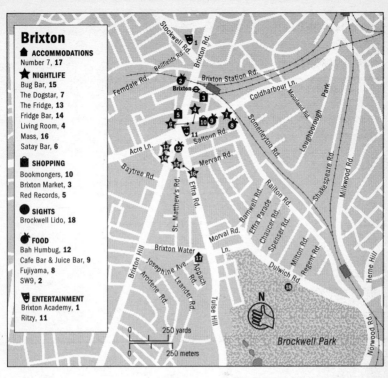

Brixton

🏠 **ACCOMMODATIONS**
Number 7, **17**

⭐ **NIGHTLIFE**
Bug Bar, **15**
The Dogstar, **7**
The Fridge, **13**
Fridge Bar, **14**
Living Room, **4**
Mass, **16**
Satay Bar, **6**

🛍️ **SHOPPING**
Bookmongers, **10**
Brixton Market, **3**
Red Records, **5**

⬤ **SIGHTS**
Brockwell Lido, **18**

🍎 **FOOD**
Bah Humbug, **12**
Cafe Bar & Juice Bar, **9**
Fujiyama, **8**
SW9, **2**

🎭 **ENTERTAINMENT**
Brixton Academy, **1**
Ritzy, **11**

Camden Town, King's Cross, & Islington SEE MAP, p. 350-351

⬤🛈 **SIGHTS**
Regent's Canal, **10** — A3
St. Pancras Old Church, **25** — B5

🏛️ **MUSEUMS**
Crafts Council, **33** — E5
The Estorick, **51** — F3
Jewish Museum
Camden, **22** — A4

🍺 **PUBS**
The Black Cap, **20** — A4
Blakes, **18** — A4
Dublin Castle, **8** — DETAIL
Duke of Cambridge, **38** — F5
Filthy MacNasty's
Whisky Cafe, **31** — E6
The King's Head, **47** — E4

🏠 **ACCOMMODATIONS**
Ashlee House, **28** — C6
Jurys Inn, **30** — E5

🎭 **ENTERTAINMENT**
The Almeida, **48** — E4
Etcetera, **23** — A4
The King's Head, **45** — E4
Little Angel Theatre, **46** — F4
The Old Red Lion, **35** — E5
Sadler's Well, **34** — E6

🛍️ **SHOPPING**
Annie's, **39** — E4
Camden Canal Market, **9** — A3
Camden Lock Market, **4** — DETAIL
The Camden Market, **11** — A3
Camden Passage, **37** — E5
Chapel Market, **32** — E5
Cybercity, **2** — DETAIL
Inverness Street
Market, **17** — A4
Mega City Comics, **16** — A4
Out on the Floor, **13** — A4
Reckless Records, **40** — E4
Stables Market, **3** — DETAIL
Vinyl Addiction, **15** — A4

🍎 **FOOD**
Candid Arts Cafe, **36** — E5
Gallipoli, **44** — E4
Gem, **50** — E3
Giraffe, **41** — E4
Le Mercury, **49** — E3
Marine Ices, **1** — DETAIL
The New Culture
Revolution, **21** — A4
Odette's Wine Bar, **6** — DETAIL
Tartuf, **42** — E4
Trojka, **5** — DETAIL

⭐ **NIGHTLIFE**
Bagleys, **26** — C5
Bar Fusion, **43** — F4
Camden Palace, **24** — A5
Cecil Sharpe House, **7** — DETAIL
Electric Ballroom, **12** — A4
Forum, **53** — A1
The Garage, **52** — E2
Jazz Cafe, **19** — A4
Scala, **27** — C5
The Water Rats, **29** — D6
WKD, **14** — A4

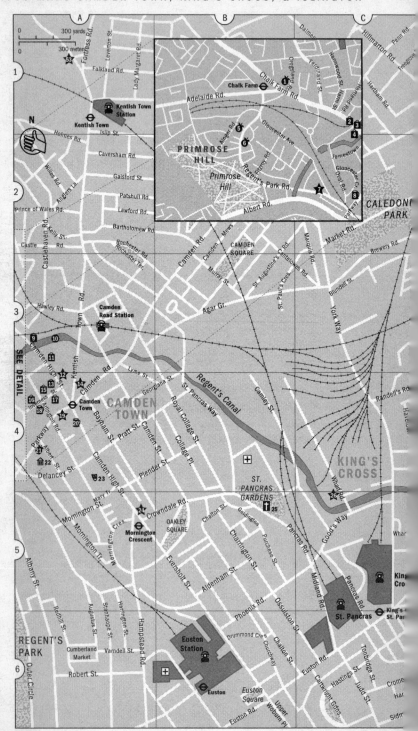

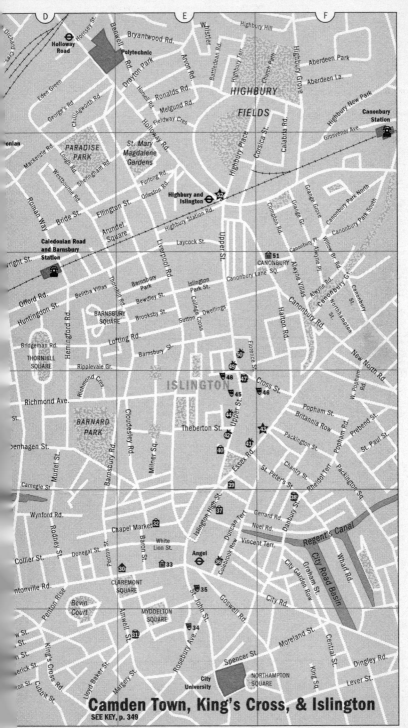

Camden Town, King's Cross, & Islington
SEE KEY, p. 349

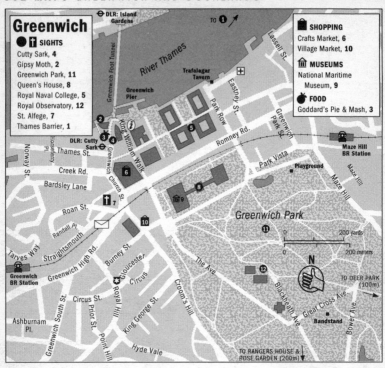

Greenwich

● ⓘ **SIGHTS**
Cutty Sark, **4**
Gipsy Moth, **2**
Greenwich Park, **11**
Queen's House, **8**
Royal Naval College, **5**
Royal Observatory, **12**
St. Alfege, **7**
Thames Barrier, **1**

🛍 **SHOPPING**
Crafts Market, **6**
Village Market, **10**

🏛 **MUSEUMS**
National Maritime
  Museum, **9**

🍴 **FOOD**
Goddard's Pie & Mash, **3**

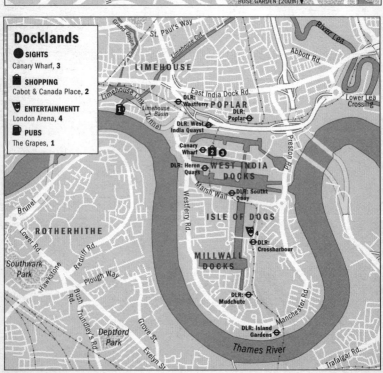

Docklands

● **SIGHTS**
Canary Wharf, **3**

🛍 **SHOPPING**
Cabot & Canada Place, **2**

🎭 **ENTERTAINMENT**
London Arena, **4**

🍺 **PUBS**
The Grapes, **1**

The East End

● SIGHTS

Bevis Marks Synagogue, **19**		A5
Brick Lane, **13**		B5
Christ Church Spitalfields, **14**		A5
East London Mosque, **16**		B5
Spitalfields Market, **10**		A4
Whitechapel Bell Foundry, **18**		B5

★ NIGHTLIFE

93 Feet East, **6**		B4
333, **32**		SD
Cargo, **33**		SD
Herbal, **31**		SD

▼ ENTERTAINMENT

Comedy Cafe, **34**		SD
Lux Cinema, **23**		SD
Spitz, **11**		A4

🏛 MUSEUMS

Geffrye Museum, **1**		A3
Lux Gallery, **22**		SD
Museum of Childhood, **37**		C3
Whitechapel Art Gallery, **17**		B5
White Cube 2, **28**		SD

🍎 FOOD

Aladin Balti House, **8**		B4
Arkansas Cafe, **12**		A4
Brick Lane Beigel Bakery, **2**		B4
Cafe 1001, **9**		B4
Grand Central, **35**		SD
Hoxton Sq. Bar & Kitchen, **24**		SD
Nazrul, **7**		B4
Yelo, **21**		SD

🛍 SHOPPING

@ work, **4**		B4
The Beer Shop, **26**		SD
Hoxton Boutique, **30**		SD
The Laden Showrooms, **3**		B4
Pauric Sweeney, **25**		SD
Petticoat Lane, **15**		A5

🍺 PUBS AND BARS

Cantaloupe, **36**		SD
Liquid Bar, **27**		SD
Prospect of Whitby, **20**		C6
Shoreditch Electricity		
Showrooms, **29**		SD
The Vibe Bar, **5**		B4

SEE SHOREDITCH DETAIL

Shoreditch
(GRID REFERENCE = SD)

0 ———— 1/4 mile
0 ———— 250 meters

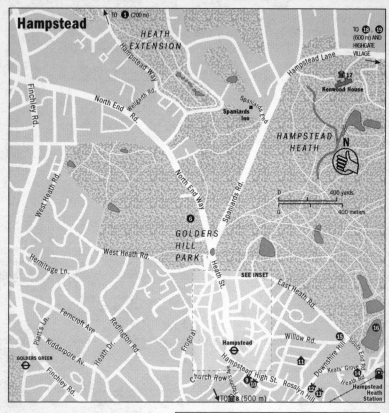

Hampstead

TO ❶ (200m)

HEATH EXTENSION

Hampstead Way

TO ⓲, ⓳ (600 m) AND HIGHGATE VILLAGE

Hampstead Lane

Finchley Rd.

North End Rd.

Wellgarth Rd.

🏛 17
Kenwood House

Spaniards End

Spaniards Inn

HAMPSTEAD HEATH

N

West Heath Rd.

North End Way

Spaniards Rd.

D 0 400 yards
0 400 meters

Hermitage Ln.

West Heath Rd.

❻

GOLDERS HILL PARK

Heath St.

SEE INSET

East Heath Rd.

Ferncroft Ave.

Redington Rd.

Willow Rd.

⓯

⓰

Platt's Ln.

Kidderpore Av.

Heath Dr.

Frognal

Hampstead

Downshire Hill

South End Rd.

GOLDERS GREEN

Finchley Rd.

Hampstead High St.

🏛 ⓫

Keats' Grove

⓮
🚇 Hampstead Heath Station

Church Row

❾ ❿

Rosslyn Hill

⓬
⓭

TO 🏛 8 (500 m)

Inset map

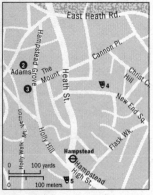

East Heath Rd.

Hampstead Grove

Cannon Pl.

The Mount

Christ Ch. Hill

❷
Adams

❸

Heath St.

🎭 ❹

New End Sq.

Holly Walk

Mt. Vernon

Holly Hill

Flask Wk.

Hampstead 🚇
Hampstead High St.

0 100 yards
0 100 meters

❺

Hampstead

● 🕴 **SIGHTS**
Admiral House, **2**
Fenton House, **3**
Golders Green Crematorium, **1**
The Grove, **19**
Highgate Cemetery, **18**
Hill Garden, **6**
Keats House, **14**
Mixed Bathing Pond, **16**
St. John's Church and Churchyard, **7**
Two Willow Road, **15**

🏛 **MUSEUMS**
Fread Museum, **8**
Iveagh Bequest, **17**

🎭 **ENTERTAINMENT**
New End Theatre, **4**
Pullman Everyman, **5**

🍴 **FOOD**
Bar Room Bar, **12**
Giraffe, **13**
King William IV, **10**
Le Creperie de Hampstead, **9**

🏠 **ACCOMMODATIONS**
Hampstead Village Guesthouse, **11**

St. John's Wood and Maida Vale

● **SIGHTS**
Abbey Rd. Crossing, **6**
Abbey Rd. Studios, **5**
Little Venice, **10**
Lord's Cricket Ground, **7**

🏛 **MUSEUMS**
Freud Museum, **1**
Saatchi Gallery, **4**

🎭 **ENTERTAINMENT**
Barge Theatre, **9**
Canal Cafe Theatre, **8**
Hampstead Theatre, **3**
Tricycle, **2**

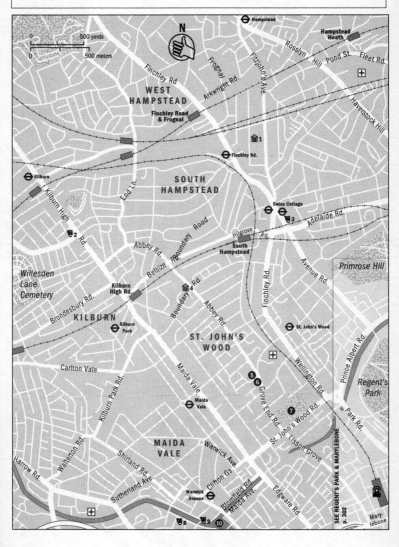

Will you have enough stories to tell your grandchildren?

<u>Yahoo! Travel</u>

CHOOSE YOUR DESTINATION SWEEPSTAKES

No Purchase Necessary.

**Explore the world with Let's Go® and StudentUniverse!
Enter for a chance to win a trip for two to a Let's Go destination!**

Separate Drawings! May & October 2002.

GRAND PRIZES:
Roundtrip StudentUniverse Tickets

✓ Select one destination and mail your entry to:

☐ Costa Rica
☐ London
☐ Hong Kong
☐ San Francisco
☐ New York
☐ Amsterdam
☐ Prague
☐ Sydney

* Plus Additional Prizes!!

Choose Your Destination Sweepstakes
St. Martin's Press
Suite 1600, Department MF
175 Fifth Avenue
New York, NY 10010-7848

Restrictions apply; see offical rules for
details by visiting Let'sGo.com or sending SASE
(VT residents may omit return postage) to the address above.

Name: _____

Address: _____

City/State/Zip: _____

Phone: _____

Email: _____

Grand prizes provided by:

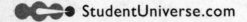

StudentUniverse.com   Real Travel Deals

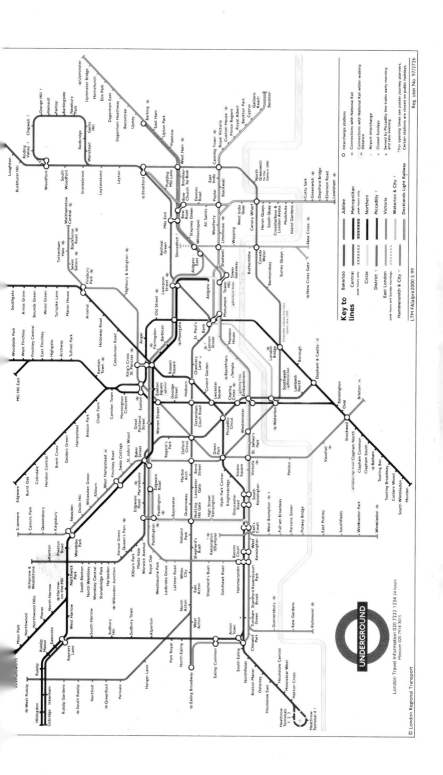

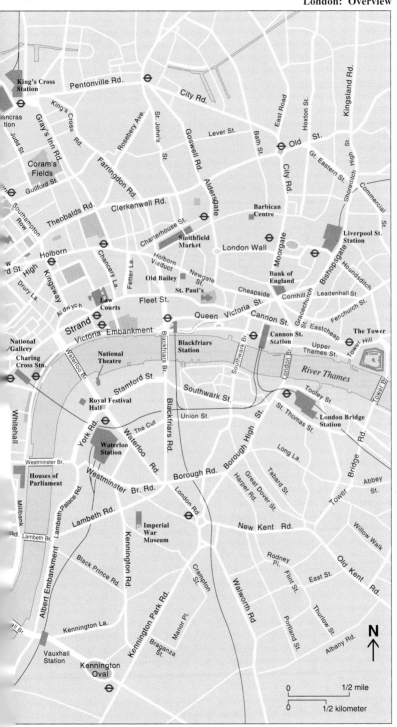

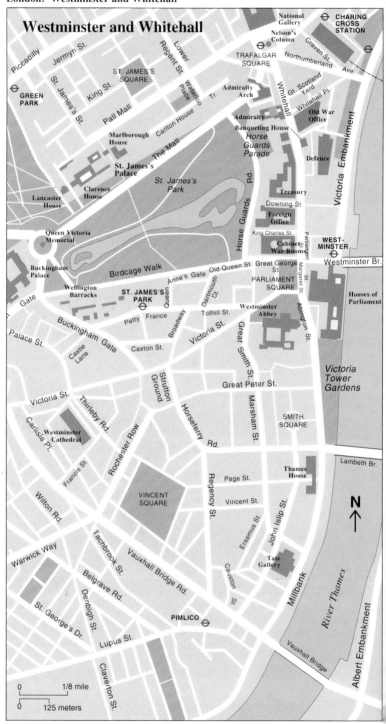

Westminster and Whitehall

National Gallery

CHARING CROSS STATION

Nelson's Column

Craven St.

TRAFALGAR SQUARE

Northumberland Ave.

Piccadilly

Jermyn St.

Regent St.

Lower

Waterloo Pl.

Tr

Admiralty Arch

Whitehall

Gt. Scotland Yard

Whitehall Pl.

Old War Office

ST. JAMES'S SQUARE

King St.

St. James's St.

Canton House Ter.

Admiralty

Banqueting House

GREEN PARK

Pall Mall

Marlborough House

The Mall

Horse Guards Parade

Defence

Victoria Embankment

St. James's Palace

Clarence House

St. James's Park

Treasury

Downing St.

Foreign Office

Lancaster House

Horse Guards Rd.

WEST-MINSTER

Queen Victoria Memorial

King Charles St.

Cabinet War Rooms

Parliament St.

Buckingham Palace

Birdcage Walk

Anne's Gate

Old Queen St.

Great George St.

Margaret St.

Westminster Br.

Wellington Barracks

ST. JAMES'S PARK

Dartmouth St.

PARLIAMENT SQUARE

Houses of Parliament

Gate

Petty France

Broadway

Tothill St.

Westminster Abbey

Abingdon St.

Palace St.

Buckingham Gate

Queen

Victoria St.

Great Smith St.

Caxton St.

Castle Lane

Strutton Ground

Great Peter St.

Marsham St.

Victoria Tower Gardens

Victoria St.

Thirleby Rd.

Rochester Row

Horseferry Rd.

SMITH SQUARE

Carlisle Pl.

Westminster Cathedral

Francis St.

Lambeth Br.

Page St.

Thames House

Wilton Rd.

VINCENT SQUARE

Regency St.

Vincent St.

John Islip St.

N

Warwick Way

Tachbrook St.

Vauxhall Bridge Rd

Erasmus St.

Tate Gallery

River Thames

Belgrave Rd.

Caulon St.

Millbank

St. George's Dr.

Denbigh St.

PIMLICO

Albert Embankment

Lupus St.

Claverton St.

Vauxhall Bridge

0   1/8 mile

0   125 meters

Soho and Covent Garden

London: Soho and Covent Garden

N ←

1/8 mile

125 meters

Southampton Row

HOLBORN

Lincoln's Inn Fields

Kingsway

ALDWYCH

Lancaster Pl.

Waterloo Br.

Cleopatra's Needle

Savoy St.

Savoy Hotel

Embankment

Victoria

Newton St.

Russell St.

Catherine St.

Wellington St.

Theatre Museum

London Transport Museum

Great Queen St.

Parker St.

High Holborn

Drury Lane

Bow St.

COVENT GARDEN

Floral Hall

COVENT GARDEN

Southampton St.

The Strand

BLOOMSBURY SQUARE

Bloomsbury Way

Royal Opera

Floral Pl.

Long Acre

St. Paul's Covent Garden

Bury

Charing Cross Station

Endell St.

Shorts Gardens

Shelton St.

Neal St.

Earlham St.

Langley St.

National Jazz Center

Garrick St.

Maiden La.

Henrietta St.

Chandos Pl.

William IV St.

New Row

Bedfordbury

St. Martin-in-the-Fields

Bloomsbury St.

Great Russell St.

St. Giles St.

High St.

Shaftesbury Ave.

Monmouth St.

LEICESTER SQUARE

St.Martins La.

TOTTENHAM COURT RD.

New Oxford St.

Tottenham Court Rd.

Rathbone Pl.

St. Barnabas in Soho

Sutton Row

Manette St.

Charing Cross Rd.

Greek St.

Frith St.

CAMBRIDGE CIRCUS

Shaftesbury Ave.

Gerrard St.

CHINATOWN

Lisle St.

Cranbourne St.

LEICESTER SQUARE

Irving St.

Orange St.

St. Martin's St.

National Gallery

Charles II Statue

SOHO SQUARE

Carlisle St.

Old Compton St.

Coventry St.

Whitcomb St.

Haymarket

Newman St.

Berners St.

Eastcastle St.

Margaret St.

CAVENDISH SQUARE

OXFORD CIRCUS

Argyll St.

Oxford St.

Rathbone Pl.

Great Chapel St.

Noel St.

Dean St.

Wardour St.

Berwick St.

Poland St.

SOHO

Lexington St.

Windmill St.

St. Anne's

Brewer St.

Glasshouse St.

PICCADILLY CIRCUS

Regent St.

Jermyn St.

Great Marlborough St.

Marshall St.

Carnaby St.

Broadwick St.

Beak St.

GOLDEN SQUARE

Piccadilly

Albemarle St.

Dover St.

Old Burlington Gardens

Clifford St.

Royal Academy

Old Bond St.

HANOVER SQUARE

St. George St.

New Bond St.

Savile Row

BERKELEY SQUARE

Berkeley St.

Regent St.

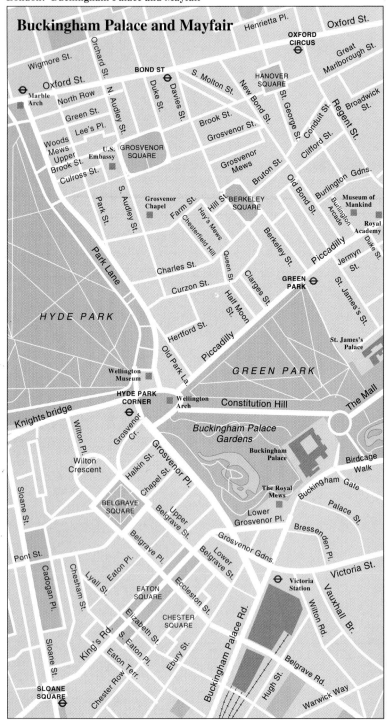

Buckingham Palace and Mayfair

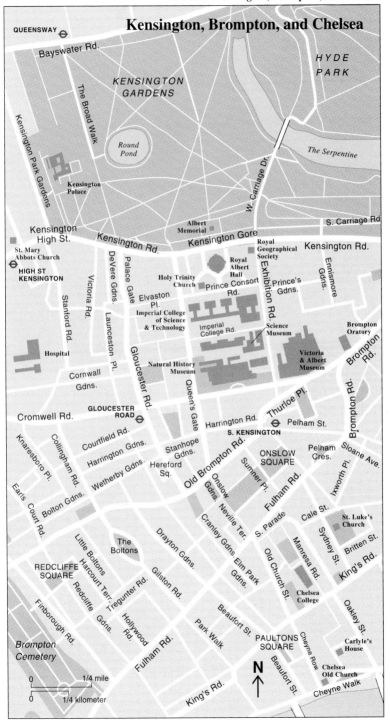

Kensington, Brompton, and Chelsea

QUEENSWAY

Bayswater Rd.

KENSINGTON GARDENS

HYDE PARK

The Broad Walk

Kensington Park Gardens

Round Pond

The Serpentine

W. Carriage Dr.

Kensington Palace

Albert Memorial

S. Carriage Rd

Kensington High St.

Kensington Rd.

Kensington Gore

Kensington Rd.

St. Mary Abbots Church

HIGH ST KENSINGTON

DeVere Gdns.

Palace Gate

Royal Geographical Society

Royal Albert Hall

Holy Trinity Church

Prince Consort Rd.

Prince's Gdns.

Ennismore Gdns.

Victoria Rd.

Stanford Rd.

Launceston Pl.

Elvaston Pl.

Imperial College of Science & Technology

Imperial College Rd.

Science Museum

Exhibition Rd.

Brompton Oratory

Hospital

Gloucester Rd.

Natural History Museum

Victoria & Albert Museum

Brompton Rd.

Cornwall Gdns.

Queen's Gate

Thurloe Pl.

Cromwell Rd.

GLOUCESTER ROAD

Harrington Rd.

Pelham St.

S. KENSINGTON

Brompton Rd.

Knaresboro Pl.

Collingham Rd.

Courtfield Rd.

Harrington Gdns.

Stanhope Gdns.

Old Brompton Rd.

ONSLOW SQUARE

Pelham Cres.

Sloane Ave.

Ixworth Pl.

Earls Court Rd.

Bolton Gdns.

Wetherby Gdns.

Hereford Sq.

Onslow Gdns.

Neville Ter.

Sumner Pl.

Fulham Rd.

S. Parade

Cale St.

Pelham Cres.

Sydney St.

St. Luke's Church

Little Boltons

The Boltons

Drayton Gdns.

Cranley Gdns.

Elm Park Gdns.

Old Church St.

Manresa Rd.

Britten St.

King's Rd.

REDCLIFFE SQUARE

Harcourt Terr.

Redcliffe Gdns.

Tregunter Rd.

Gilston Rd.

Hollywood Rd.

Chelsea College

Finborough Rd.

Beaufort St.

Park Walk

PAULTONS SQUARE

Cheyne Row

Oakley St.

Carlyle's House

Brompton Cemetery

Fulham Rd.

Chelsea Old Church

Cheyne Walk

Beaufort St.

N

King's Rd.

0   1/4 mile

0   1/4 kilometer

London: City of London

The City

Leman St.
Mansell St.
Commercial St.
ALDGATE EAST
Widegate St.
Middlesex St.
Minories
Houndsditch
ALDGATE
Aldgate
Fenchurch St. Station
Royal Mint St.
E. Smithfield
St. Katharine's Way
Tower Br. Approach
Tower Br.
TOWER HILL
Tower Hill
TRINITY SQUARE
Pepys St.
Seething La.
The Tower
Tower Pier
Liverpool St. Station
St. Mary Axe
Bishopsgate
Old Broad St.
St. Mary Axe
Lloyd's
Leadenhall St.
Fenchurch St.
Mark La.
Mincing La.
St. Olave's
St. Dunstan's
Gt. Tower St.
Lower Thames St.
All Hallows
Billingsgate Market
HMS Belfast
Sun St.
London Wall
South Pl.
FINSBURY CIRCUS
MOORGATE
Moorgate
Throgmorton Ave.
London Stock Exchange
St. Margaret's
Threadneedle St.
Gracechurch St.
Leadenhall Market
Lime St.
Cornhill
Lombard St.
St. Mary at Hill
Eastcheap
The Monument
Monument St.
MONUMENT
St. Magnus Martyr
London Br.
Chiswell St.
Ropemaker St.
Moorfields
Coleman St.
London Wall
Bassinghall St.
Lothbury St.
Bank of England
BANK
Princes St.
King William St.
St. Mary Abchurch
Walbrook
St. Mary Woolnoth
Mansion House
Poultry
St. Stephen Walbrook
Temple of Mithras
CANNON
Cloak La.
Cannon St. Station
Queen St.
Southwark Br.
River Thames
Beech St.
Silk St.
Fore St.
Barbican Centre
St. Giles without Cripplegate
Museum of London
London Wall
Guildhall
Gresham St.
Wood St.
Milk St.
King St.
St. Mary le Bow
Watling St.
Bread St.
Cheapside
MANSION HOUSE
St. Mary Aldermary
Cannon St.
Upper Thames St.
Aldersgate St.
BARBICAN
St. Bartholomew the Great
Long Lane
Little Britain
St. Martin's-Le-Grand
New Change
St. Paul's Cathedral
ST. PAUL'S
St. Andrew-by-the-Wardrobe
Queen Victoria St.
St. Benet's
Puddle Dock
Blackfriars Station
St. John St.
FARRINGDON
Cowcross St.
Smithfield Market
Gilspur St.
West Smithfield
Snow Hill
Holborn Viaduct Station
Holborn Viaduct
Old Bailey
Warwick La.
Fleet La.
Ludgate Hill
LUDGATE CIRCUS
New Bridge St.
Blackfriars Br.
BLACKFRIARS
Victoria Embankment
Clerkenwell Rd.
Hatton Garden
Greville St.
Ely Pl.
Farringdon Rd.
Farringdon Rd.
Shoe Lane
New Fetter La.
Fetter La.
St. Bride St.
Fleet St.
GOUGH SQ.
Tudor St.
Temple Ave.
Temple Church
Middle Temple La.
The Temple

1/4 mile
1/4 km
0
0